Contents

Editor's Introduction	5
Notes on Methodology	9
Global Trends	13
Armed-Group Proliferation: Origins and Consequences	14
Non-state Armed Groups and UAVs: Uptake and Effectiveness	19
ISIS Foreign Fighters after the Fall of the Caliphate	23
Human Trafficking in Conflict	31
Conflict Reports	37
1 Americas	38
Brazil (Rio de Janeiro & Ceará)	40
Colombia (BACRIMs)	51
El Salvador	60
Honduras	68
Mexico (Cartels)	76
2 Asia-Pacific	90
Myanmar (EAOs)	92
Philippines (ASG & Moro)	104
Philippines (NPA)	116
Southern Thailand	126
3 Europe and Eurasia	136
Armenia–Azerbaijan (Nagorno-Karabakh)	138
Ukraine	146

A Kashmiri school damaged after cross-border bombing in Dudhnyal, Neelum district, Pakistan

A MILF brigade commander on his farm in Datu Piang, Maguindanao

4	**Middle East and North Africa**	**156**
	Egypt (Sinai)	158
	Iraq	167
	Israel–Palestine	178
	Libya	189
	Syria	201
	Turkey (PKK)	214
	Yemen	222
5	**South Asia**	**234**
	Afghanistan	236
	India (CPI–Maoist)	244
	India (Northeast)	252
	India–Pakistan (Kashmir)	265
	Pakistan	275
6	**Sub-Saharan Africa**	**286**
	Cameroon	288
	Central African Republic	298
	Democratic Republic of the Congo	308
	Ethiopia (Communal Violence)	320
	Lake Chad Basin (Boko Haram)	329
	Nigeria (Farmer–Pastoralist)	338
	The Sahel (Mali & Burkina Faso)	347
	Somalia	360
	South Sudan	369
	Sudan (Darfur, Blue Nile & South Kordofan)	381

Index 392

Editor's Introduction

Preparing *The Armed Conflict Survey 2020* has served, once again, as a reminder of the complexity of conflict in the twenty-first century. With each edition, we observe the consolidation of trends highlighted earlier, including the substantial internationalisation of many conflicts, which increasingly often involve regional and international actors that use the battleground to pursue their rivalries. In so doing, stakes often grow higher and the strategic repercussions of events can reverberate much further afield.

For each of the 33 conflicts covered, the book provides an overview of the key developments in 2019; the events that led to the current situation; data on the conflict parties involved; the drivers of the conflict; political and military developments; and analysis of the significance of the conflict. Specifically, we delve into the consequences of the major political and military developments for human rights and the humanitarian situation, the social and economic impact of the conflict, and how it has affected relations with neighbouring and international partners. We assess the state of the conflict at the end of 2019, albeit without making predictions, and identify the trends and trajectories that will be most relevant for 2020, including prospects for conflict resolution, risks of conflict intensification or spillover, and scenarios for reconstruction. Each conflict chapter concludes with the strategic implications of the conflict locally and internationally. Complementing the analysis are conflict-specific maps and graphics to illustrate patterns and structures such as violent hotspots, armed-group networks, transitional-government structures and human-displacement data.

Snapshots for each of the six geographical regions into which conflicts are organised outline key trends, strategic implications and prospects. We endeavour to underline geopolitical and geostrategic relations and how they intersect with conflict. Examples include what Turkey's involvement in Syria means for its relationship with NATO; the impact of attacks by Baloch insurgents against Chinese interests on Islamabad–Beijing relations; or how diminishing Western engagement with the Burmese government might create room for China to expand its political influence in Myanmar.

The number of situations around the world meeting our definition of armed conflict decreased from 40 in 2015, when the *Armed Conflict Survey* was first published, to 33 in 2019. This might seem like a marked improvement, but notwithstanding the removal of some conflicts such as Kosovo and the Niger Delta, the current line-up of conflicts also reflects multiple transformations. Since 2015, we have recorded how, owing to changes in the drivers of conflicts and the relationships among armed groups, various conflicts had to be merged – as was the case for India's northeastern conflicts in the previous edition – while others were split, such as Central America's Northern Triangle. In addition to these changes, some conflicts have ended, and therefore were removed from the survey, and new ones have begun, such as in Cameroon in 2017.

Observing the morphing of some of the conflicts and the trajectory of many others brings the centrality of non-state armed groups into clear focus. We have highlighted this in three ways. Firstly, chapters include expanded profiles of conflict parties, a large proportion of which are non-state actors. Secondly, all four thematic essays are centred on aspects of the activities and nature of armed groups and the responses required to limit their pernicious effects. Finally, the 2020 Chart of Armed Conflict that accompanies the book compares the number of state and non-state parties in each conflict theatre. Notably, in 21 of 33 conflicts the number of non-state armed groups exceeds the number of state groups.[1]

Armed groups in focus

As in previous editions, we have invited experts to open the survey with thematic essays analysing emerging or evolving trends in conflict. Acknowledging that trends evolve and linger for longer than our 12-month time frame, we believe the selected topics are particularly relevant for the year at hand and will have an enduring relevance as they cover potentially growing threats and policy challenges.

This year's essays aim to provide an understanding of the changing nature of armed groups and the emerging trends that characterise their operations. In 'Armed-Group Proliferation: Origins and Consequences', Brian McQuinn warns that despite the emergence of a large number of groups in recent decades, it is the proliferation of *horizontally* structured groups that is likely to influence the direction of many conflicts. In the context of peace processes, for instance, a decentralised chain of command and involvement of multiple group leaders is likely to impede negotiations, owing to the multiplicity of voices and agendas. This challenge is well known in the context of the conflict in Mali and the wider Sahel.

Alongside the adoption of a horizontal rather than a vertical structure, adaptability and flexibility are contributing factors to groups' longevity. Experimenting with technology is a way of adapting to changing circumstances to surprise and undermine opponents. In this regard, Eleanor Beevor and Dhia Muhsin examine an area of growing concern among policymakers and security experts: the threat of armed groups using uninhabited aerial vehicles (UAVs or drones). The broader international community became acutely aware of this threat in the wake of the attack carried out by Yemen's Houthi movement (Ansarullah) in Saudi Arabia in September 2019. Despite the hype, evidence discussed in 'Non-state Armed Groups and UAVs: Uptake and Effectiveness' points to less alarming conclusions in the short term. Non-state armed groups are not currently in a position to weaponise non-military UAVs quickly or easily. Yet technological change coupled with growing experience and know-how will introduce new possibilities for armed groups and as such this remains an area of non-state activity to be monitored, especially in the case of groups receiving state backing.

Adaptability comes in many forms. In 'ISIS Foreign Fighters after the Fall of the Caliphate', Francesco Milan underlines how in the post-caliphate era, the Islamic State, also known as ISIS or ISIL, remains able to mobilise foreign fighters and exploit the networks once used to guarantee the flow of fighters to Syria and Iraq to facilitate their movement into other conflict zones. Indeed, the relocation of veteran fighters to regions such as Southeast Asia and Africa underscores ISIS's resilience at a time when Western governments face the challenge of dealing with four categories of foreign fighters, each presenting its own conundrum, while ISIS in Syria is showing signs of resurgence.

Armed groups, either ideologically or criminally driven (or both), are infamous for quickly exploiting the business opportunities presented by conflict, often for economic gain. 'Human Trafficking in Conflict' focuses on the link between the two phenomena, stressing how the increasingly prevalent protracted conflicts that displace large numbers of people create optimal conditions for human trafficking. Tuesday Reitano lists many capacity shortcomings at the local and international levels, as well as within state institutions, international organisations and NGOs. Ending the plight of trafficking victims, which warranted greater concern throughout the 2010s, appears to remain unachievable in the short and medium term.

The Chart of Armed Conflict, conflict duration and prospects for peace

In addition to presenting data on the number of parties engaged in the 33 active conflicts, this year's Chart of Armed Conflict has two other purposes. Firstly, it lists multinational missions to conflict and post-conflict countries, indicating the start date and current strength of operations and missions deployed under the aegis of the European Union, NATO, the Organization for Security and Cooperation in Europe, the UN and a number of ad hoc groupings such as the G5 Sahel Joint Force. Secondly, the Chart puts a spotlight on conflict duration. The concept of prolonged conflict and the resulting implications such as large-scale displacement have been recurrent themes in policy and conflict-analyst circles in recent years, particularly in the aftermath of the migration crisis that started in 2015. Twelve of the active conflicts started in 2009–19, while more than 60% of conflicts have been ongoing for ten years or longer. This raises questions about the prospects for conflict resolution in 2020.

Analysis in this year's *Armed Conflict Survey* suggests some glimpses of hope. Violence and hostilities have started to ease in Ukraine and Nagorno-Karabakh, and in Colombia, despite the presence and actions of FARC dissidents, the peace agreement between the government and the left-wing guerrilla group is likely to remain in place. Elsewhere, the insurgency targeting Egypt's Sinai Peninsula is losing fighting power, and violence in several African conflicts – the Central African Republic, Sudan, South Sudan and Nigeria's Farmer–Pastoralist – decreased compared to the previous year. In Pakistan, violence by the Tehrik-e-Taliban Pakistan declined, and 2019 marked the first year since 2003 without Pakistani or US airstrikes.

Most significant, however, was the lead-up to the historic deal the Taliban and the US government reached in February 2020. Following 18 months of negotiations, the agreement appeared to bring hope for the resolution of Afghanistan's nearly two-decade-long conflict (and American withdrawal) but also served as a reminder of the fragility and complexities of peace deals. Violence resumed only a few days later and there are significant hurdles to overcome regarding the role the Taliban will play in Afghan politics and society. Indeed, the challenge of implementing peace agreements remained a very tangible one in 2019, as evidence from Cameroon, the Democratic Republic of the Congo and Mali clearly indicates. The fragmentation of negotiating parties representing different factions, economic interests and agendas, often backed by different international actors, and capacity shortcomings, such as limited ability to reintegrate former armed groups into society, have proved serious obstacles to the implementation of many agreements.

Notes
[1] Brazil (Rio de Janeiro & Ceará), Cameroon, Central African Republic, Colombia (BACRIMs), Democratic Republic of the Congo, El Salvador, Ethiopia (Communal Violence), Honduras, Iraq, Israel–Palestine, Mexico (Cartels), Myanmar, Nigeria (Farmer–Pastoralist), Pakistan, Philippines (ASG & Moro), South Sudan, Southern Thailand, Sudan (Darfur, Blue Nile & South Kordofan), Syria, Turkey (PKK) and Yemen.

Notes on Methodology

The Armed Conflict Survey reviews and analyses the armed conflicts that are active worldwide every year. We define an armed conflict as a sustained military contest between two or more organised actors making purposive use of armed force. The inclusion of a conflict in the book is based on this definition and the methodology detailed below.

Armed conflicts in 2019

This year's *Armed Conflict Survey* includes 33 armed conflicts that were ongoing during the 2019 calendar year (1 January–31 December) in six world regions (Americas, Asia-Pacific, Europe and Eurasia, Middle East and North Africa, South Asia, and sub-Saharan Africa). The list of conflicts in the 2020 edition differs slightly from the 2019 edition. Firstly, the armed conflict in Ethiopia (Communal Violence) was added this year. It reflects the deterioration of relations between the federal government of Ethiopia and regional states, the deep inequality angering large sections of society, especially among the Oromo and Amhara ethnic groups, and the violent repression of social unrest. Secondly, certain conflicts have been grouped together based on common key characteristics, such as drivers or meaningful links between armed groups. Specifically, we have merged the Moro insurgency and the conflict between the Armed Forces of the Philippines and the Abu Sayyaf Group (ASG), which are now listed as Philippines (ASG & Moro). The new denomination more accurately reflects the relationship between the two phenomena and the ASG's genesis as a radical offshoot of Moro separatists. In addition, we have renamed the report 'Mali (The Sahel)' as 'The Sahel (Mali & Burkina Faso)' to reflect the regional dimension and expansion of the conflict, and the increase in conflict-related violence in northern and eastern Burkina Faso. 'Brazil (Rio de Janeiro)' is now listed as 'Brazil (Rio de Janeiro & Ceará)' to indicate that, in addition to conflict in Rio de Janeiro, the fight among criminal gangs and the security forces in the northeastern state of Ceará has escalated, and meets our criteria for inclusion as an armed conflict.

Despite the merging of conflicts in the Philippines, the unit of analysis in *The Armed Conflict Survey* remains the armed conflict itself – the military confrontation between armed actors – rather than the country in which it occurs. Most armed conflicts take place within the boundaries of a state and are therefore listed under those country names, although many do not affect the national territory as a whole. In Sudan, for example, the central state fights various armed groups in Blue Nile and South Kordofan states and in the Darfur region but, notwithstanding large protests in the capital in 2019, Khartoum has never become a theatre in these long-standing wars. Other conflicts, such as the Boko Haram insurgency, unfold across state boundaries, in this case involving territories in Cameroon, Chad, Niger and Nigeria.

Classification of armed conflicts

Conflict parties may be state or non-state actors. According to the types of actors involved and the interactions between them, armed conflicts fall into one of three categories: international (or inter-state), internal or internationalised. An *international* armed conflict takes place between two or more states (or a group of states) on the territory of one or several states, as well as the global commons. An *internal* armed conflict is fought by a government (and possibly allied armed groups) against one or more non-state actors, or between two or more non-state armed groups. An *internationalised* armed conflict is an internal conflict, in which the kernel of the dispute remains domestic, but one or more external states intervene militarily. Such involvement may include training, equipping or providing military intelligence to a conflict party, or participating in the hostilities either directly or through local proxies and sponsored actors.

Criteria for inclusion

The Armed Conflict Survey's definition of armed conflict requires combat between opposing actors. In order to be included, an armed confrontation must possess two characteristics: *duration* and *intensity*. We require an armed conflict to run for at least three months and feature violent incidents on a weekly or fortnightly basis. For wars between states – which feature substantial levels of military mobilisation, simultaneous and numerous armed clashes or significant fatalities – the duration threshold may be relaxed.

The third test for inclusion is the *organisation* of the conflict parties, namely their ability to plan and execute military operations. The scale of the attacks is not a factor in this determination – for the purpose of inclusion in *The Armed Conflict Survey*, for example, planting improvised explosive devices (IEDs) is equivalent to battlefield clashes. For armed conflicts that involve state parties, the deployment of armed forces or militarised (not regular) police is required. In the case of non-state conflict parties, the logistical and operational capacity of the group is key. This indicator includes access to weapons and other military equipment, as well as the ability to devise strategies and carry out operations, coordinate activities, establish communication between members (often based on existing social networks), and recruit and train personnel. The organisation of an armed actor does not require territorial control or a permanent base in an area. *The Armed Conflict Survey* also remains agnostic with regard to the type of organisational structure that armed groups adopt. Not all non-state groups engaged in armed conflicts have a distinct and effective chain of command, such as many of those operating in sub-Saharan Africa. Armed groups can be highly decentralised, maintain an amorphous structure, rely on a transnational network or have a global reach – a hierarchical military structure is therefore not an inclusion criterion.

The Armed Conflict Survey also applies two criteria for removal. Over time, certain armed conflicts lose the characteristics required for inclusion and are removed after two years. An armed conflict terminated through a peace agreement also ceases to be included following the military demobilisation of all conflict parties.

Methodological differences
Defining armed conflict simply as a military phenomenon rather than a legal one, *The Armed Conflict Survey* does not aim to determine the applicability of international humanitarian law to different conflict situations (as in the Geneva Conventions or the Rome Statute). Contrary to other datasets (notably the Uppsala Conflict Data Program and the Peace Research Institute Oslo's Correlates of War Project), *The Armed Conflict Survey*'s definition of armed conflict does not involve a numerical threshold of battle-related deaths.

The Armed Conflict Survey's methodology does not make distinctions based on the motivations driving an armed conflict, which may be political, ideological, religious or criminal. The book thus includes cases of internal conflicts in which only criminal organisations, rather than revolutionaries or separatists, fight each other and the state (such as in El Salvador, Honduras, Mexico and Rio de Janeiro).

Finally, *The Armed Conflict Survey* excludes cases involving the one-sided application of lethal force, terrorist attacks and public protests. Government repression, as well as ethnic cleansing or genocide, regardless of the scale, are not included if they occur outside a conflict situation, until the population displays a capacity to fight back through an armed, organised resistance, or another state wages war – as in the case of the Khmer Rouge regime in Cambodia when Vietnam invaded in 1979. Terrorist attacks may lead to the domestic deployment of armed forces, but these events are too rare to pass the intensity test. Situations with widespread but unorganised criminal activity are also excluded.

Key statistics

For each conflict, *The Armed Conflict Survey 2020* reports key statistics relevant to the context under analysis. The information in the tables at the beginning of each conflict report indicates the category of conflict (international, internal or internationalised), the start date of the conflict, and provides figures on displacement (refugees and internally displaced persons (IDPs)) and the number of people in need of humanitarian aid.

Refugees
The Armed Conflict Survey adopts the definition in Article 1A(2) of the 1951 UN Convention Relating to the Status of Refugees (also known as the Refugee Convention), according to which a refugee is a person who, 'owing to a well-founded fear of being persecuted for reasons of race, religion, nationality, membership of a particular social group or political opinion, is outside the country of his nationality and is unable, or owing to such fear, is unwilling to avail

himself of the protection of that country; or who, not having a nationality and being outside the country of his former habitual residence as a result of such events, is unable or, owing to such fear, is unwilling to return to it'. 'Refugees total' refers to the total number of refugees since the beginning of the conflict, as of the latest available date.

Internally displaced persons
The Armed Conflict Survey adopts the definition in the 1998 UN Guiding Principles on Internal Displacement, according to which IDPs are 'persons or groups of persons who have been forced or obliged to flee or to leave their homes or places of habitual residence, in particular as a result of or in order to avoid the effects of armed conflict, situations of generalized violence, violations of human rights or natural or human-made disasters, and who have not crossed an internationally recognized state border'. 'IDPs total' refers to the total number of IDPs since the beginning of the conflict, as of the latest available date.

People in need
The Armed Conflict Survey refers to people in need of humanitarian aid according to the criteria set out by the UN Office for the Coordination of Humanitarian Affairs (OCHA), which refer to basic services such as food, shelter, water and sanitation, healthcare and non-food items (such as clothing and hygiene kits). The figures refer to the latest date available.

Sources

Figures for refugees, IDPs and people in need are drawn from the sources listed in the table below.

Military data
Unless otherwise indicated, all figures related to military strength and capability, defence economics and arms equipment are from *The Military Balance*.

Key Statistics: sources			
Conflict	**IDPs**	**Refugees**	**People in need**
Brazil (Rio de Janeiro & Ceará)	n/a	n/a	n/a
Colombia (BACRIMs)	UN High Commissioner for Refugees (UNHCR), 'Global Trends: Forced Displacement in 2018'	UNHCR, 'Global Trends: Forced Displacement in 2018'	n/a
El Salvador	Internal Displacement Monitoring Centre (IDMC), Country Information: El Salvador	n/a	n/a
Honduras	IDMC, Country Information: Honduras	n/a	n/a
Mexico (Cartels)	Mexican Commission for the Defense and Promotion of Human Rights (CMDPDH)	Mexican Refugee Aid Commission, Mexican government	n/a
Myanmar (EAOs)	UN Office for the Coordination of Humanitarian Affairs (OCHA), 'Myanmar Humanitarian Needs Overview 2020', December 2019	OCHA, 'Myanmar Humanitarian Needs Overview 2020', December 2019; OCHA, 'Bangladesh: Rohingya Refugees and Host Communities Need Urgent Support', 26 April 2019; 'China Urges Kachins to Return to Myanmar and Join Peace Process', Radio Free Asia, 8 March 2019	OCHA, 'Global Humanitarian Overview (GHO), 2020'
Philippines (ASG & Moro)	Data collected by contributor for the IISS Armed Conflict Database (up to September 2019)	n/a	n/a
Philippines (NPA)	Data collected by contributor for the IISS Armed Conflict Database (up to September 2019)	n/a	n/a
Southern Thailand	n/a	n/a	n/a
Armenia–Azerbaijan (Nagorno-Karabakh)	n/a	n/a	n/a

Key Statistics: sources

Conflict	IDPs	Refugees	People in need
Ukraine	n/a	n/a	OCHA, 'GHO, 2020'
Egypt (Sinai)	n/a	n/a	n/a
Iraq	UNHCR, 'Iraq Fact Sheet', December 2019	UNHCR, 'Registered Iraqis in Jordan',15 January 2020; UNHCR, 'Turkey: Key Facts and Figures', January 2020	OCHA, 'Iraq: Humanitarian Bulletin, January 2020', 17 February 2020
Israel–Palestine	IDMC, 'Global Report on Internal Displacement', May 2019	UN Relief and Works Agency for Palestine Refugees (UNRWA), 'UNRWA in Figures', May 2019	OCHA, 'GHO, 2020'
Libya	UNHCR, Operational Portal: Refugee Situations – Libya	UNHCR, Operational Portal: Refugee Situations – Libya	OCHA, 'GHO, 2020'
Syria	OCHA, ReliefWeb Crisis Figures Data	OCHA, ReliefWeb Crisis Figures Data	OCHA, 'GHO, 2020'
Turkey (PKK)	IDMC, 'Global Report on Internal Displacement', May 2019	UNHCR, 'Mid-Year Trends 2018', January 2019	n/a
Yemen	UNHCR, Operational Portal: Refugee Situations – Yemen	UNHCR, Operational Portal: Refugee Situations – Yemen	OCHA, 'GHO, 2020'
Afghanistan	n/a	UNHCR	n/a
India (CPI–Maoist)	n/a	n/a	n/a
India (Northeast)	n/a	n/a	n/a
India–Pakistan (Kashmir)	n/a	n/a	n/a
Pakistan	n/a	n/a	OCHA, 'GHO, 2020'
Cameroon	UNHCR, Operational Portal: Refugee Situations – Cameroon	UNHCR, Operational Portal: Refugee Situations – Nigeria	OCHA, 'GHO, 2020'
Central African Republic	UNHCR, Operational Portal: Refugee Situations – Central African Republic	UNHCR, Operational Portal: Refugee Situations – Central African Republic	OCHA, 'GHO, 2020'
Democratic Republic of the Congo	UNHCR, Operational Portal: Refugee Situations – DRC	UNHCR, 'DR Congo Fact Sheet', December 2019	OCHA, 'GHO, 2020'
Ethiopia (Communal Violence)	UNHCR, Operational Portal: Refugee Situations – Ethiopia; UNHCR, 'Ethiopia Refugee Response Plan 2020–2021'	n/a	OCHA, 'GHO, 2020'
Lake Chad Basin (Boko Haram)	UNHCR, Operational Portal: Refugee Situations – Nigeria	UNHCR, Operational Portal: Refugee Situations – Nigeria	OCHA, 'GHO, 2020'
Nigeria (Farmer–Pastoralist)	n/a	n/a	n/a
The Sahel (Mali & Burkina Faso)	UNHCR, Operational Portal: Refugee Situations – Mali	UNHCR, Operational Portal: Refugee Situations – Mali	OCHA, 'Humanitarian Needs Increase in Burkina Faso/Mali/Niger', 19 November 2019
Somalia	UNHCR, Operational Portal: IDP Situations – Somalia	UNHCR, Operational Portal: Refugee Situations – Horn of Africa Somalia	OCHA, 'GHO, 2020'
South Sudan	UNHCR, Operational Portal: Refugee Situations – South Sudan	UNHCR, Operational Portal: Refugee Situations – South Sudan	OCHA, 'GHO, 2020'
Sudan (Darfur, Blue Nile & South Kordofan)	OCHA, Sudan – Internally Displaced Persons – IDPs; UNHCR: Global Focus: Sudan	UNHCR, 'Sudan Country Refugee Response Plan January 2020–December 2020'; UNHCR, Operational Portal: Refugee Situations – Sudan	OCHA, 'GHO, 2020'

GLOBAL TRENDS

A MILF Brigade Commander on his farm in Datu Piang, Maguindanao

Armed-Group Proliferation: Origins and Consequences

More non-state armed groups have emerged in the last eight years than in the previous eight decades.[1] During this period the Islamic State, also known as ISIS or ISIL, has attracted inordinate global concern, diverting attention from a trend that will define conflict in the coming decade: the proliferation of armed groups. These groups are built around highly adaptive alliances of smaller-scale units with diffuse leadership and authority. They act more like disruptive start-ups than standard corporations. By contrast, ISIS was organised like the centralised Marxist insurgencies of the late twentieth century, such as FARC in Colombia, Maoist groups in Nepal and India and the New People's Army in the Philippines.

The territorial defeat of ISIS, which functioned as a quasi-state, illustrates a shortcoming of its more formal organisational model. By contrast, armed insurgencies in Afghanistan and Iraq persist despite years of direct combat with US forces. Similarly in the Sahel, French forces aligned with Malian, Chadian and other local militaries continue to combat what often appears to be a nebulous constellation of jihadi forces. The loss of its caliphate may prompt ISIS to abandon its vertical structure in favour of a more horizontal one. Decentralised authority can be an advantage during times of insurgency and active combat – yet it can become a liability in peace negotiations, when the multiplicity of groups can impede dialogue and progress, or in peacetime, when groups' common cause may give way to competition for dominance or hinder state reassertion. Shifting alliances of armed groups require peacemakers to develop new methods of engaging and including local commanders in peace talks.

Libya, summer 2011

In 2011, small groups of fighters took up arms against Colonel Muammar Gadhafi across Libya in dozens of distinct armed revolts. In Misrata, Libya's third-largest city, the conflict began with hundreds of groups, many with fewer than 20 fighters, fighting an urban guerrilla campaign. These micro-groups outmanoeuvred government forces, merging, splintering, and devising new tactics and organisational structures. After defeating Gadhafi's security battalions downtown, however, these highly adaptive smaller groups were no match for traditional government tactics and armour in the open fields surrounding the city.[2] To address this challenge, the leaders of these small units negotiated alliances, uniting smaller units and dramatically increasing their firepower.[3] The commanders of many new alliances, often elected by the group, announced their formation on Facebook, in part to counter Libyan government claims of military victory.

Local commanders formed alliances with leaders they trusted, either because of relationships that predated the fighting or ones that were forged on the front lines. Once negotiated, the new coalitions continued to coordinate with NATO airpower and other insurgent groups in the city, attacking government forces in waves. Coalitions of such groups went on to defeat Gadhafi's security brigades.[4] The groups gradually developed closer ties and functioned more like a single organisation. But authority remained highly decentralised: sub-commanders did not cede their authority or autonomy, maintaining individual responsibility for fundraising, recruitment and weapons procurement.

Insurgents with centralised structures enjoy greater coordination and decision-making efficiency. However, these same features make them vulnerable to disruption, especially if the group's entire leadership is targeted. The loss of a leader of a horizontally organised group with decentralised authority has little effect on the group's functionality. This adaptability and resilience may come at the cost of organisational efficiency and military coordination, but often more than offsets that cost. The failure of the US military to defeat the Taliban – an integrated but militarily decentralised organisation – in Afghanistan illustrates the point.

Alternative models of insurgent organisation

Western ideals of organisation – and particularly military command and control – can blind analysts and practitioners to the capacity and benefits of horizontally organised insurgents. Observers of the conflicts in Libya and Syria, for example, have often concluded that insurgents were merely disorganised or chaotic due to an absence of strict hierarchies and top-down decision-making.[5] In fact, giving that appearance was actually an explicit strategy.[6] In Libya, for instance, assaults on government forces were typically carried out by hundreds of groups attacking at once. This tactic allowed key groups to hide among others, obscuring overall strategies until it was too late for the government to react.

Three features of horizontally organised armed groups are essential to understanding their approaches: leadership structure, decision-making and network strength. Decentralising military, political and administrative authority to lower-level commanders protects the organisation against 'decapitation strikes', as the absence of an operational chain of command reduces the disruption caused by the death of a senior leader.[7] The merely advisory role of the senior leader also allows that position to be more easily filled by another leader. And, although local or mid-level commanders wield a great deal of operational authority, the large number of them reduces the potential for adversaries to effectively target enough leaders to significantly impact a group.

Decision-making in a horizontally organised group is more deliberative and consensus-oriented than it is in hierarchical groups. Senior leaders make decisions after extensive consultation with mid-level commanders. This arrangement requires local commanders to be in regular contact with one another and to consult and negotiate on strategic issues.

Network strength is a more subtle and complicated matter. The relationship between sub-commanders in groups built around coalitions is highly personalised and egalitarian. These groups are therefore best understood as social networks. The interpersonal nature of such networks amplifies the role of a sub-commander's reputation, which becomes key to their unit's status. This can foster competition for prestige, recruits and resources, which can destabilise the group. While this dynamic can weaken networks, it also helps increase the long-term survival of the alliance by weeding out weak or ineffective commanders. Leaders of local al-Qaeda affiliates in Mali, for instance, have risen to command the regional branch through these evolving alliances.[8]

For similar reasons, alliances among decentralised armed groups can be fluid. If a local commander concludes that another insurgent group is on the rise, he may defect with his entire unit (usually about 50–100 fighters). Over time, this creates a natural-selection process whereby the most effective groups survive. Characterising such re-alignments as 'group fragmentation' may imply weakness when in fact a group is not losing strength and may even be gaining it.

Armed groups in current conflicts
Libya

In Libya circa 2011, hundreds of small-scale insurgent units defeated the government's forces. Each city produced its own groups. Political leaders, however, were able to form a single, unified organisation, the National Transitional Council (NTC), which became the face of the uprisings despite having no direct command over armed groups. The fighters' loyalty remained first and foremost to their original unit.[9] But this did not impede their capacity or willingness to coordinate their efforts with either their alliance partners or the hundreds of other groups fighting on the front lines.

During the Misrata uprising, attacks involved hundreds of groups advancing simultaneously, and were coordinated with NATO airstrikes.[10] Most fighters were unaware that these attacks were planned by only 15–20 commanders.[11] These leaders would gather the night before, review the GPS coordinates of all the insurgent groups along the front line, and use Google Earth to plan the attack. Messages would then be sent along the front lines communicating the time of the attack and the furthest point to which groups should advance, as coordinated with NATO. Select commanders would coordinate by VHF radio to ensure the key strategic points were taken while the rest of the groups simply advanced forward.

The decentralised and varied nature of these groups was an asset during urban fighting in Misrata, and in more conventional fighting scenarios, greater coordination was both possible and required. It became a liability, however, for consolidating peace and building a functional state that could ensure a monopoly on the use of force. Immediately following the war, the NTC ministries of defence and the interior put most of these groups on the government payroll, but with no consensus on how to transform them into a state military; most continued to operate independently and resisted efforts to unify and reform them. Two dynamics played out in parallel. Owing to local circumstances and solidarity, Misratan commanders continued to meet regularly after Gadhafi's death to manage security issues and political change in the city. Elsewhere, however, competition among small and medium-sized groups contributed to the descent of the country into civil war. Starting in 2015, Khalifa Haftar, a leading commander in eastern Libya, formed the Libyan National Army (which was renamed the Arab Libyan Armed Forces). Despite its name, it is a coalition of armed groups rather than an integrated force. He has, however, attracted significant foreign support and resources, which has emboldened him to attack Tripoli in a bid to take over the country.

Syria

The most striking feature of the Syrian conflict is the sheer number of armed groups involved. The Carter Center and other monitoring groups recorded the presence of thousands of armed actors and military councils in the ranks of the rebellion, the jihadi groups and ethnic organisations as well as pro-government militias, totalling over 250,000 fighters across the country. These groups continually collapsed, merged and splintered.

As in the Libyan conflict, in Syria a distinct split developed between political and military leadership. Beginning in March 2011, grassroots organisations coordinated non-violent protests across the country. Ostensibly modelled on Libya's NTC, attempts to form a national political opposition from hundreds of opposition parties, human-rights groups and diaspora associations took place by way of various international conferences. But Syrian opposition leaders were never able to consolidate power or legitimacy across the political spectrum, domestically or internationally. As a result, attempts to form centralised political or military leadership, such as the Syrian National Council or the Supreme Military Council of the Free Syrian Army, failed.

The organisation of armed groups in Syria mirrored the country's political and sectarian divisions.

In the government camp, local militias were formed, encouraged by intelligence officials; initially, they played a self-defence role, freeing up conventional manpower for offensive operations. Over time, however, these militias, either grouped under the banner of the National Defence Forces or operating in conjunction with conventional units, assumed a greater combat role. They reported either to Syrian or Iranian security officials; they often joined regime campaigns as junior partners, but at times also competed with them and developed their own economic and political interests. It was only when the rebel challenge to the regime of Bashar al-Assad was decisively defeated that the government took steps to reform, integrate and at times dismantle pro-regime militias.

In parallel, rebel groups were initially made up of soldiers who had defected from the army and joined up with highly localised neighbourhood-protection militias embedded in pre-existing community networks. The intensification of the fighting, international military support from the West and funding from private donors in Gulf countries gradually altered the community-based character of these groups. There were calls and incentives for unification. Coalitions emerged, especially of Islamist factions (such as the Islamic Front) and of southern rebel groups (the Southern Front), but these consisted of joint operations rooms rather than unified leadership, command-and-control and pooling of resources. The Free Syrian Army remained, as the Carter Center explained, 'more of an idea than a cohesive entity'.[12] On the battlefield, given the regime's firepower superiority and its organisational coherence, the rebels' horizontal organisation proved to be a strategic limitation, preventing the rebellion from mounting countrywide campaigns or sharing resources.

In contrast, the People's Protection Units (YPG), the main Kurdish militia, which received considerable US backing in the fight against ISIS, is a vertically structured organisation. The YPG formed a coalition known as the Syrian Democratic Forces (SDF) with Arab rebel groups across eastern Syria; these groups were horizontally structured.

In both the Libyan and Syrian conflicts, social media facilitated direct funding from wealthy individuals, fuelling the proliferation of small-scale groups on a local and regional basis. As the conflicts dragged on and funds dried up, many groups formed umbrella organisations to consolidate military and political influence and in some cases meet Western government conditions for support.[13] The structure of the armed opposition to the Assad government remained extremely decentralised, complicating any power-sharing accord. It was only when Turkey intervened in Syria, from 2016, that rebel groups in northern Syria began to unify under Turkish guidance. The effort has intensified since then, driven primarily by Turkish interests.

Implications for humanitarian and peacemaking actors

The trend towards horizontally structured armed groups has produced a far higher number of insurgents than those operating in the civil wars of the 1980s and 1990s.[14] The more groups that are active in a conflict zone, the more complex the conflict environment and the more intractable the war. States with already limited reach beyond major cities will become weaker, and local communities will feel compelled to fill the security vacuum. The resulting militias, such as the vigilante groups in Nigeria that coalesced to protect communities from Boko Haram, are likely to evolve horizontally. The flexibility and local adaptability of such armed groups pose unique challenges for peacemaking and post-conflict reconciliation. Additionally, Western governments' reduced political, military and development engagement in North Africa and the Middle East stands to accelerate the process of proliferation.

Humanitarian policy

For humanitarian agencies, the most serious consequences of organisational shifts in armed groups are the increased danger they pose for staff in the field and the fact that they complicate access to communities in need. Shifting coalitions and areas of control, and rivalries between sub-commanders, present field staff with an extraordinarily unpredictable environment. Local commanders of hierarchical groups generally respect their superiors' decisions and allow agencies to deliver humanitarian supplies. But senior leaders of armed groups built around coalitions have neither the authority nor the inclination to decide on issues that might appear to undermine the authority of local commanders. Humanitarian agencies must therefore negotiate with dozens of local commanders instead of one or two senior leaders, requiring them to dedicate significantly more time to networking with these groups and therefore also creating risks of entanglement and compromise. Larger humanitarian organisations like the International Committee of the Red Cross (ICRC) have the resources and specialised staff to handle this demand, but many smaller organisations do not and are no longer able to access these areas. Competition between local commanders also presents a danger. An agreement between a commander and a humanitarian organisation will not necessarily hold between the same organisation and other commanders. Indeed, successful negotiation with one commander might prompt another to dispute that decision in order to assert his authority and undermine the other commander's reputation. Humanitarian agencies have reported having to negotiate with scores of groups just to travel short distances.

International mediation

Decentralised insurgencies have limited the trajectory of international mediation policy. Lessons learned during the 1980s and 1990s in successful negotiations in South Africa, El Salvador, Northern Ireland and Bosnia–Herzegovina involved armed groups with centralised structures. Those lessons are not generally applicable to conflicts involving horizontally organised armed groups, insofar as they are predicated on the assumption that group leaders speak for and thoroughly control a group's membership.

One approach is to wait until there is sufficient consolidation among armed actors to fit existing approaches to mediation. But as the Syrian case demonstrates, that may never occur, and therefore this approach might ultimately prove futile. The theoretical solution is city-based dialogues involving multiple mediators operating continuously among women's groups, youth associations, local notables and military commanders for months, even years, with an eye to establishing a national consensus. Practically, however, most organisations lack the capacity, resources or persistence required to sustain such an effort. Furthermore, a unified international position would be needed to achieve political progress, but regional and international unity has proven elusive in recent conflicts in the Middle East and North Africa. Even allied nations such as France, Italy and the United Kingdom, for example, favour different factions in Libya. Accordingly, it seems likely that for some conflicts, at least in the short and medium term, mediators will have to adopt the more limited objective of bringing the foreign states fuelling these conflicts to the table. In certain cases, this approach may see regional powers help broker deals among the parties.

Notes

[1] The most-cited databases on armed conflict compiled by the Uppsala Conflict Data Program (UCDP) have documented hundreds of armed groups since the Second World War. By contrast, the Carter Center and others have recorded the emergence of thousands of armed groups since the onset of the civil war in Syria alone. Add to this the number of armed groups in Libya and the total far exceeds the UCDP sum. See Thérése Pettersson and Kristine Eck, 'Organized violence, 1989–2017', *Journal of Peace Research*, vol. 55, no. 4, July 2018, pp. 535–47; The Carter Center, 'Syria Countrywide Conflict Report #2', 20 November 2013; Brian McQuinn, 'After the Fall: Libya's Evolving Armed Groups', *Small Arms Survey*, 2012.

[2] 'Libyan rebels claim Misrata', Associated Press, 15 May 2011.

[3] Brian McQuinn, 'History's Warriors: The Emergence of Revolutionary Battalions in Misrata', in Peter Cole and Brian McQuinn (eds.), *The Libyan Revolution and its Aftermath* (London: Hurst, 2015), pp. 229–55.

[4] Brian McQuinn, 'Armed Groups in Libya: Typology and Roles', *Small Arms Survey Research Notes*, no. 18, June 2012.

[5] Anne Barnard, 'As Syria's Revolution Sputters, a Chaotic Stalemate', *New York Times*, 27 December 2014.

[6] For examples in Syria, see Jerome Drevon, 'The Jihadi Social Movement (JSM): Between Factional Hegemonic Drive, National Realities, and Transnational Ambitions', *Perspectives on Terrorism*, vol. 11, no. 6, December 2017, pp. 55–62. For examples in Libya, see McQuinn, 'History's Warriors: The Emergence of Revolutionary Battalions in Misrata'.

[7] Jenna Jordan, 'When Heads Roll: Assessing the Effectiveness of Leadership Decapitation', *Security Studies*, vol. 18, no. 4, December 2009, pp. 719–55.

[8] Nicolas Desgrais, Yvan Guichaoua and Andrew Lebovich, 'Unity is the exception. Alliance formation and de-formation among armed actors in Northern Mali', *Small Wars & Insurgencies*, vol. 29, no. 4, August 2018, pp. 654–79.

[9] McQuinn, 'After the Fall: Libya's Evolving Armed Groups'.

[10] Eric Schmitt and Steven Lee Myers, 'Surveillance and Coordination with NATO Aided Rebels', *New York Times*, 21 August 2011.

[11] McQuinn, 'History's Warriors: The Emergence of Revolutionary Battalions in Misrata'.

[12] The Carter Center, 'Syria Countrywide Conflict Report #2', p. 5.

[13] Ghaith Abdul-Ahad, 'How to Start a Battalion (in Five Easy Lessons)', *London Review of Books*, vol. 35, no. 4, 21 February 2013, pp. 13–14.

[14] See endnote 1.

Non-state Armed Groups and UAVs: Uptake and Effectiveness

Policymakers and security experts are increasingly concerned about what non-state armed groups (NSAGs) – including terrorist organisations – might do with uninhabited aerial vehicles (UAVs), commonly known as drones, now that they have become commercially available. Critically, however, NSAGs cannot weaponise non-military UAVs quickly or easily, and generally face a steep learning curve. By way of comparison, the construction and employment of improvised explosive devices (IEDs) during the Iraq and Afghanistan wars was gradual and depended not only on the commercial availability of the technology but also the transfer of technical expertise within and among NSAGs and the efficient production of the devices. The additional complication of delivering the munitions aerially makes the UAV challenge qualitatively greater than the IED one. It is unlikely that NSAGs will be able to use UAVS to strike moving targets effectively in the near future, particularly when using commercial off-the-shelf (COTS) systems.

Known uses of UAVs by NSAGs

Use of UAVs by NSAGs is geographically uneven. While increasingly common in conflicts in the Middle East and North Africa, it is rare elsewhere for a variety of reasons. While COTS UAVs are now available almost anywhere in the world, affordability and ease of access still vary significantly. This is among the reasons why the Middle East has comparatively higher numbers of COTS UAVs being used by NSAGs than regions such as Central Africa. Geography is another factor: UAVs are of limited use in heavily forested areas, or in places with very high winds. Perhaps the key inhibiting factor, though, is limited knowledge and expertise. Terrorist attacks using UAVs in several countries have either failed operationally or been interdicted at the planning stage. Japanese cult Aum Shinrikyo once tried to use a remote-controlled helicopter to disperse sarin gas in an assassination attempt, but the helicopter crashed and the vaporisation system caught fire.

The group reverted to simpler dispersion methods.[1] Individuals have also been convicted of planning to use UAVs in foiled terrorist attacks in the US, the United Kingdom and Italy.[2]

In Ukraine, state forces as well as insurgents with the benefit of expert Russian guidance have adapted increasingly sophisticated COTS UAVs but used them mainly for intelligence, surveillance and reconnaissance (ISR) purposes to minimise risks to manned aircraft. Both sides are experimenting with weaponised UAV systems and have made design improvements throughout the war. For instance, earlier weaponised UAVs deployed by separatists in the Donbas consisted of a grenade tied to a string, detonated by the pilot shaking the UAV until the firing pin loosened. In 2017, however, Ukrainian forces recovered an adapted COTS UAV that used a photocell release mechanism to trigger the grenade.[3]

Similarly, until recently drug cartels in Latin America had largely limited their use of UAVs to aerial smuggling. However, in July 2018 in Baja California, Mexico, a cartel dropped IEDs from a UAV onto a state official's residence, though the devices appeared to be designed to intimidate rather than to actually explode. In October 2017 in Guanajuato, Mexico, a weaponised quadcopter with operable IEDs and a remote detonator was seized in a vehicle stop.[4]

Sub-Saharan African and Asian NSAGs appear to have made little use of UAVs. Nigeria-based Boko Haram is rumoured to possess UAVs, but there is no substantiated open-source intelligence about its use of the devices.[5] Somalia's al-Shabaab has extensive financial resources, making millions of dollars each year from the illegal charcoal trade alone, and the group's geographical proximity to Yemen and known links to illicit trade networks would presumably ease its acquisition of UAVs. They are also well suited to the group's targeting of urban areas. But al-Shabaab apparently prefers to rely on more conventional terrorist tactics and methods, possibly calculating that the investment of time and money to develop a UAV capability would not yield commensurately superior results. The group may also realise that while a UAV attack on civilians would certainly cause alarm, it would be unlikely to result in large-scale destruction or mass casualties. A UAV attack may become a more attractive option where an NSAG seeks to psychologically intimidate a target population while limiting casualties.

Use of UAVs in the Middle East

Across Iraq, Israel, Lebanon, Saudi Arabia, Syria, the United Arab Emirates (UAE) and Yemen, UAVs have functioned as instruments of signalling and propaganda, and to some extent as 'a poor man's air force'.[6] There are three primary reasons. Firstly, state actors have facilitated the transfer of UAV systems and their constituent components to NSAGs, at times relying on illicit trade networks. Secondly, COTS UAVs have been widely available in the region. Thirdly, significant knowledge transfer from both state actors and non-state experts has afforded some NSAGs practical self-sufficiency in UAV production and operation.

Lebanese Hizbullah is the most prominent example. In 2002, Iran supplied Hizbullah with the *Ababil* UAV system.[7] Two years later, the group expanded its arsenal by acquiring the *Mirsad-1* – believed to be a modified version of Iran's *Mohajer* UAV. Hizbullah's use of the latter to enter Israeli airspace for a 20-minute reconnaissance mission in 2004 marked the first known deployment of a UAV by an NSAG. Hizbullah Executive Council member Nabil Qaouk declared that the mission was intended to signal Hizbullah's ability to respond in kind to Israeli extraterritorial incursions into Lebanon.[8] That same year, Hizbullah Secretary-General Hassan Nasrallah stated that the *Mirsad-1* could carry 40 kilograms of explosives.[9] In 2012, Hizbullah deployed an *Ayoub* UAV over Israel's Negev desert for ISR purposes, reportedly capturing images of Israel's Dimona nuclear facility. Although the Israelis destroyed the UAV shortly thereafter, the episode imparted Tehran's ability to target strategically important Israeli assets through Hizbullah at a time when Israel was targeting Iran's nuclear programme. Nasrallah effectively communicated the geostrategic value of Hizbullah's UAV arsenal to Iran by stating that the UAV had been assembled in Lebanon but was of Iranian origin.

More recently, Iran has transferred UAVs to another strategic ally: Yemen's Houthi movement (Ansarullah). In September 2019, Ansarullah claimed responsibility for the attacks on Saudi Arabian oil infrastructure at Abqaiq and Khurais. The attack involved UAVs and cruise missiles and did significant damage, cutting Saudi oil production by about half for more than a week. Riyadh blamed Iran for the attacks, as did Washington, given the sophistication of the attacks. Irrespective of these particular attacks, the wider use of UAVs by Ansarullah is incontrovertible. According to the 2018 United Nations Panel of Experts report on Yemen, in 2016 the UAE Presidential Guard seized a truck that contained 'at least six complete *Qasef*-1 UAVs and some components for up to another 24 UAVs'.[10] The UN Panel of Experts traced the components of the *Qasef*-1 to a range of sources, including Indian entities as well as Chinese and Ukrainian manufacturers.[11] Although Iran disavowed any policy of transferring arms to Yemen, the gyroscope of the *Qasef*-1 matched that of the Iranian *Ababil*-3 UAV, which had been recovered from use in Iraq, in design, dimensions and capability.[12] Iran has provided the *Yasir* ISR UAV to Kataib Hizbullah and Harakat al-Nujaba – two Iraqi Shia militias that form part of Iraq's Popular Mobilisation Units – to help locate and target Islamic State, also known as ISIS or ISIL, units and assets.[13] The *Yasir* is reportedly a reverse-engineered version of the Boeing Insitu *ScanEagle*.

Hizbullah has used COTS systems in Syria, in 2016 deploying a munition-rigged quadcopter against a Syrian opposition position in Aleppo.[14] COTS systems offer a cheaper alternative to systems such as the *Mirsad-1* and the *Ayoub*, and are more expendable and easily replaceable. In 2017, the Houthis began releasing infographics showcasing the range of UAVs in their possession. Among them was the *Rased* – a COTS system known commercially as the Chinese-made *Skywalker* X8. This system, while not a weaponised platform, has featured significantly in Ansarullah's propaganda, in which the commercial system has been styled to look indigenously produced.

Reports indicate that ISIS has also built its own UAV systems.[15] The value of these in terms of ISR and the psychological effect on enemy forces has been significant. The first known deployment of a COTS quadcopter by ISIS was in Syria in 2014, as part of an ISR operation.[16] In 2016, it deployed UAV-borne IEDs against Kurdish Peshmerga fighters in Iraq, killing two.[17] ISIS also procured hobbyist COTS systems and repurposed them, using plastic tubes as launchers to propel makeshift IEDs or 40 mm munitions.[18]

Accumulated expertise has made the group's use of UAVs more efficient. As the battle for Mosul progressed in 2017, ISIS developed increasing accuracy in the control and navigation of COTS systems and greater experience with munitions-release systems.[19] Its UAV operations attained greater precision as they moved from imagery acquisition for propaganda production, to ISR for tactical purposes, to weaponisation. However, towards the end of 2017, ISIS faced significant financial limitations. More critically, Chinese UAV maker DJI – from which ISIS acquired most of its COTS systems – established a 'geofencing' software protocol to prevent its UAVs being used across some areas of Iraq and Syria.[20]

ISIS improvised. Also found in Mosul were makeshift, plastic, fixed-wing UAVs and remote-controlled helicopters, which ISIS deployed to overcome financial costs, navigational barriers and a scarcity of resources.[21] In Syria, the bomblet-strapped UAVs deployed by opposition forces that targeted Russia's air base in Khmeimim in January 2018 were constructed from plywood and very simple GPS antennae for navigation, bound together with tape.[22] Owing to their use of satellite navigation through preset waypoints, they constitute a plausible – albeit less capable – alternative to the DJI systems. More broadly, their low cost and replaceability make them a sensible choice for NSAGs with limited resources.

The transfer of knowledge of UAV construction and operation from state and non-state entities to NSAGs has also helped concentrate UAV use in the Middle East. Hizbullah UAV operators were reportedly trained in Iran by the Islamic Revolutionary Guard Corps (IRGC).[23] In addition, the IRGC and Hizbullah have worked in tandem on UAV operations in Syria.[24] There is evidence that UAV construction and piloting is becoming an increasingly specialised role within Middle Eastern NSAGs. In 2017, recovered ISIS documents revealed standardised maintenance and operational practices for its UAV programme, and English-language procurement and acquisition lists for UAV parts, COTS systems and modifications.[25] Additionally, all ISIS personnel operating in its UAV factories were foreign, suggesting a focused recruitment drive for UAV specialists. In a similar vein, in November 2019 the Syrian jihadist group Hayat Tahrir al-Sham sought to enlist sophisticated aerial-reconnaissance operators.[26] The goal of such efforts would be to internalise and perpetuate expert knowledge within the organisation.

Satellite navigation: an accelerant of capability?

The use of UAVs poses significant operational challenges even to NSAGs with outside assistance. While UAVs may be guided manually with a high degree of precision by a person close to the target, the operator must be skilled and remains exposed to considerable risk. Operating at greater range complicates the targeting and deployment process, as it requires further technical input via 'line-of-sight' communications, which in turn are limited by the curvature of the Earth and by geographical features such as hills. To operate beyond line-of-sight ranges, some form of datalink is required, but that calls for placing ground-based relays close to the target, which may be strongly defended.

Satellite navigation, however, provides a more straightforward – and less technologically taxing – means of targeting. As noted, ISIS and other Syrian rebel forces have employed GPS antennae in low-cost UAVs.[27] By presetting navigational waypoints for UAVs to follow en route to their targets, NSAGs can rely on satellite navigation without requiring operator exposure or datalinks. Such a dispensation reduces the need for expertise in operating the UAV.

Conclusion

NSAGs' use of armed UAVs has empowered them, but the threat posed by such use has not reached its peak. Adoption of UAVs by NSAGs for ISR purposes is also an ongoing challenge, as valuable targeting information can be gained by using commercial UAVs to support conventional attacks. Weaponised UAVs will probably continue to proliferate, but unevenly and selectively. The explosive payload that non-military UAVs can carry is small compared to that which can be placed in, for example, a car. If an NSAG possessing only adapted commercial UAVs is aiming for maximum destruction, it is unlikely to use a UAV. However, an NSAG wishing to attack a relatively vulnerable fixed target could make effective use of a UAV. Furthermore, the propaganda value of a UAV attack is substantial, which makes the devices a tempting option for NSAGs seeking political attention. Technological change will introduce new possibilities but, to take full operational advantage of those, NSAGs will need time to develop corresponding technical expertise.

Notes

1. Larry Friese with N.R. Jenzen-Jones and Michael Smallwood, 'Emerging Unmanned Threats: The use of commercially-available UAVs by armed non-state actors', Armament Research Services, February 2016; 'Chronology of Aum Shinrikiyo's CBW Activities', Middlebury Institute for International Studies at Monterey, 2001.
2. Friese with Jenzen-Jones and Smallwood, 'Emerging Unmanned Threats: The use of commercially-available UAVs by armed non-state actors'.
3. Scott Crino and Andy Dreby, 'Drone Technology Proliferation in Small Wars', Small Wars Journal, 3 October 2019.
4. Parker Asmann, 'Are Armed Drones the Weapon of the Future for Mexico's Cartels?', InSight Crime, 15 August 2018; Christopher Woody, 'Drones appear to be taking on a bigger, more dangerous role in Mexico's criminal warfare', Business Insider, 25 October 2017.
5. Dionne Searcey, 'Boko Haram Is Back. With Better Drones', *New York Times*, 13 September 2019.
6. 'The air force of the poor', SRF, 14 September 2019.
7. Ronen Bergman, 'Hezbollah stockpiling drones in anticipation of Israeli strike', Al-Monitor, 15 February 2013.
8. 'Hezbollah sends first reconnaissance drone into Israeli territory', AP Archive, YouTube, 23 July 2015.
9. 'Explained: Unmanned aircraft', *Guardian*, 15 July 2006.
10. United Nations Panel of Experts on Yemen, 'Letter dated 26 January 2018 from the Panel of Experts on Yemen mandated by Security Council resolution 2342 (2017) addressed to the President of the Security Council', p. 154.
11. Ibid., p. 157.
12. Ibid., p. 156.
13. Austin Michael Bodetti, 'How Iranian-Backed Shia Militias Got US Drones', Offiziere.ch, 6 June 2017.
14. David Axe, 'Hezbollah Drone is Warning to the US', Daily Beast, 17 August 2016.
15. Kelsey D. Atherton, 'What We Know About ISIS's Scratch-built Drones', Popular Science, 7 November 2016.
16. Ibid.
17. Michael S. Schmidt and Eric Schmitt, 'Pentagon Confronts a New Threat from ISIS: Exploding Drones', *New York Times*, 11 October 2016; Don Rassler, Muhammad Al-`Ubaydi and Vera Mironova, 'The Islamic State's Drone Documents: Management, Acquisitions, and DIY Tradecraft', Combating Terrorism Center at West Point, 31 January 2017.
18. Don Rassler, 'The Islamic State and Drones: Supply, Scale, and Future Threats', Combating Terrorism Center at West Point, July 2018, pp. 3 and 9; Peter Layton, 'Commercial drones: Privatising air power', *Interpreter*, 27 September 2017.
19. Nick Waters (@N_Waters89), 'Here it is. Every drone strike published by Islamic State in 2017. (I believe.) 208 strikes, 450+ images & videos. This was based on a year of leveraging every source possible to collate this data. Free to use with credit. Lets [sic] see what we learned: https://t.co/iRnQUHTMmJ', 18 January 2018, Tweet.
20. David Grossman, 'DJI Deactivates Its Drones in Parts of Iraq and Syria', *Popular Mechanics*, 27 April 2017.
21. Tom Westcott, 'Death from above: IS drones strike terror in "safe" areas of Mosul', Middle East Eye, 10 August 2017.
22. Nick Waters, 'The Poor Man's Air Force? Rebel Drones Attack Russia's Airbase in Syria', Bellingcat, 12 January 2018.
23. Eugene Miasnikov, 'Terrorists Develop Unmanned Aerial Vehicles: On "Mirsad 1" Flight Over Israel', Center for Arms Control, Energy and Environmental Studies at Moscow Institute of Physics and Technology, 6 December 2004.
24. 'Hezbollah drone operations celebrated in museum', Arabian Aerospace Online News Service, 4 February 2019.
25. Rassler, Al-`Ubaydi and Mironova, 'The Islamic State's Drone Documents: Management, Acquisitions, and DIY Tradecraft'.
26. Elizabeth Tsurkov (@Elizrael), 'New Hayat Tahrir al-Sham internal recruitment announcement for its aerial reconnaissance unit. Unlike recruitment calls for combat armies, special forces, sniper & artillery units, this notice includes among its criteria high intelligence & demands a 6-months [sic] commitment.', 16 November 2019, Tweet.
27. Waters, 'The Poor Man's Air Force? Rebel Drones Attack Russia's Airbase in Syria'; Rassler, Al-`Ubaydi and Mironova, 'The Islamic State's Drone Documents: Management, Acquisitions, and DIY Tradecraft'.

ISIS Foreign Fighters after the Fall of the Caliphate

With the fall of Baghouz, the last Syrian village controlled by the Islamic State (also known as ISIS or ISIL) in March 2019, the Syrian Democratic Forces (SDF) officially declared 'the destruction of the so-called Islamic State organisation'.[1] But while the Islamic State as a *state-like* organisation has indeed been destroyed, ISIS as a terrorist organisation remains robust.

Since mid-2017, military advances achieved by the United States-led Combined Joint Task Force engaged in *Operation Inherent Resolve* (CJTF–OIR), the anti-ISIS campaign in Iraq and Syria, had already pushed ISIS to abandon conventional fighting and overt control of territory to revert back to insurgency-like strategies,[2] eventually compromising its ability to hold territory but only degrading its ability to fight. In early 2019, US estimates put the number of local and foreign ISIS fighters still active around the Middle Euphrates River Valley at 2,000, with an estimated flow of 50 new foreign fighters entering the area to join ISIS ranks each month.[3]

The flow of foreign fighters moves in multiple directions, further compounding the problem: if one of ISIS's critical lifelines comes from the movement of jihadists *into* the organisation, the international community's efforts to tackle the phenomenon also have to deal with the flow of foreign fighters attempting to return to their countries of origin, and with those attempting to relocate *across* areas where ISIS is still present. Even more problematic is the lack of coordination so far demonstrated by governments involved in these tasks. A short-term, wait-and-see international response to the management of captured foreign fighters has left countries of origin more, rather than less, vulnerable. As Turkey's military advance under the banner of *Operation Peace Spring* has put the country in charge of thousands of ISIS detainees in northern Syria, Turkish President Recep Tayyip Erdogan has been using unilateral repatriations of European and American foreign fighters for diplomatic leverage.[4]

Given the phenomenon's multidirectional flow and the range of pathways available to aspiring and veteran foreign fighters, it is possible to group ISIS foreign fighters into four categories. Firstly, 'new foreign fighters' and 'remainers' are either those attempting to reach Iraq, Syria or another ISIS branch (*wilayat*) around the world from their own country, or ISIS veterans who remained in Iraq and Syria after the fall of the caliphate. Secondly, 'relocators' are those who have moved to other *wilayat*. Thirdly, 'captured' are those who are currently detained, either in their countries of origin or abroad, as well as those who have been repatriated after capture. Finally, 'returnees' and 'untracked' are those who have returned to their home countries undetected or without being prosecuted or charged, or who are expected to attempt to do so.

Each of these categories poses challenges of its own. While Western governments grapple with the thorny issue of how to deal with their citizens currently detained as foreign fighters in Syria and Iraq, the flow of veteran fighters to other locations, such as Southeast Asia and Africa, underlines ISIS's resilience as an organisation. Meanwhile, the fragile security situation in Syria and Iraq might effectively revive it at its core.

The rise of ISIS foreign fighters between 2013 and 2018

The international community responded urgently to foreign fighters joining ISIS as the organisation expanded its presence in Iraq and Syria. The United Nations Security Council (UNSC) passed Resolution 2178 in September 2014 and Resolution 2396 in December 2017. Among other things, these resolutions provided a definition of 'foreign terrorist fighters';[5] encouraged member states to strengthen their traveller risk-assessment and screening procedures; and, most importantly, urged all countries 'to intensify and accelerate the exchange of operational information regarding actions or movements' of suspected or known foreign fighters, stressing the international dimension of the problem and the need for transnational cooperation.[6]

Individual states face numerous and complex challenges in dealing with the movement of foreign fighters. Identifying aspiring foreign fighters attempting to leave is a complex task. To avoid raising suspicions, those who are trying to leave will reach conflict zones through 'transit' countries from which they will then be helped into their final destination by local fixers or ISIS smugglers. The Istanbul–Gaziantep–Kilis route into Syria, for example, has led thousands of foreign fighters from around the world into the country, becoming known as the 'Jihadi Highway'.[7] Prosecuting those who have returned from conflict zones and been charged with being foreign fighters is hard. Collecting evidence on their actions in the caliphate and gathering enough intelligence to present in court have both proven difficult.[8] Lastly, taking charge of those foreign fighters who have been captured abroad does not always seem to be a priority for governments of the countries from which they originated.

Over the years, ISIS put together the 'most operationally experienced, lethally skilled and highly networked group of jihadis to date'.[9] Particularly since the official establishment of the caliphate in June 2014, there has been exponential growth in the number of ISIS foreign fighters in Iraq and Syria, from 6,000 in 2013,[10] to an estimated 20,000 foreign fighters in 2015,[11] up to more than 40,000 in 2017, according to UN data.[12]

After the Islamic State proclaimed the establishment of the caliphate, new *wilayat* were declared under ISIS control. In 2014, the organisation's expansion reached parts of Egypt, Yemen, Saudi Arabia and Algeria. In January 2015, a group of Afghan and Pakistani jihadist groups joined ISIS under the banner of Wilayat Khorasan, while in June 2015, various insurgent groups of the North Caucasus pledged their allegiance to ISIS, forming Wilayat al-Qawqaz. This put Russia directly in ISIS's crosshairs, as demonstrated a few months later by the attack on the Russian Metrojet flight over Sinai that killed 224 people, the vast majority Russian.[13]

While territorial control over *wilayat* in Libya and Afghanistan was quickly lost, in 2017 the so-called 'Siege of Marawi' demonstrated ISIS's growing strength in Southeast Asia. A town of 200,000 inhabitants located on an island in the Southern Philippines, Marawi was captured by 900 jihadists, with 40 foreign fighters leading combat operations. After five months of intense urban fighting, the Armed Forces of the Philippines eventually regained control – ISIS, however, had already achieved an important propaganda victory, putting the Philippines more firmly on the jihadist map and driving at least 100 new foreign fighters to join its militias in the country.[14]

Temporary achievements in Southeast Asia, however, contrasted with the rapid decline of the caliphate's presence in the Middle East: the expansion of CJTF–OIR operations against the heartland of the caliphate meant that, by February 2018, ISIS had lost over 98% of its formerly controlled territories in Iraq and Syria, with most of its foreign fighters either dead, fighting in the last pockets of resistance or fleeing.

While the eventual collapse of the caliphate has deprived ISIS of a territory it could directly control, the organisation has quickly reverted to its insurgency roots, scattering across eastern Syria and Iraq, and attempting to regroup and take back the initiative. In one of his last messages to ISIS fighters, then-leader Abu Bakr al-Baghdadi released an audio message in September 2019, calling on all fighters to continue their war: 'From [Afghanistan] to Iraq to Yemen, to Somalia to western and central Africa, eastern Asia, northern Africa: sacrifice your lives if you have to.'[15]

New foreign fighters and remainers

The flow of foreign fighters has turned to a trickle compared to 2013–17, owing to factors including the absence of a physical safe haven for fighters to reach (i.e. the caliphate) and stricter international controls. However, the mobilisation of foreign fighters towards Iraq and Syria has not stopped. The most recent CJTF–OIR estimates say that, as of mid-2019, 'ISIS likely retains between 14,000 and 18,000 "members" in Iraq and Syria, including up to 3,000 foreigners'.[16] Recruitment from outside Iraq and Syria is ongoing, with the constant arrival of new recruits adding to the challenge of fully eradicating ISIS from those countries.[17]

Quantifying ISIS foreign fighters still operating between Iraq and Syria is no small task. Militants are once again adopting insurgent tactics. They maintain a minimal military footprint and overall visibility, operate mainly in rural and remote areas and rely on safe houses and tunnels to stay 'below the radar'. New foreign fighters remain a main lifeline in this context.[18]

Research carried out on European foreign fighters shows how, contrary to expectations, the vast majority have not returned to their country of origin after ISIS was put on the back foot by the CJTF–OIR military advance. While many have been captured by anti-ISIS forces, a large proportion of surviving foreign fighters likely remained in ISIS's last pockets of resistance to 'fight to the death',[19] either out of ideological commitment or because the strong military presence around ISIS territories made leaving the area undetected much more difficult than in the past.[20]

While new foreign fighters and remainers represent the most visible manifestation of the foreign-fighter phenomenon, strategic challenges related to relocators, returnees and captured foreign fighters are becoming increasingly pressing. As former chairman of the US Joint Chiefs of Staff General Joseph Dunford highlighted, 'the flow of foreign fighters, the ability to move resources, and the ideology that allows these groups to operate'[21] are the connective tissue that allows ISIS to survive – and the flow of foreign fighters *into* Syria and Iraq is only one aspect of a broader problem.[22]

Relocators

So-called relocators, or foreign fighters who have left one front-line to join the fight elsewhere, are particularly important because their mobility enables ISIS to evade direct confrontation and to strengthen recruitment efforts across the world. ISIS reportedly relocated at least 5,600 fighters out of Iraq and Syria during 2014–17,[23] but estimates on the overall number of fighters that have relocated are unreliable.[24]

Significant relocation trends warrant attention, however, especially when considering group, rather than individual, relocation. One of the most substantial contingents in this category is from the North Caucasus. 2015 estimates put the overall number of Russian ISIS fighters active in Iraq and Syria at 4,000–5,000,[25] a large number of whom are Chechen and Dagestani veteran jihadists[26] who pledged allegiance to the caliphate and moved their armed struggle to Syria due to the de-escalation of the conflict at home.[27]

Other notable relocation waves have taken place in response to ISIS's strategic needs and direct calls. In 2015, the organisation's media outlets asked militants to join the fight in Libya. Its local militias were preparing a military offensive to expand the territory that their *wilayat* controlled there, while also enticing Sudanese volunteers to enter Libya via smuggling routes with the promise of a salary.[28] In the same year, ISIS spokesperson Abu Muhammad al-Adnani 'repeatedly called for Muslims to emigrate to other "provinces" abroad including Yemen, the Arabian Peninsula, Afghanistan, and West Africa'.[29]

In 2017, as pressure on ISIS militias in Iraq and Syria started to mount, other *wilayat* stepped in to take charge of coordinating attacks abroad and to welcome the foreign fighters who could not circumvent security forces to enter Syria. In addition, thousands of ISIS fighters fled from ISIS-held locations in Syria, mainly into Turkey and then on to other destinations, often negotiating their withdrawals with their enemies.[30] Over that period, the propaganda victory brought by the 2017 Siege of Marawi, coupled with the difficulties in reaching Iraq and Syria, paved the way for the Philippines, Indonesia and Malaysia to become priority relocation destinations for veteran foreign fighters.[31]

Monitoring and challenging the flow of relocators presents important and specific operational challenges for governments tracking their national foreign fighters abroad. These fighters' evasive techniques include transiting through various countries and sometimes temporarily resettling in them. Journeys from one front-line to another can take several months and take in various countries of residence, making multilateral intelligence sharing and cooperation critical in combatting the flow of relocators. Accordingly, the role of Interpol has become of fundamental importance in tackling the mobility of foreign fighters, so much so that UNSC Resolution 2396 (2017) has recognised Interpol's contribution in addressing the challenge posed by foreign fighters, while UNSC Resolution 2462 (2019) formally 'encourages Member States to make the best use of Interpol policing capabilities, such as relevant databases and analytical files'.[32]

Captured foreign fighters

The long-overlooked question of how to deal with captured foreign fighters is now becoming a pressing issue, as surrendering fighters and their families are massing in large numbers in SDF-controlled prisons. Despite appeals from the UN for the international community to increase its coordination efforts,[33] governments are avoiding taking charge of the repatriation, trial, detention and eventual reintegration of thousands of ISIS affiliates.[34]

UNSC Resolution 2178 (2014) provides a definition of 'foreign terrorist fighter' and thus created a legal category that member states can use to develop domestic legal frameworks to prosecute individuals who travel abroad to participate in terrorist acts. Many national approaches have emerged, but none has yet successfully addressed the 'difficulty of securing a criminal conviction'.[35] Prosecutors face major difficulties in finding evidence on individuals who operated in war zones.[36]

As of September 2019, 17,000 prisoners charged with terrorism offences were held in Iraqi prisons.[37] While most were ISIS fighters, the tally also included their wives and children. Until mid-October, the SDF alone held another 10,000 prisoners in 'pop-up prisons' in Syria. Of these, 2,000 were foreign fighters,[38] 500 women (wives or widows of foreign combatants), 'more than 1,000 children associated with the foreign ISIS fighters in their custody' (as of the beginning of 2019),[39] and 'thousands of children above the age of 12 – considered to be of "fighting age" – ... held in incommunicado detention'.[40]

The SDF's inability to manage such large groups of prisoners was already apparent after the US began reducing its military presence from the beginning of 2019,[41] and Turkish declarations of a possible military advance into SDF-held territories further exacerbated the problem,[42] with SDF representatives stating that they may have to release a large number of ISIS detainees in the event of such an offensive.[43] As a consequence, the US[44] – which has only an estimated 272 ISIS affiliates of its own[45] – took a leading role in coordinating the response and committed 'to assist in repatriation of foreign ISIS fighters to their home countries and to identify potential alternatives for long-term detention of those who cannot be repatriated'.[46]

The sudden withdrawal of all US military forces from northern Syria in October 2019, and the subsequent incursion of Turkish forces into SDF-held territories, however, saw the situation quickly spiral out of control: many SDF units were repositioned away from ISIS detention facilities to the front-lines, leaving prison camps severely undermanned.[47] As the Turkish military advance progressed, Turkey took control of several detention facilities; the chaos ensuing from the transition facilitated the escape of an unspecified number of ISIS fighters, with at least 76 jihadists reportedly joining Turkey-backed Syrian militias operating in northern Syria.[48]

Controlling these detention camps is a double-edged sword for Turkey, as it gives President Erdogan a bargaining chip with Western governments while further intensifying international scrutiny. Unfazed by the responsibility, ahead of an official visit to the US in November Erdogan and his minister of the interior stated they were going to repatriate European foreign fighters that were held by Turkish security forces 'in 72 hours',[49] in a move that echoes the recurrent threat of 'opening the gates' and letting Syrian refugees currently located in Turkey into the EU.[50] In mid-November, the first repatriation by Turkey saw a British foreign fighter returned to UK soil.

With one of the largest foreign-fighter contingents in Europe,[51] and 250–300 captured British foreign fighters currently held in Syria,[52] the UK's 'not-in-my-backyard' response is just one example of how returning captured foreign fighters have become a contentious political and diplomatic issue. Once captured, dual-nationality foreign fighters have been stripped of their UK citizenship, in line with legislation previously passed. The Canadian government lamented in August 2019 that in this way the UK was 'offloading its responsibilities' to other countries.[53] In a similar fashion, during an official visit to the UK, US Secretary of State Mike Pompeo stressed the need for all European countries to 'work to take back their foreign fighters and continue to hold those foreign fighters'.[54] In response, UK Defence Secretary Ben Wallace made the claim that 'ministers would be guilty of "rendition" if the government brought British ISIS fighters and their families back from Syria against their will'.[55]

Returnees and untracked foreign fighters

Returnees and untracked foreign fighters are the most concerning category for those in counter-terrorism circles.[56] There are, however, nuances in the degree of risk that returnees and untracked foreign fighters pose to their countries of origin, as not all of them are committed to continue fighting. According to 2017 estimates, 5,600 foreign fighters from around the world have returned home, including 1,200–2,000 fighters that left the EU to join ISIS in Iraq and

Syria and are now back in their countries of origin.[57] In the UK, at least 400 of the estimated 800 returnees remain unaccounted for. Of those who have been identified, only 40 have been prosecuted; the majority have been included 'in rehabilitation schemes'.[58] According to then UK home secretary Sajid Javid, as of February 2019, 'all ISIS fighters who re-entered the UK had been investigated and "the majority have been assessed to pose no or a low security risk"'.[59]

From a European perspective, the problem has two dimensions: the mobility of foreign fighters *into* and *within* the EU. Operations by Interpol and the European Border and Coast Guard Agency (Frontex) in September 2019 identified 'more than a dozen' foreign fighters attempting to enter the EU from Algeria, Morocco and Tunisia. They also demonstrated that coordination and intelligence sharing[60] are a critical asset even in monitoring foreign fighters' mobility within the EU. Despite pledges by European institutions to prioritise the fight against ISIS and the threat of foreign fighters, threat perception and political priorities vary significantly among individual governments, as does the manpower dedicated to tracking and monitoring returnees. Almost half of the European foreign fighters who reached Iraq and Syria originated from only a handful of EU countries. This lack of effective coordination facilitates the mobility of foreign fighters within the Union.[61]

Outside the EU, the problem is particularly significant for those countries whose foreign fighters left to acquire combat experience and grow within the ISIS ranks, only to bring the fight back home. That is the case for a large proportion of Tunisian and North Caucasian foreign fighters.[62] The Bardo National Museum and Sousse attacks in 2015 and the Battle of Ben Guerdane[63] in 2016 revealed how well developed the connections among North African ISIS militants have become. The flow of foreign fighters into Libya created a significant security threat for Tunisia as a substantial number of Tunisian jihadists were, and still are, committed to return to Tunisia to fight.[64] As for Russia, the ongoing jihadist insurgency in the North Caucasus is a well-established security priority.[65] Moscow's strategy has focused on turning a blind eye to foreign fighters' departures while targeting them in Syria and preventing their return to Russia. Official Europol reports cite an article in the Russian newspaper *Novaya Gazeta* which suggests that Russian security services might have proactively facilitated the outflow of North Caucasian jihadists away from Russia into Turkey (en route to Syria) to reduce the risk of a violent escalation within its borders, and then applied even stricter border controls to prevent their return.[66]

Strategic implications

While the potential threat from returning fighters has occupied much of the media and decision-makers' attention, research has shown that the risk of direct action (i.e. a terrorist attack) carried out by returning foreign fighters is historically quite low. Only a minimal share of those who return plot or carry out further terrorist activities:[67] a pivotal 2013 study on the issue of returnees identified that only one in nine returning foreign fighters commits to carrying out acts of domestic terrorism.[68] The risk remains, however, that these fighters may inspire terrorist attacks or would-be foreign fighters upon their return.

Moreover, the effectiveness of controls over 'new' foreign fighters has led to counter-intuitive results. A new, under-investigated category has emerged, the so-called 'frustrated travellers' – aspiring foreign fighters who have been detected before they managed to leave their country, or somehow failed to reach their destination. These individuals have resorted in several cases to improvised and rather primitive terrorist operations in their home countries, such as a lorry attack in Sweden and a series of stabbings targeting security personnel in France.[69]

In the short term, relocators will continue to have the option to transfer to *wilayat* around the world, but not the opportunity to revive a state-like organisation such as the caliphate. Since mid-2019, ISIS has been reorganising some of its key Asian *wilayat*, potentially to strengthen their ability to operate autonomously and maximise targeted-recruitment efforts. The Afghanistan–Pakistan–India triangle in particular seems of growing interest for the organisation, especially given the power vacuum in areas along smuggling routes across the Afghanistan–Pakistan border.[70]

In Southeast Asia, the Philippines has become central to ISIS's propaganda narrative, particularly after the Siege of Marawi. But the organisation's actual presence across the region is quite limited and disorganised: attacks such as the Sri Lanka Easter bombings in April 2019 demonstrate ISIS's reach while also highlighting how isolated its units are:[71] The region therefore seems more suited to hosting smaller and fairly autonomous jihadist groups, rather than a united front under the ISIS banner – even more so since the collapse of the caliphate has significantly reduced the resources and manpower available.[72]

Although ISIS's presence in Libya is consolidated, it is also fairly isolated from other *wilayat*, making it unfit to become the new hub for a caliphate in North Africa and relegating it to be more of 'a regional hub than a strategic fallback, as evidenced by the growing ties between Libya provinces and the Sinai Province'.[73] Key cities and strategic areas are constantly contested by a range of state and non-state military actors, meaning ISIS's presence in the country is rather nomadic and making it difficult to create effective governance institutions.[74]

Critically, it is the humanitarian situation of foreign fighters in Syria coupled with the political situation in Iraq that might actually provide, once more, the fundamental hotbed for the resurgence of ISIS. Makeshift prisons in which 10,000 individuals,[75] including veteran jihadists and their families, survive in hardship offer an ideal environment for exacerbating existing grievances, and to potentially breed a new generation of ISIS militants. In addition, the political tensions that have been shaking Iraq since October 2018 might provide breathing space for ISIS's insurgency as well as its re-emergence as a state actor.

Notes

1. Rodi Said, 'Islamic State "caliphate" defeated, yet threat persists', Reuters, 23 March 2019.
2. Jennifer Cafarella with Brandon Wallace and Jason Zhou, 'ISIS's Second Comeback: Assessing the Next ISIS Insurgency', Institute for the Study of War, June 2019, pp. 19–25.
3. United States Department of Defense Office of Inspector General, 'Operation Inherent Resolve and Other Overseas Contingency Operations: Lead Inspector General Report to the United States Congress, October 1 2018 – December 31 2018', February 2019, p. 7.
4. Norimitsu Onishi and Elian Peltier, 'Turkey's Deportations Force Europe to Face its ISIS Militants', *New York Times*, 17 November 2019.
5. Defined as 'individuals who travel to a State other than their States of residence or nationality for the purpose of the perpetration, planning, or preparation of, or participation in, terrorist acts or the providing or receiving of terrorist training, and the financing of their travel and of their activities', United Nations Security Council Resolution 2178 (2014), p. 2.
6. UNSC Resolution 2178 (2014), p. 4.
7. Deborah Amos, 'A Smuggler Explains How He Helped Fighters Along "Jihadi Highway"', NPR, 7 October 2014.
8. UNSC Counter-Terrorism Committee Executive Directorate, 'The Challenge of Returning and Relocating Foreign Terrorist Fighters: Research Perspectives', March 2018, p. 13.
9. Lydia Khalil, 'Sri Lanka's Perfect Storm of Failure', *Foreign Policy*, 23 April 2019.
10. Anne Barnard and Eric Schmitt, 'As Foreign Fighters Flood Syria, Fears of a New Extremist Haven', *New York Times*, 8 August 2013.
11. Peter R. Neumann, 'Foreign fighter total in Syria/Iraq now exceeds 20,000; surpasses Afghanistan conflict in the 1980s', International Centre for the Study of Radicalisation, 26 January 2015.
12. UNSC, 'Greater Cooperation Needed to Tackle Danger Posed by Returning Foreign Fighters, Head of Counter-Terrorism Office Tells Security Council', 28 November 2017.
13. Don Rassler, 'Situating the Emergence of the Islamic State of Khorasan', *CTC Sentinel*, vol. 8, no. 3, 2015; International Crisis Group, 'The North Caucasus Insurgency and Syria: An Exported Jihad?', 16 March 2016, p. i.
14. Rohan Gunaratna, 'The Siege of Marawi: A Game Changer in Terrorism in Asia', *Counter Terrorist Trends and Analyses*, vol. 9, no. 7, 2017; Zam Yusa, 'Philippines: 100 foreign fighters joined ISIS in Mindanao since the Marawi battle', *Defense Post*, 5 November 2018.
15. Louisa Loveluck and Mustafa Salim, 'ISIS leader Baghdadi urges followers to continue attacks, storm prisons in purported new recording', *Washington Post*, 16 September 2019.
16. US Department of Defense Office of Inspector General, 'Operation Inherent Resolve: Lead Inspector General Report to the United States Congress, April 1 2019 – June 30 2019', July 2019, p. 2.
17. US Department of Defense Office of Inspector General, 'Operation Inherent Resolve and Other Overseas Contingency Operations: Lead Inspector General Report to the United States Congress, October 1, 2018 – December 31, 2018', p. 7.
18. *Ibid.*, pp. 32–3.
19. Rik Coolsaet, 'Anticipating the Post-Daesh Landscape', EGMONT – The Royal Institute for International Relations, October 2017.
20. Europol, 'European Union Terrorism Situation and Trend Report 2018', June 2018.
21. 'Foreign fighters continue to join ISIS in Syria, US Joint Chiefs chair says', *Defense Post*, 16 October 2018.
22. US Joint Chiefs of Staff, 'Dunford: Chiefs of Defense Counter-ISIS Meeting "Historic"', 25 October 2017.
23. Cafarella with Wallace and Zhou, 'ISIS's Second Comeback: Assessing the Next ISIS Insurgency', p. 23.
24. UNSC Counter-Terrorism Committee Executive Directorate, 'The Challenges of Returning and Relocating Foreign Terrorist Fighters: research perspectives', CTED Trends Report, March 2018, p. 9.
25. Joana Cook and Gina Vale, 'From Daesh to "Diaspora": Tracing the Women and Minors of Islamic State', International Centre for the Study of Radicalisation, July 2018; Charles Lister,

'Returning Foreign Fighters: Criminalization or Reintegration?', Brookings Doha Center, August 2015, p. 2.

[26] Between 600 and 900 Dagestanis had reportedly moved to Syria by 2015, while by 2017 the number had increased to 1,200. Figures for Chechen jihadists were 450 in 2015 and 600 in 2017. Mark Youngman and Cerwyn Moore, '"Russian-Speaking" Fighters in Syria, Iraq and at Home: Consequences and Context', Centre for Research and Evidence on Security Threats, November 2017, p. 7.

[27] International Crisis Group, 'The North Caucasus Insurgency and Syria: An Exported Jihad?', p. 6.

[28] Shima D. Keene, 'Extremist Migration: A Foreign Jihadist Fighter Threat Assessment', Strategic Studies Institute, May 2019, p. 16. Overall, between 2012 and 2018, 2,600–3,500 individuals attempted to join ISIS in Libya. Aaron Y. Zelin, 'The Others: Foreign Fighters in Libya', Washington Institute for Near East Policy, January 2018, p. 3.

[29] Cafarella with Wallace and Zhou, 'ISIS's Second Comeback: Assessing the Next ISIS Insurgency', p. 14.

[30] *Ibid.*, p. 23.

[31] Zachary Abuza and Colin P. Clarke, 'The Islamic State Meets Southeast Asia', *Foreign Affairs*, 16 September 2019.

[32] UNSC Resolution 2396 (2017), 21 December 2017; UNSC Resolution 2462 (2019), 28 May 2019.

[33] 'Islamic State captives "must be tried or freed", says UN's Bachelet', BBC News, 24 June 2019.

[34] Tanya Mehra and Cristophe Paulussen, 'The Repatriation of Foreign Fighters and Their Families: Options, Obligations, Morality and Long-Term Thinking', International Centre for Counter-Terrorism, 6 March 2019; Kathy Gilsinan, 'Europe Has Turned Its Back on Its ISIS Suspects', *Atlantic*, 5 July 2019.

[35] UNSC Counter-Terrorism Committee Executive Directorate, 'The Challenges of Returning and Relocating Foreign Terrorist Fighters', p. 13.

[36] Christophe Paulussen and Kate Pitcher, 'Prosecuting (Potential) Foreign Fighters: Legislative and Practical Challenges', International Centre for Counter-Terrorism, January 2018, pp. 23–7.

[37] Loveluck and Salim, 'ISIS leader Baghdadi urges followers to continue attacks, storm prisons in purported new recording'.

[38] US Department of Defense Office of Inspector General, 'Operation Inherent Resolve: Lead Inspector General Report to the United States Congress, April 1 2019 – June 30 2019', p. 23.

[39] US Department of Defense Office of Inspector General, 'Operation Inherent Resolve and Other Overseas Contingency Operations: Lead Inspector General Report to the United States Congress, October 1 2018 – December 31 2018', p. 23.

[40] UN Commission of Inquiry on Syria, 'Escalating violence and waves of displacement continue to torment civilians during eighth year of Syrian conflict', 11 September 2019.

[41] Karen DeYoung, Louisa Loveluck and John Hudson, 'US Military Announces Start of Syria Withdrawal', *Washington Post*, 11 January 2019.

[42] US Department of Defense Office of Inspector General, 'Operation Inherent Resolve and Other Overseas Contingency Operations: Lead Inspector General Report to the United States Congress, October 1, 2018 – December 31, 2018', p. 5.

[43] Hwaida Saad and Rod Nordland, 'Kurdish Fighters Discuss Releasing Almost 3,200 ISIS Prisoners', *New York Times*, 20 December 2018.

[44] Felicia Sonmez and Michael Brice-Saddler, 'Trump says Alabama woman who joined ISIS will not be allowed back into US', *Washington Post*, 21 February 2019.

[45] Cook and Vale, 'From Daesh to "Diaspora": Tracing the Women and Minors of Islamic State', p. 18.

[46] US Department of Defense Office of Inspector General, 'Operation Inherent Resolve and Other Overseas Contingency Operations: Lead Inspector General Report to the United States Congress, October 1, 2018 – December 31, 2018', p. 24.

[47] US Department of Defense Office of Inspector General, 'Operation Inherent Resolve: Lead Inspector General Report to the United States Congress, July 1, 2019 – October, 2019', November 2019, p. 40.

[48] Aki Peritz, 'The Coming ISIS Jailbreak', *Foreign Affairs*, 23 October 2019; Lara Seligman, 'Turkish-Backed Forces Are Freeing Islamic State Prisoners', *Foreign Policy*, 14 October 2019; 'Former IS militants reportedly join Turkey-backed Syria groups', BBC Monitoring, 10 November 2019.

[49] Carlotta Gall, 'Turkey Vows to Send ISIS Militants Home', *New York Times*, 8 November 2019; Carlotta Gall, 'Erdogan Warns That Turkey Will Keep Deporting ISIS Detainees', *New York Times*, 12 November 2019.

[50] David Gauthier-Villars, 'Turkey's Erdogan Threatens EU With Wave of Refugees if It Doesn't Support Syria Offensive', *Wall Street Journal*, 10 October 2019.

[51] Cook and Vale, 'From Daesh to "Diaspora": Tracing the Women and Minors of Islamic State', p. 17.

[52] Dan Sabbagh, 'Britain must repatriate Isis fighters, warns US defence secretary', *Guardian*, 6 September 2019.

[53] Dan Sabbagh, 'Jack Letts stripped of British citizenship', *Guardian*, 18 August 2019.

[54] 'U.S. expects every country to take back foreign fighters: Pompeo', Reuters, 8 May 2019.

[55] Ashley Cowburn and Lizzie Dearden, 'Ministers could be "guilty of rendition" if UK brings back Isis fighters from Syria, says defence secretary', *Independent*, 1 October 2019.

[56] Colin P. Clarke and Amarnath Amarasingam, 'Where Do ISIS Fighters Go When the Caliphate Falls?', *Atlantic*, 6 March 2017.

[57] Keene, 'Extremist Migration: A Foreign Jihadist Fighter Threat Assessment', p. 8; Richard Barrett, 'Beyond the Caliphate: Foreign Fighters and the Threat of Returnees', The Soufan Center, October 2017, pp. 12–13.

[58] Bill Gardner, 'Britain has "by far the highest rate of returning jihadi fighters in Europe"', *Telegraph*, 27 June 2019.

[59] Lizzie Dearden, 'Only one in 10 jihadis returning from Syria prosecuted, figures reveal', *Independent*, 21 February 2019.

[60] Interpol, 'Foreign terrorist fighters detected during INTERPOL maritime border operation', 19 September 2019.

[61] Oldrich Bures, 'EU's Response to Foreign Fighters: New Threats, Old Challenges?', *Terrorism and Political Violence*, advance online publication, pp. 3–9.

[62] Zelin, 'The Others: Foreign Fighters in Libya', pp. 9–10; Youngman and Moore, '"Russian-Speaking" Fighters in Syria, Iraq and at Home: Consequences and Context'.

63 Tarek Amara and Patrick Markey, 'Border attack feeds Tunisia fears of Libya jihadist spillover', Reuters, 13 March 2016.

64 R. Kim Cragin, 'Preventing the Next Wave of Foreign Terrorist Fighters: Lessons Learned from the Experiences of Algeria and Tunisia', *Studies in Conflict and Terrorism*, February 2019.

65 Youngman and Moore, '"Russian-Speaking" Fighters in Syria, Iraq and at Home: Consequences and Context'.

66 Europol, 'North Caucasian fighters in Syria and Iraq & IS propaganda in Russian language', 10 November 2015, pp. 14–15.

67 Daniel Byman, 'Measuring the Threat from Foreign Fighters', in IISS, *Armed Conflict Survey 2016* (Abingdon: Routledge for the IISS, 2016), pp. 34–40.

68 Thomas Hegghammer, 'Should I Stay or Should I Go? Explaining Variation in Western Jihadists' Choice between Domestic and Foreign Fighting', *American Political Science Review*, vol. 107, no. 1, 2013, p. 10.

69 Robin Simcox, 'When Terrorists Stay Home: The Evolving Threat to Europe from Frustrated Travelers', *CTC Sentinel*, vol. 12, no. 6, July 2019.

70 Amira Jadoon and Andrew Mines, 'Taking Aim: Islamic State Khorasan's Leadership Losses', *CTC Sentinel*, vol. 12, no. 8, September 2019.

71 Abuza and Clarke, 'The Islamic State Meets Southeast Asia'; Harsh V. Pant and Kabir Taneja, 'ISIS's New Target: South Asia', *Foreign Policy*, 2 May 2019.

72 Quinton Temby, 'Cells, Factions and Suicide Operatives: The Fragmentation of Militant Islamism in the Philippines Post-Marawi', *Contemporary Southeast Asia*, vol. 41, no. 1, 2019, pp. 115–16.

73 Katerine Bauer (ed.), 'Beyond Syria and Iraq: Examining Islamic States Provinces', Washington Institute for Near East Policy, November 2016, p. 47.

74 Andrea Beccaro, 'ISIS in Mosul and Sirte: Differences and similarities', *Mediterranean Politics*, vol. 23, no. 3, 2018, pp. 410–17.

75 US Department of Defense Office of Inspector General, 'Operation Inherent Resolve: Lead Inspector General Report to the United States Congress, April 1 2019 – June 30 2019', pp. 23–4.

Human Trafficking in Conflict

Two events in 2014 – Boko Haram's abduction of 276 Chibok schoolgirls in Nigeria[1] and the rape, forced marriage and genocide of the Yazidis by the Islamic State, also known as ISIS or ISIL, in Iraq[2] – put the issue of human trafficking in conflict firmly on the international agenda. In September 2015, United Nations member states adopted Sustainable Development Goal 8.7, which pledged to end all forms of human trafficking, and the intersection between the crime and conflict has been raised at the UN Security Council (UNSC) on a number of occasions.

In November 2018, the UNSC 'reiterated its deep concern' regarding the lack of progress in combatting human trafficking in areas affected by conflict.[3] While the political commitment is nominally in place, a number of broader political factors compromise the response to human trafficking in practical terms. Firstly, conflict compounds the complexity of the challenge of human trafficking in any context. Secondly, as conflicts become increasingly protracted and funding for humanitarian assistance falls short, meeting the specialised needs of trafficking victims becomes unrealistic. Finally, and most pertinently, people displaced by conflict are acutely vulnerable to this form of exploitation. Some governments in countries that the unprecedentedly large population of global refugees and asylum seekers seek to reach or transit – such as those of Austria, Egypt, Hungary, Italy, Turkey, the United Kingdom and the United States – have seized on migrants' increasing mobility to bolster insular, anti-immigrant political agendas, restricting the influx of migrants in highly militarised ways and increasing their susceptibility to human trafficking and other forms of criminal exploitation.

A complex phenomenon

A protocol to the UN Convention against Transnational Organized Crime provides a broad definition of human trafficking:

> [T]he recruitment, transportation, transfer, harbouring or receipt of persons, by means of the threat or use of force or other forms of coercion, of abduction, of fraud, of deception, of the abuse of power or of a position of vulnerability or of the giving or receiving of payments or benefits to achieve the consent of a person having control over another person, for the purpose of exploitation.[4]

The forms of human trafficking in a conflict setting cover a wide range of exploitative acts (see Figure 1), which has created substantial ambiguity for policymakers, humanitarian and development practitioners and law-enforcement and criminal-justice actors over what does and does not amount to trafficking in persons.

As to the Central African Republic, for example, the term would need to encompass:

- forced recruitment of men, women and children into armed groups for the purposes of fighting, labour, sexual services or forced marriage;
- forced begging perpetrated by gangs and street children against other street children and people with disabilities;
- forced marriage of women and girls to non-armed actors (e.g. parents or relatives of perpetrators);
- forced labour of adults and children in remote mines (to extract diamonds and gold);
- commercial sexual exploitation of women and children;
- domestic servitude in private homes;
- migration-based exploitation of potential asylum seekers and refugees in Cameroon, Chad, the Democratic Republic of the Congo and Sudan;
- trafficking for the purposes of organ removal; and
- hereditary and traditional forms of slavery perpetrated against Pygmy communities.

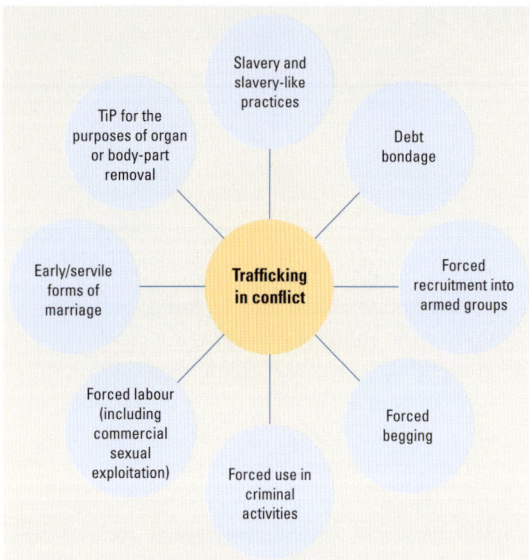

Figure 1: Forms of trafficking included as trafficking in conflict (TiP = trafficking in persons)

The list demonstrates the wide range of victims and perpetrators, the geographic spread of crimes and the scope of factors that could make people vulnerable to abuses that reasonably fall under the heading of human trafficking. In many areas afflicted by conflict, there is considerable controversy over the labelling of some traditional and cultural practices, such as early marriage or the use of child labour, as trafficking (and therefore as crimes).

These forms of trafficking in persons (apart from the first of the above categories) predated conflict, which compounds the complexity. Conflict, however, amplifies pre-existing forms of exploitation.[5] The breakdown of state capacity and the rule of law increases standing vulnerabilities and facilitates pre-existing human-trafficking practices, while potentially introducing new forms of trafficking. Insecurity gives rise to overwhelming levels of desperation and need, shortages in necessary goods, low levels of oversight and service-provider fatigue. These realities can make distinguishing between abuses of power and outright trafficking difficult. For example, in the camps for internally displaced persons (IDPs) in Nigeria, women and children have felt compelled to provide sexual services to officials and militia personnel in exchange for food.[6]

Conflict actors in need of manpower and financing find the coercive co-optation of local populations an easy solution to both challenges. Forced marriage, for instance, has become a means of both controlling local populations and exacting reprisals against enemies, while also swelling the labour force and providing an incentive to soldiers to remain loyal. ISIS-affiliated groups have reportedly forced female migrants to marry fighters, and in Somalia al-Shabaab sometimes uses forced marriage to cement relationships between clans.[7]

In conflict zones, where capacity and resources are short, neither the government nor domestic civil society is well placed to enforce the rights and remedies to which the victim would typically be entitled under national or international law. Conflict scenarios also impede the ability of NGOs and international organisations to carry out effective checks on the conduct of state and non-state parties to the conflict. Many people affected by violence may not be sufficiently informed to identify themselves as victims of human trafficking specifically, or to realise that remedies or protection may be available to them. For instance, people who have lived for extended periods under violent and coercive governance by local non-state armed groups, such as those in communities controlled by al-Shabaab, may not recognise labour exploitation or forced conscription as trafficking crimes.

For international actors attempting to address cases of trafficking in persons, conflict places an additional burden on a system already overwhelmed by other humanitarian, development and reconstruction challenges. Furthermore, the needs and entitlements of trafficking victims can extend long beyond the duration of a conflict, imposing long-standing obligations on national governments and their international partners and fuelling intergenerational grievances that render peace and justice difficult to attain.

Humanitarian crises requiring internationally led responses have increased in number and duration over the past decade. In turn, the numbers of people in need and targeted for assistance have also grown, not least due to mass displacement resulting from conflict. At the end of 2018, 70.8 million people worldwide had been forcibly displaced, including 13.6m during the previous year alone.[8] The funding to meet these rising needs is failing to keep pace. Only 59.4% of the US$26.75 billion pledged for humanitarian needs in 2019 was received (see Figure 2). Therefore, adding the obligation of responding to the specialised needs of victims of trafficking to

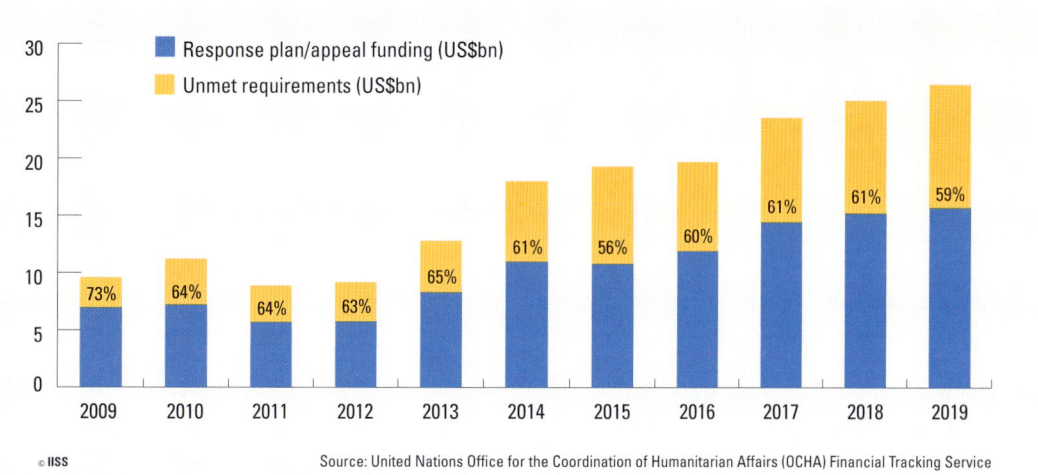

Figure 2: Trends in UN consolidated humanitarian-response plans/appeal requirements.[9] The percentage labels shown in each bar represent the global-appeal coverage for each year.

the already over-burdened and under-resourced responsibilities of the humanitarian community seems unrealistic, particularly if those needs were not generated by the conflict itself.

International law vs national agendas

Considerations of human-trafficking risks cannot be restricted to the immediate conflict zone but must also be extended to those fleeing conflict and violence, as these people have long been known to demonstrate heightened vulnerability to criminal exploitation. There are several landmark pieces of international legislation regarding the rights of those seeking refuge in foreign countries. The Universal Declaration of Human Rights, adopted in 1948, guarantees the 'right to seek and to enjoy in other countries asylum from persecution'. The same right is reiterated in numerous pieces of regional and national legislation, including the American Convention on Human Rights (article 22), the Cartagena Declaration on Refugees, the African Charter on Human and Peoples' Rights (article 12.3), the Arab Charter on Human Rights (article 28) and the European Convention on Human Rights (articles 2, 3 and 5).[10] The core principle of the 1951 Convention Relating to the Status of Refugees is '*non-refoulement*', which obliges states not to return a refugee to 'the frontiers of territories where his life or freedom would be threatened' (article 33).[11] The 1984 Convention against Torture and Other Cruel, Inhuman or Degrading Treatment or Punishment (article 3), as well as many regional and domestic courts, interpret *non-refoulement* as a protection against torture.

However, these foundational pieces of legislation and the obligations that they enshrine were devised at a time when the scale of migration and the number of people seeking international protection was far smaller. They were not designed to accommodate the immense flows of refugees currently under way nor the protracted nature of the displacement that is now occurring. Thus, if the applicable principles were to be upheld in their entirety, they would have far greater costs than their drafters contemplated. It follows that certain measures of deterrence against refugee flows on the part of receiving states, which have in fact arisen, were practically inevitable. This point is not meant to minimise or brush aside the immense human tragedy that has resulted from mass displacement and the inability of states, international organisations and NGOs to address it, but rather to recognise that they cannot be expected to readily and effectively address the contemporary challenge with extant legal and administrative tools.

Marginal progress has been made in reframing the challenge. While non-binding, the UN's Global Compact on Refugees (promulgated on 17 December 2019) 'represents the political will and ambition of the international community as a whole for strengthened cooperation and solidarity with refugees and affected host countries',[12] and was, with its sister compact on migration, intended to mark the start of a new order for migrants and refugees, aligned to the principles of the UN's Sustainable Development Goals. However, sufficient political consensus could not be reached to negotiate a binding instrument, and a number of states – including the US, Hungary and Israel – refused to sign.

Debates on the issues of migration and displacement are becoming more divisive, as migrants and refugees are increasingly considered security, economic and cultural threats. Meanwhile, the migration problem is getting worse as the drivers of displacement proliferate, and populations on the move are subject to multiple forms of criminal exploitation and abuse, including human trafficking, with little protection or recourse.

According to the UN Office on Drugs and Crime's (UNODC's) 'Global Study on Homicide 2019', the homicide rates of several countries south of the US are among the highest in the world.[13] In 2019, homicides in Mexico jumped to the highest levels on record, with 34,582 murders recorded.[14] Pervasive violence and insecurity (including extortion, kidnapping and rape as well as murder) has resulted in mass displacement in the region. Venezuela's political and security crisis has caused more than 4.6m people to flee the country,[15] while hundreds of thousands of people from the Northern Triangle (El Salvador, Guatemala and Honduras) have sought asylum in the US and Canada, driven from their homes by the violence of street gangs and organised-crime groups. Particularly in the Americas, protecting children from violence is a primary incentive for migration, and the migrant population there disproportionately consists of women and children. Beginning in mid-October 2018, several semi-organised groups of migrants, originating mainly in Honduras and El Salvador, embarked on the journey to the US via Guatemala and Mexico. The largest of these so-called 'caravans' included an estimated 7,000 people, of which 2,300 were children.[16] Criminal groups kidnap more than 20,000 migrants each year, with migrant women at risk of being sold into prostitution.[17]

In Turkey, large numbers of Syrian refugees, migrants and displaced persons have become pawns in proxy wars and the geopolitical manoeuvrings of major powers. At the close of 2019, Turkey hosted 3.6m Syrian refugees.[18] Ankara has signalled that it would forcibly resettle more than 1m refugees back into northern Syria. When Turkish President Recep Tayyip Erdogan encountered European Union opposition to Turkey's incursion into northern Syria – intended in part to facilitate the return of refugees – he warned Brussels that 'if you try to describe our operation as an invasion, we will do what's easy for us: we will open the doors and send 3.6m refugees to you'.[19] Refugees in Turkey fearful of being returned are also turning to criminal groups for alternatives, hoping to seek asylum in Europe before the options close entirely. Smuggling and trafficking rings have been actively circling the refugee populations in Turkey since the height of the migrant crisis in 2016, often with the involvement or protection of Turkish organised-crime groups.[20] In May 2019, the Turkish police arrested 20 members of a trafficking ring in four Turkish provinces. The police investigation determined that this single group could have been responsible for moving thousands of migrants out of Turkey. The trafficking ring was charging €3,000–5,000 (approximately US$3,300–5,500) per person for the journey, despite the relatively small chance asylum seekers now have of achieving refugee status in Europe.[21]

In Libya – a long-standing gateway for migration between Africa and Europe – thousands of migrants have been detained in official and unofficial centres, where they are subject to extortion, kidnap for ransom, forced labour and, in the case of female migrants, trafficking for sexual exploitation and forced prostitution.[22] Militia groups turned to the smuggling trade as early as 2012, and in the subsequent five years became increasingly professional and efficient at transporting migrants.[23] The funding from migrant smuggling as well as extortion, prostitution and the actual sale of people into bonded labour has financed conflict in Libya during its protracted and halting political transition.[24]

Despite UNSC resolutions on the topic, UN and EU sanctions against human traffickers and plentiful resources from international donors, international efforts have not substantially ameliorated the problem. A major reason is the hardening of national immigration policies. In response to febrile domestic political environments, many migrant-destination states have acted to prevent irregular migration. Hungarian Prime Minister Viktor Orbán, for example, has claimed that 'migration is not a solution but a problem … not medicine but a poison'[25] and has threatened to use force against migrants to prevent their transit across Hungary's borders.[26] In Europe – including some influential EU members, such as Austria and Italy – turning away and even mistreating migrants has become a prevalent strategy for deterring people from attempting to emigrate. EU search-and-rescue patrols in the Mediterranean ended in March 2019. Some EU states have worked to obstruct the volunteer sea-rescue operations run by non-profit groups, preventing them from making rescues[27] and closing European ports to migrant-rescue boats.[28] Perversely, the EU-funded and -trained Libyan coastguard has in some cases transferred detained migrants into criminal networks for a fee.[29] The US, for its part, has sought to instil fear in irregular migrants with targeted deportation campaigns and forced detention and child separation at the border.

Such policies are arguably counterproductive as well as inhumane, insofar as they could exacerbate underlying refugee problems. To the extent that these policies reduce or eliminate safe and legitimate options for refugees and asylum seekers, they increase their vulnerability to, and perpetrators' incentives to engage in, various forms of exploitation. Unable to gain asylum, migrants have increasingly taken desperate measures, frequently placing themselves in the hands of smugglers to make risky border crossings. The US–Mexican border is a case in point. With US security forces deployed on one side of the border and Mexican security forces on the other, attempting to make that crossing has become expensive, deadly or both. The fee to smugglers has reportedly tripled to around US$10,000 and migrant deaths have been rising.[30]

In 2019, the Missing Migrants Project run by the International Organization for Migration recorded 520 deaths along the US–Mexico border and a further 115 earlier along the route.[31] The actual number of fatalities is likely to be far greater.

The global cost

Conflicts, and especially protracted conflicts that displace large numbers of people, create optimal conditions for human trafficking. Migrants moving irregularly, either with or without the assistance of smugglers, are extremely vulnerable to different forms of exploitation. Expecting states or humanitarian workers in conflict scenarios to significantly curtail trafficking and provide adequate care and protection for its victims is unrealistic due to chronic shortfalls in capacity and resources, the severity of conditions on the ground, and the sheer number of refugees and displaced persons. Furthermore, international organisations and NGOs have been unable to deliver on the various pledges or recommendations made since 2014 or to enforce the rights of asylum seekers, refugees or victims of human trafficking. Beyond that, national policies have increasingly left migrants, refugees and asylum seekers vulnerable to predatory actors by denying them access to safe havens and pathways to resettlement. Unless international or national efforts to directly address the drivers of irregular migration ramp up significantly – which appears unlikely in the short term – the risks to vulnerable people in or fleeing conflict zones are not likely to improve.

Notes

1. 'Nigeria Chibok abductions: What we know', BBC News, 8 May 2017.
2. Human Rights Watch, 'Human Rights Watch Submission to the Committee on the Elimination of All Forms of Discrimination Against Women (CEDAW) of Iraq's periodic report for the 74th Pre-Sessional Working Group (11–15 March 2019)', March 2019.
3. United Nations Security Council, 'Report of the Secretary General on trafficking in persons in armed conflict pursuant to Security Council resolution 2388 (2017)', S/2018/1042, 21 November 2018, p. 1.
4. See UN Office of the High Commissioner for Human Rights (OHCHR), 'Protocol to Prevent, Suppress and Punish Trafficking in Persons, Especially Women and Children, Supplementing the United Nations Convention Against Transnational Organized Crime', Article 3, adopted 15 November 2000.
5. Lucia Bird and Tuesday Reitano, 'Trafficking in persons in conflict contexts: what is a realistic response from Africa?', ENACT, June 2019.
6. Amnesty International, 'They Betrayed Us: Women Who Survived Boko Haram Raped, Starved, and Detained in Nigeria', 24 May 2018, p. 61.
7. Field research conducted on al-Shabaab engagement in clan groups in two regions within Somalia, October–December 2017.
8. UN High Commissioner for Refugees (UNHCR), 'Global Trends: Forced Displacement in 2018', 20 June 2019, p. 2.
9. UN Office for the Coordination of Humanitarian Affairs Financial Tracking Service, 'Appeals and response plans 2019', accessed 6 January 2020.
10. Inter-American Commission on Human Rights, 'American Convention on Human Rights', 22 November 1969; Colloquium on the International Protection of Refugees in Central America, Mexico and Panama, 'Cartagena Declaration on Refugees',

22 November 1984; Organisation of African Unity, 'African (Banjul) Charter on Human and Peoples' Rights', 27 June 1981, OAU Doc. CAB/LEG/67/3 rev. 5, entered into force on 21 October 1986; League of Arab States, 'Arab Charter on Human Rights', 22 May 2004; Council of Europe, 'European Convention on Human Rights', 4 November 1950, amended Convention entered into force on 1 July 2010.

[11] UNHCR, 'Convention Relating to the Status of Refugees', Article 33, 28 July 1951, entered into force on 22 April 1954.

[12] UNHCR, 'Part II: Global compact on refugees', A/73/12 (Part II), 13 September 2018, p. 1.

[13] UN Office on Drugs and Crime, 'Global Homicide Report 2019', September 2019. See, for example, p. 14 of the 'Executive Summary'.

[14] Executive Secretariat of the National Public Security System (SESNSP), Mexico, 20 January 2020.

[15] As of November 2019. See Joint UNHCR–International Organization for Migration Special Representative for Venezuelan refugees and migrants, 'US$1.35 billion needed to help Venezuelan refugees and migrants and host countries', 13 November 2019.

[16] Annie Correal and Megan Specia, 'The migrant caravan: What to know about the thousands travelling north', *New York Times*, 26 October 2018.

[17] Anjali Fleury, 'Women Migrating to Mexico for Safety: The Need for Improved Protections and Rights', UN University Institute on Globalization, Culture and Mobility (UNU-GCM), Policy Report no. 03/08, 2016, p. 7.

[18] As of 31 December 2019. See UNHCR, 'Syria Regional Refugee Response: Turkey', last updated 5 March 2020, accessed 16 March 2020.

[19] Dorian Jones, 'Erdogan plays refugee card as criticism mounts over Turkey's Kurdish offensive', Voice of America, 10 October 2019.

[20] Tuesday Reitano and Mark Micallef, 'Breathing space: the impact of the EU–Turkey deal on irregular migration', IIS Paper 297, Institute for Security Studies, November 2016.

[21] Sinem Koseoglu, 'Turkey police bust human trafficking ring, arrest smugglers', Al-Jazeera, 29 May 2019.

[22] Arezo Malakooti, 'The Political-Economy of Migrant Detention in Libya: Understanding the players and the business models', Global Initiative Against Transnational Organized Crime, April 2019, p. 7.

[23] Mark Micallef, 'The Human Conveyor Belt: trends in human trafficking and smuggling in post-revolution Libya', Global Initiative Against Transnational Organized Crime, March 2017.

[24] Tuesday Reitano and Mark Micallef, 'Human Smuggling and Libya's political end game', Institute for Security Studies, December 2017.

[25] 'Hungarian prime minister says migrants are "poison" and "not needed"', *Guardian*, 27 July 2016.

[26] 'Hungary would have to "use force" to fend off new wave of migrants: PM', Reuters, 17 October 2019.

[27] Filip Warwick, 'NGO ship rescues Europe-bound migrants in Mediterranean', DW, 23 April 2018.

[28] Louise Miner, '"The ports remain closed," Italy's Matteo Salvini warns migrant rescue NGO', Reuters, 19 March 2019.

[29] Benjamin Bathke, 'Libya's coast guard picks up nearly 500 migrants in region surrounding Tripoli', InfoMigrants, 20 September 2019.

[30] Dave Philipps, 'Arrest of Marines Suspected of Smuggling Migrants Points to Lucrative Trade', *New York Times*, 26 July 2019.

[31] IOM, Missing Migrants Project, accessed 16 March 2020, https://missingmigrants.iom.int.

CONFLICT REPORTS

Houthi loyalists participate in a tribal gathering in Sanaa, Yemen

1 Americas

Brazil (Rio de Janeiro & Ceará)	40	Honduras	68
Colombia (BACRIMs)	51	Mexico (Cartels)	76
El Salvador	60		

A migrants' camp on the Mexican border in Matamoros, Tamaulipas State, Mexico, near the US border

Key trends

- Conflicts in the region continued to be predominantly criminal in nature and remained very violent, even escalating in some instances. A militarised approach prevailed, often leading to unintended consequences as a result of heavy-handedness and allegations of human-rights violations.

- Criminal gangs in Central America, particularly the MS-13, further consolidated their political power and engagement with local communities.

- Urban conflict is on the rise in Brazil, and Ceará State is now included in this survey as a result.

Strategic implications

- Central American governments' inability to reduce conflict and related illegal migration to the US undermined relationships with neighbouring countries and the US, a key partner against violent gangs.

- The economic impact of conflict was substantial, particularly as the prevalence of criminal economies and outbound migration contributed to economic depression in countries such as El Salvador.

Prospects

- The peace agreement between Colombia and FARC is unlikely to collapse despite the actions of FARC dissidents.

- Elsewhere in the region, the likelihood of fruitful negotiations with armed groups remained slim.

BRAZIL (RIO DE JANEIRO & CEARÁ)

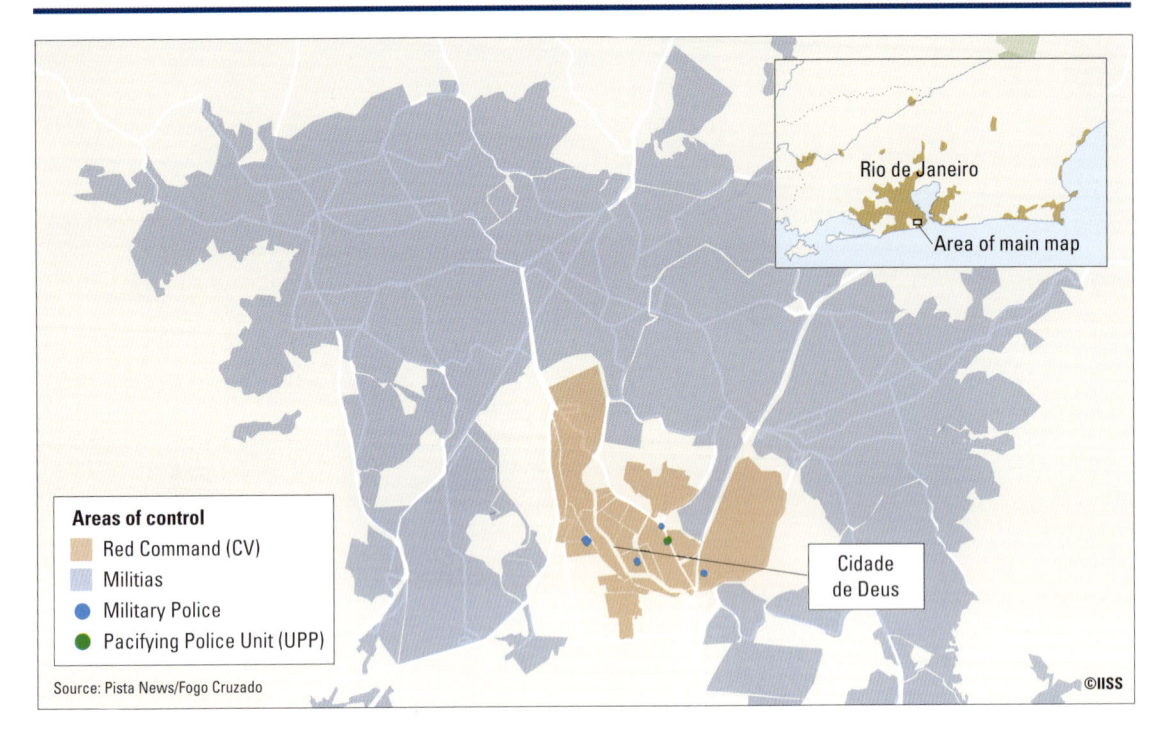

Areas of control
- Red Command (CV)
- Militias
- Military Police
- Pacifying Police Unit (UPP)

Source: Pista News/Fogo Cruzado

Overview

The conflict in 2019

January 2019 saw the inauguration of President Jair Bolsonaro, with the former army captain and congressman promising to enact hardline security policies and end corruption. Former federal judge Wilson Witzel became governor of Rio de Janeiro State in January and likewise pledged to crack down on crime.

Violence among the gangs and between gangs and the police continued in 2019 in Rio, but according to official statistics, the state registered its lowest number of homicides since 1991, when data started being collected.[1] There were 3,995 homicides in the state compared to 4,950 in 2018, a drop of 19.3%. However, there were 1,810 cases of police-involved killings throughout the year, an average of five per day – the highest such total since official records began in 1998.[2] Witzel was harshly criticised for encouraging human-rights abuses through his 'shoot on sight' rhetoric, as well as for failing to tackle the militias and corrupt police.

In the northeast, especially in Ceará State and its capital city Fortaleza, violence was severe. In spite of authorities' efforts, the gangs' territorial advance continued in 2019, even into protected indigenous territories. The gangs also conducted something resembling a joint operation: between 2 January and 4 February, the First Command of the Capital (PCC), Guardians of the State (GDE) and Northern Family (FDN) gangs conducted 283 attacks on public facilities and buses to protest changes in the prison system that aimed to house prisoners from different gangs together.

The conflict to 2019

In Rio de Janeiro, gang violence in its current form originated in the 1980s as rival gangs fought to

Key statistics	
Type	Internal
Start date	Early 1990s
IDPs total	Not applicable
Refugees total	Not applicable
People in need	Not applicable

conquer territory or to gain control over illicit economies, including drugs, extortion and unlicensed services (such as public transportation, natural-gas provision and cable TV). The militias, which carry out extortion, killings and service provision, formed in the first decade of the 2000s, though these groups have their origins in the extermination squads active during Brazil's military regime in the 1960s and 1970s.

In 2008, then-security secretary José Mariano Beltrame announced a 'pacification' policy centred on establishing Pacifying Police Units (UPPs) in the *favelas* (supported by police interventions) which would regularly patrol the area and build relations with the local communities. The programme led to a significant reduction in violence. According to state-government figures, from 2007 to 2014, intentional homicides plunged by 65.5% in areas with UPPs, whereas in the municipality as a whole the number fell by 42.5%. The overall metropolitan numbers registered similar improvements. The initial success of the programme led the state government to open several new UPPs, including in some of the city's largest *favelas* such as Rocinha and Alemão. From 2015, however, the programme gradually declined due to overstretch in terms of personnel, training and budget. Human-rights abuses by UPP officers, accompanied by a gradual increase in homicide numbers, also sapped support for the UPP project.

The decline of the UPP project led to a drastic rise in violence in Rio, with gangs fighting one another to take control of territory. The number of people killed by firearms in the state of Rio increased by 9.8% between 2016 and 2017, compared to a national rise of 6.8% over the same period.[3] During 2018, organised crime consolidated its control over Rio de Janeiro, despite a (still ongoing) federal military intervention, although the inter-gang conflict between the three main criminal factions – Red Command (CV), Pure Third Command (TCP) and Friends of Friends (ADA) – nearly eradicated the ADA. Gun violence escalated, with an average of 26 shootings per day occurring in the metropolitan area in 2018.[4] The number of militias, whose members often included former and off-duty police, also increased in this period.

Armed violence reached Ceará State later than in other parts of Brazil. Data gathered by local media outlet *O Povo* recorded the arrival of Rio's CV in Fortaleza, the state capital, in 1993, with São Paulo's PCC arriving in the 2000s. Since 2005, members of local gangs GDE and FDN began contesting control of the state with the national gangs. In 2015, the CV and PCC broke their near-20-year alliance, leading to a surge in violence in Ceará State: between 2016 and 2017, the number of people killed by firearms soared by 61.6%. After a spate of attacks in 2017 between incarcerated members of the CV and the PCC in the nearby state of Amazonas, which resulted in executions of inmates, Ceará's prisons maintained physical barriers between inmates of different gangs, but this measure was overturned in 2019.

Key Conflict Parties

Military Police (PMERJ/PM)

Strength
44,313 members.

Areas of operation
Rio de Janeiro.

Leadership
Commander-in-chief is Colonel Rogério Figueiredo de Lacerda.

Structure
The PMERJ is accountable to the Rio state government. Its hierarchy is similar to that of the army and its members are reserves for the armed forces. Specialised squads subordinate to the Special Operations Command (COE) include Battalion of Special Police Operations (BOPE), Battalion of Actions with Dogs (BAC), Riot Police Battalion (BPChq), Tactical Group of Motorcyclists (GTM) and the Aeromobile Group (GAM).

History
Created in May 1808. Current structure introduced in July 1974.

Objectives
Main public security force tasked with fighting organised criminal groups, entering *favelas*, executing arrest warrants or searching for suspects based on intelligence from other government bodies.

Opponents
Organised-crime groups and militias.

Affiliates/allies
Unofficially, some militias and gangs (such as the TCP).

Military Police (PMERJ/PM)

Resources/capabilities
Weapons currently used include IMBEL *ParaFAL* battle riffle 7.62 mm and the IMBEL IA2 assault rifle. In 2019, the Rio state government spent R$11.5 billion (US$2.5bn) on security, of which R$730 million (US$160m) was spent on policing (the PMERJ).

Red Command (CV)

Strength
3,000 to 8,000 members in Rio and 16,000 outside the state. More than 9,000 in Ceará.

Areas of operation
Rio de Janeiro, Acre, Amapá, Alagoas, Ceará, Distrito Federal, Pará, Rio Grande do Norte, Rondônia, Roraima, Mato Grosso and Tocantins. Also Paraguay, Bolivia and Colombia. Traditionally headquartered in the Alemão *favela* complex in the northern area of Rio.

Leadership
Marcinho VP and Elias Maluco remain in power, although both have been in prison for many years.

Structure
The CV has a decentralised structure: 'area leaders' are in charge of neighbourhoods and *favelas*. 'Managers' are responsible for drug-dealing spots, which are secured by 'soldiers' who fend off threats by other dealers or the police. 'Scouts' keep watch for potential risks and warn 'soldiers'.

History
CV is the oldest and largest gang in Rio de Janeiro. It was formed around 1979 in a maximum-security prison in Ilha Grande off the southern coast of Rio de Janeiro. CV has been involved in transnational drug trafficking since the 1980s, importing cocaine from Colombia. Its activity declined after a UPP was established in the Alemão *favela* complex in November 2010, but it has since grown again in prominence.

Objectives
CV aims to maintain and expand its operating area to other neighbourhoods in Rio and other states. It imposes rules on behaviour, limits locals' freedom of movement and extorts small businesses.

Opponents
Rio: PMERJ, TCP, ADA, Militia, PCC. Brazil: Bonde dos 13, Guardiões do Estado, Sindicato do Crime, Mafia Tocantinense, Comando Classe A, Bonde dos 30, União do Norte, PCC. Ceará: FND, GDE.

Affiliates/allies
Ceará: Guardiões do Estado, Família do Norte. Brazil: Primeiro Comando Catarinense. Rio: None.

Resources/capabilities
Equipped with large numbers of handguns, AK-47s, bazookas and grenades.

Pure Third Command (TCP)

Strength
Not known.

Areas of operation
Rio de Janeiro.

Leadership
BatGol, Peixão.

Structure
TCP has a decentralised structure: 'area leaders' are in charge of neighbourhoods and *favelas*. 'Managers' are responsible for drug-dealing spots, which are secured by 'soldiers' who fend off threats by other dealers or the police. 'Scouts' keep watch for potential risks and warn 'soldiers'.

History
Since 2016, TCP has acquired partial control over several *favelas* and established itself as the second-most powerful criminal organisation in Rio after CV (excluding the vigilante militias). The TCP was created from the union in 2002 of dissidents from ADA and TC (Third Command, formed in the 1980s) after the death of Uê (expelled from CV for treason) and the arrest of Celsinho da Vila Vintém (head of ADA). During 2017 and 2018, the rapid decline of ADA led many ADA members to the TCP.

Objectives
Maintain the areas currently under their control and expand their operating area to other neighbourhoods in Rio de Janeiro and other states. TCP pays bribes to the police in order to avoid confrontation and receive inside information. TCP also has evangelical Christian members, who attack and expel followers of African-based religions from their areas.

Opponents
CV, ADA, militias, PMERJ.

Affiliates/allies
PCC.

Resources/capabilities
Weapons include pistols, rifles, bazookas and grenades.

Friends of Friends (ADA)

Strength
Not known.

Areas of Operation
Rio de Janeiro.

Leadership
Celsinho da Vila Vintém, one of the gang's founders.

Structure
ADA has a decentralised structure: 'area leaders' are in charge of neighbourhoods and *favelas*. 'Managers' are responsible for drug-dealing spots, which are secured by 'soldiers' who fend off threats by other dealers or the police. 'Scouts' keep watch for potential risks and warn 'soldiers'.

History
Created in 1994, ADA has suffered heavy losses in recent years in clashes with the CV and, to a lesser extent, the TCP. By the end of 2018, ADA retained control of only two areas in the city of Rio, but maintains communication with PCC, Brazil's largest and wealthiest criminal organisation.

Objectives
Maintain the few areas currently under their control in Rio de Janeiro city and expand their operations to other neighbourhoods, especially outside the Rio metropolitan area.

Opponents
CV, TCP, militias, PMERJ.

Affiliates/allies
PCC, TCP.

Resources/capabilities
Guns, pistols, rifles, bazookas and grenades.

Militias (various)

Strength
Not known (no estimates), although the Justice League is the largest and most organised of the militias.

Areas of operation
Rio de Janeiro and particularly in the areas of Campo Grande, Paciência and Santa Cruz, in western Rio, as well as Seropédica and Nova Iguaçu in Baixada Fluminense (north of Rio).

Leadership
The Justice League is led by Wellington da Silva Braga, also known as 'Ecko', one of 2018's most-wanted men in Rio. Brothers Jerominho and Natalino Guimarães, the League's founders, remain influential. There are other, smaller militia groups, but their leadership is unclear.

Structure
The structure of the militias mirrors that of the gangs – area leaders, managers and soldiers – although at a different scale. Leaders control more than one neighbourhood/region and managers are responsible for a region or neighbourhood. Soldiers, unlike in drug groups, operate from well-placed positions (such as police stations). 'Killers' are responsible for executions.

History
The Rio militias were formed by former or current police officers (mostly from the PMERJ), firefighters and prison guards, and expanded rapidly during the 2000s. The militias claim to provide security, but also traffic in drugs and extort, abduct and kill locals.

Objectives
Expand business (providing internet, gas and van services) and gain political influence. Many militia members hold public offices in municipalities.

Opponents
ADA, CV.

Affiliates/allies
TCP.

Resources/capabilities
Since militia members are often law-enforcement agents, they have access to the same weapons as those agencies, especially .40 calibre pistols and various types of rifle.

First Command of the Capital (PCC)

Strength
30,000.

Areas of operation
All Brazil, except the states of Goias, Maranhao, Parana and Rio Grande do Sul. Also Paraguay, Argentina, Peru, Venezuela, Bolivia, Colombia, Portugal, Holland, South Africa.

Leadership
The leader is Marcos Willians Herbas Camacho, alias Marcola, who took over the leadership in 2002, although he has been in prison since 1999 and is currently held at the Federal Prison of Porto Velho in Rondônia State.

Structure
The PCC is highly organised, with a CEO and strategic Deliberative Council (13 members); Board of Directors (three members); Administrative Board; Legal Board; State Board; Economic Board; Institutional Relations Board; and HR. The structure on the street is 'manager'; 'soldier'; 'scout'; 'killer'.

History
The PCC was created by eight inmates on 31 August 1993 in prison in Taubaté city. In 2006, after Marcola and 760 other prisoners were transferred to another prison, inmates rebelled in 74 state prisons and there were coordinated attacks on police officers, vehicles, jails and public buildings. More than 500 people were killed within a week.

First Command of the Capital (PCC)

Objectives
The PCC aims to deepen and entrench its position of power in Brazil and beyond, although they lack money-laundering expertise to expand their business as quickly as they would like.

Opponents
Rio: PMERJ, TCP, ADA, CV.
Ceará State: Northern Family, Guardians of the State.

Affiliates/allies
Rio: TCP, ADA.

Resources/capabilities
The average revenue of the PCC is US$100m per year. The gang uses pistols, rifles, bazookas and grenades.

Guardians of the State (GDE)

Strength
According to the government and *O Povo* newspaper, there are 6,000 members in Ceará State. According to the group's founders, however, the actual number is somewhere between 20,000 and 35,000.

Areas of operation
Ceará State.

Leadership
Yago Steferson Alves dos Santos (alias Yago Gordão), Francisco de Assis Fernandes da Silva (alias Barrinha) and Francisco Tiago Alves do Nascimento (alias Tiago Magão) are known as the 'final counsellors' in the organisation.

Structure
The GDE has a Governing Body with 13 'counsellors' and an Overseeing Board operating as a court for internal gang affairs. The structure on the street is decentralised: 'area leaders' are in charge of neighbourhoods and *favelas*. 'Managers' are responsible for drug-dealing spots, which are secured by 'soldiers'. 'Scouts' keep watch for potential risks.

History
The GDE was created from a dispute inside the PCC in Ceará in late 2015, when local leaders decided to create an autonomous organisation. Initially, the group acted together with the PCC and CV, but in 2016, alliances fell apart. Currently the largest organisation in Ceará, GDE is known for ostentation, cruelty, excessive violence and child recruitment.

Objectives
According to the gang's statute, their main goal is 'resisting the oppression' from gangs in other states and from the government.

Opponents
CV, PCC, FND, CVN.

Affiliates/allies
None.

Resources/capabilities
The GDE uses pistols, rifles, bazookas and grenades.

Northern Family (FDN)

Strength
Around 700 members in Ceará State. There is no official estimate of the number of members in the state of Amazonas, but the Federal Police deems the FDN the third-largest gang in Brazil.

Areas of operation
Ceará and Amazonas states.

Leadership
Gelson Lima Carnaúba (alias Gê) and José Roberto Barbosa (alias Zé Roberto da Compensa).

Structure
FDN has a decentralised structure: 'area leaders' are in charge of neighbourhoods and *favelas*. 'Managers' are responsible for drug-dealing spots, which are secured by 'soldiers' who fend off threats by other dealers or the police. 'Scouts' keep watch for potential risks and warn 'soldiers'.

History
FDN was created by Carnaúba and Barbosa, and became widely known after prison massacres in Manaus in 2015. That year, the FDN, together with the CV, carried out murders of PCC leaders; efforts by the state to broker a truce foundered. The FDN owns a state-level champion soccer team and operates the 'Solimões route', used to transport cocaine produced in Bolivia and Peru through rivers in the Amazon region.

Objectives
Expand and consolidate control of drug-trafficking routes in the Amazon region.

Opponents
PCC, ADA, GDE, Primeiro Grupo Catarinense, CV.

Affiliates/allies
Okaida.

Resources/capabilities
The FDN uses pistols, rifles, bazookas and grenades.

Drivers

Criminal competition over drug distribution

The gangs' desire to establish and expand drug-trafficking territories and routes is one of the main drivers of armed violence in Brazil. In the 1980s, the transnational empire of Pablo Escobar's Medellín Cartel lowered prices for cocaine, making it available to a much larger pool of customers. The large ensuing revenues, in conjunction with the proximity of some *favelas* (such as Rocinha) to the wealthy areas in the South Zone of Rio, helped the rise of rival criminal organisations involved in the drug trade. In order to take and control territory – meaning more drug-selling points and more negotiating power with international smugglers – the gangs began to fight more frequently and more violently. Clashes between CV and its main drug-trafficking competitor, the TCP, have been a major source of gang-on-gang violence over the past decade.

It took longer for violence to reach its current levels in Ceará State, but once Ceará's strategic significance was realised – Brazil's northeast is one route through which drugs reach Africa and Europe – criminal gangs from the country's southeast seized the opportunity to expand their business and export routes. More criminal actors brought heighted competition for drug-dealing spots and routes, leading to increased violent contestation, especially after 2015. According to the Atlas of Violence – an annual report from leading Brazilian security researchers Applied Economic Research Institute (IPEA) and Brazilian Forum of Public Security – Ceará had the highest increase in homicide rate of any state in 2017.

Social and racial inequality

Social inequality triggers armed violence in Brazil's cities. Brazil is an extremely unequal country, still facing an unresolved legacy of slavery. Extreme poverty has been on the rise since 2015, with 15.2m people living in extreme poverty as of December 2018. Poverty disproportionately affects the states in northern and northeastern Brazil; black- or brown-identifying Brazilians; and Brazilians who lack formal education or who attended only primary school. Meanwhile, the number of millionaires in Brazil reached 259,000 in 2019, up 19% from 2018, according to Credit Suisse's Global Wealth Report.

In 2017, 75.5% of Brazil's homicide victims were black or brown, according to the Atlas of Violence 2019, which is based on official data from the Information System on Mortality, part of the Ministry of Health. The homicide rate of blacks increased by 33% between 2007 and 2017 (the most recent data available), while in the same period, the increase in intentional lethal violence against non-blacks increased by 3.3%. The study also showed substantial growth in the murder rate of black Brazilians in some states: between 2007 and 2017 there was an increase of 207.6% in the murder rate of black Brazilians in Ceará, compared to 11.5% in Rio.

Lack of public services and unemployment

Neighbourhoods far from the centres of cities receive less investment and fewer public services, forcing residents to rely on third parties. In Rio, criminal organisations exploit this need in the market by providing (and controlling) many services, such as internet, gas and public transportation. This provides the gangs with another form of income in addition to drug trafficking and entrenches their control in the *favelas*.

Unemployment also drives the conflict. In 2019, the average unemployment rate was 11.9%, compared to 12.3% in 2018, with 12.6m unemployed, according to the IBGE (Brazilian Institute of Geography and Statistics), while the number of self-employed workers stood at 24.2m, the majority of whom (19.3m) had no CNPJ, or official business identification number, indicating a precarious economic existence.[5] In Rio, the jobless rate reached 15%, while in Ceará it hit 11%.[6] Drug trafficking offers the prospect of short-term gains for young people, especially those without access to education, enabling the gangs to find recruits easily.

Corruption and poor law enforcement

Brazil has been plagued by widespread corruption and impunity. Every Rio de Janeiro governor since 1998 has been arrested on corruption charges. The architect of the UPP strategy, former governor Sérgio Cabral, is now in prison on corruption charges, and one of its major backers, businessman Eike Batista, has been arrested twice.

The efficacy of the law-enforcement agencies in bringing criminals to justice is also a contributing factor in the violence. On the one hand, the perpetrators of crimes are rarely convicted, leading to a climate of impunity. According to the Atlas of Violence 2019, there is no nationwide calculation of the rate of completed crime investigations, but for the states in which this is measured, it averages between 10% and 20%. The Atlas also found that nationwide investigation rates are low because 'the system is … obsolete and overloaded, due to a lack of resources'. Investigations are often started only after arrests are made. On the other hand, the militarised tactics of the PMERJ in Rio (especially the special-operations unit BOPE) have drawn allegations of human-rights abuses, including the extrajudicial executions of suspects, creating a climate of mistrust and fear among the local residents.

Political Developments

Witzel's hardline approach in Rio

Wilson Witzel assumed office as governor of Rio on New Year's Day 2019 and outlined his confrontational security approach during his inauguration speech, stating that 'organised crime can no longer have the freedom to carry weapons of war and be treated romantically as people who didn't have opportunities'. On 20 August, he seemingly granted law-enforcement officers a permit to kill on sight, stating that 'whoever carries a rifle will be slaughtered'. The use of gunfire from helicopters in police operations became a recurring feature of police operations under Witzel's administration.

Witzel quickly set about implementing a raft of new security measures that reduced civilian oversight and granted the police a freer hand. In January – six months ahead of his own stated timeline – he wound down the Rio de Janeiro State Secretary of Security (SESEG), which facilitated civilian oversight of the police, folding its responsibilities and staff under the authority of the police, while the Institute of Public Security (ISP), formerly run by a civilian, was also transferred to police control in 2019. The reorganisation of the SESEG effectively halted more than 700 lawsuits against police officers without establishing new institutions which could conclude the prosecutions.

Witzel also rescinded a measure that protected police officers responsible for investigating their peers in the Civil and Military Police, which previously allowed internal-affairs officers to choose where to work so as to avoid contact with those they were investigating. After Witzel also abolished a financial incentive aimed at reducing killings by police in Rio, the number of people killed by the police increased, few of which were later investigated.[7]

Controversial prison measures in Ceará

A new prison secretariat was created in January in Ceará, and new Secretary Luís Mauro Albequerque immediately implemented a controversial measure that suspended the separation of inmates belonging to rival gangs inside prisons, which unleashed a series of attacks across the state.

Key Events in 2019

Political events

- **1 January**: President Jair Bolsonaro and Rio Governor Wilson Witzel take office.
- **7 January**: Ceará: 20 CV and GDE leaders are transferred to federal prisons.
- **11 January**: Rio: Dissolution of SESEG and creation of the secretaries of Civil Police and Military Police.
- **14 January**: Ceará: State government offers rewards in exchange for information about attacks.

Military/Violent events

- **2 January**: Ceará: GDE, PCC and FDN launch attacks across the state in protest against prison measures.
- **4 January**: Ceará: National Public Security Force personnel deployed to contain a wave of criminal attacks.
- **6 January**: Rio: In response to the killing of an officer, the PMERJ launch an operation in six *favelas*.
- **21 January**: Rio: Militia-led massacre results in nine people dead and four wounded.
- **8 February**: Rio: Thirteen people executed in Fallet-Fogueteiro *favela* by police.

Military Developments

Rio de Janeiro

Several statistics revealed a greater police presence in clashes in Rio in 2019, although this is partly explained by the fact that federal forces had supervised the state's public security in 2018. According to Rio's Security Observatory, between March and October 2019 there was a 37% increase in the number of police operations compared to the same period the previous year. Between January and October 2019, there were 6,434 shootings or shoot-outs in the Rio de Janeiro metropolitan region, 30% of which occurred in the presence of police officers. During the same period in 2018, there were more shootings (8,014), but fewer occurred with the participation of state agents (20%).

In many cases, police involvement translated into high numbers of deaths. In the first half of 2019, police killed 881 people in the state of Rio de Janeiro.[8] (Significantly, none of these fatalities occurred in militia areas, as militias are often comprised of current or former police officers.) According to Fogo Cruzado, a Brazilian data platform that collects reports of shootings, in 2019 there were 67 massacres (defined as three or more people killed in the same incident) in the Rio metropolitan region, totalling 251 deaths. Police were involved in 52 of these cases, killing 192 people. (In 2018, there were 53 massacres with 209 deaths; 35 of these had police participation and resulted in 141 deaths.)

In August 2019, six civilians were killed over five days of police operations, while a baby under the age of two was injured. In response to the killings, State Secretary of State Cleiton Rodrigues stated: 'The governor and the state government deeply regret all these deaths. These and all the others that may happen.'

On 20 September, an eight-year-old girl, Ágatha Félix, was shot dead by a police officer in the Alemão *favela* complex. The PMERJ sought to deflect blame on Twitter, stating: 'On Friday night, 9/20, UPP Fazendinha police officers were attacked from various points in the community simultaneously. The team retaliated against the aggression. Soon after they were informed that a resident was injured in the locality "Estofador".' It was later revealed that there had been no attack on police officers and that the police officer had fired at a motorcyclist who had not stopped at a police checkpoint.

Hundreds of people took to the streets to protest Ágatha's killing, while the social-media tag #ACulpaÉDoWitzel (Witzel's fault) was used in numerous tweets that criticised the governor's security policies. Amnesty International condemned the killing, while the Inter-American Commission on Human Rights, part of the Organisation of American States (OAS), called for those responsible to be brought to justice.

Ceará State

In January and September, CV and GDE joined forces to confront the state government over proposed prison reforms that would desegregate inmates from rival gangs in prison. The scale of the attacks stunned state authorities: within a month, criminal groups carried out 283 attacks against public buildings, buses, fuel stations and other targets. Some 56

---

26 September
Ceará: In response to state-wide attacks, 506 prisoners are transferred to different prisons.

21 October
Ceará: Physical contact between visitors and inmates in maximum-security wings is banned.

8 May
Rio: Eight people killed by police at the Maré *favela* complex.

29 June
Rio: A clash between traffickers and militiamen kills four and wounds 13.

August
Rio: Five youths unconnected to crime are killed by police in less than four days.

20 September
Ágatha Felix is killed by a police officer in the Alemão *favela* complex.

September
Ceará: GDE, PCC and FDN carry out 95 attacks in 16 municipalities over eight days.

4 October
Rio: Two children, aged two and four, are wounded during a police operation.

of the state's 184 cities were attacked, including 134 attacks in the state capital of Fortaleza, according to the Jangadeiro Communication System.[9] A motorway flyover was structurally damaged after one of its columns was bombed, and 12 cities lost mobile-telephone service after an explosion in a telephone centre.

In response, Ceará's government increased recruitment calls for reserve police officers and firemen; increased overtime pay for public-security officials; offered rewards for information about attacks; created a Public Security and Social Defence Fund; and regulated command of police reinforcements from other states. It also requested an emergency division of the National Public Security Force, with at least 300 troops being deployed in the state in January, rising to more than 400 by September. Some 466 people suspected of participating in the attacks were arrested. Still, there was a spate of 95 attacks across the state in September as inmates demanded better treatment in prisons.

Despite these waves of attacks, a non-aggression pact between the gangs contributed to a significant drop in the number of homicides in Ceará, from 4,518 in 2018 to 2,257 in 2019. The number of killings by police also fell, from 221 to 136, with 28 occurring in January (the period of the attacks), compared to 25 in January 2018.

Impact

Human rights

On 6 May, the Human Rights Commission of Rio de Janeiro's state legislature filed complaints against Witzel's security policies to both the United Nations – where the complaint assessed that Witzel's tactics were becoming 'increasingly militarised, with the use of drones, helicopters and armoured cars, as well as sniper techniques' – and also to the OAS, where the commission described the tactics as bearing characteristics of 'crimes against humanity, the death penalty and torture'. Both institutions sent letters to the Brazilian government questioning Witzel's security policies, to which the federal government responded by affirming its 'commitment to the protection of human rights in public security activities'.

In September, after Ágatha's murder, the Brazilian public defender and the Rio de Janeiro chapter of the Brazilian Bar Association also denounced Witzel's policies. In September, opposition parties filed a suit against Witzel at Brazil's Superior Court of Justice, claiming that police committed crimes with the 'approval, encouragement, and promotion' of the governor.

In Ceará, Governor Camilo Santana has been criticised by his own party for considering use of an anti-terrorism law against the criminal groups, with critics warning that this could be used to target activists as well. The Human Rights Council of Ceará State published a call by 34 groups from Ceará and six other Brazilian states for authorities to guarantee human rights after the council received complaints of police carrying out home invasions, violence, alleged evidence tampering and arbitrary arrests. On 15 February, Brazil's federal anti-torture body released a report that accused the Ministry of Women, Family, and Human Rights of preventing prison inspections after the Ceará prison crisis, and said it forwarded this complaint to Brazil's attorney general and special citizens-rights prosecutor, as well as the UN.[10] The anti-torture body subsequently found that Ceará inmates had been exposed to 'collective punishments' and 'generalised torture' in three state prisons, and denounced the 'complete lack of transparency' about the real situation inside the prisons (including overcrowding, health, lack of communication and restricted rights of visitation).[11]

Humanitarian

The state's militarised response to gang control often focuses on short-term tactical objectives instead of long-term efforts to create institutions, provide services and offer stable governance in marginalised areas. This has meant that any progress on security has usually been short-lived and there has been no meaningful improvement in the conditions of people's lives.

Deaths of young women (12 to 17 years old) increased by 90% in the Ceará state capital Fortaleza between 2017 and 2018, compared to a 35% drop in homicides of young men over the same period. In 2019, due in large part to the alliance between the gangs, there was a 66.7% drop in deaths of young women in the period to November 2019, compared to the same period in 2018, from 60 to 20. However, the threat to young women remained prominent, with women targeted due to their connection to members of rival gangs as friends, relatives or boyfriends. Some were forced to move to a different neighbourhood for their own safety.

At the street level, the pervasive violence and heavy-handed tactics of the police resulted in many innocent people being killed. In Rio, between January and November of 2019, uncoordinated actions with little basis in intelligence resulted in 45 people killed by stray bullets – five of them children. The same period in 2018 saw 31 killed in the same way, three of whom were children.

Economic
According to a statement by Carlos von Doellinger, president of IPEA, in May 2019 outlays on public safety and private security cost the equivalent of 6% of Brazil's GDP, or approximately R$400bn (US$120bn).[12]

The economy of Ceará was significantly impacted by the violence. Tourism accounts for 70% of Ceará's GDP, and the state receives more than 2m (mostly Brazilian) tourists annually, but the January attacks by gangs severely disrupted business. Buses were burned and property destroyed across the state, while the capital city's hotel-occupation rate – usually about 85% in January, a summer-holiday month – was only around 65% in 2019.

Relations with neighbouring and international partners
Witzel repeatedly blamed violence in Rio on arms trafficking from Paraguay, saying he intends to file a complaint against Paraguay at the UN and may impose a security lockdown on the Brazil/Paraguay border.

Of the Brazilian gangs, the PCC will continue to operate with international partners. The São Paulo gang uses Brazilian ports for the export of drugs, which European gangs take to Africa and even Asia. In January 2015, the police and the MPE (state prosecutor's office) discovered accounts in China and the United States that were being used to launder money from the PCC, highlighting the international reach of the gang.[13] The gang's international ambitions are further demonstrated by reports of the PCC recruiting foreign members.[14] Prosecutors have alleged that at least two Spaniards, one Swiss and several Portuguese may have been recruited by the PCC.

Trends

Political trajectories
Soon after taking office, Brazilian President Jair Bolsonaro and Rio de Janeiro Governor Wilson Witzel broke their alliance. Witzel intends to run for president, hoping that his hardline security policies will win popular approval. This means that it is unlikely that Witzel will modify or ameliorate his tough stance against crime in the near future, given that it is likely to be the backbone of his putative election campaign in the future.

In the more immediate future, democratic institutions are at risk with Bolsonaro, whose belligerent approach, coupled with ineffective measures and political crises, has alienated allies such as Government Secretary General Carlos Alberto dos Santos Cruz, former commander-general of the UN peacekeeping mission UNSTAMIH, who claimed to have been bullied by Carlos Bolsonaro, the son of the president and a councillor in Rio de Janeiro, as well as by Olavo de Carvalho, Bolsonaro's political guru. The increasing grip of the armed forces, which at the end of 2019 controlled eight of the 22 ministries of the Bolsonaro government, also points to a continuing drift towards more hardline security policies and fewer civilian checks and balances.

Conflict-related risks
Municipal elections will be held in 2020 in Brazil. In Rio de Janeiro, the TRE (Regional Electoral Court) assumes that there is a risk that the activities of the militia and trafficking will have an impact on the electoral process (which decides the appointment of mayors and councillors).[15] The agency is conducting a mapping of electoral zones to list instances of homicides and coercions that occurred in the last elections to try to prevent them from recurring. In 2019, ten people in political office were shot in the metropolitan region of Rio de Janeiro, seven of whom died. Some of the deaths are still being

investigated, while others have already been linked to the militia.

Prospects for peace

The state legislature approved a bill in Rio that provides for the end of the UPPs throughout the state, but it is dependent on the governor's approval (still pending). Of the 38 units that came into operation in Rio, 19 have been extinguished or remodelled, despite the fact that many police want the programme reactivated. However, as of December 2019, no comprehensive alternative strategies have been presented. Without a comprehensive peace strategy to replace the UPP programme (now in legislative limbo), violence will likely persist in Rio. Ceará's cycle of violence is also set to continue after the re-election of hardline Governor Camilo Santana in October 2018 for another four-year term.

More generally, the causes of violence remain unaddressed by the state and federal authorities in both Rio de Janeiro and Ceará, who prefer to focus on security-based policies. But despite this security emphasis, lack of funding of police intelligence remains a key concern, with investments in intelligence representing only 0.5% of public spending on security, while little has been done in relation to integrated databases or cooperation agreements with other countries. In the absence of effective public policies based on police intelligence work, conflict mediation and prevention of the social drivers of crime, the cycle of conflict and violence will likely be perpetuated.

Strategic implications and global influences

Without serious attention to the use of intelligence to combat organised crime, criminal groups in neighbouring countries are likely to continue to enjoy the same access to drug and arms routes through Brazil that are currently in operation, with the continued internationalisation of the PCC. This will likely spread the networks of organised crime, along with violence, even further in the coming years.

Notes

[1] Carolina Heringer, 'Homicídios dolosos no Rio têm menor patamar desde 1991; mortes pela polícia chegam ao nível mais alto', *O Globo*, 21 January 2020.

[2] Sonia Bridi, James Alberti and Monica Reolom, 'Em 2019, uma em cada três pessoas assassinadas no Rio de Janeiro foi morta por policiais', *O Globo*, 19 January 2020.

[3] Institute of Applied Economic Research (IPEA) and the Brazilian Public Security Forum (FBSP), '2019 Atlas of Violence 2019', 2019.

[4] 'Região metropolitana do Rio registrou quase 10 mil tiros em 2018', Fogo Cruzado, 13 January 2019.

[5] FIESP, 'Desemprego fica em 11% em dezembro, mas ainda atinge 11,6 milhões, diz IBGE', 10 February 2020.

[6] Cristina Boeckel, 'Número de desempregados bate recorde no RJ, diz IBGE', *O Globo*, 16 May 2019; 'IBGE: taxa de desemprego é de 10,9% no Ceará', *O Povo*, 15 August 2019.

[7] Matheus Rodrigues and Felipe Grandin, 'Ações policiais com 3 mortos ou mais no RJ batem recorde em 2019', *O Globo*, 16 October 2019.

[8] Sérgio Ramalho, 'Polícias mataram 881 pessoas em 6 meses no RJ. Nenhuma em área de milícia', UOL, 20 August 2019.

[9] 'Onda de ataques no Ceará: Veja o número atualizado de ações de facções criminosas', *Tribuna do Ceará*, 4 February 2019.

[10] Bruno Fonseca, 'Ministério de Damares é acusado por órgão de combate à tortura de impedir inspeção em presídios do Ceará', Publica, 15 February 2019.

[11] Mecanismo Nacional de Prevenção e Combate à Tortura, 'Relatorio missão ao estado do Ceará', 2019.

[12] John Paul Saconi and Bernardo Mello, 'Custo da violência chega a 6% do PIB do Brasil, dizem organizadores do Atlas da Violência', *O Globo*, 5 June 2019.

[13] Alexandre Hisayasu, 'PCC 10 anos: 2: o poder geográfico', *Estadão*, 2016.

[14] Fernanda Odilla, 'PCC "batiza" estrangeiros no grupo de olho na expansão do tráfico de drogas na Europa', BBC, 1 August 2018.

[15] Ana Luiza Albuquerque, 'Milícia e tráfico ameaçam eleições municipais no Rio', *Folha De S. Paolo*, 1 March 2020.

COLOMBIA (BACRIMs)

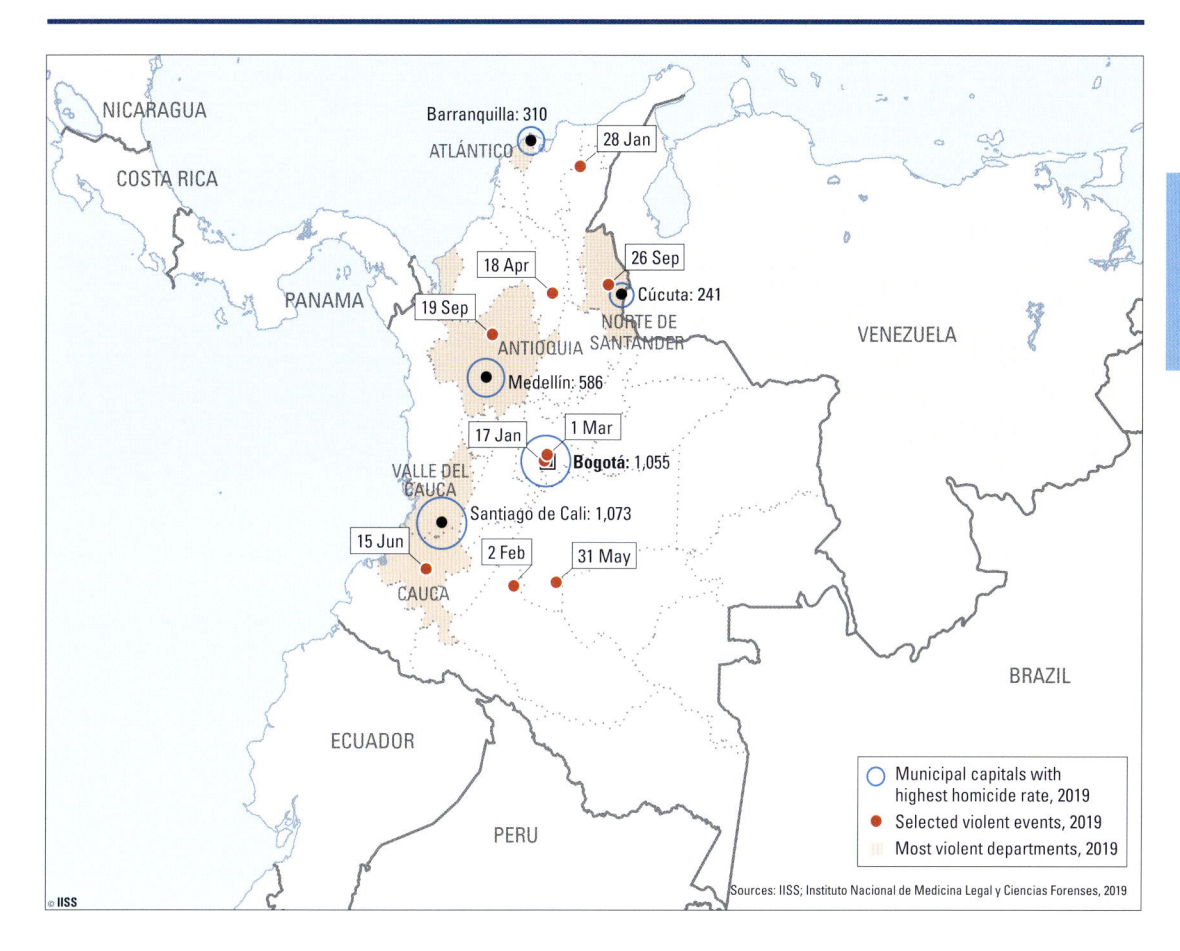

Overview

The conflict in 2019
Fighting between the Colombian security forces and armed groups and BACRIMs ('*bandas criminales*' or criminal gangs) increased in 2019, despite the successful implementation of the 2016 peace agreement between the government and the Revolutionary Armed Forces of Colombia (FARC). President Iván Duque, a right-wing politician and hardline critic of the peace agreement with FARC, took a stronger approach than his predecessor against illegal groups. His actions led to a 53% increase in armed clashes between the Colombian armed forces and illegal armed groups since 2018, a 26% increase in apprehensions of members of armed groups and an 11% increase in deaths during security operations between January and September of 2019 compared to the previous year.[1]

The conflict in Colombia is no longer an ideological struggle for political power. Only pockets of localised violence persist, mostly in rural areas, with Valle del Cauca, Antioquia, Cauca, Norte de Santander and Atlántico the most violent departments in 2019. The challenge facing the Colombian

Key statistics

Type	Internationalised
Start date	1964 (FARC); 1965 (ELN)
IDPs total (December 2018)	7,816,500
Refugees total (December 2018)*	310
People in need	No data

*In addition to 1,171,552 displaced Venezuelans.

state is a large-scale and highly sophisticated network of drug-trafficking organisations either cooperating or fighting for control of territories and drug-trafficking routes. Venezuela's economic and political collapse and the subsequent migrant and humanitarian crisis placed further strain on the Colombian government, which struggled to control its borders in 2019. This created a haven for guerrillas and criminals, who expanded their operations across the border and made Venezuela one of the main drug-trafficking routes towards the United States.

The National Liberation Army (ELN) – the only remaining guerrilla group – continued to be the most active armed group in 2019, followed by FARC dissidents and the Gulf Clan. The ELN revamped its criminal activities after the failure to reach a peace agreement with the Colombian government in 2018 and mainly targeted oil infrastructure. Following a terrorist attack in Bogotá in January 2019 that killed 22 police cadets, Duque confirmed that talks would not resume. FARC's former commander Iván Márquez and other leaders abandoned the 2016 peace agreement, accusing the government of breaking the deal. On 29 August 2019, they announced the creation of a new dissident faction and officially returned to the armed struggle. Colombia's security and defence policy therefore continued to focus on counter-insurgency and counter-narcotics operations.

The conflict to 2019

A decade of political violence known as La Violencia (1948–58), a civil war between the Conservative and Liberal parties, resulted in at least 200,000 civilian deaths. That war ended when the two parties agreed to alternate in government and to present a joint National Front candidate in elections to restrict the participation of other political movements. Political exclusion, socio-economic challenges and the international Cold War context encouraged the armed struggle and the guerrilla war in particular. FARC was founded in 1964, followed by the ELN in 1965 and the Popular Liberation Army (EPL) in 1967. These guerrilla groups were motivated by Marxist–Leninist ideals of social revolution and had the common objectives of fighting against the privatisation of natural resources and for the representation of the rural poor.

In the 1980s, rural landowners began to organise right-wing paramilitaries to protect themselves from the guerrillas. The largest, the United Self-Defence Forces of Colombia (AUC), was an umbrella organisation of paramilitary groups that formally disbanded in 2006, but its dissolution led to the formation of splinter groups that later turned into large criminal organisations, most notably the Gulf Clan.

Peace negotiations between the Colombian government and FARC began in September 2012 and ended with a peace agreement signed on 24 August 2016. A revised peace deal was signed on 24 November 2016, sent directly to Congress and not submitted to a second referendum (a referendum to ratify the first deal was unsuccessful). Both houses ratified the revised text, ending 52 years of civil war. FARC completed its demobilisation in August 2017 – 11,000 fighters and collaborators demobilised and delivered more than 8,000 weapons to United Nations monitors.[2]

Despite the successful peace process, the state still does not control former insurgent zones, where several criminal organisations have filled the void left by FARC and assumed control of illegal activities. In Antioquia, Arauca, Cauca, Chocó and Putumayo departments – remote areas rich in natural resources, coca plantations and cocaine-production sites – criminal groups continue to fight the state, the ELN and each other for control of territory and the drug-trafficking routes.[3] Additionally, several FARC splinter groups have remained active and are gaining strength. Though none of these pose an existential threat to the Colombian state, they undermine the presence of state authorities. Confrontations negatively impact local communities, with serious humanitarian consequences including forced displacement.

Key Conflict Parties

Colombian armed forces

Strength
Colombia has the third-largest armed forces in the western hemisphere in terms of active personnel, behind the US and Brazil. The army is the largest branch with 223,150 personnel, followed by the navy with 56,400 and 13,650 in the air force.

Areas of operation
Presence throughout the country but limited in some rural departments.

Leadership
Commander-in-Chief President Iván Duque, Minister of Defence Carlos Holmes Trujillo García, General Commander Gen. Luis Fernando Navarro Jiménez.

Structure
National Army of Colombia, Navy, Air Force and Naval Infantry.

History
Originated in the 1770s and 1780s with the Army of the Commoners. In 1781, the Liberating Army was created during the independence movement of 1810 against the Spanish Empire. The military forces were consolidated after 7 August 1819 with the triumph in the Battle of Boyacá.

Objectives
Main military branch involved in the armed conflicts against the BACRIMs.

Opponents
ELN, FARC dissidents, Gulf Clan, EPL and other smaller criminal organisations.

Affiliates/allies
The National Police (PNC) is in charge of public security. Not technically part of the armed forces, the PNC has been controlled and administered by the Ministry of National Defense and has had a highly militarised structure since 1953. It comprises 180,000 uniformed personnel.

Resources/capabilities
In 2019, Colombia's defence budget was US$10.5 billion, or 3.9% of Colombia's GDP.

FARC dissidents

Strength
1,500–2,500 guerrilla fighters.

Areas of operation
Various groups spread over 16 departments, with particularly strong presence in Caquetá, Guaviare, Meta, Putumayo and Vaupés.

Leadership
The leaders of the most important dissident fronts are Miguel Botache Santillana (alias 'Gentil Duarte'), Nestor Gregorio Vera Fernández (alias 'Iván Mordisco') and Géner García Molina (alias 'Jhon 40'). In late 2019, Luciano Marín Arango (alias 'Iván Márquez') created a new FARC dissident group.

Structure
Each front works independently, with ad hoc collaboration in some areas.

History
FARC dissidents rejected the 2016 peace agreement, labelling those that accepted it as traitors and themselves as the 'true FARC'.

Objectives
Overthrow the Colombian government and create a socialist state.

Opponents
Colombian armed forces and the Gulf Clan.

Affiliates/allies
ELN in the Catatumbo region.

Resources/capabilities
Drug production and trafficking are the main revenue sources, followed by kidnapping and extortion. FARC dissident fronts possess small numbers of many kinds of rifles and shotguns. The most common weapon is the AK-47 assault rifle.

National Liberation Army (ELN)

Strength
Approximately 3,000 fighters.

Areas of operation
The ELN is the last remaining guerrilla group with significant presence throughout the country. It operates in 12 states of Venezuela and nine departments of Colombia, where it has a strong presence in the northeast. Since the peace agreement with FARC, it has taken over areas previously under FARC control, particularly in the departments of Cauca and Chocó.

Leadership
Commander Nicolás Rodríguez Bautista (alias 'Gabino').

Structure
The Central Command (COCE) directs strategy and is composed of five commanders and divisions that operate independently. Additionally, the ELN has seven war fronts.

History
Founded in 1964 by a group of Catholic priests, left-wing intellectuals and students embracing liberation theology and trying to emulate Fidel Castro's Cuban revolution.

National Liberation Army (ELN)

Objectives
Overthrow the Colombian government and establish a socialist state, although now mainly focused on criminal activities.

Opponents
Colombian armed forces and the EPL in Catatumbo region and the Gulf Clan in Arauca and Valle del Cauca departments.

Affiliates/allies
FARC dissidents in the Catatumbo region.

Resources/capabilities
Drug production and trafficking are the main sources of revenue, followed by illegal mining.

Gulf Clan (also known as the Urabeños)

Strength
Approximately 4,000.

Areas of operation
Active in 17 departments, but base and territorial stronghold is the area around the Gulf of Urabá in the departments of Antioquia and Chocó.

Leadership
Leader Dairo Antonio Úsuga (alias 'Otoniel').

Structure
One-third of local cells are directly commanded by the leadership in Urabá, while the others are local criminal organisations expected to provide services or follow strategic orders when called upon.

History
Emerged from the demobilisation of the AUC paramilitary group in 2006.

Objectives
Little remains of the group's paramilitary roots and it is principally involved in criminal activities.

Opponents
Colombian armed forces, ELN and some FARC dissident fronts.

Affiliates/allies
Working with FARC dissidents in Córdoba.

Resources/capabilities
Main revenue comes from controlling the cocaine market, though the network as a whole works less as a drug cartel and more as a service provider to independent drug traffickers. It escorts shipments along international-trafficking corridors, ensures access to or protection for processing laboratories and provides storage and dispatch services on the Atlantic coast and border regions.

Drivers

Society and the state

Colombia's social, economic and political challenges have historically facilitated criminal activities. A middle-income country with a GDP of US$6,667.8 per capita in 2018,[4] Colombia is one of Latin America's most unequal countries. Approximately 19.6% of Colombians lived below the poverty line in 2018, more than one-third of whom lived in the countryside,[5] where armed groups are concentrated and most criminal activities take place.

The country faces several challenges related to corruption, including collusion between the public and the private sectors; the influence of organised crime on policy and institutions; weak state presence in remote areas; and an inefficient criminal-justice system. In Transparency International's 2019 Corruption Perceptions Index, Colombia was ranked 96th out of 180 countries.[6]

The absence of state institutions in many parts of the country, particularly rural areas, has left poor, unprotected and marginalised populations exposed to criminal and guerrilla groups, which have achieved some social legitimacy within those communities.[7]

Ideology and organised crime

For the past four decades, ideology and criminal activities have coexisted in Colombia's internal conflict, as both guerrillas and paramilitary groups have used drug trafficking to finance their activities and warfare. The demobilisation of FARC has shifted the conflict further towards purely criminal activities and increased violence between groups seeking to exploit the power vacuum and compete for territory. Organised crime pervades the country, with groups active in 28 of 32 departments. The ELN retains some remnants of ideological motivation and has an underlying objective of creating a socialist state but is also heavily involved in criminal activities.

Drug trade

In the 1970s, poor farmers in Colombia began growing marijuana as a more lucrative alternative to legal crops. Cartels, paramilitary and guerrilla

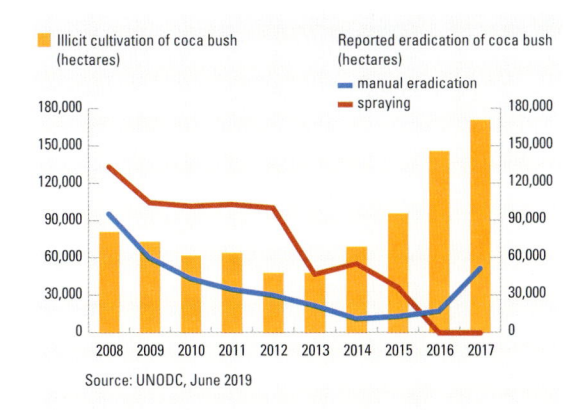

Figure 1: Coca cultivation and eradication, Colombia, 2008–17

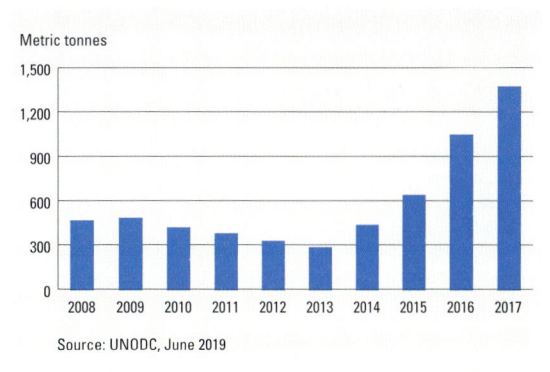

Figure 2: Potential manufacture of pure cocaine, Colombia, 2008–17

groups have been involved in drug trafficking since the coca-production boom of the 1980s. In the late 1990s and early 2000s, much of the fighting between FARC and the AUC was over control of coca plantations and trafficking routes.

Drug trafficking remains the main driver of violence in Colombia. According to the UN Office on Drugs and Crime (UNODC), estimated global manufacture of cocaine reached an all-time high of 1,976 tonnes in 2017. This represented an increase of 25% on the previous year, with Colombia accounting for an estimated 70% of production. In the same year cocaine production increased by 31% in Colombia, mainly due to a significant increase in the productive areas under coca-bush cultivation.[8] In 2018, the White House Office of National Drug Control Policy estimated that there were 208,000 hectares of coca-leaf cultivation in Colombia.[9] According to the UNODC, production is highly concentrated, with 44% of crops located in ten municipalities in 2018 (Tibú, Norte de Santander; Tumaco, Nariño; Puerto Asís, Putumayo; El Tambo, Cauca; Sardinata, Norte de Santander; El Charco, Nariño; El Tarra, Norte de Santander; Orito, Putumayo; Tarazá, Antioquia; and Barbacoas, Nariño).[10] The predominant trafficking route is along the Pacific coast, where production and manufacture are concentrated. The cocaine is trafficked from Colombia to Central America and Mexico using planes, ships and semi-submersible vessels. Mexican organised-crime groups then transport it across the border into the US. Colombia is also the main supplier of cocaine for the European market, with the drug mainly trafficked through Spain and the Netherlands.

The drug trade (including direct and indirect participation, and the taxation, administration and control of areas of production and trafficking) remains the main source of revenue for guerrilla, paramilitary and organised-crime groups. To protect their income, these groups engage in widespread human-rights abuses and undermine democratic institutions. A UNODC report of August 2019 indicated that 80% of homicides in 2018 related to the armed conflict were in municipalities where coca is produced.[11]

Political Developments

FARC leaders return to arms

On 29 August 2019, former second in command of FARC Luciano Marín Arango (alias 'Iván Márquez') – one of FARC's main ideologues who led the delegation that negotiated the 2016 agreement – announced the beginning of a new stage of armed struggle against what he called an 'exclusive and corrupt oligarchy'. Márquez accused the government of betraying the peace agreement, saying it had not followed through with pledges to develop rural areas and failed to protect former FARC members. Around 130 demobilised guerrillas have been killed since the signing of the peace deal.[12]

Márquez is the highest-ranking FARC dissident to have returned to arms. Other senior and influential commanders joined him, including Seuxis Paucias Hernández Solarte (alias 'Jesús Santrich') and Hernán Darío Velásquez (alias 'El Paisa'), who was once the commander of FARC's strongest military wing, the Teófilo Forero Column. Márquez announced that he would seek an alliance with the ELN. Jaime Arias (alias 'Uriel'), leader of the ELN operating in Chocó, publicly celebrated the return to arms of Márquez, Santrich and El Paisa, hinting at a possible alliance.

Impact of the Venezuelan crisis

Venezuela's economic, political and social collapse has shifted criminal dynamics on the Colombia–Venezuela border where several criminal groups, including the ELN and FARC dissidents, are active. Venezuela serves as a key route for drugs trafficked by Colombian organised-crime groups and destined for markets in the US and Europe. As a result, the border is becoming one of the most important organised-crime areas in the region.

Military Developments

ELN resilience

The ELN expanded its activities to several parts of the country, demonstrating its resiliency against government attacks, strengthening its control over specific territories and attempting to consolidate its regional monopoly over illegal activities. It was the group involved in the most confrontations with Colombian security forces in 2019. Its influence increased substantially, particularly in regions where it had shared a presence with FARC. It also continued to expand its operations to Venezuela.

On 17 January 2019, the ELN claimed responsibility for a car-bomb attack on a police academy in Bogotá that killed 23 people (including the attacker) and injured 68 – the deadliest attack on the capital since 2003. The ELN justified the attack as a response to bombings by the Colombian government against its camps during the unilateral ceasefire. In response, Duque suspended the peace dialogue with the ELN and said that the Colombian security forces had revamped their activities against the group. The death of Yovanni Bello Oliverio (alias 'Guacharaco'), the main ELN leader in the Lower Cauca region of Antioquia Department, was reported on 29 June. Another faction leader, Navides Chilhueso Noscué (alias 'Tigre Indio'), was killed during a confrontation on 15 June.

The government also inflicted serious damage on the Heroes y Martires de Anori bloc, one of the ELN's oldest factions, leaving it without clear leadership. The armed forces captured Juan Gabriel Villa Quiroz (alias 'Gabino'), the bloc's second in command, in February, and its commander Norberto de Jesús Arango Loaiza (alias 'el Perro') on 19 September after a confrontation in the Antioquia Department.

Death of EPL leader

Luis Antonio Quiceno Sanjuan (alias 'Pácora'), the chief commander of the EPL, was killed on 26 September during a joint police and army operation

Key Events in 2019

Political events

26 January
The Prosecutor's Office confirms arrest warrants for senior ELN members for their involvement in the 17 January attack in Bogotá.

4 February
ELN commander 'Pablo Beltran' reiterates that the ELN is open to a new peace dialogue.

9 July
The Supreme Court issues an arrest warrant for the former FARC leader Seuxis Paucias Hernández Solarte (alias 'Jesús Santrich').

Military/Violent events

17 January
The ELN attacks the General Santander Police School in Bogotá with a car bomb, killing 23 people and injuring 68.

2 February
The armed forces bomb a FARC dissident group camp in Caquetá Department, killing the group leader and nine other fighters.

18 April
Armed forces kill the leader of the Alfredo Gómez Quiñonez Front of the ELN (alias 'Juan').

30 April
Colombian troops on the border with Venezuela are quartered as a result of a military uprising in Venezuela.

31 May
Mario López Córdoba (alias 'Negro Edward'), the leader of the Gulf Clan in Meta Department, is killed in a bombing.

in Sardinata, Norte de Santander Department.[13] This was a heavy blow to the EPL, which lost several other important figures in 2019 and has been losing ground to the ELN in its base in the Catatumbo region since 2018. The EPL only has around 500 guerrilla fighters, but it is considered extremely violent and dangerous. Pácora's death created a leadership vacuum that could lead to a potential degradation and further criminalisation of the group. A weakened EPL could also enable the ELN to continue expanding its military capacity – it has gained considerable tactical and territorial advantage over the EPL since the war between the two groups started in 2018.

Impact

Human rights

The forced recruitment of minors has changed according to the new dynamics of the conflict. Historically, minors were forced into the ranks of the guerrillas and paramilitaries, but are now recruited for other purposes: as members of criminal gangs, as hit men, extortionists and drug dealers, and as workers of illicit crops. Forced recruitment is now happening in urban and rural areas, as opposed to mostly rural areas. According to a recent report, between January and September 2019 forced recruitment of minors increased by 41.6% compared to the previous year, and Bolívar, Córdoba and Antioquia departments had the highest recruitment rates. Separately, 80 social leaders were murdered in 2019 and threats against them reportedly increased by 31%.[14]

Humanitarian

Disputes over control of drug production and increasing levels of violence forced many communities in rural areas to abandon their homes. On 23 January the UN Office for the Coordination of Humanitarian Affairs (OCHA) reported that at least 700 people had been displaced in Tumaco, Nariño as a result of clashes between armed groups. Between January and October 2019, Colombia's Ombudsman's Office reported 58 major instances of forced displacement, affecting 15,140 people (5,126 families).[15] The department most affected by displacement was Nariño, followed by Córdoba, Valle del Cauca, Norte de Santander and Chocó.

Economic

The number of coca plantations in Colombia has decreased but cocaine production increased to record levels during 2017–18.[16] A UNODC report published in August 2019 estimated that production increased from 1,058 tonnes in 2017 to 1,120 in 2018. This increase was due to the fact that coca crops are increasingly concentrated in areas more suitable for farming; the use of new production technologies facilitating higher yields; and the fact that farmers are using modern equipment and improved agricultural techniques.[17] During 2019, the Colombian government eradicated more than 81,000 hectares of coca, reaching its eradication target for the year.[18] The policy appeared to

---

29 August
Three high-ranking FARC leaders, including Iván Márquez, announce that they will resume the armed struggle.

26 September
In a video statement, the commanders of the 18th Front of FARC dissidents accept Márquez as leader.

25 November
A judge orders the release of Salvatore Mancuso, the former paramilitary leader who led the demobilisation of paramilitary group the AUC.

5 December
The government announces the eradication of 81,000 hectares of coca-leaf plantations, surpassing its yearly goal of 80,000.

15 June
Navides Chilhueso Noscué (alias 'Tigre Indio'), head of an ELN faction, is killed in a confrontation with state forces in El Tambo, Cauca Department.

20 August
1,350 soldiers are deployed to Cauca Department to help with the humanitarian crisis caused by confrontations between illegal armed groups.

22 August
President Duque confirms that Colombian forces captured Carlos Mario Úsuga David, former chief of finance of the Gulf Clan and brother of the group's leader Dairo Antonio Úsuga (alias 'Otoniel').

26 September
One of the EPL's main leaders, Luis Antonio Quiceno Sanjuan (alias 'Pácora'), is killed in a joint police and army operation.

be a success, but according to Colombia's High Commissioner for Peace Miguel Ceballos, replanting rates were estimated at 50–67%.[19] As a result, Colombia is facing a 'balloon effect', by which drug production moves from one region to another as well as increasing.

Trends

Political trajectories
Though a heavy blow to the peace process, the return to arms of senior FARC commanders is unlikely to make the agreement collapse or attract other demobilised FARC fighters. It is doubtful that Márquez carries the political weight to unify the rest of the FARC dissident groups. While he seems motivated by an ideological struggle, many other dissident groups are driven by profit and will continue to focus on controlling and participating in the drug economy. Additionally, several senior FARC dissident leaders see Márquez as the principal architect of the peace accord and a traitor to the cause.

Márquez has stated his intention to create an alliance with the ELN, and Jaime Arias (alias 'Uriel'), commander of the ELN's Western War Front, applauded his return to armed struggle. The ELN has become Colombia's most prominent guerrilla group since FARC demobilised and has already reached non-aggression pacts with FARC's former 36th Front in Bajo Cauca and the 33rd Front in Norte de Santander.[20] Any alliance between the groups would immediately expand the territory and revenues of both groups and could develop into a relatively coordinated and powerful military cooperation. The FARC and the ELN have generally fought each other rather than worked together, in most cases over territory and control of drug-trafficking routes. According to Bogotá think tank Fundación Ideas para la Paz (FIP), an alliance between Márquez and the ELN would be difficult to realise at a national level, but it could happen in some areas.[21]

Conflict-related risks
The death of Pácora, the EPL's main political and military leader, is a victory for the government but also for the ELN, which has been at war with the EPL since 2018. As well as a potential collapse of the EPL, another consequence could be an economic, military and territorial strengthening of the ELN, which is likely to push for control of other municipalities contested by the EPL, including Teorama, El Tarra, Hacarí, Playa de Belén and Sardinata, all of which are in the Catatumbo region. This area is key for criminal groups because it is the location of the country's largest coca-crop harvests and is in a remote area on the border with Venezuela that provides access to key drug-trafficking routes.[22]

The government increased its operations against the ELN with relative success, capturing or killing several leaders of the group in 2019. However, the operations have not inflicted long-term damage on the organisation's revenue sources or operational capacity, and the group has expanded its activities to new territories within Colombia and Venezuela. It is likely to increase its criminal activities and expand its power and control of territory in 2020.

Despite the increase in clashes between the government and illegal groups in 2019, there have been some security and social improvements in specific areas. According to data from FIP, if trends continue, there will be a 45% decrease in victims of forced displacement, a 27% reduction in homicides of social leaders and a 40% decrease in aggressions against former guerrilla fighters during 2019 compared to the previous year.[23] Although conflict between illegal groups will continue during 2020, humanitarian costs might be reduced.

Prospects for peace
In a Gallup poll in January 2019, 64% of Colombians thought that negotiations between the Colombian government and the ELN should resume.[24] However, Duque has shown few signs of intending to re-establish peace talks. On 13 December 2019, he reiterated that the ELN must cease all criminal activities and release all hostages in order to resume peace talks. The ELN has seemingly made no attempts to reduce its criminal activities and is expanding its territorial control. The government and the ELN distrust each other and further peace talks therefore appear unlikely in 2020.

Increasing cocaine production
Despite the government reaching its eradication target for 2019, cocaine production is at an all-time

high. The voluntary coca-substitution programme, which involves the substitution of illicit crops and the transition to a government-supported legal economy, has had limited success but remains the country's best option to reduce coca production in 2020.[25] The government needs a long-term policy to convince farmers to plant alternative crops. The challenge is not only in building legality in the areas where illicit crops are produced, but in strengthening the legitimacy of the state, which needs the active participation of local actors. Experts have suggested that the best way to stop cocaine trafficking is to attack the production chain, either by seizing inputs needed to make the drug or by destroying laboratories.[26]

Strategic implications and global influences

Heightened tensions between the Colombian and Venezuelan governments are set to remain in 2020. Duque has intensified the offensive against FARC dissident factions, the ELN and other illegal groups, but accused Venezuelan President Nicolás Maduro of sheltering and supporting the criminal organisation. In response, Maduro declared an 'amber' alert and announced military exercises at the border. The Venezuelan government claimed to have deployed as many as 150,000 troops in addition to tanks and missile-defence batteries in September.[27]

Colombian intelligence shows that both ELN and FARC dissidents are active in Venezuelan territory and use the neighbouring country as a haven from attacks by the Colombian armed forces, a situation that is not set to change in 2020.[28] This situation enables criminal groups to strengthen their military position, and Venezuela provides easy routes for drug trafficking.

Notes

[1] Fundación Ideas para la Paz (FIP), 'Dinámicas de la confrontación armada y afectación humanitarian: Balance enero–septiembre 2019', 12 November 2019.

[2] Immigration and Refugee Board of Canada, 'Colombia: The Revolutionary Armed Forces of Colombia (Fuerzas Armadas Revolucionarias de Colombia, FARC), including demobilization of former combatants; information on dissident groups, including number of combatants, areas of operation, activities and state response', 18 April 2018.

[3] The Inter-American Dialogue, 'Two Years In, Is Peace Taking Hold in Colombia?', 16 November 2018.

[4] World Bank, 'GDP per capita (current US$) – Colombia'.

[5] Sergio Garcia Hernandez, 'El 19,6% de los colombianos vive en pobreza multidimensional', AA, 13 July 2019.

[6] Transparency International, 'Corruption Perceptions Index 2019', January 2020.

[7] Joel Gilin, 'Understanding the causes of Colombia's conflict: Weak, corrupt state institutions', *Colombia Reports*, 13 January 2015.

[8] United Nations Office on Drugs and Crime (UNODC), 'World Drug Report 2019: Executive Summary', June 2019.

[9] White House Office of National Drug Control Policy (ONDCP), 'ONDCP Reports Cocaine Production in Colombia is Leveling Off', 26 June 2019.

[10] UNODC, 'Colombia: Monitoreo de territorios afectados por cultivos ilícitos 2018', August 2019.

[11] *Ibid*.

[12] 'Will Colombia return to war?', *The Economist*, 5 September 2019.

[13] Maria Alejandra Navarrete and Laura Alonso, 'Colombia's EPL Faces Bleak Prospects After Death of Pácora', Insight Crime, 1 October 2019.

[14] FIP, 'Dinámicas de la confrontación armada y afectación humanitarian: Balance enero–septiembre 2019'.

[15] Defensoria del Pueblo, Colombia, 'Boletín informativo enero-octubre de 2019', 9 October 2019.

[16] Jo Parkin Daniels, 'Colombia continues to break records for cocaine production, report says', *Guardian*, 19 September 2018.

[17] UNODC, 'Colombia: Monitoreo de territorios afectados por cultivos ilícitos 2018'.

[18] Juan Carlos Garzon Vergara, '¿Cómo lograr la reducción de cultivos ilícitos en 2020?', FIP, 7 January 2020.

[19] Juan Camilo Jaramillo, 'Half of All Destroyed Coca Crops Replanted in Colombia', Insight Crime, 29 October 2019.

[20] Juan Diego Posada, 'Major Implications of Former FARC Leadership Returning to War', Insight Crime, 29 August 2019.

[21] Gideon Long, 'Colombia heads back towards its violent past', *Financial Times*, September 2019.

[22] Amy Braunschweiger, 'Interview: The War in Colombia's Catatumbo Region', Human Rights Watch, 8 August 2019.

[23] FIP, 'Dinámicas de la confrontación armada y afectación humanitarian: Balance enero–septiembre 2019'.

[24] Julia Zulver, Annette Idler and Juan Masullo, '¿Verá Colombia un acuerdo de paz con el ELN en 2019?', Open Democracy, 7 January 2019.

[25] Juan Carlos Garzon Vergara, 'Los desafíos de la sustitución de cultivos ilícitos y las opciones para enfrentarlos', FIP, 4 April 2019.

[26] Colombian Observatory of Organized Crime, 'Colombia's Drug Strategy Paradox – Less Coca Crops, More Cocaine', Insight Crime, 6 August 2019.

[27] International Crisis Group, 'Containing the Border Fallout of Colombia's New Guerrilla Schism', 20 September 2019.

[28] 'Ex-FARC Mafia: Colombia's Criminal Army Settling Down in Venezuela', Insight Crime, 4 September 2019.

EL SALVADOR

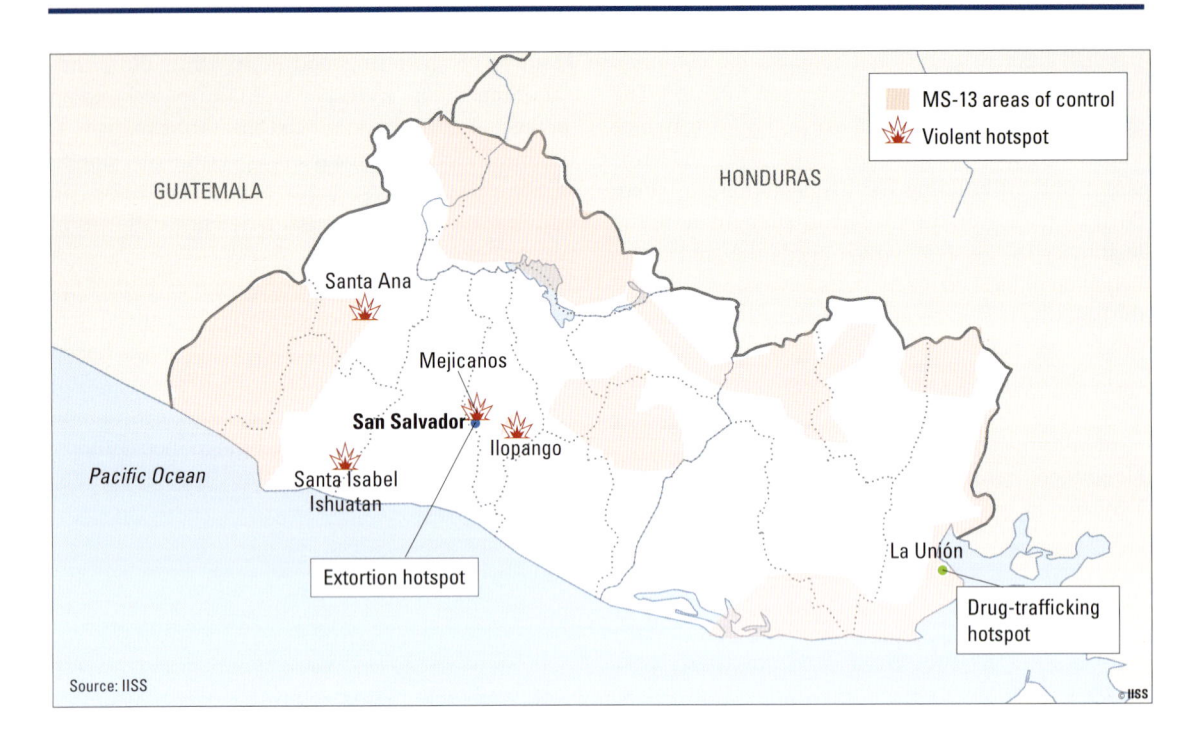

Overview

The conflict in 2019

The conflict in El Salvador ebbed and flowed in 2019, with the Mara Salvatrucha (MS-13) gang serving as the primary offensive actor. The MS-13 consolidated power in their territories and made inroads into the cocaine-transport business. The gang did not, however, expand its territorial reach, as there are few spaces left to occupy. Their efforts focused instead on political and economic goals. A series of public disclosures made in an historic trial of its members showed the MS-13's growing political strength, gained in part through negotiating with parties across the political spectrum. MS-13 testimonies publicly revealed that the gang exchanged votes for money and obtained direct access to formal state structures, including the police.[1]

During the first half of the year, homicides dropped as presidential and legislative election campaigns were under way and the MS-13 was negotiating with all major parties. Political newcomer Nayib Bukele defeated the traditional parties of the right and left which had alternated in power since 1988. The Bukele administration moved on multiple fronts: restructuring the nation's security apparatus and naming hardliners to key law-enforcement leadership positions; unveiling a 'Territorial Control Plan' to extend the government's reach into 17 municipalities formerly controlled by the MS-13; expanding the size of the armed forces and the police force (and raising their salaries); and initiating infrastructure projects in areas controlled by the MS-13. Bukele also declared a state of emergency that gave the police more freedom to counter the MS-13.

Key statistics

Type	Internal
Start date	2003
IDPs total (December 2018)	246,000
Refugees total	No data
People in need	No data

The conflict to 2019

The MS-13's presence in El Salvador, and the rest of Central America, began in the mid-1990s following the mass deportation of gang members from the United States, and California in particular. The conflict in El Salvador originally centred on fighting between the two main gangs, the MS-13 and the Barrio 18, as well as both gangs against the state. Over time though, the MS-13 grew in both organisational capacity and membership, which helped expand the group's territorial reach.

The dynamic fundamentally changed in 2012 when the two gangs agreed on a truce. The MS-13 used the truce's two-year duration to consolidate and strengthen its operations, which it refocused against the Salvadoran state. The MS-13's multi-pronged strategy successfully expanded its power by engaging more aggressively in transporting cocaine, enhancing the quality of its weapons, hiring military trainers and moving its financial holdings to legitimate investments. Conversely, the Barrio 18 remained relatively stagnant. It has since weakened significantly and does not pose the same threat to the state as the MS-13.

The conflict in El Salvador is a series of daily, running firefights rather than pitched battles between forces. The fighting, as shown by the homicide distribution, is heaviest in the areas of greatest economic benefit from drug trafficking and other criminal activities. There are fewer homicides in areas where there is little territorial advantage for gangs or criminal groups to operate. MS-13 members live in the areas they control and interact regularly with the civilian population, often through non-violent means. However, given the ongoing operational necessity of extorting local businesses, the gangs remain deeply unpopular in El Salvador, unlike their counterparts in Honduras.

Key Conflict Parties

The MS-13

Strength
Estimates of MS-13 membership in El Salvador range from 17,000 to 60,000.[2]

Areas of operation
The MS-13 is active in some 205 of the nation's 262 municipalities and has implemented a rural-expansion strategy. Efforts by the state to combat the gang's territorial control have been successful in limiting its operations in 17 municipalities.

Leadership
The gang is run by a national leadership (*la ranfla histórica*), which sets the overall policies and strategies from prisons throughout El Salvador. Faced with internal fissures, the *ranfla histórica* has devolved some decision-making power to the *ranfla libre,* or the gang leadership that is not in prison.

Structure
The *ranfla* is the prison-based senior leadership. Below them are the *palabreros* (those who delegate orders), *programas* (groups of *clicas*) with semi-autonomous leadership across multiple neighbourhoods; *clicas* are highly compartmentalised units at the street level.

History
The MS-13 began operations in El Salvador and the rest of Central America in the mid-1990s following the mass deportation of gang members from California. Until the 2012 'truce' with the government and rival gangs, the MS-13 had no discernable strategy, but it has since developed into a significant political and military actor.

Objectives
The MS-13's primary objective is to undermine the reach of the Salvadoran state, due both to the gang's ethos of expansion and a desire to displace traditional, entrenched cocaine-transport groups.

Opponents
The state is the MS-13's primary opponent, including the national police, and increasingly the armed forces. The MS-13's historical opponent, the Barrio 18 gang, is now significantly weaker.

Affiliates/allies
The MS-13 structures in Honduras and Guatemala, the Sinaloa Federation in Mexico.

Resources/capabilities
The MS-13's resources come from extortion, protecting cocaine loads, kidnapping, murder-for-hire and money laundering. The gang's armoury features a growing number of new weapons, including *Dragunov* sniper rifles, Uzis, rocket-propelled grenades and a small number of light anti-tank weapons. The members whose groups transport cocaine have better access to financial resources.

The National Civil Police (PNC)

Strength
The PNC has approximately 19,000 members; the force has increased by 1,500 members since 2018.[3]

Areas of operation
The PNC and its military counterparts operate throughout the country, with priority given to the 17 municipalities declared zones of strategic interest after Bukele took office in June 2019.

Leadership
Mauricio Antonio Arriaza Chicas, who has served his career in the police force, is the PNC Director General.

Structure
The security force tasked with countering the MS-13 is comprised of three anti-gang units comprised of approximately 600 special-forces troops and 400 PNC officers.

History
Created in 1992 and operating under the Ministry for Public Security, the PNC acts as the primary law-enforcement agency for El Salvador.

Objectives
The PNC is primarily responsible for internal threats, including combatting gangs and organised crime. PNC anti-gang units are tasked with targeting the non-incarcerated MS-13 leadership and restricting the communications capabilities of the prison leadership.

Opponents
The MS-13, Barrio 18 and other smaller criminal groups in El Salvador.

Affiliates/allies
The PNC collaborates with El Salvador's armed forces, especially since June 2019, when Bukele announced that 1,000 new troops would support anti-gang operations, with the promise of another 1,000 by the end of the year.[4]

Resources/capabilities
The specialised units combine the use of helicopters, armoured cars and assault rifles, offsetting in part the PNC's lack of heavy weapons.

Drivers

Impunity and lack of state legitimacy
Rule-of-law challenges, rampant corruption and economic stagnation create the conditions for the MS-13 to thrive, while deeply undermining state legitimacy. El Salvador is also among the countries in the hemisphere with the highest level of impunity. An estimated 95% of murders go unpunished, a significant statistic in a country with one of the highest homicide rates in the world.[5]

Meanwhile, the MS-13 has created both the perception and reality that it is an effective parallel government. This has resulted in a corresponding delegitimisation of the state, where the government, having lost the monopoly on the use of force, is viewed as having abandoned the population or being too incompetent and corrupt to combat the gang. In some cases, where MS-13 territorial control resulted in decreases in violence, the gang is viewed as a more legitimate governing force than the state and engenders more trust than the police.

Porous borders
Porous borders across the Central American region offer enormous advantages for the gang's survival and growth. When MS-13 members are threatened by state forces in El Salvador, they can easily move to safe harbour in neighbouring Honduras or Guatemala, where the gang maintains a significant presence. The MS-13 also moves money, weapons and drugs among the three countries with impunity, all while increasing revenues and sharing political and military lessons learned. This tendency accelerated in 2019 and provided the MS-13 with a significant strategic advantage over both the state and rival gangs in securing territorial control.

Migration
The increasing number of deportations of Salvadoran nationals from the US has significant security implications in El Salvador. Figures for 2019 show a significant increase from 2018. In the first nine months of the year, 14,194 Salvadorans were deported from the US and another 12,157 were deported from Mexico while en route to the US.[6] Recent deportees – many of whom are unacquainted with their country of birth – face limited job opportunities and lack community bonds, thus becoming easy targets for extortion or forced recruitment into the MS-13.

Political Developments

Pay-to-play political participation
In 2019, the MS-13 continued supporting candidates across the political spectrum, and its pay-to-play strategy bore fruit. The MS-13 now has an ally in the president's Cabinet and thus improved communication channels with the government.[7] The gang also strengthened its capacity to channel increased drug-trafficking revenues into campaign financing for municipal elections. In June, for instance, the gang's candidates for mayor won in at least six of the MS-13's municipal strongholds. As a result, the MS-13 now controls several municipal boards.

Political negotiations
The MS-13 episodically negotiated with the government in a clandestine manner in 2019, which led to spikes of visible violence alternating with non-violent periods when the gang was pressing for concessions. On 31 July, El Salvador recorded zero homicides for the first day in a decade, and August was the least violent month since 2010. Bukele claimed credit for the decline in violence, but it was more likely due to negotiations between the government and the MS-13. Either way, violence rapidly decreased in the first months of Bukele's administration. Then, on 20 September, there were 19 homicides recorded, almost four times the daily average for 2019, as the gang pressed for improved prison conditions for the MS-13's leadership. The government was anxious to demonstrate the homicide rate was at historic lows and reportedly negotiated with the gang to drop homicides in exchange for improved conditions, including access to mobile phones in prison.

Heavy-handed security policies
The Bukele administration maintained the 'extraordinary measures' of the previous government, which included the prolonged isolation of incarcerated gang leaders and the suspension of hearings, visitations and access to telephones. In 2018, the United Nations declared these measures a violation of human rights. Bukele also introduced tougher measures in 2019, such as deciding to mix members from different gangs in the same prisons. Prison director Osiris Luna defended the measure in June 2019, stressing that 'we have put all the terrorist groups in the same prison … We will show them that they have to respect the state.'

Departure of the Salvadoran population
Salvadorans continue to flee their homes as a result of violence. While the MS-13's territorial control often brings a decline in homicides, the gang usually remains a predatory force in the community and brings other types of violence that drive people to leave. In some instances, families left after middle-school- and high-school-age children were forcibly recruited by the MS-13. In other instances, women and children fled after being victims of sexual abuse by gang members or other groups. Finally, the constant extortion of small community businesses forces people from their homes, in particular those who can no longer pay the demanded fees.

Asylum deal with US
On 20 September 2019, the US and El Salvador signed an agreement that would, if enacted, force Central American asylum seekers who travel through El Salvador to request asylum there rather than the United States. This could thus further entrench the negative security dynamics associated with outward and returned migration. However, in December, Bukele said that El Salvador would not be able to implement the deal and through 2019, only Guatemala had begun receiving returned asylum seekers under a similarly signed agreement.

Military Developments

Homicide rates continue to fall
Given the nature of the gang's presence and activities, assessing the levels of violence engendered by the conflict is a difficult challenge. Homicides are an imperfect but quantifiable measure. In 2019, the homicide rate was approximately 36 people per 100,000 (2,383 homicides in total), a high rate in global terms but low in El Salvador's recent

historical context.[8] Homicide rates have fallen over the past four years and in 2019 hit their lowest level in a decade (on average 4.4 per day, compared to a high of 17.6 per day in 2015), down more than 28.7% compared to 2018.[9]

A superficial interpretation of this data might suggest that the conflict is steadily becoming less violent. Such figures, however, are not necessarily indicative of an improving situation. Forced disappearances increased slightly in 2019, with more than 2,300 reported cases through September, suggesting that violent crimes, and specifically violent deaths, are not decreasing but simply being carried out in more clandestine ways. The gangs used the same tactic during the 2012–14 truce to make the homicides appear to drop sharply when in fact the rate remained relatively constant.

Revamped mandate for PNC
The PNC in 2019 acquired improved body armour and additional transportation and communication equipment, as well as developed better intelligence to target MS-13 leaders and financial structures. Before Bukele was elected president, the PNC's primary operational methodology was to enter a community in force, arrest as many gang members as possible, carry out raids on drug-selling centres and then retreat. Bukele's Territorial Control Plan aims to fundamentally change that dynamic by maintaining a permanent law-enforcement presence in 17 key municipalities and forcing the MS-13 to abandon the territory. Bukele's entire public-security plan is set to cost US$575.2 million between 2019 and 2021.[10] However, these funds have not yet been fully approved by the Legislative Assembly. It is not clear whether the strategy will succeed – similar efforts in the past have had some short-term results before ending in failure.

MS-13 consolidation
The MS-13 worked hard in 2019 to consolidate its hold on territories that could be retaken by the state while acquiring military training, new weapons and encrypted communications. Many of the prioritised municipalities targeted by Bukele's public-security plan are in and around El Salvador's capital, which remains disputed territory and where violence continues to spike. That said, the MS-13 also began to consolidate territory in less traditional regions such as La Unión in El Salvador's southwestern coastal region, where there was less of a state-security presence.

This capacity development over recent years has originated mostly from hiring the services of military or police members, as was revealed in the high-profile trial of MS-13 members. In a sting known as *Operation Cuscatlán* in early 2018, 426 individuals associated with the gang were arrested and later jointly tried. In October, a cooperating witness (who is referred to as 'Noe') testified that he and other members of the MS-13 had also received six months of sniper training by an unnamed military member and that each class cost the gang only US$500. While other disclosures (including details on the former ruling political party's negotiations) were also described, the revelations about the MS-13's military-style training was new information.

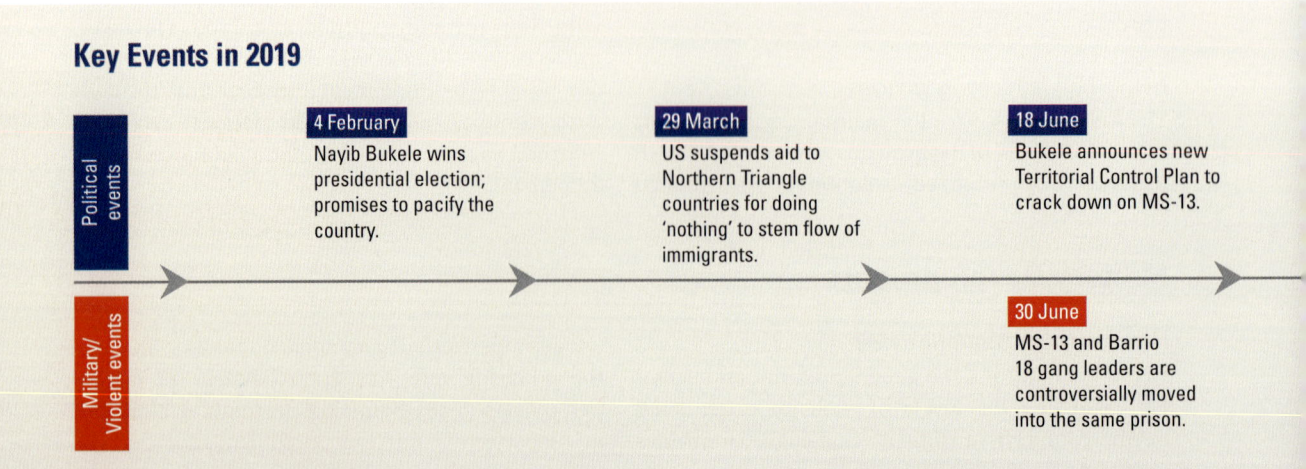

Key Events in 2019

Political events

4 February
Nayib Bukele wins presidential election; promises to pacify the country.

29 March
US suspends aid to Northern Triangle countries for doing 'nothing' to stem flow of immigrants.

18 June
Bukele announces new Territorial Control Plan to crack down on MS-13.

Military/Violent events

30 June
MS-13 and Barrio 18 gang leaders are controversially moved into the same prison.

Impact

Human rights
Reports of human-rights violations, particularly by security forces, are increasingly common. The PNC and armed-forces personnel have been accused of, and in some cases charged with, carrying out extrajudicial executions. In August 2019, a report released by El Salvador's Office for Defense of Human Rights within the Public Prosecutor's Office found that 116 individuals had been killed extrajudicially between 2014 and 2018.[11] Allegations of excessive use of force and extrajudicial killings continued in 2019, with Bukele adopting a hardline approach to combatting the gangs.

Humanitarian
The gang's structural reliance on violence as the primary instrument of social control is the main driver in both internal and external migration. Interviews conducted in the three main Salvadoran cities and with human-rights monitoring groups indicate that the phenomenon of people abandoning their homes because of gang presence and human-rights abuses grew in 2019. Additionally, the number of Salvadorans apprehended at the US southern border in the fiscal year 2019 almost doubled to more than 89,000 individuals compared to the previous fiscal year.[12]

Social
The Salvadoran government returned to the *mano dura* (iron fist) strategy of increasing repression, interspersed with tactical negotiations, while the MS-13 continued to extort the civilian population. The results of these tactics are periods of less violence but also few real efforts to address the underlying causes of insecurity. This lack of coherence in policy and discourse further discredits the state and gives the MS-13 an opportunity to capitalise on institutional delegitimisation. Internal displacement due to gang violence (or the threat of it) continues to grow, fuelling migration to the north and disrupting the country's social fabric.

Those affected by violence rarely report crimes, particularly in rural areas where the MS-13 has been expanding its drug-trafficking operations. In rural areas, access to the state or formal oversight bodies is even more difficult than in urban centres. The violence remains largely in the shadows, leaving victims with no viable options to seek redress or justice. As a result of its successes in fighting the state, the MS-13 is consolidating its territorial control and bringing violence to historically non-violent regions, further eroding state legitimacy.

Economic
The violence has driven down foreign and national investment and depressed job creation in key economic sectors, such as tourism. El Salvador's real GDP growth remained below 3% in recent years and was projected at 2.5% for 2019.[13] More than 75% of the nation's commerce and trade operate outside the formal sector.[14] As a result, Salvadorans often work for less than minimum wage, with no protection or benefits and no chances of improving their economic conditions. In addition, the gang's tactic of extorting both formal and informal

---

12 July — Bukele requests an additional US$158 million from National Assembly for the second phase of the Territorial Recovery plan.

31 July — First homicide-free day in El Salvador in a decade.

17 September — The largest mass trial of MS-13 members begins, with 263 accused of homicide, extortion and kidnapping.

20 September — President Bukele and President Trump sign Administration Cooperation Agreement or migration-cooperation plan.

20 September — MS-13 kills 19 people across El Salvador to pressure government in negotiations.

12 December — 373 of the 426 MS-13 members in the historic *Operación Cuscatlán* trial are found guilty.

15 December — Bukele says he may not be able to implement migration-cooperation plan.

businesses significantly limits the possibility of economic expansion throughout the country. The MS-13's increasing willingness to invest resources in the electoral process will likely further undermine the local and national body politic – already deeply corrupt and transactional – and undermine the climate of stability needed to attract foreign investment.

Relations with neighbouring and international partners

The US is El Salvador's primary ally in combatting the MS-13, but uncertainty over the continuation of US economic and military aid under the Trump administration has weakened the historic partnership. Humanitarian aid was suspended for five months in 2019, though it was subsequently reinstated. The bilateral relationship was further shaken given the ongoing accusations of corruption by Bukele and allegations of human-rights abuses perpetuated by the new police leadership.

Regionally, while El Salvador has cordial relations with Honduras and Guatemala – as both neighbours are also combatting the MS-13 – there is also only a limited exchange of intelligence between countries. By contrast, the MS-13 is effective at establishing collaboration with regional and international partners. Its primary allies are its branches in Honduras, Guatemala and the US. These relationships allow the MS-13 to move across borders easily, learn from the experiences of other MS-13 groups and expand its criminal portfolio. Also, the MS-13 in El Salvador is increasingly collaborating with the Sinaloa Federation in Mexico for the shipment of cocaine to the US.

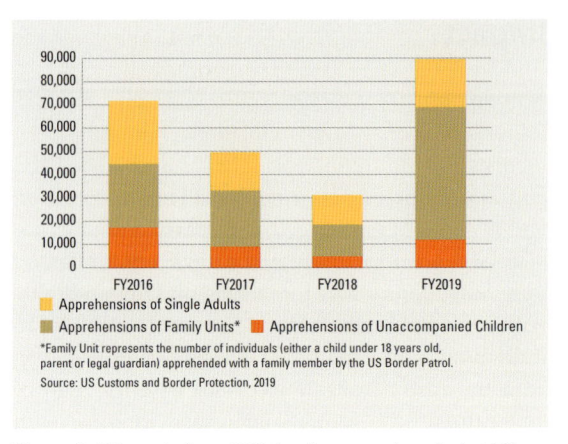

Figure 1: Migrants from El Salvador apprehended at US southern border, fiscal years 2016–19

Trends

Political trajectories

Negotiations between the gang and the government, which were historically denied in public, will likely continue as the Bukele administration seeks to show progress in addressing violence. Unlike his predecessors, Bukele remained popular in 2019, allowing him to successfully make the case for increased public spending on PNC personnel, equipment, salary increases and training. If Bukele – who constantly uses social media to promote his agenda and ideas – maintains his popularity, he may be able to change the conflict in the medium term. For the MS-13, the gang successfully consolidated its control throughout the country in 2019, but there are still a few areas where it can expand. The most disputed areas will likely be the Pacific coast – where maritime drug-trafficking networks operate – and the northern corridor from Morazán to the Guatemalan border – where land routes for transporting cocaine operate.

Conflict-related risks

The MS-13 can significantly expand its revenues if it displaces the traditional, locally based cocaine- and weapons-transport networks, while maintaining close ties to El Salvador's major political parties. The gang has previously tried and failed in such expansion efforts, but the group's military capacity and sophistication have grown significantly in the past three years. These additional revenues would allow the gang to continue purchasing better weapons, hire more professional military trainers and improve its communications through more secure technologies.

Migration, and the increasing deportation of Salvadorans from the US, will continue to complicate the already difficult social and security situation in El Salvador. This trend will significantly worsen if the asylum deal agreed with the US in September 2019 is implemented, which would force migrants from other countries – who had first passed through Salvadoran territory – to apply for asylum in El

Salvador rather than the US. Given these factors, the humanitarian crisis in El Salvador will deepen and continue fuelling insecurity.

Prospects for peace

By the end of 2019, the conflict in El Salvador was in a state of stagnation, with both sides increasing their combat capabilities but neither having the ability to win decisively. Informal negotiations may continue between the MS-13 and the government episodically, particularly when either side seeks short-term tactical concessions or temporary advantages. The government has demonstrated that it has the capacity to temporarily retake territory from the MS-13, but not the ability to hold territory in the long term. At the same time, the MS-13 has the ability to confront the PNC and its military-support structures, but not to undertake a decisive military action that would fundamentally alter the status quo. The likelihood of negotiations ending the conflict are thus limited, as both sides are poised to continue the same approach, but with better armaments and more financial resources.

Strategic implications and global influences

The strategic implications of the ongoing conflict are both national and regional. The government will continue to be challenged in its ability to govern due to the MS-13's ability to control territory. At the regional level, the flow of migrants toward the US will likely continue, though significantly fewer Salvadorans are arriving to the US southern border than migrants from Honduras. Bukele has been vocal about pursuing a closer security partnership with the US, while taking a cooler stance with China.

As a result, China has not made major advances in developing its proposed Special Economic Zone (SEZ) announced under the previous Salvadoran administration. In the short term, the US will remain the main provider of security funding and training to El Salvador. Bukele's stance on increasing migration-enforcement efforts and collaboration with the US won praise from the Trump administration and allowed for already programmed foreign aid to be unblocked and begin to flow again. However, in December Bukele said El Salvador lacked the capacity to implement the migration deal, and the ramifications of his statements are yet to be felt. Finally, El Salvador's recognition of China over Taiwan in 2018 (under former president Sánchez Ceren) and China's willingness to supply aid, weapons, and training could affect the conflict in the future.

Notes

[1] Norberto Paredes, 'MS13: 5 claves para entender el "histórico" juicio de los pandilleros de la Mara Salvatrucha en El Salvador', BBC News, 11 October 2019.

[2] The lower estimates include only hommies, or full-fledged members, who are less than one-third of the overall gang affiliates. Higher estimates include members who served as paid lookouts, messengers and retail crack and cocaine vendors. IBI Consultants interviews with National Police anti-gang unit members and MS-13 members, January to October 2018.

[3] Ministerio de Justicia y Seguridad Pública, 'La nueva promoción está formada con énfasis en policía comunitaria'.

[4] Jorge Beltrán Luna, 'La Fuerza Armada reclutará mil soldados para reforzar seguridad', El Diario de Hoy, 7 July 2019.

[5] Christine Wade, 'El Salvador's Legacy of Impunity Hampers Its Ongoing Fight Against Corruption', World Press Review blog, 12 July 2018.

[6] 'Cifra de salvadorenos deportados se dispara un 53% hasta septiembre de 2019', La Prensa Gráfica, 21 October 2019.

[7] Interviews with MS-13 senior leadership, El Salvador, July 2019.

[8] 'El Salvador no registró ningún homicidio el día 4 de enero', Univision, 5 January 2019.

[9] 'El Salvador sentences gang members; murder rate dropping', Associated Press, 17 August 2019.

[10] Ministerio de Hacienda, 'Propuesta de Financiamiento Plan de Control Territorial', 2019.

[11] 'Ejecuciones extrajudiciales en El Salvador: el informe en que el Estado reconoce por primera vez está práctica por parte de la policía', BBC News, 29 August 2019.

[12] US Customs and Border Protection, 'U.S. Border Patrol Southwest Border Apprehensions by Sector for Fiscal Year 2020', 2019.

[13] International Monetary Fund, 'El Salvador', data as of 22 May 2019.

[14] José Afane, 'El Sector Informal', La Prensa Gráfica, 22 July 2019.

HONDURAS

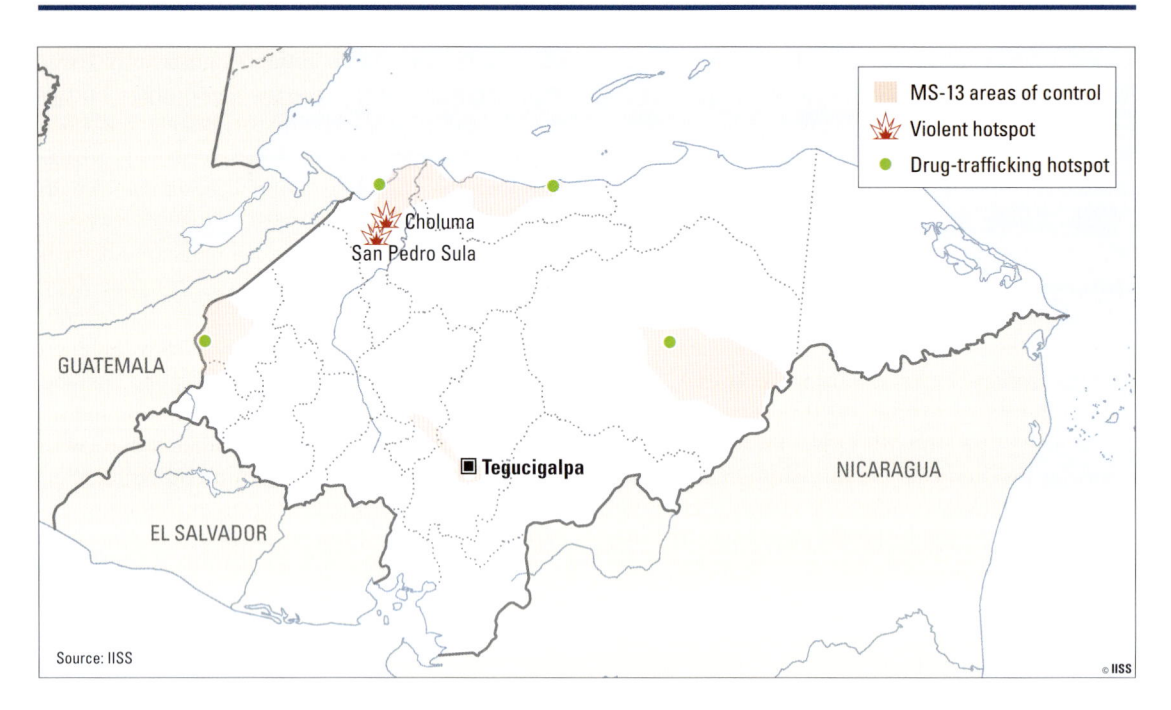

Overview

The conflict in 2019

The conflict in Honduras escalated in 2019, as the Mara Salvatrucha (MS-13) transnational gang significantly expanded its territorial control, particularly around the city of San Pedro Sula, the nearby Atlantic coastal regions and the informal border crossings to Guatemala. With assistance from former police officers, who provided the gang with training and members, the MS-13 established itself as a major player in the cocaine-transportation business, including holding a near monopoly on the internal drug market of cocaine, crack and 'krispy'.[1]

The MS-13, in the turmoil of the regional immigration crisis, also diversified its portfolio into the smuggling of migrants moving through Mexico and the United States' southern border. This put the gang in direct contact with different Mexican drug-trafficking organisations (DTOs), who may allow migrants to transport drugs across the US border in lieu of paying additional smuggling fees. The MS-13 began using sophisticated tunnelling structures, equipped with air vents, generators and beds, in the hills around San Pedro Sula, both to hide drugs and for protection from police raids – a tactic likely copied from the Sinaloa Cartel.

The MS-13 consolidated its political power in many areas, thanks to the community-level goodwill generated following its decision to stop extorting local businesses, and the further erosion of the Honduran government's legitimacy after allegations that President Juan Orlando Hernández had ties to cocaine trafficking.[2] The allegations were given further credibility when a key witness claiming to have records of the president's drug-trafficking involvement was gunned down in a maximum-security prison and all his belongings disappeared. Increased political power and

Key statistics

Type	Internal
Start date	2002
IDPs total (December 2018)	190,000
Refugees total	No data
People in need	No data

revenues from migrant smuggling allowed the gang to enhance its military capabilities, control key informal border crossings and expand operations into Mexico. Such security challenges are coupled with an increase in homicides for the first time in several years.[3] This increase is likely a combination of ineffective Honduran security forces and the MS-13's social restructuring.

The conflict to 2019

Much like the Salvadoran branch of the gang, MS-13 operations in Honduras began only after the mass deportation of gang members from the US, and specifically California, in the 1990s. As the gang was not necessarily born out of strong organisational structures, the MS-13 did not initially operate as a transnational organisation. Until recently, the gang's Honduran branch had few ties to significant drug-trafficking operations, rarely engaged in political matters, maintained relatively stable territorial divisions and demonstrated no clear military prowess. Since 2016, however, the Honduran branch of the MS-13 has become the most innovative and successful MS-13 branch in Central America, developing significantly more sophisticated political and military structures to counter the Honduran state.

In addition to direct political participation, the gang has worked diligently and successfully to diversify its criminal portfolio by engaging in new regions where territorial control is a strong competitive advantage. It has also continued to acquire new technologies for communication and new methodologies – such as tunnelling – that have increased its operational security and viability in drug-trafficking operations. This new political confidence is due in part to the gang's ongoing recruitment of highly trained police officers forced out of the national police force after allegations of corruption or human-rights abuses.

Key Conflict Parties

The MS-13

Strength
The gang has 8,000–12,000 full members and around 40,000 recruits in training, as lookouts and as messengers. These figures are up slightly from 2018 and do not include long waiting lists of would-be recruits.

Areas of operation
They operate in most of the country, though their territorial control is concentrated in San Pedro Sula, Puerto Cortes, Omoa in the north as well as Copán along the border with Guatemala.

Leadership
Senior MS-13 leadership figures remain in prison, though few are identified. Carlos Alberto Álvarez (AKA Cholo Houston) and Dimas Aguilar (AKA Taca el OSO) are considered key leaders. Secondary leaders operate in very decentralised manners.

Structure
The *ranfla* is the prison-based senior leadership. Below them are the *palabreros* (those who delegate orders), *programas* (groups of *clicas*) with semi-autonomous leadership across multiple neighbourhoods; clicas are highly compartmentalised units at the street level. The *jefe de clica* is responsible for their group's finances and criminal activity.

History
The MS-13 began operations in Honduras in the mid-1990s following the mass deportation of gang members from California. Until 2016, the gang's Honduran branch was relatively unorganised. Since then, it has become the most innovative and successful of the MS-13 groups in Central America.

Objectives
The MS-13's primary objective is to gain control of key cocaine-trafficking and migrant-smuggling routes, to dominate local drug markets and to create an alternative state structure to the Honduran government. It seeks also to dominate informal border crossing, diversify its criminal portfolio, and expand into the production of cocaine, cocaine hydrochloride (HCL) and synthetic drugs.

Opponents
The Honduran government, smaller gangs (e.g. Calle 18, Chirizos and Ponce) and extrajudicial paramilitary groups.

Affiliates/allies
The MS-13 structures of El Salvador and Guatemala, and the Sinaloa Cartel in Mexico.

Resources/capabilities
Proceeds from cocaine trafficking, migrant smuggling and drug sales provide the gang with a yearly income of tens of millions of US dollars. Other localised revenue sources include investments in motels, car lots, private-security firms, buses and public transportation. Advanced tunnelling techniques have allowed the gang to protect their operations and store goods.

Policía Militar de Orden Público (Military Police of Public Order, or PMOP) and Fuerza Nacional Anti-Maras y Pandillas (National Anti-Gang Force, or FNAMP)

Strength
The PMOP has 4,300 members – increased from 4,000 in 2018. The FNAMP has 5,000 members.[4]

Areas of operation
The whole national territory, with a focus on areas with high gang and drug-trafficking presences, including Tegucigalpa, San Pedro Sula, Palmerola and Copán – usually major urban centres or areas with formal or informal border crossings.

Leadership
The leader of the PMOP, under the ministry of defence, is Major-General Manuel de Jesús Aguilera. The leader of the FNAMP, under the police, is Lieutenant-Colonel Amílcar Hernández.

Structure
PMOP has eight combat battalions and one canine battalion. The FNAMP has not publicly defined its operational structure.

History
PMOP is a somewhat controversial hybrid military-police force, created in 2013 to combat gangs. It conducts highly militarised operations and has been accused of human-rights abuses, such as excessive use of force.[5] The FNAMP was created in July 2018 as a new inter-agency force to combat gangs, primarily the MS-13.

Objectives
Retake territory from the MS-13 and decapitate its operational structures while combatting transnational organised crime and drug trafficking.

Opponents
The MS-13, other smaller gangs and local DTOs.

Affiliates/allies
The national police, the TIGRES special-forces unit of the police, the military and US military/police trainers.

Resources/capabilities
Total military budget: US$306.9 million, increased from US$281.9m in 2018. Line items of budgets have not been published publicly.

Drivers

The conflict stems from endemic poverty, corruption, political disenfranchisement and widespread impunity. These factors, combined with a weak overall state capacity, the electoral crises (of 2006, 2013 and 2017) and the ongoing allegations of drug trafficking at the highest levels of government, have led to a legitimacy crisis for Honduras's democratic institutions. Honduran residents must choose between an ineffective state and a violent – though increasingly less brutal – gang, without many alternative options. The MS-13 is gaining legitimacy as an alternative governance provider in many areas of the country, further undermining state legitimacy.

Poverty
Poverty and a lack of economic opportunities continue to drive the conflict, the most visible result of which is forced migration towards the US. Approximately 56% of the population in Honduras lives in poverty, with approximately 17% living in extreme poverty, the highest rate in Latin America after Haiti.[6] The World Bank estimates that 77% of Hondurans worked in the informal economy in 2017 (the latest statistics available) and were thus deprived of the security and benefits guaranteed in the formal sector.[7] The state has consistently failed to deliver job opportunities or economic growth. With jobs increasingly scarce in rural areas of the country, individuals move to urban areas and encounter the MS-13, often for the first time. Lacking community ties, internal migrants become easy targets for extortion and violence. This cycle only exacerbates an already bleak economic situation. In many cases, and for young men particularly (only about 10% of the MS-13's fully fledged members are women), working for the MS-13 is one of the few viable employment options.

Corruption and impunity
High levels of corruption and impunity are key drivers of the conflict. Increasingly, high-profile corruption cases fail to receive sentences, while lower-level cases are not fully investigated. The Inter-American Commission on Human Rights estimates that the impunity rate in Honduras is between 95% and 98%. At least 153 attorneys were murdered between 2002 and 2018, while many more have received death threats while attempting to prosecute cases.[8] At least 63 Honduran journalists were killed during the same period.[9] In October 2019, in the most high-profile case of the year, President Hernández's brother and confidant, Tony, was convicted of cocaine trafficking in the US. Days later, the

primary witness to his case was assassinated inside a maximum-security prison while guards looked on. President Hernández's brother's conviction and the subsequent murder rocked Hondurans' trust in their president and in the state.

Electoral crises

Another driver of the conflict is the recurrence of electoral crises that have eroded the state's political legitimacy. Disputed election results in 2006 and a *coup d'état* in 2009 preceded likely fraudulent results in 2013 and significantly discredited the electoral process. In November 2017, President Hernández's victory – likely the result of more significant fraud – further delegitimised both the state and the current administration.[10] The October 2019 conviction of President Hernández's brother – who exercised significant influence with the president – on charges of international drug trafficking, exposed a key link between the Hernández family and illicit activities, increasing the attractiveness of the MS-13 as an alternative governance structure.

Disputed border control

The MS-13's efforts to control key informal border-crossing points has fuelled the conflict at the regional level. The gang's expansion in 2019 aimed at gaining control of key routes for the transit of illicit products on the southern border with Nicaragua, the northern and western borders with Guatemala and El Salvador, and parts of the Guatemala–Mexico migrant border crossings. The strategy of forcibly evicting the state or other armed groups from those crucial nodes, and the need to fend off attempts by rivals to retake the territory, led to a sharp rise in violence in all three border regions.[11] This violence further displaced residents, exacerbating an already bleak economic and security situation for Hondurans, particularly those living along the Atlantic coast and in border communities.

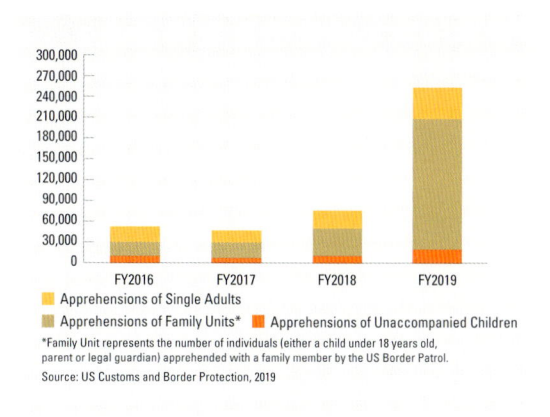

Figure 1: Migrants from Honduras apprehended at US southern border, fiscal years 2016–19

Family Unit represents the number of individuals (either a child under 18 years old, parent or legal guardian) apprehended with a family member by the US Border Patrol.
Source: US Customs and Border Protection, 2019

Political Developments

Political protests and attacks

The MS-13 continued to engage in both political participation and targeted attacks against security forces in 2019 – consolidating its presence and visibility on the national political scene. The gang participated in multiple violent mass mobilisations against the administration of President Hernández, including protests in May, where the US Embassy's entrance in Tegucigalpa was torched. While the Hernández government suffered from a significant erosion of legitimacy, the MS-13 benefitted from its decision to halt the extortion of small businesses in their areas of control, as well as to ban rape and violence in the communities under its control.

The MS-13 enforces these rules of engagement with the community systematically, while it seeks to provide social services and implement rudimentary judicial structures. As a result, it has gained growing trust within many communities. One indicator of the pay-off for this increased social engagement is that Hondurans now commonly refer to MS-13 as *La Mara Buena* (the Good Gang). This positive title is in direct contrast to common references to both rival gangs and the government. Such a development does not imply that the gang is no longer violent or does not make use of arbitrary punishments. It only indicates that the MS-13's behaviour is less abusive than that of other groups, including Honduran law-enforcement and military forces.

Migrant smuggling

The MS-13 has increasingly provided human-smuggling services. Thanks to its internal military consolidation and structural reforms, the gang has grown to be a disciplined group, capable of organising reliable services to smuggle migrants into Mexico – and in some cases all the way to the US border. Some of the organisers of the 2018 migrant caravans have been forced to abandon their operations or to work as employees for the gang. In interviews with migrants who returned to Honduras, the gang was described as the only organisation that would deliver people at the agreed-upon price with no attempts to renegotiate along the way. At the US–Mexico border, the MS-13 introduces migrants to Mexican criminal groups with whom they negotiate their way into the US, either for cash payments or in exchange for cocaine-trafficking services.

Migrant-smuggling services provide a significant new revenue stream to the MS-13 and give the gang an opportunity to interact with Mexican criminal groups which may eventually assist them in establishing a more robust drug-trafficking partnership. At the same time, this new relationship has displaced significant parts of the traditional political and criminal structures in Honduras, which revolved around migrant-smuggling at border crossings into El Salvador and Guatemala.

Military Developments

In 2019, violent incidents in Honduras were largely single-victim homicides or assassinations of small groups of people (three or four). Overall, there were 4,133 homicides in Honduras, a rate of 42.8 murders per 100,000 inhabitants.[12] Moreover, for the first time in at least five years, the homicide rate has actually increased in Honduras: this represented an increase of 300 homicides on the previous year.[13] The province of Cortés, where the MS-13 is fighting for control of maritime shipping routes, was the most violent region.[14] These statistics do not include unreported killings by gangs, police and criminal groups, where victims are dismembered or clandestinely buried. This widespread, seemingly unpredictable, violence creates an atmosphere of instability over broad areas of the country and contributes to a feeling that the MS-13 can provide protection from violence in areas under its control.

The 'social turn' of the MS-13's activity in Honduras has resulted in a steady decrease of homicides, despite the minor uptick in 2019. In 2011 the murder rate in Honduras was approximately 85 deaths per 100,000 residents – among the highest in the world.[15] However, homicides are also often an unreliable indicator of the conflict and should not be understood as a sign of an improving security situation. In the areas of MS-13 control, the rates of homicides and other violent crimes often drop because the gang has achieved military victory and no longer needs to kill people to occupy the territory.

In December, prison riots erupted in El Porvenir and Tela, killing 37 inmates. The government declared a state of emergency in the prison system, with Assistant Security Minister Luis Suazo saying that the MS-13 had ordered the attacks.[16]

Key Events in 2019

Political events

24 May
The public prosecutor, with investigators from the Organisation of American States, announces the first major 'narco-politics' case over the state granting contracts to DTOs.

Military/Violent events

January
The MS-13 in Honduras expands into at least two communities in Mexico to smuggle migrants and traffic cocaine – establishing direct contact with Mexican DTOs.

30 April
Clashes between police and marchers protesting new austerity measures include the burning of municipal offices and widespread looting in Tegucigalpa.

Impact

The impact of the conflict in Honduras manifests in three primary ways: the weakening and delegitimisation of state institutions, the mass exodus of migrants towards the US and the humanitarian effects of territorial and political expansion by the MS-13 within the country.

Human rights

Throughout 2019, Human Rights Watch documented several human-rights violations in Honduras, including police abuse and corruption, an increasingly violent crackdown on non-violent protests, and attacks on advocates and lawyers.[18] The Inter-American Court for Human Rights has described Honduras as one of the 'most hostile and dangerous countries for human-rights defenders'.[19] From 2001 until November 2019, 229 journalists and lawyers were murdered in Honduras, and the impunity rate for the crimes was 91%, consistent with the national average for homicides.[20] Violent crime remained rampant. Prisons continued to be severely overcrowded (17,712 prisoners were held in prisons with capacity for 8,000 people), lacking in services, violent and often under the direct control of the MS-13.[21]

Humanitarian

Hundreds of thousands of people left Honduras in 2019 to seek asylum or economic opportunities in the US. The primary causes for the exodus were gang violence, food insecurity caused by negative climatic fluctuations and a lack of employment opportunities. More than 330,000 Hondurans were apprehended along the US southern border in fiscal year 2019, or approximately 4% of the Honduran population.[22] In addition, thousands of internally displaced people flee the violence and relocate mostly in urban areas, but do not report their cases to the government. The Internal Displacement Monitoring Centre estimated that, as of December 2018, approximately 190,000 Hondurans had been internally displaced (approximately 950 more than the previous year and about 2% of the population). Given that only a small number of people register with the United Nations refugee offices, the real number is likely much higher.

Economic

After growing 4.8% in 2017 and 3.7% in 2018, GDP is projected to grow 3.3% in 2019. The ongoing violence, extortion of large foreign and national companies and investors, and the lack of government capacity and legitimacy led to the 'emergence of two mutually reinforcing cycles in the country: 1) a high crime–low growth cycle; and 2) an immigration/remittance flows–low growth cycle.'[23] This means that, with high crime levels tamping down economic growth, the pressure to migrate to the US to earn money grows. Rather than leading to economic investment, remittances are often a primary source of income to avoid hunger and extreme poverty for family members who remain in Honduras.

---

1 June
A violent protest against the government with MS-13 participation sees significant property destruction and the burning of tyres at the entrance of the US Embassy.

9 June
Five people are massacred in Omoa Beach, the largest targeted massacre of the year.[17]

18 October
Tony Hernández is convicted of drug trafficking in New York, setting off riots against the president.

27 October
A key witness in Tony Hernández's case is assassinated. He claimed to have ledgers proving drug payments to the president.

3 November
Opposition leaders form an alliance to remove President Hernández from power by whatever means necessary, including a national strike.

20–22 December
37 are killed in gang violence across two prisons. A government official blames the MS-13.

Relations with neighbouring and international partners
The government's primary ally in combatting the MS-13 is the US. However, ongoing accusations of corruption and human-rights abuses within Honduras – up to the level of the Honduran president – have made the relationship more tense. In addition, uncertainty over the continuation of US economic and security aid under President Donald Trump's administration – including the suspension of aid for five months in 2019 – weakened the two nations' historic partnership. While Honduras maintains cordial political relations with El Salvador and Guatemala (and while both neighbours are also combatting the MS-13), the three Northern Triangle countries do not boast significant intelligence-sharing capabilities or the ability to conduct joint operations. The MS-13's primary allies are its branches in El Salvador, Guatemala and the US. These relationships allow it to move across borders easily, learn from the experiences of other MS-13 groups and expand criminal activities. The MS-13 is increasingly allied with the Mexican Sinaloa Cartel for the shipment of cocaine through Mexico and into the US.

Trends

Political trajectories
The MS-13's political trajectory over the past three years has been rapidly ascendant and successful. The gang is learning how to exercise direct political control in territories where it operates while simultaneously displacing state power. The political trajectory of the Hernández administration has been downward since the president's likely fraudulent re-election in 2017, with the situation further exacerbated by his brother's drug-trafficking conviction in October 2019, which linked the president to criminal activities. In September, an important group of senior police and military officials publicly asked Hernández and top military commanders to resign following allegations of massive institutional corruption. While the revolt was tamped down, it was an important indicator of the government's fragile hold on its combat forces.

Conflict-related risks
The participation of the MS-13 in mass protests in May showed the gang's ability to put the Hernández government under siege and to appear as a potentially viable partner in a new political coalition. If pursued further, these political aspirations would likely prompt a robust military response by the government against the MS-13 in heavily populated areas, which would in turn lead to many civilian casualties. The MS-13 has also established itself as a successful DTO with the economic resources to launch more sustained and sophisticated military attacks on security forces.

Prospects for peace
Prospects for peace are slim given that the MS-13 has no incentive to negotiate in a substantive way and the government has publicly vowed not to negotiate in any way with the gang. In contrast to El Salvador, there is no evidence that the Honduran government has negotiated with the MS-13 to date. As the gang's revenues increase – thanks to the growing cocaine-transport business, its entry into migrant-smuggling services and its monopoly on the local drug market – its members will likely become better trained and better armed. The government, particularly if it opts to maintain strong relations with the Trump administration in Washington, will have to respond with force. A scenario where the MS-13 would be willing to give up territory, political power and economic resources to a government that is perceived as weak and illegitimate seems highly unlikely.

Strategic implications and global influences
The strategic implications of the conflict are both national and regional. On the national level, the government will face a growing crisis of governance and legitimacy. On a regional level, the flow of migrants toward the US will likely continue, as it represents the only escape left to a desperate population seeking security and economic survival. The flow of migrants out of Honduras will likely affect Guatemala, with the impending implementation of an asylum-cooperation agreement (which would require migrants en route to the US to apply first for protections in Guatemala, El Salvador or Honduras).

It also has a destabilising effect on Mexico, where people are now warehoused in camps waiting for asylum hearings in the US. Neither country has the resources to deal with the crisis or migrants there. The unrest in Honduras and the consolidation of the MS-13 as a cross-national criminal organisation will keep the Central America–Mexico–US corridor in turmoil for the foreseeable future, while continuing to weaken the legitimacy and capacity of the Honduran government.

Notes

[1] Krispy is a marijuana derivative sold in blocks and laced with chemicals. In interviews the drug was described as much more powerful than marijuana, and is favoured by criminal groups because it is more addictive and sells at much higher prices.

[2] On 18 October 2019, Juan Antonio 'Tony' Hernández, brother of President Juan Orlando Hernández, was convicted in the Southern District of New York on multiple counts of drug trafficking, weapons trafficking and related offences. During the trial key witnesses directly linked the president to his brother's drug-trafficking structure and to taking money from cocaine cartels for his campaigns. This strengthened the perception that the president operates on behalf of certain cocaine cartels and that his administration lacks legitimacy. See 'Former Honduran Congressman Tony Hernández Convicted in Manhattan Federal Court of Conspiring to Import Cocaine Into the United States and Related Firearms and False-Statement Offenses', US Attorney's Office, Southern District of New York, 18 October 2019.

[3] 'Homicidios en Honduras han aumentado en relación con el 2019', *El Heraldo*, 28 October 2019.

[4] Presidencia de Honduras, 'Miembros de la PMOP son héroes del order público', Prensa Oficial, 29 August 2019.

[5] 'Situación de derechos humanos en Honduras', Inter-American Commission on Human Rights, 27 August 2019.

[6] World Bank, 'Honduras Overview', 10 October 2019.

[7] World Bank, 'Informal employment (% of total non-agricultural employment) – Honduras, 2006–2017', September 2019.

[8] 'Alrededor de 153 abogados han sido asesinados en Honduras entre 2002 y 2018', *El Nuevo Diario*, 3 December 2018.

[9] 'Periodistas asesinados en Honduras', *Pasos de Animal Grande and Comisionado Nacional de los Derechos Humanos (CONADEH)*, 2017.

[10] Sarah Kinosian, 'Call for fresh Honduras election after President Juan Orlando Hernández wins', *Guardian*, 18 December 2017.

[11] Interviews with MS-13 senior leadership, Honduras, June 2018. The description of the battles for control of the key crossing point to Guatemala came from MS-13 senior leaders in a visit to the crossing points in June 2018. The strategy of moving to rural areas and controlling key crossing points was described in multiple interviews with the MS-13 and police units in San Pedro Sula, Omoa and the Honduras–Guatemala Copán region.

[12] 'La tasa de homicidios en Honduras aumenta por primera vez tras el declive iniciado en 2012', Notimérica, 26 December 2019.

[13] *Ibid.*; 'Homicidios en Honduras han aumentado en relación con el 2019'.

[14] '57 masacres se han registrado este 2019 en Honduras, según el OV-UNAH', Tiempo Digital, 9 November 2019.

[15] World Bank, 'Intentional Homicides (per 100,000)', 2018.

[16] Marlon González, 'Graft, gangs, bad conditions fuel Honduran prison killings', Associated Press, 23 December 2019.

[17] '57 masacres se han registrado este 2019 en Honduras, según el OV-UNAH', Tiempo Digital, 9 November 2019.

[18] Human Rights Watch, 'Honduras events of 2018', 2019.

[19] *Ibid.*

[20] 'Mas del 90% de crímenes de peridistas y abogados están impunes en Honduras', EFE, 15 February 2019.

[21] 'Al menos dos muertos en un motín en una cárcel de alta seguridad de Honduras', eldiario.es, 30 June 2019.

[22] United States Department of Homeland Security Customs and Border Protection, 'US Border Patrol Southwest Border Apprehensions by Sector Fiscal Year 2019', 2019.

[23] World Bank, 'Honduras Overview'.

MEXICO (CARTELS)

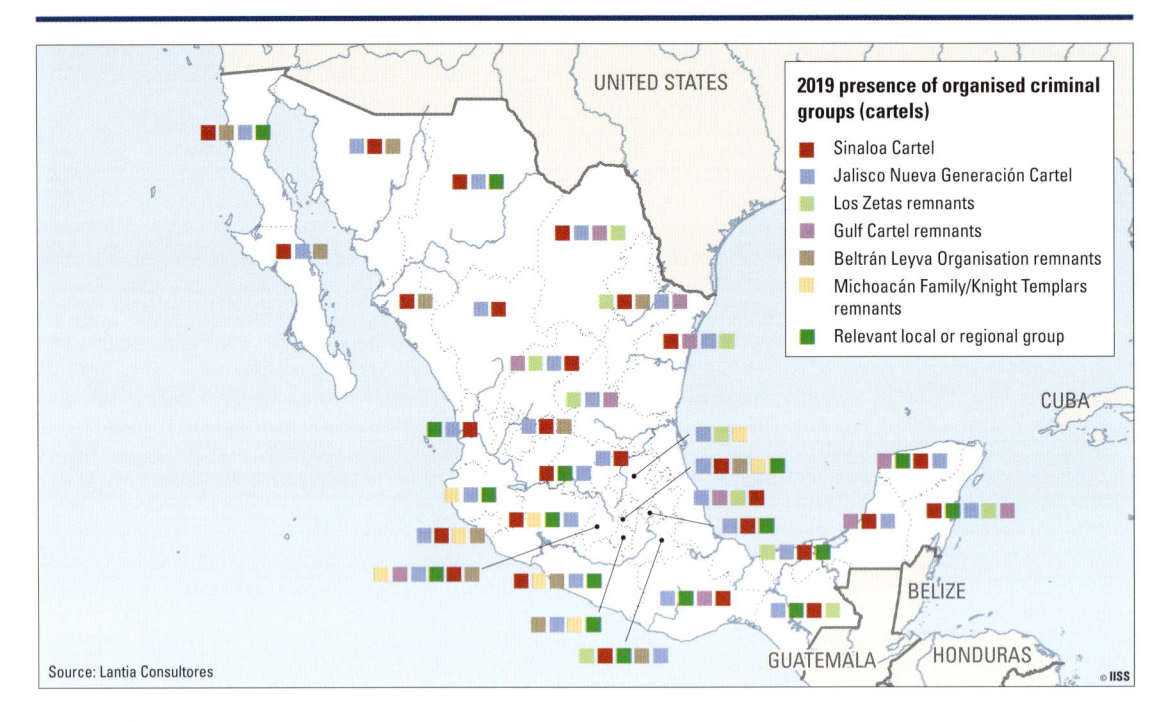

2019 presence of organised criminal groups (cartels)
- Sinaloa Cartel
- Jalisco Nueva Generación Cartel
- Los Zetas remnants
- Gulf Cartel remnants
- Beltrán Leyva Organisation remnants
- Michoacán Family/Knight Templars remnants
- Relevant local or regional group

Source: Lantia Consultores

Overview

The conflict in 2019

The conflict among the major drug-trafficking organisations (DTOs) and between the DTOs and the Mexican state continued to generate high levels of violence and widespread human-rights abuses in 2019. According to official figures from the Mexican government, in 2019 there were 29,421 intentional homicides, a 1.1% increase from 2018, at a rate of 23.24 per 100,000 inhabitants, a marginal increase from 2018.[1] On 17 October, the 'Battle of Culiacán' saw the National Guard (GN) apprehend and then release Ovidio Guzmán, son of Joaquín 'El Chapo' Guzmán and a senior figure in the Sinaloa Cartel. The leading Mexican government official overseeing the 'war on drugs' between 2007 and 2012, former secretary of public security Genaro García Luna, was arrested in the United States on 9 December. He is accused of protecting the Sinaloa Cartel.

Immediately after taking office on 1 December 2018, President Andres Manuel López Obrador (popularly known as 'AMLO') announced changes in the government's strategy to combat DTOs: a shift of focus from war to peace. He criticised the militarised approach of the two previous presidents, Felipe Calderón and Enrique Peña Nieto, and stated that US assistance (through the Mérida Initiative, a security-cooperation agreement) should be reoriented to social programmes and to combat poverty. On 31 January 2019, López Obrador announced that 'there is no longer a war against drug traffickers' and launched instead a 'war on corruption', recognising this as one of the engines that facilitated the growth of common and organised crime.

López Obrador's headline security policy was the creation of the GN to tackle organised crime. The new force includes military personnel from the army, the navy and the Federal Police (particularly the Scientific Division and the Intelligence Division),

Key statistics

Type	Internal
Start date	2006
IDPs total (31 December 2019)	364,000
Refugees total (31 December 2019)	66,915
People in need	Not applicable

with reassignment beginning in January 2019. Congress passed the National Guard Act on 27 May, and the GN was officially established.[2] The Secretary of Security and Citizen Protection (SSPC), a civilian, leads the GN and oversees its military commander. Its two main missions in 2019 were to curtail fuel theft (mainly between January and March) and to detain migrants from Central America, with approximately 20,000 personnel deployed between June and December to Mexico's northern and southern borders. This was at the behest of US President Donald Trump, who had threatened to impose tariffs unless Mexico took action to curb illegal migration to the US.

Despite the promised demilitarisation, during 2019 military personnel oversaw a variety of non-military tasks, among the most prominent of which were the construction of a new airport and banking facilities, the transportation of fuel and monitoring of pipelines, the distribution of medicines and textbooks, securing ports and the containment of migrants. The armed forces were thus empowered within the cabinet.

Notwithstanding these changes, however, and broad support for López Obrador, 68% of Mexicans believed that the government was failing to reduce organised crime and violence.[3] At the end of November 2019, 44% of the population still wanted drug trafficking to be fought, even if that generated more violence, and only 35% of Mexicans supported negotiating with DTOs.[4]

The conflict to 2019

Since the beginning of the 1970s, Mexican criminal groups trading in cocaine from South America have appeared and gradually strengthened. During the twentieth century, large DTOs were in control of specific regions and operated under a common Pax Mafiosa that limited violence contestation. The political party in office, the Institutional Revolutionary Party (PRI), had agreements and protection rackets in place with DTOs, especially the Sinaloa Cartel. Confrontations arose once the PRI lost power in 2000 after 70 years in office and these agreements no longer held.

On 10 December 2006, Calderón declared Mexico's war on drugs. The situation escalated when the Mérida Initiative began in October 2007. The Mérida Initiative is the second Mexico–US military-cooperation agreement in support of the war on drugs. Under this initiative, the US has transferred US$2.88 billion to Mexico between 2008 and 2019.[5] The 2020 requirement is US$76.3 million.[6]

With US support, the Mexican government designed a strategy to combat DTOs similar to that applied against terrorist groups in the Middle East; one centred on high-value targets, aiming to capture leaders and decapitate their organisations.[7] By the end of Peña Nieto's tenure in December 2018, 110 of the 122 criminal leaders wanted by the governments of Mexico and the US had been captured.[8] The unintended consequences of this strategy were the fragmentation of DTOs and the diffusion of many more groups across the Mexican territory, and a rise in the number of casualties, both within the DTOs and among the civilian population. Although ascertaining the number of fatalities that have resulted from the contestation among the DTOs and between the DTOs and the government is impossible for several reasons, the overall number of fatalities – while not all conflict-related – indicate a rising level of violence in Mexico between 2007 and 2019.[9]

Key Conflict Parties

Criminal DTOs

Sinaloa Cartel

Strength
Approximately 500 leaders, a business-support force of 5,000 money-laundering entrepreneurs and a soldier/killers force of 30,000.

Areas of operation
Headquartered in Culiacán, Sinaloa, but present in all 32 states. Its main partners are in Colombia, where the cocaine it traffics is produced. Outside Mexico, the Cartel is active in Asia, Central America, Europe and Canada. In the US, it has an important presence in California; Colorado; El Paso, TX; and New York.

Sinaloa Cartel

Leadership
Historical leader El Chapo was captured in 2016 and imprisoned for life in the US in 2019. His number two is Ismael 'El Mayo' Zambada, who is currently fighting for leadership with El Chapo's sons, Ovidio and Archibaldo.

Structure
Hierarchical organisation, with three sub-divisions: finance/business, logistics for drug transportation and military.

History
Preceded by the Guadalajara Cartel, co-founded in the late 1970s by leader Rafael Caro Quintero. In the 1990s, following the peace processes in Central America, ground transit of cocaine began on a large scale. In the mid-1990s, El Chapo became leader of the Sinaloa Cartel, opened routes from Guatemala to Mexico and the Tijuana route, and forged alliances with the Medellín Cartel in Colombia. At his trial in New York in mid-2019, El Chapo was charged with ten crimes and ordered to give up US$12.6bn in forfeiture. For 20 years the cartel focused on cocaine, but is currently diversifying into heroin, methamphetamine and fentanyl.

Objectives
Control drug markets (of cocaine and methamphetamine in particular), including production networks in Colombia, distribution in Central America and Mexico, and consumption in the US.

Opponents
Other DTOs, including the Gulf, the Tijuana and the Juarez cartels. The Mexican navy's and army's intelligence and special forces. The US's Drug Enforcement Administration (DEA) and Defense Intelligence Agency (DIA).

Affiliates/allies
Many subordinate medium-sized and small DTOs at the regional level. Many corrupt Mexican officials are partners. A large number of Sinaloa governors are suspected to support the cartel.

Resources/capabilities
High-powered weapons, such as the Barrett M107 sniper rifle, anti-aircraft missiles and a large fleet of drug-transportation planes. At his sentencing, the judge calculated El Chapo's personal wealth at more than US$12bn.

Jalisco New Generation Cartel (CJNG)

Strength
5,000 members globally.

Areas of operation
Headquartered in the city of Guadalajara, Jalisco, with a presence in 25 states, particularly Jalisco, Michoacán, Colima, Nayarit, Guerrero and Guanajuato. It also controls the Pacific ports of Manzanillo and Lazaro Cardenas, where chemicals from China enter Mexico. According to the DEA, it has rapidly expanded in the US, where it has a solid presence in 35 states and in Puerto Rico.

Leadership
The main leader is Nemesio Oseguera Cervantes, commonly known as 'El Mencho'.

Structure
El Mencho successfully co-opted all regional leaders of the Michoacán Family and the Knights Templar to control the laboratories in the Michoacán mountains.

History
Formed in 2011 in Guadalajara, Jalisco, CJNG initially produced methamphetamine in rural laboratories in Jalisco and Michoacán. In 2012–13, it expanded to Veracruz. Since 2015–16 its influence has grown throughout the country, thanks in part to gaps left after the government successfully targeted other DTOs (the Michoacán Family, the Knights Templar, Los Zetas and the Sinaloa Cartel).

Objectives
Fully replace the Sinaloa Cartel at the helm of Mexico's criminal networks.

Opponents
Sinaloa Cartel, Los Zetas, Mexico's Federal Police and the special forces of the navy and the army.

Affiliates/allies
Demobilised members of the Michoacán Family and the Knights Templar, as well as large numbers of collaborating peasants.

Resources/capabilities
Estimated capital of US$1bn from the sale of methamphetamine and fentanyl as well as the extortion of merchants and money-laundering activities in Guadalajara.

Los Zetas

Strength
Unknown. A decentralised organisation, the cartel was hit hard by the government between 2012 and 2016.

Areas of operation
Tamaulipas State, mainly along the border with Texas, as well as Coahuila, Nuevo León, Veracruz, Tabasco and the area along the border with Guatemala.

Leadership
Founded by Heriberto Lazcano, former member of the Mexican army. Since 2013, 33 of its main leaders have been arrested or killed in combat by military forces.

Los Zetas

Structure
Horizontal, decentralised structure that works as a large business with multiple criminal activities. Unsuccessful at drug trafficking, its cells carry out extortions and kidnappings, collect criminal taxes from merchants and traffic migrants from Central America to Texas.

History
Originally the armed wing of the Gulf Cartel, drawing most of its members from the Mexican and Guatemalan armies. Notorious for perpetrating mass violence against the civilian population and migrants. Between 2010 and 2012, the navy undertook a major military offensive to dismantle the 'Gulf Corridor', which weakened the group significantly. It is the DTO against which the Mexican government has been most successful.

Objectives
Control criminal activity in the Gulf of Mexico states.

Opponents
CJNG, Gulf Cartel and the special forces of the Mexican navy.

Affiliates/allies
Criminal networks in Tamaulipas State.

Resources/capabilities
Migrant smuggling and criminal taxes on merchants.

Gulf Cartel

Strength
Between 3,000 and 5,000 full-time members.

Areas of operation
Operates and controls territories in Tamaulipas State, particularly the border area with Texas, including strategic border cities, such as Nuevo Laredo, Reynosa and Matamoros.

Leadership
The current leader is Homero Cárdenas Guillén. Many former leaders have been killed in combat or detained and extradited to the US.

Structure
Unstable, with fragmented leadership.

History
The second-oldest DTO in the country, smuggling alcohol, weapons and drugs across the US border since the 1940s. After forging a partnership with the Colombian Cali Cartel in the 1990s, the group focused on introducing cocaine to the US market. It has undergone many changes of leadership, with its internal structure destabilised by fragmentation – particularly the violent separation of Los Zetas in 2010.

Objectives
To smuggle drugs on the Texas–Tamaulipas border and control drug trafficking in the northeast US.

Opponents
Los Zetas, CJNG and the special forces of the Mexican army and navy.

Affiliates/allies
Closely linked to Tamaulipas State's governors (three former governors have been charged in Texas) and criminal networks.

Resources/capabilities
Approximately 5,000 full-time members, and many Tamaulipas businessmen who support the cartel in laundering money.

Beltrán Leyva Organisation (BLO)

Strength
Approximately 1,000 members.

Areas of operation
The cartel's main activity is in the states of Guerrero and Morelos, and the Mexico City–Acapulco highway. The group controls poppy production and the export of heroin from Iguala (Guerrero) to Chicago, IL.

Leadership
Founded by brothers Arturo, Alfredo, Carlos and Héctor Leyva – Arturo was killed and the other three imprisoned, with Héctor later dying.

Structure
Based around vertically organised cells. After the death or imprisonment of the four brothers, seven local criminal groups emerged in Guerrero State: Cartel Independiente de Acapu, Guerreros Unidos, Los Ardillos, Los Granados, Los Mazatecos, Los Rojos and Los Ruelas Torres.

History
Originally from Sinaloa. A breakaway group of the Sinaloa Cartel formed in 2008 and moved to the South Pacific – Acapulco (Guerrero State), Morelos and Mexico State.

Objectives
Control heroin traffic in the South Pacific and from Mexico to Chicago.

Beltrán Leyva Organisation (BLO)

Opponents
Sinaloa Cartel, CJNG and the special forces of the Mexican army.

Affiliates/allies
An estimated 100,000 peasants who grow poppies in Guerrero.

Resources/capabilities
Profits from the sale of heroin in the US, and from criminal activities such as extortion and kidnapping in Mexico.

Michoacán Family/Knights Templars

Strength
The Michoacán Family became powerful with the production of methamphetamines, importing chemical precursors from China. After the government conducted a major offensive between 2013 and 2016, the cartel's current strength is estimated at 300 members. Following the capture of its first leaders, the Michoacán Family became the Knights Templar in 2013–14, under the leadership of Servando Gomez.

Areas of operation
The surviving criminal cells moved to Guanajuato, Guerrero and Mexico State.

Leadership
Leader Servando Gómez was arrested in 2015 by the Federal Police.

Structure
Organised into independent cells.

History
Founded by Nazario Moreno in 2005, the organisation was practically dismantled by Mexican government forces between 2013 and 2016. Initial recruitment was based on a religious discourse. Between 2006 and 2012, the group built a broad network of collaborators among the population, bought a large number of local politicians on the Pacific coast of Michoacán and ran methamphetamine labs in the mountains.

Objectives
The organisation engages in a great deal of criminal activity beyond drug trafficking. It aims to control mining and agricultural production (of avocados for export to the US) in Michoacán State; the port Lazaro Cardenas (for smuggling the chemical base for producing methamphetamine); and the theft of fuel in Guanajuato State.

Opponents
Sinaloa Cartel, CJNG, Los Zetas, the Federal Police and the special forces of the Mexican army.

Affiliates/allies
A large number of collaborating peasants.

Resources/capabilities
The revenue from criminal taxes on economic activities.

Tijuana Cartel (a.k.a. Arellano Felix Family Organisation)

Strength
It has between 2,000 and 3,000 members in the city of Tijuana. Since 2018 its strength has increased again. The cartel is a bi-national, cross-border organisation operating between Tijuana and San Diego, CA.

Areas of operation
Tijuana; San Diego; Los Angeles, CA.

Leadership
Benjamin Arellano Felix and his brothers Ramón, Eduardo, Luis Fernando, Francisco, Carlos and Javier – all imprisoned in California jails.

Structure
Groups of young people are divided into gunmen and middle-class youth who have visas to cross the border and export the cocaine. Their leaders are family members.

History
During the 1980s and 1990s, the Arellano Felix brothers controlled the north of the country, and transported drugs across the border through tunnels, migrants, and people walking and driving. The Tijuana Cartel is one of the groups which perpetrates the most violence against the population. In 2018 the intentional-homicide rate in Baja California was 79.43 per 100,000 inhabitants, and in 2019 it was 72.77 per 100,000, the second highest in the country.[10]

Objectives
Control drug trafficking from Baja California to California, US.

Opponents
Sinaloa Cartel, the special forces of the Mexican army and US intelligence services at the border which cooperate with the Mexican authorities.

Affiliates/allies
Many people cross the border daily with small amounts of drugs.

Resources/capabilities
Revenue from the cross-border cocaine trade.

Juarez/La Línea Cartel

Strength
Between 4,000 and 5,000 members. A bi-national, cross-border organisation operating between Ciudad Juárez and El Paso.

Areas of operation
North Chihuahua; North Sonora; Southwest Texas; Las Cruces and Albuquerque, NM; and Tucson, AZ.

Leadership
It was founded by Amado Carrillo Fuentes in the 1990s. His brother Vicente Carrillo Fuentes directs it from prison.

Structure
In Ciudad Juárez, there are three local cartels: La Línea, Los Artistas Asesinos and Los Aztecas. Between the three of them, they fight over cocaine shipments to be exported to El Paso, Texas.

History
The cartel was founded by Amado Carrillo Fuentes, the 'Lord of the Heavens', in the 1990s; Carrillo orchestrated the smuggling of drugs in small planes at low altitude, which went undetected by radars. It began to fight with the Sinaloa Cartel for control of the Central Mexican and the US-highway trafficking routes. The cartel is controlled from jail by Vicente Carrillo Fuentes, brother of Amado.

Objectives
Control drugs crossing from Ciudad Juárez to El Paso, and into New Mexico and Arizona, and drug trafficking to the northeast US.

Opponents
Los Zetas, CJNG, the special forces of the Mexican army and the DEA.

Affiliates/allies
Groups of young people are divided into gunmen and middle-class youth who have visas to cross the border.

Resources/capabilities
The proceeds from drug trafficking.

Government forces

Secretariat of National Defence (SEDENA) – Army and Air Force

Strength
214,157 members at the outset of 2019;[11] 165,461 at the end of 2019, after 48,696 were transferred to the GN between January and December.[12]

Areas of operation
Operates across the whole country but concentrates its forces in the north and the Pacific region: in Tamaulipas, Chihuahua, Baja California, Coahuila, Sonora, Michoacán, Jalisco and Guerrero.

Leadership
General Luis Crecencio Sandoval heads SEDENA. General Jesús Hernández González heads the air force.

Structure
Since 1939 the Mexican federal government has had two defence ministries: SEDENA, which includes the army and the air force, and the Secretariat of the Navy (SEMAR). The army is divided into 12 military regions and 46 military zones. The air force is divided into four air regions. The General Staff of National Defence is divided into eight sections. The second section (intelligence) and the seventh section (combatting drug trafficking) focus on DTOs.

History
The Ministry of War and the Navy was created in 1821 to supervise the army, navy and air force. In 1939 it was divided into Secretariat of National Defence and Secretariat of the Navy.

Objectives
Provide internal security and fight drug trafficking.

Opponents
DTOs.

Affiliates/allies
Secretariat of the Navy (SEMAR), GN and special-forces combat group GAIN (Drug Trafficking Information Analysis Group), which is in charge of capturing DTO leaders. Also supported by the National Intelligence Centre (CNI) and the Attorney General's Office, as well as foreign governments through cooperation programmes (e.g. the Mérida Initiative with the US).

Resources/capabilities
Infantry, armoured vehicles and combat helicopters. 2019 budget: US$4.92bn.

Secretariat of the Navy (SEMAR)

Strength
57,824 personnel in June 2019,[13] with 7,486 transferred to the GN over the course of the year.[14]

Areas of operation
The country's coasts, divided into the Pacific and Gulf of Mexico–Caribbean zones.

Leadership
Admiral José Rafael Ojeda.

Secretariat of the Navy (SEMAR)

Structure
Divided into General (70%) and Naval Infantry Corps (marines; 30%), which operate in eight naval regions and 18 naval zones (12 in the Pacific and six in the Gulf and Caribbean). The marines' special forces also combat criminal groups in the country's interior.

History
Created in 1821. SEMAR separated from the army in 1939.

Objectives
Defend Mexico's coasts, strategic infrastructure (mainly oil platforms in the Gulf of Mexico) and the environment at sea, and fight piracy.

Opponents
DTOs, particularly those that traffic people through the coasts, from South and Central America, and those that transport drugs via sea from Colombia and Venezuela.

Affiliates/allies
SEDENA, GN and CNI. Cooperates with US Coast Guard at the border.

Resources/capabilities
Fast vessels for interception, exploration and intelligence; supported by naval aviation. 2019 budget: US$1.67bn.

National Guard

Strength
92,090 personnel as of December 2019, drawn from the army and military police (35,232), navy and naval police (6,871), Federal Police (14,768), SEDENA (13,464) and SEMAR (615).[15]

Areas of operation
Across the whole country. Mexico, Jalisco, Michoacán, Oaxaca and Mexico City were the states with most GN troops in 2019.

Leadership
Headed by Secretary of Public Security and Citizen Protection (SSPC) Alfonso Durazo. Commanded by General Luis Rodríguez Bucio, Retd.

Structure
Three inter-institutional groups – Federal Police, Army and Navy – and 266 deployment regions. By December 2019, 150 were covered and had regional coordinators. The plan is to have 266 regional coordinators on the ground by the end of 2023.

History
Began operating on 11 January 2019, by presidential order. The law gives GN personnel the authority to stop suspected criminals on the streets.

Objectives
Reduce the level of violence in the country and combat DTOs. So far, the GN has mainly monitored highways to prevent the passage of undocumented people and the theft of fuel.

Opponents
DTOs and medium-sized criminal organisations.

Affiliates/allies
Army, navy, and local and municipal police.

Resources/capabilities
Resources from the defunct Federal Police, including their helicopter teams and equipment such as assault rifles. Relies on intelligence from the army, the navy and the CNI.

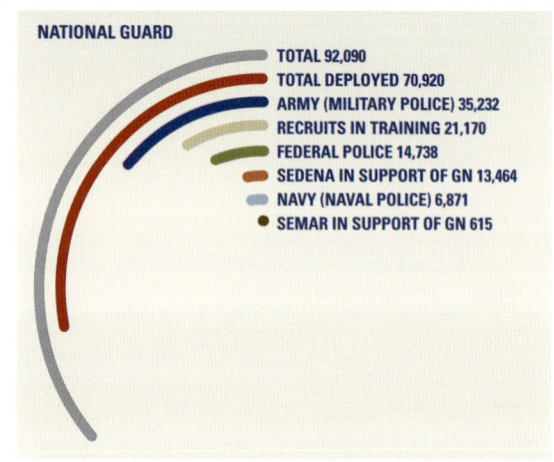

NATIONAL GUARD
- TOTAL 92,090
- TOTAL DEPLOYED 70,920
- ARMY (MILITARY POLICE) 35,232
- RECRUITS IN TRAINING 21,170
- FEDERAL POLICE 14,738
- SEDENA IN SUPPORT OF GN 13,464
- NAVY (NAVAL POLICE) 6,871
- SEMAR IN SUPPORT OF GN 615

FEDERAL POLICE
- TOTAL 38,550
- WITHDRAWN, JANUARY–NOVEMBER 2019* 23,812
- TRANSFERRED TO GN, NOVEMBER 2019 14,738

*Federal Police personnel are in a process of gradual retirement after the body ceased to exist following the passage of the National Guard Act on 27 May 2019. Those who decided to stay now operate in the GN uniform. At the close of 2019, there was an ongoing labour dispute.

Source: SESNSP

Figure 1: Federal internal-security forces

Drivers

Geography and drugs

Mexico is located between Colombia to the south and the US to the north. Colombia is the largest producer of cocaine in the world, and the US is the largest consumer of cocaine and synthetic drugs. The vast revenues available through drug trafficking have driven cartel activity and brought the DTOs into conflict with each other and with the Mexican and US governments. Violence arises from competition between different DTOs and their links with Colombian cocaine exporters, and from the fights over shipments when drugs are unloaded from the air or sea to cross the Mexico–US border. The free sale of arms on the southern border of the US provides DTOs with significant firepower with which to assail other DTOs and the government.[16]

Mexican cartels use violence to discipline their members, to prevent them from cooperating with government officials and betraying the cartel, or to prevent them from working for other DTOs. They also use violence to extort businesspeople into trafficking drugs or laundering money; to threaten politicians and military, police and customs officials; and to force migrants to traffic drugs across the US border. Since the advent of the war on drugs in 2007, DTOs have fought each other for territory, particularly in border cities such as Juárez and Tijuana. These two cities are among the most violent in the world.

The legal transit of people between Mexico and the US has increased since the advent of the North American Free Trade Agreement (NAFTA) in 1994, with an average of one million people crossing the border every day. The two countries lack the capacity to check goods containers, and the border is also riddled with tunnels, many of them built by the Sinaloa Cartel:[17] this is one of the reasons why it will be difficult for Trump's proposed wall to be successful in stopping drugs and migration. In addition, some Mexican criminal organisations have also carried out human-trafficking activities, primarily Los Zetas.[18]

Corruption and impunity

DTOs have infiltrated state and local governments, particularly many state and county law-enforcement agencies. They can operate openly and with impunity, bribing or killing public officials, police chiefs, mayors and judges when needed to pursue their objectives. A weakened justice system and widespread corruption have greatly hampered Mexico's efforts to fight DTOs. The 2018 Global Impunity Index reported that in Mexico 93.7% of crimes go unreported and only 17.1% of those accused of homicides are imprisoned.[19] Corruption not only erodes the country's security and justice mechanisms, but is estimated to cost Mexico circa 10% of its GDP.[20]

Poverty, inequality and migration

Poverty indirectly drives drug-related violence in Mexico, where two out of every five people (52.4m) live in poverty. Working for or with DTOs can offer the opportunity to earn a significantly higher income. Additionally, as of August 2019, 56.3% of the working population worked in the informal economy.[21] Such a high level of informality makes money laundering and corruption extremely hard to prove. DTOs hold the majority of their earnings in cash flow, making it very difficult to measure their financial power. López Obrador has committed to fighting these socio-economic roots of violence with policies to improve the conditions of the poor.[22] Whether this strategy is successful will only become evident in the long term.

The desperate economic situation of some in Mexico has driven them to attempt to migrate to the US, leaving them vulnerable to exploitation. Some Mexican DTOs, such as Los Zetas, have developed a business in trafficking people from Central America to the US, using the same highways as for drug trafficking. Los Zetas, exploiting the severe corruption of Guatemalan and Mexican officials, kidnap and extort migrants. This has generated significant violence, especially towards women and child migrants. It has become a serious security problem for Mexico, informed US security and migration policy and led the US to collaborate with the Mexican army and GN.

Political Developments

Domestic developments

López Obrador's first major political act was the abandonment of the war on drugs and the promise of a change in strategy to combat the DTOs, on 31 January. (His criticism of the prior strategy was that it resulted in the expansion of the territories where DTOs fight each other and caused thousands more victims among the civilian population.) His political party, the National Regeneration Movement (MORENA), was able to pass a major reform with the creation of the GN, owing to it controlling both parliamentary chambers (with 259 of 500 deputies and 60 of 128 senators). With 56,182 personnel transferred from the armed forces, the GN numbered 92,090 personnel by November.

At the same time, López Obrador declared a 'war on fuel theft', which Pemex (the state oil company) estimates affects up to 10% of the total sales of petrol in the country.[23] Carried out through the drilling of illegal oil pipelines, fuel theft relies on a complex network of corruption linking Pemex officials and employees with criminal organisations.

This anti-corruption campaign has focused on key public officials in the Calderón and Peña Nieto administrations. In the most prominent cases of the year, in July arrest warrants were issued for former Pemex director Emilio Lozoya (implicated in the Odebrecht scandal), who fled the country, and in October Supreme Court Justice Eduardo Medina Mora resigned after the Mexican Financial Intelligence Unit announced in June that he was under investigation. And, on 9 December, García Luna – who had designed the war-on-drugs strategy under the Calderón administration and led the Federal Police – was arrested in Dallas, TX, on charges of collaborating with the Sinaloa Cartel and receiving US$5m in bribes. At least six state governors have been incarcerated on counts of corruption and collaboration with the DTOs, including those from Tamaulipas, Coahuila, Chihuahua and Veracruz.

Mexico–US relations

From May 2019, at the behest of the Trump administration and with the negotiation of the new US–Mexico–Canada Agreement (USMCA) in jeopardy, the army, navy and GN built a system of migrant control in southern Mexico.

On 26 November, Trump announced plans to designate Mexican DTOs as terrorists; López Obrador responded to this perceived interventionism with 'cooperation, yes; intervention, no', and Trump later announced that the plans would be suspended. On 5 December, US Attorney General William Barr visited López Obrador in Mexico to discuss border security. On 6 December, the governments of Mexico and the US signed a commitment to reactivate the High-level Security Group (GANSEG), in order to strengthen security-cooperation mechanisms. This confirmed the cooperation of Mexico's GN in controlling the trafficking of Central American migrants. The revised USMCA, a free-trade pact to replace NAFTA, was signed on 10 December. With these agreements, Mexico and the US reconfirmed their status as strategic partners not only in trade, but also in security, justice and defence.

Key Events in 2019

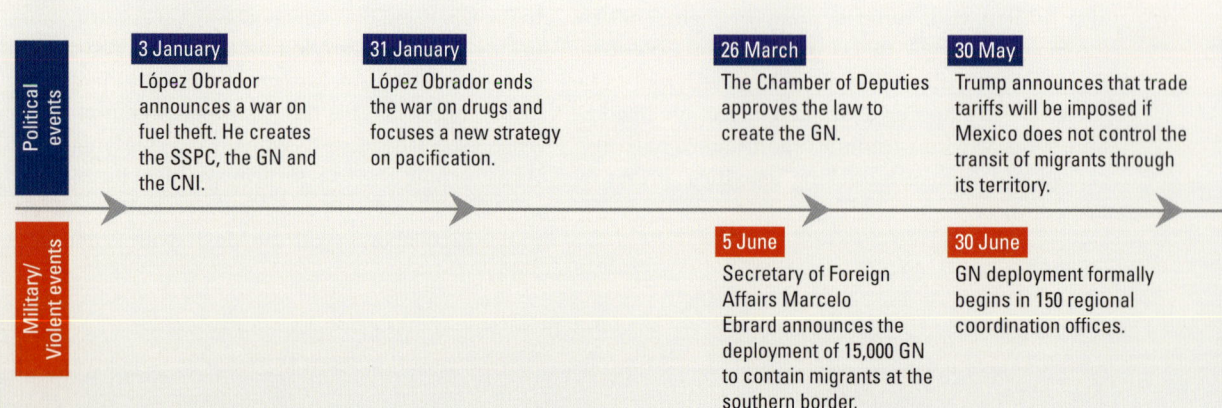

Political events

3 January — López Obrador announces a war on fuel theft. He creates the SSPC, the GN and the CNI.

31 January — López Obrador ends the war on drugs and focuses a new strategy on pacification.

26 March — The Chamber of Deputies approves the law to create the GN.

30 May — Trump announces that trade tariffs will be imposed if Mexico does not control the transit of migrants through its territory.

Military/Violent events

5 June — Secretary of Foreign Affairs Marcelo Ebrard announces the deployment of 15,000 GN to contain migrants at the southern border.

30 June — GN deployment formally begins in 150 regional coordination offices.

Military Developments

Reorganisation of security forces

In 2019, López Obrador undertook to change the structure of Mexico's security and defence apparatuses by dismantling the Federal Police and reducing its personnel and reforming the functions of the Secretariat for Home Affairs (SEGOB). Previously in control of the Federal Police, the reformed SEGOB is now only in charge of the National Institute of Migration (INAMI), religious affairs and human rights, while the newly created Secretariat of Security and Citizen Protection (SSPC) controls the civil-intelligence system and the CNI.

During 2019, the army and navy have also been readapting their forces to the new internal-security missions. Circa 52,000 troops from the army and air force were permanently assigned to public security and the fight against drug trafficking. As a result, the army carried out many non-military tasks – such as supporting the GN in fighting fuel theft, helping administer the rural programme 'Sowing Life' and assisting the population affected by natural disasters – which diminished its capacity to fight the DTOs. In the navy, the Naval Intelligence Unit (UIN) was strengthened with US support, while the marines and the Fuerzas Especiales (FES), the special-operations unit, continue to support the fight against the DTOs. By the end of the year, however, this new security strategy had come under heavy criticism, due mostly to the failure of the military operation against the Sinaloa Cartel on 17 October and the assassination of the LeBaron family on 4 November.

The Battle of Culiacán

After the Mexican government captured Ovidio Guzmán in Culiacán, Sinaloa on 17 October (following an extradition order by the US in 2018), the Sinaloa Cartel initiated a series of acts of sabotage and attacks throughout the city against military and civilian vehicles, attacking a military helicopter and threatening to attack military-family housing facilities. The Battle of Culiacán lasted four hours, after which the government freed Guzmán in order to prevent civilian deaths. Durazo acknowledged the failure of the military operation, one of the most prominent such failures since the start of the war on drugs in 2007.

LeBaron family assassination

Weeks later, a Juarez Cartel commando killed nine members of the LeBaron family (a very famous business family in northern Mexico) in northern Sonora, close to the Mexico–US border – territory disputed with the Sinaloa Cartel. Three women and six children died. The massacre caused a double crisis for the Mexican government, both with the US, because the family had US nationality, and at the national-political level. For the first time, Mexico permitted FBI agents to participate in the investigation.

---

1 July
López Obrador announces that his security policy has not yielded results.

1 August
Trump announces that the flow of migrants has decreased and thanks Mexico for its cooperation.

17 October
Government forces capture El Chapo's son, Ovidio Guzmán, in Culiacán, Sinaloa. The Battle of Culiacán ensues.

4 November
A Juarez Cartel commando kills nine members of the LeBaron family in Sonora, close to the US border. The FBI later joins the investigation.

6 December
Trump suspends the designation of Mexican DTOs as terrorists.

9 December
García Luna is arrested in Dallas.

10 December
The revised USMCA is signed in Mexico City.

Impact

Humanitarian
The new strategy promoted by López Obrador since January, based on amnesties, pardons and trying to promote negotiations with criminal leaders to reduce violence, did not bear fruit by the end of 2019. Violence has increased, with an increase in overall homicides, murders of journalists,[24] murders of women, kidnappings for ransom and cases of human trafficking.[25] The dedication of security forces – principally the GN and the army – to overseeing border controls (at the behest of the US) limited the government's ability to provide a robust response to the DTOs. This empowered the DTOs, such as the Sinaloa Cartel, as was evident on 17 October. Meanwhile, the contestation over fuel theft meant an increase in violence in states such as Guanajuato, which was the most violent in the country in 2019, with 2,775 intentional homicides.[26]

López Obrador's strategy of decreased direct engagement with the DTOs was called into serious question with the security crisis that began in October with the Battle of Culiacán and continued with the massacre of the LeBaron family on 4 November in Sonora. 1 December was the most violent day of the year, with the press reporting 127 people killed.[27]

Relations with neighbouring and international partners
During 2019, Mexico's security reforms caused confusion within the US security establishment. Cooperation continued, but the Trump administration did not have full confidence in López Obrador. Added to this was the issue of migration to the US from Central America, with Mexico acting to quell the flow after Washington exerted significant pressure. While security relations are good between the two countries, there is mutual distrust. Mexico's detention of migrants has also brought it into diplomatic conflict with the countries of Central America.

Trends

Increasing violence of DTOs and militarisation
The Battle of Culiacán demonstrated that the DTOs have the capacity to make credible threats of mass killings against the civilian population whenever the state threatens their activities. Though López Obrador's security response has so far proven highly inadequate, he has reiterated that it will not change, despite pressure from civil society, the armed forces and the US government. If the upward trend in violence continues in 2020, intentional homicides will rise to more than 30,000 per year (though not all conflict-related), with additional humanitarian consequences such as mass displacement.

The media, and analysts of the war on drugs, have criticised López Obrador for the absence of a strategy to combat criminal groups. The launch of the war on fuel theft and the dismantling of the Federal Police led to an increase in the use of military personnel, and to Guanajuato becoming the most violent state in the country in 2019, feeding into the significant militarisation of public security. With reform of the country's security system continuing in 2020, López Obrador's administration has handed primary responsibility for public security to the armed forces.

Rebuilding the Mexico–US partnership
The new system of migrant control established in 2019 will offer a common framework for Mexico and the US to address cross-border migration, one of the most sensitive political issues at play, going forward. This, and the improvement in relations signalled by the signing of the USMCA, will ensure continued cooperation between the two governments in fighting organised crime. However, the short term will see little done by the US to tackle the liberalised sale of high-powered weapons on the border – an important factor destabilising Mexican internal security – with Trump rather continuing to focus on immigration control.

Despite differences in the ideologies of the two presidents, with López Obrador broadly on the left and Trump on the right, both have pointed out that neighbourliness is the key to solving common problems. The US will need Mexico to cooperate

Legalisation of cannabis and opium poppies

In 2018, the Mexican Supreme Court of Justice ruled the country's prohibition of the personal consumption of cannabis unconstitutional. This opened the debate during 2019 in the Senate and the Chamber of Deputies over the legalisation of the drug. A large number of forums were held to discuss the legalisation of the medical and recreational use of cannabis, and to propose a General Law on the Production, Trade and Consumption of Cannabis. A number of changes to the General Health Law were also proposed across these forums. The different initiatives coincide on the need to eliminate prohibitionist regulation and change existing laws according to a focus on human rights, public health, sustainable development, and peace and security. The law is planned to be approved in April 2020. The approach is similar to that of Uruguay, where the state controls and grants permits for cannabis production and trade. Similarly, in the state of Guerrero, it has been proposed that the cultivation and trade of opium poppies also be regulated, because there are many peasants who make a living from such production. Senator Manuel Añorve proposed that an amnesty be granted to the estimated 120,000 peasants who grow poppies in Guerrero, the idea being that this would serve to reduce the violence caused by poppy cultivation and the shipment of heroin to the US. Civilian groups such as Mexico United Against Crime, which is leading a major campaign on the issue, maintain that legalisation would reduce violence and that the state would benefit from the collection of taxes.

Security and elections, 2020–21

The US will have a presidential election in November 2020. Mexico will hold mid-term elections for the Senate and Chamber of Deputies in July 2021. With the US Senate acquitting him in his impeachment trial, Trump will run for re-election. In this US presidential campaign, the issue of Mexico and migration does not seem to be as important as in the 2016 election cycle, following agreements reached by the governments during 2019 for a new degree of coexistence on economic and security matters. In the case of Mexico, the issue of increased violence is one of López Obrador's fundamental concerns. If he does not manage to reduce violence and control the DTOs, his high popularity among the Mexican population could decline.

Notes

[1] Executive Secretariat of the National Public Security System (SESNSP), 'Incidencia Delictiva Del Fuero Común 2019', 20 March 2020; SESNSP, 'Número de delitos por cada 100 mil habitantes 2015–2020', 20 March 2020.

[2] 'Ley de la Guardia Nacional. Texto vigente', *Diario Oficial de la Federación*, 27 May 2019.

[3] Alfredo Corchado, 'Mexico stands by Lopez Obrador, poll says, even as violence soars, economy crumbles', *Dallas Morning News*, 1 December 2019.

[4] Ibid.

[5] Congressional Research Service, 'Mexico: Background and U.S. Relations', 2 May 2019, p. 20.

[6] Ibid., p. 20.

[7] Brian J. Phillips, 'How Does Leadership Decapitation Affect Violence? The Case of Drug Trafficking Organisations in Mexico', *Journal of Politics*, vol. 77, no. 2, April 2015.

[8] Victoria Dittmar, 'The Mexico Crime Bosses Peña Nieto's Government Toppled', Insight Crime, 24 September 2018.

[9] Reporting on conflict-related homicides is made challenging by such factors as the massive proliferation of criminal groups in the last decade, the severe difficulty in sorting low-level informal murder from organised-crime murder and a lack of scrupulous reporting. A dataset of homicides allegedly related to organised crime from 2006 to 2010 was published on the presidential web page in January 2011. Met with criticism from local attorney offices and the press, the federal government stopped publishing official data on homicides related to organised crime in the country. Mexico has two official data sources on homicides: the first, gathered by the National Institute of Statistics and Geography (INEGI), provides the total number of homicides (dataset up to date to December 2018); the second, gathered by the SESNSP, provides open case files for total, intentional and non-intentional homicides and was available up to February 2020 at time of press. Additionally, some newspapers (such as *Reforma* and *Milenio*) and civil-society organisations have collected information and released their own estimates of executions and homicides related to organised crime.

[10] SESNSP, 'Número de delitos por cada 100 mil habitantes 2015–2020'.

[11] President of the United Mexican States, 'Informe de Gobierno 2018–2019', 1 September 2019, p. 22.

[12] SESNSP, 2019.
[13] President of the United Mexican States, 'Informe de Gobierno 2018–2019', p. 22.
[14] SESNSP, 2019.
[15] Ibid.
[16] The US Ambassador to Mexico, Christopher Landau, acknowledged that the US is co-responsible for the violence in Mexico, owing to the high demand for drugs and the free sale of weapons in the US. Jorge Martinez, 'US is responsible for violence: Landau', *Milenio*, 2 December 2019.
[17] Kristine Phillips, 'As Trump pushes for a wall, authorities keep finding drug tunnels under the U.S.–Mexico border', *Washington Post*, 15 January 2019.
[18] Parker Asmann, 'Nearly 50 Groups Active in Human Trafficking in Mexico: Report', Insight Crime, 7 August 2017.
[19] Juan Antonio Le Clercq Ortega and Gerardo Rodríguez Sánchez Lara, (eds.), 'La impunidad subnacional en México y sus dimensiones IGI-MEX 2018', *Índice Global de Impunidad México*, April 2018.
[20] According to the Organization of American States and the Centre on Environmental, Economic and Social Policy. See María Amparo Casar, 'Costos de la Corrupción', October 2016.
[21] According to INEGI's National Survey of Occupation and Employment. See Lozano, 'Mucho combate a la pobreza, pero en México 4 de cada 5 la padecen'.
[22] See President of the United Mexican States, 'Plan Nacional de Desarrollo 2019–2024', 30 April 2019.
[23] 'Tras la tragedia: crece el Huachicol', *Reforma*, 12 January 2020.
[24] Committee to Protect Journalists, 'Killed since 1992', accessed 30 March 2020.
[25] SESNSP, 'Incidencia Delictiva Del Fuero Común 2019'.
[26] Ibid.
[27] 'Fue 1 de diciembre día más violento del sexenio', *Reforma*, 2 December 2019.

2 Asia-Pacific

Myanmar (EAOs) 92
Philippines (ASG & Moro) 104
Philippines (NPA) 116
Southern Thailand 126

Citizens prepare to vote in Cotabato City, southern Philippines

Key trends

- In Myanmar, violence intensified and peace negotiations made no progress. Similarly, the conflict between the Philippines and the New People's Army (NPA) escalated and talks at government level ended permanently.
- Incidents in Southern Thailand remained low level, but the Barisan Revolusi Nasional (BRN) proved able to strike outside its main operational area, including in Bangkok.

Strategic implications

- The Abu Sayyaf Group (ASG) in the Philippines remained the most active extremist group in the region, but the risk of ISIS resurgence in Southeast Asia calls for the strengthening of naval and intelligence cooperation among neighbouring states.
- ISIS struggled to infiltrate the ethno-nationalist conflict in Southern Thailand, but anti-Muslim attitudes might encourage recruitment.

Prospects

- As Western countries struggle to engage with Myanmar, China's influence on its politics is likely to increase.
- The resumption of peace talks with the NPA is unlikely.
- Worsening ethnic and religious animosity in Thailand does not bode well for a long-term solution to the conflict.

MYANMAR (EAOS)

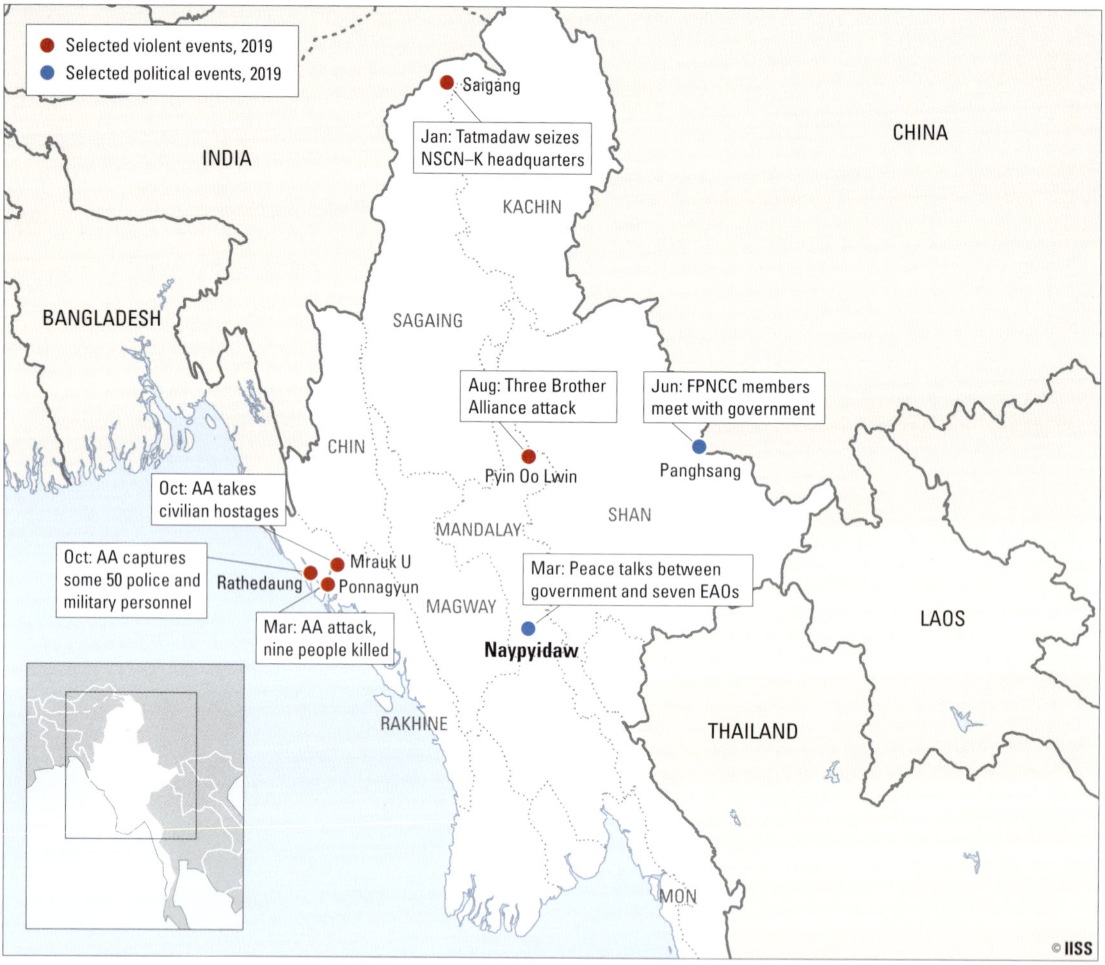
Selected violent events, 2019
Selected political events, 2019
Saigang
Jan: Tatmadaw seizes NSCN–K headquarters
INDIA
CHINA
KACHIN
BANGLADESH
SAGAING
Aug: Three Brother Alliance attack
Jun: FPNCC members meet with government
CHIN
Pyin Oo Lwin
Panghsang
Oct: AA takes civilian hostages
SHAN
MANDALAY
Oct: AA captures some 50 police and military personnel
Mrauk U
Rathedaung
Ponnagyun
Mar: Peace talks between government and seven EAOs
MAGWAY
LAOS
Mar: AA attack, nine people killed
Naypyidaw
RAKHINE
THAILAND
MON
© IISS

Overview

The conflict in 2019

Fighting in Rakhine State occupied centre stage in the conflict in 2019, with violence intensifying across more townships. The campaign of the Myanmar armed forces (Tatmadaw) against the Arakan Army (AA) led to more clashes in the first half of the year than in all of 2018, according to the Myanmar Institute for Peace and Security (MIPS), with the most incidents in March (102) and August (170), exceeding every monthly total of 2018.[1] The increased number of clashes reflect the AA's guerrilla-style tactics of hit-and-run attacks, as well as abduction of government and military personnel, and its reduced reliance on fixed positions compared to other ethnic armed organisations (EAOs). The Tatmadaw's conflict with the AA therefore differs from that with many other EAOs.

Key statistics

Type	Internal
Start date	1949
IDPs total (31 December 2019)	273,922
Refugees total (31 December 2019)	1,000,000
People in need (31 December 2019)	986,000

In December 2018, the Tatmadaw declared a unilateral, four-month ceasefire in the Northern Command in Kachin State, the Northeastern, Eastern and Central Eastern Commands and the Triangle Command in Shan State, covering most active hostilities in Myanmar except for those with the AA in Rakhine State, where the Tatmadaw aimed to concentrate forces. Although the ceasefire mostly held until June, when fighting erupted in northern Shan State, peace negotiations did not advance, and a 21st Century Panglong Peace Conference (21CPC) did not take place in 2019. Instead, confidence in the Nationwide Ceasefire Agreement (NCA) process deteriorated, as the participation of the Karen National Union (KNU) and the Restoration Council of Shan State (RCSS) stalled.

Despite condemnation of the abuses in Rakhine State, the government enhanced its list of international friends, signed new arms deals and undertook a successful wave of defence diplomacy. These developments exposed the limits of Western influence in the lead-up to the 2020 elections, and on the conflict's future trajectory. The importance of defending Myanmar against international criticism for the domestic audience became apparent in December, when State Counsellor Aung San Suu Kyi appeared at the International Court of Justice (ICJ), where a case accusing Myanmar of genocide was being heard, to 'defend the national interest'.[2]

The conflict to 2019

The ethnic Bamar majority took control of independent Burma in 1948 following the signing of the Panglong Agreement in 1947, which laid the foundations for an administrative and financial framework regulating the coexistence of dozens of minority ethnic groups. Dissatisfaction with the implementation of the agreement led to the formation of numerous EAOs.

Following a *coup d'état* in 1962, General Ne Win's regime attempted to 'Burmanise' the country, provoking further armed backlash from ethnic minorities. A second coup in 1988 against Ne Win's Burmese Socialist Programme Party installed a new junta that ushered in market-oriented reforms and negotiated ceasefire agreements with some EAOs, which gained limited territorial control. In 1989, the junta changed the country's name to Myanmar. At the same time, following a mutiny, the Communist Party of Burma (CPB) collapsed, ending a long-running military and political campaign across the country's northeast. The United Wa State Army (UWSA) integrated much of the CPB's arms and manpower and continued the struggle. Despite periodic ceasefires, fighting between the Tatmadaw and non-ceasefire EAOs continued throughout the 2000s.

The 2008 military regime drafted a new constitution, ushering in a period of political change. Elections for national and regional legislatures in 2010, followed by a new presidential administration in 2011, generated optimism and paved the way for dialogue and the NCA. Though 15 EAOs agreed on an initial draft, only eight signed the final NCA text in 2015 – the All Burma Students' Democratic Front (ABSDF), the Arakan Liberation Party (ALP), the Chin National Front (CNF), the Democratic Karen Benevolent Army (DKBA–5), the Karen National Liberation Army–Peace Council (KPC), the KNU, the Pa-O National Liberation Organisation (PNLO) and the RCSS.

The landslide victory of Aung San Suu Kyi's National League for Democracy (NLD) party in the 2015 elections brought hope for expansion of the NCA. Despite some success in initiating political dialogue through the 21CPCs, beginning in August 2016, the peace process stalled. The complex power-sharing arrangement between the Tatmadaw and the government complicated attempts to broaden the peace process. In 2018, two smaller EAOs – the Lahu Democratic Union and the New Mon State Party (NMSP) – signed the NCA. However, the same year, the two largest signatories – the KNU and the RCSS – suspended their participation.

The history of violence in Rakhine State, which has led to the rise of various Rakhine nationalist armed groups including the AA, is crucial to understanding how the conflict in Myanmar evolved in 2019. The conflict's roots in this area date back to 1784–85 when the Bamar Kingdom invaded and defeated what was then the Arakan or Rakhine Kingdom. Rakhine resistance and nationalism has remained strong since independence through the various Arakan armed groups fighting the government, including the Arakan People's Liberation Party, National United Party of Arakan and the Arakan National Liberation Party. In the 2015 elections, the Arakan National Party (ANP) won the most seats in the state, but was denied power by the NLD, which nominated a non-ANP chief minister who then formed a non-ANP cabinet. These 'betrayals' have emboldened the AA, a small but growing armed force with support from larger northeastern EAOs, to lead an offensive against the Tatmadaw in Rakhine State in 2018 and 2019.

Key Conflict Parties

Non-state armed groups, militias and the Tatmadaw populate Myanmar's crowded conflict environment. There are more than 100,000 armed personnel attached to EAOs in Myanmar.[3] These groups vary in size, capability and ceasefire status. Militias are formed by local communities or by private interests, and often protect illicit businesses. Accurate numbers for militia membership are even murkier, with an often-cited study suggesting that there may be up to 180,000 members spread across 5,000 groups.[4]

Tatmadaw (Myanmar armed forces)

The Tatmadaw has been the primary actor in Myanmar since 1962. Despite the country's much-lauded 'transition' away from the junta-led regime, the Tatmadaw maintains effective control over the country. The 2008 military-drafted constitution ensures its dominance over the civilian government, reserving a quarter of parliamentary seats for members of the armed forces and thus the ability to veto legislation. Similarly, the Tatmadaw commander-in-chief appoints the ministers of defence, border affairs and home affairs. The progress since the 2010 transition is the result of a carefully managed process by the Tatmadaw, and not of Aung San Suu Kyi's charismatic leadership or popular pressure.

The Tatmadaw is estimated to comprise 406,000 active personnel. Since 2011 Senior General Min Aung Hlaing has doubled down on Myanmar's military modernisation,[5] which has included acquiring new materiel and reducing the Tatmadaw's overall size as well as producing the first defence white paper in 2016. A history of poor-performing procurements from China has led to acquisitions from a range of new suppliers, including Israel and Ukraine.[6]

Ethnic armed organisations (EAOs)

There are some 135 recognised ethnic groups in Myanmar, most of which have been engaged in armed conflict at some point since independence.[7] Alliances have been fluid, both as a result of the Tatmadaw's divide-and-rule tactics and due to disputes between ethnic groups over territory. Some EAOs have turned into Tatmadaw-commanded Border Guard Forces or militias, while others have grown in strength through the production of narcotics or support from external actors. The EAOs therefore do not form a unified bloc against the Tatmadaw; they are a highly heterogeneous group with both competing and converging interests.

An uncomfortable truth in the conflict is that an EAO's survival and prospect of peace comes through strength and deterrence against the Tatmadaw, as the UWSA – the most capable of these groups – has effectively shown. Since the most recent peace process has stalled, EAOs have sought to strengthen their negotiating position, either by acquiring weapons or by making powerful allies. One recent example is the AA, which, allied with the Kachin Independence Army (KIA) and the Northern Alliance, displayed in a recent recruitment video an elite Barrett MRAD sniper rifle and a US-made M60 machine gun.

Overview of ethnic armed organisations active in Myanmar

EAO	Umbrella group	Date NCA signed (if signed)	Previous ceasefires (if any)	Strength (approximate)	Alliances (current)	Opposition (active)	Activity location
All Burma Students' Democratic Front (ABDSF)	NCA–S	2015	2013	400	KIA, KNU	Tatmadaw	Kachin State, Karen State, Shan State

Overview of ethnic armed organisations active in Myanmar

EAO	Umbrella group	Date NCA signed (if signed)	Previous ceasefires (if any)	Strength (approximate)	Alliances (current)	Opposition (active)	Activity location
Arakan Liberation Party/Arakan Liberation Army (ALP/ALA)	NCA–S	2015	2012	<100	KNU	Tatmadaw	Karen State, Rakhine State
Chin National Front (CNF)	NCA–S	2015	2012	200		Tatmadaw	Chin State
Democratic Karen Benevolent Army/Klo Htoo Baw Battalion (DKBA–5)	NCA–S	2015	2011	1,500	KNU, KPC	Tatmadaw	Karen State
Kachin Independence Organisation/Kachin Independence Army (KIO/KIA)	FPNCC; Northern Alliance		1994	12,000	AA, MNDAA, NDAA, SSA–N, TNLA, UWSA	Tatmadaw	Kachin State
Karen National Union (KNU)	NCA–S	20159	2012	5,000	DKBA–5, KPC	MNLA, Tatmadaw	Bago Region, Karen State, Tanintharyi Region
Karen National Union/Karen National Liberation Army–Peace Council (KPC)	NCA–S	2015	2007	200	DKBA–5, KNU	Tatmadaw	Karen State
Karenni National Progressive Party (KNPP)			2005, 2012	600		Tatmadaw	Kayah State
Lahu Democratic Union (LDU)	NCA–S	2018		<200		Tatmadaw	Shan State
Myanmar National Truth and Justice Party/Myanmar National Democratic Alliance Army (MNTJP/MNDAA)	FPNCC; Three Brother Alliance; Northern Alliance			2,000	AA, KIA, NDAA, SSA–N, TNLA, UWSA	Tatmadaw	Shan State
National Socialist Council of Nagaland–Khaplang (NSCN–K)			2012	500	National Socialist Council of Nagaland–Isak Muivah (India) (NSCN–IM)	Tatmadaw	Northeast India (Manipur, Nagaland), Sagaing State
New Mon State Party/Mon National Liberation Army (NMSP/MNLA)	NCA–S	2018	1995, 2012	800		KNU, Tatmadaw	Mon State
Palaung State Liberation Front/Ta'ang National Liberation Army (PSLF/TNLA)	FPNCC; Three Brother Alliance; Northern Alliance			6,000	AA, KIA, MNDAA, NDAA, SSA–N, UWSA	Pansay militia, SSA–S, Tatmadaw	Shan State

Overview of ethnic armed organisations active in Myanmar							
EAO	Umbrella group	Date NCA signed (if signed)	Previous ceasefires (if any)	Strength (approximate)	Alliances (current)	Opposition (active)	Activity location
Pa-O National Liberation Organisation/ Pa-O National Liberation Army (PNLO/PNLA)	NCA–S	2015	2012	400		Tatmadaw	Shan State
Peace and Solidarity Committee/National Democratic Alliance Association–East Shan State (PSC/NDAA)	FPNCC		2011	4,000	AA, KIA, MNDAA, NDAA SSA–N, TNLA, UWSA	Tatmadaw	Shan State
Restoration Council of Shan State/Shan State Army–South (RCSS/ SSA–S)	NCA–S	201510	2012	8,000		SSA–N, Tatmadaw, TNLA	Shan State
Shan State Progress Party/Shan State Army– North (SSPP/SSA–N)	FPNCC		1989	8,000	AA, KIA, MNDAA, NDAA, TNLA, UWSA	SSA–S, Tatmadaw	Shan State
United League Army/Arakan Army (ULA/AA)	FPNCC; Three Brother Alliance; Northern Alliance			7,000	KIA, MNDAA, NDAA, SSA–N, TNLA, UWSA	Tatmadaw	Chin State, Kachin State, Rakhine State, Shan State
United Wa State Party/ United Wa State Army (UWSP/UWSA)	FPNCC		2011	1989, 2011	30,000	AA, KIA, MNDAA, NDAA, SSA–N, TNLA	Tatmadaw	Wa State
Wa National Organisation/ Wa National Army (WNO/WNA)			1997	<200	UWSA (as of 2017)	Tatmadaw	Shan State

Drivers

Geography and exclusion

Myanmar's geography has historically made it difficult to govern. Lowland populations living along the alluvial plains of the Irrawaddy River and Delta have long attempted to rule over borderland people, with limited success.[11] The rugged terrain of these border areas separated their inhabitants from Myanmar's 'strong centres of state formation'[12] and left them outside the lowland kingdoms' and the Tatmadaw's control for much of the country's history. These geographical realities have resulted in border people being largely excluded from public services and the workings of the state, and ultimately fostered further resentment. These sentiments continued in 2019.

Unequal access to services, endemic corruption and poor governance continued to drive the conflict. Rural people make up approximately 70% of the population, the majority still relying on subsistence farming. Greater discussion about decentralisation of public services is gaining traction and would be a boon for ethnic and rural populations. This is most notable in the government's ambitious plans for universal healthcare. According to one recent report, the most vulnerable townships were located in areas of conflict or natural disaster and had low levels of education, sanitation and literacy, as well as poor access to government services.[13] These areas, largely comprising ethnic minorities, disproportionately witnessed conflict in 2019 compared to other townships. The election of the NLD party in 2015 brought hopes of swift reforms, but these soon gave way to renewed distrust and resentment of the Tatmadaw and government.

In 2019, the three EAOs that formed the Three Brother Alliance fought to ensure their territorial security and inclusion in the peace process. The three EAOs have been excluded from the main peace process by the Tatmadaw and often fight together. Much of the violence by the AA, MNDAA and TNLA aimed to maintain key alliances with the large EAOs that they rely on for support. Unlike other EAOs, the AA and TNLA traditionally do not control a large, defined territory from which to generate income. Support for the AA, however, grew in Rakhine State in 2019. The group has capitalised on grievances created by the NLD government's poor management of relations with the Rakhine population. Remittances and support from outside Myanmar in 2019 began to reshape how the AA is funded and could change its capabilities.

Illicit economies

Historical mistrust of Burmese military regimes and decades of conflict have led many of these contested areas to maintain separate economies or rely on neighbouring countries and their populations for military support and commerce. Illicit goods, particularly narcotics including opium and methamphetamine or *yaba*, have been a mainstay of some EAOs' financing. Myanmar remains the world's second-largest opium-poppy grower, with 37,300 hectares under cultivation in 2018 according to the United Nations Office on Drugs and Crime (UNODC). As the opium trade has declined the methamphetamine trade has boomed. The UNODC reports that the use of methamphetamine has increased annually, with seizures of methamphetamine tablets increasing from ten million in 2013 to over 100m in 2018.[14] Some EAOs have used their control over the drug trade to successfully barter for peace, leveraging or relinquishing their involvement for benefit in negotiations.[15]

Neighbouring countries

China was the most prominent external actor shaping the course of the conflict in Myanmar in 2019. Chinese investment in Myanmar increased: in the first half of the year, mainland Chinese and Hong Kong money accounted for 84 of the 134 newly approved foreign investments, an increase of about 140% from that source.[16] Development of large-scale projects carrying the Belt and Road Initiative label continued, and included further details agreed in April on cooperation for the China–Myanmar Economic Corridor (CMEC). Military ties also improved as Senior General Min Aung Hlaing met with Chinese President Xi Jinping and Chinese military leaders in Beijing. Influential Chinese state support for the Federal Political Negotiation and Consultative Committee (FPNCC) – a political negotiation team formed by seven EAO non-signatories to the NCA – continued. State and non-state actors in Bangladesh, India, Laos and Thailand have previously supported non-state armed groups operating in border areas. Ethnolinguistic similarities across border populations support exchanges and financial or military support. To varying degrees, this continued in 2019.

Political Developments

The power-sharing arrangement between the Tatmadaw and the NLD government underwent further transformation in 2019 following a continued backlash from Western governments, many of which had been vocal supporters of the NLD's Aung San Suu Kyi. In January, the Tatmadaw claimed that the State Counsellor had demanded a response to AA attacks in Rakhine State. The statement greatly exaggerated the power of Suu Kyi, who does not command the military, but it nevertheless angered the Rakhine population. This likely helped swell AA ranks in 2019 and may precipitate a fall in support for the NLD in the state in the 2020 elections.

The overriding goal of the peace process for EAOs is to establish a federal system in which they hold a degree of autonomy. The desired degree of autonomy varies between groups. Importantly, in early 2019, both the AA and the UWSA called for a confederation of states, rather than a federal state.

The UWSA used its 30th anniversary to call for recognition of the Wa self-administered zone as an autonomous ethnic state.[17] Importantly for prospects for peace, the UWSA leads the FPNCC. The UWSA is heavily influenced and supported by Chinese state actors, including the People's Liberation Army, and it is often characterised as a prefecture of China.[18] In January, AA Commander-in-Chief Major General Twan Mrat Naing noted that his group also wanted a confederation of states, highlighting the UWSA's ambitions. These calls are an affront to the Tatmadaw, which stresses that the integrity of the Union and the centrality of Naypyidaw are non-negotiable. They also further destabilised an already uncertain peace process.

EAOs appeared to be waiting until after the 2020 elections to work on the peace process with a new government. However, the discord between NCA signatories in 2019 did not inspire hope for the post-election peace process. In May, at a special summit of NCA signatories in Chiang Mai, Thailand, the KNU, the largest EAO signatory, announced its intention to leave the Peace Process Steering Team (PPST), the decision-making and negotiating body of EAO signatories. Vying for more power and a level of autonomy in decision-making more commensurate with its size, the KNU proposed a new but similar structure, the Peace Process Consultative Meeting (PPCM). At the meeting's conclusion, in an effort to retain the KNU's cooperation in the PPST, it was agreed that PPST and PPCM structures would work in parallel. In August the KNU returned to the peace process after largely internal rifts challenged its participation in the NCA. The move improved the prospects of the PPST, but continued jostling for position among EAOs in the NCA – both at the negotiating table and in inter-EAO territorial skirmishes – suggests that ceasefire agreements, let alone the peace process, still have a long way to go in 2020.

In July, the NLD government attempted to amend the constitution, the first such attempt in four years, with 4,000 proposed changes. Following this failed bid, in October, Suu Kyi declared that the NLD would again attempt to amend the constitution if it won another term in the 2020 elections.[19] While this is a popular proposal across Myanmar, the Tatmadaw's resolve to remain in control means that change to the constitution is unlikely. The assassination of the NLD's constitutional lawyer U Ko Ni in 2017 highlighted the deep-seated resistance to constitutional change.[20]

Military Developments

Solidarity between EAOs weakened in 2019. The Northern Alliance members – the AA, KIA, MNDAA and TNLA – largely respected the Tatmadaw's unilateral ceasefire, turning their back on their usual ally the AA and allowing the military to concentrate forces in Rakhine State. Fighting therefore intensified in the first quarter of the year between the AA and Tatmadaw in Rakhine State, around the previously popular tourist site Mrauk U, with the Tatmadaw deploying fighter jets and helicopters.

Key Events in 2019

Political events

- **February** — NCA signatory meetings continue informally.
- **21 March** — Some success during peace talks in Naypyidaw involving seven EAOs. The AA attends.
- **11 April** — The Tatmadaw commander-in-chief meets with members of China's Central Military Commission, thanking them for their support.
- **14–18 May** — Internal EAO tensions mount during the Peace Process Steering Team NCA signatory summit in Thailand.

Military/Violent events

- **1 January** — Fighting between the AA and Tatmadaw intensifies in Rakhine State.
- **29 January–5 February** — The Tatmadaw seizes the NSCN–K headquarters, earning praise from India.
- **9 March** — The AA attacks a police outpost in Ponnagyun township, Rakhine State, killing nine people.
- **9 April** — Fighting continues between the AA and Tatmadaw around Mrauk U, Rakhine State.
- **May** — Tatmadaw–AA fighting continues in Rakhine State. The unilateral ceasefire holds in northeastern Myanmar.

The use of anti-vehicle improvised explosive devices (IEDs) and anti-personnel mines continued in 2019, particularly in northern Rakhine and Shan states. The use of civilians as cover increased, particularly by the AA. This, combined with Tatmadaw clearance operations in civilian areas, resulted in civilian casualties. In October a German tourist was killed by a landmine in northern Shan State. There were 13.5 IED and mine incidents on average per month in 2018, according to the MIPS. In 2019 (up to October), there were 12.8 incidents per month; this figure is significant given that it does not include three of the most intense months of fighting (October–December), and contains a period of unilateral ceasefire across most of the country. The AA also carried out an increased number of kidnappings in late 2019, including of government representatives and Tatmadaw forces.

As in previous years, EAOs concentrated many attacks along the Lashio–Muse highway in 2019, confirming the continuing tactical significance of the area. The group that can maintain control or, at least, create instability along this key China–Myanmar trade route can have more leverage in negotiations. On 15 August, a small group of fighters from the AA, MNDAA and TNLA attacked the Defence Services Technological Academy in Pyin Oo Lwin with 107-mm rockets and killed 15 people.[21] The attack took place at the seat of the Myanmar military, a designated Tatmadaw white- or safe-zone in Mandalay Region.[22] Five days of skirmishes followed, the Tatmadaw responding with heavy artillery and an attack helicopter. This was one of the most embarrassing incidents for the Tatmadaw in years and demonstrated the vulnerability of targets around the country and the potential reach of EAOs. If EAOs were to expand these tactics to target Tatmadaw or government sites in urban environments – hitherto such incidents have been sporadic and largely avoided Burman-majority areas – the conflict would enter a new and dangerous chapter.

India–Myanmar relations improved in 2019, including supportive, if not explicitly cooperative, targeting of cross-border armed groups. In an important operation for the India–Myanmar security relationship, the Tatmadaw seized the NSCN–K headquarters in Saigang Region in January. This was widely seen as a quid pro quo for New Delhi's support for Tatmadaw operations against the AA. Further direct attacks by the Tatmadaw on NSCN–K in May pushed the group to near irrelevancy in the peace process, yet it maintained that it would not sign the NCA.

Impact

Human rights

Allegations of human-rights abuses were rife in 2019, particularly during fighting between the AA and Tatmadaw in Rakhine State. State and non-state armed actors continued to employ forced recruitment, extortion and other types of harassment. In June the Tatmadaw rejected an International Criminal Court prosecutor's call for an investigation

---

18 June — FPNCC members meet in Panghsang to discuss bilateral ceasefire agreements with the government.

26 July — Singapore extradites six members of the AA to Myanmar.

10 September — The Union Peace Conference is postponed until 2020.

11 December — Aung San Suu Kyi defends the Tatmadaw's actions in Rakhine State at the ICJ.

10 December — The US imposes new sanctions on senior military leaders, including Tatmadaw Commander-in-Chief Senior General Min Aung Hlaing.

15 August — The Three Brother Alliance attacks the Defence Services Technology Academy in Mandalay Region.

September — Fighting between the Three Brother Alliance and the Tatmadaw continues in northern Shan State.

26 October — The AA captures some 50 police and military personnel in Rakhine State. The Tatmadaw rescues 15.

12 November — The Tatmadaw refuses a prisoner swap with the AA. Prisoners include Tatmadaw soldiers and Chin State Member of Parliament U Hwei Tin.

27 November — The NMSP and the Tatmadaw, both signatories to the NCA, clash near the Thailand–Myanmar border.

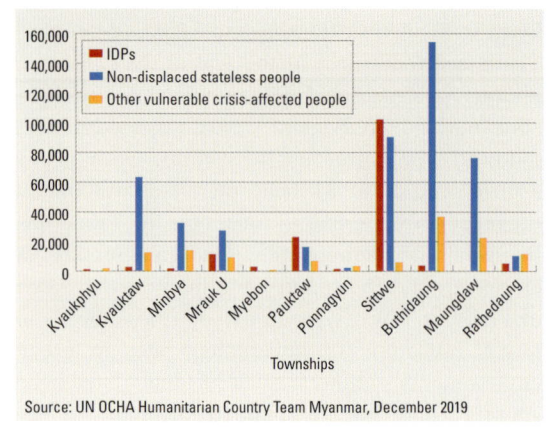

Figure 1: People in need in Rakhine State

Source: UN OCHA Humanitarian Country Team Myanmar, December 2019

into alleged crimes against the Rohingya population. In the same month, the Chin Human Rights Organisation called on the AA to release 52 Chin civilians, including 17 children. In December, State Counsellor Aung San Suu Kyi defended the Tatmadaw's actions in Rakhine State at the ICJ.

Humanitarian

In December 2019 the UN Office for the Coordination of Humanitarian Affairs (OCHA) estimated that 986,000 people were in need of assistance.[23] Hundreds of Arakanese and Chin fled to Bangladesh following clashes between the AA and Tatmadaw in early 2019. Between January and October more than 23,000 people were temporarily displaced in northern Shan State by conflict, and a further 32,000 were displaced in Rakhine and Chin states between March and May due to fighting between the AA and Tatmadaw.[24] By the end of 2019, OCHA estimated that some 750,007 people in Rakhine State were in need of humanitarian assistance – of whom 154,760 were internally displaced persons (IDPs), 470,000 were non-displaced stateless people and 125,247 were other vulnerable crisis-affected people.[25] People were also reported to be in need of humanitarian assistance in Chin (4,279 people), Kachin (160,834), Karen (10,621) and Shan (59,917) states.[26]

Attempts to facilitate the voluntary repatriation of 3,000 Rohingya refugees failed in 2019. Of the 3,000 who were vetted by Myanmar and declared eligible to return to temporary housing, none accepted the conditions of the voluntary return. They demanded that citizenship and safety guarantees be in place first.

Social

Freedom of the press suffered in 2019, as Myanmar dropped to 138th place in the World Press Freedom Index.[27] Disinformation on social media and to a lesser extent in traditional media remained high and rumours continued to fuel conflict – in late 2018 Facebook admitted that it had been used to spread hate speech.[28] A government blackout of the internet in Rakhine State in late June remained in place until the end of the year. Aid groups cautioned that a continued shutdown may harm livelihoods and worsen the humanitarian crisis. In May, two local Reuters journalists, who were arrested in 2017 for reporting on the situation of the Rohingya population, were released from prison. They were awarded the Pulitzer Prize for their work on exposing atrocities in Rakhine State. While their release was significant for press freedom in the country, it was perhaps more important in demonstrating that international pressure on Myanmar can still achieve some desired outcomes.

The country also fell 31 places to 150th in the Women, Peace and Security Index, a Georgetown University initiative that measures performance in women's education, inclusion, employment and discrimination. The index cited that a rate of organised violence resulting in deaths of women rose to 1.60 deaths per 100,000, one of the worst in the region. A Protection and Prevention of Violence against Women bill has been under development by the government since 2013 but remained mired in debate around definitions of violence – in 2019 the EU provided €5m (US$5.54m) for the Women and Girls First Programme to support such initiatives.

Myanmar's health system remained plagued by poor infrastructure and discrimination. Poor education standards in rural and ethnic areas have resulted in fewer rural and ethnic people entering tertiary education to become doctors and nurses, leading to an over-representation of the Bamar people in these professions.[29] In a sign of the challenges ahead, Chikugunya, a mosquito-borne viral disease with a significant mortality rate, returned in 2019 after no cases had been reported since 2011. Plans to upgrade Public Health Emergency Operation Centres across the country with surveillance and response mechanisms, including field epidemiologists and rapid response teams, have the potential to improve health security nationwide, as well as build trust and increase prosperity in vulnerable areas. To be successful this initiative will require cooperation between ethnic groups and the central government, as well as a significant building of capacity and resources.

Economic
The faltering peace process, continuing instability and the loss of confidence in the government left the economy weaker than earlier forecasts predicted. Still, the economy rebounded in 2019 from a sluggish 2018. In June the World Bank projected real GDP growth of 6.5% in 2018–19 and 6.7% in 2020–21. Inflation, a key concern in 2018, fluctuated in 2019 – declining to 6.1% in January but rising again to 7.9% in March following food and fuel price increases.[30] Insurance-sector liberalisation made headway when in November five insurance firms, including British Prudential and US Chubb, received licences to operate in Myanmar. Less than 5% of the population are insured in any way.

Relations with neighbouring and international partners
Relations with China remain the most important for Naypyidaw and were strengthened in 2019 following Western criticism of the atrocities perpetrated by the Tatmadaw in Rakhine State. India's presence was also felt in Tatmadaw operations against the NSCN–K headquarters in Sagaing Region – a group on New Delhi's terrorist list and affiliated with similar groups in India. Also, India's Look East policy, which aims to refocus the country's foreign policy towards Southeast Asia, saw Myanmar acquire a *Kilo*-class submarine from India.

Bangladesh also played a more active role in Myanmar in 2019, although the relationship between the two countries was strained. Dhaka has sought to find solutions as an increasingly disgruntled citizenry grows frustrated with hundreds of thousands of Rohingya refugees living in camps in Cox's Bazar. In January Myanmar government spokesperson Zaw Htay stated that the AA and Arakan Rohingya Salvation Army had established bases in Bangladesh, a claim Dhaka vehemently denied.[31]

Trends

Political trajectories
The late 2018 shift of control of the General Administration Department to the Ministry of the Office of the Union Government demonstrated an important change in the Tatmadaw and indicated that the military is gradually relinquishing some direct control over state affairs not pertaining to security. This trend continued in 2019 and is likely to do so in 2020, with further discussions on decentralising non-security administrative functions, such as public health. In Myanmar's wider power politics, however, the impact of these changes should not be overblown. The Tatmadaw still holds ultimate control over the state and will do so for the foreseeable future. Also, delegating decisions on non-security matters allows the Tatmadaw to focus on military objectives, which will increase its control and freedom of manoeuvre in conflict areas.

Conflict-related risks
Two conflict-related risks loomed large at the end of 2019 – food security and climate change. The spread of African swine fever (ASF) across the region and Myanmar may have implications for the conflict. UN Food and Agriculture Organization data for China, Mongolia and Vietnam suggested that at least 10% of pigs were culled or died from the disease in 2019.[32] Pork products are a major source of protein in many parts of Myanmar and key to supporting smallholder producers. Food insecurity and related food-price spikes can have significant impacts on their livelihoods and the conflict. Wage and income insecurity is associated with pull factors for recruitment to armed groups or criminal activity to substitute lost livelihoods, as well as increased civilian unrest. Crisis-related food insecurity was estimated to affect 734,000 people in 2019.[33] The impact of ASF or other catalysts for food insecurity could increase this number and lead to a deterioration in the conflict situation.

According to the Global Climate Risk Index 2019, Myanmar has been the third-most-affected country by climate change over the past 20 years.[34] The Global Facility for Disaster Reduction and Recovery estimated expected losses from natural hazards to cost US$185m annually.[35] With poor preparedness and mitigation policies, it will remain at significant risk of climate-change-related events in the short and medium term, with detrimental consequences on livelihoods and conflict dynamics.[36]

Prospects for peace

The intensification of the fighting in Rakhine State led to a period of relative calm in the conflict-affected areas of northeastern Myanmar, particularly Kachin and northern Shan states, where the Tatmadaw extended unilateral ceasefires. Despite the opportunities that these truces provided for advancing the peace process with EAOs, few gains were made. All parties' desire for peace and dialogue will likely remain weak prior to the 2020 elections and the installation of the next government.

Until a resolution to the Rohingya crisis is found, the Tatmadaw will continue to fear refoulement and armed insurgency on its western border. There may be greater political space to explore opportunities for resolution after the 2020 elections; however, without a significant change in the situation on the ground and sentiment towards the Rohingya minority population more broadly in Myanmar, a solution is unlikely to emerge soon. Resettlement of Rohingya refugees in Rakhine State, where the population remains hostile, would lead to a return to pre-2018 levels of violence. Bangladesh has little capacity to provide livelihoods to the Rohingya outside the current arrangement in camps in Cox's Bazar. Yet, the longer the Rohingya refugees stay in such squalid conditions, with few prospects of improvement or resolution, the more likely it is that extremist views will gain traction.

Strategic implications and global influences

China weighs heavily in all aspects of Myanmar's politics and will continue to do so in the long term. The award in 2019 of contracts to two Chinese firms to supply 1,040 MW of emergency electricity to Myanmar renewed concerns over Myanmar's energy security and China's role in the country's electricity supply. More broadly, Beijing's attempts to push through the CMEC exerted pressure on the fighting in Rakhine State, home to the port of Kyaukphyu, which China needs to access the Bay of Bengal. The August offensive by the Three Brother Alliance, across the Lashio–Muse route at the heart of the CMEC, however, showed that EAOs can disrupt China's ambitions to expand trade in Myanmar. The offensive coincided, either deliberately or opportunistically, with a similar but less successful AA offensive in Rakhine State, indicating that even the smaller EAOs can disproportionately affect the country's stability. These vulnerabilities may force the Tatmadaw to engage in new dialogue with the 'troublesome three', a strategy it has so far been reluctant to pursue.

As Western governments find engagement with Myanmar more difficult in the wake of the Rohingya crisis, China's influence will grow, particularly with regard to the peace process and its support for the FPNCC. During a meeting with members of China's Central Military Commission and Joint Staff Department, Senior General Min Aung Hlaing praised Beijing as an 'eternal friend' and 'strategic partner' to Myanmar.[37] A pragmatic Tatmadaw understands that a broader base of diplomatic support for Myanmar would permit greater domestic agility and growth; in the medium to long term, the current warming with Beijing will therefore likely be balanced with other actors.

Notes

[1] Myanmar Institute for Peace and Security, 'Peace and Security Brief', vol. 3, no. 10, October 2019.

[2] Moe Thuzar, 'Myanmar at the ICJ: Intent and Implications', ISEAS–Yusof Ishak Institute, 22 November 2019.

[3] Maung Aung Myoe, 'The Soldier and the State: The Tatmadaw and Political Liberalization in Myanmar since 2011', *South East Asia Research*, vol. 22, no. 2, 2014, pp. 244–5.

[4] See John Buchanan, 'Militias in Myanmar', The Asia Foundation, July 2016; Min Zaw Oo, 'Understanding Myanmar's Peace Process: Ceasefire Agreements', Catalyzing Reflection, Swiss Peace Foundation, February 2014, p. 33. The exact strength of the militia may be 'unknowable'.

[5] Andrew Selth, '"Strong, Fully Efficient and Modern": Myanmar's New Look Armed Forces', Griffith Asia Institute, Regional Outlook, no. 49, 2016.

[6] Jeff M. Smith (ed.), *Asia's Quest for Balance: China's Rise and Balancing in the Indo-Pacific* (Lanham, MD: Rowman & Littlefield, 2018).

[7] Elliot Brennan and Min Zaw Oo, 'Peace, Alliance and Inclusivity, Ending Conflict in Myanmar', Brookings Institution, 1 April 2016.

[8] Estimates vary widely but are based on various independent sources.

[9] The group suspended its participation in the NCA-mandated process in 2018 and in 2019.

[10] The group suspended its participation in the NCA-mandated process in 2018 and in 2019.

[11] Willem van Schendel, 'Geographies of Knowing, Geographies of Ignorance: Jumping Scale in Southeast Asia', *Environment and Planning D: Society and Space*, vol. 20, no. 6, 2002, pp. 647–68.

[12] Ibid.

[13] Humanitarian Assistance and Resilience Programme Facility and the Myanmar Information Management Unit, 'Vulnerability in Myanmar: A Secondary Data Review of Needs, Coverage and Gaps', June 2018.

[14] UNODC, 'Synthetic Drugs in East and South-East Asia: Trends and Patterns of Amphetamine-type Stimulants and New Pscyhoactive Substances', March 2019.

[15] See Michael Jonsson, Elliot Brennan and Christopher O'Hara, 'Financing War or Facilitating Peace? The Impact of Rebel Drug Trafficking on Peace Negotiations in Colombia and Myanmar', *Studies in Conflict & Terrorism*, vol. 39, no. 6, January 2016, pp. 542–59.

[16] Yuichi Nitta, 'Myanmar investment inflows double from China as deals surge', *Nikkei Asian Review*, 18 July 2019.

[17] Paul Keenan, 'A Dangerous Precedent: The UWSA and Statehood', EBO Background Paper no. 3, June 2019.

[18] Ibid.

[19] Wataru Suzuki and Yuichi Nitta, 'Suu Kyi: Myanmar constitution must change for "complete democracy"', *Nikkei Asian Review*, 23 October 2019.

[20] Elliot Brennan, 'U Ko Ni's assassination a symptom of deepening divisions in Myanmar', *Interpreter*, Lowy Institute, 31 January 2017.

[21] International Crisis Group, 'A Violent Push to Shake up Ceasefire Negotiations', Asia Briefing no. 158, 24 September 2019.

[22] 'At least 14 dead in unprecedented Northern Alliance attacks', *Frontier Myanmar*, 15 August 2019; 'Focal Points: TNLA, MNDAA and AA Launch Coordinated Attacks, Conflict Likely to Escalate', Myanmar Institute for Peace and Security, 24 August 2019.

[23] OCHA Humanitarian Country Team in Myanmar, 'Humanitarian Needs Overview Myanmar', 20 December 2019.

[24] Ibid.

[25] Ibid.

[26] Ibid.

[27] Reporters Without Borders, 'Myanmar', 2019 World Press Freedom Index, 2019.

[28] Alexandra Stevenson, 'Facebook Admits It Was Used to Incite Violence in Myanmar', *New York Times*, 6 November 2018.

[29] Tin Aung et al., 'Rural and urban disparities in health-seeking for fever in Myanmar: findings from a probability-based household survey', *Malaria Journal*, vol. 15, article no. 386, 25 July 2016.

[30] World Bank, 'Myanmar Economic Monitor: Building Reform Momentum', June 2019.

[31] Myanmar Institute for Peace and Security, 'Peace and Security Brief', vol. 3, no. 2, February 2019; Jesmin Papri, 'Bangladesh: No ARSA, Arakan Militant Bases in Country', *BenarNews*, 9 January 2019.

[32] UN Food and Agriculture Organization, 'ASF situation in Asia update', Agriculture and Consumer Production Department, 9 January 2020.

[33] OCHA Humanitarian Country Team in Myanmar, 'Humanitarian Needs Overview Myanmar'.

[34] David Eckstein, Marie-Lena Hutfils and Maik Winges, 'Global Climate Risk Index 2019: Who Suffers Most from Extreme Weather Events? Weather-related Loss Events in 2017 and 1998 to 2017', Germanwatch, December 2018.

[35] Global Facility for Disaster Reduction and Recovery, 'Myanmar', 2019.

[36] See Elliot Brennan, 'Climate Change and Security Threats in Southeast Asia', in Ashok Swain, Joakim Öjendal and Anders Jägerskog (eds.), *Handbook of Security and the Environment* (Cheltenham: Edward Elgar, 2020–forthcoming).

[37] Nan Lwin, 'Myanmar Military Chief Thanks Beijing for Support on Rakhine Crisis', *Irrawaddy*, 10 April 2019.

PHILIPPINES (ASG & MORO)

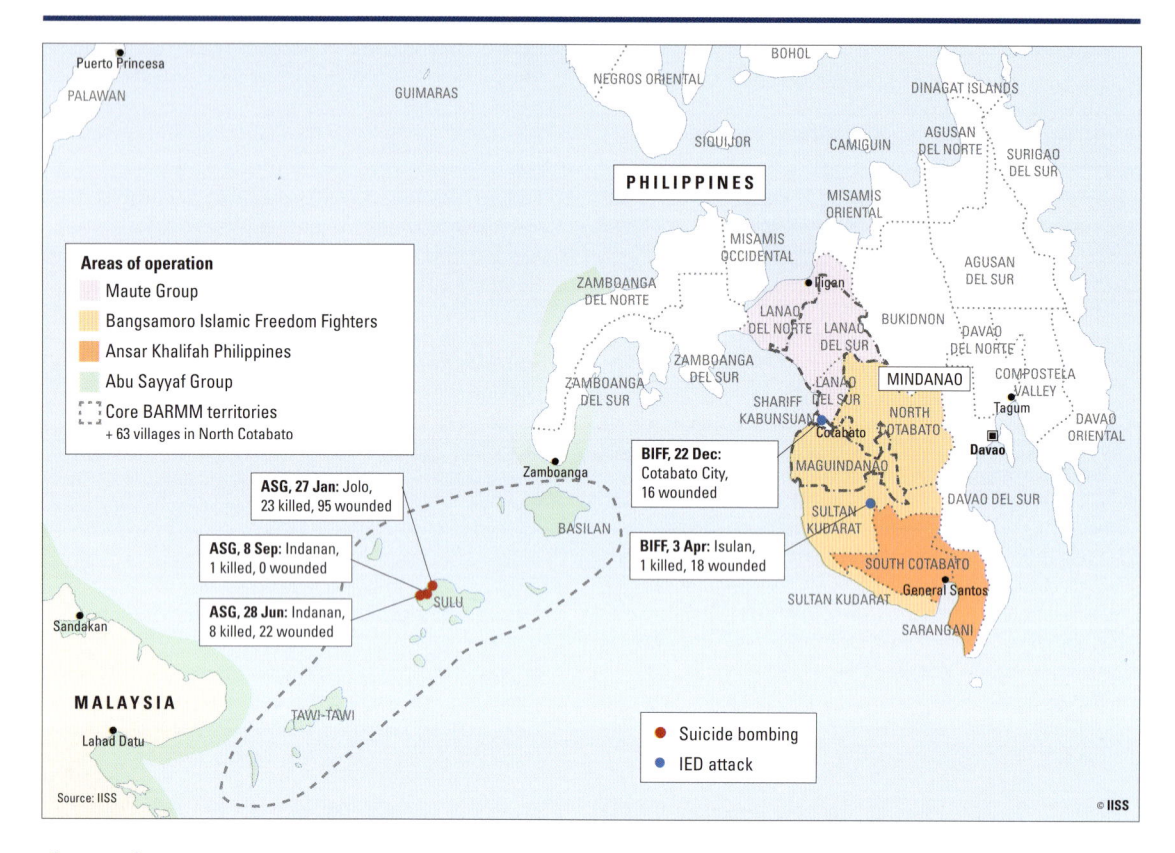

Overview

The conflict in 2019

The peace process between the Philippine government and the Moro Islamic Liberation Front (MILF) was concluded in 2019 after residents of western Mindanao voted to ratify the Bangsamoro Organic Law (BOL) in a two-stage referendum held in Muslim-majority areas on 21 January and 6 February. The bill created the Bangsamoro Autonomous Region in Muslim Mindanao (BARMM), replacing the Autonomous Region in Muslim Mindanao (ARMM), in place since 1989. MILF chairman Al Haj Murad Ebrahim was selected to lead the 80-member Bangsamoro Transition Authority (BTA), which will govern the entity and oversee the demobilisation of more than 30,000 MILF rebels before the first BARMM parliamentary elections are held in 2022.

Meanwhile, the Armed Forces of the Philippines (AFP) continued to confront groups aligned with the Islamic State, also known as ISIS or ISIL, that are opposed to the BOL, damaging the capabilities of the Maute Group (MG) and the Bangsamoro Islamic Freedom Fighters (BIFF).

The AFP also launched offensives against the Abu Sayyaf Group (ASG) in its maritime strongholds but the group demonstrated its resilience and adaptability and reclaimed its position as the most active extremist group in the Philippines. An ISIS-affiliated Sulu-based ASG faction led by Hatib Hajan Sawadjaan rose to prominence, carrying out three high-profile suicide-bomb attacks in 2019 and

Key statistics

Type	Internal
Start date	October 1972
IDPs total (September 2019)	64,574
Refugees total	Not applicable
People in need	Not applicable

engaging in regular shoot-outs with government forces in Patikul and Banguingui on the island of Jolo.

The AFP and the Philippine National Police (PNP) deployed greater resources and naval assets to combat the ASG in Basilan, Sulu and Tawi-Tawi, while the continued presence of ISIS members meant that Mindanao remained under martial law until the end of 2019. The rebuilding of Marawi city proceeded slowly, causing frustration among displaced residents and raising fears of a boost in recruitment for terrorist groups.

The conflict to 2019

The modern-day Moro insurgency began in 1972 after earlier armed uprisings by Moro Muslim rebels against Spanish and American colonisers. The Moro National Liberation Front (MNLF) was the first group to launch an armed uprising against Manila for an independent Moro homeland, fuelled by perceived political, economic and cultural oppression. The MNLF was later displaced as the foremost actor in the conflict by the MILF, which emerged as a splinter organisation in 1977. Both groups signed peace accords with the government (see Table 1), which reduced the frequency and intensity of violent clashes. The 1976 Tripoli Agreement between the MNLF and the government of Ferdinand Marcos promised autonomy but collapsed amid a dispute over which areas to include. A significant breakthrough came in 1989 with the establishment of the ARMM, covering the provinces of Basilan, Lanao del Sur, Maguindanao, Sulu and Tawi-Tawi. MNLF founder Nur Misuari served as ARMM governor for five years after his group signed a final peace agreement, the Jakarta Accord of 1996.[1] The MNLF has since declined in strength.

The MILF fought the AFP regularly in the 1990s but entered its own negotiations with the government in 1996. In 2014, it signed the Comprehensive Agreement on the Bangsamoro (CAB) during the administration of Benigno Aquino III, which promised expanded autonomy in return for demobilisation. The CAB was a precursor to the 2018 BOL, signed by MILF leader Ebrahim and President Rodrigo Duterte, which provided the legislation for the proposed BARMM to replace the ARMM.

While the MILF and MNLF have laid down their weapons in pursuit of autonomy via dialogue, several extremist groups opposed to the peace process have emerged since 1990. The ASG, formed in 1991, is the most well established, and notorious for piracy attacks, kidnappings and beheadings. More recently the BIFF, MG and Ansar Khalifah Philippines (AKP) have emerged. In May 2017, an ISIS-affiliated coalition of these four groups laid siege to the city of Marawi, leading Duterte to place Mindanao under martial law. The AFP defeated the militants after five months, ending the siege, although martial law remained in place. In 2018, the ASG retreated to its outlying island bases of Basilan, Sulu and Tawi-Tawi, while the MG declined in relative strength and the BIFF clashed with the AFP regularly in western Mindanao.

Key Conflict Parties

Armed Forces of the Philippines (AFP)

Strength
142,350 regular combatants across the army, navy and air force, with a reserve paramilitary force of 50,000 serving in Citizen Armed Force Geographical Units (CAFGUs).

Areas of operation
Operates nationwide. Headquarters, Camp Aguinaldo, is in Quezon city, Metro Manila.

Leadership
Led by Chief-of-Staff Lt-Gen. Noel Clement, who was appointed by President Duterte in September 2019.[2]

Structure
Divided into six area unified military commands, which include the Western Mindanao Command (AFP–WMC). Battalions are usually 500-strong.

History
Established in December 1935 after the passage of the National Defence Act, during the US colonial period. Passed to Philippine control following independence in 1946.

Objectives
Aims to maintain peace with the MILF and MNLF, while carrying out proactive operations targeting ISIS-affiliated groups. Often launches airstrikes targeting militant hideouts in conjunction with ground operations.

Opponents
ISIS-linked groups in Mindanao: AKP, ASG, BIFF, MG. Also opposed to the communist New People's Army (NPA), which operates nationwide.

Armed Forces of the Philippines (AFP)

Affiliates/allies
Aided in anti-ISIS raids and law-enforcement operations by the PNP. The MILF and MNLF – both former enemies of the AFP – provide intelligence support to the AFP in offensives targeting ISIS.

Resources/capabilities
Access to combat tanks and a fleet of armoured trucks, while the air force makes use of rapid-attack aircraft, transport planes and helicopters. The AFP uses pistols, high-powered rifles and artillery in anti-ISIS operations.

Abu Sayyaf Group (ASG)

Strength
400 active members (estimate).

Areas of operation
Maritime provinces of Basilan, Sulu and Tawi-Tawi. Limited presence on the Zamboanga peninsula and active along the coastline of Malaysia's eastern state of Sabah.

Leadership
No overall leader. Most influential figure is Hatib Hajan Sawadjaan, who commands an ISIS-affiliated faction in Sulu. Radullan Sahiron is another senior leader in Sulu, while Furuji Indama leads the ASG in Basilan.

Structure
No centralised command structure or decision-making body. Divided into a network of loosely linked cells arranged primarily along clan and family lines.

History
Formed in 1991 by radical Islamist preacher Abdurajak Abubakar Janjalani. The ASG has fought the military for three decades and has become notorious for piracy attacks and kidnappings in the Sulu Sea.

Objectives
Fought to establish an Islamic state in western Mindanao since 1991. In 2014, (now-deceased) former ASG chief Isnilon Hapilon pledged allegiance to ISIS, and most ASG factions remain allied to the group. Now seeks the establishment of an ISIS-style caliphate in the Philippines.

Opponents
AFP, PNP. The MILF and MNLF are also opposed to the ASG and have become increasingly vocal critics of its radical outlook since it aligned with ISIS.

Affiliates/allies
ISIS's central branch in Syria, and loosely aligned to three other ISIS-affiliated groups in the southern Philippines: AKP, BIFF and MG.

Resources/capabilities
Deploys speedboats in piracy operations and maritime kidnappings, while its fighters use automatic rifles and improvised explosive devices (IEDs) in attacks on the military and civilians. Suicide bombings became a signature tactic in 2019.

Ansar Khalifah Philippines (AKP)

Strength
Fewer than 50 active fighters (estimate).

Areas of operation
Southern Mindanao provinces of Sarangani and South Cotabato.

Leadership
Unknown. Founder Mohammad Jaafar Maguid was killed in a gun battle with police officers in 2017.

Structure
No centralised leadership structure. The military regards the AKP as a local-level criminal actor rather than a regional jihadist threat.

History
Formed in 2014 and has played only a minor supporting role in attacks – including the 2017 Marawi siege and a string of bombings in 2018 – alongside larger jihadist groups such as the MG and BIFF. AKP militants have also engaged government forces and police officers in small-scale shoot-outs.

Objectives
Affiliated to ISIS and aims to establish an Islamic caliphate in Mindanao.

Opponents
AFP, PNP. Moderate Moro rebel groups, the MILF and MNLF, also oppose the AKP and have cooperated with the AFP in operations against ISIS-aligned groups.

Affiliates/allies
Pledge of allegiance to ISIS; loosely aligned to three local ISIS affiliates operating in Mindanao: ASG, BIFF and MG.

Resources/capabilities
Small firearms, and has perpetrated IED attacks alongside the BIFF.

Bangsamoro Islamic Freedom Fighters (BIFF)

Strength
Fewer than 300 active fighters (estimate).

Areas of operation
Western Mindanao provinces of Maguindanao, North Cotabato and Sultan Kudarat.

Bangsamoro Islamic Freedom Fighters (BIFF)

Leadership
Loosely commanded by ISIS-linked jihadist Abu Toraife (also known as Esmael Abdulmalik), who leads the most radical of the BIFF's three factions.

Structure
Thought to have no centralised leadership structure, and divided into three factions. In 2019, the AFP said the factions were forced into a 'tactical alliance' in response to sustained battlefield pressure.

History
Formed as a splinter group of the MILF in 2010 when its founder, Ameril Umbra Kato, grew frustrated at the MILF's decision to drop a demand for independence in favour of autonomy. Fought in the 2017 Marawi siege and has since clashed regularly with the AFP in central Maguindanao.

Objectives
Aims to secure an independent homeland for Moro Muslims in the form of an ISIS-style caliphate. Also aims to disrupt the government–MILF peace process by launching bomb attacks in major urban centres.

Opponents
AFP, PNP, MNLF. The MILF is also opposed to the BIFF despite being its parent group and has clashed with BIFF militants regularly.

Affiliates/allies
Pledged allegiance to ISIS in 2014 and has cooperated with several local ISIS-affiliated groups in Mindanao: AKP, ASG and MG.

Resources/capabilities
Counts foreign fighters from Indonesia and Malaysia among its ranks and uses high-powered rifles to target the AFP and PNP. Uses IEDs to attack government forces and civilian targets.

Moro Islamic Liberation Front (MILF)

Strength
More than 30,000 active members serving in its Bangsamoro Islamic Armed Forces (BIAF). The entire fighting force is set to be demobilised by 2022 under the terms of a 2014 peace agreement with the government.

Areas of operation
Western Mindanao, although most fighters remain encamped within a network of MILF bases. Headquarters, Camp Darapanan, is in Maguindanao province.

Leadership
Led by chairman Al Haj Murad Ebrahim, who also serves as the interim chief minister of the BARMM.

Structure
Centralised and hierarchical organisation, which for decades has operated like a conventional military. Undergoing a transition from a rebel group to a political party and has formed the United Bangsamoro Justice Party (UBJP) to contest BARMM parliamentary elections from 2022.

History
Founded in 1977 by Hashim Salamat after breaking away from the MNLF and fights the government to secure expanded autonomy for Moro Muslims in Mindanao. It has largely avoided combat with the AFP since signing a preliminary peace deal in 2014.

Objectives
Initially advocated a fully independent Moro state. In the late 1990s it started peace talks with Manila, seeking autonomy via political dialogue.

Opponents
ISIS-affiliated groups: AKP, ASG, BIFF and MG. The MNLF, as the MILF's parent organisation and rival, also occasionally clashes with the MILF at the local level.

Affiliates/allies
In recent years, the MILF has cooperated with the AFP to tackle ISIS-aligned groups in Mindanao. The AFP was formerly a staunch adversary of the MILF, but demobilised MILF fighters will now form Joint Peace and Security Teams (JPSTs) alongside AFP personnel and PNP officers.

Resources/capabilities
Access to high-powered automatic rifles and grenade launchers, but these will be decommissioned by 2022.

Moro National Liberation Front (MNLF)

Strength
Fewer than 10,000 active fighters. The MNLF's strength has declined since the 1970s when it had 30,000 fighters during the dictatorship of Ferdinand Marcos.

Areas of operation
Western Mindanao and the Sulu islands.

Leadership
MNLF founder Nur Misuari still leads a 3,000-strong faction in Sulu and remains an influential figure. Yusop Jikiri, considered a more moderate figure, leads another major faction and serves as MNLF chairman and spokesman.

Structure
Initially centralised but splintered after signing peace agreements with the government in 1976, 1989 and 1996.

Moro National Liberation Front (MNLF)

History
Formed as a splinter of the now-defunct Muslim Independence Movement (MIM) in 1972, with the aim of forging an independent Moro state in western Mindanao. Has fought the AFP on and off for 48 years.

Objectives
No longer advocates full Moro independence. The group is broadly supportive of the government–MILF peace process but has not been involved in formal talks. Misuari, however, remains a vocal critic and President Duterte has sought to engage him amid fears that his faction could prove disruptive.

Opponents
Four ISIS-linked groups in Mindanao: AKP, ASG, BIFF and MG. The MILF is a major rival but the two sides rarely resort to violence.

Affiliates/allies
Formally allied with the government having signed a final peace agreement in 1996. Tensions in government–MNLF relations remain.

Resources/capabilities
Regularly ambushed government troops in the countryside and raided major towns in previous decades. It has not engaged in major clashes with the AFP since the Zamboanga siege of 2013, but remains a powerful, dormant actor in the conflict with access to a network of bases and automatic rifles.

Maute Group (MG)

Strength
Fewer than 25 members (AFP estimate) but still considered a threat amid reports of ongoing recruitment. Before the Marawi siege of 2017 it had up to 1,000 fighters. Most were killed in the siege.

Areas of operation
Active in the northwestern Mindanao provinces of Lanao del Norte and Lanao del Sur, particularly around Lake Lanao.

Leadership
No leader since Abu Dar – also the 'emir' of ISIS in Southeast Asia – was killed during an army offensive in March 2019.

Structure
No defined structure. Remaining fighters operate in small cells.

History
Founded by brothers Abdullah and Omar Maute in 2010–11 and espoused an extreme form of Salafi–Wahhabi ideology more often associated with jihadi groups in the Middle East. The MG led the 2017 siege of Marawi in which its senior leaders were killed and capabilities damaged.

Objectives
Aims to forge an ISIS-style Islamic caliphate in Southeast Asia, centred on Mindanao.

Opponents
AFP, PNP. The MILF is also opposed to the MG and has provided the AFP with intelligence, and occasionally engaged MG militants in gun battles.

Affiliates/allies
Has pledged allegiance to ISIS and is loosely tied to Mindanao's three other ISIS-affiliated groups: AKP, ASG and BIFF.

Resources/capabilities
Thought to possess only a small cache of rifles.

Drivers

Oppression of Moro Muslim population
The roots of the conflict lie in the oppression of the Moro Muslim population, who account for one-fifth of residents on the Catholic-majority island of Mindanao. Moro rebels led uprisings against Spanish and US rule during the colonial period and resisted Japanese rule during the Second World War. Despite having lived in western Mindanao since the arrival of Arab traders in the Sulu islands in the 1300s, the Moros have been denied an independent homeland by two former colonial powers and the Philippine state after 1946. Christian migration to Mindanao is a major cause of resentment because it allegedly erodes traditional Moro identity and culture. The absence of full political control over land and resources has fuelled feelings of historical injustice for generations.

Poverty and underdevelopment
Economic marginalisation has long been a driver of recruitment for Moro rebel groups. Moro-majority provinces are among the most deprived in the Philippines, despite being home to fertile soils suitable for agriculture and rich in natural resources such as hydropower, timber, gold and mineral deposits. The central government and large

multinational firms accrue a significant proportion of profits from these resources while inadequate infrastructure and limited service provision restrict development in western Mindanao. Figures from the Philippine Statistics Authority (PSA) revealed in April 2019 that 63% of residents and 55.4% of families in the ARMM were living in poverty – markedly higher than the national averages of 21% and 16.1%.[3] In the provinces of Basilan and Sulu (home to the ASG) and Lanao del Sur (home to the MG) the poverty rate exceeded 72% in early 2018, making militancy a credible alternative option for many young men.[4]

The growth of Islamist extremism
The global spread of ISIS since its emergence in Iraq and Syria in 2014 served as a more recent trigger for violence in the southern Philippines, transforming what was for decades a local separatist struggle into a more complex conflict with links to transnational jihadism. ISIS inspired sympathetic militant groups in Southeast Asia to fight for a regional caliphate. This project threatened to materialise in 2017 when a coalition of jihadist groups based in Mindanao, which had pledged allegiance to former ISIS leader Abu Bakr al-Baghdadi, overran the city of Marawi with the help of foreign fighters from Indonesia and Malaysia. This attempt to seize and govern territory was defeated after a five-month war, but ISIS's ideology remains prevalent in Mindanao. Brutal methods associated with ISIS and its predecessor al-Qaeda have driven conflict dynamics in 2019, with the ASG launching a series of high-profile suicide bombings. ISIS-linked jihadists from the wider region have also travelled to Mindanao, boosting the recruitment pool.

A fractured Moro separatist movement
A history of splintering within the once-centralised Moro separatist movement has prolonged the conflict. Initially led by the hierarchical and dominant MNLF, a series of ideological disagreements and personality clashes since the late 1970s resulted in the formation of breakaway groups and sub-factions, each altering the dynamics of the conflict and leading to fresh violence. Out of the MNLF and its own splinter – the MILF – emerged more radical groups such as the ASG, the BIFF and the MG. Splits have centred on whether the uprising should be more secular or Islamist in nature, and whether the Moros should accept political devolution or pursue independence. In recent years, opposition to the government–MILF peace process has galvanised radical offshoots to revive their campaigns within a conducive climate of lawlessness, sustained via decades of separatism and clan warfare in Mindanao.

Political Developments

Government–MILF accord ratified via public vote
The BOL, signed by Duterte and MILF chairman Ebrahim in 2018, was ratified by voters in western Mindanao through a two-stage referendum held on 21 January and 6 February. The outcome was described as a 'landslide victory' by Ebrahim, with 1.54 million people voting in favour and 198,750 voting against.[5] The public approval for the BOL established a new autonomous Muslim-majority region, the BARMM, to replace the 20-year-old ARMM. The new region covers the existing ARMM provinces of Basilan, Lanao del Sur, Maguindanao, Sulu and Tawi-Tawi in addition to Cotabato City – which will be the official BARMM seat of government – and 63 villages in North Cotabato.

While the result was unanimous and no irregularities were reported, aspects of the referendum were controversial because of the way votes were counted. Voters in Sulu rejected the BOL by a narrow margin of 163,526 votes against to 137,630 in favour, yet Sulu's votes were included as part of a collective total from the five former ARMM provinces, meaning the province was forced to join the BARMM.[6] Residents in Isabela City, six municipalities in Lanao del Norte and four villages in North Cotabato also rejected the BOL, but these areas were not forced to accede as they were not part of the ARMM. The formation of the BARMM represents the end of a 23-year peace process between the government and the MILF and ensures expanded autonomy for the region. The BARMM will be governed by an elected parliament and will receive an annual US$1.3 billion block grant from Manila, in addition to 75% of tax receipts from its territories. The region will also benefit from a greater proportion

Table 1: Peace agreements between Philippine government and Moro insurgent groups

Date	Agreement	Signatories	Goals	Result
1976	Tripoli Agreement	Government–MNLF	Intended to facilitate the creation of a self-governed Moro region	Collapsed. Hostilities with the MNLF resumed
1989	Autonomous Region in Muslim Mindanao (ARMM)	Government–MNLF	Autonomous region covering Basilan, Lanao del Sur, Maguindanao, Sulu and Tawi-Tawi. MNLF chief Nur Misuari was ARMM governor 1996–2001	Remained in place for 20 years but was plagued by alleged corruption. Replaced by a new Moro region in 2019
1996	Jakarta Accord	Government–MNLF	Designed to end conflict between the AFP and the MNLF	Largely held. Ended large-scale fighting with MNLF insurgents
2014	Comprehensive Agreement on the Bangsamoro (CAB)	Government–MILF	Stipulated that the MILF would disarm in return for expanded autonomy	Precursor deal. Led to progress in 2018 and 2019 deals
2018	Bangsamoro Organic Law (BOL)	Government–MILF	Provided the legislation needed for an expanded Moro autonomous zone	Successful. BOL was passed by Congress of the Philippines and ratified through a public vote in 2019
2019	Bangsamoro Autonomous Region in Muslim Mindanao (BARMM)	Government–MILF	A new autonomous region to replace the ARMM. Covers the five ex-ARMM provinces, Cotabato City and 63 North Cotabato villages	Implementation phase. The MILF is leading a three-year transition ahead of elections of a BARMM parliament in 2022

of revenue from natural resources including gold, timber and minerals.

Ebrahim to lead Bangsamoro transition

Until the first elections to the BARMM parliament are held in 2022, the 80-member BTA will govern the region during a transition period. Duterte appointed veteran MILF chair Ebrahim to lead the BTA on 19 February, ahead of the formal inauguration of the BARMM on 29 March. While the BTA is predominantly made up of MILF members, a few seats were reserved for members of the rival MNLF and representatives of ethnic-minority groups. The UBJP, founded by the MILF in 2014, intends to run in the 2022 elections in the hope that the ex-MILF leadership will secure a public mandate to administer the region.

Duterte seeks deal with MNLF founder Misuari

The MNLF was not involved in the BOL-centred peace talks but is broadly supportive of the BARMM. Duterte made repeated efforts in 2019 to accommodate MNLF founder Nur Misuari, who has been a disruptive, unpredictable figure in the past

Key Events in 2019

Political events

- **January–February**: Residents of western Mindanao vote to ratify the BOL.
- **22 February**: President Duterte appoints MILF chairman Al Haj Murad Ebrahim as interim chief of the BTA.
- **4 March**: The demobilisation of 30,000 MILF combatants begins.

Military/Violent events

- **27 January**: Two ASG suicide bombers attack a cathedral in Jolo, Sulu province, killing 23 people.
- **11–13 March**: The AFP launches a major offensive targeting the BIFF in central Maguindanao province.
- **14 March**: MG leader Abu Dar is killed along with three other militants during a clash with AFP soldiers.
- **31 May**: Major fighting breaks out between the AFP and ASG in Patikul town, Sulu province, killing six ASG militants.

and is more sceptical about the BARMM than his colleagues. After a series of meetings with Misuari, Duterte's chief peace adviser Carlito Galvez remarked in August 2019 that the president was open to the creation of a separate MNLF-controlled autonomous area or the appointment of MNLF figures to senior positions in the BTA.[7] On 28 August, Duterte announced the creation of a coordinating committee to hold talks with the MNLF, while Ebrahim vowed in September to work with Misuari to unite the Bangsamoro people. On 14 December, panels representing the government and the MNLF met for initial talks in Davao and agreed to cooperate to fully implement commitments made in a 1996 peace deal, reducing tension between the two sides.

ISIS-linked groups remain opposed to the BARMM

All four of Mindanao's ISIS-affiliated groups remained opposed to the BARMM. Despite a suicide-bomb attack by the ASG on 27 January – timed to cause maximum disruption between the two BOL voting days – the second poll went ahead as planned, with a turnout of 75%. However, the rejection of the BOL by voters in Sulu – an ASG heartland – has raised fears that resentment towards the new region could boost recruitment to the armed groups. ISIS-affiliated groups may also benefit from rising frustration among residents still displaced by the 2017 Marawi siege, amid stalling reconstruction efforts.

The ASG is considered the most radical of the ISIS-affiliated groups. In 2019, the government maintained its long-held position of not negotiating with the group and the ASG displayed no willingness to initiate talks. On 2 September, the BARMM interim government formed a committee to negotiate with two of the three factions of the BIFF, led by Imam Bongos and Ustadz Karialan, but ruled out talks with the most extreme Abu Toraife faction.

Military Developments

MILF demobilisation and disarmament begins

With the ratification of the BOL in February 2019, the MILF began to demobilise, according to the 2014 CAB. The process was formally initiated when Duterte signed an executive order on 24 April, triggering the CAB's Annex on Normalization, under which the MILF must decommission its 30,000 fighters in three stages before 2022. Around one-third of MILF BIAF personnel and one-third of an estimated 6,000–7,000 BIAF firearms had been demobilised by the end of 2019. Former MILF rebels were set to form JPSTs with AFP soldiers and PNP officers, and the first batch of 219 rebels completed training on 28 August. In total, 3,000 ex-rebels were set to serve alongside 3,000 AFP troops and PNP officers in more than 200 JPSTs, which the AFP–WMC chief said would 'significantly reduce the manoeuvre space' of the BIFF.[8]

The MILF did not clash with government forces during 2019, abiding by the terms of the CAB and previous ceasefires. However, the group occasionally fought against the BIFF in Maguindanao

27 August
President Duterte orders the creation of a coordinating panel for peace talks with the MNLF.

7 September
1,060 former MILF insurgents surrender 940 firearms in Sultan Kudarat, Maguindanao province.

28 June
Two ASG suicide bombers attack an AFP camp in Indanan, Sulu province, killing eight people.

25–30 July
The AFP launches an offensive targeting the BIFF in Shariff Saydona Mustapha town, Maguindanao province, killing 15 militants.

4 October
BIFF militants attack a MILF camp in Shariff Saydona Mustapha town, Maguindanao province, leaving seven MILF rebels and four BIFF fighters dead.

8–11 November
The AFP launches an assault against the BIFF in Mamasapano town, Maguindanao province, killing 17 BIFF militants.

22 December
BIFF militants attack a military truck in Cotabato City, Maguindanao province, wounding 16 people.

province, and some of its members participated in localised inter-factional clashes centred around clan loyalties.

AFP offensives degrade ISIS affiliates on mainland Mindanao

The AFP maintained pressure on ISIS-aligned groups in western Mindanao in 2019. Duterte first imposed martial law in the region in response to the Marawi siege of May 2017 and then extended it repeatedly on the advice of AFP and PNP commanders. Martial law expired on 31 December 2019 after Duterte opted not to renew it for a fourth time, amid the receding threat level from ISIS affiliates. Regular airstrikes throughout the year targeted BIFF hideouts in rural areas of Maguindanao and North Cotabato, killing scores of militants and severely damaging the group's operational capabilities. Major anti-BIFF offensives took place in March, July and November. In April, sustained AFP pressure reportedly forced the BIFF's three remaining factions to enter a 'tactical alliance', cease large-scale operations and turn to guerrilla tactics such as ambushing military personnel by roadsides using IEDs.[9] The AFP also targeted remnants of the MG in Lanao del Sur, where the group's leader, Abu Dar, was killed on 14 March in the town of Tubaran.[10] His death left the group without a leader and on 15 October the AFP said that the MG had fewer than 25 members, a drastic decline from its pre-Marawi strength of 1,000.[11]

ASG rebounds amid high-profile suicide attacks

The ASG retreated to its island hideouts after the defeat in Marawi but in 2019 it rebounded to become the most active of the four ISIS-affiliated groups. ASG fighters clashed with the AFP frequently in Sulu, around the town of Patikul and on the nearby island of Banguingui. Smaller-scale clashes also occurred in the neighbouring maritime provinces of Basilan and Tawi-Tawi.

A faction with close ties to ISIS, commanded by Hatib Hajan Sawadjaan, gained global notoriety after a double suicide bombing targeted a cathedral in Jolo on 27 January, leaving 23 people dead and 95 wounded.[12] A second double suicide attack struck an army base in Indanan on 28 June, killing eight people,[13] while a third blast at a military camp in the same town on 8 September killed only the bomber.[14] ISIS claimed responsibility for the attacks, two of which were carried out by Indonesian citizens and one by a Moroccan national, raising concerns that the ASG may be harbouring foreign fighters in Sulu, Basilan and Tawi-Tawi. On 31 August, the WMC chief said that around 60 foreign terrorists were likely present in Mindanao. This assertion gained further traction on 5 November when AFP troops manning a checkpoint in Jolo killed two ASG-linked Egyptian militants.[15]

While smaller ASG factions led by Radullan Sahiron in Sulu and Furuji Indama in Basilan remain active, the faction commanded by Sawadjaan in Sulu, known as Ajang-Ajang, represents the greatest security threat. Following the death of Abu Dar, Sawadjaan is considered the emir of ISIS in Southeast Asia and, in advocating suicide bombings in Mindanao, threatens to open a dangerous new front in the conflict. In the second half of 2019, the AFP deployed greater resources and naval assets in the waters around Sulu in ongoing operations against the group, which Duterte promised to 'wipe out'.[16]

Impact

Humanitarian and human rights

AFP–BIFF clashes in Maguindanao and North Cotabato resulted in localised displacement, particularly during sustained aerial assaults by the military. An offensive against the BIFF in mid-March forced 30,295 people from 6,000 families from their homes in 22 Maguindanao villages,[17] while 8,911 people fled during the 14 March offensive that killed MG chief Abu Dar.[18] In late July, 10,150 people from 1,691 families were displaced along the Maguindanao–North Cotabato border during a week-long anti-BIFF campaign.[19] AFP–ASG fighting caused localised displacement on a smaller scale in Basilan and Sulu.

The conflict affected the education system for limited periods. Classes were suspended for several days in 13 schools in Pikit, North Cotabato on 26 July because of AFP–BIFF fighting, while 200 teachers refused to attend work in Basilan the previous week amid an ASG kidnapping threat.

ISIS-affiliated armed groups targeted civilians directly with bombs and indiscriminate attacks. The ASG was primarily responsible for atrocities, beheading villagers suspected of being army informants. On 6 February, the group shot dead a logger in Maluso after he failed to recite passages of the Koran. On 31 May, Dutch hostage Ewold Horn was killed as he attempted to flee his captors in Patikul.

The slow pace of rehabilitation in Marawi also had humanitarian implications, with the UN Office for the Coordination of Humanitarian Affairs (OCHA) reporting in June that 66,000 residents remained displaced after the 2017 siege.[20] More than 10,000 of these internally displaced persons (IDPs) moved out of evacuation centres and into government-provided temporary housing on 10 July, with the National Housing Authority (NHA) building 4,852 temporary shelters by the end of 2019. Task Force Bangon Marawi (TFBM), charged with rebuilding the city, aims to complete reconstruction by December 2021 and TFBM chief Eduardo del Rosario repeated throughout the year that the project was on target. On 26 September, the BTA created a special committee to monitor the rehabilitation of Marawi. It does not possess legal powers but serves as an 'oversight and accountability mechanism' for the TFBM.[21] Demolition of buildings in the central Banggolo district only began in February and with much unexploded ordnance still to be cleared, the TFBM's target looked optimistic at best.

Martial law remained in place in Mindanao throughout 2019, and while it reduced fighting in some areas, freedoms remained limited. On 24 May, human-rights group Karapatan said that it had recorded 93 extrajudicial killings, 35 cases of torture and 1,450 illegal arrests since the measure was first imposed.[22]

Social and economic

The establishment of the BARMM has afforded Moro Muslims a new autonomous status and greater control over their own affairs. This constitutes the beginning of a process of correcting what Duterte termed 'historical injustices' centred on economic and political marginalisation.[23] Symbolic moves, such as the adoption of a Bangsamoro flag, which will be flown over all public buildings in the BARMM, and the appointment of MILF chairman Ebrahim as BTA chief served to reduce identity-based tensions between Muslim communities and the central government.

However, political decentralisation must translate into economic growth if the poorest in society are to benefit from the new institutional arrangements. Corruption was a persistent problem in the ARMM, with Moro politicians accused of abusing their power to accumulate wealth. On 11 August, Ebrahim called for 'moral governance' in the new region and added that politicians must 'sacrifice personal gains' for 'good government to thrive'.[24] The interim administration pledged to implement strict financial-transparency mechanisms to avoid a repeat of past issues.

The BTA hopes to boost agricultural production and productivity in the BARMM. In January, Agriculture Secretary Emmanuel Piñol revealed plans to turn the MILF's former headquarters, Camp Abubakar, into a banana plantation after the government signed a deal with two foreign companies; meanwhile, in May the Department of Agriculture said it would form a ten-year master plan with the BTA to increase farm productivity, improve irrigation and build farm-to-market roads to tackle poverty.[25]

Relations with neighbouring countries

Cooperation between the Philippines, Indonesia and Malaysia continued in the Sulu and Celebes sea region to combat the threat of piracy, maritime kidnappings and the movement of ISIS-linked foreign fighters seeking to join the ASG. The neighbours held regular trilateral naval and aerial patrols in the region, while Malaysia maintained a dawn-to-dusk curfew for civilian vessels in waters off the Eastern Sabah Security Zone (ESSZ) aimed at reducing the risk of fishermen being seized by the ASG.

The US remains a close ally of the Philippines in its battle against ISIS, and on 15 August signed a deal with the PNP to finance the construction of a new regional counter-terrorism training centre in Cavite.

Trends

Political trajectories
The conclusion of the government–MILF peace process and replacement of the ARMM with the BARMM offer a renewed chance for political stability in western Mindanao, amid a significant reduction in tensions between Moro communities and the central government. The three-year implementation period gives the BTA interim administration time to refine its governance structures and procedures ahead of parliamentary elections set for 2022. Public support will be vital to ensure the legitimacy of the new self-governance structures. In 2020, the government will likely continue to engage MNLF founder Misuari to ensure he remains supportive of the BARMM.

Conflict-related risks
The ASG currently represents the greatest security threat in western Mindanao, making the provinces of Sulu, Basilan and Tawi-Tawi high-risk areas for foreign firms. The threat of piracy attacks and kidnappings in the Sulu and Celebes seas will continue to disrupt maritime trade routes and lead most major shipping companies to avoid the area.

The risk that ISIS-aligned groups based on mainland Mindanao, in the provinces of Maguindanao, North Cotabato and Lanao del Sur, might rebound will persist in 2020. The most likely scenario in this regard is the BIFF and MG replenishing their ranks and launching more ambitious attacks against civilian and AFP targets. Reduced AFP vigilance after martial law is lifted or recruitment among displaced residents of Marawi might aid those efforts.

Prospects for peace
The approval of the BOL and the establishment of the BARMM effectively ended the mainstream Moro insurgency. However, this institutional shift will change little on the ground, as the MILF and the MNLF have not fought the military on a sustained basis for the past decade. The MILF's commitment to disarm is genuine and the process is on track but forging a longer-term peace will depend on the successful reintegration of ex-MILF fighters into mainstream society and the economic dividends of the BARMM.

ISIS-affiliated groups on mainland Mindanao, which continue to fight for independence or an Islamic caliphate, have been subdued over the past year. The manpower and capabilities of the MG and BIFF have dwindled dramatically since the Marawi assault, while AKP remnants are inactive. The largest threat emanates from the ASG and suicide bombings, but it is geographically restricted to remote, outlying islands, which will limit the spread of this new tactic. The integration of ex-MILF rebels into JPSTs alongside the AFP and PNP should have a stabilising effect and will help with efforts to confront ISIS-affiliated groups.

Strategic implications
The Philippines and its neighbours will remain on alert for a resurgence of ISIS activity in the region, despite the death of its leader Abu Bakr al-Baghdadi in 2019. ISIS may look to shift its focus to Southeast Asia and other regions with a history of Islamist militancy after the defeat of the caliphate in Syria. Mindanao's ISIS-linked groups retain ambitions to create an independent state governed by extreme Islamist ideology. Regional cooperation in the naval and intelligence spheres will be key to guard against the growth of radical groups and the movement of foreign fighters. Indonesia and Malaysia will continue to be at risk of lone-wolf attacks by ISIS sympathisers unable to reach ISIS-linked groups in Mindanao.

Notes

[1] Michael Hart, 'Deciphering the jihadist threat to Mindanao's Moro peace process', IISS Blogs & Podcasts, 20 May 2019.

[2] Lt-Gen. Felimon Santos Jr took over as chief of staff on 4 January 2020.

[3] Philippine Statistics Authority, 'ARMM Poverty Statistics', 17 April 2019; Ralf Rivas, 'Philippine poverty incidence down in first half of 2018', Rappler, 10 April 2019.

[4] Philippine Statistics Authority, 'ARMM Poverty Statistics', 17 April 2019.

[5] Pia Ranada, 'Comelec: Bangsamoro Organic Law "deemed ratified"', Rappler, 25 January 2019.

[6] Llanesca Panti, 'Sulu voters reject BOL', GMA News, 23 January 2019.

7. Catherina S. Valente, 'Duterte open to creation of MNLF region', *Manila Times*, 21 August 2019.
8. Bong Garcia, 'Security team deployment will constrict BIFF movements', *SunStar Zamboanga*, 28 August 2019.
9. Rene Acosta, 'Fierce AFP campaign forces BIFF, faction to forge alliance', BusinessMirror, 7 April 2019.
10. Carmela Fonbuena, 'Leader of Isis in Philippines killed, DNA tests confirm', *Guardian*, 14 April 2019.
11. 'Military remains "careful" as Maute "remnants" continue to recruit members', CNN Philippines, 15 October 2019.
12. 'Jolo cathedral bombing death toll rises to 23', GMA News, 4 February 2019.
13. Roel Pareño, 'Sayyaf faction tagged in Sulu bombing', *Philippine Star*, 30 June 2019.
14. 'Suspected suicide bomber attacks Sulu military camp', Rappler, 8 September 2019.
15. 'Two suspected suicide bombers from Egypt killed in Philippines', Al-Jazeera, 6 November 2019.
16. Genalyn Kabiling, 'Duterte to AFP, PNP: Finish off Abu Sayyaf', *Manila Bulletin*, 7 July 2019.
17. Edwin O. Fernandez, 'Maguindanao clashes displace 30,000 villagers', *Philippine Daily Inquirer*, 15 March 2019.
18. 'Clashes in southern Philippines displace around 50,000 people', Xinhua, 22 March 2019.
19. Taher Solaiman, 'At least 1,600 families flee as Army pursues BIFF in Cotabato, Maguindanao', *Philippine Daily Inquirer*, 31 July 2019.
20. OCHA, 'Philippines: Mindanao Humanitarian Situation', 19 June 2019.
21. Carolyn O. Arguillas, 'BTA creates Special Committee on Marawi; UXOs cleared by end of October', Minda News, 29 September 2019.
22. Jigger J. Jerusalem, 'Groups slam gov't for failure to address HR violations under martial law', Davao Today, 24 May 2019.
23. Republic of the Philippines Presidential Communications Operations Office, 'President Duterte to Moros: Take advantage of BARMM to "correct" historical injustices', 29 March 2019.
24. Ali Macabalang, 'BARMM chief calls for a moral gov't', *Manila Bulletin*, 11 August 2019.
25. Karl R. Ocampo, '10-yr agriculture master plan for BARMM readied', *Philippine Daily Inquirer*, 6 May 2019.

PHILIPPINES (NPA)

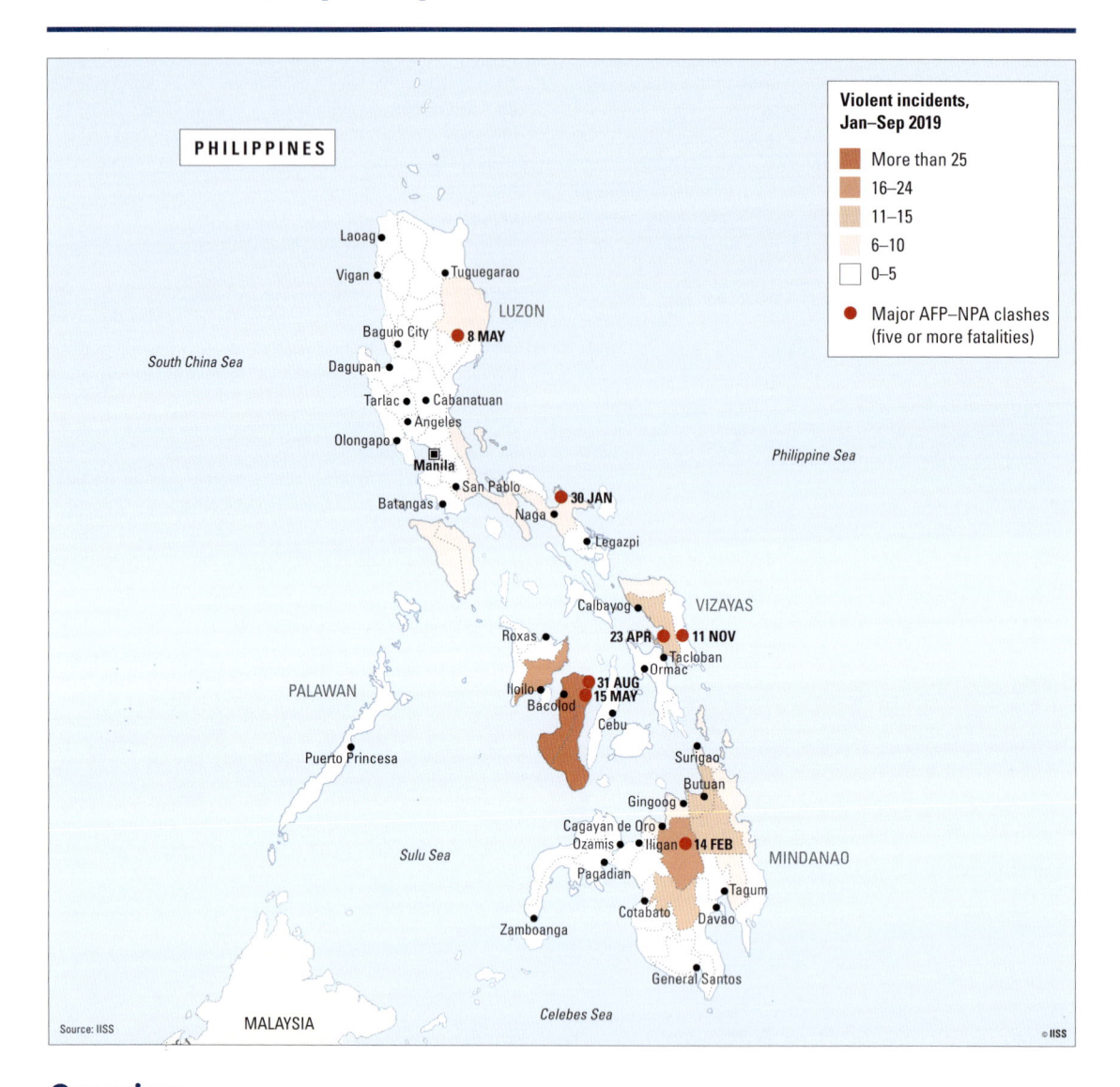

Overview

The conflict in 2019

Absent a national peace dialogue, fighting between the New People's Army (NPA) and Philippines' government forces continued in 2019. The NPA was most active in eastern Mindanao, Samar and Negros Island, where it regularly clashed with the Armed Forces of the Philippines (AFP) and Philippine National Police (PNP). The group also attacked government forces in rural areas nationwide using improvised explosive devices (IEDs) and high-powered rifles, with civilian bystanders often caught in the crossfire. It continued to exercise de facto control over villages in the countryside via intimidation and the collection of 'revolutionary taxes', and to harass non-compliant firms and individuals.

No formal negotiations between the government and the National Democratic Front of the Philippines (NDFP) – which represents the NPA and its parent organisation, the Communist Party of the Philippines (CPP), in talks with Manila – have taken place since President Rodrigo Duterte proclaimed the end of the peace process in November 2017.

Any prospect of reviving talks ended on 21 March 2019, when Duterte disbanded his negotiating panel and reiterated that during his presidential term (due to expire in 2022), talks with the NDFP were 'permanently terminated'. The government announced that it would instead form local peace panels within civilian-led task forces to engage directly with rebel commanders, bypassing the CPP–NDFP leadership. By the end of the year, 17 Regional Task Forces (RTFs) had been established but the initiative remained at an early stage.

The conflict to 2019

The post-independence communist rebellion in the Philippines began with the founding of the NPA as an armed wing of the CPP in 1969. Left-wing student activist Jose Maria Sison had established the CPP the previous year as a successor to the Hukbalahap communist movement, which had organised armed uprisings against US colonial rule and Filipino elites after the Second World War. Firmly rooted in Marxist–Leninist–Maoist ideology, the CPP–NPA has waged a guerrilla-style insurgency for the last five decades in remote rural areas across the country, with the aim of overthrowing the government and replacing it with a socialist political system led by the working class.

The NPA was at its strongest in the mid-1980s during the dictatorship of Ferdinand Marcos, when it gained widespread public support and its ranks swelled to around 26,000 fighters. Large-scale violence between the NPA and the military took place during the Marcos era, mainly in the countryside. Public support for the NPA declined in the post-1986 democratic era and the conflict has fluctuated since, with periods of intensified violence interspersed with peace talks.

The NDFP, established in 1973, has represented the CPP–NPA in talks with successive administrations led by Corazon Aquino, Fidel Ramos, Joseph Estrada, Gloria Macapagal Arroyo and Benigno Aquino III, but to little avail. After Duterte's election in 2016, both sides declared separate unilateral ceasefires and four rounds of formal negotiations were held in Oslo, Rome and Amsterdam. Talks collapsed in February 2017 amid renewed rebel attacks and a cancelled prisoner amnesty. Duterte labelled the CPP–NPA a domestic terrorist organisation and ordered the termination of the peace process in November 2017. In 2018, several months of back-channel talks failed to revive formal negotiations and fighting has since flared.

Key statistics

Type	Internal
Start date	March 1969
IDPs total (September 2019)	10,458
Refugees total	Not applicable
People in need	Not applicable

Key Conflict Parties

Armed Forces of the Philippines (AFP)

Strength
142,350 regular combatants across the army, navy and air force, with a reserve paramilitary force of 50,000 serving in Citizen Armed Force Geographical Units (CAFGUs).

Areas of operation
Operates nationwide. Headquarters, Camp Aguinaldo, is in Quezon city, Metro Manila.

Leadership
The AFP is led by Chief-of-Staff Lt-Gen. Noel Clement, who was appointed by President Duterte in September 2019.[1]

Structure
The AFP is divided into six area unified military commands, with the Eastern Mindanao Command (AFP–EMC) primarily responsible for fighting the NPA in its southern heartlands, and the Central Command (AFP–CC) in the Visayas.

History
Established in December 1935 after the passage of the National Defence Act, during the US colonial period. Passed to Philippine control following independence in 1946.

Objectives
Aims to defeat the NPA militarily by 2022 and expressed its support in 2019 for Duterte's plan to hold peace talks with NPA commanders at the local level while encouraging rebels to surrender. Pursues a reactive anti-NPA strategy but also launches airstrikes in response to intelligence reports.

Armed Forces of the Philippines (AFP)

Opponents
NPA. Also fights several ISIS-affiliated groups that operate in western Mindanao.

Affiliates/allies
Aided in anti-NPA raids and law-enforcement operations by the PNP. Also cooperates with the Revolutionary Proletarian Army–Alex Boncayao Brigade (RPA–ABB) against the NPA and is training ex-RPA–ABB rebels as local defence forces.

Resources/capabilities
Access to combat tanks and a fleet of armoured trucks, while the air force makes use of rapid-attack aircraft, transport planes and helicopters. Uses pistols, high-powered rifles and artillery in anti-NPA operations.

New People's Army (NPA)

Strength
Around 4,000 active fighters nationwide (AFP estimate). Numbers have declined significantly since the early 1980s, when it had around 26,000 members during the Marcos dictatorship.

Areas of operation
Most active in eastern Mindanao. In the Visayas, high levels of NPA activity have been recorded in the provinces of Negros Occidental, Negros Oriental and Samar in 2019. Also present in rural areas across the country.

Leadership
Led by its founder, Jose Maria Sison, from self-imposed exile in the Netherlands. NPA fighters are led by a network of local ground commanders.

Structure
The NPA is the armed wing of the CPP and is represented in formal peace talks by the NDFP. The three groups are often referred to collectively as the CPP–NPA–NDFP. NPA rebels operate via small guerrilla-style armed units.

History
Formed in 1969, shortly after the founding of the CPP. It has fought the AFP for 50 years, with clashes centred on rural areas. Peace negotiations have failed under six presidents in the post-1986 democratic era.

Objectives
The CPP–NPA's ideology has remained unchanged since the 1960s. The group deploys anti-colonial and anti-US rhetoric denouncing capitalism and Filipino elites, vowing to fight a 'Protracted People's War' for a socialist government. It does not govern territory but exercises de facto control in its rural strongholds via a system of extortion enforced through violence and threats.

Opponents
AFP and PNP. Often targets the RPA–ABB (made up of former NPA members) in raids and ambushes.

Affiliates/allies
No known affiliates. The NPA has received funds and weapons from China and like-minded Maoist insurgent groups based abroad.

Resources/capabilities
Arsenal consists of high-powered rifles looted from military bases and firearms seized from private security guards during raids on businesses. The group also deploys IEDs in ambushes targeting military and police vehicles.

Revolutionary Proletarian Army–Alex Boncayao Brigade (RPA–ABB)

Strength
Thought to have fewer than 500 members and is largely inactive but maintains a cache of firearms for defensive purposes.

Areas of operation
Present in the Western Visayas. In the late 1990s the group operated in Manila and cities across Luzon, Negros Island and the Visayas.

Leadership
The RPA–ABB was led by Nilo dela Cruz and Arturo Tabara when it signed a peace deal with the government in 2000. Tabara was killed during a clash in 2004. Current leader is unknown.

Structure
During its early years – as part of the NPA – the ABB consisted of hit squads of up to four snipers who would carry out targeted killings of NPA opponents.

History
The ABB was established in 1984 as the NPA's urban assassination unit but split in the early 1990s over an ideological dispute. It merged with the RPA in 1997 to form the RPA–ABB. The RPA–ABB signed a peace agreement with Manila in 2000.

Objectives
Under the NPA's leadership, the ABB was tasked with assassinating military personnel, police officers and government officials in urban areas. The RPA–ABB initially espoused a Maoist ideology mirroring that of the CPP–NPA, but it now has no overarching aim or strategy and is disarming.

Opponents
The NPA regards the RPA–ABB as an enemy and considers its leaders to have betrayed the communist cause, and occasionally attacks RPA–ABB personnel.

Revolutionary Proletarian Army–Alex Boncayao Brigade (RPA–ABB)

Affiliates/allies	Resources/capabilities
Has cooperated with the AFP since signing a peace deal in 2000. Some former RPA–ABB fighters underwent AFP training in 2019 to defend their communities from NPA attacks.	Thought to retain access to rifles and other light weaponry.

Drivers

The CPP–NPA's enduring ideology
Unlike many insurgent groups, the CPP–NPA's ideology has remained remarkably consistent. Through a campaign of armed resistance, the insurgents aim to overthrow the government and replace it with a socialist system predicated on Marxism–Leninism–Maoism. Sison outlined the movement's core principles in *Philippine Society and Revolution* (1970), which laid the foundations for the CPP's anti-capitalist and anti-imperialist stance. He still serves as the CPP–NPA's main leader. The CPP–NPA has maintained a high degree of ideological unity, making it resistant to splintering and enabling it to endure for five decades. Its refusal to compromise on altering the Philippine system of government has limited its ability to negotiate a peace agreement, however.

Geographical dispersal of NPA fighters
The NPA is active in at least 69 of the 81 provinces of the Philippines, making it difficult to contain and ultimately defeat in an expansive maritime nation of more than 7,000 islands. NPA fighters are widely dispersed at both national and local levels and wage most attacks in remote areas away from major towns and cities. Operating in densely forested, mountainous and inaccessible terrain is a strategic choice, based on Sison's idea of geographical decentralisation and guerrilla-style campaigns, as detailed in his *Specific Characteristics of our People's War* (1974). The leader wanted the NPA to be difficult to defeat via conventional means, resilient to both detection and major offensives. NPA fighters operate in small groups and move frequently, using a network of temporary bases to maximise this effect.

Rural poverty and underdevelopment
Poverty and underdevelopment have long fuelled grievances against the government in the Philippines, sustaining the NPA's support and recruitment in rural areas. Lack of access to land and natural-resource revenue are key drivers of the conflict in eastern Mindanao, where the NPA is strongest. Weak governance, poor infrastructure and inadequate service provision in the region have created an environment in which armed groups can firmly embed themselves in and recruit from economically marginalised communities. Societal inequalities are high and many residents of deprived rural areas view the NPA as fighting for their core interests. The International Fund for Agricultural Development (IFAD) recorded at the end of 2016 that 34.9% of the Philippines' 55 million rural citizens lived in poverty, compared to 13.2% of 45m urban citizens.[2] State-led development initiatives in the past decade, such as the Philippine Development Plan (PDP), have resulted in strong economic growth at the national level but only marginally reduced poverty in the countryside.[3]

Failed peace dialogue under Duterte
The failure of the peace process under Duterte has served as a more recent trigger for the violence. As the first president to come from insurgency-plagued Mindanao, Duterte's election in 2016 led to renewed hopes of a negotiated settlement. Yet, after four rounds of dialogue halted the hostilities between August 2016 and February 2017, Duterte refused to release political prisoners – a key demand of the CPP leadership – talks collapsed and fighting resumed. The decision to formally terminate the process in November 2017 sparked a further intensification, which has persisted amid an ongoing war of words, threats and fiery rhetoric between Duterte and Sison. The deteriorating relationship between the government and the CPP compounded a long-standing lack of trust and failed talks under six successive administrations.

Political Developments

Duterte dissolves peace-negotiation panel

The start of 2019 offered little sign that the peace process would be revived. On 1 January, Sison said that the NDFP's priority in 2019 would be to forge a 'broad united front' to 'work for the ouster of the Duterte regime'.[4] Defence Secretary Delfin Lorenzana responded that talks would not resume amid threats from Sison, and reaffirmed that any future negotiations would be dependent on the NPA meeting a list of preconditions, including an end to rebel attacks and extortion, the encampment of NPA fighters and a commitment from the CPP not to seek participation in a coalition government. On 21 March, Duterte announced the 'permanent termination' of talks and disbanded the government's peace-negotiation panel, led by Silvestre Bello, with immediate effect, stating that the NDFP could 'talk to the next president'.[5] Despite this assertion, on 23 December Duterte proposed holding a one-on-one meeting with Sison in a final attempt to revive the peace process, but only on the condition that Sison returned to Manila from exile. Sison ruled out returning and said that he would only be willing to meet Duterte in a neighbouring country. As of the end of 2019, no such arrangement for a meeting had been made, and the peace process remained terminated.

Shift towards local-level dialogues

With national-level talks scrapped, the government's chief peace adviser Carlito Galvez announced in March that 'inclusive' local peace panels – within civilian-led task forces set up to bring together all local stakeholders, including military and community representatives – would be formed to engage NPA commanders at the provincial level, bypassing the CPP and NDFP leadership, which presidential spokesman Salvador Panelo said had lost control of fighters on the ground.[6] Galvez said that the idea was based on peace bodies in Colombia that comprise a wide range of stakeholders on all sides. A key part of the plan involved persuading fighters to surrender through the government's Enhanced Comprehensive Local Integration Program (E-CLIP), which provides financial and livelihood assistance. Duterte also pledged to assist ex-rebels in securing housing, training and employment. In a speech in Davao on 16 July, he encouraged rebels to 'return to mainstream society' and act as 'responsible, productive, peaceful and law-abiding citizens'.[7] Between January and September, 826 members of the NPA surrendered voluntarily, turning in their weapons in return for livelihood support through the E-CLIP scheme.

By the end of 2019, 17 Regional Task Forces to End Local Communist Armed Conflict (RTFs–ELCAC) had been formed in addition to smaller task forces at the provincial, municipal, city and village levels. A National Task Force (NTF–ELCAC) was created to coordinate them and met in Manila in November. Commenting on the initiative, National Security Adviser Hermogenes Esperon said that Duterte had outlined his plan to tackle the 'roots of the insurgency' in 'conflict-prone communities' via 'enhanced programmes and harmonised efforts to provide for basic needs such as housing, water,

Key Events in 2019

Political events

- **21 March**: Duterte announces the termination of talks with the NDFP and disbands the government's peace-negotiating panel. The formation of local peace panels is announced.
- **1 June**: The foreign secretary says that EU countries must gain government approval before assisting Philippine NGOs.

Military/Violent events

- **30 January**: Six NPA insurgents are killed in a clash with AFP personnel in Tinambac, Camarines Sur province.
- **14 February**: NPA insurgents attack an AFP base in Malaybalay, Bukidnon province. Two AFP soldiers and four NPA rebels are killed.
- **30 March**: 14 NPA insurgents are killed in coordinated AFP–PNP raids on NPA hideouts in Negros Oriental province.
- **23 April**: NPA rebels detonate an IED in Calbiga, Samar province, killing six AFP soldiers.
- **15 May**: Five NPA rebels are killed in a clash with AFP soldiers in Calatrava, Negros Occidental province.

Table 1: Timeline of the peace process

Peace talks between the government and the NPA since President Duterte came to power in 2016

Date	Event
Jun 2016	Duterte inaugurated as president of the Philippines, having promised on the campaign trail to revive the national-level peace process with the National Democratic Front of the Philippines (NDFP).
Aug 2016	First round of formal government–NDFP talks held in Oslo. Both sides implement separate unilateral ceasefires and agree to further talks.
Oct 2016	Second round of formal government–NDFP talks held in Oslo. The parties agree on a framework for social and economic reform in rural areas.
Jan 2017	Third round of formal government–NDFP talks held in Rome. Dialogue on a joint ceasefire breaks down but unilateral ceasefires are maintained.
Feb 2017	Duterte refuses to release political prisoners. Clashes between the Armed Forces of the Philippines (AFP) and the NPA break out after insurgent attacks. Both sides terminate their unilateral ceasefires.
Apr 2017	Fourth round of formal government–NDFP talks held in Amsterdam. Little progress is made, and no joint ceasefire is announced.
May 2017	Duterte cancels a fifth round of government–NDFP talks amid NPA attacks on AFP troops and the NPA's continued collection of 'revolutionary taxes'.
Nov 2017	Duterte signs proclamation No. 360, formally ending the government–NDFP peace process. He labels the Communist Party of the Philippines (CPP) and the NPA 'terrorist organisations'.
Jun 2018	Informal government–NDFP negotiations fail to revive the peace process, amid disagreement over preconditions and the proposed venue for talks.
Mar 2019	Duterte disbands his peace-negotiating panel, led by Silvestre Bello. He says the NDFP can 'talk to the next president' after his term ends in 2022.

education and healthcare'.[8] This rhetoric indicated a shift towards addressing the drivers of recruitment in NPA-affected regions. Yet, notably, Esperon added that 'focused military operations' against the NPA would continue.

Pressure on CPP 'front organisations'

Duterte repeatedly accused humanitarian groups of serving as fronts for the CPP and accused them of diverting money to the NPA. In March, the government asked the EU to 'stop the flow of funds to communist terrorist front organisations' after alleging that Belgian donations to several non-governmental organisations (NGOs) had unwittingly ended up with the CPP.[9] The EU, which listed the CPP–NPA as a terrorist group in 2002, requested further information and pledged to launch an investigation. In early April, AFP spokesman Brig.-Gen. Antonio Parlade claimed that the CPP had at least 252 'member organisations' across 39 countries

---

18 July — NPA rebels allegedly torture and execute four captured PNP officers in Ayungon, Negros Oriental province.

28 August — An arrest warrant is issued for CPP leader Sison over the 1985 Inopacan massacre.

31 August — Five NPA insurgents are killed in a clash with AFP soldiers in Escalante, Negros Occidental province.

26 October — The AFP launches airstrikes that destroy an NPA camp in Las Navas, Northern Samar province and reports inflicting heavy casualties.

11 November — Six IEDs explode during a gun battle between the AFP and NPA in Borongan, Eastern Samar province, killing six AFP soldiers.

19 November — The NTF–ELCAC meets for a joint command conference to discuss government strategy to tackle the NPA insurgency.

13 December — NPA rebels ambush a PNP vehicle in Borongan, Eastern Samar province, killing a PNP officer and two civilians.

serving as fronts designed to secure international funding.[10] On 1 June, Foreign Secretary Teodoro Locsin announced that EU member states must gain official clearance from the Department of Foreign Affairs before donating to NGOs in the Philippines.

Rising government–CPP hostility

Relations between the government and the CPP–NDFP soured further in 2019 amid a public war of words between Duterte and Sison. On 14 March, Sison described Duterte as 'crazy' for insisting on a set of preconditions for talks, which would amount to 'political suicide' for the CPP.[11] In June, the CPP responded to a jibe from Duterte that communism is 'outdated' by saying 'it is Duterte's ideology, fascism, that is old and rotten'.[12] In August, a Manila court issued an arrest warrant for Sison over his alleged role in the 1985 Inopacan massacre, while the PNP asked INTERPOL in September to issue a 'red notice' for the detention of Sison, who lives in self-imposed exile in the Netherlands. Sison described the charges as politically motivated and reiterated that he would not return to the Philippines. Amid growing animosity, both Duterte and Sison declared in September that there was no chance of the peace process resuming.

Military Developments

Escalating violence in eastern Mindanao and Visayas

Fighting escalated in 2019, with the NPA targeting AFP and PNP personnel on a near-daily basis in the countryside. The violence was most intense in eastern Mindanao and the Visayan provinces of Negros Occidental, Negros Oriental and Samar. In addition to IED attacks and roadside ambushes, NPA fighters engaged in spontaneous gunfights with AFP personnel on patrol in remote regions, while urban rebel hit squads known as 'sparrow units' targeted soldiers in towns and cities.

Most clashes were brief and resulted in between one and four casualties, while several incidents led to multiple deaths and gained national attention. Six rebels were killed in an encounter with the AFP in Camarines Sur on 30 January, while on 14 February four rebels and two soldiers were killed during an NPA attack on a military outpost in Bukidnon. Another six AFP soldiers were killed in an IED explosion in Samar on 23 April, while five rebels were killed in a shootout with the army in Negros Occidental on 15 May. On 18 July, the NPA allegedly tortured four PNP officers in Negros Oriental before shooting them dead in execution-style killings. That incident provoked widespread public outrage, leading Duterte to offer a bounty, which he later raised to US$97,000, for the capture or killing of the rebels involved.[13] In other major clashes, five rebels were killed in a battle with the AFP in the province of Negros Occidental on 31 August and six soldiers died in an IED blast in Eastern Samar in November.

Table 2: Key events on Negros Island in 2019	
Date	Event
26 Jan	Members of a suspected NPA 'sparrow unit' shoot dead the police chief of Bacolod city.
30 Mar	Joint AFP–Philippine National Police (PNP) raids across Negros Oriental lead to the deaths of 14 suspected NPA rebels.
1 Apr	An AFP–NPA clash in Moises Padilla displaces at least 1,700 residents from their homes.
27 Apr	The AFP deploys 150 troops and three armoured vehicles to Moises Padilla after NPA attacks.
8 May	NPA rebels attack a Revolutionary Proletarian Army–Alex Boncayao Brigade (RPA–ABB) resettlement site in Kabankalan, killing two RPA–ABB fighters.
15 May	AFP troops clash with the NPA in Calatrava, leaving five rebels dead and three soldiers injured.
18 Jul	NPA insurgents shoot dead four police officers after ambushing their vehicles in Ayungon.
8 Aug	The AFP clashes with the NPA in Himamaylan, leaving three insurgents and an AFP soldier dead.
31 Aug	AFP soldiers clash with the NPA in Escalante, leaving five rebels dead and three soldiers injured.
31 Oct–1 Nov	Two days of joint AFP–PNP raids result in the arrest of at least 40 NPA rebels and seizure of 32 firearms.

There was a surge in violence in Negros Island throughout the year, which led the AFP to boost resources there. On 30 March, a series of coordinated joint AFP–PNP raids on suspected NPA hideouts in Negros Oriental resulted in the killing of 14 rebels and the seizure of 53 firearms. In August, after a spate of shootings linked to the NPA, Duterte ruled out placing the island under martial law, saying that the 'unbridled killings' did not constitute the full-scale rebellion required by the constitution to impose the measure.[14] Instead, the AFP formed a new joint task force (JTF–Negros) in September to bolster anti-NPA offensives.

Defeating jihadists remained the AFP's priority in 2019, diverting attention and resources from fighting the NPA in eastern Mindanao. The AFP launched some airstrikes and coordinated ground offensives against the NPA, but its approach remained mainly reactionary, in contrast to the more active strategy pursued against groups aligned with the Islamic State, also known as ISIS or ISIL, in western Mindanao and the Sulu islands.[15] As a result, the NPA guerrilla warfare persisted at similar levels to 2017, when the peace process first faltered.

Demobilised RPA–ABB rebels undergo training

The RPA–ABB, mostly inactive since signing an accord with the government in 2000, maintained a low-key presence in the Western Visayas region. The group no longer fights the AFP, and 560 of its members demobilised and turned in their firearms in early September 2019 across the provinces of Capiz, Iloilo and Negros Occidental. Former RPA–ABB fighters are set to be trained by the AFP to become a local civilian defence force and will be issued with guns to protect their communities from the NPA. The first batch of 27 former rebels finished training in November and received M16 rifles and a living allowance.[16]

The group did not initiate any attacks in 2019, but its members were subjected to a series of bandit-style attacks by the NPA. On 8 May, around 30 heavily armed NPA fighters attacked an RPA–ABB resettlement site in Negros Occidental, killing two RPA–ABB members and seizing firearms. The NPA also shot dead a former senior commander of the RPA–ABB in an ambush on 4 October.

Impact

Human rights

Fears rose in 2019 that Duterte was intensifying efforts to silence human-rights critics. Political opponents accused the government of 'red-tagging' (falsely labelling individuals as communist insurgents or supporters) as part of a widening crackdown on left-wing and humanitarian organisations.[17] In a high-profile case, the National Union of Peoples' Lawyers (NUPL) complained of military harassment after leaflets were distributed alleging it had ties to the NPA.[18] The practice of naming and intimidating groups with alleged links to the communist movement was associated with former dictator Marcos and has been revived under the Duterte administration. In addition to lobbying the EU over alleged funding for CPP-linked charities, on 5 November an AFP intelligence chief publicly named 18 alleged CPP–NPA fronts in a presentation to Congress including the charity Oxfam, church groups and women's advocacy groups.[19]

Rising instability on Negros Island brought accusations of vigilante killings and concerns over impunity for AFP personnel. Amid a series of shootings of left-leaning individuals by unidentified gunmen, the PNP vowed in August to investigate the alleged presence of an anti-communist vigilante group, known as Kagubak, on the island.[20] After the government announced the death of 14 NPA rebels in joint AFP–PNP raids on 30 March, the CPP claimed that many of those killed were not NPA fighters, but red-tagged farmers.[21] PNP Chief General Oscar Albayalde insisted the victims were armed insurgents who opened fire on his officers.[22] The AFP also linked the NPA to a spate of assassinations in Negros Oriental in June and July and accused the rebels of continuing to recruit child soldiers in Mindanao, some as young as 12.[23]

Humanitarian

In 2019, temporary displacements occurred near the sites of AFP–NPA encounters, with residents usually able to return home once fighting subsided. In the largest of these incidents, on 22 June, 1,500 people from 230 households fled fighting in Manjuyod,

Negros Oriental.[24] The NPA maintained a firm stranglehold and de facto control over communities in rural areas through extortion, threats and intimidation. The group killed local opponents – including ex-rebels, town councillors, village chiefs, tribal leaders and suspected military informants – in drive-by shootings after convicting them of crimes against the rebel cause in its People's Courts. At least 44 opponents were killed in targeted assassinations by the NPA during January–September 2019.

Social and economic
Collection of 'revolutionary taxes' by the NPA continued to restrict economic growth in the countryside, where non-compliant businesses were targeted in raids and arson attacks. Firms in the mining, agricultural, construction and energy sectors were targeted most often because the group views multinational corporations with suspicion and condemns firms that damage the environment. In June, the NPA vowed to launch tactical offensives to stop the construction of the Kaliwa Dam in Quezon[25] and on 22 August it threatened to shut down coal-fired power plants after a raid in Misamis Oriental.[26]

Relations with neighbouring and international partners
The NPA insurgency is a purely internal conflict, with no neighbouring countries involved. The development partner likely to be most affected by the latest developments is the EU. Its member states are considering demands from Manila to halt donations to charities allegedly linked to the CPP–NPA. CPP chair Sison is in exile in the Netherlands, where he maintains that his status as a 'recognised political refugee' will protect him from extradition, and he is unlikely to return to his home country to engage in talks or face criminal charges.[27]

Trends

Political trajectories
Tension between the two sides is set to persist. Relations between the government and the CPP have been strained since the collapse of peace talks in 2017 and continued to worsen in 2019 amid the public war of words between Duterte and Sison. The CPP will likely continue its attempts to discredit the government through press statements critical of economic and development policies, and Duterte's leadership style. The CPP's threat to forge a 'broad coalition' to oust Duterte, however, is a gross overstatement.[28] From exile, CPP leaders have little influence on national politics.

Conflict-related risks
Conflict continued at a similar intensity to recent years in eastern Mindanao, where the presence of the NPA dented prospects for foreign investment and faster economic growth in rural areas. There was a spike in attacks in Negros Island in 2019, and violence in the region could potentially escalate in 2020 if the military is unable to stem killings by the NPA and vigilante groups. The training of RPA–ABB rebels as community-defence volunteers could boost stability at the local level but may also provide a new target for NPA attacks. Luzon is the region least affected by the insurgency, but AFP–NPA clashes persist in rural areas, where civilians are at risk of displacement and being caught in the crossfire.

Prospects for peace
Lack of trust and persistent hostilities indicate that there is little prospect of the national-level peace process being revived under Duterte. Duterte's offer in late December of a one-on-one meeting with Sison is unlikely to materialise. Previous disagreements over preconditions, the return of Sison from exile and whether talks should be held in the Philippines or a neutral country, remain unresolved and represent a barrier to formal dialogue. A history of broken promises and failed ceasefires also reduces the prospect of national-level talks restarting. Localised talks may reduce violence in some areas and encourage insurgents to surrender through the E-CLIP programme, but rebel recruitment continues and the NPA retains its strength despite AFP offensives. The NPA's nationwide presence means that ending the conflict will not be possible without a ceasefire and a peace accord signed by its political bodies, the CPP and NDFP.[29]

Notes

1. Lt-Gen. Felimon Santos Jr took over as chief of staff on 4 January 2020.
2. IFAD, 'The Republic of the Philippines: COSOP results review', 31 December 2016.
3. 'Govt admits failure to reduce poverty', Manila Times, 17 February 2014.
4. 'Duterte ouster Reds' 2019 priority: Sison', ABS–CBN News, 2 January 2019.
5. E.J. Roque, 'Duterte permanently ends peace talks with Reds', Philippine News Agency, 21 March 2019.
6. Catherine S. Valente, 'Duterte to form new peace panel to talk to Reds', Manila Times, 22 March 2019.
7. Nestor Corrales, 'Duterte calls on task force vs insurgency to "work doubly hard"', Inquirer, 16 July 2019.
8. Ruth Abbey Gita-Carlos, 'Duterte wants focus on "conflict-prone" areas to stop insurgency', Inquirer, 19 November 2019.
9. 'CPP foreign funding revealed; PH asks Belgium, EU to stop cash flow', Manila Bulletin, 6 March 2019.
10. Francis Wakefield, 'AFP official unmasks CPP fronts, networks', Manila Bulletin, 5 April 2019.
11. 'Joma says Duterte "must be crazy" for asking NPA to drop their guns', GMA News, 14 March 2019.
12. NDFP, 'Fascism–Duterte's ideology–is old and rotten', NDFP statement, 21 June 2019.
13. Adrian Stewart, 'Bounty for Negros cops' killers now P5 million', Panay News, 2 August 2019.
14. Arianne Merez, 'Palace rules out martial law in Negros for now', ABS–CBN News, 6 August 2019.
15. Michael Hart, 'Deciphering the jihadist threat to Mindanao's Moro peace process', IISS Blogs & Podcasts, 20 May 2019.
16. '27 ex-RPA-ABB rebels complete basic military training', Sunstar Bacolod, 10 November 2019.
17. Nick Aspinwall, 'In the Philippines, activists increasingly face a "living hell"', The Lowy Institute, 15 February 2019.
18. Lian Buan, 'Duterte admin dismisses red-tagging petition as "implausible"', Rappler, 18 July 2019.
19. Alan Robles, 'Safety fears after Philippines names Oxfam a front for communist terror', South China Morning Post, 10 November 2019.
20. Aaron Recuenco, 'PNP to probe anti-communist death squad in Negros Oriental', Manila Bulletin, 29 August 2019.
21. '14 killed in NegOr; NPA claims they were farmers', Sunstar Cebu, 30 March 2019.
22. 'Albayalde on 14 slain farmers: They "fought back" during arrest', Manila Times, 1 April 2019.
23. Anna Felicia Bajo, 'NPA recruits as young as 12 in Northern Mindanao, CARAGA – military', GMA News, 6 September 2019.
24. Department of Social Welfare and Development, Government of the Philippines, 'DSWD DROMIC Report #1 on the Armed Conflict in Manjuyod, Negros Oriental', 25 June 2019.
25. Communist Party of the Philippines, 'NPA-Quezon, Supports the People's Opposition to Kaliwa Dam Project, Vows to Launch More Tactical Offensives!', NPA statement, 10 June 2019.
26. 'Rebels threaten to halt operation of power plants in South', Mindanao Examiner, 22 August 2019.
27. Jofelle Tesorio, 'Joma Sison says summons from Manila "malicious", "futile"', ABS–CBN News, 13 February 2019.
28. Rambo Talabong, 'CPP taps students of 10 Manila universities for Red October plot – Galvez', Rappler, 6 October 2018.
29. Michael Hart, 'Collapsed Talks Lead Philippines to Seek New Approach with NPA', Asia Sentinel, 10 April 2019.

SOUTHERN THAILAND

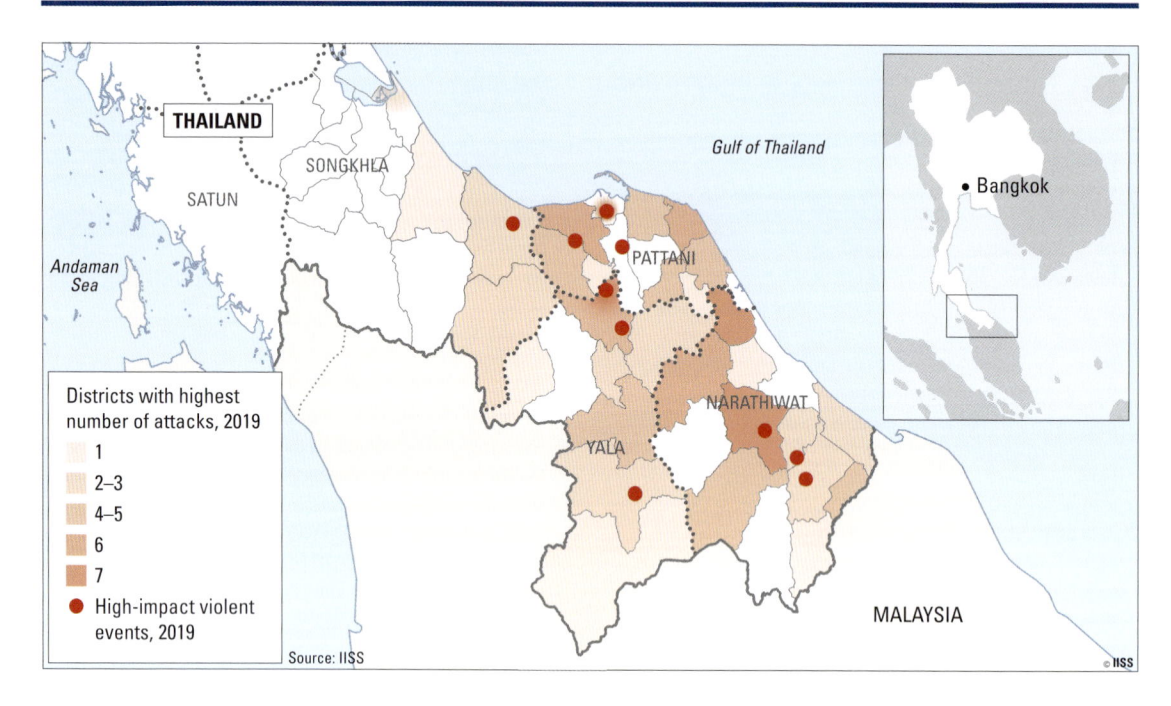

Overview

The conflict in 2019

On 5 November 2019, insurgents in Southern Thailand conducted their deadliest attack against security forces in decades, killing 15 people, including Village Defence Volunteers, police personnel and civilians, at a checkpoint in Yala province. Although there were other high-profile attacks during the year – the killing of two Buddhist monks at a temple in Narathiwat province in January and a series of small improvised explosive device (IED) attacks in Bangkok in August – the number of violent incidents remained relatively low. This was in line with the trend of decreasing attacks and fatalities since 2016.

After the March general election, incumbent Prime Minister Prayut Chan-o-cha, who led the military coup in 2014, returned to office to head a civilian administration after five years of military rule. The new government was formed with the approval of King Maha Vajiralongkorn. In the newly elected parliament, the leading opposition parties, Pheu Thai and Future Forward, strongly criticised the government, including on issues such as human rights and constitutional reforms relating to the conflict in southern Thailand. At the end of the year, Future Forward faced multiple threats of dissolution, including for allegedly planning the overthrow of the monarchy.[1]

Peace negotiations between the government and insurgent groups made little progress in 2019. However, towards the end of the year Malaysian facilitators reported that the most active insurgent group, the Barisan Revolusi Nasional (BRN), had participated in initial talks and the Thai government's new lead negotiator, Gen. Wanlop Rugsanaoh, reaffirmed efforts to end the conflict.[2]

Several high-profile incidents in 2019, including the death of a suspected insurgent in custody in August and a judge attempting suicide after

Key statistics

Type	Internal
Start date	4 January 2004
IDPs total	Not applicable
Refugees total	Not applicable
People in need	Not applicable

presiding over a case that was allegedly subject to judicial interference in October, highlighted ongoing human-rights issues and public grievances against the military. There were also several retaliatory killings targeting religious leaders and civilians on both sides of the conflict.

The conflict to 2019

The Malay ethno-nationalist insurgency and rejection of assimilation into the Thai state has driven decades of conflict in southern Thailand. An insurgent raid on an army base in Narathiwat province that killed four soldiers in January 2004 marked the beginning of the current phase of armed conflict.

Separatists seek independence for the region of the former kingdom of Patani, which spans the Thai provinces of Narathiwat, Yala and Pattani, and parts of northern Malaysia. Militant attacks peaked in May 2007, when an average of four people were killed each day.[3] There were also high levels of internal migration, particularly of Buddhist civilians, to safer areas, including Hat Yai, Songkhla province. At that time, Thai authorities began to acknowledge that the BRN was responsible for most of the violence, not the Patani United Liberation Organisation (PULO), which they previously targeted. Militant violence has disproportionately targeted Buddhist civilians, particularly monks and teachers, but has recently shifted to include Muslim civilians and local army 'collaborators', as well as security personnel and paramilitary soldiers.[4]

Two large-scale incidents in 2004 are frequently cited as motivation for insurgents resorting to violence and remain powerful rallying symbols for the insurgency: the storming of the Krue Se Mosque in April and the Tak Bai massacre in October. In the former, security forces killed 32 militants who had retreated to the mosque in Pattani. In the latter, 85 protesters were killed in Narathiwat's Tak Bai district, most of whom suffocated in lorries while being transported to detention.[5]

Militant attacks and total fatalities have declined since 2016 but in December 2018 the BRN carried out a string of IED attacks after Malaysian facilitators put pressure on its leadership to join relaunched peace negotiations.

Key Conflict Parties

Royal Thai Armed Forces, Fourth Army Region

Strength
About 58,000 regular soldiers in the conflict theatre in 2019.

Areas of operation
Headquartered in Nakhon Si Thammarat province, the Fourth Army Region is responsible for Thailand's southern region.

Leadership
Gen. Apirat Kongsompong is the commander-in-chief of the Royal Thai Army. Lt-Gen. Pornsak Poonsawat is the commander of the Fourth Army Region.

Structure
The Southern Border Provinces Administrative Centre (operating under the Ministry of Interior) oversees security and development in the region, reporting to the military-dominated Internal Security Operations Command (ISOC– operating under the Prime Minister's Office), which has extensive powers under martial law.

History
The Thai army was formed in 1874 and shaped by counter-insurgency campaigns starting in the 1960s. Since 1932, it has led 19 coups, 12 of which were successful (the last was in 2014).

Objectives
The military seeks to preserve the current political order, increasingly under the control of the monarchy. In southern Thailand, pacification is its primary goal.

Opponents
The BRN. Civil-society and rights groups criticise military actions in the region and opposition parties Pheu Thai and Future Forward reject military influence at a national level.

Affiliates/allies
The military is closely aligned with the monarchy. The ruling military-led Palang Pracharath Party leads a coalition of 19 parties and enjoys the support of the country's richest family conglomerates.

Resources/capabilities
Royal Thai Army soldiers are equipped with light arms purchased from the United States, other NATO member states and Israel. Aircraft including attack helicopters and armoured vehicles are principally sourced from the US.

Royal Thai Border Patrol Police

Strength
The number of auxiliary forces stationed in the south fluctuates. Estimated strength in 2019 was 58,000.

Areas of operation
Forces are stationed along borders across the country, including in southern Thailand, where they operate across the region.

Leadership
Police Lt-Gen. Wichit Paksa is the force's commissioner. The police and subsidiary forces are legally under the Ministry of Interior, but in practice they are subordinate to the military and the ISOC.

Structure
The police coordinate paramilitary forces including *thahan phran* (hunter/soldier) rangers and the Volunteer Defence Corps (*or sor*).

History
Formed in the 1950s with the help of the Central Intelligence Agency (CIA) and has served as a front-line force in counter-insurgency operations since. The Volunteer Defence Corps was founded in 1954.

Objectives
Trained to protect Thailand's borders against illegal entry, drug and other trafficking.

Opponents
Counter-insurgency efforts in the south are linked to drugs and weapons trafficking by criminal networks.

Affiliates/allies
Royal Thai Armed Forces.

Resources/capabilities
Paramilitary platoons have heavy-weapons teams and aerial units at the regional level. The force also received counter-insurgency training from US special forces.

Village Defence Volunteers (*chor ror bor*) and Village Protection Volunteers (*or ror bor*)

Strength
The number of auxiliary forces stationed in the south fluctuates but estimates in 2019 placed the strength at near that of conventional forces.

Areas of operation
Locally recruited to serve in their own communities.

Leadership
Village militias are commanded by officers from the police or military. Supervision is often poor.

Structure
Organised in squads of about ten volunteers stationed at village checkpoints, often alongside regular police personnel.

History
The Village Protection Volunteers was established under Queen Sirikit's direction in 2004. Original deployment plans involved recruiting 30 militia members in each village in the south.

Objectives
Militia volunteers are paid a small monthly stipend to provide local security support.

Opponents
BRN and Runda Kumpulan Kecil (RKK).

Affiliates/allies
Support military and police forces in the region.

Resources/capabilities
Volunteers are typically more lightly armed than other forces, in some cases with shotguns, and undergo about ten days of training.

The Barisan Revolusi Nasional–Coordinate (BRN–C) and its affiliate Runda Kumpulan Kecil (RKK) comprise the majority of active militants, although many identify simply as juwae (fighter). Members of the BRN are part of the Majlis Syura Patani (MARA Patani) (Patani Consultative Council) umbrella group, which has sporadically negotiated with the government since 2015. Members of PULO also are involved with MARA Patani, although the group no longer fields active militants.

Barisan Revolusi Nasional (BRN) (Patani Malay National Revolutionary Front)

Strength
Approximately 3,000.

Areas of operation
Narathiwat, Pattani and Yala provinces, as well as the four southeastern districts of Songkhla province. More infrequent attacks have targeted Bangkok and tourist centres in the south.

Leadership
The BRN is led by an executive council, known as the Dewan Pimpinan Parti. Sama-ae Kho Zari succeeded Dulloh Waemanor as secretary-general in 2019. A network of religious teachers leads the BRN–C and recruits from *pondok* Islamic religious schools.

Barisan Revolusi Nasional (BRN) (Patani Malay National Revolutionary Front)

Structure
Five organisational units covering political work and recruitment, economic and financial affairs, women's affairs, youth (*pemuda*), and the armed groups, known as the Pejuang Kemerdekaan Patani (Patani Freedom Fighters) who are organised in a loose, cell-like structure.

History
Founded in 1963 and subsequently split into the BRN–Coordinate (BRN–C), the BRN–Congress and the BRN–Ulema by 1984, the first of which is the most dominant.

Objectives
The long-term goal is the independence of the historical kingdom of Patani. The short-term tactic is to make the region ungovernable.

Opponents
Royal Thai Army, associated security forces and 'collaborators' in the region.

Affiliates/allies
Political elements of the BRN have allied with PULO and other groups under MARA Patani and previous coalitions.

Resources/capabilities
Light weapons including assault rifles such as M16s, often stolen from security forces, and small to medium-sized IEDs.

Runda Kumpulan Kecil (RKK) (Small Patrol Units)

Strength
Approximately 500.

Areas of operation
Narathiwat, Pattani and Yala provinces, as well as the four southeastern districts of Songkhla province. More infrequent attacks have targeted Bangkok and tourist centres in the south.

Leadership
The RKK is loosely organised in a cell-like structure subordinate to the BRN–C.

Structure
Organised in cell-like structure consisting of five to ten members in a village.

History
The BRN–C founded the RKK in the early 2000s and it consisted of members who had been trained in Indonesia, in most cases while studying there.

Objectives
The long-term goal is independence. The short-term tactic is to make the region ungovernable.

Opponents
Royal Thai Army, associated security forces and 'collaborators' in the region.

Affiliates/allies
Tactical arm of the BRN–C.

Resources/capabilities
Light weapons and small to medium-sized IEDs.

Drivers

Malay ethno-nationalist identity

The ethno-nationalist insurgency in southern Thailand is ideologically rooted in the historical kingdom of Patani, which was formally absorbed into the kingdom of Siam by the Anglo-Siamese Treaty of 1909. The Malay identity for the majority in the region predates the union with Siam by hundreds of years. Although data on area demographics is incomplete and undocumented cross-border migration to and from Malaysia is common, estimates in 2018 suggested that 85% of residents in Narathiwat, Pattani and Yala provinces self-identify as ethnically Malay.

Insurgent demands have traditionally centred on the establishment of an independent state in southern Thailand, although the historical kingdom of Patani also included areas of present-day Malaysia. While the pragmatic reality of establishing such a state remains questionable, the appeal continues to act as a rallying cry, with the call for an independent Patani, or 'Patani Merdeka', invoked in propaganda materials. Many southern residents, for example, wrote 'merdeka' on their ballots during the March 2019 election.[6]

Islamic religious identity is also integral to conceptions of Patani-Malay ethnicity across the region. Perceived threats to that combined identity have a strong religious dimension. As a result, policies of assimilation into 'Thai' identity involve a perceived surrender of faith, culture and ethnicity. In 2019, the targeting of Muslims and civilians by security forces – particularly a planned surveillance programme at a university, SIM card registration requirements and a DNA register for army recruits in the region – elicited numerous protests and accusations of religious discrimination.[7]

Assimilation efforts and 'Thainess'
Assimilation policies pursued by various governments in Bangkok implemented over decades, including the promotion of Buddhism as the state religion and the state-sponsored migration of Thai-Chinese to the region, have also contributed to alienation. Government school curricula have been traditionally taught in Thai rather than native Malay, holding back learning outcomes in the region[8] and fuelling resentment among local communities.

Student achievements in the south consistently fall short of national standards, with many students attending *pondok* Islamic religious schools rather than government schools. In early 2019, the Immigration Bureau targeted 600 privately run *pondok* schools for allegedly hosting foreign Muslim students and serving as recruitment centres for the insurgency.[9]

Despite some efforts by the army and the current military-led government to build relations with Muslim leaders in the region, senior leaders have reinforced the concept of 'Thainess' to define national unity, portraying themselves as protectors of Buddhism, the monarchy and a conception of citizenship based on mono-cultural traits.

Economic and political marginalisation
Insurgent spokespeople consistently cite alienation from the state and discrimination by local governments, particularly in education and employment opportunities, as reasons for their grievance. Muslim residents in the region are on average significantly poorer than Thai Buddhists in the same area and populations in nearby provinces, while Malay Muslims often refer to unemployment and other social problems as the most common drivers for joining the insurgency.[10]

Political Developments

In July 2019, incumbent Prime Minister Prayut, the former army chief who led the 2014 coup, formed a civilian government after a contested election in March, in which his pro-military Palang Pracharath Party won fewer parliamentary seats than the opposition Pheu Thai Party. Prayut's return to the premiership was accomplished only after a difficult coalition-building process, which included retroactively apportioning seats to smaller parties, which then joined the ruling coalition. The result means continuity in the security and negotiating strategies vis-à-vis the insurgency.

King Maha Vajiralongkorn affirmed his support for the government, lending legitimacy to the former coup leaders and the continuation of their security policies. In October 2019, the army filed sedition charges against six opposition leaders, including Thanathorn Juangroongruangkit, the leader of the Future Forward Party, who discussed the possibility of amending the 2017 military-sponsored constitution to devolve more powers to the region as a potential solution to the conflict in southern Thailand.[11] Army commander Gen. Apirat Kongsompong classified the discussion of

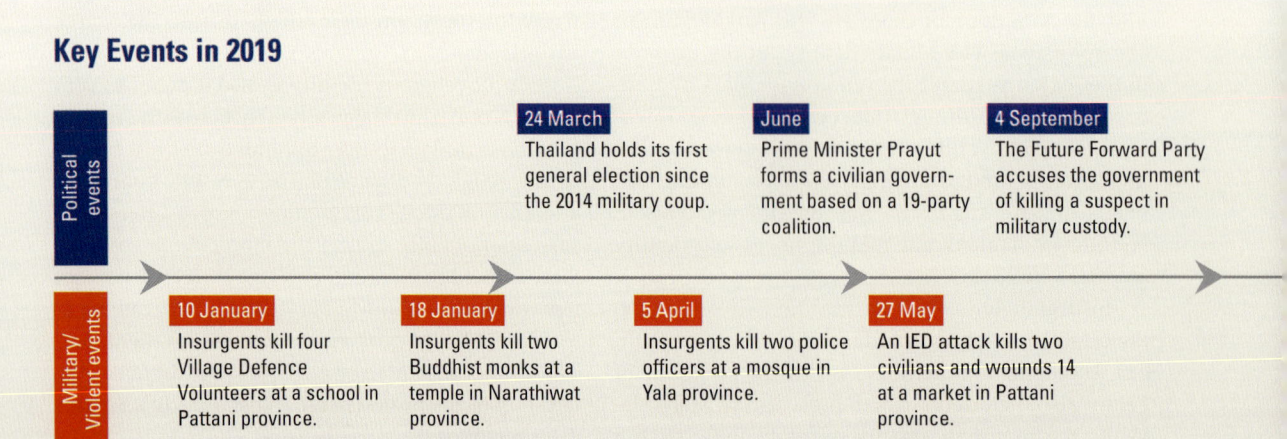

Key Events in 2019

Political events

24 March — Thailand holds its first general election since the 2014 military coup.

June — Prime Minister Prayut forms a civilian government based on a 19-party coalition.

4 September — The Future Forward Party accuses the government of killing a suspect in military custody.

Military/Violent events

10 January — Insurgents kill four Village Defence Volunteers at a school in Pattani province.

18 January — Insurgents kill two Buddhist monks at a temple in Narathiwat province.

5 April — Insurgents kill two police officers at a mosque in Yala province.

27 May — An IED attack kills two civilians and wounds 14 at a market in Pattani province.

the constitution as an attack on the monarchy and linked Thanathorn to a resurgent communist insurgency.[12] By the end of 2019, the Constitutional Court of Thailand was considering disbanding the Future Forward Party, including for allegedly trying to overthrow the monarchy.

In June, a large-scale reorganisation of the ISOC expanded the number of agencies and areas of responsibility under its purview. The new command, which assumes some of the roles of the former junta's governing body (National Council on Peace and Order), may monitor and intervene in civil society, including at the local-government level. The loosely defined 'national security' mandate grants the ISOC particularly large scope in the southern provinces under the state of emergency first implemented in 2005 and renewed every three months since then.[13]

For most of 2019, insurgent groups sent conflicting signals about their willingness to engage in the peace negotiations. In January, Sama-ae Kho Zari, a reputed hardliner, became the new secretary-general of the BRN, and is believed to have led the uptick in violence in November 2019.[14] MARA Patani chief negotiator and BRN member Sukree Hari resigned in May 2019 and later told the media that the Thai government was insincere in negotiations.[15]

At the beginning of the year, peace talks seemed likely to break down, with the BRN rejecting participation and MARA Patani's complaints, but there were signs of possible initial progress in the last few months of 2019. The outgoing chief of the Council for National Security, Gen. Wanlop Rugsanaoh, announced in September that he would assume the role of Thai chief negotiator in a relaunch of the negotiations. At the end of November, he held his first press conference to announce renewed efforts to bring the BRN to the negotiating table, although he admitted that the government did not have a new approach to the peace process.[16] Several days later, Malaysian authorities said the BRN had met Thai officials in Berlin following a series of 'back-channel' conversations.[17]

Military Developments

The relatively low level of violence continued for most of the year, although one attack in early November inflicted more casualties on government forces than any other attack in recent history. On 5 November, at least 20 insurgents ambushed two checkpoints in Sai Buri district, Pattani province, killing 15 people, including security officials, civilians and pro-government militia forces. The checkpoint was guarded mostly by locally recruited and lightly armed Village Defence Volunteers, who have been increasingly targeted because they are considered part of the state apparatus. Authorities believe the attack was in retaliation for the extrajudicial killings of two suspected insurgents in the same district two weeks prior,[18] but the attacks could also have been motivated by the death of a suspected insurgent in military custody on 25 August.

26 September
Malaysia's Prime Minister Mahathir says the Thai government will never agree to autonomy in the south.

3 October
The army files sedition charges against opposition leaders over a meeting in Pattani province.

4 October
A judge's attempted suicide in a courtroom incites calls for judicial reform.

11 October
Army chief Apirat describes the opposition as 'communists' and a threat to the monarchy.

25 December
The Constitutional Court says it will rule on the potential dissolution of the Future Forward Party on 21 January 2020.

23 July
Insurgents kill four security personnel at an outpost in Pattani province.

2 August
Eleven IEDs wound four people in Bangkok during an ASEAN summit.

5 November
Insurgents kill 15 people, including security personnel and civilians, at checkpoints in Yala.

16 December
Soldiers kill three unarmed civilians in Narathiwat province.

Figure 1: Conflicting signals: timeline of insurgent developments

Date	Description	Date	Description
16 Jan	Reputed hardliner Sama-ae Kho Zari is announced as BRN secretary-general.	17 Jul	Sukree criticises the government for failing to sign agreements and 'just pretending in negotiations, playing for time'.
23 Jan	Self-identified BRN representative 'Dr Fakis' denies the group was responsible for the killings of two monks at a temple in Narathiwat province.	16 Aug	Senior BRN member Pak Fakir says the group met a Thai delegation in the first talks since 2015, but the government declines to comment.
3 Feb	MARA Patani delays negotiations until after the March election after a perceived slight by Thai negotiators in Kuala Lumpur.	29 Nov	Thai authorities say Kho Zari was behind recent violence, including the 5 November attack that killed 15 people in Yala province.
13 Mar	BRN member Abdul Karim Khalib marks group's 59th anniversary by urging the international community to help resolve the conflict.	2 Dec	Malaysian officials tell the media that BRN representatives have met Thai government negotiators in Berlin following 'back-channel' contacts.
17 May	Chief MARA Patani negotiator and senior BRN member Sukree Hari resigns, citing his health, after rifts appear in the insurgent umbrella group.		

The 5 November attack prompted a security review by the military and a suggested strategic shift from outposts secured by Village Defence Volunteers to mobile patrols. An earlier operational shift in May showed increasing penetration of the countryside. The Fourth Army Region announced that specially trained soldiers would be stationed in villages to integrate with local communities.[19]

At the beginning of the year, suspected insurgents attacked a temple in Narathiwat province, killing two monks. The attack followed the killing of three imams earlier in January, which separatists attributed to 'a government or pro-government death squad'.[20]

Among attacks outside the traditional conflict theatre, 11 IEDs exploded in Bangkok during a high-level Association of Southeast Asian Nations (ASEAN) summit in August, wounding four people. Initially, the BRN denied responsibility but the government concluded that BRN militants were responsible and arrested suspects from Narathiwat province who reportedly confessed to the bombings. Despite these high-profile attacks in 2019, the insurgents' ability to recruit and retain *juwae* (fighters) remained relatively low.[21]

Impact

Civilian casualties and extrajudicial killings

Civilians constituted a significant number of fatalities in 2019. While perpetrators and motives were unclear in many cases, insurgents carried out attacks with a high risk of civilian casualties, such as the IED attack in May at a market in Pattani province that killed two. In December, security personnel killed three unarmed Muslim civilians in Yala after being fired upon by an unidentified group. Two soldiers were later charged with murder.

Throughout 2019, there was a pattern of underreported extrajudicial and revenge killings targeting civilians and religious figures, who are typically considered off-limit targets. In June, the military arrested a paramilitary volunteer, Abdul 'Hakeem' Darase, who, according to Human Rights Watch, killed 'a long list' of BRN supporters.[22] Police subsequently charged him with the murder of a village headman's wife in Yala province.

Human-rights implications

Allegations of human-rights abuses continued to damage the image of the security forces in 2019 and raised concerns about the rule of law in the southern region.

In June, the ISOC announced that residents in the southern provinces would have to register SIM cards with fingerprints and photographs, which civil-rights groups denounced as a violation of privacy rights. The ISOC and military officials justified the requirement as a necessary counter-terrorism measure given the use of mobile phones in IED attacks.

Abdulloh Esormusor, a suspected insurgent, died on 25 August while detained at a military camp in Pattani province. A preliminary investigation concluded that suffocation was a possible cause of death.[23] In September, Abdulloh's wife accused the military of having tortured her husband. Several days earlier, Deputy Prime Minister Prawit Wongsuwan – one of five Thai deputy prime ministers – had ruled out compensation for the family unless they could prove that he had not been involved in the insurgency. In a similar case, the Pattani provincial court ruled in March 2019 that authorities were not required to provide compensation to the families of four men killed by security personnel in 2015, despite a fact-finding commission concluding that the victims were not connected to the insurgency.

In early October, a judge acquitted five defendants of murder and then shot himself in the chest inside the courtroom. His court statement accused a regional justice chief of pressuring him to deliver guilty verdicts that could have led to death penalties for the defendants. A preliminary inquiry attributed the attempted suicide to 'personal stress' but public protest ensued, calling out the lack of judicial independence and denouncing trials against insurgent suspects as unfair.

Social
In 2019, security forces and the Immigration Bureau announced plans to review *pondok* schools for alleged connections to the insurgency. In September, a letter from the Special Branch Police emerged, requesting a university to monitor and report on Muslim students and campus activities. The police later described this as 'routine practice' for intelligence gathering.[24] After a backlash from Muslim leaders and academics, authorities dropped the request.

Discrimination against Muslims continued throughout Thailand and was often led by Buddhist organisations. In November, village residents in the northeast province of Khon Kaen voted 528 to six against registering a mosque as an official place of worship. Activists from the south travelled to Khon Kaen to campaign against the mosque. Similarly, the inclusion of Muslims in a video for the new national anthem elicited protests from Buddhist groups.[25]

Trends

Political trajectories
Military, economic and royalist elites linked to the 2014 military coup dominate the government formed in 2019, relying on the primacy of the monarchy, Buddhism and 'Thainess' for legitimacy. Army commander Apirat's allies are consolidating power in the upper ranks of the military at the expense of Prayut's faction. Ultra-royalist military elements will maintain power for the foreseeable future, regardless of Prayut's continued tenure as prime minister. The king's increasingly assertive role in governance and overt control of the military's upper echelons continue to raise doubts about the rule of law and democratic institutions. However, substantive challenges to the monarchy are unlikely.

The possible dissolution of the widely popular Future Forward Party by the Constitutional Court in early 2020 could weaken the government's legitimacy and increase the possibility of social instability, even though demonstrations and public protests have remained limited since the 2014 coup.

Conflict-related risks
Despite high-profile violent incidents over the year, 2019 continued the trend of relatively low levels of violence and fatalities compared to the peak in 2007. The BRN is still able to carry out coordinated attacks, including outside of the normal theatre of operations, but insurgent military capabilities remain weakened and unlikely to inflict the same number of casualties as a decade ago.

The military admitted security failures in 2019, such as vulnerabilities at temples and civil-defence outposts, but the regional strategy is broadly succeeding in keeping levels of violence relatively low. This trend will likely continue, although intensive security operations under martial law and the emergency decree could mobilise resistance to the military.

Prospects for peace
Declines in violence and insurgent capabilities will not lead to the long-term resolution of a conflict with century-old root causes. There has been little progress in addressing Malay Muslims' historical and contemporary grievances, while allegations of human-rights abuses continue to alienate communities in the region.

Islamophobic narratives from senior military leaders hamper long-term compromise, including limited regional autonomy or the recognition of cultural and linguistic diversity. While Thailand has not taken extreme collective-punishment actions against Muslims, there are signs of worsening ethnic and religious animosity that will further marginalise minorities, especially Muslims.

There are positive signs of willingness to engage in talks from both the government and insurgent sides. As in past efforts, however, disunity in both camps raises questions about good-faith negotiations and the durability of prospective agreements. In particular, the ability of MARA Patani and BRN negotiators to exert operational control over militants on the ground in the event of a possible settlement or ceasefire remains doubtful.

Strategic implications and global influences
Thailand's insurgency remains an ethno-nationalist conflict highly resistant to co-option by transnational jihadist movements. While Thai Muslims have been accused of promoting materials of the Islamic State, also known as ISIS or ISIL, there is no evidence that the possession or dissemination of jihadist propaganda has contributed to the insurgents' operations. The goals of gaining independence in the region, negotiating autonomy or achieving regional self-determination do not directly align with a transnational caliphate.

Across Southeast Asia, however, concerns about ISIS influence are growing following the group's setbacks in the Middle East. Malaysia, for example, has been a base for insurgent leaders and a cross-border refuge for militants. Given the continued conflict in southern Thailand and violence and discrimination against Muslims, the risk of terrorist recruitment and radicalisation will increase.

Notes

[1] 'Court to rule on Future Forward dissolution case next month', *Bangkok Post*, 26 December 2019.

[2] Noah Lee and Nisha David, 'Hardline Rebels May Join Southern Thai Peace Talks, Officials in Malaysia Say', BenarNews, 2 December 2019.

[3] Zachary Abuza, 'The Ongoing Insurgency in Southern Thailand: Trends in Violence, Counterinsurgency Operations, and the Impact of National Politics', INSS, September 2011, p. 4.

[4] John Funston, 'Conflict in Southern Thailand: Causes, Agents and Trajectory', ARC Federation Fellowship Islam, Syari'ah and Governance Background Paper Series, 2008, pp. 5–6.

[5] Human Rights Watch, 'Thailand: No Justice 10 Years After Tak Bai Killings', 25 October 2014.

[6] Don Pathan, 'Future Forward's Inroads in Thai Deep South Alarm Military, BRN', BenarNews, 17 October 2019.

[7] Nontarat Phaicharoen, 'Thai PM Defends Directive to Gather Data on Muslim Students', BenarNews, 17 September 2019.

[8] Adam Burke, Pauline Tweedie and Ora-orn Poocharoen, 'The Contested Corners of Asia: Subnational Conflict and International Development Assistance: The Case of Southern Thailand', The Asia Foundation, 2013, p. 24.

[9] Wassana Nanuam and Wassayos Ngamkham, 'Policing Islamic schools to secure the state', *Bangkok Post*, 25 February 2019.

[10] Burke, Tweedie and Poocharoen, 'The Contested Corners of Asia: Subnational Conflict and International Development Assistance: The Case of Southern Thailand', pp. 19, 28.

[11] 'Thai army charges opposition parties with sedition', *Jakarta Post*, 4 October 2019.

[12] Tappani Boonbandit, 'Apirat Revives Red Scare in Epic Rant Against Opposition', Khaosod English, 11 October 2019.

[13] 'Interview: Military Surveillance Turning Thailand into "1984"', Khaosod English, 9 October 2019.

[14] 'South peace chief wants BRN talks', *Bangkok Post*, 30 November 2019.

[15] 'Thailand: MARA Patani Negotiator Resigns from Deep South Peace Talks', BenarNews, 17 May 2019.

[16] 'Thai Peace Negotiator Predicts Change in Deep South Dialogue Partners', BenarNews, 29 November 2019.

[17] Lee and David, 'Hardline Rebels May Join Southern Thai Peace Talks, Officials in Malaysia Say'.

[18] 'Army hunts checkpoint attackers', *Bangkok Post*, 7 November 2019.

[19] 'Soldiers sent to live with local people in deep South', *Bangkok Post*, 21 May 2019.

[20] Don Pathan, 'Slaying of Buddhist Monks in Thai Deep South Jolts Nation', BenarNews, 22 January 2019.

[21] Anthony Davis, 'Despite big bangs, Thai Muslim rebels fading away', Asia Times, 11 November 2019.
[22] Sunai Phasuk, 'Notorious Militia Member Arrested in Southern Thailand', Human Rights Watch, 18 June 2019.
[23] 'Thai rebel suspect could have been suffocated, probe finds', Star, 28 July 2019.
[24] Pravit Rojanaphruk, 'Letter Shows Cops Asked University to Monitor Muslim Students', Khaosod English, 16 September 2019.
[25] '"Not enough monks" in anthem video', Bangkok Post, 22 May 2019.

3 Europe and Eurasia

Armenia–Azerbaijan (Nagorno-Karabakh) 138
Ukraine 146

Ukrainians gather outside the Presidential Office during a demonstration

Key trends

- Notwithstanding continued tensions and fighting, hostilities eased and violence declined in both conflicts compared to the previous year.

Strategic implications

- The conflict is highly detrimental to the economies of Armenia and Azerbaijan. The war in Donbas had a catastrophic impact on Ukraine's economy, compromising the ability of many Ukrainians to survive.
- The Nagorno-Karabakh conflict continued to have a significant humanitarian impact on civilians.

Prospects

- The likelihood of political dialogues towards peace remains moderate despite some positive steps in 2019 in both conflicts.
- In Nagorno-Karabakh the short- to medium-term risk of major violence is moderate.
- The conflicts receive limited international attention but foreign influence continues to have an impact. Conflict parties will need to factor in, among others, Russia–US and Russia–Turkey relations in their calculations.

Arctic Ocean
Norwegian Sea
North Sea
Atlantic Ocean
Mediterranean Sea
Black Sea
Caspian Sea
ICELAND
Reykjavik
NORWAY
Oslo
SWEDEN
Stockholm
FINLAND
Helsinki
ESTONIA
Tallinn
LATVIA
Riga
LITHUANIA
Vilnius
Kaliningrad(Russia)
RUSSIAN FEDERATION
Moscow
DENMARK
Copenhagen
UNITED KINGDOM
London
IRELAND
Dublin
NETHERLANDS
Amsterdam
BELGIUM
Brussels
LUXEMBOURG
GERMANY
Berlin
POLAND
Warsaw
BELARUS
Minsk
UKRAINE
Kiev
CZECH REP.
Prague
SLOVAKIA
Bratislava
AUSTRIA
Vienna
HUNGARY
Budapest
SWITZ.
Berne
FRANCE
Paris
SLOVENIA
Ljubljana
CROATIA
Zagreb
BiH
Sarajevo
SERBIA
Belgrade
MONTENEGRO
Podgorica
KOSOVO
N. MACED.
Skopje
ALBANIA
Tirana
GREECE
Athens
BULGARIA
Sofia
ROMANIA
Bucharest
MOLDOVA
Chisinau
ITALY
Rome
MALTA
SPAIN
Madrid
PORTUGAL
Lisbon
TURKEY
Istanbul
CYPRUS
GEORGIA
Tbilisi
ARMENIA
Yerevan
AZERBAIJAN
Baku
KAZAKHSTAN
Astana
UZBEKISTAN
Tashkent
TURKMENISTAN
Ashgabat
KYRGYZSTAN
Bishkek
TAJIKISTAN
Dushanbe

ARMENIA–AZERBAIJAN (NAGORNO-KARABAKH)

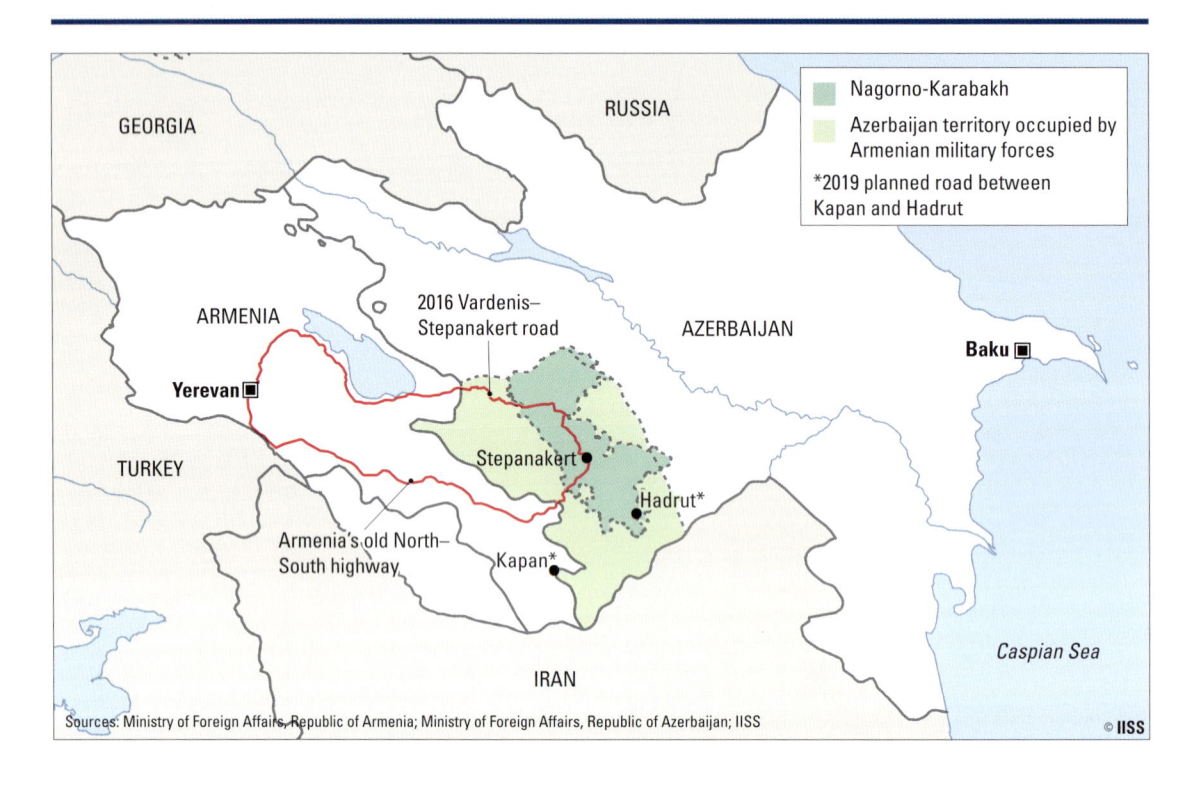

Overview

The conflict in 2019

In early 2019, hopes that Armenia's new prime minister, Nikol Pashinyan, and Azerbaijan's president, Ilham Aliyev, would find ways to reinvigorate long-stagnant negotiations fuelled anticipation of a possible shift towards de-escalating the Armenian–Azerbaijani conflict. An increased number of face-to-face meetings between senior officials in late 2018 and early 2019 resulted in limited agreements to create a communication channel between the armed forces and allow family visits to detainees. Ceasefire violations over the year were significantly fewer than in recent years and casualties due to enemy fire were among the lowest on record. Yet, by the latter half of the year, there was no indication that a revived negotiation was forthcoming, and the dynamism of earlier in the year began to dissipate. Securing domestic politics became the priority in both countries — consolidating the 'Velvet Revolution' of 2018 in Armenia and replacing 'old guard' political elites through top-down intervention in Azerbaijan.

The conflict to 2019

The Armenian–Azerbaijani conflict is a dispute over sovereignty in Nagorno-Karabakh, a mountainous area of some 4,400 square kilometres in the South Caucasus. First contested in the early twentieth century, Nagorno-Karabakh became an autonomous region in Soviet Azerbaijan in 1923, with an ethnic Armenian majority. Following the onset of Mikhail Gorbachev's perestroika policy, the Armenians of Nagorno-Karabakh mobilised in late 1987 to seek unification with Soviet Armenia. The movement was quickly radicalised by the outbreak of communal

Key statistics	
Type	Internationalised
Start date	20 February 1988
IDPs total	No data
Refugees total	No data
People in need	No data

violence between Armenians and Azerbaijanis across multiple locations from February 1988. Various efforts to contain the conflict failed during the last years of the Soviet Union's existence and large-scale hostilities followed the Soviet collapse in December 1991.

A two-year war ended in an Armenian military victory. The Russian-brokered ceasefire of 12 May 1994 left almost all of Nagorno-Karabakh under Armenian control. Armenian forces occupied a further seven districts surrounding the territory, in whole or in part. In all, some 1.2 million people — Azerbaijanis, Armenians and others — were displaced between 1988 and 1994. Many Armenian refugees resettled in Russia, with others resettling and integrating in Armenia; Azerbaijani refugees resettled in Azerbaijan, and the internally displaced population is now settled in either urban centres or newly constructed settlements across the country. In Nagorno-Karabakh, an independent republic, the Nagorno-Karabakh Republic (NKR; also known as the Artsakh Republic) was proclaimed in 1991, but to date it has not been recognised by any United Nations member state.

Unlike other post-Soviet conflicts in the 1990s, no peacekeeping forces were deployed to monitor the ceasefire along the approximately 200-km Line of Contact between Armenian and Azerbaijani forces. The Conference (later Organisation) for Security and Cooperation in Europe (CSCE/OSCE) took up the mediation of the conflict in 1992. In 1997, France, Russia and the United States were confirmed as a permanent troika leading the OSCE's Minsk Group, the body convening Armenian–Azerbaijani negotiations. While a succession of peace proposals was put forward between 1997 and 2004, none proved viable.

Key Conflict Parties

Armenian armed forces

Strength
45,000 service personnel make up a conscript force consisting of five army corps and an air force. Military service is mandatory for males between 19 and 27 years old, including dual citizens residing abroad. An increasing number of professional officers also serve.

Areas of operation
The Armenian armed forces are mainly deployed along the international border with Azerbaijan. Some 80 Armenian non-combat personnel are currently deployed in Syria in support of Russian military operations there, a signal of Armenia's continued geopolitical fidelity to Moscow.[1]

Leadership
The armed forces' commander-in-chief is Prime Minister Nikol Pashinyan, and the Minister of Defence is David Tonoyan.

Structure
Though the two structures maintain separate command chains, the Armenian army is closely integrated with the armed forces of the unrecognised Nagorno-Karabakh Republic, the Nagorno-Karabakh Defence Army.

History
Soviet Army assets and personnel located on the territory of the former Armenian Soviet Socialist Republic (ASSR) became the basis for the newly independent Republic's armed forces following the collapse of the USSR in 1991.

Objectives
The Armenian armed forces' primary objective is to secure Armenia and provide extended deterrence covering Nagorno-Karabakh and the surrounding occupied regions.

Opponents
Armed forces of Azerbaijan.

Affiliates/allies
Armenia is covered by an extended deterrent through bilateral agreements with Russia and as a founding member of the Collective Security Treaty Organisation (CSTO). The Russian military maintains a base in the western city Gyumri, close to the Turkish border, and its soldiers are also present on the Iranian border. Some 120 Armenian troops are deployed in Afghanistan with the NATO-led train, advise and assist *Resolute Support* mission.

Resources/capabilities
Although Russia has supplied large quantities of new equipment to Armenia, ageing Soviet-era systems remain in use in many units. The Azerbaijani military enjoys a clear material/numerical advantage on aggregate as a result of large-scale investment of oil and gas revenues into defence – commodities which Armenia lacks, although broad parity is observed along the theatre of the Line of Contact.

Nagorno-Karabakh Defence Army (NKDA)

Strength
The armed forces of the unrecognised Nagorno-Karabakh Republic report a strength of 18,000 to 20,000 members, though independent confirmation is unavailable.[2] Sixty-five out of every 1,000 people in Nagorno-Karabakh reportedly serve in the NKDA, the highest proportion in the South Caucasus.

Areas of operation
The NKDA is deployed in Nagorno-Karabakh and in the surrounding occupied regions, where it faces off against the opposing Azerbaijani forces.

Leadership
Despite close integration with the Armenian armed forces, the NKDA nonetheless maintains a separate operational command structure, led by Major-General Karen Abrahamyan since 2018. Its commander-in-chief is Nagorno-Karabakh's de facto president Bako Sahakyan.

Structure
The NKDA consists of a land force, air force and air-defence force.

History
Established in 1992, the NKDA united ethnic Armenian paramilitary units engaged in the conflict against Azerbaijan.

Objectives
The NKDA's primary objective is defending Nagorno-Karabakh and the surrounding territories under Armenian control against Azerbaijani forces ranged along the approximately 200-km-long Line of Contact.

Opponents
Armed forces of Azerbaijan.

Affiliates/allies
The Armenian armed forces, with whom the NKDA is closely integrated, provide the NKDA with equipment, training, personnel and logistical support.[3]

Resources/capabilities
Despite its small size, its reported level of professionalism is high, with many of its personnel experienced in insurgency tactics and capable of effectively using Nagorno-Karabakh's mountainous terrain to its advantage.

Azerbaijani armed forces

Strength
The Azerbaijani armed forces comprise 66,950 active service personnel. Military service is mandatory for able-bodied males. Upon reaching the age of 18, they must serve 18 months, or 12 months for university graduates.

Leadership
The commander-in-chief is President Ilham Aliyev. Since 2013, the Minister of Defence is Colonel-General Zakir Hasanov.

Structure
The armed forces of Azerbaijan consist of land, sea and air forces.

History
Like other post-Soviet states, Azerbaijan's armed forces were formed from the remains of the local Soviet armed forces after the USSR's collapse in 1991. Its navy was formed from the Azerbaijani fleet of the Soviet Navy stationed in the Caspian Sea.

Objectives
The primary objective of the Azerbaijani armed forces is to restore Azerbaijan's territorial integrity.

Opponents
Armed forces of Armenia, NKDA.

Affiliates/allies
Since independence, Azerbaijan's government has maintained a non-aligned foreign policy and avoided formal military alliances. Nonetheless, Turkey retains a historical role as security guarantor of Azerbaijan's Nakhichevan exclave, and the two forces cooperate closely. 120 Azerbaijani troops are deployed in Afghanistan with *Resolute Support* mission.

Resources/capabilities
Azerbaijan's armed forces have benefitted from substantial military expenditure since late 2007, and by most quantitative parameters enjoy a significant advantage over Armenia's armed forces.

Drivers

Contested borders
The root causes of the conflict lie in contested territorial allocations of the Bolshevik regime in the early 1920s, which followed a short and violent interlude of Armenian and Azerbaijani independence from 1918–20 after the collapse of the Russian Empire in 1917. The local Armenian population never accepted Nagorno-Karabakh's incorporation into Azerbaijan and periodically mobilised for unification with Armenia during Soviet rule. Soviet nationality policy encouraged the consolidation of exclusive narratives of ownership over the territory, which became mainstream in the late 1980s. The scope of territorial contestation subsequently expanded as a result of the 1992–94 war. The Armenian occupation of the territories surrounding Nagorno-Karabakh was originally conceived as a collateral war gain but became a deep-rooted claim with the construction of infrastructure in those territories, such as roads connecting Armenia and urban centres in Nagorno-Karabakh, and limited, but still politically significant, settlements.[4]

Hybrid regimes

Following the end of communist rule, hybrid regime types appeared in both Armenia and Azerbaijan (rather than the expected democratic transitions). While the new leaders exercised enough control over the electoral process to be able to extend their incumbency, they were not sufficiently dominant to enforce a controversial compromise with the rival nation. The 1994 military victory became the anchor of the Armenian political elite's legitimacy from 1998 to 2018. Natives of Nagorno-Karabakh held the presidency over this period, retaining close ties both with clients in the territory and with Russia, networked through patronage ties transcending *de jure*/de facto borders. The conflict remained a highly emotive issue in Azerbaijan as well, largely beyond the control of the state, even under more consolidated authoritarian rule than in Armenia. From the early 2000s, public discussion of peace proposals declined and nationalist rhetoric increasingly dominated the discourse on the conflict in both countries.

Regional and international diffusion

The Armenian–Azerbaijani conflict has implications for an exceptionally wide range of regional and global actors. A complex network of international partnerships creates both disincentives for escalation and a tendency to de-prioritise the resolution of this conflict (vis-à-vis other higher-order strategic interests). Armenia is formally allied with Russia and is protected by Russian extended deterrence through a number of bilateral treaties. It is also a member of Russian-led security and economic blocs the CSTO and Eurasian Economic Union (EAEU). Azerbaijan avoids formal alignment, but has a close historical, cultural and geostrategic relationship with Turkey. Turkey in turn has a conflicted historical relationship with Armenia and closed the briefly opened Turkish–Armenian border in 1993 in protest at Armenian military operations during the war with Azerbaijan. Russia is also Azerbaijan's principal arms supplier and seeks partnership with it in regional infrastructure projects. The OSCE's Minsk Group is one of the few world forums where Russian and Euro-Atlantic interests are aligned in the prevention of renewed war.

Political Developments

Following the 'Velvet Revolution' in 2018, the new Armenian political elite's primary challenge was to consolidate Armenia's democratic transition while simultaneously preventing the regrouping of the former regime, associated with the Republican Party of Armenia (RPA) and with figures central to the military victory in 1994. Armenia's new leadership balanced the projection of a more conciliatory stance in the negotiations with Baku with more populist rhetoric upholding the Armenian claim to the unrecognised republic Nagorno-Karabakh. Prime Minister Nikol Pashinyan's visit to Nagorno-Karabakh in August 2019 exposed this contradiction. Pashinyan reasserted the unity of Armenia and Karabakh during a speech in the capital Stepanakert (Khankendi in Azerbaijani), and led crowds in chants of *miatsum*, a rallying cry dating from 1988 meaning 'unification' in Armenian. This public display undercut a putative commitment to a vote on the final status of the territory, a key element in the 'Basic Principles' under negotiation since the mid-2000s.[5]

Azerbaijan denounced Pashinyan's speech as an indication of Armenian insincerity, and as a contradiction to Armenians' core demand that Nagorno-Karabakh represent itself at the negotiating table.

Azerbaijan has engaged in a faltering effort to reform its economy and diversify away from its reliance on oil and gas. Progress, however, has been halting and the country struggles with high inflation and persistent unemployment. Pre-empting public discontent – expressed in rare public protests in October 2019 – appeared to be the aim behind a series of dismissals of unpopular long-serving officials and their replacement with younger technocratic figures. These included the influential Head of the Presidential Administration, Ramiz Mehdiyev, a key figure in Azerbaijan's 'old guard'. These changes demonstrated the priority of regime security, and suggest that during this sensitive period of renewing and consolidating power there will be little scope for innovation in the negotiations process.

On 29 October 2019, the US House of Representatives recognised the First World War mass extermination of Armenians in the Ottoman Empire as a genocide. While this was an indirect outcome of deteriorating US–Turkey relations after Turkey's invasion of northern Syria, it also validated the many years of intense lobbying by Armenian-American diaspora communities. Similar campaigns are pursued by Armenian-American communities for the recognition of Nagorno-Karabakh's independence, and by Azerbaijanis for the recognition of a 1992 massacre of Azerbaijani civilians near the town of Khojaly in Nagorno-Karabakh as an act of genocide.

Military Developments

Reflecting the softened rhetoric at the beginning of the year, 2019 was significantly quieter than preceding years in terms of incidents and casualties along the Line of Contact. Particularly over the first six months of the year, the Line of Contact and the international border between Armenia and Azerbaijan were exceptionally calm.

Following deteriorating attitudes towards the peace process by mid-year, the second half of 2019 saw a slight increase in ceasefire violations, although not on the scale of recent years. There were shooting incidents in the Tavush/Tovuz area of the international border in late July and October, killing at least two, and in September, for the first time since early 2017, an Azerbaijani incursion crossed the Line of Contact. One Azerbaijani soldier – reportedly in special-forces uniform – was killed. The incident may have been related to a scheduled meeting of the Armenian and Azerbaijani foreign ministers in New York the following day. Nevertheless, four Armenian and nine Azerbaijani servicemen were reported killed in action over the year.[6]

Both Armenia and Azerbaijan continued to invest heavily in defence. Armenia's defence expenditure continued an upward trend to reach US$644m in 2019. Salaries of armed forces personnel were increased by 10%.[7] In October, Yerevan declared that this level of spending would be maintained, with the 2020 defence budget announced at US$625m.[8] In February, the Armenian authorities confirmed the purchase of four Su-30SM *Flanker-H* fighters from Russia.

Azerbaijan's military spending in 2019 was around US$1.79 billion, approximately 2.8 times

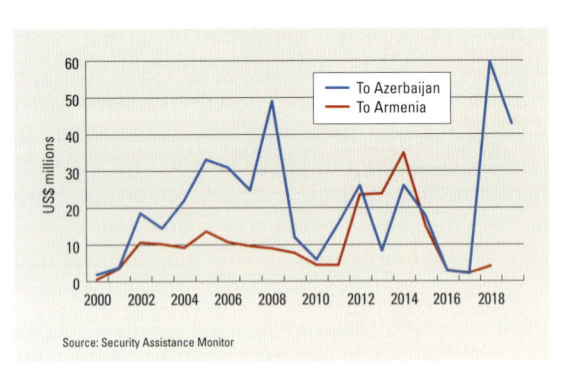

Figure 1: Security assistance from all US funding departments, 2000–19

Key Events in 2019

Political events

16 January — Armenian and Azerbaijani foreign ministers meet in Paris and reportedly agree on the necessity of preparing their populations for peace.

5 February — For the first time in several years, a journalist from one country visits the other.

29 March — Pashinyan and Aliyev meet in Vienna and commit to strengthening the ceasefire and to humanitarian cooperation.

26 July — Armenia announces the construction of a new road from Kapan in Armenia to Hadrut in Nagorno-Karabakh.

Military/Violent events

30 May–1 June — Tensions rise as each side reports servicemen killed in action.

that of Armenia. Though the overall number of ceasefire violations fell in 2019 as a result of thawing tensions at the diplomatic level, Azerbaijan's efforts to put Armenia under pressure by expanding the battlespace beyond Nagorno-Karabakh continued. This strategy was evident in the continued ceasefire violations on Armenian-held territory around the Nakhichevan exclave and along the international border. In October, Azerbaijan announced that its 2020 defence budget would be US$2.3bn, a 28% increase from 2019, suggesting the purchase of significant hardware. In addition, Azerbaijan became the third-largest recipient of US military aid after Lebanon and Jordan, with a dramatic increase to more than US$100m in assistance for fiscal years 2018 and 2019, directed at improving border control, customs offices and maritime security.[9] Conversely, US military aid to Armenia has fallen, at less than US$10m in assistance over the same period.

In September, extensive military exercises took place in Nagorno-Karabakh, reportedly involving the largest ever call-up of the territory's reserve forces. While basic conditions in the militaries across the conflict have improved, non-combat-related incidents still account for significant numbers of deaths – in 2019, considerably more than those killed in action. Armenian non-governmental organisation Peace Dialogue recorded 45 such cases in Armenia and Nagorno-Karabakh in 2019.[10] Comparable data for Azerbaijan is elusive, but 15 such cases were reported for the year to July – although the actual figure is likely to be higher.[11]

Impact

Human rights

In September, an Azerbaijani offer to exchange two of their citizens detained in Nagorno-Karabakh for two Armenians held by Azerbaijan was discussed under the auspices of the OSCE. The proposal was rejected by Armenia, however, on the basis that the two imprisoned Azerbaijanis had murdered a civilian. Though the total number of detainees held in relation to the conflict is small – three Armenians held in Azerbaijan, one Azerbaijani in Armenia and two others in Nagorno-Karabakh – such a transfer would address a pressing humanitarian issue and, as the first such operation since the 1990s, foster mutual trust.

Humanitarian

The conflict continues to have a significant humanitarian impact on civilians on all sides. In October, a construction worker was killed by shelling in Azerbaijan's northern Qazakh region. There were no reports of civilian casualties on the Armenian side in 2019, but shelling, shooting and landmines and unexploded ordnance cause direct and indirect physical, psychological, social and economic harm to civilians on all sides. Nearly 60% of landmine victims recorded in Nagorno-Karabakh are civilians.[12] For civilians living close to the Line of Contact, freedom of movement is hampered, access to pasture land and markets is restricted, and

5 August — Pashinyan calls for reunification and leads crowds in chants of *miatsum* at a ceremony in Nagorno-Karabakh.

13 August — Ceasefire violations are reported, resulting in wounded servicemen, in Tavush/Tovuz, Gegharkunik and Nakhichevan.

16 October — Aliyev announces the resignation of the Head of the Presidential Administration, Ramiz Mehdiyev.

22 September — An Azerbaijani incursion across the Line of Contact leads to one serviceman's death.

19–20 October — Small-scale protests, against the Azerbaijani government and domestic violence against women, are dispersed by security forces.

29 October — The US House of Representatives recognises the Armenian genocide in a bipartisan vote of 405 to 11.

17–19 November — Reciprocal visits by Armenian and Azerbaijani journalists take place for the first time in a decade.

provision of basic services such as healthcare and education is generally limited.

The deaths of two Karabakh Azerbaijanis as a result of a fire in communal block housing for internally displaced persons (IDPs) in Baku highlighted the precarious conditions in which many continue to live, more than 30 years on from the start of the fighting.[13] This followed a similar incident in 2018 which left dozens of displaced families homeless.[14]

Social
Whereas until the mid-2000s cross-conflict contact was regular, 'people-to-people' contact declined with the intensification of military build-up and escalatory dynamics after 2008. The societies have had both less contact with one another and more exposure to mutually exclusive narratives of conflict and identity. In 2019, for the first time in many years, journalists of each nationality visited the other country, and at least one ethnic Armenian analyst visited Azerbaijan.

Economic
The conflict continues to inhibit the economic development of both Armenia and Azerbaijan due to the need to divert significant resources to defence. An influential study on the potential economic benefits of a peaceful resolution to the Nagorno-Karabakh conflict calculated that achieving peace would permit Armenia and Azerbaijan to reduce their military spending by as much as 2% of annual GDP each. Potential for substantial further long-term gains exists in other sectors such as finance, water (particularly for Azerbaijan) and electricity (particularly for Armenia).[15]

Trends

Political trends
The primary dynamics of the Armenian–Azerbaijani conflict are domestic. In the short term, in both Armenia and Azerbaijan, domestic politics will limit the attention devoted to conflict resolution and further negotiations. In Armenia, the domestic priority will remain to consolidate the Velvet Revolution against the threat of backtracking under the influence of figures associated with the former regime, their Russian patrons and their clients in Nagorno-Karabakh. De facto presidential and parliamentary elections in the territory in mid-2020 will have a significant impact on Armenia's wider trajectory. If associates of the former RPA regime in Armenia win elections in Nagorno-Karabakh, this could strengthen authoritarian reserves across both spaces, whereas if a modernising candidate wins this will strengthen Nikol Pashinyan. The Azerbaijan ruling elite will continue to focus on consolidating its power and containing the threat of popular mobilisation, while simultaneously seeking to diversify the economy.

Conflict-related risks
Although both countries announced substantial defence budgets for 2020, confirming the uninterrupted military competition, the short- to medium-term risk of major violence is moderate. Relative equilibrium, punctuated by occasional escalatory incidents along the Line of Contact involving small-force incursions and uninhabited aerial vehicles (UAVs), is the likely trend. Formal agreements reached in May 2016, on the expansion of resources allocated to the OSCE monitoring mission and the introduction of an incident-investigation mechanism, will likely remain unimplemented.

Prospects for peace
The prospects for progress in the negotiations are limited. There is little appetite to reinvigorate negotiations based on the 'Basic Principles', yet the elaboration of alternatives remains hindered by disagreement on the format of the talks. Elite turnover has introduced a number of figures into the Armenian government with experience of informal dialogue with Azerbaijanis. Turnover in Azerbaijan meanwhile has promoted a number of technocrats, rather than ideologues, tasked with diversifying the economy. The adoption of a serious reform programme in Azerbaijan could create mutual incentives across the conflict to avoid escalation. Yet attempts to establish a denser infrastructure for dialogue beyond the executive leaders and foreign ministers will have to overcome a high degree of inertia, due to decades-long top-down negotiations.

Global and strategic implications

Regionally and globally, the policy attention devoted to the Armenian–Azerbaijani conflict will remain both limited and mediated by other policy priorities. The ongoing Syrian crisis and US–Iranian relations will continue to have tangential impacts on Armenia and Azerbaijan. The detente in Syria between Russia and Turkey, two states traditionally considered patrons to Armenia and Azerbaijan respectively, strengthens a crucial restraint on escalation in Nagorno-Karabakh. By the same token, deteriorating Russian–Turkish relations would negatively affect the conflict. US–Iranian tensions tend to benefit Azerbaijan, which is able to present itself as an American ally in harm's way and translate that position into US assistance.

Notes

[1] Joshua Kucera, 'US rebukes Armenia over Syria deployment', Eurasianet, 14 February 2019.

[2] C. W. Blandy, 'Azerbaijan: Is war over Nagorny Karabakh a realistic option?', Conflict Studies Research Centre Caucasus Series 08/17, Defence Academy of the United Kingdom, May 2008, p. 14.

[3] Ron Synovitz, '"Open Secret": Experts Cast Doubt on Yerevan's Claims over Nagorno-Karabakh', Radio Free Europe/Radio Liberty, 5 April 2016.

[4] Numbers of settlers are exaggerated on all sides. Yet even demographically limited settlement poses the problem of either relocating settler communities in the event of an agreement which envisages the return of displaced communities, or long-term reconciliation processes between the two populations.

[5] See Conciliation Resources, 'A Final Status Vote for Nagorny Karabakh: Choosing Politics?', May 2018.

[6] '2019 Ends as Most Peaceful Year in 25 Years of Ceasefire', University of Southern California Dornsife Institute of Armenian Studies, 31 December 2019.

[7] 'Armenian Government Plans Further Rise in Public Spending', Radio Free Europe/Radio Liberty Armenian Service, 30 September 2019.

[8] 'Armenia government approves defense budget for 2020', Panarmenian.net, 1 October 2019.

[9] Emil Sanamyan, 'US Allocates $100 million in Security Aid to Azerbaijan in 2018–19', University of Southern California Dornsife Institute of Armenian Studies, 17 July 2019.

[10] Peace Dialogue, 'Safe Soldiers for a Safe Armenia'.

[11] Caucasian Knot, 'CDSI reports 20 perished Azerbaijani soldiers in 2019', 23 July 2019.

[12] International Committee of the Red Cross, 'Nagorno-Karabakh conflict: Landmines, a disturbing reminder of war', 31 May 2019.

[13] 'Two Karabakh refugees killed in Baku communal housing fire', JAM News, 7 March 2019.

[14] 'Fire in Baku leaves 46 IDP families homeless', JAM News, 15 November 2019.

[15] Berlin Economics, 'The economic effect of a resolution of the Nagorno-Karabakh conflict on Armenia and Azerbaijan', June 2018.

UKRAINE

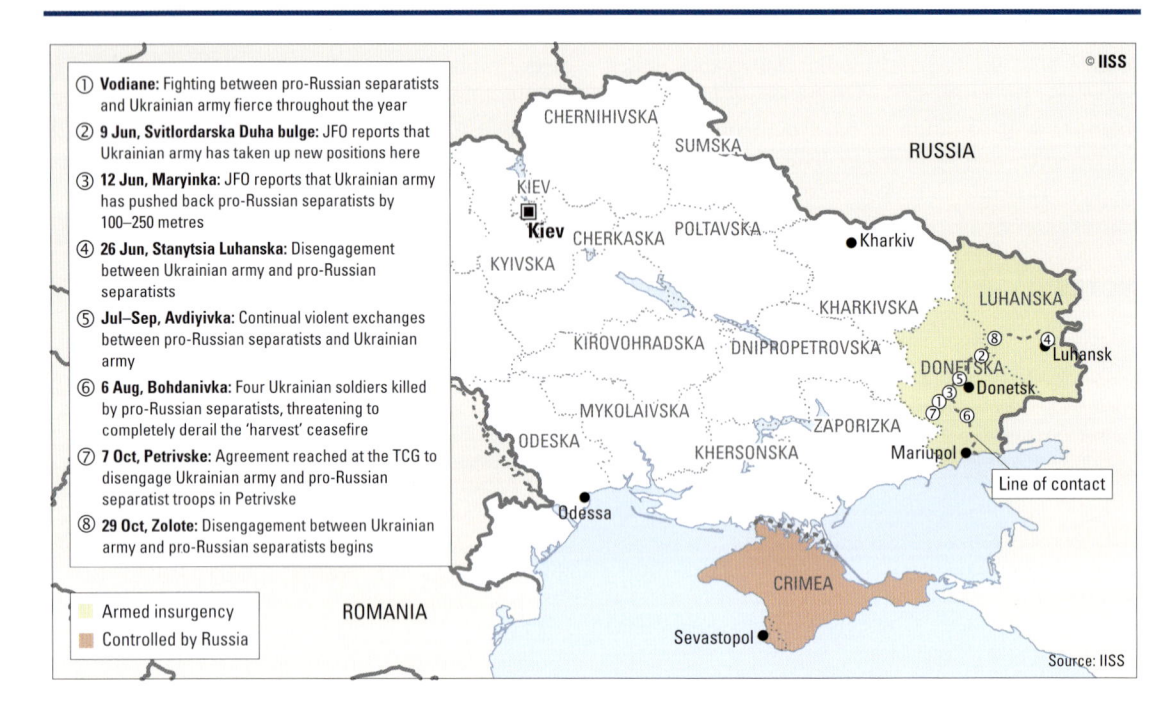

Map legend:
1. **Vodiane:** Fighting between pro-Russian separatists and Ukrainian army fierce throughout the year
2. **9 Jun, Svitlordarska Duha bulge:** JFO reports that Ukrainian army has taken up new positions here
3. **12 Jun, Maryinka:** JFO reports that Ukrainian army has pushed back pro-Russian separatists by 100–250 metres
4. **26 Jun, Stanytsia Luhanska:** Disengagement between Ukrainian army and pro-Russian separatists
5. **Jul–Sep, Avdiyivka:** Continual violent exchanges between pro-Russian separatists and Ukrainian army
6. **6 Aug, Bohdanivka:** Four Ukrainian soldiers killed by pro-Russian separatists, threatening to completely derail the 'harvest' ceasefire
7. **7 Oct, Petrivske:** Agreement reached at the TCG to disengage Ukrainian army and pro-Russian separatist troops in Petrivske
8. **29 Oct, Zolote:** Disengagement between Ukrainian army and pro-Russian separatists begins

- Armed insurgency
- Controlled by Russia

Overview

The conflict in 2019

Following the collapse of the New Year's ceasefire early in 2019, the war in the Donbas region continued, with daily engagements between the Ukrainian armed forces and pro-Russian separatists across the 500-kilometre contact line. Tensions increased at the start of the year during the electoral campaign, with then-president Petro Poroshenko implicated in a money-laundering scandal and promising the end of the war using hyper-nationalistic rhetoric.

Former comedian Volodymyr Zelensky was elected president in April with 73% of the vote. He promised to pursue a quick peace and to engage with Russia to de-escalate the conflict. However, Zelensky faced several domestic and international political crises that took his attention away from the war in Donbas. Although conflict continued throughout 2019, there were some periods of reprieve, and the harvest, Easter and holiday ceasefires all had varying degrees of success.

Despite the challenges facing the new president, there were some positive signs in the peace process. Limited demobilisation of troops from both sides of the conflict took place in the towns of Petrivske and Zolote, Donetsk oblast, and Stanytsia Luhanska, Luhansk oblast. Two significant exchanges of prisoners between the Ukrainian armed forces and separatists also took place in early September and late December. Zelensky progressed some aspects of the Minsk peace process, particularly in relation to prisoner exchanges (Article 6 of Minsk II), and his government began drafting an interpretation of the 'Steinmeier formula', designed to grant Donetsk and Luhansk some political autonomy in order to resolve the conflict. Finally, the 'Normandy Four' (France, Germany, Russia and Ukraine) met on 9 December, the first meeting of this group since October 2016,

Key statistics

Type	Internationalised
Start date	March 2014
IDPs total	No data
Refugees total	Not applicable
People in need (31 December 2019)	3,400,000

The conflict to 2019

The war between the Ukrainian armed forces and pro-Russian separatists began in 2014 in the Donbas area of eastern Ukraine, including the Donetsk and Luhansk regions. Protesters and activists seized government-controlled buildings following the removal of Viktor Yanukovych's government in February 2014 and proclaimed the Donetsk and Luhansk 'people's republics' (DPR/LPR). The Ukrainian army, with significant support from volunteer battalions recruited from nationalist and far-right protesters who had previously been involved in the 2013–14 'Revolution of Dignity' (Maidan Revolution), mobilised to engage with the pro-Russian separatists in the east. Concurrently, Russian troops without insignia were deployed throughout strategic points in the Ukrainian Crimean Peninsula on 27 February. The Crimean parliament held a referendum on 16 March that allegedly demonstrated overwhelming support for Russian accession by the Crimean people, though the conduct of the referendum was widely criticised by foreign governments. Russia formally annexed Crimea on 18 March 2014.

There have been accusations of foreign meddling on both sides throughout the conflict, most prominently Russia's support for the separatists in Donbas. There is evidence that Russia – particularly early in the conflict – provided military equipment and funding and allowed Russian volunteers to enter the Donbas region. The relationship between Russia and the pro-Russian separatists has been evolving and complex, with varying degrees of separation between these entities. Similarly, the European Union and United States have supported the Ukrainian armed forces throughout the conflict, providing training, military hardware and other assistance, with some of this aid going to far-right volunteer battalions.

Ukraine has depicted the conflict as an attempt to liberate its territories from Russian aggression, while the pro-Russian separatists have argued that they are protecting their citizens from 'fascists' in Kiev. Following early and violent exchanges between the two sides, the conflict has settled into daily exchanges of fire between the two sides across the contact line.

and issued a joint communiqué reporting some progress in important areas.

Key Conflict Parties

Ukrainian armed forces

Strength
Approximately 209,000 active military personnel in 2019, including 145,000 in the army, 45,000 in the air force and 11,000 in the navy. In August 2019 it was reported that 21,000 Ukrainians had been accepted for military service in 2019.[1]

Areas of operation
500-km contact line in the Donbas region of Ukraine.

Leadership
On 5 August 2019, President Volodymyr Zelensky appointed General Volodymyr Kravchenko as Commander of the Joint Forces in Donbas.[2]

History
Severely underprepared at the start of the conflict, the Ukrainian armed forces have undergone a significant modernisation process since 2014, mobilising a large army with advanced equipment.

Objectives
A strategy of slow gain across the Line of Contact, with 24km² of territory reportedly regained between 2018 and 2019.[3]

Opponents
Donetsk People's Republic (DPR), Luhansk People's Republic (LPR).

Affiliates/allies
US, EU, Poland.

Resources/capabilities
Ukraine spent US$2.4 billion on defence in 2013, US$2.8bn in 2017 and US$3.2bn in 2018, purchasing a large quantity of advanced military equipment including 71 fully functioning fourth-generation fighters (Su-27s and MiG-29s). The Ukrainian air force has 336 aircraft recorded, and three uninhabited aerial vehicles (UAVs). The Ukrainian army has 500 anti-tank units, 3,315 armoured fighting vehicles and 1,888 artillery pieces, which include the 155-mm self-propelled howitzer *Bogdana* and the *Vilkha* missile system, as well as *Javelin* anti-tank missiles.

Donetsk People's Republic (DPR)

Strength
Troop numbers are estimated at around 20,000 active personnel with a pool of volunteer reserves as high as 40,000, with approximately 4,000 Russian volunteers.[4]

Areas of operation
Across the contact line in the Donetsk region.

Leadership
Led by Denis Pushilin since election on 11 November 2018.

Structure
The DPR has sought to demonstrate that it can perform governmental functions in the occupied territories, and originally formed 16 specialised committees tasked with working on bills. Its parliamentary body, the People's Council, consists of various committees that hold working sessions on a semi-regular basis, to which representatives of the ministries of the DPR and experts are invited. There are also more localised governmental bodies under the People's Council, such as city administrators and 'local Soviets', which are locally based governance groups of workers, bureaucrats and government officials. The DPR has drawn up a constitution, issued its own vehicle number plates, changed the currency to the Russian rouble from the Ukrainian hryvnia and instituted Russian as the official regional language. Since 2014, the multiple militias operating across Donetsk have gradually been integrated into a main DPR force.

History
Formed by the protesters and volunteers of the 'Euromaidan' protests across Donetsk in 2014, who proclaimed the DPR in June 2014 after seizing government buildings and assets.

Objectives
The DPR has changed strategy throughout the conflict but hopes to achieve autonomy for the Donetsk region by breaking away from Kiev, either becoming a province of Russia or an independent state.

Opponents
Ukrainian armed forces.

Affiliates/allies
LPR, Russia.

Resources/capabilities
Difficult to ascertain, though much equipment was captured from Ukrainian forces and shipped from Russia.

Luhansk People's Republic (LPR)

Strength
Troops are concentrated in disparate groups and numbers are difficult to estimate, with the most recent estimate putting overall numbers at 14,000.

Areas of operation
Across the contact line, particularly in the Luhansk region.

Leadership
Leonid Pasechnik has led the LPR since local elections on 11 November 2018.

Structure
The LPR appears to be less centralised than the DPR, with several armed groups retaining power in various parts of the occupied Luhansk territory. This has tended to promote power struggles at the local level against various factions, such as an alleged coup against previous LPR leader Igor Plotnitsky in September 2016, when Gennady Tsypkalov, who briefly served as head of the LPR in May 2014, was arrested, along with Alexei Karyakin (former head of parliament) and Igor Kornet (former interior minister). In November 2017, Plotnitsky had attempted to dismiss a local commander from the LPR, but loyal troops joined a coup attempt against him, which eventually led to the appointment of Pasechnik as acting leader (previously the LPR's security minister) until confirmed in elections a year later.

History
See DPR.

Objectives
Difficult to ascertain, as different military sub-groups have different priorities. Attempts to unite some groups under one council were made in 2019.[5]

Opponents
Ukrainian armed forces.

Affiliates/allies
DPR, Russia.

Resources/capabilities
Difficult to estimate, but there are reports that the DPR has Russian-made munitions, uniforms, communication and signals equipment, and reconnaissance UAVs.

Pro-Kiev paramilitaries

Strength
Disparate groups including Azov, Dnipro and Donbas battalions. With reintegration of many of these into the Ukrainian armed forces, approximately 1,000–2,000 volunteers remain.

Areas of operation
Azov battalion active in Zolote.

Leadership
Arsen Avakov, Ukraine's interior minister, controls the Azov battalion, and Igor Kolomoisky controls the Dnipro battalion.

History
Volunteer battalions were formed following the Maidan Revolution to mobilise against pro-Russian separatists in the east.

Opponents
DPR, LPR.

Affiliates/allies
Ukrainian armed forces.

Drivers

Inequality, corruption and economic stagnation
Popular protests erupted throughout Ukraine at the end of 2013. Opposition to corruption, political nepotism, declining standards of living, increasing inequality and arguably the pivot towards Russia by the Yanukovych presidency fuelled the Maidan Revolution. Social, political and economic inequalities were the main drivers of the protests, along with desire for greater integration with the EU. Yanukovych fled the country in early 2014 and a coalition of two opposition parties, Batkivshchyna (Fatherland) and the far-right Svoboda, formed the post-Maidan government. Escalating protests and seizures of government buildings in the Donbas region echoed the tactics of the Maidan protesters. However, these protests coalesced into a separatist movement supported by Russia and fuelled by ethno-nationalist tensions, language and religious differences, anger at the way in which Yanukovych's government was deposed, and an increasingly poor economic outlook.

The new Ukrainian government mobilised the depleted Ukrainian army and nationalist volunteers from the Maidan Revolution to counter the rising threat from pro-Russian separatists in the east. The blockade of the Donbas territories by the Ukrainian government, as well as the difficulties created for Ukrainians living in non-government-controlled areas in collecting social benefits, has fostered increased disillusionment and anger with Kiev. Rising food prices, violent attacks, poor social services and degrading infrastructure in both government-controlled and non-government-controlled areas is fuelling discontent among Donbas residents.

Ukrainian nationalism
Some observers attribute the continuation of the conflict to a 'monist' interpretation of Ukrainian nationalism – a 'naturalistic, historicist and restitutive narrative of Ukrainian statehood, that sees Ukraine as finally coming together after the deviations of history', as a society bound by 'blood' and 'nation', constructed against an 'other'.[6] Russia has increasingly been constructed as this other since the late 1990s and early 2000s, as economic crises gripped the country and nationalist ideologies came to the fore. Russia has been framed as a historical aggressor to Ukrainian sovereignty, and the prevailing notion that it is supporting the pro-Russian separatists in the war in Donbas has helped further drive the violent reaction from Kiev.

Language
Political conflicts centred around language have occurred since independence. Ukraine's first president, Leonid Kravchuk, often depicted Russian speakers as 'traitors', while Leonid Kuchma informally decentralised language policy to facilitate the coexistence of Russian and Ukrainian. Viktor Yushchenko also attempted to promote the Ukrainian language at the expense of Russian. In 2012, Yanukovych supported the Kolesnichenko–Kivalov language law, which allowed any local language spoken by 10% of the population to be declared official within that region. As a result, 13 of Ukraine's 27 regions adopted Russian as a second official language. The post-Maidan government voided this law and Poroshenko made Ukrainian the language for all 'public life' in 2019.

Language politics are central to Ukraine's national elites but have contributed to deepening divisions between the east and west of the country. Indeed, instituting the Ukrainian language (or not, such as in the non-government-controlled areas) has become momentous both politically and symbolically. This has led to ramifications with Ukraine's close neighbours, such as Hungary but especially Russia. Both countries have objected to the treatment of minority languages in Ukraine on the world stage, despite a widespread practice of 'non-accommodating bilingualism', by which most people speak the language they prefer, Ukrainian or Russian.

Geopolitics
The conflict in Donbas has been construed as a new geopolitical power play between the West (primarily the US and EU) and Russia. Ukraine's location between the EU and Russia has indeed been a factor in prolonging the war and the economic crisis but depicting Russia as the only driving force is too simplistic. The Euromaidan protests were sparked by dissatisfaction with Yanukovych, but the international media characterised them as 'Euromaidan', with desire for greater integration with the EU a central cause.

Political Developments

Presidential and parliamentary elections
Following a tense and divisive political campaign, Zelensky won the presidential election on 21 April 2019, defeating incumbent Poroshenko with 73% of the vote (Poroshenko won 24%). Poroshenko portrayed himself as a 'strong man' who could defeat the pro-Russian separatists in the east, after introducing martial law across Ukraine at the end of 2018 in response to the Kerch Strait closure. He was also accused, together with top army officials, of accepting kickbacks for obtaining contraband military parts at inflated prices. An attempt to impeach him failed, but his popularity plummeted nonetheless, after mass protests in Kiev.

Zelensky's election raised hopes of a political solution to the war in Donbas. However, his tenure has so far faced significant political disruptions. The day after his inauguration on 21 May, he issued a decree to dissolve the Verkhovna Rada (parliament), which was unsuccessfully challenged in the Constitutional Court. Snap parliamentary elections on 21 July gave Zelensky's party, the Servant of the People, 254 of 424 seats – the first single-party majority in independent Ukraine. Despite some signs of progress, other international and domestic political roadblocks have hampered Zelensky's ability to move the peace process forward.

Russia–Ukraine tensions
Relations between Russia and Ukraine continued to deteriorate throughout 2019. On 24 April, Russian President Vladimir Putin signed a decree allowing residents in the areas of Donbas not under Ukrainian government control to apply for Russian citizenship through a simplified procedure, which resulted in approximately 40,000 applications for Russian passports. The move followed the planned passage of a draft law on 25 April in the Verkhovna Rada, which

Key Events in 2019

Political events

26 February — Members of the Verkhovna Rada initiate an ultimately unsuccessful impeachment proceeding against President Poroshenko over a report implicating him in money-laundering around military sales.

1 April — The Friendship Treaty between Ukraine and Russia expires.

20 May — Volodymyr Zelensky is inaugurated as president. He dissolves the national parliament, triggering new elections on 21 July, which his party wins with 43% of the vote.

11 July — President Zelensky speaks on the phone to Russian President Vladimir Putin for the first time.

Military/Violent events

23 January — A member of the Ukrainian army's 79th Air Assault Brigade is captured by the DPR.

23 February — A civilian minibus travelling across the 'grey zone' is destroyed by a landmine. Two passengers are killed.

7 March — The 'holiday' ceasefire is agreed at the TCG meeting and comes into effect at 12.00am on 8 March.

5 June — The TCG agrees on a limited disengagement of Ukrainian and pro-Russian separatist forces at Stanytsia Luhanska checkpoint, Luhansk region.

stipulated the mandatory use of the Ukrainian language by government agencies, self-governing areas and other spheres of public life.[7] Poroshenko signed the draft law into official legislation on 15 May, despite condemnations by the Russian and Hungarian governments.

On 25 May 2019, the UN International Tribunal for the Law of the Sea ruled that Russia must release three Ukrainian vessels and 24 Ukrainian sailors captured in November 2018. Tensions spiked again in June 2019 after international investigators named three Russians and one Ukrainian as responsible for the downing of Malaysian Airlines Flight MH17 (destroyed while flying over eastern Ukraine in July 2014). Russia had previously denied all involvement in the incident.

Steps towards peace
The Trilateral Contact Group (TCG: Ukraine, Russia and the Organisation for Security and Cooperation in Europe–OSCE) was the main forum for peace discussions in 2019 and made some progress. The TCG has met almost monthly, and is divided into thematic groups that hold discussions on issues of security, political reintegration and economics. On 2 July the TCG announced steps to dismantle fortifications on both the Ukrainian army and pro-Russian separatist sides in Stanytsia Luhanska in Luhansk. Repairs were also finalised on a bridge connecting government- and non-government-controlled areas on 20 November, a significant development envisioned in the original Minsk peace processes. Disengagement occurred in three areas during 2019 as a result of the work of the TCG, with Ukrainian and pro-Russian separatists withdrawing from Stanytsia Luhanska, and Zolote and Petrivske in Donetsk oblast. The TCG's work also led to a prisoner swap. On 7 September, 277 prisoners were exchanged in the first exchange since the beginning of the war: 69 Ukrainians held in the occupied territories, and 208 people held in Ukrainian government-controlled prisons.

The Normandy Format (involving France, Germany, Russia and Ukraine) was revived in Paris on 9 December, having not met since October 2016. It is regarded as more 'high-level' discussions on the overall peace process. Leaders of the four participating countries agreed to a 'full and comprehensive implementation' of a ceasefire in eastern Ukraine and an 'all-for-all prisoner exchange' by the end of 2019, and three additional disengagement zones by March 2020. Following this meeting, a major prisoner exchange occurred on 29 December. Ukraine released 124 people, and pro-Russian separatists released 76 to Ukraine.

US domestic controversies
Zelensky became involved in an impeachment process against US President Donald Trump, which diverted attention from the conflict in Donbas and may undermine his diplomatic work. Evidence emerged in September suggesting that Trump ordered the withholding of US$250 million of previously approved military assistance to Ukraine to pressure Zelensky to investigate the Ukrainian gas company Burisma Holdings' executive Hunter Biden, the son of US Democrat presidential-nominee candidate Joe Biden. On 14 May 2019, Trump's personal attorney Rudy Giuliani had cancelled a trip to Kiev, during which he was to meet with Ukraine's prosecutor to discuss Burisma and Hunter Biden.

---

30 August — US President Donald Trump halts US$250m of military assistance to Ukraine, which is later authorised for release on 12 September.

23 September — US President Trump is accused of pressuring President Zelensky to investigate Hunter Biden for domestic political gain.

1 October — President Zelensky announces that his government is preparing a law on special status for Donetsk and Luhansk.

20 November — The Stanytsia Luhanska Bridge is completed, connecting government- and non-government-controlled areas.

9 December — The Normandy Four summit convenes in Paris.

29 December — The Ukrainian military and pro-Russian separatists complete a major prisoner swap.

21 July — The 'harvest' ceasefire commences at 12.01am Kiev time.

11 September — Three volunteer battalions hand in their weapons to Ukrainian police.

28 October — The Ukrainian military introduces a 'yellow regime' in government-controlled areas of Donbas, permitting the military to use 'special means' to detain people, check identity documents and enter private property.

11 November — Disengagement by Ukrainian forces and pro-Russian separatists is completed at Petrivske, Donetsk and Zolote, Luhansk.

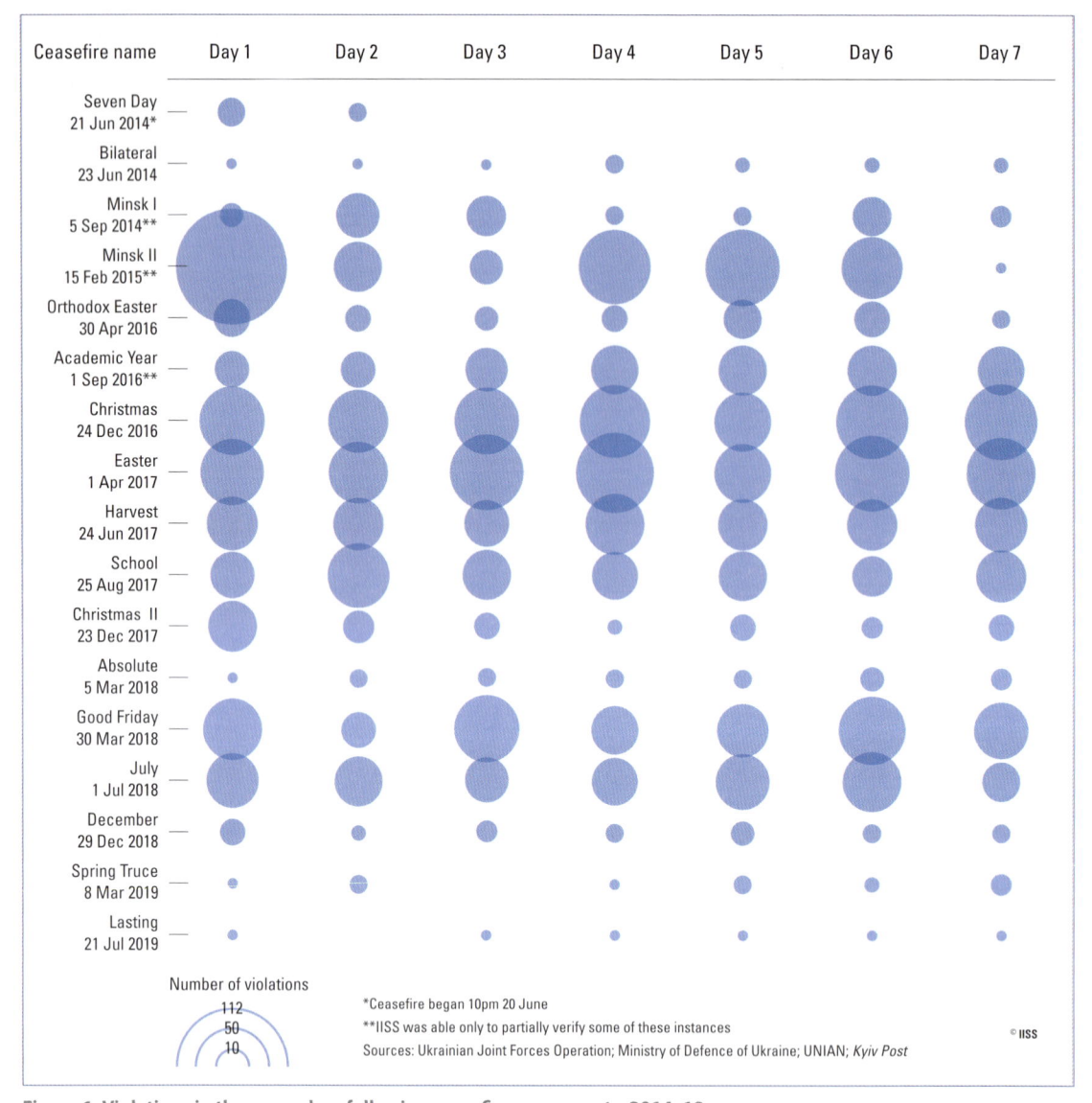

Figure 1: Violations in the seven days following ceasefire agreements, 2014–19

Military Developments

Ceasefire failures
Ceasefires have generally been negotiated throughout the Donbas region and across the contact line. The 'New Year' ceasefire between the Ukrainian army and pro-Russian separatists negotiated on 27 December 2018 by the TCG came into effect on 29 December but quickly broke down at the beginning of 2019. Although the number of attacks across the contact line declined to 27 in the first week of January, from 30–40 attacks per week just before, this had returned to pre-ceasefire levels by early February. At the UN Security Council meeting on 12 February, representatives expressed concern at the stalling peace negotiations in the Minsk format, and at the escalating humanitarian cost of the conflict. The 'holiday' ceasefire agreed by the TCG on 7 March also failed: despite an immediate reduction in daily attacks, the intensity of the conflict was back to pre-ceasefire levels by the end of March, and four civilians had been killed by April.

The most significant ceasefire of 2019 was the indefinite 'harvest' ceasefire agreed by Ukrainian and Russian representatives on 18 July and implemented on 21 July from 12.01am Kiev time. Violent exchanges between the Ukrainian army and pro-Russian separatists and civilian casualties decreased but the situation deteriorated by late August with intensified fighting and deaths on both sides. Despite the attempts at ceasefires and disengagement throughout 2019, the UN Human Rights Monitoring Mission in Ukraine reported that 26 civilians were killed and 136 injured between 1 January and 15 November 2019.[8]

Territorial gains

Ukraine's Joint Forces Operation (JFO) reported territorial gains by the Ukrainian army throughout the year, but these were not independently verified. On 11 April 2019, the JFO reported that Ukrainian units advanced in the 'grey zone' of Donbas, securing a 'large piece' of territory, but provided no details on its location or strategic significance.[9] On 9 June, the JFO reported that Ukrainian troops 'took up new positions on Svitlodarska Duha bulge' – a strategic location east of Donetsk at the centre of the military struggle of the last two years – but offered no further information. On 12 June, the JFO reported that the Ukrainian army pushed back pro-Russian separatists around Maryinka (Donetsk region) by 100–250 metres.[10]

Limited disengagement

At a meeting on 5 June, the TCG agreed on the first phase of disengagement in the Luhansk region, by which Ukrainian and pro-Russian separatist forces would pull back from the Stanytsia Luhanska checkpoint. On 26 June, the Ukrainian army and pro-Russian separatists complied, though two weeks later than planned. OSCE representatives confirmed that the disengagement was carried out successfully without incident. The removal of weapons and demining of the area was completed on 22 August.

At its 1 October meeting, the TCG agreed that all forces would disengage from the village of Petrivske and the town of Zolote on the contact line in Donbas, as agreed in the Minsk agreements of September 2016. On 27 October, war veterans with the Azov battalion stationed in Zolote refused to follow the disengagement orders from Zelensky's office, leading the JFO to announce that the soldiers were in the area illegally and would be disciplined.[11] Disengagement from Zolote finally began on 29 October. It was finalised on 1 November and mutual withdrawal was completed on 11 November. Despite these positive steps, plans for further disengagement of soldiers near the village of Bohdanivka were unsuccessful.

Impact

Human rights

The Office of the UN High Commissioner for Human Rights (OHCHR) has documented hundreds of human-rights violations committed by the DPR and LPR authorities, as well as the Ukrainian government, which has failed to adequately investigate conflict-related abuses and crimes that occurred during the 2014 Maidan protests and subsequent events, particularly the violent disturbances in Odessa. The Ukrainian government has repeatedly been accused of restricting freedom of expression and information, and of suppressing media freedom.

Humanitarian

Of the approximately 5m people living along the contact line in Donetsk and Luhansk, approximately 784,660 were registered as internally displaced persons (IDPs) at the end of 2019.[12] However, the total number of IDPs across Ukraine estimated by the Ukrainian Ministry of Social Policy (approximately 1.4m[13]) is generally considered an overestimate by humanitarian organisations as it includes residents who are no longer displaced but need to remain in the IDP database in order to receive benefits.[14]

Social

The hardships many Ukrainians face, particularly those living near the front lines, have exposed deepening social divides. The increasing militarisation of the state has led to a general increase in violence, and the increasingly nationalist rhetoric has in turn facilitated ostracism of and numerous violent attacks against minorities and marginalised communities.[15]

These attacks were more prominent in 2018, but significant violent incidents occurred in 2019, such as the stabbing of Roma activist Naufal Khamdani in October. An increase in domestic violence has also been reported near the front lines[16] (though it is difficult to obtain verifiable quantitative data), along with a higher incidence of negative coping strategies by citizens such as prostitution, under-heating and meal withholding.[17]

Economic
The war in Donbas is having a catastrophic impact on Ukraine's economy and is compromising the ability of many Ukrainians to survive. The immediate consequences of the war included years of macroeconomic contraction and an increasing poverty rate. World Bank statistics indicate that 10% of the population was impoverished in 2015, but by mid-2019 the poverty rate had decreased to approximately 5%, pre-war levels. It is, however, unlikely that these statistics include the entire population in non-government- and government-controlled areas. For many families, approximately half the monthly household expenditure – roughly 4,105 Ukrainian hryvnias (US$170.82) – goes on food, and the cost of utilities has almost doubled since the start of the war, now standing at approximately 1,200 hryvnias (US$49.94) a month.[18]

Trends

Prospects for peace
Zelensky's election and the majority his party commands in the Verkhovna Rada suggest that he might have the legislative and executive power necessary to make progress towards peace in Ukraine. Increased engagements between Zelensky and Putin in 2019, culminating in the first face-to-face meeting at the 9 December Normandy Format meeting, may indicate a willingness from both sides to negotiate and potential positive implications for conflict resolution, as Putin often speaks on behalf of the pro-Russian separatists and has the power to restrain them. The political controversy over Trump's attempt to influence Zelensky has, however, diverted attention from the conflict and may undermine Zelensky's diplomatic work.

The latest ceasefire has largely collapsed, resulting in deaths on both sides. The daily clashes that followed the collapse will likely continue, with little prospect for either side to gain significant territory or breach the relatively stable line of contact.

However, some of the most positive developments in easing hostilities in Donbas took place in 2019, including the disengagement from key positions – Zolote and Petrivske, Donetsk and Stanytsia Luhanska, Luhansk – by both sides, along with associated limited demining and reconstruction, especially around Stanytsia Luhanska. This demobilisation was outlined in the Minsk peace processes and has only been implemented in 2019, but it is an encouraging sign that more positive developments could soon happen.

Regular meetings of the TCG yielded good results and the continuation of this format seems assured. The prisoner exchanges and explorations of further exchanges, as well as the limited demobilisation, were positive, important steps. The Ukrainian government is reportedly preparing political concessions to the DPR and LPR along the lines of the 'Steinmeier formula', which proposes elections in the separatist areas and the subsequent award of a 'self-governing status' for the territories, though the Ukrainian government controls the border with Russia. However, the proposal has faced significant domestic opposition, with thousands marching against it in Kiev during September and October. Decisions by Zelensky that appear too lenient towards the separatists could risk sparking violent protests. A political solution was not formally proposed by the Normandy Format process, which was relaunched on 9 December, but there may be further discussion on this topic at the next meeting, scheduled for March 2020.

Strategic implications
The new Ukrainian government seems to have realised that a military solution to the conflict is not possible. Giving greater political autonomy to the Donbas area may provoke a reaction from the US, which has been vocal against 'Russian imperialism' in the region and would oppose a position that seemed to appease the separatists. The risk, though not high, remains of a more direct intervention from

Russia in the case of a looming military collapse of separatist forces. Neither side will be able to accrue sufficient territorial gains to achieve a military victory in the near future.

Notes

1. 'Over 21,000 people accepted for military service in Ukraine in 2019', 112UA, 9 August 2019.
2. Illia Ponomarenko, 'Zelensky appoints new top military commander in Donbas', *KyivPost*, 5 August 2019.
3. Nolan Peterson, 'After 4 Years of a Frozen Conflict, Ukrainians Slowly Retake Ground From Russian Forces', Daily Signal, 13 May 2019.
4. 'Around 3–4 thousand Russian volunteers fighting for Donetsk People's Republic militia', TASS, 28 August 2014.
5. Richard Arnold, 'Russian-Backed Luhansk Authorities Enlist Help of Local Cossacks', Jamestown Foundation, 16 July 2019.
6. Ilya Prizel, 'Nation-Building and Foreign Policy', in Sharon L. Wolchik and Volodymyr Zviglyanich (eds.), *Ukraine: The Search for a National Identity* (Lanham, MD: Rowman & Littlefield, 2000), pp. 11–29: 13; Richard Sakwa, *Frontline Ukraine: Crisis in the Borderlands* (London: I.B. Tauris, 2015), p. 15.
7. See Law of Ukraine, 'On ensuring the functioning of the Ukrainian language as a state language', Verkhovna Rada (BBR) Bulletin, 25 April 2019, no. 21, p. 81.
8. Office of the United Nations High Commissioner for Human Rights, 'Report on the human rights situation in Ukraine 16 August to 15 November 2019', 12 December 2019.
9. UNIAN Information Agency, 'Gaining ground: Ukraine Army advances in Donbas "gray zone"', 11 April 2019.
10. UNIAN Information Agency, 'Ukrainian troops get close to Donetsk – JFO HQ', 12 June 2019.
11. UNIAN Information Agency, 'Donbas war veterans to stay in Zolote in defiance of government's disengagement plans', 26 October 2019.
12. UN High Commissioner for Refugees (UNHCR) Ukraine, 'Registration of Internal Displacement', 10 January 2020.
13. *Ibid.*
14. Internal Displacement Monitoring Centre, 'Ukraine: Figure Analysis – Displacement Related to Conflict and Violence', May 2019.
15. Mila O'Sullivan, '"Being strong enough to defend yourself": Untangling the Women, Peace and Security agenda amidst the Ukrainian conflict', *International Feminist Journal of Politics*, vol. 21, no. 5, April 2019; Tetyana Bureychak and Olena Petrenko, 'Heroic masculinity in post-soviet Ukraine: Cossacks, UPA and "Svoboda"', *East/West: Journal of Ukrainian Studies*, vol. 2, no. 2, pp. 3–27.
16. Teah Pelechaty, 'Violence against women remains silent epidemic in Ukraine', *KyivPost*, 16 July 2019; Organisation for Security and Cooperation in Europe (OSCE) Special Monitoring Mission to Ukraine, 'Gender Dimensions of SMM Monitoring', 1 January 2017–1 November 2018', December 2018.
17. OSCE Special Monitoring Mission to Ukraine, 'Gender Dimensions of SMM Monitoring', 1 January 2017–1 November 2018'.
18. State Statistics Service of Ukraine, 'Structure of total expenditure', 2019.

4 Middle East and North Africa

Egypt (Sinai)	158	Libya	189	Yemen	222
Iraq	167	Syria	201		
Israel–Palestine	178	Turkey (PKK)	214		

Syrian Democratic Forces fighters withdraw from near the Turkish border, Amuda, Syria

Key trends

- Conflicts in the Middle East remain highly regionalised and internationalised; rivalries among external powers play out across the region.
- The US-backed Syrian Democratic Forces (SDF) liberated the last ISIS-held territory in Syria. ISIS adapted by resorting to insurgency tactics, in both Syria and Iraq.
- Iraq's post-ISIS stabilisation is tentative. By 2019, a large protest movement upended Iraqi politics, while US–Iran tensions also played out in the Iraqi arena.
- In Libya, a new, more brutal phase of civil war began, with more direct involvement of regional rivals.
- Egypt contended with regular attacks in the Sinai Peninsula although the insurgency began to lose its strength.
- Israeli dominance and unilateralism shaped the trajectory of the Israel–Palestine conflict.

Strategic implications

- Syria is likely to remain an exporter of instability in the foreseeable future and to continue drawing external interference.
- Turkey's intervention in Syria isolated the country from its regional interlocutors and NATO allies. Russia attempted to fill the diplomatic vacuum created by the sudden withdrawal of US forces from northern Syria.
- The influence of pro-Iranian militias, the weakness of the central government and US–Iran tensions put the stability of Iraq at risk.
- Many global powers see the conflict in Libya as an opportunity to expand their strategic influence in the Mediterranean.

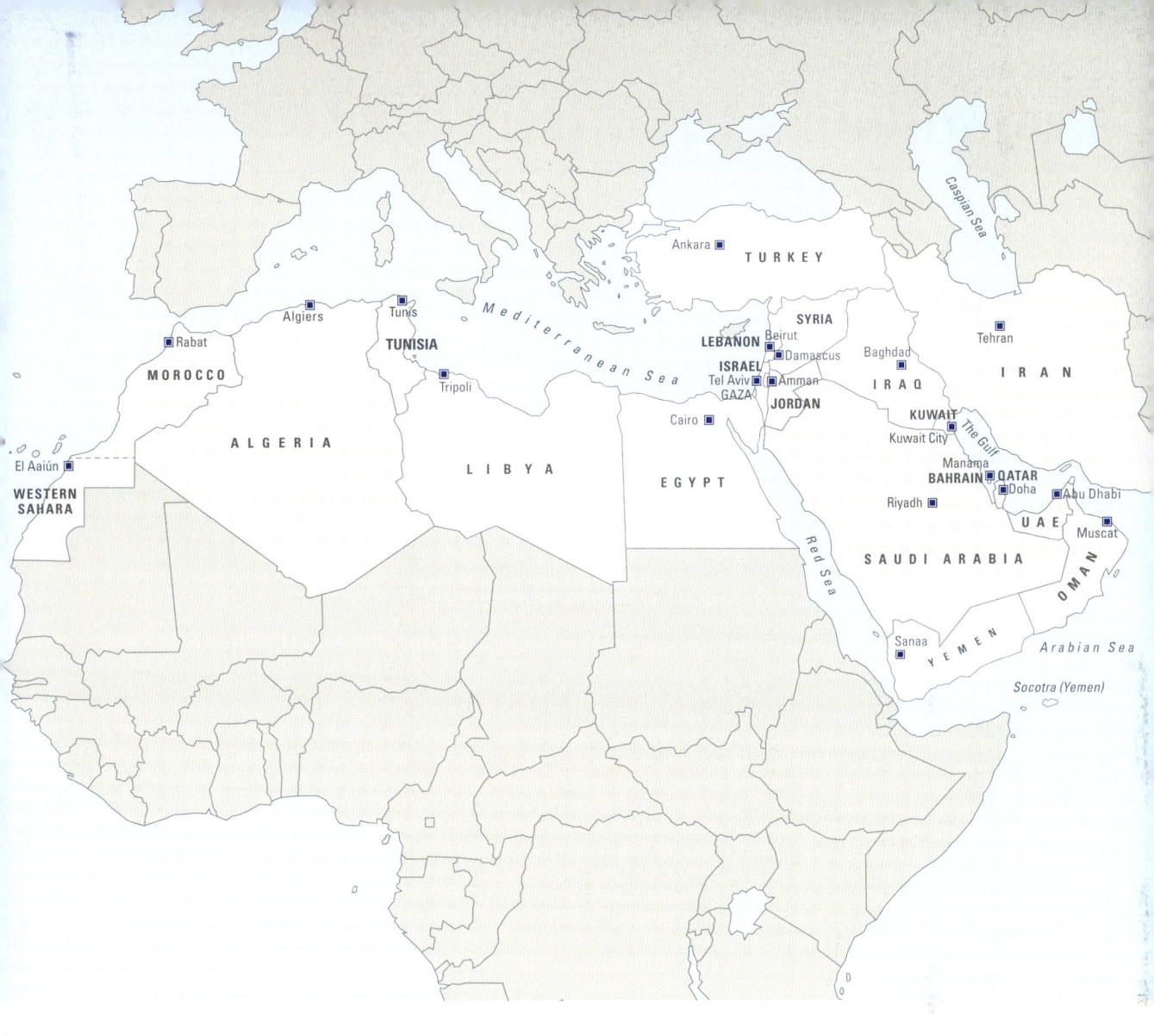

- The Saudi-led coalition came under greater scrutiny in 2019, from the US and UK in particular.
- President Trump's pro-Israeli policies alienated Palestinians and undermined the United States' role as negotiator.

Prospects

- While a comprehensive and inclusive political settlement in Syria remains elusive, a new insurgency is brewing in southern Syria. The resurgence of ISIS is already under way.
- A lull in hostilities in northern Syria is possible, but prospects for peace are non-existent in the short term. Turkish forces in Syrian areas are creating tensions with local communities and fuel low-intensity conflict.
- A return to large-scale territorial control by ISIS is unlikely, but without adequate counter-insurgency efforts, Iraq will struggle to eliminate remaining militants.
- The Saudi-led coalition's declining appetite for war in Yemen suggests a potential peace settlement more expansive than the Stockholm Agreement envisaged.
- Increased fragmentation in Libya raises concerns over a possible partition. Proxy wars are unlikely to end soon.

EGYPT (SINAI)

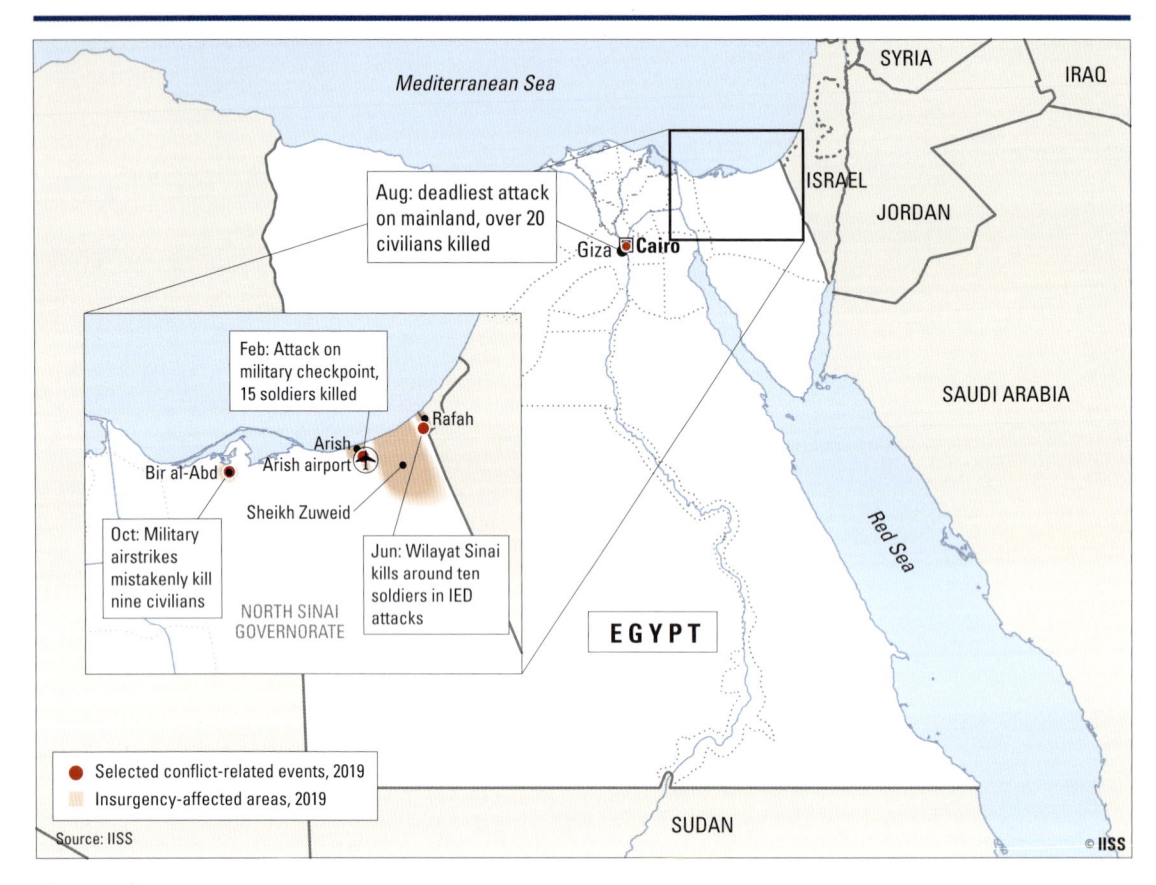

Map annotations:
- Aug: deadliest attack on mainland, over 20 civilians killed
- Feb: Attack on military checkpoint, 15 soldiers killed
- Oct: Military airstrikes mistakenly kill nine civilians
- Jun: Wilayat Sinai kills around ten soldiers in IED attacks
- Locations: Bir al-Abd, Arish, Arish airport, Sheikh Zuweid, Rafah, North Sinai Governorate

Legend: Selected conflict-related events, 2019; Insurgency-affected areas, 2019
Source: IISS

Overview

The conflict in 2019

In 2019, the conflict in North Sinai remained largely unchanged from previous years and levels of violence continued to fluctuate. The areas of eastern North Sinai remained the flashpoint for insurgent violence, despite the Egyptian army expanding its zone of control and exclusive military 'buffer zones'.

Despite the hailed success of *Operation Sinai* and a drawdown of over 50,000 troops from the area, attacks continued on a weekly basis. Attacks were more common in 2019 but had a lower impact and inflicted fewer casualties than in previous years. In the summer, militants launched numerous attacks on security outposts and major infrastructure in the peninsula, causing prolonged power outages. Several attacks occurred throughout the year and claimed the lives of dozens of security officials, beginning with an improvised explosive device (IED) attack on a military checkpoint near Arish airport in February that killed up to 15 soldiers. An increase in suicide attacks and kidnappings by the Islamic State, also known as ISIS or ISIL, led to more civilian casualties, particularly among the Coptic Christian community in Sinai. Though far from being extinguished, the insurgency's strength in the peninsula has waned.

The Egyptian army responded with airstrikes and raids on alleged hideouts in cities where

Key statistics

Type	Internal
Start date	January 2011
IDPs total	Not applicable
Refugees total	Not applicable
People in need	No data

insurgents were active – Arish, Rafah and Sheikh Zuweid. Quarterly statements from the military spokesperson set the number of militants killed in 2019 at more than 220, but reports remained vague on the casualties among security forces. In addition, dozens of tunnels along the Gaza–Rafah border were destroyed.

Following the troop drawdown in October 2018, some movement restrictions were relaxed, but the Sinai Peninsula remains heavily militarised. Night-time curfews are still imposed periodically, fuel and other services remain sparse, and schools and universities are yet to resume a full schedule. Civilian use of some vehicles, notably 4×4 trucks and motorcycles, remains banned throughout North Sinai.

The conflict to 2019

Armed insurgencies have operated in Sinai for decades. When the Arab Spring protests began in Egypt in January 2011 and the police withdrew from the streets, armed groups in North Sinai governorate took advantage of the security vacuum. They first attacked a controversial pipeline near Arish that supplied gas to Israel and subsequently attacked it 13 more times during 2011–13, eventually forcing the authorities to halt gas exports to Israel. Armed groups launched at least four cross-border attacks into Israel, mostly using rockets, and killed an Israeli soldier in a shooting in 2012 (before the fence along the border was completed).

After the *coup d'état* in 2013 reinstated military rule in Egypt, armed groups in the Sinai Peninsula began to more aggressively target both military positions (killing soldiers at checkpoints, for example) and state interests (targeting a bus of Korean tourists in South Sinai governorate in 2014 and downing a Russian MetroJet plane in 2015).

Following a pledge of allegiance to ISIS in November 2014, Wilayat Sinai, the ISIS affiliate in North Sinai, has led the insurgency. The insurgency originally focused on the eastern areas of Arish, Sheikh Zuweid and Rafah in North Sinai, but spread to the western city of Bir al-Abd in recent years, and a small number of attacks recorded in South Sinai in 2017 suggested a spillover in those areas. At its peak in July 2015, the ISIS insurgency battled the Egyptian army for control of Sheikh Zuweid city.

The Sinai Peninsula has been in a state of emergency since September 2013.[1] Since then, the Egyptian military has sought to extinguish the insurgency by establishing control over the area through military designated zones, where it deployed significant numbers of troops – up to 75,000 troops during *Operation Sinai* in 2018. Although the number and impact of insurgent attacks diminished significantly, North Sinai remains a breeding ground for insurgents.

Key Conflict Parties

Egyptian Armed Forces

Strength
438,500 active armed personnel, with 470,000 in reserve (army: 310,000 active officers).

Areas of operation
North Sinai, militarised triangle (Halayeb/Shalateen), Western Desert and Salloum border (the western border with Libya).

Leadership
Supreme Council of the Armed Forces (SCAF), led by Defence Minister Maj.-Gen. Mohamed Zaki.

Structure
The SCAF consists of the army, air force and navy; paramilitary forces are formed under the Ministry of Interior.

History
Founded in 1820. The SCAF has been in its current form since the Free Officers Coup led by Gamal Abdel Nasser in 1952. Since then, Egypt has been under de facto military rule, with consecutive military officers serving as president (except the 2012–13 period when Egypt was led by Muslim Brotherhood leader Muhammad Morsi).

Objectives
The SCAF controls border security, and all national-security threats coming from abroad. Since 2013 it has taken full control over the situation in North Sinai where a low-level insurgency by jihadist militants has continued against the Egyptian state. Following 2014 legal amendments to land control, the SCAF now has direct and sole control of all border demarcations up to 60 kilometres inland. It controls border outposts, including within the country between the mainland and the Sinai Peninsula, and connecting roads southwards and westwards.

Egyptian Armed Forces

Opponents
ISIS (Wilayat Sinai), Ansar Bayt al-Maqdis (ABAM), Muslim Brotherhood, Lewaa al-Thawra and Hassm.

Affiliates/allies
EU, France, Germany, Israel, Russia and the US.

Resources/capabilities
The SCAF does not publicise its defence budget. An estimated 2–3% of GDP (approximately US$7.5 billion–11.1bn) is allocated to defence, which includes the US$1.3bn in Foreign Military Financing received annually from the US.

Directorate of Military Intelligence (Egypt – DMI)

Strength
Unknown, although within the military hierarchy the ascension of Abdel Fattah Al-Sisi to the presidency has strengthened the DMI within the armed forces and provided a larger mandate for the intelligence branch since 2013.

Leadership
Maj.-Gen. Khaled Megawer, since December 2018.

Structure
Unknown.

History
Founded in 1952 and led by Gamal Abdel Nasser. The DMI has been a 'coup-proof' mechanism for the Egyptian military and its leaders since its inception. Sisi led the DMI from 2010 until 2012, and his presidency now adds to its heightened status. It has been accused of conducting extrajudicial killings of alleged militants in the Sinai Peninsula, in partnership with local Bedouin groups (2017).

Objectives
Protect the state, military intelligence and Sisi from any attack; monitor foreign threats towards Egypt (alongside the General Intelligence Services). Sisi announced Sinai as a top priority for the DMI in 2019.

Opponents
Wilayat Sinai.

Affiliates/allies
Egyptian Armed Forces, General Intelligence Services.

Resources/capabilities
Unknown, although current leader Megawer has launched a new Military Intelligence Reform plan, unveiled in April 2019, albeit with little detail.

Wilayat Sinai (ISIS affiliate)

Strength
Estimated 1,500–2,000 militants. Announcements by its news site Amaq have suggested that an increasing number of foreign fighters have joined, notably jihadists coming from Gaza.

Areas of operation
North Sinai governorate in the Sinai Peninsula (the group has also claimed several attacks in mainland Egypt, notably against Coptic Christians and places of worship).

Leadership
As of June 2019, Wilayat Sinai is led by Abu Jafar al-Ansari (*nom de guerre*). It pledged allegiance to the new ISIS leader, Abu Ibrahim al-Hashimi al-Qurayshi, in November 2019.[2]

Structure
Unknown, although some evidence suggests training camps in Sinai and Gaza. Several jihadists are known to have travelled to Syria for training, suggesting that periodically the ISIS leadership structure plays a significant role in the Sinai insurgency.

History
Formed out of the Sinai militant group ABAM. ABAM's militant activity increased following the 2011 uprising that removed Hosni Mubarak. In November 2014, the group split with just over half of its members believed to have pledged allegiance to ISIS, creating Wilayat Sinai.

Objectives
Overthrow the state and establish an Islamic caliphate, which perceives modern nation-states as lacking legitimacy. Wilayat Sinai has accordingly depicted security forces and the president as apostates.

Opponents
Egyptian Armed Forces, wider Egyptian security forces, Israel, non-Sunni Muslims and non-Muslims.

Resources/capabilities
Unknown, although anecdotal evidence suggests most income is received via economic smuggling between the Sinai Peninsula and Gaza through tunnels. The group also benefits from an active weapons-smuggling war economy bringing weapons from Libya into Sinai, via routes that go through the Nile Valley and Upper Egypt/Red Sea. Some funds are believed to have occasionally been sourced from the ISIS leadership in Iraq and Syria.

Drivers

Marginalisation and economic insecurity

The violence in Sinai originates from the peninsula's long-standing marginalisation and neglect. Israel occupied Sinai in 1967 and the region only returned to Egyptian control in 1981 after the Camp David Peace Accords. The agreement included a clause that Sinai ought to remain demilitarised, which left the region vulnerable to the establishment of smuggling routes and other illicit activities. Networks of underground tunnels between North Sinai and the Gaza Strip flourished after 2007, when Egypt and Israel began imposing a blockade against the occupied territory.

Sinai's Bedouin population has faced systematic discrimination and been deprived of the rights enjoyed by other Egyptians.[3] Government investment has been concentrated in the south of the peninsula, where a lucrative tourist industry has flourished, but the rest of the province has not benefited from private capital flows or public-development programmes.[4] Since the closure of the region to outsiders in 2013, the situation has deteriorated further, with residents unable to move around freely or conduct business – despite commitments from the military promising over EGP5bn (around US$3.1bn) in spending and redevelopment plans for the governorate. This includes the rebuilding of major cities such as Rafah and Sheikh Zuweid, now destroyed by the conflict, but also new developments alongside the coast, such as the Arish Port Development programme.[5]

In 2019, the Egyptian military formally inaugurated the Sinai Redevelopment Plan – which followed the broader nationwide economic reform plans initiated in 2016 – and promised to invest in rebuilding homes, rejuvenating cities and ports, and invigorating the economy in North Sinai. Owing to the volatile security situation, the lucrative investment plans have been awarded to companies owned by the Egyptian security forces and coincided with mass spending in arms and security equipment, including ground, air and sea bases along Egypt's most sensitive borders. The most prominent of these investment plans included the New Rafah City – an expansive new social-housing programme surrounding what is still Rafah city along the Egypt–Gaza border – and the development of Arish Port.

Political grievances

Notwithstanding Wilayat Sinai's ideological objectives, the insurgency is rooted in domestic grievances, particularly against the armed forces, the violent tactics of which Wilayat Sinai frequently uses as a justification for its activities. The insurgency depicts many attacks as a way to avenge prisoners, acts of torture or deaths, and the general marginalisation of the community in the Sinai Peninsula, which originally resulted in it gaining some support among civilians in Sinai. The general hostility of the Sinai population towards the armed forces emerged in response to the 'eradication approach' adopted to remove dissent and opposition since the military's return to power in 2013. In Sinai particularly, the view that the armed forces and political leadership are serving US and Israeli interests while neglecting the local population exacerbates such grievances.

Political Developments

In 2019, President Abdel Fattah Al-Sisi continued to consolidate his power, extending control over all arms of the Egyptian state. Despite considerable opposition, he pushed through constitutional amendments in April 2019 that could enable him to remain in office until 2030. According to the National Electoral Commission, more than 27 million Egyptians (just over 44%) participated in the referendum on the amendments – some 23m voted in favour and just 2m against.[6] Sisi now rules over the judiciary, the legislature, the civilian bureaucracy and the armed forces, which the amendments designate as the 'protectors of the state'. The president appoints judges to the Supreme Constitutional Court and several other lower courts, as well as the prosecutor-general and many members of the newly reinstituted upper house (the Council of Sheikhs).

Throughout 2019 hundreds of citizens, activists, journalists and dissidents were arrested and jailed across the country including in the Sinai Peninsula, with regular reports of torture. A sustained media blackout in the area makes it impossible to verify numbers or reports emerging from North Sinai. While the military contended that it arrested hundreds of alleged militants and killed at least 220, there is no way to verify both the circumstances and the nature of these numbers.

Further sowing discontent, in June 2019, former president Morsi died suddenly in prison. Just days later, his youngest son (24) died at home of a suspected heart attack. Alongside an increasing number of reports of torture emerging from those in detention, the United Nations found that prison conditions were contributing to the deteriorating health conditions of detainees, and may well have been a factor in Morsi's death.[7] The treatment of other political prisoners, such as Abdelmonein Aboul Fottouh and Hisham Geniena, remained a focal point for presidential opposition.

Anger over years of austerity imposed by Sisi's reform package with the IMF spilled over late in 2019. After yet another round of fuel-subsidy cuts in August 2019, a wave of small protests erupted across the country on 20 September. Fuelled by a 'tell-all' series of videos uploaded to Facebook by a disgruntled military contractor, Mohamed Ali – who described in detail the corrupt practices in the state and military institutions, including among the president and his family – thousands took to the streets. A severe security crackdown meant that the protests were short-lived but still represented the first challenge to the regime since 2013.

Military Developments

Under Sisi, there have been rolling security reshuffles on a scale not seen since the military first took power in 1952, including in the SCAF, the ministries of interior and defence, the intelligence apparatus and lower security branches such as national security, and these continued in 2019. Maj.-Gen. Khaled Megawer became director of military intelligence (DMI) in December 2018, while other generals, notably Deputy Minister of Defence Maj.-Gen. Mohamed el-Keshky, were quietly removed from the SCAF either into early retirement or to civilian ministries. In late 2019, Sisi was forced to respond to long-standing criticism of his inner circle and supposed nepotism. He appears to have privately acknowledged the detrimental effect his eldest son had in the general-intelligence apparatus and announced that he would send him as military attaché to Moscow, although sources close to the military apparatus suggested this plan was changed owing to personal opposition to the move within the president's family.

Overall, Sisi has continued to expand the military's purview over various state portfolios, mainly economic. Through the establishment of dozens of military companies, he has awarded state contracts for development plans in North Sinai,[8] notably Arish Port and New Rafah City. No details were available on the value of the investments because of the highly securitised state of the region. The military argues that the investments are aimed at rehousing citizens displaced by insurgent violence.[9]

Key Events in 2019

Political events

- **4 February**: A military court sentences eight people to death for their involvement in a 2014 plot to assassinate Sisi in Mecca.
- **23 April**: Sisi wins a referendum on constitutional amendments that could help him remain in power until 2030.
- **12 June**: An Egyptian military court issues sentences (from three years to life in prison) for 296 individuals allegedly involved in a 2014 plot to assassinate Sisi.

Military/Violent events

- **16 February**: Militants assault an army checkpoint near Arish airport, causing at least 15 casualties. Seven militants are killed.
- **18 February**: A suicide bomber kills three police officers in an attack near Al-Azhar Mosque, Cairo. Three attacks in Giza kill two security officials.
- **4 June**: Wilayat Sinai kills around ten soldiers in IED attacks near Rafah.
- **26 June**: Militants kill eight security-forces members in three attacks on checkpoints near Arish.

Impact

Human rights
State repression and human-rights abuses under Sisi have reached unprecedented levels. Sustained attack on rights and freedoms has resulted in harmful legislation including the criminalisation of foreign funding and the activities of independent journalists and academics. In 2018, a cyber-crime law was passed, and drafts of a 'fake news' law that would criminalise anything the state deems as false or as jeopardising national security are currently under parliamentary review. In the aftermath of the September protests, at least 4,300 people were arrested, journalists were systematically targeted and reports of torture increased.

Humanitarian
Since the insurgency in Sinai began, the army has isolated the region and cut off access to the rest of the country, including via the control of vehicle movement over the main land crossing (Ahmed Hamdi Tunnel) and by banning the passage of motorcycles and 4×4 trucks. After a peak in 2017, the flow of Coptic Christians escaping Wilayat Sinai violence to the Delta region has slowed significantly. Continued curfews on movement between villages across North Sinai mean there is little opportunity for targeted civilians to flee. Forced displacement is still largely contained to neighbouring towns and villages.

Social and economic
Egyptians continue to struggle with economic hardship following the budget-reform package agreed with the IMF in 2016. The programme, which ended in August 2019, supported budget reforms but slashed civilian incomes and increased the prices of staple items. While the prices of fuel and electricity are now set at international rates, gas consumption is expected to increase and household costs to decrease, supported by large deposits discovered in 2015 and now in production (Zohr gas fields). The continued military dominance of the economy, however, is preventing growth, while foreign and domestic direct investment (non-oil/gas) continues to contract month on month.

Corruption accusations surrounding the president and his family and within military institutions are exacerbating already turbulent social dynamics. Egyptian society is generally still polarised along Islamist/non-Islamist lines, but the support that brought Sisi to power in 2013 has largely dissipated, giving way to broad-based frustration and anger. The tensions that led to the 2011 uprising remain unaddressed or are growing. Unmanaged population growth and youth unemployment are increasing challenges.

Relations with neighbouring and international partners
Sisi has re-engaged Egypt's foreign policy by forging strong relations with Gulf states, notably the United Arab Emirates (UAE) and Saudi Arabia, and allying with anti-Islamists such as General Khalifa Haftar in the war in Libya. Despite European countries trying to persuade Egypt to halt its support for Haftar, Sisi is unlikely to oblige.

---

17 June
Former president Muhammad Morsi dies in detention.

19 June
Wilayat Sinai announces a new leader, Abu Jafar al-Ansari.

20 September
Anti-government protests break out across six governorates. Over 4,300 people are arrested.

8 November
A UN report says that poor prison conditions contributed to Morsi's death.

30 June
Wilayat Sinai announces the execution of three alleged Egyptian military spies, reportedly related to the kidnapping of civilians in mid-June.

3 July
Major attacks on infrastructure in Central Sinai cause a mass power outage that lasts for ten days.

5 August
A VBIED attack on a cancer hospital in Imbaba kills over 20 civilians in Cairo's largest terror attack in two years.

27 September
Wilayat Sinai attacks a checkpoint in Bir al-Abd, killing seven soldiers and one civilian.

9 October
The Egyptian military conducts airstrikes on alleged military hideouts in Bir al-Abd, mistakenly killing nine civilians.

Ethiopia's construction of the Grand Ethiopian Renaissance Dam (GERD) upstream on the River Nile continues to threaten Egypt's longer-term sustainability, owing to the possibility of reduced access to the Nile's fresh water, on which Egypt relies heavily. A recent flurry of diplomacy placed the issue firmly on national and international agendas and Egypt has engaged the US, a close ally, to support mediation. While constructive discussions have taken place on filling times for the reservoir behind the dam, US-mediated talks did not bring about an official agreement and Ethiopia indicated that it planned to fill the reservoir in August 2020.

Sisi continued to pursue economic plans with Russia, despite warnings of sanctions from the US if Egypt concludes any arms deals. Although the US–Egypt relationship remains Sisi's highest priority, he continued to signal strong commitment to strengthen Egypt's security relationship with Russia, which is made highly lucrative by plans to develop the Dabaa Nuclear Plant and to seal economic deals around the Suez Canal Economic Zone.

Furthermore, although Sisi enjoys a good relationship with US President Donald Trump, both his foreign and domestic policy have come under increased scrutiny from the US Congress and the Department of State. The allocation of US$1.3bn in Foreign Military Financing (FMF) annually means that the US remains a key partner in the fight against the insurgency. Beyond specific intelligence support that is shared between Egyptian and US military commands, the US Congress has continued to question the use of US-made weapons in the battle in Sinai, and is now placing more pressure on Egypt to respond to calls for end-line monitoring of US equipment in the area. The scrutiny comes after a 2017 video leak purportedly showed several military officials performing extrajudicial killings of alleged militants. (In August 2017, the US government withheld a portion of the FMF, in part over the question of monitoring of equipment.) As such, new language is being suggested for forthcoming FMF legislation that will directly require scrutiny of Egyptian military activity in the Sinai Peninsula and potentially put pressure on the relationship.

Trends

Political trajectories

The political disruption caused by the protests and accusations of corruption in September 2019 is expected to continue. Sisi has already anticipated that local elections – which have not been held since the 2011 uprising – will be further delayed until 2021. However, parliamentary elections are due in 2020 for both the House of Representatives and the newly introduced Council of Sheikhs. The president has been largely unhappy with the performance of the current parliament and has reportedly delegated the national-security apparatus to engineer a more pliant and less disruptive parliament for the next term. Crackdowns on political opposition, civilian dissidents, independent media and civil-society organisations are set to increase as elections approach, entrenching the repression that has so far defined the regime – threats and intimidation to silence opposition voices short of severe punishments so as to avoid the attention of the international community. The recent raids and arrest of several journalists from independent news outlet Mada Masr in November invoked considerable condemnation from a number of international allies, including the EU and the US.

Conflict-related risks

The conflict in North Sinai remains limited to the cities of Arish, Rafah and Sheikh Zuweid and neighbouring areas within the governorate, and levels of violence remain low. Although armed militancy moved towards the west and ensnared cities such as Bir al-Abd in 2019, spillover into other parts of the country was limited. Sporadic attacks in the mainland continue, but their scale and effects have not reached the levels of the attacks on Coptic Christian worship sites in 2017. The collapse of ISIS in Syria and Iraq has not led to the predicted large-scale migration of foreign fighters to the Sinai Peninsula, although some fighters have used its smuggling routes to move into Libya.

Prospects for peace

Conflict resolution remains highly unlikely in the Sinai Peninsula. The long-standing drivers of violence remain unchanged. Wilayat Sinai retains the loyalty of its ranks as well as the capacity to recruit. The main challenge to the armed insurgency will come from revamped counter-terrorism efforts as the Egyptian security forces respond to international criticism for lack of results, mostly from the US. The appointment of Megawer – a powerful figure within the armed forces with significant operational experience in Sinai – as the head of the DMI signals an increased focus on traditional counter-terrorism. Continued community relations, improved living standards and freedom of movement in North Sinai will be crucial to the success of this strategy.

Strategic implications and global influence

The conflicts in Libya and in Gaza will continue to dominate Egypt's domestic-security concerns. The main factors affecting the dynamics of violence in North Sinai will be the crossing of Palestinian fighters into Sinai, the construction of tunnels into Gaza and the border closure at Rafah. Weapons smuggling from Libya and continued militant activity in eastern Libya will continue to have spillover effects in the Western Desert and Nile Valley areas of mainland Egypt.

Sisi will remain at the forefront of international mediations for conflicts across the Middle East, having successfully portrayed himself as a stable leader in an unstable region. He has been aided by the staunch support of the Gulf states, primarily the UAE and de facto leader Muhammad bin Zayed Al Nahyan, and will continue to promote this image through partnering with the EU to curb migration and hosting large-scale international economic conferences – for example, the annual Invest in Africa, the global and Arab youth forums, and the Egyptian Petroleum Show. The recent creation of the Eastern Mediterranean Gas Forum, endorsed by regional partners (except Turkey) and the US, will continue to allow Sisi to promote Egypt as a regional gas hub and an attractive emerging market for investment.

Notes

[1] The nationwide state of emergency was invoked in 2014. Despite the 2014 Constitution essentially making a state of emergency renewable only once, and lasting a full period of six months, Sisi has kept the country under a full state of emergency by merely allowing it to lapse for a day, and then ordering parliament to approve a new state of emergency. In addition, he has also amended the State of Emergency Law to allow for strengthened powers to be devolved from institutions to the presidency, notably the nomination of courts and judges. Currently the State Security Supreme Courts oversee most criminal cases in Egypt, of which the judges are directly appointed by the president and his delegated authority. These courts have historically overseen foreign-espionage cases, in periods where the country is not under a state of emergency.

[2] Abu Ibrahim al-Hashimi al-Qurayshi was the name initially given as Abu Bakr al-Baghdadi's replacement. It emerged in January 2020 that this was a *nom de guerre* and the ISIS leader's name is Amir Mohammed Abdul Rahman al-Mawli al-Salbi.

[3] Generally, Bedouins in the Sinai region have been deemed second-class citizens and find it difficult to access the mainland. This has led to many not holding Egyptian national identification, marginalised employment opportunities and minimal state investment or development in the region. Generally, levels of poverty and illiteracy remain much higher in the Sinai Peninsula (particularly North Sinai, with the south of the peninsula reaping rewards from the tourism industry) than anywhere else in the country.

[4] The percentage of Egyptians living in extreme poverty rose to 32.5% in 2018, according to official data from the state-owned Central Agency for Public Mobilization and Statistics (CAMPAS), an increase of almost 5% since 2015. Egypt sets the poverty line higher than the World Bank (US$1.9/day), at US$1.3/day. See '32.5% of Egyptians live in extreme poverty: CAPMAS', Egypt Today, 1 August 2019. Although figures are not available for each province, and Sinai in particular, it is believed the Bedouins are much poorer than Egyptians in the mainland. Recent announcements in 2019 included an ambitious US$315m development plan for the Sinai Peninsula, an increase of 75% on investment levels for 2018. No real data is available for prior years, particularly under the Mubarak regime, but investment is believed to be minimal.

[5] 'Skepticism looms over Egypt's plan to develop Sinai', Al-Monitor, 1 September 2019; Egypt Maritime Transport Sector, 'Arish Port Development Plan' (official site).

[6] This number is contested by most independent observers including media and diplomatic missions who monitored the vote. In addition, complaints of interference in the process were rife. Diplomats reported that they were denied access to polling stations, that no texts of the amendments were available at polling stations, that the state deliberately misled voters, and that the offer of 'Ramadan boxes' was used for vote-buying.

[7] See UN News, 'Egypt: "Credible evidence" that "brutal" prison conditions prompted Morsi's death, thousands more at risk', 8 November 2019.

[8] As the port-development plan continues, the Al Sokhna trading port in the mainland is a significant part of this project, and a significant element of Sisi's broader Red Sea security policy. Currently, DP World has new contracts to complete a second container terminal at Sokhna by March 2020. Other contractors include China Harbour Engineering Company, which is constructing the pier and the refining works. Rawad Engineering Company has been brought in to undertake

infrastructure works, which are due to be completed in March 2020. The Arish Port is owned by the Ministry of Defence, under the naval forces. The total cost of the development is estimated at EGP1.2bn (US$76.5m); see ECO Group, 'El-Arish Port Master Plan', 2020. The General Authority for the Suez Canal Economic Zone (led by a military general) is expected to finance and implement the development, management and operation of the port. See Menna A. Farouk, 'Sisi transfers control of northern Sinai port to army for security reasons', Al-Monitor, 24 July 2019.

[9] Tacitly admitting that there has been significant displacement, a claim the military and presidency have yet to officially deny.

IRAQ

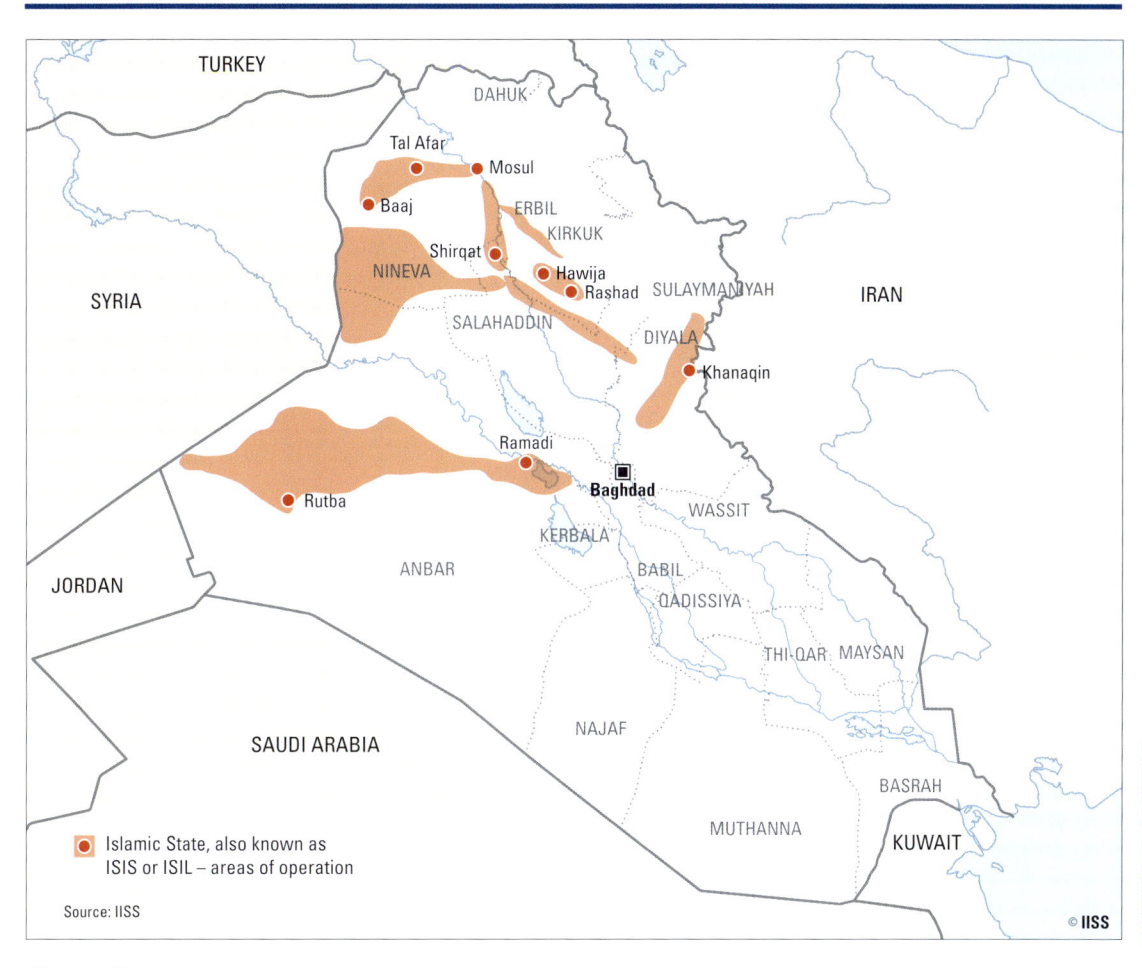

Islamic State, also known as ISIS or ISIL – areas of operation

Source: IISS

Overview

The conflict in 2019
In December 2017, then Iraqi prime minister Haider al-Abadi announced the defeat of the Islamic State, also known as ISIS or ISIL, in Iraq. In March 2019, the US-backed Syrian Democratic Forces (SDF) announced the liberation of Baghouz, the last territory in Syria held by the group. ISIS has adapted to its loss of territory by reforming as a covert network organisation using insurgency tactics – a process evident in Iraq in the past two years. In response, the Iraqi government and its international partners shifted to a counter-terrorism and counter-insurgency strategy focused on clearing areas previously under ISIS control and dismantling terrorist cells.

Meanwhile, reconstruction efforts proceeded slowly – a low priority for a government that struggled for months to form a cabinet after elections in 2018. ISIS exploited this lack of progress, launching attacks in rural and mountainous regions, particularly in Anbar, Diyala, Kirkuk, Nineva and Salahaddin provinces. These attacks mirrored

Key statistics

Type	Internationalised
Start date	20 March 2003
IDPs total (31 December 2019)	1,414,632
Refugees total* (31 December 2019)	209,159
People in need (31 December 2019)	4,100,000

*Number of Iraqi refugees in Turkey and Jordan.

ISIS's pre-2014 insurgency strategy: they targeted members of the security forces, federal police, local government and tribal chiefs, and mainly consisted of setting up fake checkpoints and hijacking trucks.

Iraq's political landscape reflected this continued instability. In October, protests against the government's inability to tackle corruption and provide jobs and basic services spread in Baghdad and several southern cities. Like the 2018 protests in Basra, demonstrators demanded reform and the security forces responded with violence, resulting in at least 500 deaths by December.[1] The protests marked the greatest internal-security challenge since 2017. Alongside the protests, Iraq was caught up in heightened tensions between the US and Iran at the end of the year.

The conflict to 2019

Iraq has been the site of multiple overlapping conflicts since the US-led invasion in 2003. A sectarian civil war, anti-government insurgencies, intra-Shia paramilitary violence and Kurdish forces have all challenged the authority of the Iraqi government and its international partners. Since 2014, however, the war with ISIS – a Sunni jihadist insurgent group that emerged from al-Qaeda in Iraq and Jama'at al-Tawhid wal-Jihad led by Abu Musab al-Zarqawi – has been the main conflict in the country.

On 4 June 2014, ISIS launched a major offensive in northern Iraq and took Tikrit and Mosul, Iraq's second-largest city, within days. The Iraqi security forces partially disintegrated as a result, allowing Kurdish paramilitaries (Peshmerga) to take control of Kirkuk, the strategically vital and oil-rich province at the heart of the territorial dispute between the Iraqi government and the Kurdistan Region of Iraq (KRI).

In October 2014, the rapid advance of ISIS prompted the US and 30 coalition partners to form the Combined Joint Task Force (CJTF) and launch *Operation Inherent Resolve* to 'degrade and destroy' ISIS in both Syria and Iraq. The operation provided air support, materiel, intelligence cooperation and training to the Iraqi security forces and the Peshmerga to retake territory from ISIS. By the end of November 2017, all major towns and cities in Iraq had been retaken.

The rout of the national security forces by ISIS in 2014 prompted Ayatollah Ali al-Sistani, Iraq's leading Shia figure, to issue a religious edict calling on Iraqis to volunteer for the security forces. Various existing Shia paramilitary groups used this fatwa to expand their recruitment and operational role and became an important auxiliary force in the war against ISIS. These groups, many of which have close ties to Iran's Islamic Revolutionary Guard Corps (IRGC), acquired a legally recognised status as the Popular Mobilisation Units (PMU). With the territorial defeat of ISIS, the question of the future of these increasingly politicised groups has resurfaced.

Key Conflict Parties

Iraqi armed forces

Strength
191,000.

Areas of operation
Areas previously held by ISIS, including Anbar, Diyala, Nineva and Salahaddin provinces.

Leadership
Caretaker Prime Minister Adil Abdul-Mahdi (commander-in-chief), Minister of Defence Najah al-Shammari, Minister of Interior Yaseen al-Yasiri.

Structure
The Iraqi armed forces consist of the army, air force and navy. In the fight against ISIS, the army has cooperated with the Federal Police and Counter-Terrorism Service. The army reports to the Ministry of Defence, the Federal Police to the Ministry of Interior and the Counter-Terrorism Service to the Prime Minister's Office.

History
The capture of Tikrit and Mosul by ISIS in 2014 led to the partial disintegration of Iraqi forces. The forces have been rebuilt with the assistance of the US-led coalition but remain insufficiently equipped for counter-insurgency tasks.

Objectives
Defeating ISIS and ensuring security across the country. Since the territorial defeat of ISIS Iraqi forces have focused on eliminating remaining cells in rural areas.

Opponents
ISIS.

Affiliates/allies
Kurdish Peshmerga, Combined Joint Task Force–*Operation Inherent Resolve*.

Resources/capabilities
A range of conventional land, air and naval capabilities including armoured fighting vehicles, anti-tank missile systems, artillery and fixed- and rotary-wing aircraft.

Combined Joint Task Force–*Operation Inherent Resolve* (CJTF–OIR)

Strength
The exact number of coalition forces in Iraq is unknown, but the US, the largest component of the coalition, has approximately 5,000 personnel.

Areas of operation
Working in tandem with Iraqi armed forces, areas previously held by ISIS, including Anbar, Diyala, Nineva and Salahaddin provinces.

Leadership
US Central Command: Commanding General Lt-Gen. Paul LaCamera.

Structure
The US leads the CJTF–OIR, which brings together 30 coalition partners.

History
Established in October 2014 when the US Department of Defense formalised ongoing military operations against ISIS.

Objectives
Fight ISIS in Iraq and Syria, through airstrikes in support of Iraqi and Kurdish forces. Ground forces are deployed as trainers and advisers.

Opponents
ISIS.

Affiliates/allies
Iraqi armed forces, Kurdish Peshmerga.

Resources/capabilities
Air support (airstrikes complementing military operations by Iraqi armed forces) and artillery.

Popular Mobilisation Units (PMU)

Strength
Approximately 100,000.

Areas of operation
Areas previously held by ISIS including Anbar, Nineva, Diyala and Salahaddin provinces, and areas of southern Iraq, particularly the shrine cities of Najaf and Karbala.

Leadership
Formally under the Prime Minister's Office and technically directly answerable to the prime minister, the most prominent groups have some autonomy, such as the Badr Organisation and its leader Hadi al-Ameri, and Asaib Ahl al-Haq and its leader Qais al-Khazali.

Structure
Approximately 40–60 paramilitary units under the umbrella organisation. Formally, the PMU are a branch of the Iraqi security apparatus, but each unit is organised around an internal leader, influential figures and fighters.

History
Formed in 2014 when Grand Ayatollah Ali al-Sistani called upon Iraqi men to protect their homeland against ISIS, the PMU brought together new and pre-existing groups. In 2016, the units were formally recognised as a branch of the Iraqi security apparatus, but recent attempts to consolidate and centralise them met with limited success.

Objectives
Initially emerged to fight ISIS. Some units have evolved into political entities.

Opponents
ISIS.

Affiliates/allies
Iraqi armed forces, Iran's Islamic Revolutionary Guard Corps (IRGC).

Resources/capabilities
Capabilities differ between units. Those supported by Iran receive arms and training from the IRGC, including heavy weapons and small arms.

Islamic State, also known as ISIS or ISIL

Strength
14,000–18,000 in Iraq and Syria, including members and fighters.[2]

Areas of operation
Active predominantly in Iraq's northern and central provinces in mountainous and desert areas. Most attacks in 2019 were launched in the governorates of Anbar, Baghdad, Diyala, Kirkuk, Nineva and Salahaddin.

Leadership
Led by Abu Bakr al-Baghdadi until he was killed in October 2019 and replaced by Amir Mohammed Abdul Rahman al-Mawli al-Salbi (known by the *nom de guerre* Abu Ibrahim al-Hashimi al-Qurayshi).[3]

Structure
Operates as a covert insurgent network across Iraq, using a largely autonomous sleeper-cell structure. Its central command remains in place, but greater autonomy is granted to local cells across the country to facilitate an insurgent campaign.

History
Originated in Iraq around 2003 but proclaimed itself a separate group from al-Qaeda in Iraq, fighting to create a caliphate during the Syrian civil war. In 2014–17, ISIS controlled extensive territories and governed more than eight million people in Syria and Iraq. It has now lost all its territory, since 2017 in Iraq and since March 2019 in Syria.

Islamic State, also known as ISIS or ISIL

Objectives
Maintain a presence across Anbar, Kirkuk and Nineva provinces, harass the Iraqi security forces and the PMU, punish Sunni partners of the Iraqi security forces and PMU. ISIS continues to fight and project ideological influence globally. In Iraq it operates through decentralised, guerrilla-style insurgent tactics, with hit-and-run attacks, kidnappings and killing of civilians, and targeted assassinations of Iraqi armed forces.

Opponents
Iraqi security forces, PMU, Kurdish Peshmerga.

Affiliates/allies
ISIS fighters in other countries.

Resources/capabilities
Carries out attacks through shootings and explosions, using small arms, cars, improvised explosive devices (IEDs) and mortar bombs.

Kurdish Peshmerga

Strength
Approximately 150,000 personnel.

Areas of operation
Kurdistan Region of Iraq (KRI)

Leadership
Nechirvan Barzani (commander-in chief), Shoresh Ismail Abdulla (minister of Peshmerga affairs), Lt-Gen. Jamal Mohammad (Peshmerga chief of staff).

Structure
A Kurdish paramilitary force, acting as the military of the Kurdish Regional Government and Iraqi Kurdistan. While remaining independent, operates officially as part of the Kurdish military system. Split between political factions, the dominant ones being the Kurdistan Democratic Party (KDP) and the Patriotic Union of Kurdistan (PUK).

History
Began as a Kurdish nationalist movement in the 1920s and soon developed into a security organisation. Following the ISIS advance, the Peshmerga took disputed territories in June 2014, including Kirkuk, which were retaken by Iraqi security forces in August 2017.

Objectives
Ensure security in the KRI. During 2019, this has meant fighting ISIS.

Opponents
ISIS.

Affiliates/allies
CJTF–OIR, Iraqi armed forces.

Resources/capabilities
Poorly equipped, lacking heavy weapons, armed vehicles and facilities. The US has provided some financial assistance and light weapons such as rifles and machine guns. US assistance in 2019 has been mostly training.

Drivers

Patronage, corruption and sectarianism
Iraq has a patronage-based system of government that relies on the country's vast oil reserves. The political elite uses rents from oil extraction to reward allies, pursue personal projects and resolve disputes, rather than to fund public goods and services. Jobs in the public sector, with better pay and benefits, are awarded based on party connections or to address public discontent: announcement of more positions in the already bloated public sector are the usual response to protests over poor job opportunities. As a result, incompetence and corruption are systemic, exacerbated by the country's underdeveloped banking sector.

In this system, those without the right connections are often marginalised and denied employment opportunities and access to public services including clean drinking water and stable electricity supply. The legitimacy of central government has been eroded and this has encouraged people to join militias and insurgent groups to gain both dignity and a livelihood. The patronage system also exacerbates antagonism between Iraq's main sects, as most parties are organised along Shia, Sunni or Kurdish lines. Political patronage channels jobs, contracts and services towards certain groups and away from others, thus encouraging sect-based political mobilisation. Sunni grievances at what is perceived as sect-based discrimination and socio-economic marginalisation have facilitated recruitment to insurgent groups.

ISIS has exploited these sectarian divisions. A breakdown in the relationship between Iraq's Sunni community and the Iraqi government allowed the insurgency to gain a foothold in Sunni-majority cities in Iraq's western Anbar province following widespread civil unrest in these areas in 2012–13. ISIS then used these positions to launch attacks in Fallujah, Mosul and Tikrit in 2014. Since its defeat in 2017, sect-based politics has gradually diminished, and a more nationalistic tone has emerged.

Socio-economic challenges

The ISIS insurgency and falling global oil prices (oil accounted for 90% of government revenues and more than half of Iraq's GDP in 2018[4]) caused at least five years of economic hardship in Iraq. Facing a demographic youth bulge, the country also struggles to provide employment opportunities, particularly for graduates. Rapid urbanisation, internal displacement and high unemployment all contribute to socio-economic dislocation that feeds alienation and radicalisation, in turn driving the conflict.

Geopolitical rivalries

Multiple overlapping geopolitical rivalries intersect with Iraq's local conflict. Iran provides materiel and training to and has close ties with numerous Shia paramilitary groups and political parties, including the Islamic Dawa Party, Badr Organisation and Asaib Ahl al-Haq. Turkey established a military camp at Bashiqa, Nineva governorate, and trained a 3,000-strong force under former Nineva governor Atheel al-Nujaifi. At various times since 2003, both Syria and the Gulf states provided support to Sunni insurgents in Iraq.

Geopolitical rivalries have also eroded Iraq's capacity to build a coherent, unified state and security apparatus. The Iran–US and Iran–Saudi rivalries contributed to the proliferation of non-state paramilitaries that continue to challenge the government's monopoly over the legitimate use of force in its territory. The US and Iran vie for influence over Iraq's political institutions and security forces, even running competing organisational networks within the Ministry of Interior. The Iran–Saudi rivalry has also dragged Iraq's conflicts into wider regional confrontations, with several of Iraq's Iran-backed Shia paramilitary groups fighting in support of Bashar al-Assad in Syria.

Political Developments

Iran–US and regional tensions

Iraq was caught between Iran and the US again in 2019, with tensions reaching new heights. Tehran and Washington strived to bring Baghdad under their sphere of influence, while Iraqi officials struggled to maintain a balance between their relationship with both. In March, in an attempt to limit Iranian influence, the US Treasury added Harakat Hezbollah al-Nujaba, an Iran-allied group within the PMU, to its sanctions list. In April, US President Donald Trump announced the designation of the IRGC as a foreign terrorist organisation.

Despite pressure from both the US and Iran for Iraq to diminish ties with the other, stability in the country is dependent on an Iran–US equilibrium in which Baghdad does not take sides. Iraq depends on Iran for energy and goods, and on the US for military training and counter-terrorism and counter-insurgency operations. US support has been essential in the fight against ISIS, during which the Iraqi security forces conducted several operations with US assistance. Forgoing its relationship with either country would damage Iraq's security, and its political and economic stability.

Role of the PMU

The role of the PMU is a point of contention between Iran and the US. The largest and most powerful paramilitary groups are linked to Iran, and the US is concerned that this could strengthen Iran's influence in Iraq. Within Iraq, there are two dominant positions in the debate on the future role of the PMU. The first advocates for their autonomy, enabling them to function alongside the army as a separate entity. The second proposes their integration into the armed forces, under the Ministry of Defence, or into the federal police, under the Ministry of Interior.

On 1 July, Prime Minister Adil Abdul-Mahdi decreed the integration of the PMU into the armed forces or the federal police, ordering that the names of all PMU groups should be replaced with military designations, and that all economic offices, checkpoints and other PMU locations should be closed. The units that did not wish to follow these directives should disband or transition into political parties. The deadline was 31 July, but by the end of the year, Chairman of the Popular Mobilisation Committee Falih al-Fayyadh had registered only the closure of a few economic offices.

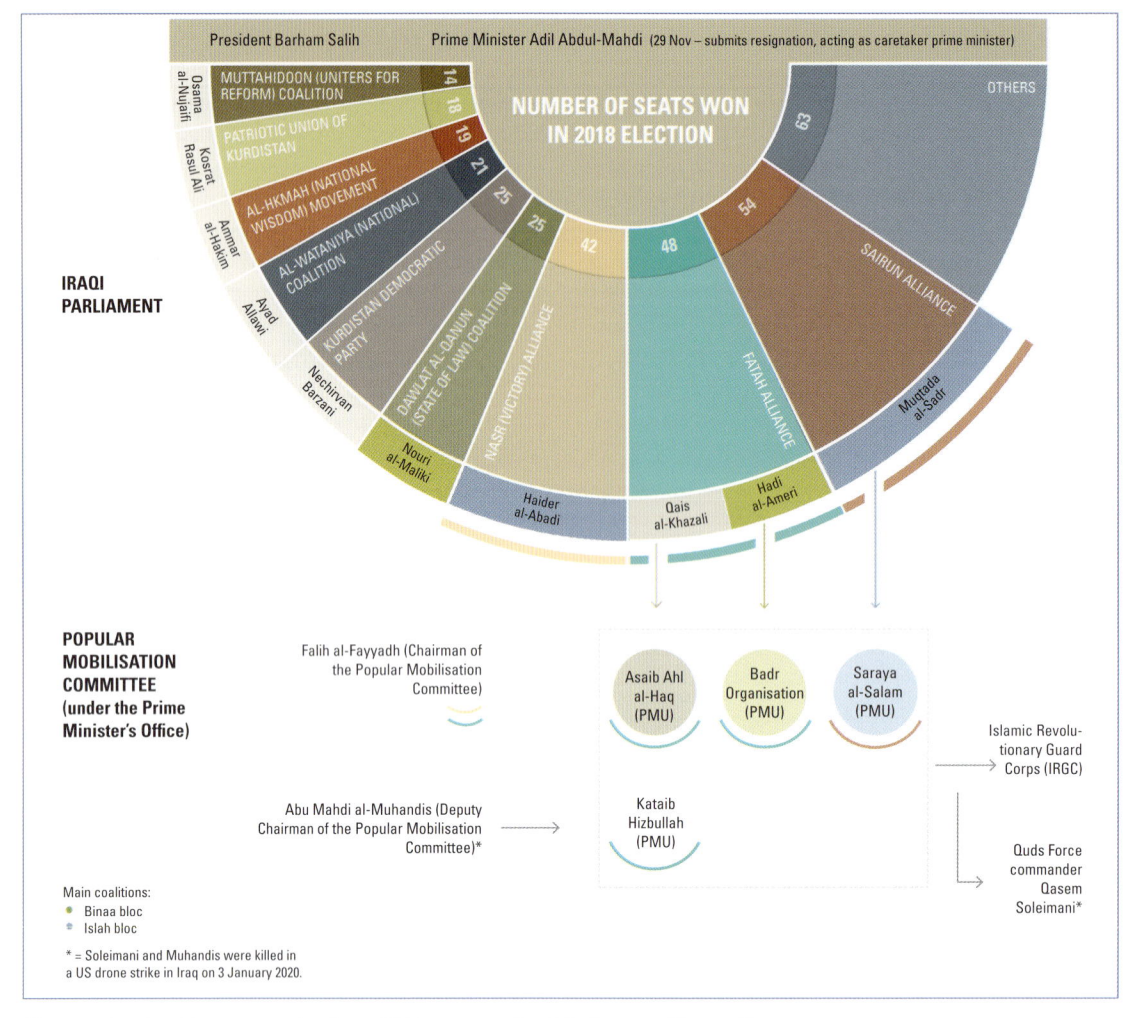

Figure 1: Iraqi parliamentary elections, 2018: seats and political–paramilitary alliances

Previous prime ministers had also called for the integration of paramilitary units, the most recent attempt being that of Haider al-Abadi in March 2018. Little has changed in practice, however, mostly because governments are weak and rely on coalitions with many conflicting interests (particularly in the case of Abdul-Mahdi). As a result, Iraqi officials have yet to present a plan for the integration. The decrees call for integration but fail to outline how such measures would be implemented.

Protests and instability
In October 2019, Iraqi citizens poured onto the streets of several cities to voice anger and dissatisfaction towards the government. Protests began peacefully in Baghdad on 1 October and spread to other cities in the south, including Diwaniya, Nasiriyah, Hilla and Najaf. Demonstrators called on the government to provide basic services and tackle corruption. The security forces responded with heavy-handed tactics, using tear gas and live ammunition to disperse the protests, with fatalities reaching over 500 by December, according to the Iraqi Ministry of Health.[5]

The grievances of the protesters were like those that had sparked previous demonstrations. Lack of job opportunities for a burgeoning youth population, rampant corruption and provision of essential services are persistent causes of discontent in Iraq. Unlike previous rounds of protests, however, those in 2019 were spontaneous and decentralised, not controlled by a specific leader or party. Protesters did not call for reform as they had previously, but rather demanded a complete overhaul of the current political system.

Shia cleric Muqtada al-Sadr, who has often incited protests, supported the protesters from the start and eventually officially sided with them by withdrawing his Sairoon coalition from government on 26 October. Abdul-Mahdi announced reforms, including ministerial changes and amendments to the constitution and electoral laws. Protesters were not satisfied by the promise of reforms and demanded a change in the political system and leadership, including Abdul-Mahdi's resignation, which was subsequently announced on 29 November.

On 24 December, the Iraqi parliament passed changes to the electoral legislation, allowing voters to elect individuals rather than choosing from party lists, in an attempt to address protesters' concerns and make elections fairer. However, protesters highlighted that this move maintained the current political class with which they were dissatisfied. Protests continued as parliament was tasked with electing a new prime minister, with Abdul-Mahdi maintaining a 'caretaker' position. On 26 December, after the Iraqi parliament's biggest bloc, Binaa, nominated the current governor of Basra Asaad al-Eidani for the position, President Barham Salih said that he was 'ready to resign' rather than accept the nomination of a candidate the protest movement rejected.

Military Developments

ISIS insurgency

After the loss of its territory in Iraq in 2017, ISIS retreated to remote areas with rough terrain and avoided major battlefield engagements, resorting to the insurgency tactics of its earlier years. This shift led the group to focus on hit-and-run and suicide attacks in the areas it once controlled, including Anbar province, particularly the Jazeera desert, Nineva province and the Makhmur mountains, Diyala province and the Hamrin mountain range, and the areas of Kirkuk and Salahaddin.

As a result, the frequency of ISIS attacks was much lower in 2019 than in previous years, but its selective targeting meant that the threat of attacks remained high. Its main targets were the Iraqi security forces, including the army and the federal police, with ambushes or hit-and-run attacks against patrols and checkpoints. On 21 October, ISIS militants killed two members of the Iraqi security forces and wounded three others in an attack on checkpoints in the Allas oilfields, northern Salahaddin province.[6] The insurgents also targeted members of the PMU and their families, as well as local leaders, including tribal leaders and governors of towns and cities. On 13 April, ISIS militants targeted a PMU checkpoint in Khanaqin, Diyala province, injuring four members of the PMU.[7] Civilians were also targeted, with car bombs or suicide attacks in cities including Mosul, Kirkuk and Baghdad, in the latter of which Shia areas were targeted. On 20 September, ISIS militants detonated a bomb on a bus at a checkpoint north of Karbala, an important city for Shia Muslims, killing 12 people.[8]

The Iraqi security forces continued with efforts to clear ISIS militants from the desert regions of Anbar province and the mountainous areas of Nineva and Diyala provinces but faced numerous challenges. Firstly, for years these forces were trained and equipped to conduct battlefield operations and defeat ISIS territorially, and they found themselves ill-equipped for counter-insurgency operations. Secondly, the already overstretched forces found it difficult to reach and maintain a presence in the remote areas where ISIS cells exist. Thirdly, the forces fighting militants were often divided, with the army, federal police, counter-terrorism service and the PMU differing in their preferred method of fighting. Coordinated joint operations were often disjointed and incoherent, particularly between counter-terrorism forces and the PMU.

Regional tensions

Various incidents in May pointed to a tense atmosphere in the region. Iran was thought to be responsible for the incidents on 12 May in which two Saudi Arabian oil tankers, a Norwegian oil tanker and an Emirati bunkering ship were damaged off the Fujairah coast in the Gulf of Oman, and on 14 May, when Yemen's Ansarullah launched a drone attack on a Saudi oil pipeline. On 15 May, the US evacuated all non-emergency staff from its embassy in Baghdad and consulate in Erbil. On 18 May, ExxonMobil evacuated its foreign staff from

Basra. On 19 May, a rocket was fired into Baghdad's Green Zone, near the US Embassy, an attack later claimed by a previously unknown armed group, Operations of Martyr Ali Mansour, which denied any connection to Iran. On 13 June, the US accused Iran of attacking a Japanese oil tanker and a Norwegian oil tanker near the Strait of Hormuz. On 18 June, a rocket was fired onto a military base east of Mosul hosting US military troops. The following day another rocket was fired on the Burjesia site in Basra that houses the headquarters of international oil companies including ExxonMobil. There were no immediate claims of responsibility. On 24 September, rockets fell again in Baghdad's Green Zone near the US Embassy, with no group claiming responsibility.

Tensions between the US and Iran-allied groups, particularly Kataib Hizbullah, reached a new peak in the final week of 2019. On 27 December, a rocket attack on the K1 military base in Kirkuk killed an American contractor and wounded at least four military personnel. Kataib Hizbullah was suspected of being responsible. Two days later the US conducted airstrikes on bases belonging to Kataib Hizbullah, killing 25 of its fighters in Qaim, Anbar province. On 31 December, supporters of the group raided the US embassy in Baghdad's Green Zone in protest against the strike.

Impact

Human rights
In the fight against ISIS, civilian casualties decreased in 2019 compared to 2018, reflecting an overall decline in civilian deaths since the territorial defeat of ISIS in Iraq in 2017.[10] However, the violence against protesters in October resulted in at least 500 fatalities by the end of the year, an unprecedented figure in post-2003 Iraq for non-terrorist-related incidents.

Trials and investigative hearings of suspected ISIS militants, including foreign fighters, continued in 2019 and attracted international attention. Human-rights groups have criticised Iraq's handling of ISIS suspects, with Iraqi and Kurdish authorities being accused of arbitrary detentions, unfair trials and the use of torture to obtain confessions. Since Western states showed little willingness to repatriate their foreign fighters, Iraqi President Barham Salih announced that suspects would all be tried under Iraqi law. Iraq's counter-terrorism legislation allows for the death penalty if an individual is found to be a member of a terrorist organisation, regardless of having committed any acts.

Humanitarian
Reconstruction efforts or humanitarian responses were not priorities for the Iraqi government in 2019, particularly in relation to internally displaced persons (IDPs). Funds for humanitarian programmes were particularly low, with only US$295 million of the US$701m needed to assist IDPs and vulnerable communities received by 15 September 2019, according to the UN.[11] The lack of funding

Key Events in 2019

Political events

- **24 February**: The SDF hand over 280 ISIS detainees to Iraq, including 14 French citizens.
- **14 April**: The trials begin of 900 people accused of being members of ISIS.
- **15, 18 May**: The US pulls all non-emergency staff from its embassy in Baghdad and consulate in Erbil. ExxonMobil then evacuates its foreign staff from West Qurna oilfield.
- **23–24 May**: Protests take place in Basra against lack of jobs. Protests in Baghdad call for Iraq not to take sides despite increasing US–Iran tensions.

Military/Violent events

- **29 January**: Iraqi airstrikes kill six ISIS militants near Rutba, Anbar province.
- **6 March**: ISIS militants kill seven members of the PMU in an ambush near Makhmur, Erbil province.
- **4 April**: Iraqi airstrikes kill 14 ISIS militants in Wadi Qarah, Kirkuk province.
- **15 May**: Muqtada al-Sadr calls on supporters to protest in Najaf. Mall guards fire at demonstrators, killing four.
- **19 May**: A *Katyusha* rocket is fired into Baghdad's Green Zone and falls near the US Embassy, causing no casualties.

added to the ongoing scaling down of education projects, including the closure of learning centres in displacement camps in Nineva.

Social

The transfer of the fight against ISIS to desert and mountainous areas eased the social impact of the conflict in less remote areas. With the help of the UN, many schools, universities and educational institutes were reopened in urban centres, including Nineva University, which enrolled 5,000 students for the 2019–20 academic year.

However, access to water and electricity remained a problem throughout the country, with power outages continuing in various cities, including Baghdad where some households went for hours without electricity in the summer. The Iraqi electricity sector's operable capacity in 2019 was estimated at 18 GW, while demand was expected to have reached 24 GW.[12] Basra province in particular continued to lack clean water, due to neglect and mismanagement of water infrastructure and reserves by the local authorities.[13]

Economic

Iraq's economy struggled to recover, although there was some improvement for the first time since the defeat of ISIS in 2017. GDP grew at 4.8% in the first half of 2019,[14] compared to the 1% contraction of 2018 and the 4% contraction of 2017.[15] The growth was mainly due to an increase in crude-oil production, an expansionary fiscal policy and a rise in non-oil economic activity, partly as a result of increased rainfall.

Relations with neighbouring and international partners

Iraq continued to pursue a friendly relationship with both Iran and the US and strived to replicate its neutrality among other powers in the region, including Saudi Arabia and Turkey. On 20 April, officials from its six neighbouring countries (Iran, Jordan, Kuwait, Saudi Arabia, Syria and Turkey) gathered for a summit hosted by Speaker of Parliament Mohammed al-Halbusi, with the objective of encouraging cooperation and debate despite the conflicting positions. However, Iraq was in no position to mediate major regional or international crises such as Iran–US tensions.[16]

Trends

Political trajectories

The mass protests in Iraq exposed the unstable nature of its political system. Demonstrators rejected Abdul-Mahdi's proposed reforms, which they saw as simply continuing previous approaches and ultimately unable to address the structural causes of their discontent. The violence against protesters fuelled anger further. The withdrawal of Muqtada al-Sadr's Sairoon coalition from government heightened the political fragility, while protests showed little sign of subsiding unless the existing system was completely overturned with new elections leading to constitutional reform. Following Abdul-Mahdi's resignation, Iraqi legislators faced the

1 July
The prime minister issues a decree integrating the PMU into the Iraqi armed forces.

October–November
Protests take place in Baghdad and several cities in southern Iraq against corruption and lack of basic service provision. Security forces respond with violence, killing at least 200 people in one month.[9]

29 November
Prime Minister Adil Abdul-Mahdi submits his resignation.

24 December
Parliament passes significant changes to the electoral law.

15, 17, 19 June
Mortar shells and rockets are fired at three Iraqi bases hosting US forces.

20 September
ISIS detonates a bomb in a bus near the holy city of Karbala, killing 12 people.

3, 27 November
Protesters attack the Iranian consulate in Karbala and Najaf respectively.

27 December
A rocket attack on the K1 military base in Kirkuk kills an American contractor. Iranian-linked Kataib Hizbullah is suspected of being responsible.

29 December
The US conducts airstrikes on bases belonging to Kataib Hizbullah, killing 25 of its fighters in Qaim, Anbar province.

difficult task of finding a candidate who both the largest political blocs and the dissatisfied public would approve. Salih's announcement of his readiness to resign on 26 December was a direct result of this difficulty. Promising signs, such as the passing of amendments to electoral legislation, establishing electoral districts and allowing voters to vote for individual candidates, pointed towards meaningful change. However, while the legislation was passed, it remained unlikely to be implemented soon, due to the fragmented state of parliament and the members' inability to appoint a prime minister, leaving the country leaderless.

Conflict-related risks
A large-scale retake of territory by ISIS is unlikely. The population in the Sunni-majority areas of Iraq's central and northern provinces do not support an ISIS-led alternative to the state as they did in 2014. This attitude is reflected in the lack of widespread protests in those areas. ISIS militants will nonetheless continue their insurgent efforts, targeting key groups associated with the state. Amid political instability, however, an ISIS resurgence does remain a possibility in certain pockets of Iraqi territory, particularly the mountainous regions of Nineva and Diyala, as well as the desert areas in Anbar. Militants may capitalise on popular dissatisfaction to recruit fighters and gain supporters among marginalised communities.

Prospects for peace
With the territorial defeat of ISIS in 2017, peace in Iraq became more attainable, but the path remains long. Several challenges remain to Iraq's long-lasting stability. Firstly, ISIS will continue to pose a security risk, albeit a diminished one. Iraqi security forces will continue to conduct operations aimed at clearing the areas ISIS previously held. Without an adequate counter-insurgency strategy, sufficient resources and proper cohesion and coordination, Iraqi security forces will struggle to defeat the remaining militants. Secondly, political instability will continue, amid attempts to reconstitute the government and install a more legitimate political leadership in the wake of protests. Finally, slow reconstruction and economic development will continue to fuel popular dissatisfaction if the government fails to prioritise the provision of basic services.

Strategic implications and global influences
While the level of conflict declined in 2019, political instability remained rife, which had both domestic and international implications. Protesters criticised the domestic political system, while also calling for the expulsion of foreign powers from Iraq. These demands were directed at both Iran and the US. However, it is unlikely that this anger will translate into drastic changes in the short to medium term. Iraq relies heavily on Iran and the US for security, goods and resources, and needs the cooperation of both to ensure its own stability. Despite its efforts to distance Iraq from Iran, the US is aware that Baghdad is dependent on energy imports from Iran and is unlikely to end sanctions exemptions that allow Iraq to receive these imports. Nonetheless, the prominence of Iran-allied groups in the Iraqi political and security scene will lead to further tensions between Iran and the US manifesting in Iraq. Iraq's relationship with these two competing external powers is key to ensuring stability in the country in the near future.

Notes

[1] Human Rights Watch, 'Iraq: State Appears Complicit in Massacre of Protesters', 16 December 2019.
[2] US Department of Defense Office of Inspector General, 'Operation Inherent Resolve: Lead Inspector General Report to the United States Congress', 1 April 2019–30 June 2019.
[3] The name initially given as Baghdadi's replacement was Abu Ibrahim al-Hashimi al-Qurayshi. It emerged in January 2020 that this was a *nom de guerre*.
[4] World Bank Group, 'Iraq Economic Monitor: From War to Reconstruction and Economic Recovery', Spring 2018.
[5] Human Rights Watch, 'Iraq: State Appears Complicit in Massacre of Protesters'.
[6] 'Islamic State attack kills two security forces near northern Iraqi oilfields', Reuters, 21 October 2019.
[7] Loaa Adel, '4 paramilitary fighters injured by ISIS attack on Khanaqin', Iraqi News, 13 April 2019.
[8] 'ISIS claims blast that killed 12 near Iraq's Karbala', *National*, 22 September 2019.
[9] 'Death toll rises in Baghdad protests, military declares curfew in Iraqi capital', France24, 28 October 2019.
[10] United Nations Security Council, 'Implementation of Resolution 2470 (2019) – Report of the Secretary-General', 5 August 2019.

[11] United Nations Security Council, 'Implementation of Resolution 2470 (2019) – Report of the Secretary-General', 22 November 2019.

[12] 'Solving Iraq's electricity crisis', Castlereagh Associates, 30 May 2019.

[13] Human Rights Watch, 'Basra is Thirsty: Iraq's Failure to Manage the Water Crisis', 22 July 2019.

[14] World Bank, 'Iraq's Economic Update – October 2019', 9 October 2019.

[15] World Bank, 'GDP per capita growth (annual %) – Iraq'.

[16] Iraqi officials have avoided referring to themselves as mediators, rather, as Abdul-Mahdi stated, they are 'trying to defuse the crisis'. Qassim Abdul-Zahra, 'Iraqi PM says he want to end tensions between Iran and US', Associated Press, 21 May 2019.

ISRAEL–PALESTINE

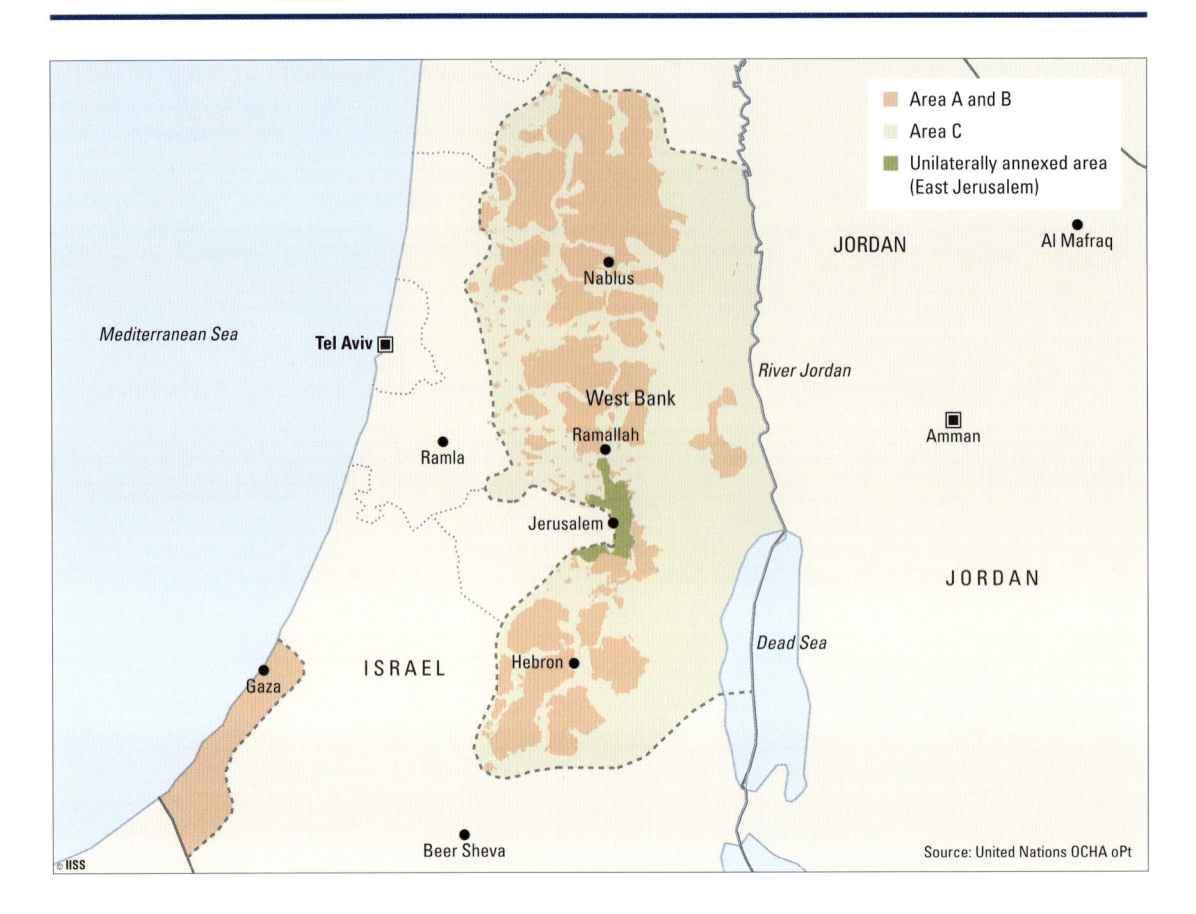

Overview

The conflict in 2019

The Israel–Palestine conflict continued unabated in 2019. In May, fighting in the Gaza Strip escalated rapidly in the worst outbreak of violence since the war of 2014. Violence also characterised the protests of Gaza citizens, which have taken place on a weekly basis since the 'Great March of Return' in March 2018, aimed at highlighting the dire economic situation in the Strip and demanding the right of return for Palestinian refugees. According to B'Tselem, an Israeli human-rights organisation, Israeli security forces were responsible for the deaths of 216 Palestinians protesters in the period up until June.[1]

Besides the intermittent clashes in the Gaza Strip, lone-wolf attacks by Palestinians against Israeli civilians and security personnel in the West Bank and Jerusalem raised tensions and heightened inflammatory rhetoric throughout the Israeli elections. Settler violence also increased in the midst of promises by Prime Minister Benjamin Netanyahu to extend Israeli sovereignty to all West Bank settlements, in addition to the Jordan Valley. These promises, made prior to both the April and September elections, coincided with governmental approval for an expansion of West Bank settlements.

Key statistics

Type	Internal
Start date	November 1947
IDPs total (December 2018)	238,000
Refugees total (February 2019)	5,545,540
People in need (31 December 2019)	2,400,000

Against the backdrop of the increasing alignment between the United States and the Israeli administrations, and a fragmented European Union, prospects of an effective peace process remained slim.

The conflict to 2019

The Israel–Palestine conflict began with the outbreak of a civil war in November 1947, a day after the United Nations' adoption of the partition plan that called for the creation of a Jewish state alongside a Palestinian state. The civil war was followed by an official war in May 1948, when the armies of Syria, Egypt, Transjordan and Iraq, along with contingents from other Arab countries, attacked the newly founded state of Israel after the formal termination of the British Mandate. The war resulted in the displacement – including through force – of between 650,000 and 1 million Palestinians from their homes inside what became the 1948 borders. A further 50,000 Palestinians were internally displaced within Israel.

The 1948 War did not put an end to regional and domestic conflict. In two successive wars (1967 and 1973), Israel defeated a coalition of Arab states led by Egypt and Syria. During the 1967 Six-Day War, Israel captured the West Bank, the Gaza Strip, East Jerusalem and the Golan Heights. The dire socio-economic effects of Israel's ongoing military occupation subsequently led to the outbreak of two Palestinian uprisings, known as Intifadas, in 1987–93 and 2000–05; three Israeli military operations in Gaza (2008–09, 2012 and 2014); and intermittent waves of violence and terrorist attacks.

Despite numerous pledges over the years, final-status negotiations, as set out in the Declarations of Principals encapsulated in the 1993 Accords (Oslo I), have so far failed to materialise. A peace initiative led by then-secretary of state John Kerry faltered in 2016, leading Kerry to conclude that the prospects for the creation of a Palestinian state were negligible.[2] Future negotiations look likely to be further complicated by both Israel's constant settlement expansion in the West Bank and East Jerusalem and the inter-Palestinian political rivalry between Gaza-based Hamas and the West Bank-based Palestinian Authority (PA).

Key Conflict Parties

Israel Defense Forces (IDF)

Strength
As of 2019, the IDF had a standing strength of 169,500 personnel, with a further 465,000 in reserve.

Areas of operation
West Bank, Gaza, Lebanon, Syria and Iraq.

Leadership
In January 2019, Aviv Kochavi replaced Gadi Eisenkot as chief of staff and will serve a three-year term.

Structure
The IDF is divided into three service branches: ground forces, navy and air.

History
The IDF was founded in 1948 from the paramilitary organisation Haganah, which fought during the 1948 War.

Objectives
Israel's defence policy prioritises homeland defence, but Israel's anti-Iran strategy became increasingly overt in 2019, with strikes targeting Iranian positions in Syria and, allegedly, Iraq, to curb Iranian weapons transfers and military build-ups.

Opponents
Hamas, Hizbullah, Iran, Iran-backed groups.

Affiliates/allies
The IDF maintains close military relations with the US. In 2016, the two governments signed a new ten-year Memorandum of Understanding (MOU), covering fiscal years 2019–28, under which the US pledged to provide US$38 billion in military aid to Israel.[3]

Resources/capabilities
The IDF relies on sophisticated equipment and training. It has a highly capable and modern defence industry, including aerospace; intelligence, surveillance and reconnaissance (ISR); and counter-rocket systems. It is also believed to have an operational nuclear-weapons capability, though estimates of the size of such arsenal vary. The IDF can operate simultaneously in the West Bank, Gaza, Lebanon, Syria and Iraq.

Hamas

Strength
Hamas's military wing, the Izz al-Din al-Qassam Brigades (IDQ), which consists of eight separate units, is estimated to comprise around 15,000–20,000 fighters trained in urban warfare.

Areas of operation
Gaza Strip, Israel, West Bank.

Leadership
In 2017, Yahya Sinwar replaced Ismail Haniyeh as head of Hamas, with the latter taking over as chief of the central Political Bureau.

Structure
Hamas's internal political leadership exercises ultimate authority; other wings and branches, including IDQ, follow the strategy and guidelines set by Hamas's Consultative Council and Political Bureau.

History
Founded in 1987 by members of the Muslim Brotherhood in the Palestinian Territories, Hamas is the largest Palestinian militant Islamist group. It has been designated a terrorist group by the US and the EU, but many Palestinians view it as a legitimate popular resistance group.

Objectives
Hamas's original charter called for the obliteration or dissolution of Israel, but Haniyeh stated in 2008 that Hamas would accept a Palestinian state within the 1967 borders. This position was confirmed in a new charter in 2017, which stated that Hamas's struggle was with the 'Zionist project'.

Opponents
Israel, Palestinian Islamic Jihad (periodically), Salafi jihadi groups, Fatah-led Palestinian Authority (PA).

Affiliates/allies
Hamas relies on financial support and arms and technology transfers from its main regional backer, Iran. A 2019 report found that Iran had agreed to increase its funding to Hamas by US$24m a month (to the total tune of US$30m) in exchange for intelligence on Israeli missile stockpiles.[4]

Resources/capabilities
The IDQ's capabilities include artillery rockets, mortars and anti-tank systems. Israel's military actions have periodically degraded the command and the physical infrastructure of Hamas but seemingly have had little effect on the long-term ability of the IDQ to import and produce rockets and other weapons.

Palestinian Islamic Jihad (PIJ)

Strength
The al-Quds Brigades, the armed wing of the PIJ, consists of approximately 6,000 combatants.

Areas of operation
Gaza Strip.

Leadership
In September 2018, Ziad al-Nakhalah replaced Ramadan Abdullah Shallah as PIJ's secretary-general following his election by the leadership council. Since its exile from Lebanon, PIJ's leadership has operated from Syria.

Structure
PIJ is governed by a 15-member leadership council. In 2018, in the first elections since 1980, PIJ elected nine new members to the council, who represent PIJ members in the West Bank, the Gaza Strip, Israeli prisons and abroad.

History
PIJ was established in 1979 by Fathi Shaqaqi and Abd al-Aziz Awda, who were members of the Egyptian Muslim Brotherhood until the late 1970s. Among the Gaza-based militant groups, PIJ poses the greatest challenge to Hamas's authority in the Strip and has derailed unofficial ceasefire agreements between Hamas and Israel.

Objectives
PIJ aims to establish a sovereign, Islamic Palestinian state within the borders of pre-1948 Palestine. Since the late 1980s, PIJ has carried out suicide-bombing attacks and, in the past decade, fired rockets into Israeli territory, at times in coordination with Hamas. PIJ refuses to negotiate with Israel and does not seek political representation within the PA.

Opponents
Israel and, periodically, Hamas.

Affiliates/allies
PIJ's primary sponsor is Iran, which has provided the group with millions of dollars of funding in addition to training and weapons. Since the leadership's relocation to Damascus in 1989, the Syrian regime has also offered military aid and sanctuary to PIJ.

Resources/capabilities
PIJ has increased the size of its weapons cache by producing its own rockets. Nakhalah has stated that PIJ has the ability to fire more than 1,000 rockets daily for a month in the event of a new war. Analysts, however, estimate that PIJ has some 8,000 rockets in its stockpile.[5]

Drivers

Land disputes and settlement issues
The origins of the Israel–Palestine conflict lie in the inter-communal violence in Mandatory Palestine (1920–48) between Jews and Palestinians. Increased Jewish immigration from the late nineteenth century, in addition to incompatible nationhood pledges made by contemporary Western superpowers, heightened land disputes.

These diverging national objectives largely centred on presumed religious and historical rights to the same territory and singular claims to the holy city, Jerusalem.

The UN's adoption of the Partition Plan in November 1947, which was accepted by Zionist leaders but rejected by the Palestinian leadership, led to the outbreak of a civil war in Palestine. Military operations in turn exacerbated pre-existing territorial disputes. The 1967 War resulted in the Israeli occupation of East Jerusalem, the West Bank, the Gaza Strip and the Golan Heights. Since then, Israel has strived to keep the Palestinian Territories under its control; in 1980 and 1981 it passed laws formally annexing East Jerusalem and the Golan Heights, respectively. With the nation-state law (adopted in July 2018), the Knesset designated Jerusalem the 'complete and united' capital of Israel.

The occupation of the West Bank also heralded the beginning of Israel's settlement policy. The Allon Plan (named after the then Israeli minister of labor Yigal Allon) was based on the doctrine that sovereignty over large swathes of Israeli-occupied territory was necessary for Israel's defence, and became the framework for the settlement policies implemented by successive Israeli leaders. Since 1967, more than 140 Israeli settlements have been established across the West Bank and East Jerusalem (with circa 640,000 people), although settlements are illegal under international law, violating Article 49 of the Fourth Geneva Convention of 1949.

The PA sees the settlements as proof of Israel's lack of commitment to a two-state solution. This perception has been reinforced by the fact that although some Israeli administrations have attempted to restrict or reverse the movement of settlers – then-prime minister Ariel Sharon forcibly evacuated some 8,800 settlers from the Gaza Strip in 2005 – settlements continue to proliferate. The Israeli government outlawed the construction of additional settlements in the West Bank in the mid-1990s, but dozens of unauthorised outposts have since been established. Constant settlement growth has fragmented and dramatically reduced the territory foreseen for an independent Palestinian state as part of the 1993 Oslo Accords. The two-state solution based on pre-1967 borders has therefore become increasingly difficult to realise.

Palestinian economic malaise

Failed peace negotiations have enabled ongoing Israeli control over the Palestinian economy. Restrictive import and export policies, in addition to the territories' reliance on foreign aid and Israeli management of Palestinian taxes and import duties, have had a devastating effect on the Palestinian economy and further eroded Palestinian–Israeli relations. Palestine's trade deficit has grown substantially over the past two decades. Israeli products have free access to the Palestinian markets while Palestinian exports to Israel are subject to a wide range of restrictions. A UN report in 2016 concluded that the Palestinian economy is impeded by 'restrictions on the movement of people and goods; the systematic erosion and destruction of the productive base; loss of land, water and other natural resources'.[6] A World Bank report in 2014 found that these same restrictions in Area C of the West Bank led to approximately US$800m in lost government revenue for the PA each year.[7]

Under the 1994 Paris Protocol, which governs Israeli–Palestinian economic relations, Israel is supposed to collect value-added tax, import duties and other taxes on the PA's behalf and transfer them on a monthly basis. The PA is highly dependent on these tax revenues; they account for approximately 63% of its budget and 15% of its GDP. Under a law adopted by the Israeli Knesset in February 2019, Israel started deducting about 7% (approximately US$138m) of the PA's monthly tax revenues – the equivalent of the amount that, according to the Knesset, the PA hands over to Palestinians convicted of terrorism. PA President Mahmoud Abbas subsequently announced that he would henceforth refuse all tax revenues, a decision which had major financial repercussions for the West Bank economy and the Palestinian public sector. In July 2019, Abbas also declared that he would cease all security coordination with his Israeli counterparts in response to Israel's non-compliance with the Paris Protocol.

Since 2007, Israel and Egypt have imposed a crippling economic blockade on the Gaza Strip, resulting in a shortage of basic products, including food, medical supplies, fuel and construction materials. This situation led to a proliferation of smuggling tunnels under the border with Egypt. After ousting Egypt's then-president Muhammad Morsi, General Abdel Fattah Al-Sisi dismantled most of the tunnel complex that supplied Gaza, destroying almost 1,500 tunnels between 2013 and 2014. The combination of the collapse of the 'tunnel economy' (controlled and taxed by the Hamas government), the continuation of the Israeli embargo (together with restrictions on Gazan farmers and fishermen) and Hamas's bad governance has had a devastating effect on the local economy and the population's well-being. In October 2019, the World Bank reported that the unemployment rate in the Gaza Strip had increased by almost four percentage points in the second quarter of the year to reach 47%;[8] unemployment among those aged under 26 stood at 69% in 2018.[9] Public despair resulting from socio-economic hardship not only precipitates outbreaks of violence, but can also be the subject of violent retorts. Hamas resorted to force as a means to curb expressions of internal criticism in early 2019, when protesters sought to highlight the high cost of living and the increase in taxes on goods imposed by the ruling group.

Political Developments

Israel's settlement policy
The Israeli government's settlement policy continues to represent a serious obstacle to peace. In late 2019, 427,800 settlers were living in the West Bank across 132 settlements and 121 outposts, constituting approximately 14% of the entire West Bank population. In addition, some 215,000 Jews live in East Jerusalem across 13 Israeli neighbourhoods and 13 settlements inside Palestinian neighbourhoods.[10] In August 2019, the Israeli government approved an additional 2,304 housing units in the West Bank and regularised three outposts retrospectively.[11] One of these outposts, Mevo'ot Yericho, is slated to become the sixth official settlement since the Oslo Accords, as per a cabinet decision of September 2019. Some 805 tenders were issued by the Housing Ministry for the construction of housing units in East Jerusalem, in accordance with plans approved since 2017 to increase the density of built-up areas. Meanwhile, in the period to 31 October 2019, Israel demolished 70 housing units across the West Bank, leaving 197 people homeless.[12] In the same period, it demolished 155 Palestinian housing units in East Jerusalem, compared to 59 in the whole of 2018.[13]

Netanyahu's hardline electioneering
In an attempt to secure his political survival, Netanyahu adopted fringe ideas advocated by far-right-wing parties, such as Tkuma. Prior to the April and September 2019 elections (the latter being held after Netanyahu failed to form a government after the April elections), Netanyahu promised to annex the West Bank upon his re-election. A pre-election survey conducted in March 2019 found that such a move would garner support among voters for Zionist centre-left parties, such as Labor and Meretz, which have traditionally advocated for the two-state solution, indicating a broad political move to the right.

Key Events in 2019

Political events

- **January**: Hamas rejects US$12m in Qatari aid after Israel imposes new conditions on the funds entering the Gaza Strip.
- **February**: PA President Mahmoud Abbas returns tax revenues – representing 65% of the PA's budget – to Israel.
- **25 March**: Trump announces a formal recognition of Israeli sovereignty over the Golan Heights.
- **9 April**: Legislative elections result in a tie between Netanyahu's Likud party and Benny Gantz's Blue and White party.
- **July**: Abbas announces that Palestinians will no longer abide by agreements with Israel made over the past 25 years.

Military/Violent events

- **4–5 May**: Militants in Gaza and Israeli security forces clash, leaving four Israelis dead together with more than 20 Palestinians.

In September, following additional rocket attacks, political and military sources confirmed that Netanyahu sought to go to war in the Gaza Strip in an attempt to postpone the general elections in order to secure his political survival in the midst of ongoing corruption investigations (under Israeli law, prime ministers are not required to resign if charged with a crime). In November, after months of deliberations, Netanyahu was indicted on charges of fraud, bribery and breach of trust – the first-ever charges against a sitting Israeli prime minister.

Failed peace negotiations

US President Donald Trump's long-anticipated peace plan, composed by his son-in-law Jared Kushner and dubbed the 'deal of the century', did not result in a breakthrough in the peace negotiations. The US-sponsored Manama conference, which took place in June and sought to highlight the potential economic benefits of a solution to the Israel–Palestine conflict, did not include any Israeli or Palestinian officials. While Palestinian attempts to implement a large-scale regional boycott of the conference failed, key participants refused to endorse the economic-assistance plan in the absence of a viable political proposal.

While the US has never been perceived as an unbiased broker, the Trump administration has implemented far-reaching, pro-Israeli policies that have undone his predecessors' work and alienated the Palestinian leadership, eroding the credibility of the United States' role in negotiations. US attempts to coerce Palestinian leaders to the negotiating table have also proved ineffective: ongoing US cuts to Palestinian aid, including the termination of US Agency for International Development (USAID) assistance in February 2019, did not result in the PA agreeing to concessions or bring about Palestinian engagement.

PA's lack of legitimacy, climate of corruption

With no elections held since 2006, Abbas remained the primary decision-maker and partner for the international community in 2019, despite a clear lack of popular support. A poll conducted in September 2019 found that 61% of Palestinians in both the West Bank and Gaza would like to see the octogenarian leader step down.[14] The Palestinian political establishment remains marred by corruption charges. In June, an anonymous report revealed Abbas's approval of salary hikes (67%) and the provision of other benefits to Palestinian cabinet members, despite the widespread economic hardship. The leaked document was met with outrage across the West Bank and further undermined the PA's legitimacy and efficiency.

---

17 September
No clear winner in Israel's second election. Both parties' attempts to form a government fail.

4 October
Abbas decides to accept the majority of Israeli-collected tax revenue.

18 November
US Secretary of State Mike Pompeo states that Israeli settlements are not 'per se, inconsistent with international law'.

21 November
Israel's attorney general indicts Netanyahu for bribery, fraud and breach of trust.

December
A third Israeli election is announced for March 2020 after Blue and White and Likud fail to form a coalition government.

18 August
Following rocket fire from Gaza, Israeli forces kill three Palestinians. Hamas denies any involvement.

Table 1: Timeline of previous peacemaking initiatives

Peace Talks and Official Accords	Date	Negotiators/Mediators	Achievements
Madrid Conference	1991	Co-sponsored by the US and USSR. Hosted by Spain. Participation of Israeli and Palestinian–Jordanian delegations.	Palestinians were part of a joint Palestinian–Jordanian delegation. Direct and multilateral negotiations followed the conference.
Oslo Accords	1993–95	Israeli prime minister Yitzhak Rabin and chairman of the Palestinian Liberation Organization (PLO) Yassir Arafat. Mediation of US president Bill Clinton and the Norwegian Ministry of Foreign Affairs.	Declaration of Principles on Interim Self-Government Arrangements (Oslo I) signed in Washington on 13 September 1993. Interim Agreement on the West Bank and the Gaza Strip (Oslo II) was first signed in Taba, Egypt, on 24 September 1995 and then in Washington on 28 September 1995. Mutual recognition of the State of Israel and the PLO. The Palestinian Authority (PA) was created and tasked with limited self-governance over the West Bank and the Gaza Strip.
Wye River Memorandum	1998	Israeli Prime Minister Benjamin Netanyahu and PLO chairman and PA president Arafat. Mediation of US president Clinton.	Negotiations held in Maryland, US, 15–23 October 1998, were aimed at resuming the implementation of the 1995 Oslo II Accord. The agreement was signed in Washington on 23 October 1998.
Sharm el-Sheikh Memorandum	1999	Israeli Prime Minister Netanyahu and PLO chairman and PA president Arafat. Overseen by US secretary of state Madeleine Albright. Witnessed and co-signed by Egyptian president Hosni Mubarak and King Abdullah II of Jordan.	The Sharm el-Sheikh Memorandum on the Implementation Timeline of Outstanding Commitments of Agreements Signed and the Resumption of Permanent Status Negotiations was signed on 4 September 1999.
Camp David Summit	2000	Israeli prime minister Ehud Barak and PLO chairman and PA president Arafat. Peace meetings brokered by US president Clinton.	No solution was reached that could satisfy both Israeli and Palestinian demands. Talks ended without an agreement.
Taba Summit	2001	Israeli minister of foreign affairs Shlomo Ben-Ami and Palestinian diplomat Saeb Erekat. Mediation of US president Clinton.	Held in Taba, Egypt, on 21–27 January, following the collapse of the Camp David Summit talks. US president proposed 'The Clinton Parameters' (including the 'Land Swap' principle). Talks ended without an agreement.
Roadmap for Peace	2002	Proposed by the Quartet on the Middle East (EU, Russia, UN and US). PA President Mahmoud Abbas and Israeli prime minister Ariel Sharon. Mediation of US president George W. Bush.	The Quartet outlined the principles of a Roadmap for Peace, including an independent Palestinian state. The final text of the Roadmap, mainly drafted by the US administration, was released on 30 April 2003.
Sharm el-Sheikh Summit	2005	Israeli prime minister Ariel Sharon, PA President Abbas, Egyptian president Mubarak and King Abdullah II of Jordan.	After a series of meetings, the Israeli and Palestinian participants reaffirmed their commitment to the 2002 Roadmap.
Annapolis Conference	2007	Organised and hosted by US president Bush. Israeli prime minister Ehud Olmert and PA President Abbas. Foreign delegations included the Arab League, China, the EU and Russia.	Held on 27 November at the US Naval Academy of Annapolis, Maryland, to revive the peace process and implement the 2002 Roadmap. Negotiations continued after the conference but ended in September 2008 without an agreement.
Bilateral talks	2010	Israeli Prime Minister Netanyahu and PA President Abbas. Mediation of US president Barack Obama, represented by US secretary of state Hillary Clinton.	Talks were held in Washington and Sharm el-Sheikh to revive the peace process, ending in September 2010 when the partial Israeli moratorium on settlement construction in the West Bank expired and the Palestinian leadership refused to continue the negotiations.

Table 1: Timeline of previous peacemaking initiatives

Peace Talks and Official Accords	Date	Negotiators/Mediators	Achievements
Bilateral talks/ The Kerry Initiative	2013–14	Israeli minister of justice Tzipi Livni and Palestinian diplomat Erekat. Mediation of US secretary of state John Kerry and US special envoy Martin Indyk.	Held in Washington, Jerusalem and Hebron. The parties were given nine months to reach a final-status agreement. On the day of the deadline, 29 April 2014, negotiations collapsed.
Manama Summit	2019	US-sponsored workshop in Manama, Bahrain. Israeli and Palestinian government representatives refused to attend.	The US presented its 'Peace to Prosperity' plan for economic investment in the West Bank and the Gaza Strip based on a US$50 billion investment fund, but repeated delays in the US publication of its peace plan meant that the required political framework to implement the plan was lacking by the time of the conference. No economic pledges were made by key participants, including Gulf Arab states, to offer the required funding for the plan.

Military Developments

Clashes in Gaza

The March of Return protests continued on a weekly basis throughout 2019 along the fence separating the Gaza Strip from Israel, with occasional demonstrations on the beach next to the perimeter fence in northern Gaza. The rallies often turned violent; protesters, at times, resorted to burning tyres and throwing stones, incendiary balloons and Molotov cocktails. In response, Israel has used live ammunition, high-velocity bullets and tear gas. In early 2019, the UN found that the IDF had violated international human-rights law in the Gaza Strip by using excessive force to counter the protests.[15] More than 8,000 Palestinians were injured by live ammunition in the period ending 31 July 2019, while according to Gaza's Health Ministry 313 Palestinians were killed by Israeli fire up to October.

Sporadic rocket attacks from the Gaza Strip and Israel have hampered informal ceasefire agreements between Hamas and the Israeli government. In May 2019, violence escalated in the worst fighting since the 50-day war in 2014. After a sniper wounded two Israeli soldiers and Gazan armed groups reportedly launched 600 projectiles into Israeli territory over two days, Israel levelled the homes of several militant commanders, including Hamas and Islamic Jihad members, and launched attacks on individuals allegedly responsible for terrorist activities. According to health officials, 23 Palestinians and four Israelis were killed, including more than a dozen civilians.[16]

Gaza's rocket fire seemingly served political purposes. In late March, two weeks before Israel's highly contested parliamentary elections, a rocket launched from Gaza hit a house northeast of Tel Aviv. The outbreak of violence in May preceded Israel's Memorial and Independence Day celebrations and the Eurovision song contest in Tel Aviv, which put additional pressure on the prime minister to reduce tensions and address socio-economic grievances. The ceasefire brokered by Egypt and the UN in May included measures to ease the acute economic crisis in the impoverished enclave.

Clashes in West Bank

The summer of 2019 witnessed a substantial rise in the number of (attempted) attacks and violent clashes between Palestinian protesters and Israeli forces across the West Bank. Some of the tensions derive from religious disputes over Jewish presence on the Temple Mount on Tisha B'Av; Netanyahu's threats of an Israeli annexation of parts of the West Bank; and Trump's pro-Israel policy. At times, Israeli forces utilised excessive force against protests, including the use of live fire. In July, a nine-year-old boy was reportedly shot in the head. The UN Office for the Coordination of Humanitarian Affairs (OCHA) also reported a sharp increase in violent clashes between Palestinian youths and Israeli security forces in East Jerusalem; as of 21 August 2019, these clashes had resulted in the killing of one Palestinian and the injury of 137 Palestinians and four Israeli police personnel.[17]

Daily violence

During the year, violence occurred on a daily basis in the Palestinian Territories. Since 2015, the conflict has been characterised by Israeli settler violence against Palestinian civilians, and by Palestinian lone-wolf knife, vehicle and gun attacks against Israeli civilians (mostly settlers) and security forces. While (attempted) terror attacks have also occurred in West Jerusalem and Tel Aviv, violence has mainly occurred in the West Bank and East Jerusalem. Israeli settler violence against Palestinians remained at a high level in 2019. Israel's security agency, Shin Bet, documented 295 incidents of what it termed 'Jewish terror' in 2018.[18] According to the UN, settler violence against Palestinians in the West Bank has been rising since the beginning of 2017. This surge originates partly from an inadequate response by Israeli law enforcement, resulting from a failure to investigate – and prosecute – perpetrators.

Impact

Human rights

Israel continues to enforce severe and discriminatory measures against Palestinians, including restrictions on the right of movement within the West Bank and travel between the West Bank and the Gaza Strip, into East Jerusalem and Israel, and abroad. Daily life in the West Bank is further complicated by Israeli road closures, which constitute a method of collective punishment. In June and July 2019, B'Tselem documented the closure of two West Bank villages for 20 and 29 days respectively, in response to youth throwing stones. Israeli and Egyptian restrictions on movement out of Gaza equally harm the civilian population, including by limiting approval of permit applications from Palestinians seeking medical treatment outside of Gaza to 'exceptional humanitarian cases'.

The PA's repressive form of governance has also hampered the daily lives and opportunities of Palestinians. Restrictions on free press and the application of a carrot-and-stick policy have sought to curtail Palestinian journalists from exposing societal flaws. Human-rights groups have repeatedly shed light on extrajudicial arrests and the persecution of journalists who oppose Fatah-led government policies. At times, the arrests have targeted journalists suspected of supporting Hamas.

Humanitarian

Regular outbreaks of violence between Gaza's Islamist rulers and Israel, together with infighting among Palestinian factions, have affected public facilities and worsened an already precarious humanitarian situation. In 2019, the UN reported a surge in humanitarian needs since March 2018 (coinciding with the outbreak of the March of Return protests) and raised concerns about the failing health system. Ongoing power cuts and contaminated drinking water worsened by population growth, low rainfall and poor maintenance have further deteriorated living conditions in the enclave.

The Trump administration's imposition of aid cuts also contributed to the worsening humanitarian situation in the Palestinian Territories in 2019, forcing non-governmental organisations to end programmes, cut staff members and halt important infrastructure projects. The decision to cease all USAID assistance in January 2019 exacerbated an already dire situation. Prior to the announcement, USAID had provided critical food aid to more than 180,000 Palestinians in the West Bank and Gaza. Plans to fund a water and sanitation-improvement programme in Gaza were halted, as were a multimillion-dollar sewage network and a US$1.4m school facility already under construction in the West Bank, despite objections from US officials involved in the efforts. In May, the effects of Trump's decision in 2018 to cancel US funding to the United Nations Relief and Works Agency for Palestine Refugees (UNRWA) also became clear, with the UN warning of a food crisis in Gaza, where more than a million people rely on food aid.[19] The UN also noted that the funding crisis was crippling an overburdened healthcare system and impeding access to limb-saving treatment, among other services.

Trends

Prospects for peace

The Israel–Palestine peace process is mired in a hazardous stalemate. The governmental crisis in Israel, following two elections in one year, has relegated the Israeli–Palestinian situation down the order of urgency. At the same time, the belief in a peace deal based on the premises of the Oslo Accords has substantially subsided. Only 34% of respondents to a pre-election survey backed the two-state solution in 2019, compared to 60% of respondents surveyed in 1993.[20]

The inter-Palestinian political struggle has equally hampered the possibility of any effective mediation. The Fatah–Hamas division, despite repeated brokering attempts by Egypt, enables Israel and its allies to invoke the infamous 'no partner for peace' narrative to justify the absence of mediation. A new initiative aimed at ending the Hamas–Fatah split (supported by eight Palestinian factions) in October 2019 is unlikely to address the challenges that impeded the implementation of past reconciliation agreements. While new parliamentary elections might offer a democratic solution to the impasse, it is unclear whether Abbas plans to set a date or whether he would respect the results.

Strategic implications and global influences

Multilateral mediation has long been considered key to achieving a resolution to the Israel–Palestine conflict. Nevertheless, it is unlikely that traditional brokers will be able to overcome past ideological and policy challenges and conduct a constructive mediation in 2020. The cuts to Palestinian aid, the closure of the Palestine Liberation Organization (PLO) mission in Washington and the merger of the US Consulate General diplomatic mission in Jerusalem with the US Embassy preclude the Trump administration from acting as an effective broker. Despite an increased normalisation of ties between Israel and Arab states, the Arab commitment to the Palestinian cause – including the establishment of an independent state as envisaged in the 2002 Arab peace deal – has not yet been forsaken. The failure of the US-sponsored Manama Summit to generate any economic pledges or overt endorsements thus indicated Arab, and particularly Gulf, reticence in backing an undefined political plan.

Consumed by the Brexit process, a far-right political surge and foreign-policy challenges, the EU is equally unlikely to take a proactive approach to the resolution of the conflict. The nomination of Josep Borell as High Representative for Foreign Affairs and Security Policy is set to maintain the troubled relationship his predecessor had with Israel. Known for his pro-Palestine and pro-Iran stances, Borell may exacerbate perceptions of the EU as a biased mediator, while sustaining the United States' role as Israel's preferred interlocutor in the Middle East peace process.

Notes

[1] 'Security forces make deadly use of crowd control weapons in Gaza', B'Tselem, 6 August 2019.

[2] Jeremy Diamond and Elise Labott, 'Secretary of State John Kerry: Two-state solution in "serious jeopardy"', CNN, 28 December 2016. See also Harriet Sherwood, 'Kerry: Two Years Left to Reach Two-State Solution in Middle East Peace Process', *Guardian*, 13 April 2013.

[3] This MOU replaced a previous $30bn ten-year agreement, which ran through FY2018. Congressional Research Service, 'U.S. Foreign Aid to Israel', 7 August 2019, p. 5.

[4] Anna Ahronheim, 'Iran increases Hamas funding in exchange for intel on Israel missiles', *Jerusalem Post*, 8 August 2019.

[5] Shlomi Eldar, 'Behind Egypt's gift to Islamic Jihad', Al-Monitor, 21 October 2019.

[6] United Nations Conference on Trade and Development, 'Report on UNCTAD Assistance to the Palestinian People: Developments in the Economy of the Occupied Palestinian Territory', 2017, p. 9.

[7] Orhan Niksic, Nur Nasser Eddin and Massimiliano Cali, 'Area C and the Future of the Palestinian Economy', World Bank, 17 July 2014, p. 5.

[8] World Bank, 'The World Bank in West Bank and Gaza', 1 October 2019.

[9] 'Forced Unemployment', B'Tselem, 6 June 2019.

[10] Peace Now, 'New 2018 Population Data for Israelis in the West Bank', 2 October 2019; Peace Now, 'Settlements Data: Jerusalem', 2019.

[11] Peace Now, '2,304 Settlement Units Promoted, 3 Outposts Regularized', 4 August 2019.

[12] 'Statistics on demolition of houses built without permits in the West Bank (not including East Jerusalem)', B'Tselem, 4 November 2019.

[13] Twenty-five owners demolished their own homes after receiving demolition orders. 'Statistics on demolition of houses built without permits in East Jerusalem', B'Tselem, 24 October 2019. See also Peace Now, 'Jerusalem Municipal Data Reveals Stark Israeli–Palestinian Discrepancy in Construction Permits in Jerusalem', 12 September 2019.

[14] 'Poll: More than 60% of Palestinians want Abbas to quit', *Middle East Monitor*, 18 September 2019.

[15] UN, 'Accountability Needed to End Excessive Use of Force Against Palestinian Protesters in Gaza, Says Special Rapporteur on the Situation of Human Rights in the OPT', 5 March 2019.

[16] Almog Ben Zikri et al., 'Palestinian Report: Israel and Hamas Reach Cease-fire; Israeli Army Lifts Restrictions', *Haaretz*, 6 May 2019.

[17] UN Office for the Coordination of Humanitarian Affairs (OCHA), 'Casualties', https://www.ochaopt.org/theme/casualties.

[18] Loveday Morris and Ruth Eglash, 'Attacks by Israeli settlers surge as West Bank tensions boil', *Washington Post*, 6 March 2019.

[19] UN, 'Gaza blockade causes "near ten-fold increase" in food dependency, says UN agency', 13 May 2019.

[20] Grace Wermenbol, 'Netanyahu's fifth term: The end of the two-state solution', Atlantic Council, 15 April 2019.

LIBYA

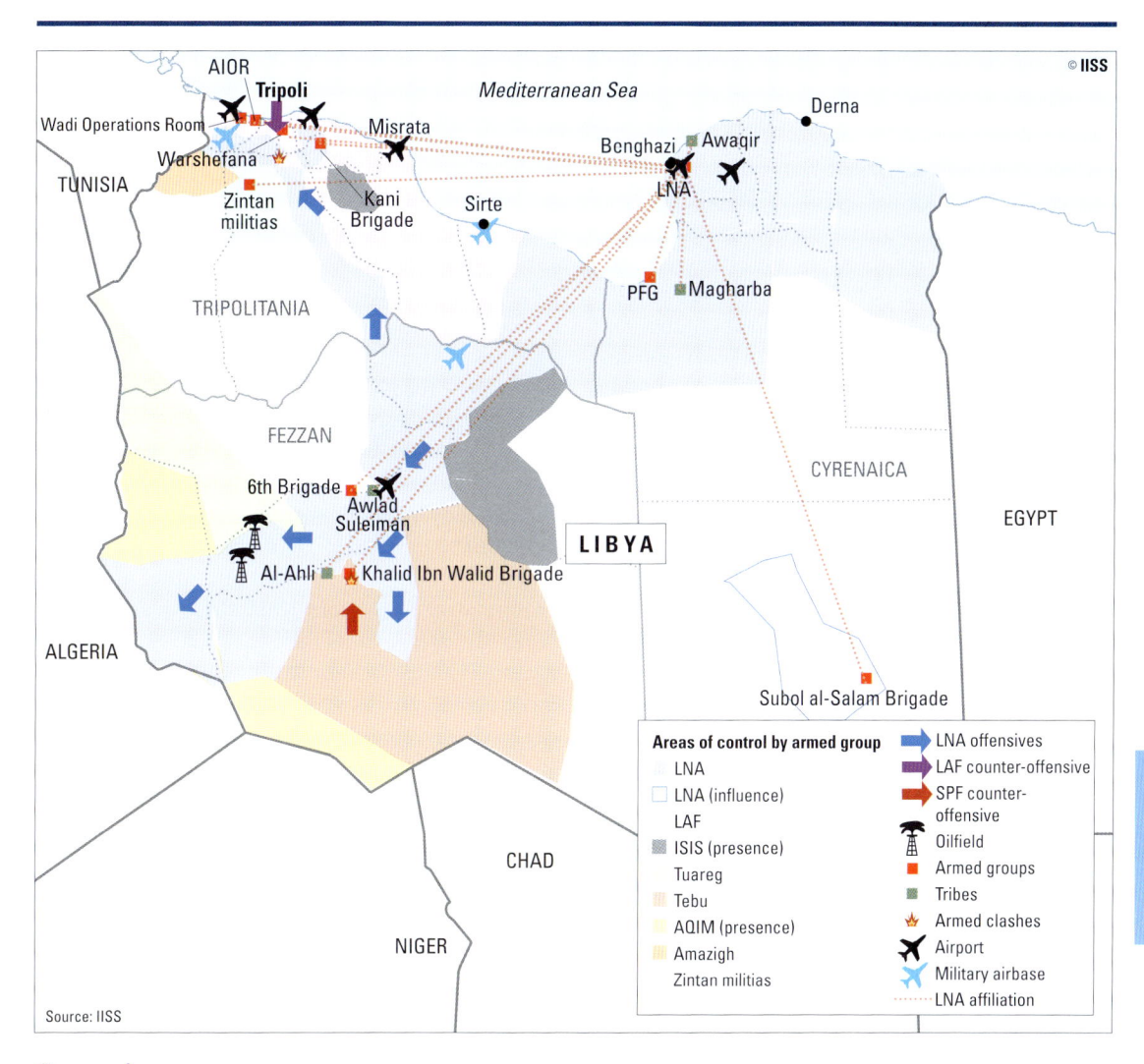

Overview

The conflict in 2019

In 2019, the conflict in Libya escalated from low-intensity fighting into a major confrontation. The launch of *Operation Flood of Dignity* by Field Marshal Khalifa Haftar precipitated the third phase of Libya's civil war, following the 2011 revolution and the 2014 fight between Haftar's *Operation Dignity* and the revolutionary *Operation Libya Dawn*.

In April, following a successful military campaign in the south, Haftar moved on to the capital, Tripoli, and plunged the country into this new phase of the civil war, undermining the different reconciliation attempts of the UN and various state actors (including the United Arab Emirates (UAE)) and exposing the full extent of external interference in Libyan affairs. As foreign powers, including Russia and Turkey, significantly increased their diplomatic, economic and military support to their proxies, Libya gradually became an arena for regional and international powers to fight, project their influence and test new military technology.[1] The United States resumed airstrikes against the Islamic State (also known as ISIS or ISIL) in the second half of the year, confirming the group's successful regrouping in the south and its renewed capability.

Haftar's attack on Tripoli was a turning point. In attempting to reunite Libya under his command, the general contributed instead to its fragmentation, exacerbating tribal and ethnic divisions and reviving the presence of mercenaries and non-state armed groups (NSAGs), especially in the south of the country. Neither the Libyan National Army (LNA) nor the 'Libyan Armed Forces' (LAF, supporting the Government of National Accord, or GNA) could secure control in southern Tripoli. The resulting stalemate deepened the rift between the east and the west of the country, and between rival political and economic institutions. Both the attack on Tripoli and the subsequent military developments indicated the foreign powers' loose control over their proxies in Libya. This, together with the deep distrust between rival parties, suggests that the conflict will not end soon.

The conflict to 2019

In 2011, mass protests and an international intervention precipitated a regime change in Libya that ousted Muammar Gadhafi, who had ruled the country for 42 years. The inability of the transitional authorities to rebuild state institutions led to protracted violence during the transition and exacerbated existing political, social, economic and military fissures. Increasing insecurity and a proliferation of armed groups led to a second civil war in 2014 that forced the House of Representatives (HoR, the parliament which resulted from the election of that year) to leave Tripoli and move to Tobruk.

The second phase of the civil war polarised the country, accelerated its fragmentation and created a breeding ground for terrorist organisations. It also deepened the conflict between revolutionary and counter-revolutionary forces, effectively splitting the country in two. Since then, Tripoli and the western region have been under the control of revolutionary groups and militias from the capital and the cities of Misrata and Zintan. In the eastern part of the country, the LNA, with the support of Egypt and the UAE, gradually extended its influence across the entire Cyrenaica region, taking control of Benghazi in 2017 and Derna in 2018.

The Libyan Political Agreement (LPA), signed in Skhirat, Morocco, in December 2015, had established the GNA with the goal of uniting a divided country. But four years later, the government of Prime Minister Fayez al-Sarraj has not been endorsed by the HoR (which is backing the rival Interim Government, led by Prime Minister Abdullah al-Thinni, in the east) and is still struggling to maintain control in Tripoli. Internal resistance to the Action Plan of the UN Special Representative of the Secretary General (SRSG) to Libya, Ghassan Salamé, led to increasing diplomatic activism by France, Italy and the UAE, exposing growing international divisions over Libya.

Internally, Libya's division is enshrined in the parallel institutions in the eastern and western parts of the country, with the National Oil Corporation (NOC) and the Central Bank of Libya (CBL) having two rival branches in Tripoli and the east. This fragmentation poses a major challenge to reconciliation and sustains centrifugal forces present since the second phase of the Libyan civil war.

Key statistics

Type	Internationalised
Start date	February 2011
IDPs total (30 November 2019)	355,672
Refugees total (31 December 2019)	46,453
People in need (31 December 2019)	880,000

Key Conflict Parties

Libyan Armed Forces

Strength
Armed groups and militias affiliated to the GNA in Tripoli and defending the capital from Haftar's offensive have been considered part of the LAF, the Libyan prospective military, opposed to the LNA. Given the undisclosed number of militias joining in to defend Tripoli and the undefined relation between these groups and the central command in the capital, it is impossible to determine the exact strength of the LAF.

Areas of operation
Southern Tripoli front line, near the disused International Airport: in Ain Zara, Aziziya, Qasr Ben Ghasir, Sawani and Tajoura. The LAF has also carried out airstrikes against LNA positions, particularly on the Watiya and Jufra air bases.

Leadership
As head of the Presidency Council (PC) – which presides over the GNA – Prime Minister Sarraj is supreme commander of the LAF. The chief of staff is Maj.-Gen. Mohammed al-Sharif, who replaced Maj.-Gen. Abdulrahman al-Tawil following the LNA's advance in southern Libya in early 2019. However, the real power lies in the hands of the commanders of the military zones. Maj.-Gen. Osama al-Juwaili (western military zone) and Maj.-Gen. Mohammed al-Haddad (central military zone) ensure the GNA enjoys the support of powerful militias from Zintan and Misrata, which also joined forces to defend Tripoli. In January, the appointment of Ali Kana (a former officer under Gadhafi's regime and prominent leader of the Tuareg minority) as commander of the southern military zone failed to halt the LNA's military advance in southern Libya but indicated the GNA's willingness to court ethnic-minority groups there.

Structure
The militias in Tripoli represent the backbone of the LAF's initial response to Haftar's advance. Building upon the experience of the Tripoli Protection Force (TPF, which included the Abu Salim Brigade, the Bab al-Tajoura Brigade, the Nawasi Brigade and the Tripoli Revolutionaries Brigade, or TRB), militias in Tripoli rallied in defence of the GNA. The Special Deterrence Force (SDF, a Tripoli militia now part of the GNA Ministry of the Interior) initially maintained some distance from the TPF. However, following clashes with the LNA in September, it took part in the defence of Tripoli, even though there are some doubts about its stance due to its Salafist-Madkhalist orientation, common to the core of the LNA. Militias from Misrata, Zawiya and Zintan also took part. The participation of Misrata militias was crucial, as these groups are considered the most powerful in Libya (it is estimated that there are more than 200 militias in Misrata, with a total of 18,000 fighters).

History
In the aftermath of Haftar's offensive on Tripoli most of the armed groups and militias in the city and western Libya rallied in support of the GNA. The GNA took advantage of this cohesion and tried to integrate most of them into its prospective army.

Objectives
Repel the LNA's offensive on the capital and thwart Haftar's plan to take control of the country. The GNA has presented the LAF as a fresh attempt to forge Libya's new military, following unsuccessful efforts to disarm and demobilise militias and unite the country's divided army at successive meetings held in Cairo. While the outcome of the conflict is still uncertain, it is highly unlikely that powerful armed groups would voluntarily accept disarmament, demobilisation and reintegration (DDR) programmes and relinquish their coercive powers.

Opponents
The LNA and its allies; terrorist groups such as ISIS and al-Qaeda in the Islamic Maghreb (AQIM); Sudanese armed groups and mercenaries fighting alongside the LNA.

Affiliates/allies
Armed groups opposing the LNA's offensive in western and southern Libya, including Tebu militiamen of the South Protection Force (SPF); Chadian rebel forces active in Libya, such as the Front pour l'alternance et la concorde civile au Tchad (FACT), the Conseil du Commandement Militaire pour la Salut de la République (CCMSR), the Rassemblement des forces démocratique (RFD), the Union des Force pour la Démocratie et le Développement (UFDD) and the Union des Forces de la Résistance (UFR).

Resources/capabilities
The coalition of groups in control of Tripoli takes advantage of unrestricted access to the political and economic institutions in the capital. In particular, the cartel of militias in Tripoli has been responsible for the pervasive corruptive practices that help sustain the war economy in Libya. These include human trafficking, fuel smuggling, fraudulent letters of credit and the exchange of foreign currency on the black market.

Libyan National Army

Strength
The LNA, also known by its official name of the Libyan Arab Armed Forces (LAAF), is composed of about 25,000 fighters, but the regular army is made up of some 7,000 troops. The 106th Brigade is the largest unit, exceeding 5,000 fighters.

Areas of operation
After seizing Benghazi and Derna, the LNA extended its territorial control in southern Libya in early 2019. In April, Haftar launched the Tripoli offensive, making considerable inroads in western Libya and taking control of Gharyan, Sabratha, Tarhouna and the Watiya air base. Nevertheless, the LNA has so far not been able to make further progress along the southern Tripoli front line, losing Gharyan to GNA-affiliated forces in June.

Leadership
While the president of the HoR, Agila Saleh, is supreme commander, the real power is in the hands of Haftar, appointed field marshal in 2016. Maj.-Gen. Abdul Razzaq al-Nazhuri is the chief of staff. Other important figures include Gen. Abdel Salam al-Hassi and Oun al-Furjani, chief of staff of Haftar's office.

Structure
The LNA includes the Saiqa Special Forces, led by Wanis Bukhamada and comprising 3,500 fighters; the 106th Brigade, led by Khaled Haftar, son of Gen. Khalifa Haftar, who succeeded his brother Saddam; the 166th Brigade, led by Ayoub Furjani, Khalifa Haftar's son-in-law; and the 101st Brigade, led by Captain Mohamed Absayat al-Zway and made up mainly of fighters from Ajdabiya. About 18,000 fighters are considered auxiliary forces, including Sudanese forces, tribal militias and other armed groups such as the eastern and central branches of the Petroleum Facilities Guards (PFG). The LNA also relies on the support of relevant eastern tribes, such as the Awaqir, despite relations with tribal actors often being controversial.

History
In 2014, Haftar launched *Operation Dignity* against Islamist factions in Benghazi. In 2015, the HoR gave legitimacy to *Operation Dignity*, leading to the establishment of the LNA, which is not recognised as the legitimate Libyan military by Haftar's opponents.

Objectives
Against a backdrop of deteriorating security, especially in Benghazi, the LNA was established to fight against Islamist and terrorist groups responsible for attacks, targeted assassinations and the absence of the rule of law. However, as time passed, Haftar extended the definition of terrorist groups to include revolutionary militias and other armed groups that opposed his rule. Given its strong anti-Islamist background, the LNA has often been considered a secularist force in Libya. In the eyes of several counter-revolutionary regimes in the region, it was instrumental in cracking down on terrorist and Islamist groups, including the Muslim Brotherhood. Nevertheless, some groups inside the LNA have a Salafist orientation and the influence of the Madkhali doctrine has grown.

Opponents
Islamist groups and terrorist organisations, such as the Muslim Brotherhood, the Benghazi Defence Brigades (BDB), AQIM and ISIS; revolutionary groups, such as the militias in Misrata, Tripoli and Zintan; the GNA and its affiliates; Tebu armed groups in southern Libya; Chadian rebel forces.

Affiliates/allies
The LNA can rely on the support of affiliated military units in the west and south, including approximately 2,500 fighters in Zintan and several tribes in the south, including the Awlad Suleiman and the al-Ahali. The co-optation of local and tribal militias has been crucial in explaining the LNA's military advance in 2019, as shown by the cases of the Kani Brigade in Tarhouna, the Anti-ISIS Operation Room (AIOR) in Sabratha and the Arab tribes in Murzuq (al-Ahli) and Sabha (Awlad Suleiman).[2] Madkhalist and Salafist armed groups like the Tariq Ibn Ziyad Brigade (led by Omar Mraje) and the al-Tawhid Brigade also operate under LNA control. In Kufra, the Subol al-Salam Brigade, led by Abdel Rahman Hashim al-Kilani, has been affiliated since 2015. It is a Madkhali-Salafist group of approximately 300 fighters, mostly from the Zway tribe. In Sabha, the LNA relies on the Sixth Brigade, mainly composed of Awlad Suleiman fighters. Led by Gen. Salem al-Attaybi, the group shifted its allegiance from the GNA to the LNA in May 2018. Sudanese rebel forces and paramilitaries such as the Sudan Liberation Movement/Army–Minni Minnawi (SLM/A–MM) and the Sudan Liberation Movement/Army–Abdel Wahid al-Nur (SLM/A–AW) and the Rapid Support Forces (RSF) have reportedly backed the LNA.

Resources/capabilities
The establishment of the Military Investment and Public Works Authority has provided additional sources of revenue. The LNA's involvement in Libya's economic activities, so far limited to the areas under its control in the east, is in line with the model established in Egypt by President Abdel Fattah Al-Sisi, who offered an influential role to the military. However, as in Egypt, the oversized role played by the armed forces in economic activities often leads to corruption and illegalities. Recent reports highlighted the involvement of the LNA and affiliated armed groups in illicit activities, such as human trafficking, arms and fuel smuggling and selling scrap metal.

ISIS – Libya

Strength
Different estimates exist of the number of ISIS militants active in Libya. On 26 August 2019, UN Secretary-General António Guterres reported between 500 and 700 ISIS militants but, following the latest US airstrikes in September, US Africa Command (AFRICOM) said that ISIS's presence has been reduced to fewer than 150 members.[3]

Areas of operation
ISIS maintains a presence in the areas south of Sirte, between Bani Walid, Waddan and Jufra, from where it launched a series of high-profile attacks on Tripoli in 2018. The fighting in 2019 has offered the group the opportunity to extend its reach in southern Libya, where it has taken advantage of the instability, porous borders and lawlessness. The most recent US airstrikes against ISIS occurred in Murzuq, showing the group's extended area of operation.

Leadership
The group is led by Mahmoud al-Barasi, also known as Abu Musab al-Libi. Barasi was targeted by US airstrikes in southern Libya in September 2019. His current fate is unknown.

Structure
In 2014 the organisation announced the establishment of three *wilayat* (provinces) in the three historical regions of Libya: Wilayat al-Barqa in Cyrenaica, Wilayat al-Fizzan in Fezzan and Wilayat al-Tarablus in Tripolitania. Despite the distinction between the three branches being confirmed by claims of responsibility (for instance, Wilayat Tarablus claimed the attack against the Corinthia hotel in Tripoli in January 2015), ISIS maintained a centralised structure in Libya. Recent attacks have been claimed without any reference to the different regional branches.

History
ISIS emerged in Libya in 2014, when it was able to gain a foothold in the eastern city of Derna. Eventually, ISIS's local affiliate was forced to withdraw following clashes with the Abu Salim Martyrs Brigade, an Islamist militia with alleged ties to al-Qaeda and which was part of the Derna Protection Force (DPF), an umbrella group of Islamist and revolutionary militias active in the city. ISIS found more fertile ground in Sirte, where in 2015 it established its presence, taking advantage of the marginalisation of the city by Libyan authorities. ISIS seized neighbouring towns such as Nawfaliya and Harawa, taking control of the Ghardabiya air base and threatening Misrata. Following clashes on the outskirts of Misrata, in May 2016 the GNA launched an offensive against Sirte. Misrata militias comprised the backbone of *Operation Solid Structure*, which took control of ISIS's stronghold in December 2016 with the crucial support of US AFRICOM, which launched 495 airstrikes during the operation. The resumption of hostilities in 2019 meant conditions were favourable for the resurgence of ISIS, whose Libya province represented one of its most significant outposts in 2015–16.

Objectives
A return to the position the group held in 2015–16, when it took control of Sirte and nearby areas. Despite ISIS being severely weakened by *Operation Solid Structure* and US AFRICOM's frequent airstrikes, the resumption of hostilities in April 2019 provided it with an opportunity to re-establish its presence. Since then attacks claimed by ISIS have increased, particularly in remote areas of central and southern Libya. Nevertheless, in the short term, it is highly unlikely that the group can take control of territory.

Opponents
The GNA and affiliated militias; the LNA and its local allies; the Muslim Brotherhood and other moderate Islamist groups (including Sufi followers); third parties engaged in the fight against terrorism (the US in particular).

Affiliates/allies
The group has always had a confrontational stance toward other terrorist organisations in Libya. However, since its defeat in Sirte, reports suggest that ISIS is collaborating with other jihadist groups, including AQIM. This limited cooperation has been instrumental in allowing ISIS to regroup and re-establish its presence in central and southern Libya.

Resources/capabilities
ISIS militants have seized trucks carrying fuel and gained revenue from imposing taxes on human traffickers and arms smugglers. The group has also resorted to kidnapping for ransom.

Drivers

The attack on Tripoli and the personalisation of Libyan politics

The LNA military offensive against Tripoli returned the armed confrontation in Libya to levels unseen since 2014. *Operation Flood of Dignity* (a codename referring to Haftar's *Operation Dignity* in 2014) confirmed Haftar's objective to control the whole country – often reiterated in interviews and public appearances – while also disrupting negotiations and reconciliation efforts a few weeks before the National Conference organised by the UN Support Mission in Libya (UNSMIL).

Haftar planned a rapid takeover that would have completed his project to unite the country by force and overcome the internal challenges faced by the GNA – its inability to rein in militias inside and outside Tripoli, and to take advantage of its control over the economic institutions in the capital. The plan did not succeed, however. Only a few armed groups backed the offensive, which further backfired once rival militias in western Libya decided to join forces to resist.

The attack demonstrated the strong personalisation of Libyan politics, a major driver of the conflict colouring all aspects of the public debate.[4] The authoritarian leadership of Haftar and the surprising resilience of Sarraj represent serious obstacles to the peace process. Talks were already difficult due to Haftar's rejection of any civilian oversight over the military, on which Sarraj had insisted. However, their positions became irreconcilable following the April offensive, when they both ruled out any further talks. Their hardening positions thwart international attempts to help agree a ceasefire and resume negotiations.

The pervasive presence of foreign NSAGs

The eight-year conflict has fragmented state authority at both the central and local levels. The resulting proliferation of militias has furthered lawlessness and impunity and in turn attracted rebel and opposition forces with ethnic ties to minority groups in Libya from neighbouring countries. These foreign groups have taken advantage of porous borders in the south and the remoteness of the Fezzan region to regroup, train and profit.

The conflict took an increasingly sectarian tone by drawing Libyan ethnic minorities into the fighting. The LNA has increasingly targeted the Tebus (scattered along the borders with Chad, Niger and Sudan) due to their proximity to the Chadian rebels operating in Libya, who were the initial targets of the early 2019 offensive in the south. Whereas the LNA claimed to have neutralised several terrorists from ISIS and AQIM (suggesting that these two terrorist groups, once considered rival organisations, collaborate), its opponents and Tebu representatives accused Haftar's forces of systematic destruction, marginalisation and ethnic cleansing against the Tebus.

Third parties increase support to their proxies

Operation Flood of Dignity intensified foreign meddling, as all regional powers increased support to their proxies in Libya. Haftar attacked Tripoli a few days after meeting Saudi King Salman bin Abdulaziz Al Saud and Crown Prince Mohammed bin Salman

Key Events in 2019

Political events

- **27 February**: Haftar and Sarraj meet in Abu Dhabi, agreeing to end the transitional period and hold elections.
- **27 March**: Haftar visits Riyadh to meet with King Salman and Crown Prince bin Salman.
- **9 April**: Salamé postpones the National Conference that was to be held in Ghadames on 14–16 April.
- **22 May**: After meeting French President Emmanuel Macron in Paris, Haftar says conditions for a ceasefire are not met.

Military/Violent events

- **15 January**: LNA announces a military operation to remove criminal gangs, ISIS militants and mercenaries from the south.
- **22 February**: LNA announces that it has taken Murzuq after clashes with Tebu militias under the SPF.
- **4 April**: LNA advances to Tripoli, taking control of Gharyan and Tarhouna but failing to take Gate 27.

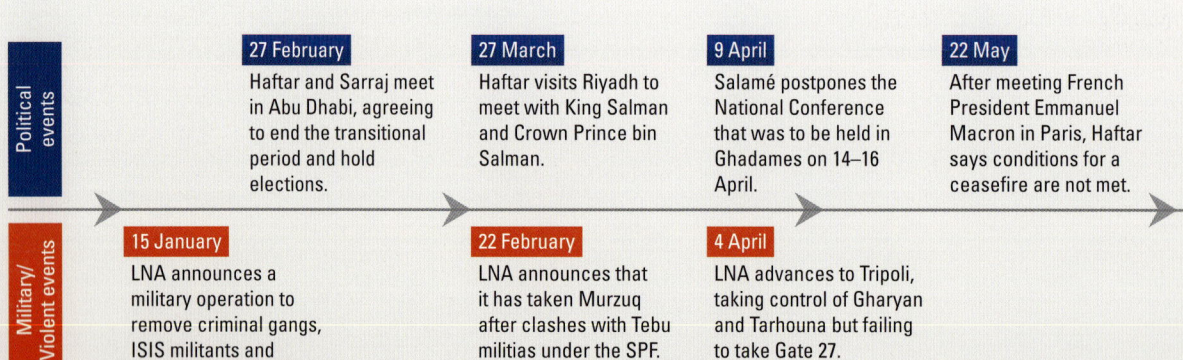

in Riyadh. Several observers made a direct connection between the meeting and the offensive, suggesting Saudi financing of the LNA.[5]

Haftar also relied on the support of more traditional allies. In 2019, the UAE increased its military footprint in Libya, already displayed by the establishment of the al-Khadim air base near Benghazi.[6] It also provided air cover to the LNA with Chinese-made *Wing Loong* II uninhabited aerial vehicles (UAVs) armed with *Blue Arrow* 7 missiles. The presence of French forces alongside the LNA was confirmed in June, when Paris was forced to admit ownership of the anti-tank *Javelin* missiles found in an LNA military base in Gharyan seized by GNA-affiliated forces.

The GNA's resistance to Haftar's offensive would not have been possible without Turkey's support. Ankara increased its involvement in Libya after being excluded from the high-level informal meeting in Palermo, Italy, in 2018 attended by both Haftar and Sarraj. It provided the LAF with Turkish-made *Bayraktar* TB2 UAVs to counter the LNA's aerial superiority. Following a shipment of *Kirpi* armoured personnel carriers to the port of Tripoli, Turkish President Recep Tayyip Erdogan did not deny having violated the arms embargo and expressed full support for the GNA.

Jordanian-made *al-Mared* 8x8 and *al-Wahsh* 4x4 armoured personnel carriers arrived also in the LNA's hands, confirming the intensification of a regional proxy war in Libya, which further complicates reconciliation attempts.

Political Developments

The power struggle in Tripoli
The political crisis in Algeria and the approaching elections in Tunisia represented important factors that pushed Haftar to move towards Tripoli. Both Algiers and Tunis were supportive of the GNA and Sarraj, but internal developments distracted both of them from the Libyan crisis.

Haftar also took advantage of military and political infighting in Tripoli to launch his offensive. As fighting resumed between the Kani Brigade and the TPF in January, members of the PC started to squabble over the replacement of the Administrative Control Authority (ACA) head Nasr Ali Hassan and the appointment of two new Libyan Investment Authority (LIA) board members. The infighting undermined the authority of PC head and GNA Prime Minister Sarraj.

Accused of unilateral decision-making, abusing power and a conflict of interest, Sarraj also faced the internal opposition of three PC members (Ahmed Maiteeq, Abdulsalam Kajman and Fathi al-Majbari). The dispute worsened the dysfunction inside the nine-member PC, which had already suffered from the resignation in 2017 of vice-president Musa Al-Koni, and been boycotted by Ali Gatrani, Omar al-Aswad and al-Majbari. The dispute showed Sarraj's increasing isolation and also affected civilian–military relations in the capital, with the TPF saying that it would only obey the PC's orders when decisions were taken unanimously.

---

17 July
Benghazi HoR member Seham Sergiwa, critical of Haftar, is abducted.

10 August
The GNA and LNA agree on a UN-proposed truce for Eid al-Adha.

27 November
Turkey strikes a deal with the GNA on military cooperation and delimitation of maritime boundaries in the Eastern Mediterranean.

26 June
LNA loses control of Gharyan following a surprise attack by LAF.

2 July
LNA is blamed for an airstrike on a migrant detention centre in Tajoura that kills 53 and injures over 130.

4 August
LNA UAV strike in Murzuq kills 43 and injures 51.

29 September
AFRICOM carries out the fourth airstrikes in ten days against ISIS in southern Libya, reportedly killing 43 militants.

LIBYAN ARMED FORCES (LAF)

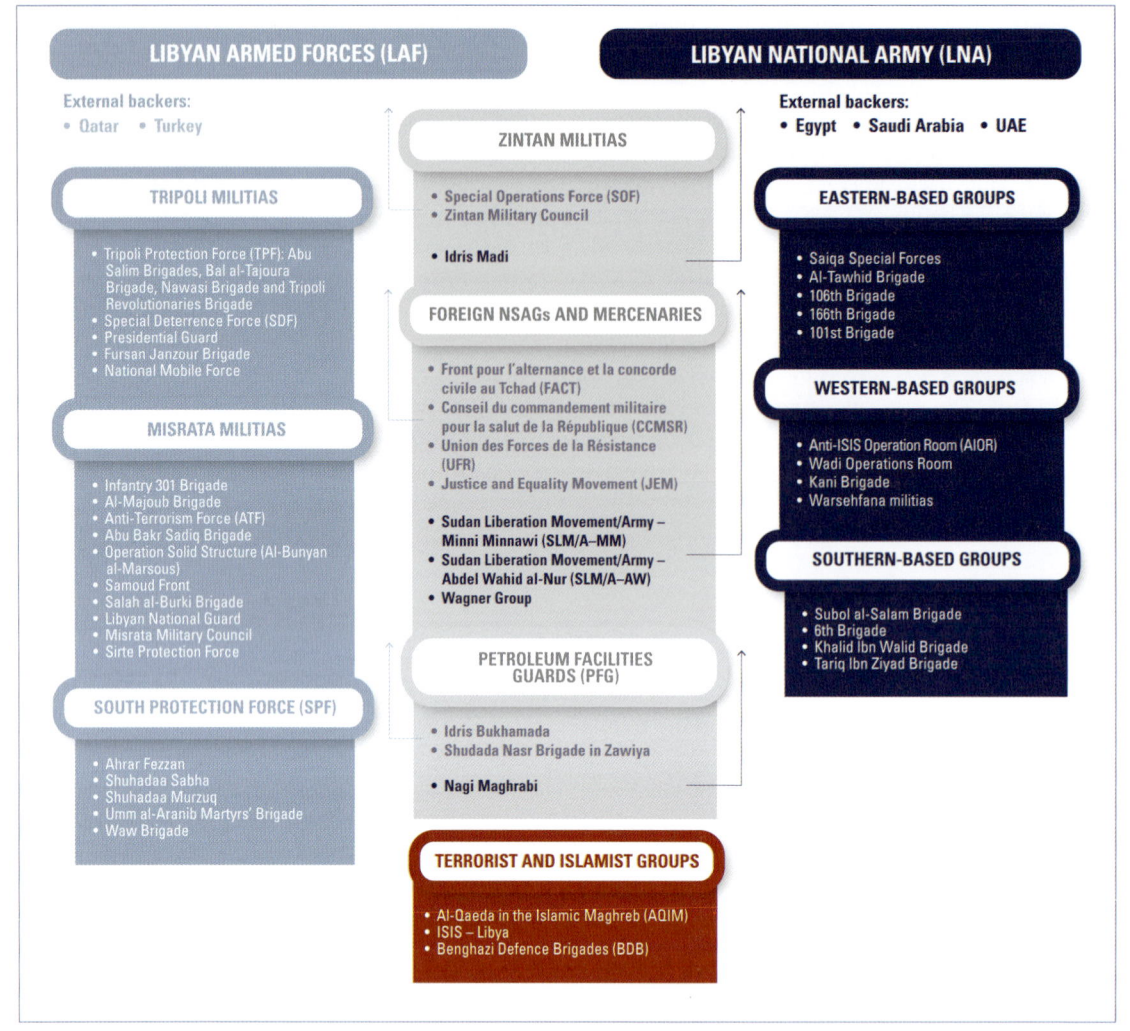

External backers:
- Qatar
- Turkey

TRIPOLI MILITIAS
- Tripoli Protection Force (TPF): Abu Salim Brigades, Bal al-Tajoura Brigade, Nawasi Brigade and Tripoli Revolutionaries Brigade
- Special Deterrence Force (SDF)
- Presidential Guard
- Fursan Janzour Brigade
- National Mobile Force

MISRATA MILITIAS
- Infantry 301 Brigade
- Al-Majoub Brigade
- Anti-Terrorism Force (ATF)
- Abu Bakr Sadiq Brigade
- Operation Solid Structure (Al-Bunyan al-Marsous)
- Samoud Front
- Salah al-Burki Brigade
- Libyan National Guard
- Misrata Military Council
- Sirte Protection Force

SOUTH PROTECTION FORCE (SPF)
- Ahrar Fezzan
- Shuhadaa Sabha
- Shuhadaa Murzuq
- Umm al-Aranib Martyrs' Brigade
- Waw Brigade

ZINTAN MILITIAS
- Special Operations Force (SOF)
- Zintan Military Council
- Idris Madi

FOREIGN NSAGs AND MERCENARIES
- Front pour l'alternance et la concorde civile au Tchad (FACT)
- Conseil du commandement militaire pour le salut de la République (CCMSR)
- Union des Forces de la Résistance (UFR)
- Justice and Equality Movement (JEM)
- Sudan Liberation Movement/Army – Minni Minnawi (SLM/A–MM)
- Sudan Liberation Movement/Army – Abdel Wahid al-Nur (SLM/A–AW)
- Wagner Group

PETROLEUM FACILITIES GUARDS (PFG)
- Idris Bukhamada
- Shudada Nasr Brigade in Zawiya
- Nagi Maghrabi

TERRORIST AND ISLAMIST GROUPS
- Al-Qaeda in the Islamic Maghreb (AQIM)
- ISIS – Libya
- Benghazi Defence Brigades (BDB)

LIBYAN NATIONAL ARMY (LNA)

External backers:
- Egypt
- Saudi Arabia
- UAE

EASTERN-BASED GROUPS
- Saiqa Special Forces
- Al-Tawhid Brigade
- 106th Brigade
- 166th Brigade
- 101st Brigade

WESTERN-BASED GROUPS
- Anti-ISIS Operation Room (AIOR)
- Wadi Operations Room
- Kani Brigade
- Warsehfana militias

SOUTHERN-BASED GROUPS
- Subol al-Salam Brigade
- 6th Brigade
- Khalid Ibn Walid Brigade
- Tariq Ibn Ziyad Brigade

Figure 1: Conflict parties' relations

Unsuccessful international initiatives

Operation Flood of Dignity not only undermined the UN Action Plan, but also disrupted reconciliation attempts by regional and international powers. Haftar's military campaign in southern Libya delayed SRSG Salamé's revised Action Plan as endorsed by the 2018 Palermo Conference, which included a National Conference in early 2019 and general elections to follow.

As the UN failed to convince rival parties to resume dialogue, regional powers took the lead in negotiations. Following attempts by France and Italy in 2018, on 27 February Haftar and Sarraj met in Abu Dhabi, a major sponsor of Haftar. In the presence of Salamé, they reportedly agreed on the need to hold general elections and unify Libyan institutions. The vague formula adopted and the lack of a time frame and details about the meeting raised immediate suspicions. Recriminations followed when the LNA advanced to Tripoli and both sides accused each other of reneging on the agreement.

In order to break the political, military and diplomatic stalemate, Salamé revisited his Action Plan once again. After a P3+3[7] meeting in Paris, the G7 meeting in Biarritz, France, in August endorsed the proposed three-step approach for Libya, including a ceasefire, an international conference with the main countries involved in the conflict and an inter-Libya conference facilitated by the UN and the African Union (AU). The German government expressed its intention to host the international conference. However, the absence of a ceasefire and the intensification of foreign meddling on the ground continued to challenge Berlin's diplomatic initiative.

Military Developments

Haftar's southward push

Before launching its offensive on Tripoli, the LNA moved southwards to secure its supply lines. On 15 January, LNA spokesperson Ahmed al-Mismari announced the start of a military operation to restore order and the rule of law in the south, and specifically to remove foreign militias, criminal gangs and terrorists responsible for the increasing lawlessness. The population in the marginalised Fezzan region welcomed the LNA's advance, which it saw as a way to end kidnappings, abductions and impunity and restore public services. In January and February the LNA peacefully took control of several cities (including Ghat, Qatrun, Sabha and Umm al-Aranib) and oilfields (El Feel and Sharara).

The seizure of the oilfields was possible only after negotiating with armed groups (mainly composed of Tuareg militiamen) that are part of the southern branch of the PFG.

In an attempt to resist Haftar's southern advance and entice the Tuareg population into the GNA camp, the PC appointed Kana, who is Tuareg, commander of the southern military zone. The strategy failed as the Tuareg chose to negotiate the peaceful handover of the fields with the LNA.

The GNA was not alone in leveraging ethnic divisions in the south. The LNA relied on Arab tribes in its advance. In Murzuq, for example, the only area where Haftar's forces faced considerable obstacles, the LNA joined forces with the al-Ahli tribe. These opportunistic alliances led to resentment by other minorities (including the Tebus), significantly disrupting social coexistence in the region.

Flood of Dignity *and* Volcano of Rage

The LNA's campaign in the south prepared the ground for the move toward the capital. On 4 April, Haftar's forces launched *Operation Flood of Dignity*. They rapidly took control of Gharyan and Tarhouna, where the Kani Brigade joined them and became the LNA's 9th Infantry Brigade. Pushing from the south, LNA units also took control of the disused Tripoli International Airport, making significant inroads in the southern outskirts of the capital.

Haftar had planned a joint advance from the west of Tripoli, where he could rely on LNA-affiliated groups based in Sabratha, but operations on the western front failed when militias in Zawiya halted the offensive at Gate 27, a checkpoint 27 kilometres west of Tripoli. Once militias from Misrata and Zintan mobilised to defend the capital, the TPF posed significant resistance in southern Tripoli. The Western militias' joint action offered Sarraj a window of opportunity to regroup and launch a counter-offensive codenamed *Operation Volcano of Rage*. The successful cooperation of armed groups under the command of the PC made Sarraj increasingly reluctant to return to the negotiating table.

The fighting on the southern outskirts of Tripoli continued in the following months, but the front line did not change significantly, with the exception of the fall of Gharyan on 27 June, when the LAF's surprise attack forced the LNA to withdraw. As the military stalemate continued, both the LNA and the LAF increasingly resorted to airstrikes using warplanes and UAVs and expanded the areas of operation to other parts of Libya, including Jufra, Misrata and Sirte. The use of UAVs in particular drew foreign forces (notably the UAE and Turkey) deeper into the fighting, with significant consequences for the civilian population.

Impact

Humanitarian consequences

The military stalemate after the Tripoli offensive led to an increase in the use of low-cost military technology provided by foreign backers. The LAF and the LNA resorted to UAVs for intelligence, surveillance and reconnaissance operations and airstrikes, significantly increasing civilian casualties. UAV strikes were carried out not only along the front line in southern Tripoli, but also in other parts of the country, including the remote south. On 2 August, an LNA UAV strike targeted Murzuq's town hall, killing 43 people and injuring 51.[8]

The fighting had significant humanitarian consequences. According to UNSMIL and the UN High Commissioner for Human Rights, 284 civilians were killed and 363 injured in 2019;[9] around 2,000 combatants are reported to have been killed.[10] At least 149,315 people were displaced over the course of the year since 4 April.[11] As of 30 November, there were 355,672 internally displaced persons (IDPs) in Libya.[12]

The fighting affected civilian infrastructure, including water-pumping stations, pipelines and airports. In May, groups affiliated with the LNA attacked the Great Man-Made River water system in al-Shwayrif and disrupted the water supply to Tripoli.[13] UNSMIL denounced the frequent airstrikes and the shelling of Mitiga International Airport in Tripoli as possible violations of international humanitarian and international human-rights law.

The UN mission also condemned the increasing number of abductions in eastern Libya and called on the relevant authorities to collaborate in obtaining the release of the victims. The case of HoR member Seham Sergiwa, abducted by an armed group affiliated to the LNA on 17 July, was particularly important. Sergiwa, whose whereabouts are still unknown, had previously been critical of Haftar's offensive in Tripoli.

The fighting did not spare humanitarian operators, and field hospitals, ambulances and paramedics were frequently targeted. In October UNSMIL said it had recorded more than 58 attacks against health workers and facilities in 2019.[14]

Looming partition

Operations *Flood of Dignity* and *Volcano of Rage* contributed to Libya's fragmentation and raised concerns about a possible partition of the country. The offensive on Tripoli deepened the regional divide between east and west. Following Haftar's attack, the centrifugal push extended to political institutions, with HoR members who opposed the offensive meeting in Tripoli and calling for the replacement of Haftar and HoR President Saleh.[15] The establishment of the Cyrenaica Society by the GNA in July and the eastern branch of the Brega Petroleum Marketing Company by the Interim Government in September represented further steps towards the disintegration of the country.

Egypt's cautious approach and increasing regional instability

As Algeria and Tunisia turned their focus to internal affairs, Egypt was left with significant room for manoeuvre in Libya. President Sisi had backed the LNA since the launch of *Operation Dignity* in 2014. He met again with Haftar in Cairo immediately after the start of the Tripoli offensive. It was expected that Egypt would take advantage of the changing regional context and its presidency of the AU to advance its interests in Libya and back Haftar's quest for power, continuing its fight against Islamist groups and challenging Turkey's influence.

However, as the fighting continued, Egypt took a more cautious approach than other regional partners. Cairo continued to provide political and military support to Haftar's offensive, but increasingly pushed for a political solution, especially after the LNA's first setbacks on the ground. The loss of Gharyan confirmed Haftar's inability to seize Tripoli without significant backing from his regional partners. As the LAF mounted a counter-offensive, the prospect of Haftar retreating eastward raised fears that the LNA could collapse – a significant security threat for Egypt. Sceptical since the beginning about Haftar's move on Tripoli, Cairo would have preferred to maintain the status quo, with the LNA securing its western border against Islamist and terrorist groups' infiltration attempts.

Haftar's military adventure also had implications for Libya's southern neighbours. The military campaign in the south pushed several foreign NSAGs out of Libya, increasing the security risk for neighbouring countries, as shown by French airstrikes on CCMSR and UFR vehicles in Chad in February.[16]

Trends

Political changeover to break the deadlock

At the end of 2019 the prospects for peace in Libya appeared dim. Both Haftar and Sarraj have refused negotiations with each other and international attempts to move the reconciliation process forward have not produced results. It is likely that the strong personalisation of Libyan politics will continue to prevent direct talks between the two sides.

Replacement of the two leaders cannot be ruled out, especially in the GNA camp, where Sarraj already faces significant internal opposition. The outcome of the fighting in Tripoli will determine the succession process, with Misrata and Zintan positioned to benefit from their decisive support of the GNA. The risk is a repeat of the 2014 clashes between powerful militias in Tripoli that would not easily renounce access to revenues from political and economic institutions.

This scenario could also affect the rebuilding of the military, jeopardising the LAF experiment. The fighting in Tripoli has provided the glue for different and sometimes rival militias to coalesce around the GNA. Once the fighting is over, the infighting in western Libya could resume, leading to an abortive process for the composition of the GNA's prospective army.

The cohesiveness of the LNA could also come under stress. Haftar's leadership has been uncontested so far, but also divisive. Despite attempts to groom his sons, the general does not have credible successors. Relations with affiliated tribes (especially the Awaqir) are often strained due to different priorities, and military developments on the ground frequently result in dismissals and arrests, showing the authoritarian nature of Haftar's rule.[17]

The collapse of the LNA or the failure of the LAF would have dire consequences. The façade of stability that both groups have in their own areas of control partially mends the political, social and economic fragmentation. The ongoing fighting and the resistance of these groups to DDR indicate that the time is not ripe to restore the state's monopoly on the use of force and that such an option will be possible only once a comprehensive peace deal is reached.

Russia's and Turkey's expanding influence

The personalisation of politics has also affected the work of the UN in Libya. Accused of having contributed to legitimising Haftar internationally, Salamé faces opposition from both sides, while regional organisations push for his replacement.[18] The September 2019 cabinet reshuffle in Italy and the apparent rapprochement between Paris and Rome offer him one more opportunity to get his road map back on track.

Many global powers will see the conflict as an opportunity to extend their strategic influence in the Mediterranean. In the absence of a ceasefire and an agreed road map to solve the crisis, foreign meddling will continue to intensify, potentially turning into open intervention. As the political crisis in Algeria continues and the new Italian government takes a more removed foreign-policy approach, the GNA is consistently pushed towards Turkey. The 27 November military agreement between Ankara and Tripoli paved the way for a direct intervention by Turkey in Libya, even though the joint deal between the two on the delimitation of maritime boundaries demonstrated the real nature of Turkey's interests. For President Erdogan, assisting the GNA is instrumental to more pressing energetic and geo-economic needs.

On the other hand, Russia's more visible involvement raises concerns, also considering Moscow's peculiar strategy of diversification. While the presence of Russian mercenaries from the Wagner Group fighting alongside the LNA has been confirmed, indicating Russia's preference for Haftar, commercial interests with the GNA and attempts to reach out to political outsiders such as Muammar Gadhafi's son, Saif al-Islam Gadhafi, indicate Moscow is exploring options to reap the benefits from the crisis. Its policy towards Libya raises important questions about US strategy (or the lack thereof), with contradictory messages from the US State Department and President Donald Trump highlighting divergent approaches. The US administration seems to be focused exclusively on fighting ISIS, adopting a counter-terrorism narrative, which fatally ignores the political, economic and social drivers of the conflict.

Notes

1. 'Proxies battle over Tripoli', *Africa Confidential*, vol. 60, no. 16, 9 August 2019.
2. Emaddin Badi, 'General Hifter's southern strategy and the repercussions of the Fezzan campaign', Middle East Institute, 7 March 2019.
3. Carla Babb, 'VOA Interview with US AFRICOM Spokesman', Voice of America, 25 October 2019.
4. 'Libya's unhealthy focus on personalities', International Crisis Group, Briefing no. 57, 8 May 2018.
5. Jared Malsin and Summer Said, 'Saudi Arabia promised support to Libyan warlord in push to seize Tripoli', *Wall Street Journal*, 12 April 2019.
6. In September, news of seven UAE soldiers killed abroad – hours after an airstrike launched by the LAF against the Jufra air base – suggested the broader involvement of the UAE in the Libyan conflict. See 'Yemen or Libya? Six Emirati soldiers "mysteriously" die in action', *New Arab*, 15 September 2019.
7. P3: France, the UK and the US, three permanent members of the United Nations Security Council with direct interest in the Libyan crisis. The other three members of the group are Egypt, Italy and the UAE.
8. The victims were representatives of conflict parties engaged in negotiations for a ceasefire. The conflict in Murzuq between the SPF and the LNA-affiliated al-Ahli tribe had resumed in the summer, prompting the intervention of the LNA and, allegedly, of UAE UAVs.
9. UN High Commissioner for Human Rights, 'Press Briefing on Libya', 20 December 2019.
10. Patrick Wintour, 'Libya peace talks to go ahead in Berlin despite ceasefire setback', *Guardian*, 14 January 2019; Leela Jacinto, 'Can Europe, caught scrapping or napping, mend its credibility at Berlin talks on Libya?', France 24, 18 January 2020.
11. International Organization for Migration (IOM), Displacement Tracking Matrix, 'Tripoli Update', 9 January 2020.
12. UNHCR, Operational Portal: Refugee Situations: Libya.
13. The vulnerability of the water supply system was also highlighted by the Man-Made River Authority in an annual report published in May, in which it said that it had suffered 106 attacks in 2018. Forty-two of the attacks (40% of the total number) were reported on the Hasawna–Jafara system, followed by the Ghadames–Zuwara–Zawiya system with 36 attacks. See Safa al-Haraty, 'MMRA annual reports reveals more than 100 attacks on the water system during 2018', Libya Observer, 13 May 2019.
14. In July, UNSMIL reported more than 38 attacks against health facilities and medical personnel, resulting in 11 deaths and more than 33 injuries.
15. The breakaway faction of the HoR also elected its speaker, Sadiq el-Kehili.
16. It also suggested strict coordination between the LNA and France, wary of the potential destabilisation of one of its allies in the Sahel.
17. As occurred to Gen. Abdulsalam al-Hassi, commander of the LNA's Tripoli Operations Room, following the defeat in Gharyan in June.
18. During a meeting of the UN General Assembly, the AU reportedly asked for Salamé to be replaced, calling for the establishment of a joint UN–AU Special Representative to Libya. The appointment of an African envoy would have represented a diplomatic victory for the AU, which frequently complains of having been excluded from peace talks in Libya.

SYRIA

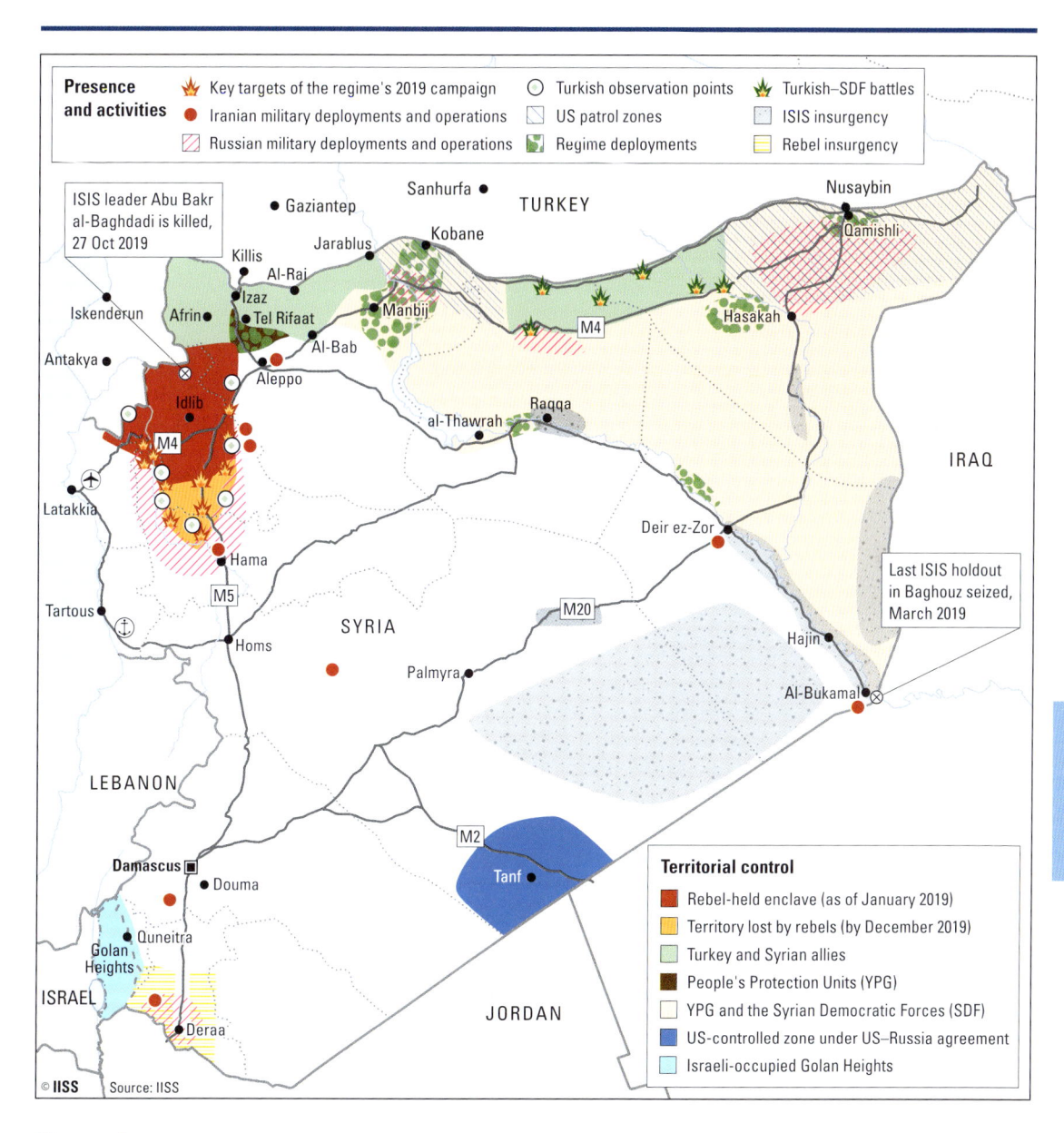

Overview

The conflict in 2019

The intense, complex and multidimensional conflict in Syria continued throughout 2019, constantly morphing in ways that affected and implicated local and regional actors. In addition to local forces, Iran, Israel, Russia, Turkey and the US conducted regular military operations in Syria. Given this intense international competition, the influence of the various political processes, including the UN talks in Geneva but also bilateral tracks, was marginal at best. The willingness of the warring parties to use force shaped events and dynamics on the ground.

Backed by Russia and Iran, the regime of Bashar al-Assad launched in the spring a strong push to capture Idlib, the last rebel-held enclave where Islamist groups backed by Turkey and jihadi factions mounted a ferocious defence. The battle for Idlib, ongoing by late 2019, created yet another humanitarian catastrophe.

Simultaneously, the international campaign to retake territory held by the Islamic State, also known as ISIS or ISIL, came to an uneasy end when Kurdish-led forces, supported by the US, seized the last ISIS holdout of Baghouz in eastern Syria in March. ISIS insurgent cells remained active in eastern areas, however, and the international community struggled to address the fate of jailed jihadis and their families. Dominant Kurdish militia the Kurdish People's Protection Units (YPG), the primary component of the Syrian Democratic Forces (SDF), was entrusted with administering a large and ethnically diverse area but faced an array of powerful enemies.

Against Western wishes, Turkey intervened against the YPG in October over concerns about Kurdish empowerment and possible autonomy and established a security zone along parts of the Syrian–Turkish border. A partial US withdrawal prompted a rush by the Assad regime, Iran-affiliated militias and Russia for control of strategic areas in northeastern Syria and created a controversy in the US over the perceived abandonment of Kurdish partners.

The conflict to 2019

The Syrian uprising of 2011, born from political and social grievances against the authoritarian and sectarian rule of the Assad regime, morphed into a complex set of intractable conflicts that have pulled in regional and international powers. The conflict has created the largest humanitarian crisis in the Middle East to date, generating large waves of refugees and fuelling Islamic extremism.

The core struggle has been between the regime, aided by Iran and Russia, and an array of opposition forces, backed by Western and Arab governments as well as Turkey. The fragmentation and radicalisation of rebel forces, combined with Western reluctance to provide game-changing weaponry, prevented the opposition from scoring political and military victories and weakened it during failed political talks. In contrast, the regime obtained significant Iranian assistance, including the deployment of Shia militias from across the region.

The 2015 Russian intervention secured the survival of the shaky Assad regime. The loss of Aleppo

Key statistics
Type	Internationalised
Start date	March 2011
IDPs total (31 July 2019)	6,100,000
Refugees total (31 December 2019)	5,560,393
People in need (31 December 2019)	11,000,000

in December 2016 debilitated the mainstream opposition. It gave Moscow a decisive say in Syria's future: Russia has alternatively brokered settlements and deployed massive firepower and has orchestrated diplomacy to rehabilitate the Assad regime. As a result, Western and Arab countries ended military and political support for the remnants of the rebellion in 2017.

In parallel, the rise of ISIS – the jihadi group that captured Syria's northeast and Iraq's northwest in 2014, then mounted international terrorist attacks – compelled the US and allied forces to intervene militarily from 2014. The US partnered with the YPG, the main Kurdish militia that formed a coalition with Arab rebel forces, to defeat ISIS. Supported by US airpower, intelligence, funding and special forces, the YPG succeeded in ending ISIS's territorial control, but the organisation reverted to insurgent tactics. To contain the YPG's ambitions, Turkey has supported Arab proxy militias. It has consequently intervened three times in Syria, capturing territory in the northwest in 2016 and 2018, and in the northeast in 2019.

Syria has also served as an arena for the Iran–Israel conflict. Tehran has built military infrastructure in Syria to threaten Israel, which has responded by conducting frequent airstrikes across Syrian territory to destroy Iranian arms shipments and logistical facilities.

The key drivers of the conflict remain unaddressed. The isolation and rigidity of the regime, economic collapse and the emergence of a war economy prevented political reconciliation and large-scale reconstruction. Ongoing government repression and dire living conditions make the return of refugees and internally displaced persons (IDPs), who account for nearly 50% of the population,[1] implausible in the near future.

Key Conflict Parties

Syrian Arab Army (SAA)

Strength
200,000 (estimate).

Areas of operation
Across Syria.

Leadership
President Bashar al-Assad (commander-in-chief), Gen. (retd) Ali Abdallah Ayoub (defence minister), Gen. Salim Harba (chief of staff).

Structure
The Syrian security apparatus consists of competing agencies, including within the SAA. The SAA is divided between regional commands, elite units and strike forces. Key elite units such as the Republican Guard and the 4th Division fall under the command of Maher al-Assad, the president's brother. Other units, such as the Tiger Force, respond to either Russian or Iranian commanders. The SAA also includes the 5th Corps, a unit formed of former rebels. To compensate for its shrinking ranks, the SAA encouraged the growth of pro-regime militias during the height of the war. Since 2017, and with Russian support, an effort has been made to integrate or dissolve these militias, and to reorganise and equip the SAA.

History
Founded during the French mandate, the SAA has played a key role in Syrian politics since 1963. Minority groups were traditionally over-represented in its ranks and in the officer corps, and many senior officers belonged to Arab nationalist parties, including the Ba'ath Party. Since 1970, the SAA has been dominated by Alawite officers, from which sprung the Assad dynasty.

Objectives
Defend the Assad regime, capture territory across Syria, integrate pro-regime militias.

Opponents
NLF, YPG/SDF, HTS, Turkish Armed Forces, Israel Defense Forces.

Affiliates/allies
Russia, Iran, local militias (National Defence Forces (NDF) and Local Defence Forces (LDF)).

Resources/capabilities
The SAA has an ageing air force and helicopter fleet, but airpower has given the regime a fighting edge. It has used chemical weapons repeatedly since 2012, with the last proven instance in 2018. It benefits from significant Russian and Iranian financial, military, organisational and tactical support.

Russian Armed Forces

Strength
2,500 (estimate).

Areas of operation
Across Syria.

Leadership
Gen. Sergey Shoygu (minister of defence), Gen. Valery Gerasimov (chief of the general staff), Gen. Andrey Serdyukov (commander of all Russian forces in Syria).

Structure
The Russian mission in Syria combines ground forces, special forces, attack aircraft and bombers, an air-defence component and military intelligence. Russian mercenaries operate alongside conventional units.

History
Since its intervention in 2015, Russia has shaped the Syrian battlefield, playing a crucial strategic and operational role to shore up and reorganise Syrian government forces. Russia helped Assad capture key areas including Aleppo, Ghouta, Deraa, Homs and other regions. In 2017, Russia focused on combating ISIS in eastern Syria. It has also countered Turkish power in Syria and sought to contain Iranian ambitions. It has suffered casualties in the dozens, though the total number is unclear.

Objectives
Protect the Assad regime, defeat rebel and Islamist groups, counter US dominance, counter Turkish ambitions.

Opponents
NLF, HTS, ISIS, Turkish Armed Forces, US forces.

Affiliates/allies
SAA, NDF, IRGC, Hizbullah, Turkish Armed Forces.

Resources/capabilities
Russia has deployed significant air, artillery, missile and intelligence capabilities in Syria, testing new weapons and tactics. It has also deployed Russian mercenaries in front-line roles.

Islamic Revolutionary Guard Corps (IRGC)

Strength
2,000 in Syria (estimate). 20,000 affiliates in Syria (estimate).

Areas of operation
Across the country. In 2019, the emphasis was Aleppo, Al-Bukamal, Damascus and Deir ez-Zor.

Leadership
Qasem Soleimani, commander of the Quds Force (QF).[2]

Structure
The IRGC–QF maintains a significant presence inside Syria in support of the Syrian regime forces and its allied militias. QF officers lead fighters from Afghanistan, Iraq, Lebanon, Pakistan and Syria on the battlefield.

History
The IRGC–QF has been active in Syria since 2011, providing strategic, organisational and tactical advice to the Assad regime and building a network of loyal militias. IRGC officers have played front-line roles, leading battles in Homs (2012–14), Aleppo (2015–16), Deir ez-Zor (2017) and Deraa (2018).

Objectives
Ensure the victory of the Assad regime, shore up militia partners, build a military infrastructure inside Syria, contain Russian influence.

Opponents
NLF, HTS, ISIS, Israel Defense Forces, Turkish Armed Forces, US forces.

Affiliates/allies
SAA, Hizbullah, NDF, LDF, Russian forces.

Resources/capabilities
The IRGC–QF provides an array of weaponry to its allies, including anti-tank guided missiles and uninhabited aerial vehicle (UAVs), but its main contribution is command and control.

National Liberation Front (NLF)

Strength
40,000 (estimate).

Areas of operation
Idlib province, western Aleppo province, northern Hama province, eastern Latakkia province.

Leadership
Col Fadlallah al-Haji (commander and head of Liwa al-Sham rebel militia).

Structure
A coalition of rebel militias operating through joint command and operation rooms.

History
The NLF, formed in 2018, is composed of Islamist and rebel units once operating under the banner of the Free Syrian Army. Their coalition was encouraged by Turkey and motivated by the need to counter HTS, the dominant force in Idlib.
In early 2019, the NLF confronted HTS on Turkey's behalf but after it was defeated, it acquiesced to HTS hegemony and prioritised the fight against the Assad regime.

Objectives
Defend the rebel enclave of Idlib, contain HTS.

Opponents
SAA, YPG, Russia, Iran, regime militias, HTS.

Affiliates/allies
Turkey, HTS.

Resources/capabilities
Weaponry seized by or provided to anti-Assad rebel militias since 2012. It consists mostly of light weaponry, anti-tank missiles and rockets. Turkey has provided small numbers of anti-tank guided missiles, the group's most advanced equipment.

Hayat Tahrir al-Sham (HTS)

Strength
30,000 (estimate).

Areas of operation
Idlib province, western Aleppo province, northern Hama province, eastern Latakkia province.

Leadership
Abu Mohamed al-Golani.

Structure
Led by a disciplined, tightly controlled security and military leadership controlling core HTS units as well as affiliated groups.
It has a complex relationship with other groups. It has both competed and cooperated with the NLF and maintains ties with other jihadi groups such as Hurras al-Din while constraining their activities.

Hayat Tahrir al-Sham (HTS)

History
Originally an extension of al-Qaeda in Iraq and known until 2016 as Jabhat al-Nusra, HTS is a jihadi organisation that has prioritised the fight against the Assad regime over global jihad. It competed with ISIS from 2012 and fought alternatively with and against other rebel groups in northern and southern Syria. It rebranded as HTS in 2016 to signal its dissociation from al-Qaeda, but the nature of its ties to al-Qaeda remains unclear.

Objectives
Resist the Assad regime, counter and co-opt the NLF, establish a quid pro quo with Turkey, defeat ISIS in Idlib.

Opponents
SAA, YPG, Russia, Iran, regime militias, NLF, ISIS.

Affiliates/allies
NLF, Turkistan Islamic Party.

Resources/capabilities
Arsenal comprises light weaponry, rocket launchers, anti-tank guided missiles as well as a small number of mechanised vehicles. It has seized weaponry from other rebel groups, including some equipped by Turkey and Western governments. HTS has used vehicle-borne improvised explosive device (IED) and suicide bombings.
Finances itself primarily through taxation in Idlib province, thanks to its control of border crossings with Turkey, and has interfered with internationally provided humanitarian assistance.

Turkish Armed Forces

Strength
512,000. 30,000 (estimate) deployed in southeast Turkey and northern Iraq, 22,000 (estimate) deployed in Syria.

Areas of operation
Southeast Turkey, northern Iraq, northern Syria.

Leadership
President Recep Tayyip Erdogan (commander-in-chief), Gen. (retd) Hulusi Akar (minister of national defence), Gen. Yasar Guler (chief of general staff).

Structure
Turkish army units operate under the Turkish Land Forces Command and squadrons carrying out airstrikes under the Air Force Command are subordinate to the chief of general staff. Gendarmerie units reporting to the Gendarmerie Command are subordinate to the Ministry of Interior.

History
Rebuilt after the collapse of the Ottoman Empire, the Turkish Armed Forces were significantly restructured after the country joined NATO in 1951 and have grown to become NATO's second-largest armed force.

Objectives
Eradication of the Kurdistan Workers' Party (PKK) and its affiliates, support of allied militias in Syria.

Opponents
The PKK and its affiliate organisations, particularly the YPG/SDF in Syria.

Affiliates/allies
Turkey relies extensively on the SNA as a proxy and support force in northern Syria.

Resources/capabilities
Turkey's estimated defence expenditure for 2019 was almost US$14 billion.[3] Its military capabilities include air attack and intelligence, surveillance and reconnaissance (ISR) assets such as the F-16 and the *Bayraktar* TB2 UAV, armoured tanks and special-forces units.

(Turkey-sponsored) Syrian National Army (SNA)

Strength
70,000 (estimate).

Areas of operation
Northern Syria.

Leadership
The SNA is a conglomerate of dozens of militias, differing vastly in size, affiliation and ideology. Turkey oversees the SNA's military leadership. Its leader is General Salim Idriss, the defence minister of the Syrian opposition government.

Structure
SNA units are currently deployed alongside Turkish forces and operate under Turkish leadership. The SNA is divided into seven main legions, each composed of a wide array of divisions and brigades.

History
Created as a splinter group of the Turkey-backed Free Syrian Army, the SNA is composed of Syrian militants, trained and equipped by the Turkish government since 2016. In 2019, the Idlib-based and Turkey-sponsored NLF was merged into the SNA.

Objectives
Control northern Syria, notably along the Syrian–Turkish border.

Opponents
YPG/SDF, Syrian government.

Affiliates/allies
Turkish government.

Resources/capabilities
The SNA is fully reliant on Turkish support. Turkey has provided small arms and infantry vehicles, and SNA military operations have benefited from the Turkish army's fire support via artillery and airstrikes.

People's Protection Units (YPG)/Syrian Democratic Forces (SDF)

Strength
Around 100,000.

Areas of operation
Northern and eastern Syria.

Leadership
Mazlum Kobani Abdi (also known as Sahin Cilo), a former PKK senior member, is the joint military commander of the SDF and the YPG.

Structure
The SDF is dominated by the Kurdish YPG but includes other ethnic and military groups, as well as the Women's Protection Units (YPJ). The YPG and the YPJ include small numbers of international volunteers grouped into an international battalion. Other ethnic (notably Arab) groups are organised under various military formations within the SDF, mainly as military councils.

History
The SDF was created in 2015 by the YPG to coalesce Kurdish, rebel and tribal forces to counter the advance of ISIS into northern Syria. Since then, it has fought primarily against ISIS and the Turkish military, but has also been involved in firefights with Syrian government forces.

Objectives
Defeat ISIS, protect Rojava's de facto autonomy, counter Turkish and Arab Islamist ambitions, secure Western support.

Opponents
Turkey, SNA, Syrian regime.

Affiliates/allies
US, Russia.

Resources/capabilities
While it built upon the experience of its militias, since the formal creation of the SDF, the group has been equipped and trained by the US. SDF units are equipped with small arms and some infantry vehicles, and can count on Western artillery, airpower and intelligence.

Islamic State, also known as ISIS or ISIL

Strength
14,000–18,000 in Iraq and Syria, including members and fighters.[4]

Areas of operation
Across eastern Syria, notably along the Euphrates River and the Badiya desert.

Leadership
Abu Bakr al-Baghdadi (until October 2019), succeeded by Abu Ibrahim al-Hashimi al-Qurayshi.

Structure
ISIS's presence in Syria changed considerably since the 2017 loss of Raqqa and the gradual territorial defeat of the jihadi organisation. Its central command remains in place, but greater autonomy is granted to local cells across the country to facilitate an insurgent campaign.

History
After seizing the northeastern third of Syria in 2014, ISIS established a 'caliphate' across Syria and Iraq. An international coalition led by the US and partnering with the YPG and local Arab forces succeeded in reducing its territorial hold, leading to the capture of Baghouz in 2019. ISIS was combated by a vast array of forces.

Objectives
Conduct an active insurgency in eastern Syria, harass Kurdish forces to force a retreat, punish Arab partners of the YPG and the US, harass SAA and pro-Assad forces.

Opponents
SAA, NDF, SNA, HTS, US forces, Russian forces, IRGC, Hizbullah, Turkish Armed Forces.

Affiliates/allies
ISIS fighters in other countries.

Resources/capabilities
Relies on light and small weaponry and deploys insurgent tactics including suicide bombings.

Drivers

National dynamics
The Syrian conflict is rooted in decaying economic and social conditions as well as divisive and sectarian governance under the authoritarian rule of the Assad family since 1970. The structure of the regime, which relies on recruitment from the Alawite sect of Islam in the security forces and the co-optation of minorities as well as urban and upper Sunni communities, excluded and brutalised rural and poor Sunni communities. A combination of poorly managed liberal economic policies, endemic corruption, environmental challenges and polarised urban development fuelled popular discontent.

The Syrian uprising started in 2011 as part of the wave of Arab revolutions that shook the region. The systematic, large-scale repression by the regime exacerbated existing social, ethnic and sectarian tensions. Military defectors and civilian fighters formed rebel units early on, which grew quickly due to popular support and foreign assistance.

Tribal divides across Syria also played a role, with clans and tribes splitting between the regime and the opposition. Members of the small Druze and Christian communities sided with the regime or maintained an uneasy neutrality. The regime owed its survival to the unpalatable nature of the extremist presence in the rebellion's ranks, the cohesion of the officer corps and the development of pro-regime militias, and to foreign intervention.

The security vacuum and the radicalisation of parts of the rebellion also allowed extremist groups to flourish across Syria, the two most prominent being the jihadi Jabhat al-Nusra and ISIS. Each established a territorial and political presence in northern Syria and relied on experienced fighters for their respective rule. The conflict and the weakening of central authority also revived hopes of autonomy for the Kurdish community, primarily based in northern Syria. From 2012, a variety of Kurdish factions sought to assert their political and cultural rights in northern Syria, but in doing so, they clashed among each other and with Syrian Arab factions. The campaign against ISIS that began in 2014 gave the PKK-affiliated YPG the dominant role.

Regional competition

Syria's geographic position and involvement in Arab–Israeli and Arab–Iranian conflicts conferred strategic importance. The conflict was exacerbated by fierce regional competition among three sets of actors: the 'Resistance Axis' led by Iran, which sought to protect the Assad regime; the pro-Islamist alliance of Qatar and Turkey, which sought to help Islamist factions gain power; and the conservative Gulf monarchies, steered by Saudi Arabia, which sought to check Iran's reach in the Levant. Each alliance extended political cover and military support to their local partners; in the case of Iran, this included direct intervention and deployment of non-Syrian Shia militias from 2012. In part due to external assistance, the conflict has displayed a sectarian dimension, pitting Sunni rebels against primarily Alawite and Shia regime forces.

Geopolitical factors

The Syrian conflict intensified the simmering rivalry between the US and Russia. The Obama administration, nominally supportive of democratic change in the Middle East but reluctant to intervene in its conflicts, played an ambivalent role. It provided political and military support to the rebellion but not enough for a military victory for fear that Islamist factions would prevail. US diplomacy was centred on an elusive political settlement.

In contrast, a resurgent Russia saw the Syrian conflict as an opportunity to check US power and return as a strategic actor in the Middle East by securing the survival of the Assad regime. By 2016, by working with government and Iranian forces, Moscow had achieved these objectives and become the dominant external actor in Syria. The US and Russia established deconfliction mechanisms to avoid direct combat.

The systematic use of prohibited weapons and tactics (including chemical weapons) by the regime, Russia and Iran tested international humanitarian laws. Political and security interference hindered humanitarian assistance, limiting the reach of international aid organisations. The UN also struggled to maintain a meaningful and inclusive political track.

Political Developments

Domestic consolidation

The Syrian government consolidated and expanded its authority in areas it controlled and recovered, which comprised almost 70% of Syrian territory by late 2019. It did so by reorganising its military forces and integrating militias into the new security structure. New security chiefs were appointed in the key services: General Ghassan Ismail succeeded Jamil al-Hassan as head of air-force intelligence and General Hussam Luka became head of general security. General Ali Mamlouk remained the most powerful security chief, becoming Assad's key security adviser.

Regime consolidation excluded meaningful reconciliation, however. In southern Syria, the regime flouted Russian guarantees offered to rebels who had voluntarily disarmed. Amnesties offered to former rebels and civilians avoiding conscription required that they complete military service. The government maintained its outreach to minority and religious groups. In order to maintain regime cohesion but also stabilise a crumbling economy and currency, the government launched a calibrated crackdown on senior businessmen, including members of the Assad family.

Astana process

The Russia–Iran–Turkey tripartite forum remained the main setting for conflict management, as the three powers had most sway over the warring factions inside Syria, and each directly controlled militias. They met several times at presidential and ministerial levels in 2019, hashing out temporary and partial arrangements to avoid direct confrontation and agree on escalation levels.

The fate of the rebel-held province of Idlib became the focus of Astana and Russia–Turkey bilateral talks. In September 2018, both countries had agreed on a ceasefire arrangement in Idlib, which required the establishment of a demilitarised zone and the dissolution of extremist groups. However, the regime repeatedly broke the ceasefire, while extremist groups operating in Idlib resisted any attempt to disarm them. Turkey also set up observation points inside Syrian territory.

UN talks

UN envoy Geir Pedersen, in place since early 2019, launched the first round of consultations to amend the Syrian constitution as part of the political process envisioned by UN Security Council Resolution 2254, adopted in 2015. Pedersen hoped that progress on a new or amended constitution would pave the way to a comprehensive political settlement, including elections. Western countries also placed emphasis on the UN and the Geneva process, hoping that these would compensate for their lack of influence inside Syria. Russia invested in the Geneva process to showcase its intentions and obtain legitimacy for its role in Syria, to be leveraged at a later stage for financial and reconstruction assistance there.

The formation of the constitutional committee was delayed by regime stalling. Damascus resisted any such effort as a violation of Syrian sovereignty, prompting Russian intervention to secure regime participation. The constitutional committee was officially launched in October and met twice in November. It was composed of three clusters of 50 representatives, one representing the government, another the opposition and the third civil society. A core group of 45 members representing each cluster was tasked with discussing and proposing amendments. Discussions over two rounds of talks, focused on procedural and agenda matters, achieved little progress, illustrating the immense gap between regime and opposition delegations. The former insisted that it reserved the right to reject any suggested constitutional amendments.[5]

Military Developments

Major combat in Syria in 2019 was concentrated on three fronts: Idlib, the northeast and the Euphrates Valley.

Idlib

Starting in April, regime forces, supported by Russian airpower, began a large operation to capture

Key Events in 2019

Political events

8 January
Norwegian diplomat Geir Pedersen begins his tour as UN Special Envoy for Syria, stating that he will focus on the formation of the constitutional committee.

23 January
Russian President Vladimir Putin and Turkish President Recep Tayyip Erdogan meet in Moscow to discuss Syria's future and the status of Idlib.

Military/Violent events

1 January
HTS begins a campaign against rebel and Islamist rivals in Idlib. Within two weeks, it defeats them and effectively dominates the last rebel stronghold through the HTS-run Salvation Government.

11 January
The US announces the start of the withdrawal of US troops from northeast Syria.

15 January
ISIS conducts a major suicide attack in Manbij, killing 15 people.

20 January
Israel conducts a major strike against several targets in Syria, including the main Damascus airport.

the rebel-held areas of Idlib, Hama and Aleppo provinces as well as northeast Latakkia province. The goal was to reach the main highways, the M4 and M5, and seize the main urban centres of Khan Sheikhoun, Maarat al-Numan and Idlib city.

Regime forces combined regular and elite units such as the Tiger Force and the Republican Guard, as well as militias from the National Defence Forces and a small number of foreign Shia militiamen under Hizbullah command. Rebel forces included the remnants of the Free Syrian Army and Islamist factions, but the dominant force was HTS, the commanders of which led the defence.

The initial advance through southwest and southeast Idlib was frustrated by extensive rebel preparations, which imposed heavy losses on regime forces. The capture of Khan Sheikhoun in August illustrated that relentless air and artillery fire could break civilian morale and debilitate rebel defences, however. The regime's strategy was to pound and depopulate areas before capturing them, and to advance gradually. Rebel logistical lines were disrupted while regime forces were better supplied. By late 2019, the regime had captured nearly 100 towns and villages.

The race for the northeast

In October, Turkey launched *Operation Peace Spring* to establish a safe zone along the Syrian border and push back the Kurdish YPG militia.

The Turkish operation was facilitated by a US reversal. After a phone call with Turkish President Recep Tayyip Erdogan, US President Donald Trump announced the US withdrawal of the 1,000-strong US contingent from Syria, undercutting efforts by US officials to maintain an uneasy truce between Turkey and the YPG since 2017. This removed the risk of accidental US–Turkish clashes but was perceived by the Kurdish leadership as a betrayal. In a complex diplomatic choreography over several days, Turkey, the US and Russia agreed on the size of the safe zone, from which the YPG was asked to withdraw.

In the following weeks, Turkish forces operated alongside the SNA, a franchise of Islamist groups directly armed, trained and equipped by Turkey. Major fighting ended by December, by which point Turkey had occupied an area of around 4,000 square kilometres, stretching 130 km from Tel Abyad to Ras al-Ayn and reaching the M4 highway. US troops maintained a small presence in the country, deploying around oilfields in eastern Syria, while Russian troops deployed along the border.

Euphrates River Valley

ISIS mounted its last stand as a quasi-conventional force in the town of Baghouz, along the Euphrates River, in February and March. The battle was exceptionally hard and gruesome, with thousands of civilians and ISIS families stuck as the militants resisted a well-resourced campaign by the SDF supported by coalition airpower and artillery.

In the following months, however, ISIS re-emerged as a small insurgency operating in the Badiya desert, primarily against regime forces, but also conducting small attacks in the southwest and the central provinces. The killing in October by US forces of ISIS leader Abu Bakr al-Baghdadi, who hid in the province of Idlib far from his depleted forces, exemplified the shift from a strategy of territorial control and state-building to one of insurgency.

---

11 February
The defence ministers of Russia and Turkey meet to discuss security arrangements over Idlib.

25 February
Bashar al-Assad visits Iran for the first time since the beginning of the conflict, meeting with Supreme Leader Ali Khamenei and President Hassan Rouhani in the presence of Quds Force commander Gen. Qasem Soleimani.

12 March
The EU and the UN host a conference on 'Supporting the Future of Syria and the Region'.

25 March
The US recognises the Israeli annexation of the Golan Heights, occupied since 1967.

9 February
The US-backed SDF launches the battle for Baghouz, the last remaining town controlled by ISIS.

16 February
The Syrian Arab Army and Russian forces launch massive attacks against villages and towns in northern Hama and southern Idlib.

21 February
The US announces that it will maintain a residual force of 200 in northeast Syria, later increased to 500.

13 March
Syria and Russia conduct extensive air and artillery strikes against rebel and Islamist forces in Idlib despite the September 2018 security agreement between Turkey and Russia.

23 March
The SDF declares the liberation of Baghouz from ISIS control.

Impact

Human rights

The human-rights situation in Syria remained dire throughout 2019. The regime and Russia were repeatedly accused of systematic war crimes, including the deliberate targeting of civilian and medical facilities. The fate of more than 100,000 disappeared individuals[6] remained unsolved, though the regime issued death notices for prisoners who died in prison in previous years. Mass arrests were reported in southern Syria and around Damascus.

From October, concerns mounted about ethnic cleansing by Turkey and Turkish-backed Syrian groups in northeast Syria, where they sought to establish a safe zone and relocate Syrian refugees based in Turkey. Residents fled and were at times evacuated forcefully. Exactions against civilians, including killings, were reported. HTS also violated human rights in Idlib, where arbitrary arrests and executions of fighters and civilians opposed to its rule were reported.

Humanitarian

The humanitarian situation remained critical. In December the UN estimated that around 11 million Syrians required some form of assistance inside the country.[7]

Flows of internally displaced persons (IDPs) remained significant, with a total of 6.1m by mid-2019. Between October and November, more than 220,000 residents, mostly Kurds, evacuated the areas occupied by Turkey and its Arab proxies in the northeast. The largest movement of IDPs was in Idlib, where more than 700,000 civilians relocated closer to the border with Turkey throughout the year.[8]

Many Syrians were dependent on humanitarian assistance, with 6.6m counted as food insecure by December 2019[9] and around 50% of health facilities partially or totally destroyed.[10] Conditions were dismal in camps such as Atmeh, where families in Idlib sought refuge, al-Hol, where families of ISIS fighters were detained, and Rukban, where Syrian IDPs fleeing Assad resided close to the Jordanian border.

Conditions for Syrian refugees in neighbouring states (around 5.5m by the end of 2019) deteriorated due to local fatigue and pressure, inadequate funding and increasing despair. Registered returns, mostly forced or out of desperation, were fewer than 100,000 in 2019 (52,387 returned between January and July 2019).[11]

By late 2019, concern grew that the complex UN humanitarian operation would be further strained by the reduction of access through cross-border points, made possible by UN Resolution 2265, because of Russian opposition. The presence of HTS in Idlib has deterred foreign donors from funding humanitarian activities there for fear of unintended entanglements with a jihadi group.

Social

Syria's social fabric struggled to recover because of a lack of national reconciliation, continuing violence and dislocation, and extreme hardship. By August 2019 more than 2m children had no access to education, and at least 1m more were at risk of losing it.[12]

Key Events in 2019

Political events

- **4 July** — UK forces stop the *Grace*-1, a Panama-flagged supertanker carrying Iranian oil and heading towards Tartous, for violating EU sanctions on Syria.
- **1 August** — Lebanese and Iraqi officials attend for the first time and as observers the 13th round of the Astana talks, held in Kazakhstan.
- **7 August** — The US and Turkey reach an agreement on a demilitarised safe zone along the Syrian–Turkish border, but details remain scarce and implementation slow.

Military/Violent events

- **30 April** — Syrian government and Russian forces begin a campaign to retake Idlib, focusing in the first phase on the southwestern and southeastern flanks of the rebel-held province.
- **7 July** — Assad appoints new heads of the key security agencies and promotes Gen. Ali Mamlouk as assistant vice-president for security affairs.
- **1 August** — The Syrian government proposes then quickly rescinds a truce in Idlib.
- **23 August** — Syrian government forces, advancing since April in northern Hama and southern Idlib, announce the capture of key towns including Khan Sheikhoun.

Women played an increasing role in the Syrian economy, due to a shortage of men, either killed, detained, injured or abroad.

Civil-society organisations (CSOs) in rebel-held areas struggled to survive. Those in regime-captured areas were dissolved, or else were affected by cuts in Western funding and increasingly dangerous circumstances, coming under attack by the regime and jihadi groups. In regime-held areas, CSOs operated under government guidance and partnered at times with the UN. However, a consolidation of regime-affiliated CSOs and non-governmental organisations (NGOs) such as the Bustan Association was undertaken, giving first lady Asma Al-Assad's Syria Trust for Development the leading role in providing humanitarian help in regime-controlled areas.

CSOs found a more hospitable environment in Syria's northeast, where the Kurdish-dominated administration welcomed their assistance in stabilising its areas of control. NGOs operating in ISIS-liberated regions such as Raqqa obtained UN and Western funding, though the partial US withdrawal in October threatened their operations.

Economic

Syria's economic situation remained dismal, in part due to the regime's limited resources and vengeful mindset and in part to international isolation and sanctions. The Syrian currency lost more of its value, hitting a low of 1,000 lira to the dollar in late 2019 on the black market, against an official rate of 434 lira.

Aside from a few highly controversial real-estate projects in Damascus, the government did not launch or fund any large-scale reconstruction efforts. Contrary to Damascus's expectations, hopes of significant Russian, Chinese and Indian investment failed to materialise. Trade with Jordan, facilitated by the reopening in 2018 of the Nassib border crossing, remained under US$50m, from a high of US$250m before 2011.[13] The Syrian economy was also affected by the dependence on Turkey of large swathes of northern Syria, where the Turkish lira and investment became pivotal.

Escalating sanctions, notably through the passing in December of the US Caesar Syria Civilian Protection Act,[14] further isolated the Syrian economy, placing sanctions on any entity trading with regime officials and targeting financial transactions.

Relations with neighbouring and international partners

Syria remained an arena for competition between major and regional powers, as the consolidation of the Assad regime was tentative. While relations with several Arab states improved, the return of Syria into the Arab fold faced internal opposition and Western disapproval but was also complicated by Assad's insistence that the Arab League show contrition. By early 2019, the United Arab Emirates (UAE) and Bahrain had reopened their embassies but maintained a low diplomatic profile. After capturing the highways running from Palmyra to Deir ez-Zor and Al-Bukamal, Damascus sought to revive trade and transport links with Iraq, hoping that Iranian influence in Baghdad would deliver Iraqi goodwill and opportunities. By the end of 2019, though plans for railway links and a transregional electricity grid were discussed, there was little movement.

---

3 September
US President Donald Trump tweets: 'President Bashar al-Assad of Syria must not recklessly attack Idlib Province. The Russians and Iranians would be making a grave humanitarian mistake to take part in this potential human tragedy.'

16 September
The presidents of Turkey, Russia and Iran meet in Ankara to discuss the future of Syria, the formation of the constitutional committee and the status of Idlib.

17 October
US Vice President Mike Pence meets Erdogan in Ankara to negotiate a temporary ceasefire and the withdrawal of YPG forces out of the Turkish-imposed safe zone.

30 October
The Syrian constitutional committee meets for the first time in Geneva under UN auspices. Syrian Kurdish officials condemn the launch of the committee, which excludes the YPG.

31 August
Erdogan and Putin meet in Moscow, after which Russia declares a unilateral ceasefire in Idlib.

30 September
The Al-Bukamal border crossing between Syria and Iraq reopens.

4 October
The NLF and the SNA announce their merger.

6 October
The US announces the withdrawal of its troops from the Syrian–Turkish border.

9 October
Turkey launches *Operation Peace Spring* to establish a safe zone along the border.

Russia played a key role in lobbying for the regional reintegration of the Assad regime, hoping that Arab diplomatic re-engagement and investment would stabilise the country and compel Western governments to drop their opposition to the regime. However, Russia was largely unsuccessful, and its own investment in Syria was limited to the Tartous port and a phosphate mine.

Syrian influence in Lebanon, on the wane since 2005, rebounded since 2016. Assad's survival allowed Syrian allies there to play an increasing role in politics. Eager to return refugees to Syria and reopen trading routes, Lebanon moved towards normalisation of relations.

Relations with Turkey remained fraught. The Assad regime virulently criticised the Turkish occupation of Afrin and the northeastern safe zone, and Turkish support for rebel groups in Idlib, but avoided a direct confrontation, in large part because of Russian restraint. When Turkey intervened in northeast Syria, Moscow negotiated an arrangement to allow Syrian government forces to deploy in parts of the region abandoned by US forces and began joint patrols with Turkish forces.

Trends

Political trajectories

With the survival of the Assad regime certain in the short to medium term, the central question for many governments will be whether and how to engage Damascus, on what issues and to what purpose. But even as it makes a vengeful return, the regime's territorial and political control varies widely across the country, and its weak, ineffective and gravely under-resourced institutions are struggling to rebuild legitimacy and offer public services.

In the northeast, the YPG is increasingly squeezed between an inflexible Assad government, an unreliable US, an aggressive Turkey, a resurgent ISIS and possible unrest in the provinces it controls due to limited resources and local dissent. Yet a compromise with Assad, the YPG's preferred option, remains unlikely, as the former, in a position of relative strength, has shown no readiness to accommodate Kurdish self-rule.

Conflict-related risks

The risk and cost of conflict in Syria remains high. By late 2019, government forces had made major advances in Idlib and were likely to seize much of the province and the major highways, locking around 2.5m people in the northwest in dire conditions. Turkey is also conflicted about Idlib. Its fall to the regime would weaken its hand and precipitate a new refugee crisis, which would exacerbate Turkey's internal problems. Ankara will therefore face the difficult and costly choice of whether to provide more substantive support to rebel groups in Idlib and check the regime and Russian advance.

Tensions between Turkey and the YPG could lead to an intense insurgency and major fighting in northeast Syria, especially if the US completes a total withdrawal, exposing the YPG to a Turkish onslaught.

Key Events in 2019

Political events

November — The constitutional committee meets twice in November. The inconclusive proceedings end in acrimony.

10 December — Turkish, Russian and Iranian delegations meet in Nur-Sultan for the 14th round of the Astana talks, but fail to reach an agreement on Idlib.

21 December — The US enacts the Caesar Syria Civilian Protection Act of 2019, which imposes penalties and sanctions on individuals and entities dealing with the Assad regime.

Military/Violent events

14 October — The Syrian government and the SDF reach a deal allowing regime forces to return to parts of SDF-controlled areas.

22 October — The Turkish and Russian presidents meet in Sochi to agree on a Turkish safe zone in northeast Syria. Joint Turkish–Russian patrols in northeast Syria begin shortly thereafter.

27 October — ISIS leader Abu Bakr al-Baghdadi is killed during a US raid on his compound in the town of Barisha in Idlib.

24 November — The Syrian Arab Army and allied Russian forces launch a massive campaign in southern Idlib and western Aleppo, and rapidly capture territory.

Syria is also an important arena in worsening tensions over Iran. The possibility that Iran will target US troops or allies in Syria through its Syrian militias, or that an Israel–Iran escalation will engulf Syria, is significant.

While a new uprising is unlikely given the state of despair and destruction and the absence of rebel forces, an insurgency is brewing in southern Syria. Additionally, the resurgence of ISIS is already under way, mostly in Deir ez-Zor province and the Badiya desert, facilitated by local discord and regional competition.

Prospects for peace

A comprehensive and inclusive political settlement in Syria as a result of the UN process in Geneva remains elusive. As it recovered its strength, the regime showed no sign of readiness to enact reforms or reconcile with an increasingly weak and splintered opposition. The lack of international interest and attention weakens the hand of the UN envoy, who has constantly redefined what is realistically achievable. Consequently, the safe and fair return of refugees remains unlikely.

Strategic implications and global influences

Syria is likely to remain an exporter of instability in the foreseeable future and to continue drawing external interference. Multiple rivalries will shape its fate. Russia and Iran, once partners, now compete to exert political and security influence inside the regime. Turkey is locked in a complex game with Russia and is keen to protect its security interests inside the country. US–Iran and Israel–Iran tensions are also likely to affect Syria's future.

Notes

[1] United Nations High Commissioner for Refugees (UNHCR), 'Syria Regional Refugee Response', 30 January 2020; UN Office for the Coordination of Humanitarian Affairs (OCHA), '2019 Humanitarian Needs Overview' (Syria), March 2019.

[2] Soleimani was killed in January 2020 and was succeeded by Esmail Qaani.

[3] NATO Public Diplomacy Division, 'Defence Expenditure of NATO Countries (2012–2019)', 25 June 2019.

[4] US Department of Defense Office of Inspector General, 'Operation Inherent Resolve: Lead Inspector General Report to the United States Congress', 1 April 2019–30 June 2019.

[5] 'President al-Assad's interview given to al-Sourya and al-Ikhbarya TVs', SANA, 31 October 2019.

[6] Syrian Network for Human Rights, 'At Least 98,000 Forcibly Disappeared Persons in Syria Since March 2011', 30 August 2019.

[7] UN, 'Describing Vast Scale of Need, Humanitarian Official Urges Security Council to Renew Authorization for Lifesaving Cross-Border Aid Delivery in Syria', 19 December 2019.

[8] UN News, 'Syria: Civilians face "daily nightmare" in Idlib, says top UN official', 7 January 2020.

[9] World Food Programme, 'WFP Syria Situation Report #12', December 2019.

[10] World Health Organization, 'WHO Health Emergencies: Seven years of suffering: Syria facts and figures', 2020.

[11] UNHCR, 'Syria: UNHCR Operational Update, January–July 2019', 31 July 2019.

[12] UNICEF, 'Syria Crisis Fast Facts', August 2019.

[13] Nabih Bulos, 'U.S. punishes Syria with sanctions – but allies like Jordan also pay a price', Los Angeles Times, 10 September 2019.

[14] US Embassy in Syria, 'Passage of the Caesar Syria Civilian Protection Act of 2019', 20 December 2019.

TURKEY (PKK)

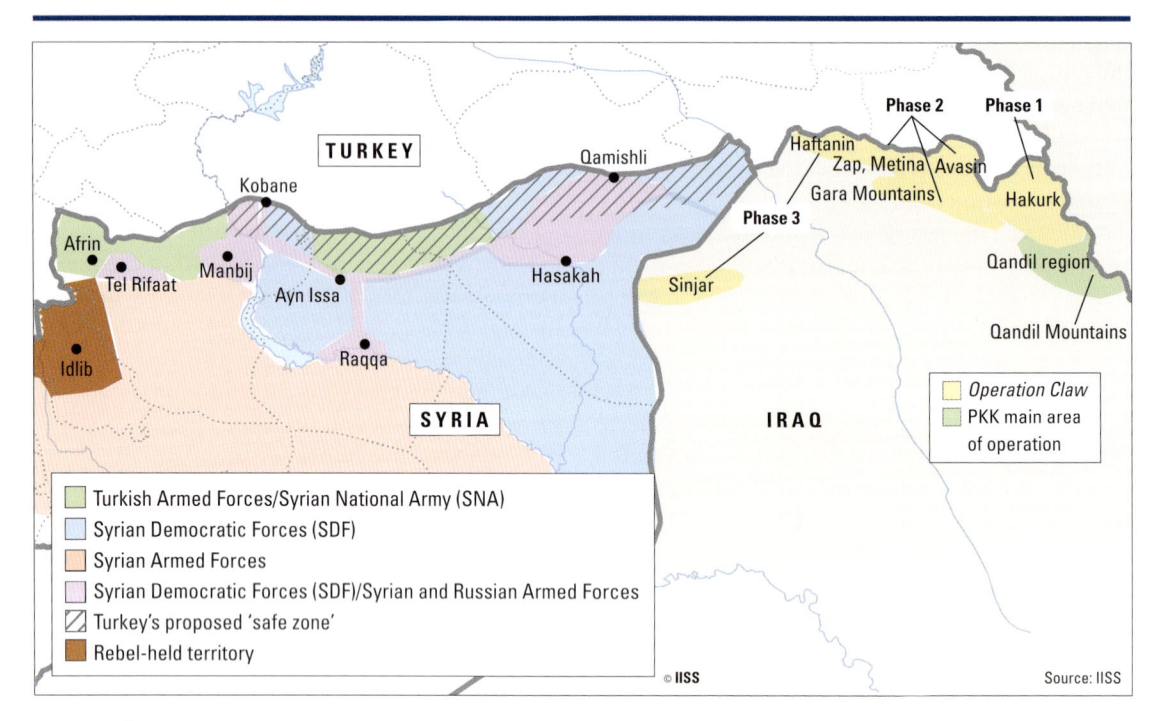

Map legend

- Turkish Armed Forces/Syrian National Army (SNA)
- Syrian Democratic Forces (SDF)
- Syrian Armed Forces
- Syrian Democratic Forces (SDF)/Syrian and Russian Armed Forces
- Turkey's proposed 'safe zone'
- Rebel-held territory
- Operation Claw
- PKK main area of operation

Source: IISS

Overview

The conflict in 2019

In 2019, the conflict between Turkey and the Kurdistan Workers' Party (PKK) continued on two front lines: in southeast Turkey against the PKK and in northern Syria against the Syrian Democratic Forces (SDF), the main combat component of which (the People's Protection Units–YPG) overlaps significantly with the PKK.

In Turkey, clashes continued throughout the year, with an estimated 80 casualties among Turkish soldiers, 280 among PKK militants and 30 among civilians. Besides recurrent PKK ambushes and operations by the security forces, significant incidents also occurred in northern Iraq, where the PKK maintains a significant presence.

Within Syria, alongside the observation mission set up by the Turkish military in 2017 around Idlib, and *Operation Olive Branch*, launched in January 2018, Turkey launched a third operation, *Operation Peace Spring*, aimed at creating an SDF-free, 30-kilometre-deep safe zone along the Syrian side of the Turkish–Syrian border. Facilitated by the withdrawal of US military personnel from northeastern Syria in October and perceived by the SDF as an existential threat to the survival of the Kurdish minority in northern Syria, the operation hastened the deterioration of the security situation in the region. The SDF remobilised and Russian and Syrian government forces advanced into territories previously controlled by the SDF in an attempt to limit Turkey's military advance.

The conflict to 2019

The low-intensity conflict between Turkey and the PKK – which is still formally recognised as a terrorist organisation by Turkey, the European Union and the United States – has persisted for more than three decades. Clashes have included

Key statistics

Type	Internal
Start date	1984
IDPs total (December 2018)	1,097,000
Refugees total (December 2018)	65,754
People in need	Not applicable

a wide range of actions from ambushes against Turkish military outposts and patrols, to fully fledged military and security operations targeting the Kurdish organisation. Since its foundation in the late 1970s, the PKK has called for the recognition of Turkey's Kurdish minority, inspired by its imprisoned founder and leader Abdullah Ocalan's vision of separation from Turkey. The organisation has adjusted its objectives to seeking political and cultural autonomy, together with ethnic recognition, within Turkey.

Historically, violent incidents have occurred mainly in southeast Turkey, where most of the Turkish Kurdish minority lives, and northern Iraq, where the PKK maintains a network of bases and training camps. In 2016, however, the conflict extended into Syrian territory, as Turkey fought against the YPG, the PKK's Syrian Kurdish affiliate and the main fighting force of the SDF. Clashes between Turkey and Kurdish units have escalated considerably since Turkey launched *Operation Olive Branch* in northern Syria to clear the Afrin district of YPG forces. In Syria, Turkish armed forces have been fighting alongside the so-called Syrian National Army (SNA), a franchise of Islamist groups directly armed, trained and equipped by Turkey.

Key Conflict Parties

Turkish Armed Forces

Strength
512,000. 30,000 (estimate) deployed in southeast Turkey and northern Iraq, 22,000 (estimate) deployed in Syria.

Areas of operation
Southeast Turkey, northern Iraq, northern Syria.

Leadership
President Recep Tayyip Erdogan (commander-in-chief), Gen. (retd) Hulusi Akar (minister of national defence), Gen. Yasar Guler (chief of general staff).

Structure
Turkish army units operate under the Turkish Land Forces Command and squadrons carrying out airstrikes under the Air Force Command are subordinate to the chief of general staff. Gendarmerie units reporting to the Gendarmerie Command are subordinate to the Ministry of Interior.

History
Rebuilt after the collapse of the Ottoman Empire, the Turkish Armed Forces were significantly restructured after the country joined NATO in 1951 and have grown to become NATO's second-largest armed force.

Objectives
Eradication of the PKK.

Opponents
The PKK and its affiliate organisations, particularly the YPG/SDF in Syria.

Affiliates/allies
Turkey relies extensively on the SNA as a proxy and support force in northern Syria.

Resources/capabilities
Turkey's estimated defence expenditure for 2019 was almost US$14 billion.[1] Its military capabilities include air attack and intelligence, surveillance and reconnaissance (ISR) assets such as the F-16 and the *Bayraktar* TB2 uninhabited aerial vehicle (UAV), armoured tanks and special-forces units.

Kurdistan Workers' Party (PKK)

Strength
30,000 (estimate).

Areas of operation
Southeast Turkey, northern Iraq.

Leadership
Imprisoned Abdullah Ocalan remains the ideological leader of the PKK. Since Ocalan's capture in 1999, Murat Karayilan has acted as leader on the ground and Bahoz Erdal as military commander.

Structure
While operating under the same command and leadership, the PKK's armed wing is divided into the People's Defence Forces (HPG) and the Free Women's Units (YJA–STAR).

History
Founded by Ocalan in 1978, the PKK has since 1984 been engaged in an insurgency campaign against the Turkish Armed Forces.

Objectives
Political and cultural recognition of the Kurdish minority in Turkey; adoption of a democratic and federalist system of governance. The PKK relies on highly mobile units, using guerrilla tactics against Turkish military targets.

Opponents
Turkish Armed Forces.

Affiliates/allies
SDF/YPG in Syria.

Kurdistan Workers' Party (PKK)

Resources/capabilities
The organisation relies on money-laundering activities and drug trafficking to generate revenues, in addition to donations from the Kurdish community and diaspora, and left-wing international support.

(Turkey-sponsored) Syrian National Army (SNA)

Strength
70,000 (estimate).

Areas of operation
Northern Syria.

Leadership
The SNA is a conglomerate of dozens of militias, differing vastly in size, affiliation and ideology. Turkey oversees the SNA's military leadership. Its leader is General Salim Idriss, the defence minister of the Syrian opposition government.

Structure
SNA units are currently deployed alongside Turkish forces and operate under Turkish leadership. The SNA is divided into seven main legions, each composed of a wide array of divisions and brigades.

History
Created as a splinter group of the Turkey-backed Free Syrian Army, the SNA is composed of Syrian militants, trained and equipped by the Turkish government since 2016. In 2019, the Idlib-based and Turkey-sponsored National Liberation Front (NLF) was merged into the SNA.

Objectives
Control northern Syria, notably along the Syrian–Turkish border.

Opponents
YPG/SDF, Syrian government.

Affiliates/allies
Turkish government.

Resources/capabilities
The SNA is fully reliant on Turkish support. Turkey has provided small arms and infantry vehicles, and SNA military operations have benefited from the Turkish army's fire support via artillery and airstrikes.

People's Protection Units (YPG)/Syrian Democratic Forces (SDF)

Strength
Around 100,000.

Areas of operation
Northern and eastern Syria.

Leadership
Mazlum Kobani Abdi (also known as Sahin Cilo), a former PKK senior member, is the joint military commander of the SDF and the YPG.

Structure
The SDF is dominated by the Kurdish YPG but includes other ethnic and military groups, as well as the Women's Protection Units (YPJ). The YPG and the YPJ include small numbers of international volunteers grouped into an international battalion. Other ethnic (notably Arab) groups are organised under various military formations within the SDF, mainly as military councils.

History
The SDF was created in 2015 by the YPG to coalesce Kurdish, rebel and tribal forces to counter the advance of ISIS into northern Syria. Since then, it has fought primarily against ISIS and the Turkish military, but has also been involved in firefights with Syrian government forces.

Objectives
Defeat ISIS, protect Rojava's de facto autonomy, counter Turkish and Arab Islamist ambitions, secure Western support.

Opponents
Turkey, SNA, Syrian regime.

Affiliates/allies
US, Russia.

Resources/capabilities
While it built upon the experience of its militias, since the formal creation of the SDF, the group has been equipped and trained by the US. SDF units are equipped with small arms and some infantry vehicles, and can count on Western artillery, airpower and intelligence.

Drivers

Turkey and Kurdish self-determination
The conflict between Turkey and the PKK is rooted in the incompatibility between the Kurdish quest for self-determination, the PKK's pursuit of political autonomy and Turkey's opposition to the recognition of the minority rights of its Kurdish population. Turkey sees any expansion of Kurdish political influence in the region as a potential threat

to its national security and, ultimately, as a threat to the unity of the country. While the PKK only represents one, albeit prominent, platform linked to the Kurdish issue, the Turkish government tends to conflate most forms of Kurdish political activism into PKK- or terrorism-related activities, further compounding tensions.

The fate of pro-Kurdish parties in Turkey is one of the most prominent examples of this dynamic. Since the 1990s, the Constitutional Court has disbanded all Kurdish parties that ran for parliamentary elections for having alleged ties with the PKK. The People's Democratic Party (HDP, Turkey's current pro-Kurdish party) focuses on a social-democratic political agenda in which the Kurdish issue is but one item rather than its defining element. Nonetheless, and despite a track record of electoral successes, HDP leaders and many of its MPs are currently imprisoned, and after the March 2019 local elections the Ministry of Interior had removed 24 HDP mayors from office by November 2019.

Influence of regional developments
Before the outbreak of the Syrian civil war in 2011, the Kurds, who live as a divided minority across national boundaries between Turkey, Syria, Iraq and Iran, reached a breakthrough achievement towards self-determination in 2005 with the constitutional recognition of the federal Kurdistan Regional Government (KRG) in northern Iraq. Despite deep political divisions among Iraqi Kurds and between the Iraqi Kurdish minority and the rest of the Kurdish political world, for many Kurds this was still a milestone development towards the creation of a Kurdish state.

The political progress of Iraqi Kurds, coupled with the turmoil caused by the ongoing US-led invasion of Iraq, also bolstered the PKK's ambitions for Kurds in Turkey, leading to a resumption of hostilities in 2010 after a five-year ceasefire. The PKK launched a stream of attacks against Turkish forces from strongholds based in the Qandil Mountains of northern Iraq, and the Turkish security forces retaliated with operations against the PKK in Turkey and northern Iraq. The Syrian civil war, and particularly the advance of the Islamic State, also known as ISIS or ISIL, in Syria in 2013–14, further aggravated the Turkey–PKK conflict, opening a cross-border front in northern Syria in addition to the long-established domestic front in southeastern Turkey. While the collapse of the Islamic State's caliphate in 2019 fostered a period of relative stability in SDF-controlled northern Syria, the sudden withdrawal of US forces in October paved the way for a new Turkish military campaign against the SDF, dragging the region back into conflict.

Political Developments

Turkey's conflict with the PKK, and the government's approach to the Kurdish issue more broadly, continued to have significant political ramifications. As the political fight between the HDP and the government continued, the HDP was the only parliamentary party that opposed Turkey's offensive into northern Syria. The number of HDP mayors removed from office and replaced by Ministry of Interior appointees had risen to 24 by November 2019, with thousands of HDP activists and members prosecuted for alleged ties to the PKK. In response, the HDP called for an extraordinary party meeting to discuss withdrawing its 62 MPs from parliament, together with the remaining mayors across southeast Turkey, to protest the government's repression. The party leadership voted against the proposal, calling for early elections instead.

The sudden withdrawal of US forces in October led to a redefinition of power relations in northern Syria, paving the way for Turkey's incursion and for President Recep Tayyip Erdogan's emboldened diplomatic approach with NATO and Russia. This readjustment also led to a 'convergence of convenience' between the SDF and the Syrian regime. Incapable of sustaining and repelling a Turkish military incursion, the SDF agreed to let Syrian (and Russian) troops enter strategic locations controlled by its forces in order to deter Turkish forces.

Lacking international support, Turkey's military advance triggered a range of negative responses from NATO allies. While Germany and France interrupted the flow of arms exports to Turkey, US President Donald Trump reacted by re-imposing tariffs on Turkish steel and freezing talks on a potential US–Turkey trade deal, stating that he was 'fully prepared to swiftly destroy Turkey's economy if Turkish leaders continue down this dangerous and destructive path'.[2] As NATO prepared to publish its defence plans for the Baltic states and Poland, Turkish representatives de facto vetoed their release, in a tit-for-tat for what Turkey perceived as NATO's double standards, including the lack of support for its military efforts in Syria and the failure to formally recognise the YPG as a terrorist organisation.

Turkey also engaged in extensive diplomatic dialogue with Russia. At the end of October, after the two countries reached an agreement on the coordination and management of military manoeuvres on the ground, the Syrian regime claimed it was making plans to take back full control in northern Syria, and that under these new arrangements the SDF would be integrated into the Syrian armed forces as a battalion – a proposal the SDF senior leadership promptly rebuffed.

Military Developments

The conflict between Turkey and the PKK expanded on all three fronts in 2019. In May, the Turkish armed forces launched a major operation (*Operation Claw*) against PKK targets in northern Iraq, which continued throughout 2019. Turkish army units, together with gendarmerie units specialised in counter-terrorism operations and supported by airstrikes by the Turkish air force, seized control of various strategically important locations along the Turkish–Iraqi border. Lack of further progress in ground operations led to a second phase. During July and August, Turkey carried out the offensive almost exclusively through airstrikes, paving the way for the third phase, initiated at the end of August, in which ground operations resumed. Throughout these three phases, Turkish forces occupied and took control of an area of 370 square kilometres. From September 2019 they attempted to push another 60 km east, towards the areas surrounding the Qandil Mountains.

In October, the Turkish armed forces, with support from the SNA, launched *Operation Peace Spring* in northern Syria to remove any remaining SDF presence and create a 30-km-deep safe zone along the Turkish–Syrian border. The international community unanimously criticised Turkey's strategy as highly destabilising for the region, as the weakening of the SDF's territorial control risked facilitating the re-emergence of the Islamic State. To avoid being overrun by the vastly superior Turkish forces, the SDF agreed to cede control of some strategic cities to Russian and Syrian troops, which took control of Ayn Issa, Hasakah, Manbij, Qamishli, Raqqa and Tel Rifaat. This agreement was intended to deter Turkey's military advance and prevent ISIS-led political and military activities from taking root again – it was not simply an act of hostility towards Turkey. At the end of October, Russia reached a separate deal with Turkey, putting its own troops in charge of guaranteeing the withdrawal of YPG forces from the 30-km section of the border Turkey was aiming to control – while also putting on the table a gradual reduction of Kurdish entities'

Key Events in 2019

Political events

17 February — Turkish security forces detain 735 individuals accused of planning a pro-Ocalan demonstration, arresting 61 of them.

15 April — Turkey's Supreme Election Council confirms that six HDP mayors who had been dismissed will not return to office.

7 May — Erdogan says that any reconciliation process with the PKK is 'out of the question'.

Military/Violent events

23 January — A Turkish airstrike kills four civilians in the village of Sheladize, 15 km into Iraqi territory, sparking violent protests.

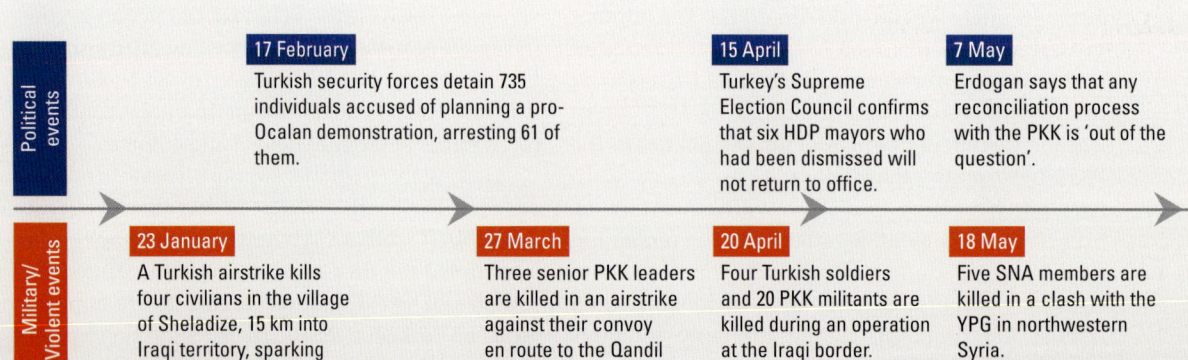

27 March — Three senior PKK leaders are killed in an airstrike against their convoy en route to the Qandil Mountains.

20 April — Four Turkish soldiers and 20 PKK militants are killed during an operation at the Iraqi border.

18 May — Five SNA members are killed in a clash with the YPG in northwestern Syria.

political influence and control over the key cities of Manbij and Tel Rifaat.

In a surprise move in October, Turkey announced that it had merged the NLF, a Turkey-backed militia operating in Idlib, into the SNA. This arrangement allowed Turkey to have a unified proxy actor in Syria, and will help Ankara to approach future negotiations on the fate of Idlib and northern Syria as part of the same deal, and to guarantee some operational and logistical continuity between the militias it supports in Idlib and the rest of the region.

Impact

Human rights
The conflict between Turkey and the PKK continued to have a significant impact on human rights in Turkey, northern Iraq and northern Syria. In Turkey, the crackdown on the pro-Kurdish HDP by the security services led to the detention of thousands of individuals alleged to have connections with the PKK, including politicians, journalists and grassroots activists. In northern Iraq, airstrikes carried out by the Turkish air force continued to cause civilian casualties, as did the conflict in northern Syria.

Humanitarian
The UN Office for the Coordination of Humanitarian Affairs (OCHA) estimated that by December 2019, 200,000 people had been displaced across northern Syria since the beginning of *Operation Peace Spring* in October. Roughly 17,500 individuals moved into Iraq by the end of November, according to the UN High Commissioner for Refugees (UNHCR).[3] The overall humanitarian situation remained dire, especially as various sections of the M4, northern Syria's main highway, were inaccessible to humanitarian convoys. The retreat of the SDF compounded the problems surrounding the detention facilities where Islamic State members and their families are held: dozens of captured fighters escaped from the facilities, but those who remained (including their families) had faced problems deriving from limited food distribution and limited access to primary-healthcare facilities since September.[4]

Social
In an extremely polarised political landscape, the launch of *Operation Peace Spring* rallied all political parties (except the HDP) in support of the armed forces, reflecting how Turkey's nationalist rhetoric had become mainstream. Isolated voices of dissent against Turkey's military actions have emerged across Turkish society but have been systematically accused of insulting the government and betraying the nation.

Economic
Up-to-date data on the economic impact of the conflict is not available, but a major trend has recently emerged in Turkey's defence budget, which has increased 24% year-on-year in 2018–19. The new deployments of Turkish armed forces in northern

24 July — INTERPOL revokes the 'red notice' request to locate and arrest PKK leaders and other key figures with ties to the YPG.

24 September — Erdogan stresses that creating a safe zone in northern Syria is necessary to avoid a new migrant crisis.

13 October — Germany and France halt arms exports to Turkey over its military operations in Syria.

16 November — Four HDP mayors are dismissed and detained on terrorism charges.

30 December — The Turkish interior minister accuses the HDP of using its offices as PKK recruitment centres.

11 June — Turkish military forces kill ten YPG members in an operation near Afrin, northwestern Syria.

25 August — Twenty-four PKK members are killed in airstrikes on both sides of the Turkish–Iraqi border.

8 September — Turkish and US troops begin conducting joint patrols along the Turkish–Syrian border.

9 October — Turkey launches *Operation Peace Spring* in northern Syria.

1 November — Turkish and Russian troops begin conducting joint patrols along the Turkish–Syrian border.

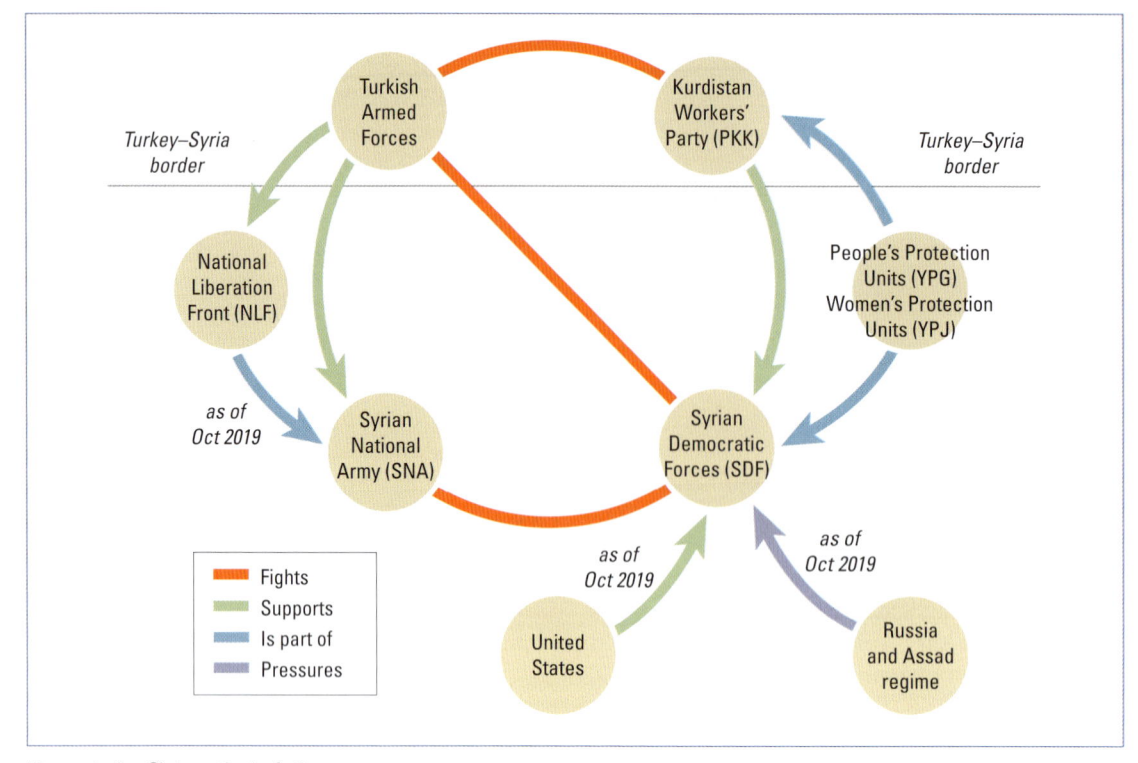

Figure 1: Conflict parties' relations

Iraq (*Operation Claw*) and northern Syria (*Operation Peace Spring*) are widely expected to push Turkey's defence spending well beyond US$20bn in 2020.

Relations with neighbouring and international partners
While Turkey's actions in Syria further isolated the country from its regional interlocutors and NATO allies, the diplomatic vacuum created by the United States' sudden withdrawal from northern Syria was quickly filled by Russia, with which Turkey increasingly cooperated despite Ankara's and Moscow's irreconcilable views on the regime of Bashar al-Assad. Relations between the Turkish government and Iraq's KRG also continued to move towards full normalisation. The KRG stepped up its anti-PKK rhetoric, while top-level visits from representatives of the two governments continued, to discuss security and energy issues, and reinforce trade and diplomatic relations.

Trends

Political trajectories
The most important political trajectories emerging from the Turkey–PKK conflict relate to Turkey–NATO and Turkey–Russia relations. The Alliance's strong opposition to Turkey's military action in Syria builds on existing frictions caused by Ankara's decision to purchase the Russian S-400 surface-to-air missile system, and the subsequent exclusion of Turkey from the US F-35 project. Turkish unilateralism is pushing the country progressively closer to Russia, and ongoing military operations in Syria offer an ideal opportunity for Turkey to further engage with Moscow. Although far-fetched, a potential solution to the stalemate in Idlib – where Turkey is in charge of demilitarising the last remaining stronghold of jihadist and other anti-regime forces – and an end to the conflict between Turkey and the SDF would bring Syria significantly closer to a resolution of its civil war.

Conflict-related risks
Absent any progress towards a political resolution of the conflict drivers, risks related to the conflict

will follow familiar paths. In Turkey, PKK attacks against security forces, and subsequent security and military operations, will continue, with a likely peak in intensity during spring and summer, when the PKK's mobility across mountain passes is higher. In northern Iraq, Turkish airstrikes will continue to target PKK hideouts and training facilities. In northern Syria, humanitarian concerns are likely to remain unaddressed, as Turkish military operations overshadowed the degree of stability the region had reached after the fall of ISIS.

Prospects for peace

The Turkish government's position on the Kurdish question remains unchanged: it is first and foremost a matter of national security dictated by the PKK's existence, and as such, it needs to be approached from a counter-terrorism perspective. Prospects for peace on the Turkish side of this conflict are, therefore, non-existent in the short term. In northern Syria, the combination of Turkey's military advance and the Russia-brokered deal for the relocation of SDF/YPG units away from the 30-km zone requested by Turkey might lead to a lull in hostilities. In the short term, however, this arrangement will still leave Turkish forces in control of important Syrian areas, creating tensions with local communities and potentially fuelling low-intensity conflict.

Strategic implications and global influence

The SDF is at the same time Turkey's main enemy in Syria and NATO's most valued partner in the country. As adamant as Turkey is in pursuing its security and strategic interests in trying to eliminate it, NATO will not cave in and side with Turkey on the Syria dossier. Doing so would jeopardise its credibility at a critical juncture for the Alliance, which is already dealing with significant internal pressure. Building on other sources of friction between NATO and Turkey, events in Syria might push Turkey further away from NATO and towards Russia. As for Syria, as coordination and cooperation between Turkey and Russia continue, finding a solution to regain control over Idlib would mark a significant turning point in Syria's civil war, and potentially cement future Turkish–Russian relations.

Notes

[1] NATO Public Diplomacy Division, 'Defence Expenditure of NATO Countries (2012–2019)', 25 June 2019.

[2] 'Trump authorises sanctions, slaps steel tariffs on Turkey', France 24, 15 October 2019.

[3] UN Office for the Coordination of Humanitarian Affairs (OCHA), 'Syrian Arab Republic: North East Syria displacement', 18 December 2019.

[4] OCHA, 'OCHA Syria Flash update #9: Humanitarian impact of the military operation in northeastern Syria', 21–24 October 2019.

YEMEN

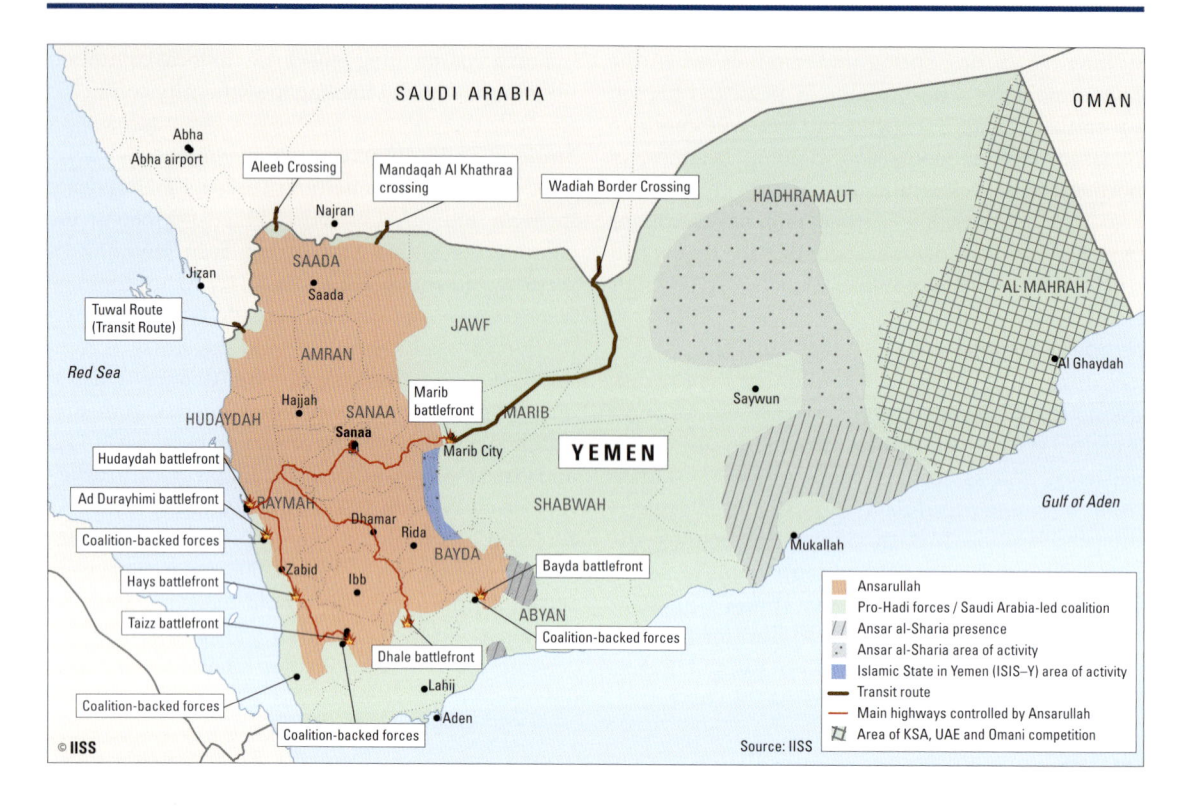

Overview

The conflict in 2019

Diplomatic and military stalemates prolonged the conflict in Yemen in 2019. The 2018 Stockholm Agreement between the Houthi movement (Ansarullah) and the Saudi Arabia-led coalition backing Yemen's president in absentia Abdu Rabbu Mansour Hadi was only partially implemented. Despite Ansarullah and the coalition redeploying their forces from Hudaydah, there were more than 30 active battlefronts in the conflict in 2019.[1] The coalition's continued aerial campaign and Ansarullah's intensification of attacks into coalition territory indicated the broader military stalemate of the conflict.

The United Arab Emirates (UAE) reduced its military involvement in Yemen in July. A volatile security situation in the Persian Gulf and the coalition's divergences over political and military investment in Yemen strengthened Ansarullah's position. The group was able to undermine not only the coalition's unity but also Hadi's claim to the presidency. This was most notably manifested by Ansarullah's missile attack against a pro-Hadi military parade in Aden in August.

Calls for secession gained more traction in the south of the country. Prominent groups within the southern secessionist movement, including umbrella organisation the Southern Transitional Council (STC), politically consolidated their military gains. They continued to contest Hadi's ability to guarantee security and clashed with forces loyal to him in Aden. This culminated in the 'Riyadh Agreement' reached between the two parties in

Key statistics	
Type	Internationalised
Start date	2014
IDPs total (21 August 2019)	3,647,250
Refugees total (31 August 2019)	353,895
People in need (31 December 2019)	24,000,000

November, which sought to create a power-sharing arrangement.

Ansarullah's targeting of critical Saudi infrastructure and reliance on uninhabited aerial vehicles (UAVs) and missiles throughout 2019 showed the group's increased effectiveness and resolve.[2] The September attack against Saudi Aramco's Abqaiq and Khurais oil-processing facilities immediately affected the global oil market. While attribution for the incident was disputed, with the United States and Saudi Arabia pointing to Iran, Ansarullah claimed responsibility. This led to the group's subsequent offer to halt offensive UAV and missile operations in exchange for the cessation of the coalition's military campaign. Back-channel talks between Ansarullah and Saudi Arabia resumed in October.[3]

The conflict to 2019

The political roots of Yemen's conflict partly stem from the country's troubled unification in the 1990s. The Yemen Arab Republic (North Yemen) and the People's Democratic Republic of Yemen (South Yemen) were integrated in 1990, but the process was left incomplete. The new country was afflicted by food insecurity in 1992, protests by the southern political elites in 1993 and a civil war in 1994. Grievances were not solved during the 22-year rule of Ali Abdallah Saleh and were only complicated by protests in the wake of the Arab Spring in 2011 and the presidential transition between Saleh and his vice president Hadi facilitated by the Gulf Cooperation Council (GCC) in 2012. As part of that process, a National Dialogue Conference (NDC) was held between March 2013 and January 2014 in an attempt to reach a political compromise among Yemen's key stakeholders. The NDC failed to forge a consensus on the federalisation of Yemen, however, and left the representatives of the southern secessionist movement and Ansarullah (of the north) unsatisfied.

When Ansarullah took over the capital Sanaa and the port city of Hudaydah in September and October 2014, Hadi was unable to control the country and was ousted by Saleh's General People's Congress (GPC) in November 2014. In January 2015, Ansarullah laid siege to the presidential palace. Hadi resigned and sought refuge in Aden but fled to Saudi Arabia in February when Ansarullah took Taizz and Aden. Following the bombing of Zaydi Shia mosques in Sanaa by the Islamic State, also known as ISIS or ISIL, in March 2015, Ansarullah leader Abdul Malik al-Houthi accused Gulf Arab states of financing terrorist acts in the Middle East.[4] With Riyadh interpreting Ansarullah's rhetoric and dominance over Yemen's north as a security threat, Saudi Arabia subsequently formed a military coalition to reinstall Hadi.

Retroactively backed by UN Security Council Resolution 2216, the Saudi-led coalition was met with fierce resistance from Ansarullah, which, allied with Saleh, could rely on the Yemeni armed forces loyal to the ex-president. The Saudi-led coalition relied heavily on airpower, land forces and mercenaries from partner states, and maritime blockades, and controlled large swathes of southern Yemen by mid-2015.

By 2016, Ansarullah had developed better military capabilities and by 2017 had increased deployment of UAVs and missiles against coalition forces and critical infrastructure. The group also managed to down a US MQ-9 *Reaper* UAV in July 2017.[5] Saleh's alliance with Ansarullah came to an end in December 2017 after a dispute over his attempt to regain power. Ansarullah also distanced itself from other anti-Hadi groups, which had provided essential financial capital.

By 2018, the STC and its affiliated forces largely had control of Aden. Despite nominally backing Hadi, the STC lacked faith in his ability to govern or support southern interests and began to call for secession.

Newly appointed UN Special Envoy for Yemen Martin Griffiths brought together representatives of Hadi and Ansarullah and by 13 December 2018 had brokered the Stockholm Agreement, which sought to establish a ceasefire in Hudaydah and the handover of Hudaydah port, Ras Isa Marine Terminal and Saleef port from Ansarullah to the UN-recognised coastal guard.

Key Conflict Parties

Ansarullah

Strength
180,000–200,000 fighters.

Areas of operation
Principally northern Yemen, including in Amran, Hudaydah, Ibb, Jawf, Mahwit, Saada, Sanaa and Taizz provinces, with clashes in Marib. Also operates along the border of Saudi Arabia, into Jizan province.

Leadership
Abdul Malik al-Houthi.

Structure
A mix of former military personnel loyal to Saleh but is largely dependent on fighters from the Zaydi Shia northern region of the country and its constituent tribes.

History
Ansarullah emerged in opposition to Saleh in the 1990s under the leadership of former parliamentarian Hussein Badr al-Din al-Houthi. Abdul Malik al-Houthi became the leader after the founder's assassination and led an insurgency in 2004 to avenge al-Houthi's death, to reform Yemen's political system and tackle corruption.

Objectives
Meaningful inclusion in Yemen's political system and expulsion of the Saudi-led coalition.

Opponents
Saudi-led coalition, Islamic State in Yemen (ISIS–Y), Ansar al-Sharia, Al-Islah, Southern Transitional Council (STC) and the Hadi government.

Affiliates/allies
Iran and Hizbullah.

Resources/capabilities
Small arms and light weapons, UAVs (intelligence, surveillance and reconnaissance (ISR); armed), missiles.

Saudi-led coalition

Strength
150,000–200,000 (air, land and naval personnel).

Areas of operation
Aden, Bayda, Lahij, Hadhramaut, Hudaydah, Mahrah, Marib, Mukallah, Shabwah and Taizz provinces as well as Saudi Arabia's Jizan province.

Leadership
Muhammad bin Salman Al Saud (crown prince of Saudi Arabia and minister of defence), Mohamed bin Zayed Al Nahyan (Crown Prince of Abu Dhabi and deputy supreme commander of the UAE armed forces).

Structure
Conventional hierarchical command-and-control structure. The coalition is a combination of ground forces supplemented by foreign mercenaries from South Sudan and Latin America, and locally trained militias.

History
Following Ansarullah's takeover of large swathes of Yemen, including Aden, in 2015, Saudi Arabia formed a coalition to restore Hadi to power and roll back Ansarullah's territorial control.

Objectives
For Saudi Arabia, to defeat Ansarullah militarily and reinstate the Hadi presidency. For the UAE, also counter-terrorism operations against Ansar al-Sharia and ISIS–Y.

Opponents
Ansarullah, ISIS–Y and Ansar al-Sharia.

Affiliates/allies
Al-Islah, Popular Resistance Forces.

Resources/capabilities
ISR assets (UAVs and satellites), fighter jets, air defences, small arms and light weapons, and tanks.

Al-Qaeda in the Arabian Peninsula (Ansar al-Sharia)

Strength
6,000–8,000.

Areas of operation
Hadhramaut and Shabwah provinces.

Leadership
Qasim al-Raymi.

Structure
Decentralised with allegiances cemented through marriages.

History
Created in 2009 when the al-Qaeda franchises in Saudi Arabia and Yemen fused. The organisation changed its name to Ansar al-Sharia in 2011. It had control of the strategically important southern city of Mukallah between 2015 and 2016 but was defeated and lost the territory after extensive counter-terrorism operations by the UAE.

Objectives
Retain territorial control and oppose Saudi Arabia, Ansarullah and the Popular Resistance Forces, and win over local tribes. Ansar al-Sharia competes with the Popular Resistance Forces and ISIS–Y for recruitment of combatants.

Al-Qaeda in the Arabian Peninsula (Ansar al-Sharia)

Opponents
ISIS–Y, Al-Islah, Ansarullah, Saudi-led coalition, Popular Resistance Forces and the STC.

Affiliates/allies
Local tribes through marriage.

Resources/capabilities
Small arms and light weapons, and improvised explosive devices (IEDs).

Islamic State in Yemen (ISIS–Y)

Strength
250–500.

Areas of operation
Across the southern provinces.

Leadership
Abu Ibrahim al-Hashimi al-Qurayshi.

Structure
Decentralised.

History
Formed in November 2014 and rejected by Ansar al-Sharia on ideological grounds, it seeks to recruit from the same demographic. ISIS–Y is in direct competition with Ansar al-Sharia for influence in Bayda. The group has exploited sectarianism towards the Zaydi Shia population in northern Yemen as a means of gathering support for anti-Ansarullah and anti-Zaydi attacks.

Objectives
Prevail over Ansar al-Sharia for regional influence and, in line with ISIS, attack Zaydi Shia groups/communities, whom it regards as out of the fold of Islam.

Opponents
Ansar al-Sharia, Al-Islah, Ansarullah, Saudi-led coalition, Popular Resistance Forces and the STC.

Affiliates/allies
ISIS (all franchises).

Resources/capabilities
Relies heavily on IEDs, small arms and light weapons.

Al-Islah

Strength
Political party, but unaffiliated militia forces fight in support of it.

Areas of operation
While not an armed group, Al-Islah is well supported across Marib and Taizz.

Leadership
Mohammed bin Abdullah al-Yadumi.

Structure
Political organisation comprising a general secretariat and executive offices.

History
The Yemeni Congregation for Reform (Al-Islah) was established in 1990 following the unification process. The political party is composed of a variety of Muslim Brotherhood affiliates alongside tribal groups and Salafi Muslims. The participation of tribal groups in support of Al-Islah has also provided the party with a mobilisation power. This has resulted in it being able to raise armed fighters, most notably in the early 2000s against Ansarullah. While the party has received backing from both Saudi Arabia and Qatar, both Saudi Arabia and the UAE have now designated it a terrorist organisation for its relationship with the Muslim Brotherhood. Despite the UAE militarily targeting Al-Islah and its affiliates, Saudi Arabia maintains a positive political relationship with it due to its support for Hadi.

Objectives
Primary objective is the restoration of Hadi's premiership, along with opposition to both Ansarullah's control of northern Yemen and the southern secessionist movement.

Opponents
Ansarullah, the UAE and the STC.

Affiliates/allies
Hadi, Saudi Arabia.

Resources/capabilities
None. However, tribes who have supported Al-Islah in the past have fought in support of the party in armed clashes.

Popular Resistance Forces

Strength
100,000.

Areas of operation
Aden, Bayda, Hadhramaut, Hudaydah, Marib, Mukallah and Taizz provinces.

Leadership
Divided between Hadi, the Saudi-led coalition, Tareq Saleh (nephew of Ali Abdullah Saleh) and local commanders.

Structure
Decentralised with different levels of cohesion among various groups.

History
The Popular Resistance Forces comprise mostly former Yemeni army members loyal to Hadi. They were the first to take up arms against Ansarullah and were later joined by the Elite Forces, Security Belt Forces, National Resistance Forces led by Tareq Saleh and Al-Islah-affiliated militias.

Objectives
To militarily defeat Ansarullah, in line with the Saudi-led coalition's goals, but do not seek to restore Hadi's legitimacy.

Opponents
Ansarullah, ISIS–Y and Ansar al-Sharia.

Affiliates/allies
Al-Islah, Saudi-led coalition and the STC. Operational assistance and support, and logistical support from Hadi's government and the Saudi-led coalition.

Resources/capabilities
ISR UAVs, small arms and light weapons, vehicles and tanks.

Southern Movement

Strength
90,000.

Areas of operation
Aden, Abyan, Shabwah, Hadhramaut, Mahrah and Lahij provinces.

Leadership
Aidarous al-Zubaidi, Ali Salem al-Beidh.

Structure
Political organisation with several affiliated armed groups operating within the Popular Resistance Forces. The Southern Transitional Council (STC) presents itself as the most prominent political representative of the southern cause.

History
The Southern Movement emerged after the 1990 unification process, when the vice president of South Yemen Ali Salem al-Beidh protested Ali Abdullah Saleh's power-sharing agreement. The movement's most organised political body, the STC, is a political umbrella grouping secessionists in the south. It is aligned with and backed by the UAE, and has benefited from the UAE's military support.

Objectives
Secession of south Yemen from the north. The movement has expressed willingness to share power, as a temporary measure, on the condition of fair representation in any future government.

Opponents
Ansarullah, ISIS–Y, Ansar al-Sharia and Al-Islah.

Affiliates/allies
Saudi-led coalition, Popular Resistance Forces. The UAE provides financial and military support, including training and equipment of affiliated armed groups.

Resources/capabilities
The UAE has provided small arms and light weapons, and light infantry vehicles.

Drivers

Regional competition

Iran views Saudi Arabia and the UAE as aggressors because of their regional policies, support and accommodation of the US, and broader posture towards Iran. Saudi Arabia holds a reciprocal view of Iran because of its regional relationships, and missile and nuclear programmes. The Saudi-led coalition has come to view Ansarullah as a conduit of Iranian power against the Persian Gulf states and frames its intervention in Yemen as a direct challenge to Iran's regional influence. Despite the fact that Iran did not support Ansarullah directly at the start of the war, it has benefited from the group's fight against the coalition because the protracted conflict has drained resources from coalition members. By 2019, Ansarullah had grown closer to Iran, and its spokesperson Mohammed Abdul-Salam met with Iranian Supreme Leader Ayatollah Ali Khamenei in Tehran in August.[6]

Historical grievances in the south

Grievances about the marginalisation of southern Yemen came to the fore with the incomplete unification process in 1990. Despite holding much of the country's natural resources, including oil, the south derived little benefit from these. Education standards dropped and civic rights deteriorated, heightening feelings of disaffection towards the north-centric and nepotistic government in Sanaa. As a result of the unification process, southern secessionist aspirations have increased over the years. The STC's opposition to the federalisation plans outlined by the NDC became a focal point of dissatisfaction with Hadi's rule in absentia and inability to guarantee security in the south.

Saleh's legacy and poor governance

The legacy of Saleh's rule indirectly drives the current crisis. The former president systematically promoted his family members into key governmental positions while at the same time profiting personally from Yemen's natural resources. Hadi's appointment in 2012 did not usher in the change that Ansarullah had expected. Much of the south backed Hadi, but disputes over his rule persisted within the secessionist movement and converged in August 2019 when forces affiliated with the STC took control of Aden.

Political Developments

The 2018 Stockholm Agreement

The 2018 Stockholm Agreement, which sought to establish a ceasefire in Hudaydah and the handover of several ports to UN-backed local entities, was partially implemented in 2019. The diplomatic accord contained three sections. The first, the Hudaydah Agreement (see table), outlined the conditions related to a ceasefire in the city of Hudaydah and the status of Hudaydah port, Ras Isa Marine Terminal and Saleef port. The second established an agreement on prisoner exchanges. The final component was a statement of understanding to improve the humanitarian situation in Taizz and de-escalate military tensions, but no progress was made in 2019 on the de-escalation of violence in the province.

On 15 April Griffiths briefed the UN Security Council and stated that Ansarullah and the Saudi-led coalition had accepted the first part of a redeployment plan for Hudaydah. Ansarullah's fighters would withdraw 5 kilometres from their positions in the port of Hudaydah. The coalition forces would reciprocate by withdrawing 1 km from their positions in the eastern area of the city.

Between 11 May and 1 June, the UN Mission to Support the Hudaydah Agreement (UNMHA) observed the implementation of first the handover of control of Hudaydah port from Ansarullah to the UN-recognised 'coastal guard' and then the cessation of Ansarullah's military activity across Hudaydah port, Ras Isa Marine Terminal and Saleef port.

STOCKHOLM AGREEMENT (HUDAYDAH AGREEMENT), 13 DECEMBER 2018 Between Ansarullah and Abdu Rabbu Mansour Hadi as backed by the Saudi-led coalition, covering the city of Hudaydah, Hudaydah port, Ras Isa Marine Terminal and Saleef port	STATUS
Immediate ceasefire in the city of Hudaydah and Hudaydah port, Ras Isa Marine Terminal and Saleef port	In progress/unclear
Mutual redeployment of forces from the city of Hudaydah and Hudaydah port, Ras Isa Marine Terminal and Saleef port	In progress/unclear
Commitment not to bring any military reinforcements into the city of Hudaydah, Hudaydah port, Ras Isa Marine Terminal and Saleef port	In progress/unclear
Commitment to remove military manifestations from the city of Hudaydah	Not implemented
Establishment of Redeployment Coordination Committee (inclusive, but not limited to members of the parties)	Implemented
Redeployment Coordination Committee to supervise and observe the redeployment of forces and monitor demining operations	Implemented
Weekly report to the UN Security Council on compliance of the parties to be submitted by the chairman of the Redeployment Coordination Committee	Implemented
UN to support the Yemen Red Sea Ports Corporation in management and inspection of the ports, including enhanced monitoring of them by the Verification and Inspection Mechanism for Yemen (UNVIM)	Implemented
UN taking the lead in supporting the Yemen Red Sea Ports Corporation in management and inspection of sites	Implemented
Strengthened UN presence across the sites	Implemented
Commitment by parties to facilitate and support work of the UN in Hudaydah	Implemented
Parties to facilitate freedom of movement of both civilians and goods throughout the city of Hudaydah and the sites, including the free movement of humanitarian aid	Not implemented
Revenues of the ports channelled to the Central Bank of Yemen through its Hudaydah branch as a contribution to the payment of salaries in Hudaydah and throughout Yemen	Not implemented
Responsibility for security across the sites transferred to local security forces	In progress/unclear

● Implemented
● In progress/unclear
● Not implemented

Source: UN Office of the Special Envoy of the Secretary-General for Yemen

The agreement also called for an immediate ceasefire in Hudaydah, but while military activity stopped in the port area, hostilities continued in the city in July, particularly in the areas of Kilo 7 and Saleh City, as the battlefronts shifted eastwards. On 18 May, less than a week after the handover from Ansarullah to the coastal guard, the coalition shelled the 50 Street area.

In September, the International Committee of the Red Cross (ICRC) facilitated Ansarullah's unilateral release of 290 prisoners.[7] The Saudi-led coalition reciprocated in November when the ICRC facilitated the release and repatriation of 128 prisoners back to Sanaa.[8] Despite this progress, both parties – as per the Stockholm Agreement – had been expected to release approximately 7,000 prisoners.[9]

Ansarullah and the Saudi-led coalition

Despite the US and Saudi Arabia blaming Iran for the attack on the Aramco facilities on 14 September, this gave Ansarullah political leverage against Saudi Arabia. The group capitalised on the incident and subsequently offered the coalition a halt on all UAV and missile attacks into Saudi Arabia conditional on the coalition's halting of military operations in Yemen. Despite a formal ceasefire not being established, back-channel negotiations between Ansarullah and the coalition subsequently started in Riyadh in October 2019 for the first time in two years. The impact of these on the conduct of war in Yemen will be highly dependent on Saudi Arabia's willingness to accept Ansarullah's political and military existence and activity. The extent to which Hadi will accommodate Ansarullah's political demands while balancing his commitments to other parties is another important factor shaping the viability of a peace process.

The STC and Hadi

Ansarullah's targeting of southern Yemen deepened the cleavage between the STC and Hadi. Following its attacks against the pro-Hadi military parade in Aden on 1 August, the STC moved to take Aden militarily, thereby further diminishing Hadi's political legitimacy. Hadi's failure to guarantee security in the south has enabled the STC to leverage its military footing politically. The Riyadh Agreement of 5 November between the southern secessionists and the government in exile yielded significant political gains for the former – a power-sharing deal whereby a new cabinet of 24 ministers would comprise 12 from the south and 12 from the north.[10] This was the first agreement of this kind reached in Yemen. However, by the end of the year, the deadline of 30 days from the establishment of the accord for the creation of the cabinet had not been met, which diminished its political value. The STC's position and Hadi's political capital within the context of the agreement were eroded in turn.

Key Events in 2019

Political events

- **17 February**: The Hadi government and Ansarullah agree on the first phase of force redeployment from Hudaydah.
- **13 March**: US Senate passes a bill to withdraw support for the Saudi-led war in Yemen.
- **17 April**: US President Donald Trump vetoes the bipartisan bill to withdraw US support for the Saudi-led war in Yemen.
- **11–14 May**: The UN observes the mutual withdrawal of forces from Hudaydah.

Military/Violent events

- **10 January**: Ansarullah assassinates Hadi's chief of military intelligence Major-General Mohammad Saleh Tamah.
- **23 February**: UAE-affiliated forces take control of an Ansar al-Sharia training camp and announce control of the Wadi Omran area in Abyan province.
- **24 March**: Militants reportedly affiliated with Ansar al-Sharia engage in an armed clash with ISIS–Y.
- **22 April**: Ansarullah's leader Abdul Malik al-Houthi issues a warning to Saudi Arabia and the UAE that it will target their cities if violence in Hudaydah persists.

Military Developments

UAE's military redeployment

In July, the UAE began relocating its forces away from Hudaydah and allowed its locally trained partners to take over. A further withdrawal occurred in Aden in October.[11] Not only did this aim to accommodate the Hadi government's issue with the UAE-backed STC's dominance of Aden, but it also carried with it two signals. Firstly, UAE Minister of State for Foreign Affairs Anwar Gargash stated that the withdrawal was intended as a 'confidence-building measure to create new momentum to end the conflict'.[12] The reduction in the UAE's force size, however, did not affect its counter-terrorism operations in Yemen. The UAE views ISIS–Y and Ansar al-Sharia as existential threats to its internal security and thus sought to refocus its intervention towards countering those threats. Secondly, the move was intended to restore international support for the UAE's foreign policy amid widespread opposition to its involvement in Yemen.

Ansarullah's air capabilities

Ansarullah's strategy of targeting enemy territory inside and outside Yemen with missiles and UAVs aims to project an image of defiance in the face of a militarily superior enemy. In January, Hadi's chief of military intelligence Major-General Mohammad Saleh Tamah was killed in a targeted operation of this kind. In July, Ansarullah held a significant military exhibition as well as targeting civilian and economic infrastructure using some of the UAV capabilities displayed, in an attempt to deter the coalition from further military action. In *Operation First Deterrence Balance* on 17 August, Ansarullah deployed ten low-flying UAVs against Aramco's Shaybah natural gas liquids (NGL)-processing facility in Saudi Arabia.[13]

The 14 September attack against Saudi Arabia's Abqaiq and Khurais oilfields resulted in a shock to global oil markets and approximately 5 million barrels per day of lost production.[14] Despite ambiguity over the launch site of the attacks, Ansarullah claimed responsibility and pointed to the use of *Quds*-1 missiles, and a 'previously unseen' UAV system, as evidence of its involvement. Irrespective of this, the US and Saudi Arabia held Iran responsible. With Saudi Arabia already viewing Ansarullah as a proxy of Iran, the prospect of an intensified cross-border military effort from Ansarullah while the possibility of a direct war with Iran loomed played on Saudi Arabian fears of uncontrollable military escalation. Ansarullah's claim of responsibility signalled its ability to complicate Saudi Arabia's threat landscape by capitalising on the incident. Despite the humiliation of the attack, Saudi Arabia found face-saving value in engaging in back-channel talks with Ansarullah following its claim of responsibility and its offer to halt UAV and missile attacks into Saudi Arabia.

---

14 May–1 June
The UN observes the full handover of the Hudaydah port, Ras Isa Marine Terminal and Saleef port to the coastal guard.

7 July
Ansarullah holds an exhibition showcasing its missile and UAV capabilities.

17 August
Ansarullah announces the appointment of an 'ambassador' to Iran.

20 September
Ansarullah offers to halt all missile and UAV attacks against Saudi Arabia in exchange for a reciprocal halt.

30 September
Ansarullah releases 290 prisoners.

23 June
Ansarullah targets Abha International Airport using a UAV, killing one person and injuring 21 others.

29 July
The Saudi-led coalition launches an airstrike on al-Thabet market in Saada province, killing ten people.

1 August
Ansarullah launches missiles against a UAE-backed military parade in Aden, killing 36 people.

9 August
Clashes erupt between STC-affiliated forces and Hadi-affiliated forces in Aden as the STC takes control of the city.

17 August
Ansarullah announces *Operation First Deterrence Balance* and deploys ten UAVs against an Aramco facility in Saudi Arabia.

Impact

Human rights

The UN's Group of Eminent Experts on Yemen reported 'a pervasive lack of accountability' on all sides in 2019.[15] The armed conflict has led to widespread exploitation of children. The UN documented sexual violence against children in Lahij province by Yemeni forces loyal to Hadi between June 2017 and 2019.[16] It also reported that the Saudi-led coalition's air campaign led to widespread human-rights violations. The Group of Experts noted that an explosion reportedly triggered by a coalition airstrike in Mawiyah district, Taizz governorate in May 2019 led to the deaths of 12 civilians, including seven boys.[17] In May, a coalition airstrike struck a building in a residential area in Sanaa, killing at least five civilians. The Group of Experts noted that there were no apparent military targets in the vicinity.[18]

Humanitarian

The ongoing conflict continued to hamper humanitarian efforts. At the start of 2018, 22.2m people required humanitarian assistance,[19] and this figure had risen to around 24m by February 2019, according to the UN Office for the Coordination of Humanitarian Affairs (OCHA) and remained at that level by the end of 2019.[20] Furthermore, 12.6m people were reported to be in acute need of improved water, sanitation and hygiene conditions.[21] Public health in Yemen remained dire. The cholera epidemic in the country continued to worsen, with 460,000 suspected cases as of July 2019, exceeding a total of 380,000 suspected cases for the whole of 2018.[22]

The sustained decline in humanitarian conditions resulted in at least 20.1m people being recorded as food insecure as of February 2019.[23] The OCHA reported that food assistance between December 2018 and April 2019 in 29 of the 45 most food-insecure districts in Yemen resulted in approximately 250,000 fewer people being food insecure.[24] The management of aid by conflict parties has exacerbated food insecurity more generally. On 21 June the UN partially suspended food aid following a dispute between Ansarullah and the World Food Programme (WFP). Ansarullah protested that the UN's use of a biometric system to identify Yemenis most in need of aid contravened Yemeni law. The UN was in fact concerned about the reported diversion of aid by senior Ansarullah officials. For the first time since September 2018, on 6 May Ansarullah allowed access to a WFP facility in Hudaydah holding 51,000 tonnes of wheat.[25] The difficulty in accessing the Red Sea Mills resulted in further delays in the delivery of perishable foodstuffs.

Notwithstanding the OCHA reporting better implementation of humanitarian operations and logistics in 2019, in December the International Organization for Migration (IOM) reported that more than 398,000 people were displaced across Yemen in 2019. The highest displacement figures were in the provinces of Hajjah, Hudaydah and Dhale, while the provinces with the least displacement were Mahwit, Mahrah and the island of Socotra, where 160 households were displaced on the island this year.[26] More than 69,000 individuals

Key Events in 2019

Political events

25 October — The STC agrees to hand over military control of Aden to the Hadi government in exchange for political concessions in negotiations as part of the Riyadh Agreement.

30 October — The UAE withdraws all troops from Aden as part of a compromise reached between the STC and the Hadi government.

5 November — The Hadi government and the STC sign the Riyadh Agreement.

28 November — 128 prisoners are repatriated to Sanaa from Saudi Arabia.

Military/Violent events

14 September — Ansarullah claims responsibility for an attack on Saudi Arabia's Abqaiq and Khurais oil facilities.

30 October — UAE forces withdraw further from Yemen, handing over operational control to Yemeni and Saudi forces.

24 December — The Saudi-led coalition shells a market in Saada province, reportedly killing 17 people.

returned to their areas of origin between September and December 2019.[27]

Social
Yemen remains a highly militarised society. The UAE's redeployment of forces in summer 2019 was enabled by training and equipping a network of local militias in the southern region. While these groups (the STC-affiliated Elite Forces, for example) are considered professional in nature, the broader availability of and ease of access to small arms and light weapons has significantly benefited other non-state armed groups and enabled ISIS–Y and Ansar al-Sharia in particular to compete for jihadist dominance of Yemen. The extensive military equipment deployed by anti-Ansarullah forces has also fed a growing black market that has become a steady source of income for individuals who have found themselves without work as a result of the war.

Economic
The World Bank estimated in October that Yemen's economy could grow by 2–2.5% per year in 2019–21 if the security situation stabilised.[28] Unfortunately, the 2018 Stockholm Agreement has not helped Yemen's economy as intended. The revenues generated by the handover of ports in 2019 should have been redirected to Yemen's Central Bank and redistributed among the governorates to pay government salaries. This redistribution, a confidence-building measure that would have also revitalised the country's commercial activity, did not occur in accordance with the agreement, however.

Relations with neighbouring and international partners
The Saudi-led coalition came under greater scrutiny in 2019. In April the US Congress voted to end military assistance to Saudi Arabia over the war in Yemen, although President Donald Trump vetoed the bipartisan resolution. Similarly, the United Kingdom's court of appeal ruled in June that the country's arms sales to Saudi Arabia were unlawful. The unpopular nature of the war, though not directly weakening the UK's relationship with Saudi Arabia, has indicated that support for the Saudi-led coalition is dwindling.

Trends

Political trajectories
It remains to be seen if the Riyadh Agreement between the STC and Hadi is tenable. The extent to which it is integrated into future peace talks and government negotiations may lead the STC to attempt to militarily seize Aden again. Ansarullah's August attack against the military parade in Aden lent credence to the claim that Hadi cannot guarantee security in the south and has thus emboldened those calling for secession. Avoiding Yemen's fragmentation will remain dependent on Hadi's willingness to accommodate and include the STC and the broader southern movement in the political dialogue with Ansarullah.

Conflict-related risks
Hadi has been unable to implement any meaningful policy in absentia and thus meet domestic humanitarian and economic needs. With few resources directed towards the reconstruction of Yemen's war-damaged sanitation and sewage infrastructure the cholera epidemic remained a major risk. The intractability of the conflict parties' hostilities and their obstruction of UN-coordinated humanitarian assistance has exacerbated this issue, as has the UN lacking sufficient funds to address the cholera crisis.[29] Member states have not upheld their promises to provide additional funds for development and this forced the UN to shut down water and sanitation programmes in four governorates.[30]

Prospects for peace
The unsuccessful implementation of the 2018 Stockholm Agreement exposed the ineffectiveness of the UN's current diplomatic strategy. The almost exclusive focus on Hudaydah prevented the UN from addressing violence in other parts of the country. With ongoing conflict between the coalition and Ansarullah in Taizz, Hadi loyalists and southern secessionists in Aden, and Ansar al-Sharia and ISIS–Y in the southern region, violence looked set to continue in 2020.

However, Ansarullah's offer to halt offensive UAV and missile attacks into coalition territory presented an alternative track towards peace in the face of the Stockholm Agreement's ineffectiveness. Reductions in appetite for the war on the part of the coalition, with talks resumed in October, suggested the potential for a broader peace settlement than the Stockholm Agreement envisioned.

Strategic implications and global influences

Given the magnitude of the attack against Saudi Arabia's Aramco facilities, the UAE's withdrawal of forces and the volatility of regional security, the implications of the war in Yemen are far-reaching. As tensions escalate in the region, Ansarullah's resilience against the coalition has underscored a higher-than-expected political and military cost in sustaining the war. In turn, this has eroded the coalition's military effectiveness against the group. With the UAE's reduced role and lack of dominance over strategic planning, Saudi Arabia's heavy-handed – but strategically ineffective – use of force may lead to greater military resistance on Ansarullah's part.

However, if tensions between Saudi Arabia and Iran persist, Saudi Arabia may recalibrate its military posture in the region, shifting military resources away from the war in Yemen. Saudi Arabia's threat perception may lead to a demotion of Ansarullah in terms of strategic priority. In this environment, the extent to which Ansarullah and Iran's relationship deepens may lead the coalition to heighten its use of force in Yemen.

Notes

[1] UN Office for the Coordination of Humanitarian Affairs (OCHA), 'Briefing to the Security Council on the humanitarian situation in Yemen', 18 July 2019.

[2] Dhia Muhsin, 'Houthi use of drones delivers potent message in Yemen War', IISS Blogs & Podcasts, 27 August 2019.

[3] Andrew England and Simeon Kerr, 'Riyadh holds talks with Houthis in effort to break Yemen deadlock', Financial Times, 11 October 2019.

[4] 'US, Israel behind Yemen terrorist attacks: Houthi leader', PressTV, 22 March 2015.

[5] Shawn Snow, 'US MQ-9 drone shot down in Yemen', Defense News, 2 October 2017.

[6] 'Iran's Khamenei backs Yemen's Houthi movement, calls for dialogue', Reuters, 13 August 2019.

[7] International Committee of the Red Cross (ICRC), 'Yemen: 290 detainees released with facilitation of the ICRC', 30 September 2019.

[8] ICRC, '128 detainees repatriated to Yemen from Saudi Arabia', 28 November 2019.

[9] 'Yemen's Houthis unilaterally release hundreds of detainees', Reuters, 30 September 2019.

[10] Simeon Kerr, 'Yemen's government agrees peace deal with southern secessionists', Financial Times, 27 October 2019.

[11] 'UAE withdraws troops from Yemen's southern port city of Aden', Al Jazeera, 30 October 2019.

[12] Anwar Gargash, 'We're proud of the UAE's military role in Yemen. But it's time to seek a political solution', Washington Post, 22 July 2019.

[13] Maher Chmyatelli and Rania El Gamal, 'Houthi drone attack on Saudi oilfield causes gas fire, output unaffected', Reuters, 17 August 2019.

[14] Pierre Noel, 'Saudi Oil Under Attack', IISS Blogs & Podcasts, 17 September 2019.

[15] UN News, 'Nowhere is safe to hide in war-torn Yemen, say UN-appointed rights experts', 3 September 2019.

[16] UN Human Rights Council, 'Situation of human rights in Yemen, including violations and abuses since September 2014, Report of the detailed findings of the Group of Eminent International and Regional Experts on Yemen', 3 September 2019, pp. 68–9.

[17] Ibid., p. 76.

[18] Ibid., pp. 110–11.

[19] OCHA, '2018 Yemen Humanitarian Response Plan, January–December 2018', 20 January 2018, p. 3.

[20] OCHA, '2019 Yemen Humanitarian Response Plan, January–December 2019', 19 February 2019, p. 7; OCHA, Yemen: Situation Report – Highlights', 5 February 2020.

[21] OCHA, '2019 Yemen Humanitarian Response Plan, January–December 2019', p. 16.

[22] OCHA, 'Yemen: Over 460K cases of cholera registered to date this year', 8 July 2019.

[23] OCHA, '2019 Yemen Humanitarian Response Plan, January–December 2019', p. 8.

[24] OCHA, 'Yemen Humanitarian Update Covering 26 July–28 August 2019', 28 August 2019, p. 2.

[25] 'UN gets access to vital grain in Yemen port city of Hodeidah', Al Jazeera, 5 May 2019.

[26] International Organization for Migration, 'Rapid Displacement Tracking (RDT) DTM-Yemen, Reporting Period: 15–21 December 2019', 22 December 2019.

[27] Ibid.

[28] World Bank, 'Yemen's Economic Update–October 2019', 9 October 2019.

[29] OCHA, 'Yemen: Over 460K cases of cholera registered to date this year'.

[30] OCHA, 'Yemen Humanitarian Update Covering 26 July–28 August 2019'.

5 South Asia

Afghanistan	236	India–Pakistan (Kashmir)	265
India (CPI–Maoist)	244	Pakistan	275
India (Northeast)	252		

A Kashmiri school damaged after cross-border bombing in Dudhnyal, Neelum District, Pakistan

Key trends

- The Indian government had some success in reducing violence and partly regaining people's trust vis-à-vis conflicts in the Northeast and with the CPI–Maoist group. In Pakistan, violence by the Tehrik-e-Taliban Pakistan (TTP) declined; 2019 was the first year since 2003 without Pakistani or US airstrikes.
- Violence intensified in several theatres, including Afghanistan, where the Taliban increased its territorial control, and in Kashmir. The latter conflict sparked an arms race between India and Pakistan.
- Multiple long-running protests and incidents of civil disobedience in the region were repressed violently by security forces.
- ISIS is active across the region and announced three South Asian provinces.

Strategic implications

- The conflict in Kashmir was discussed at the UN Security Council as it generated international concerns and became increasingly internationalised.
- Baloch insurgent attacks against Chinese interests in Pakistan put significant pressure on Islamabad and continued to frustrate Beijing (although it remains a key ally of Pakistan in the international arena).
- In Northeast India, counter-insurgency coordination between India and Myanmar was a significant military and diplomatic development.

Prospects

- Stalemate or collapse of peace talks is a strong possibility in both Afghanistan and all the Indian conflicts.
- In the Kashmir conflict a rapprochement between India and Pakistan is not on the horizon and the situation might worsen along the Line of Control.
- India's economic clout means it is unlikely to come under greater international pressure.

AFGHANISTAN

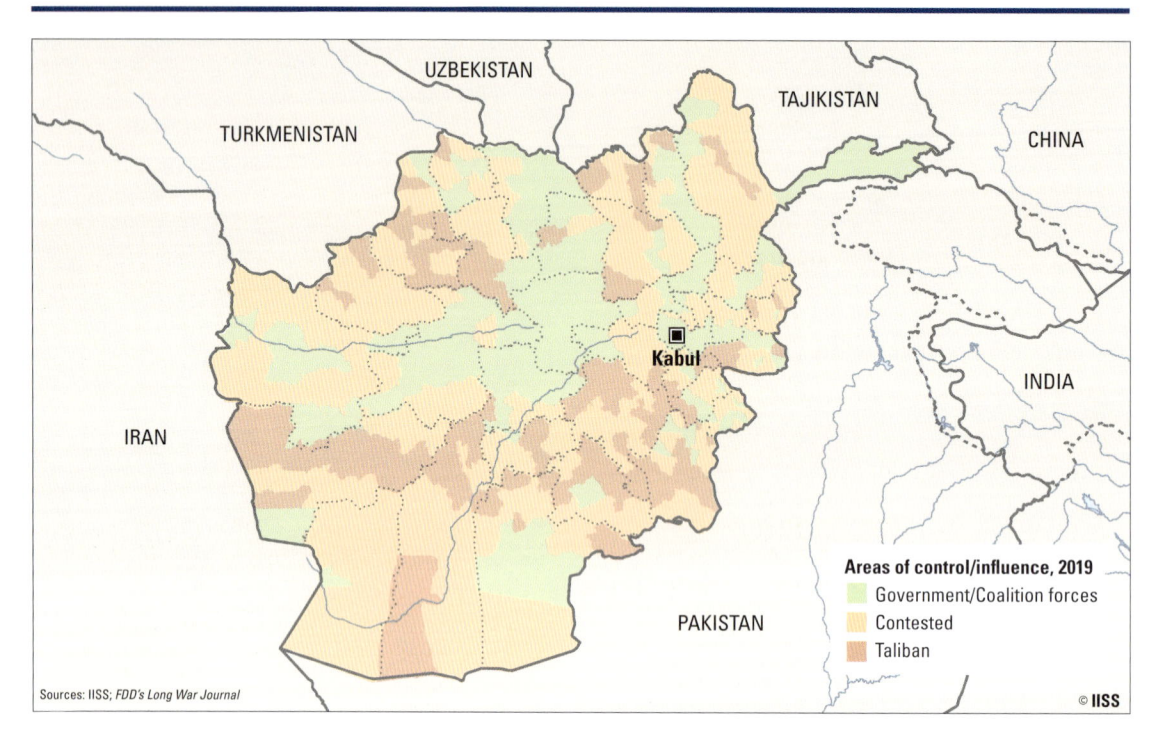

Areas of control/influence, 2019
- Government/Coalition forces
- Contested
- Taliban

Sources: IISS; *FDD's Long War Journal*

Overview

The conflict in 2019

The conflict in Afghanistan intensified in 2019, as both the United States and the Taliban sought to leverage their negotiating positions. The number of insurgent-initiated attacks increased in 2019, primarily due to increased violence in the latter half of the year as US–Taliban talks faltered.[1] The Islamic State in Khorasan Province (ISIS–KP) continued to operate and to complicate potential political solutions to the conflict.

The Afghan government planned and implemented presidential elections in September but the process was marred by logistical problems, violence, and claims of fraud and corruption. The World Bank estimated that Afghanistan's economy grew by about 2.9% in 2019, but this increase was not enough to offset negative trends, including a rise in poverty and a decline in living standards.[2]

Peace negotiations advanced significantly in 2019. Special Representative for Afghanistan Reconciliation Zalmay Khalilzad announced on 28 January that the Taliban and the US had agreed in principle to a framework deal. US President Donald Trump announced that a final meeting at Camp David had been planned but this was cancelled in September, along with talks with the Taliban. Khalilzad subsequently continued with efforts to revive the negotiations.

The conflict to 2019

The conflict in Afghanistan began with the US-led invasion in October 2001 following the 9/11 terrorist attacks. Initially, the US declared that its objectives were to destroy the al-Qaeda terrorist organisation and to overthrow the Taliban regime that had given it safe haven. With a combination of special forces

Key statistics

Type	Internationalised
Start date	7 October 2001
IDPs total	No data
Refugees total (December 2019)	2,700,000
People in need	No data

and conventional units, and a strategic partnership with the Northern Alliance (an anti-Taliban group formed in 1996), the US-led operation removed the Taliban regime from power in November 2001. As a result, the Taliban's structure and leadership quickly dissipated. In December 2001, the Bonn Conference set the groundwork for a new government led by Hamid Karzai.

The period following the invasion was relatively calm and the US planned to maintain a small footprint. This strategy inadvertently left space for local strongmen and militia leaders to fill the power vacuum and allowed the Taliban to reconstitute and reorganise in Pakistan. Taliban fighters soon began conducting more significant operations in Afghanistan, with violence increasing every year up to 2010. In response, coalition forces began increasing troop numbers and expanding their presence throughout the country. By 2006, the International Security Assistance Force (ISAF) operated in all regions of Afghanistan. The US security personnel deployed in Afghanistan reached a peak of more than 100,000 in 2010–11.[3] During the presidency of Barack Obama, troop numbers were gradually reduced to 8,600 by the time Trump took office in 2017. Trump increased troop numbers to approximately 14,000. By the end of 2019, there were 13,500 US troops in Afghanistan.[4]

Key Conflict Parties

Afghan National Defense and Security Forces (ANDSF)

Strength
Total personnel (army, air force and paramilitary forces) is 272,500. This figure is around 50,000 below the total strength in 2018, but officials say this decline resulted from an accurate purging of rosters (deleting individuals who did not exist or did not report to work regularly).

Areas of operation
Operates in all 34 provinces. Open-source information estimates that the government controls 133 districts (33.4%) and the Taliban contests 191 (47.9%). Most of these districts are rural and the government controls or contests areas where 86.4% of the population lives.[5]

Leadership
Under the command of the Islamic Republic of Afghanistan. Current president is Ashraf Ghani, the minister of defence is Asadullah Khalid and the chief of staff is Lt-Gen. Bismillah Waziri.

Structure
Organised under the minister of defence and the general staff with five corps, the 201st in Kabul, the 203rd in Gardez, the 205th in Kandahar, the 207th in Herat and the 209th in Mazar-e Sharif. Separate commands exist for the Kabul military training centre, the military academy and the general staff college.

History
Established in 2002 following the collapse of the Taliban regime. Growth was initially slow with only 27,000 troops by 2005, but increased after the Taliban resurgence. New commandos began training and entered service in 2007.

Objectives
The ANDSF took full responsibility for security in Afghanistan in 2015 after the official end of combat operations by coalition forces in 2014.

Opponents
The Taliban, ISIS–KP and other anti-government forces.

Affiliates/allies
Relies on US support through the Bilateral Security Agreement of 2014. The US continues to pay salaries for the security forces.

Resources/capabilities
Afghanistan's defence budget in 2019 was approximately US$1.98 billion. The US spent an estimated US$5bn directly on Afghan security forces in 2019 and requested US$4.8bn for 2020.[6]

Coalition forces

Strength
NATO countries and allies contribute 8,705 personnel to *Operation Resolute Support*. The US contributes another 8,000, along with an additional 5,500 to *Operation Freedom's Sentinel*.

Areas of operation
Operation Freedom's Sentinel conducts counter-terrorism missions throughout the country and *Operation Resolute Support* maintains a central command in Kabul, with supporting commands in Mazar-e Sharif, Herat, Kandahar and Laghman.

Leadership
General Austin Scott Miller has been the commander of both US forces and the NATO mission in Afghanistan since September 2018.

Structure
Coalition forces in Afghanistan are divided into two missions, US forces focusing on counter-terrorism under *Operation Freedom's Sentinel* and NATO forces focusing on training and advising under *Operation Resolute Support*.

Coalition forces

History
Coalition forces entered Afghanistan in 2001. ISAF was created at the 2001 Bonn Conference. With the conclusion of combat operations by foreign forces in 2014, ISAF became *Operation Resolute Support* and US forces transitioned from *Operation Enduring Freedom* to *Operation Freedom's Sentinel*.

Objectives
Continued support to the government in Kabul and to democratisation and development. Preventing the rise of international terrorist organisations that might use Afghanistan as a safe haven or base for operations is of greatest concern to the US.

Opponents
The Taliban insurgency, although the ANDSF are the primary actors engaging the Taliban and terrorist groups including al-Qaeda and ISIS–KP.

Affiliates/allies
39 NATO countries participate in various missions in Afghanistan. The UN also maintains a mission in country, the UN Assistance Mission in Afghanistan (UNAMA).

Resources/capabilities
The US has spent nearly US$1 trillion on the conflict in Afghanistan. The estimated annual budget for all US operations, including reconstruction efforts, is approximately US$50bn.

The Taliban

Strength
An official US report in 2019 put the number of active Taliban fighters in Afghanistan at 20,000–30,000, with an additional 10,000–25,000 joining periodically for attacks.[7] Afghan officials put the number at 74,500 in June 2018.[8]

Areas of operation
Maintains 'shadow governments' in the districts it controls throughout the country and has named shadow provincial governors in all 34 provinces. As of 2019, the group was estimated to control 74 of Afghanistan's 398 districts (18.5%) and contested the government's control in another 191 districts (47.9%), while also continuing to carry out large-scale attacks in major cities.

Leadership
Mullah Haibatullah Akhundzada took over as leader on 25 May 2016. Together with deputies Sirajuddin Haqqani (leader of the Haqqani network) and Mullah Mohammad Yaqoob (son of Taliban founder Mullah Mohammad Omar), he heads the Quetta Shura, which directs the military campaign against the Afghan government and coalition forces.

Structure
Formally, the Taliban consists of the leader and deputy leaders, executive offices, a shura (leadership council) and 12 commissions covering military affairs, political affairs, economic affairs, education, prisoners, martyrs and disabled members, as well as the Council of Ulema (Council of Senior Religious Scholars).

History
The Taliban (translated as 'the students') movement began in the Afghan refugee camps of Pakistan following the Soviet invasion and occupation. Under Mullah Mohammad Omar, the group entered the civil war in 1994 with the capture of Kandahar city. Taliban fighters quickly conquered other areas of Afghanistan and it officially ruled as an Islamic emirate from 1996 to 2001, though it never controlled the whole country.

Objectives
Since the US invasion in 2001, its main goal is the expulsion of foreign troops, the overthrow of the Kabul government (considered a foreign puppet) and the return to sharia law.

Opponents
US and other foreign forces. Also fights the Afghan government and ISIS–KP.

Affiliates/allies
Connections with a variety of other non-state armed groups in South Asia, including al-Qaeda, the Haqqani network, the Islamic Movement of Uzbekistan (IMU) and Tehrik-e-Taliban Pakistan.

Resources/capabilities
The Taliban is one of the wealthiest insurgent/terrorist organisations in the world, with an estimated annual income of around US$800 million.[9] Much of this revenue comes from the drugs trade, extortion or taxes collected in the territory it controls. Interviews with current and former fighters have shown that donations from Persian Gulf charities and wealthy individuals have increased significantly in recent years.[10]

Islamic State in Khorasan Province (ISIS–KP)

Strength
Current estimates 2,500–4,000.

Areas of operation
Primarily confined to a small region of Nangarhar province in eastern Afghanistan but has also had small presences in Logar, Zabul, Farah and Helmand provinces.

Leadership
The original leader, Hafiz Saeed Khan, was killed in a US drone strike in July 2016. Successive leaders were also killed in US strikes: Abdul Hasib in April 2017, Abu Sayed in July 2018 and Abu Sayeed Orakzai in August 2018.

Structure
ISIS–KP is an Islamist militant organisation, formally affiliated with the larger Islamic State, also known as ISIS or ISIL, of which it is the Central and South Asia branch.

History
Formed and pledged loyalty to then ISIS leader Abu Bakr al-Baghdadi in October 2014. The initial membership primarily comprised disgruntled and estranged members of the TTP.

Islamic State in Khorasan Province (ISIS–KP)

Objectives
Similar to its parent organisation in Syria and Iraq, ISIS–KP maintains both local and global ambitions: the establishment of a caliphate in Central and South Asia to be governed under sharia law.

Opponents
Mainly focuses on fighting the government in Kabul and international forces in Afghanistan, but also frequently clashes with the Taliban and other military groups in the region.

Affiliates/allies
Central ISIS organisation in Iraq and Syria.

Resources/capabilities
Since its founding in 2014, ISIS has invested several hundred thousand dollars in improving its organisation and capabilities. With the decline of its territory in Iraq and Syria, however, the core group has fewer resources to invest in foreign networks.

Al-Qaeda Central

Strength
40,000 fighters worldwide (2018 estimate) with approximately 1,000 in South Asia.[11]

Areas of operation
The alliance structure operates throughout the Middle East, North Africa, South Asia and Southeast Asia. However, al-Qaeda Central only maintains a small number of members in the mountainous region between Afghanistan and Pakistan.

Leadership
Led by Ayman al-Zawahiri since 2011. Reports indicated that Osama bin Laden's son, Hamza, was being prepared for a leadership role, but the US announced in September 2019 that he had been killed in an airstrike.

Structure
Core leadership is primarily focused on the cultivation of the group's political message of fighting the West and its global branding. Its affiliate groups often pursue local objectives independent of the goals and strategy of the central organisation. Below Zawahiri and his immediate advisers, al-Qaeda Central maintains a Shura council and committees for communications, finance and military operations.

History
Al-Qaeda was created by Arab fighters who travelled to Afghanistan and Pakistan to fight against the Soviet invasion in the 1980s. The organisation (officially formed in 1988) was initially led by Osama bin Laden, who envisioned it as a base for the global jihadist movement, to train operatives and to support other jihadist organisations throughout the world. The group was responsible for a number of high-profile terrorist attacks against the US, including the 9/11 attacks. Bin Laden was killed in a US special-operations raid in Abbottabad, Pakistan in 2011.

Objectives
Focus has always been to fight the 'far enemy'. The organisation's core belief is that in order to bring about Islamist governance in the Muslim world it would first have to destroy the West and the US, which support current Middle Eastern regimes.

Opponents
US and other Western countries supporting non-Islamic regimes.

Affiliates/allies
Currently maintains an affiliation with five groups: al-Qaeda in the Islamic Maghreb (AQIM) in North Africa, Jabhat Al-Nusra in Syria, al-Qaeda in the Arabian Peninsula (AQAP) in Yemen, al-Qaeda in the Indian Subcontinent (AQIS) in South Asia and al-Shabaab in Somalia. Also has a strong relationship with the Taliban.

Resources/capabilities
Al-Qaeda and its affiliate groups are thought to earn approximately US$300m per year (2018).[12] Al-Qaeda Central continues to receive support from charitable organisations in the Gulf region as well as from sympathetic wealthy donors.

Drivers

International intervention
Both the presence of coalition troops and other forms of covert and overt intervention in Afghan domestic affairs are key drivers of the conflict. The Taliban's key goal is the withdrawal of foreign troops. In the Asia Foundation's 2019 Survey of the Afghan People, 18.9% of respondents cited the presence of foreign troops or the international community as a reason why the Taliban continues to fight.[13] Foreign troops also give legitimacy to the cause of other insurgent groups that frequently cause collateral damage and injure and kill civilians.

Domestic and socio-economic grievances
It is unlikely that the withdrawal of foreign troops would be sufficient to end the conflict. Domestic

political and socio-economic grievances also drive the insurgency and have fuelled conflict in Afghanistan for the past 40 years. Liberal democracy, civic liberties and women's rights are difficult to reconcile with the Islamist form of governance the Taliban pursued in the 1990s and is seeking to reinstall. A negotiated peace would have to address this disconnect. Furthermore, the slow pace of domestic economic growth over the past 10–15 years is causing a rise in poverty and inequality, which could continue to drive violence even if political grievances were settled through a negotiated peace deal.

Regional support for the Taliban

A number of regional powers are involved in the domestic affairs of Afghanistan. According to former US commander in Afghanistan General John Nicholson, Russia continues to provide support and assistance to the Taliban, although it is difficult to quantify the nature and extent of this support.[14] Interviews with current and former Taliban militants have revealed that foreign financing of the group, particular from wealthy individuals from the Gulf states, has become increasingly critical for the group.[15] The Taliban also relies on safe havens in Pakistan and coordinates its operations through leadership councils in Quetta and Peshawar.

Democratic legitimacy

Limited governance and widespread corruption continue to plague Afghanistan. US counter-insurgency operations have sought to strengthen the legitimacy of the central government in the eyes of the Afghan people. According to the 2019 Asia Foundation survey, more than 80% of respondents said that corruption was a major problem. More than 65%, however, still believed the government was doing a 'good job'. In an increase from 2018, 55% had a great deal or some confidence in their provincial councils.[16]

The overwhelming majority of Afghans are still unsympathetic to the Taliban – 85.1% of respondents had no sympathy for the Taliban at all, and only 13.4% had a lot or some sympathy. Yet greater support for the government over the Taliban does not imply overall approval of the government's policies: 58.2% of Afghans said the country was moving in the wrong direction.[17] Even those who do support Taliban insurgents said they do so either because they are Muslims or because they are Afghans.[18]

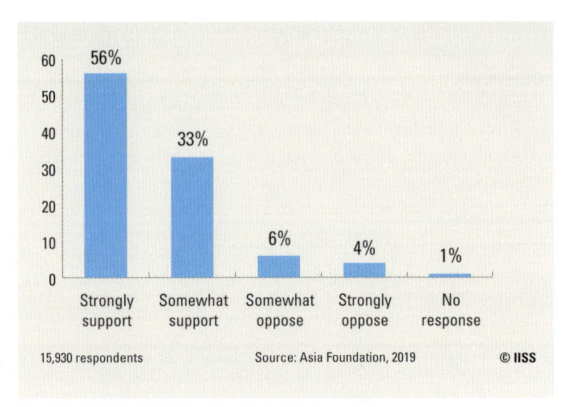

Figure 1: Support for peace talks with the Taliban

Response	Percentage
Strongly support	56%
Somewhat support	33%
Somewhat oppose	6%
Strongly oppose	4%
No response	1%

15,930 respondents. Source: Asia Foundation, 2019. © IISS

Key Events in 2019

Political events

Military/Violent events

21 January – Taliban fighters attack a military base in Maidan Shar, killing at least 126 personnel.

17 March – The Taliban captures 150 Afghan border-patrol personnel in Badghis province.

1 July – Gunmen detonate a vehicle bomb and open fire in the Wazir Akbar Khan neighbourhood in Kabul, killing approximately 45 people and wounding over 100.

Political Developments

Difficult negotiations

Since Khalilzad was appointed special representative for Afghanistan in September 2018 the US has intensified its efforts towards reaching a settlement. In 2019, unprecedented progress was made in negotiations towards a peace settlement between the US, the Afghan government and the Taliban. By September, Khalilzad announced that an agreement had been reached in principle. Trump planned for Taliban and Afghan representatives to hold a meeting at Camp David in the US to finalise the deal, but before it occurred he said the meeting had been cancelled and that the talks were 'dead'.

Informal negotiations began again in November 2019. The deal negotiated between the US and the Taliban could still be implemented if leaders in the US were to agree to it. Intra-Afghan talks remain an issue for the peace process, however. The Taliban continues to refuse to engage with the Afghan government, while Afghan President Ashraf Ghani sees a ceasefire as a necessary precondition to peace talks, something the Taliban has rejected.

Presidential elections

The crucial political event of 2019 in Afghanistan was the presidential election held on 28 September. Voter turnout was far lower than in the past with reports indicating that 20–25% of registered voters participated. Preliminary results were announced on 22 December, indicating that incumbent president Ghani won just over 50% of the vote. If Ghani is shown to have received over 50%, he will avoid a run-off election in 2020. The elections took place amid claims of corruption and lack of transparency, although more than 65.1% of Afghans declared in 2019 that they were either somewhat or very satisfied with how democracy works in Afghanistan.[19] More than 16,000 complaints were officially filed and a review process is under way.

Military Developments

Violence increased in 2019 compared to 2018, most of which was driven by the Taliban and the US attempting to increase leverage during negotiations, as well as by Taliban efforts to undermine the presidential election. Afghan security forces conducted 2,531 ground operations between January and September 2019, more than the total number of operations conducted in 2018 (2,365).[20] Civilian casualties increased as a result of increased fighting.

ISIS–KP faced significant pressure from the Taliban and US and Afghan government forces, and its territory has significantly decreased. However, the organisation remains capable of carrying out significant attacks. A suicide attack at a wedding hall in Kabul killed more than 60 civilians and injured 180 on 17 August 2019.

During the presidential election held on 28 September 2019 there was a lower level of violence

17 August
ISIS–KP carries out a suicide attack on a Shia wedding party in Kabul, killing more than 60 civilians.

7 September
US President Donald Trump cancels peace talks with the Taliban before a planned meeting at Camp David.

28 September
Presidential elections are held with some violence and substantially lower voter turnout than in previous elections.

22 December
The Independent Election Commission announces preliminary results of the presidential election with incumbent Ashraf Ghani winning 50.64% of the vote.

23 December
A US Special Forces soldier is killed, bringing total US casualties in Afghanistan in 2019 to 23.

than around the 2018 parliamentary elections, but more violence than around the presidential election in 2014. UN figures suggested that attacks targeting the electoral process caused 85 deaths and 373 injuries.[21]

During 2019, 23 US soldiers were killed and 192 wounded – the highest rate of combat casualties in the past five years.[22]

Impact

Economic
The World Bank estimated a GDP growth rate of 2.9% in 2019, an increase from 2018.[23] The national poverty rate increased from 38% in 2012 to approximately 55% in 2016,[24] and a survey in 2018 estimated the poverty level had remained relatively unchanged since 2016.[25] The population growth rate in Afghanistan was estimated at 2.14% in 2019 and the Afghan Ministry of Economy indicated that employing the large youth bulge would cause economic problems.[26]

The country still faces significant impediments to sustained development. The increase in GDP growth was mostly due to an easing of the drought that caused significant problems in 2018. Improving environmental conditions increased agricultural output in 2019, but population growth continues to strain the economy and depress per capita income.[27] The uncertainty surrounding the presidential elections also caused the Afghani to depreciate faster than other regional currencies.

Displacement
Conflict-induced displacement increased in 2019, consistent with the increase in violent events for the year. The UN recorded 446,497 new internally displaced persons (IDPs) as a result of the conflict in 2019.[28]

Trends

Stalemate set to continue
Many systemic issues point to a protracted stalemate in Afghanistan. The negotiating positions of the US, the Afghan government and the Taliban make any agreement highly unlikely to satisfy all involved.

Both the number of districts under Taliban control and the levels of violence throughout the country increased in 2019. Afghan government officials expressed satisfaction with Trump's decision to cancel the Taliban deal, but pressure to bring the conflict to an end is growing in the US. The ability of the Afghan security forces to fight will drop dramatically if or when the US withdraws from the conflict, with significant numbers of desertions likely to follow.

A short-term collapse of the Islamic Republic of Afghanistan, however, remains unlikely. Conditions are very different from the time of the Soviet withdrawal in 1989 and even then the regime survived until 1991, when economic and military aid ran out. The most likely near-term outcome, regardless of a US withdrawal, is a continued stalemate.

Uncertain prospects for peace
An alternative but less likely scenario to a protracted stalemate is a negotiated settlement. This option would be based on a power-sharing agreement aimed at integrating the Taliban into politics, but the structure and character of the Afghan government would need to be fundamentally altered to accommodate Taliban preferences. The Taliban vision of governance, based on fundamentalist Islam, is incompatible with the liberal-democratic model embraced by the current regime. Accepting it would risk mass defections among the rank and file, as foreshadowed by limited, but ongoing, desertions of disaffected fighters from the Taliban towards ISIS–KP.

It is unlikely that the Afghan population would support the government sharing power with the Taliban. Although civilians overwhelmingly want an end to the conflict, few have sympathy for the Taliban. Additionally, despite corruption and attempts to gain power outside legal channels, many influential Afghans now seek power and prestige through democratic and constitutional pathways. Those who have benefited from the established system will not want to alter it or to relinquish power to the Taliban.

Notes

1 Special Inspector General for Afghanistan Reconstruction, 'Quarterly Report to the United States Congress', 30 January 2020.
2 World Bank, 'Afghanistan Improves its Growth Despite Uncertainty', 22 January 2020.
3 Special Inspector General for Afghanistan Reconstruction, 'Quarterly Report to the United States Congress', 30 May 2018.
4 NATO, 'Resolute Support Mission (RSM): Key Facts and Figures', 2 December 2019; IISS, *The Military Balance 2020* (Abingdon: Routledge for the IISS, 2020).
5 Bill Roggio and Alexandra Gutowski, 'Mapping Taliban Control in Afghanistan', *FDD's Long War Journal*.
6 US Department of Defense, 'Defense budget overview: United States Department of Defense fiscal year 2020 budget request', March 2019.
7 US Department of Defense Office of Inspector General, 'Operation Freedom's Sentinel: Lead Inspector General Report to the United States Congress, 1 January–31 March 2019', 17 May 2019, p. 20.
8 Gulabuddin Ghubar, 'Territorial Army Cadets in Kabul for Training', ToloNews, 11 June 2018.
9 Itai Zehorai, 'The richest terror organizations in the world', *Forbes*, 24 January 2018.
10 Antonio Giustozzi, *The Taliban at War, 2001–2018* (London: Hurst, 2019).
11 Bruce Hoffman, 'Al-Qaeda's Resurrection', Council on Foreign Relations, 6 March 2018.
12 Itai Zehorai, 'The richest terror organizations in the world'.
13 The Asia Foundation, 'A Survey of the Afghan People: Afghanistan in 2019', 2019, p. 77.
14 US Department of Defense Office of Inspector General, 'Operation Freedom's Sentinel: Lead Inspector General's Report to the United States Congress, 1 January–31 March 2018', 21 May 2018.
15 Giustozzi, *The Taliban at War, 2001–2018*.
16 The Asia Foundation, 'A Survey of the Afghan People: Afghanistan in 2019'.
17 *Ibid*.
18 *Ibid*.
19 *Ibid*.
20 Special Inspector General for Afghanistan Reconstruction, 'Quarterly Report to the United States Congress', 30 October 2019, p. 68.
21 *Ibid*., p. 74.
22 Special Inspector General for Afghanistan Reconstruction, 'Quarterly Report to the United States Congress', 30 January 2020, p. 72.
23 World Bank, 'Afghanistan Improves its Growth Despite Uncertainty', 22 January 2020.
24 Asian Development Bank, 'Afghanistan GDP growth forecasts', 26 September 2019.
25 'Over 54 percent of Afghans live under poverty line: CSO', Ariana News, 6 May 2018.
26 Haseeba Atakpal, 'Afghanistan's Population Annually Grew at 2.14%: Survey', ToloNews, 11 July 2019.
27 World Bank, 'Afghanistan Improves its Growth Despite Uncertainty'.
28 UN Office for the Coordination of Humanitarian Affairs (OCHA), 'Afghanistan – Conflict Induced Displacements in 2019', 3 March 2020.

INDIA (CPI–MAOIST)

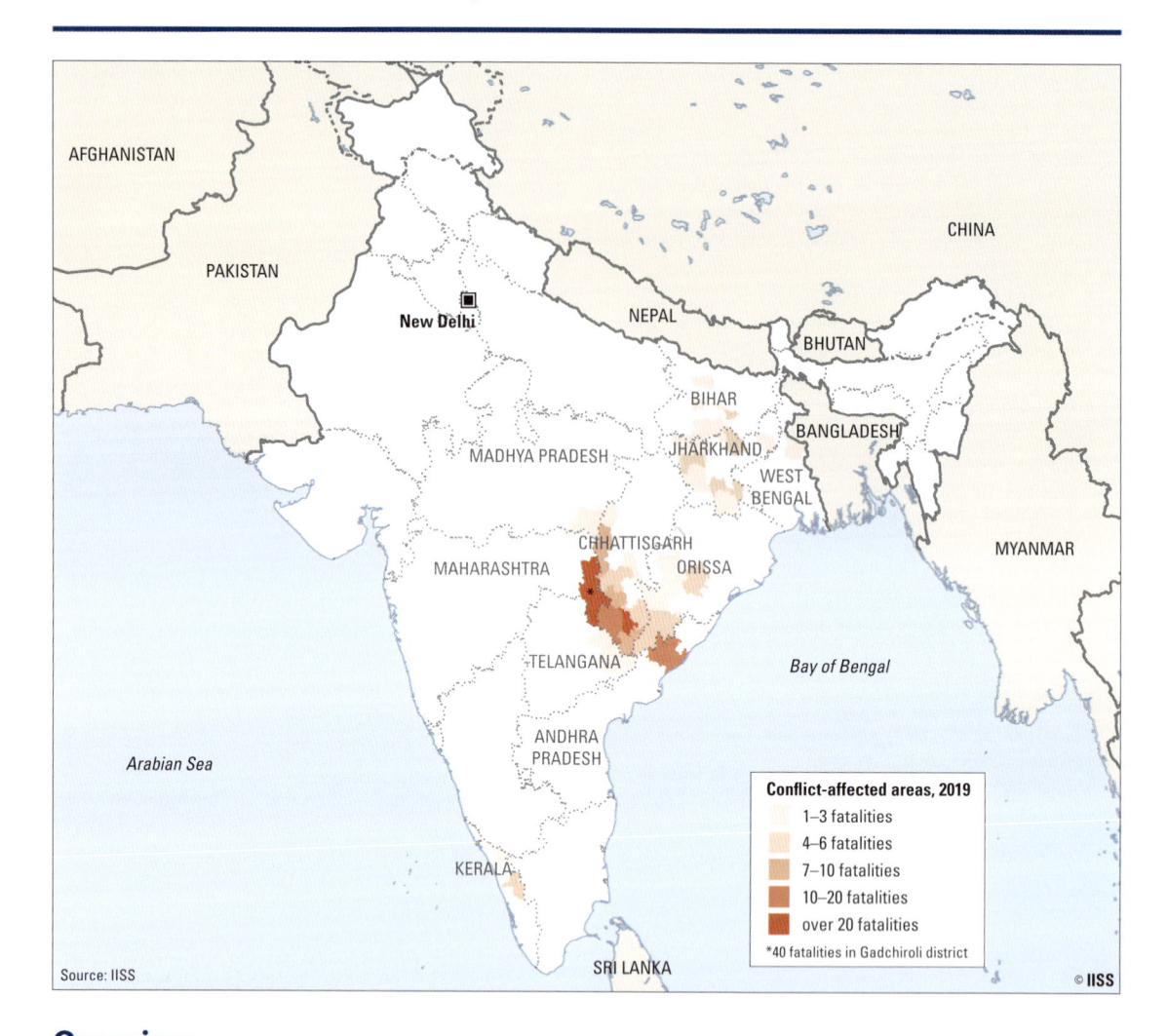

Conflict-affected areas, 2019
- 1–3 fatalities
- 4–6 fatalities
- 7–10 fatalities
- 10–20 fatalities
- over 20 fatalities

*40 fatalities in Gadchiroli district

Source: IISS

Overview

The conflict in 2019
After decades of violence, the Naxalite movement continued to fight the Indian government in 2019. The insurgency, based mainly in the rural areas of central and eastern India, led to the deaths of at least 213 people during the year, a significant decline from 2018. The Communist Party of India–Maoist (CPI–Maoist) is the most important rebel faction in the Naxalite movement. Though several groups have splintered from CPI–Maoist since its formation in 2004, none of the remaining splinter groups have posed a significant threat to government forces or civilians.

Consistent with previous years, CPI–Maoist fighters (who are commonly referred to as 'Maoists') used their mobility and expert knowledge of the terrain to evade the government's increasingly effective security operations. They also used improvised explosive devices (IEDs) to inflict losses on security patrols. In addition to clashing with government forces, CPI–Maoist targeted civilians suspected of collaborating with police forces, culminating in at least 53 executions during the year.

The Indian government relied on a large security presence and undertook economic-development programmes to counter the Maoist influence on local communities. By expanding government services and infrastructure in the 'Red Corridor' (a term commonly used to refer to territories affected by the insurgency), the government had some success in winning the loyalty of civilians who might otherwise have supported and concealed insurgents.

The conflict to 2019
CPI–Maoist reached the height of its power in the early 2010s when it controlled and governed vast swathes of 'liberated' territory. The counter-insurgency began gaining ground in 2014 and continued into 2019. Since 2014, insurgents have experienced significantly higher fatality rates than security forces, and Maoist fighters and commanders have surrendered in large numbers in exchange for amnesties and financial incentives. CPI–Maoist has publicly acknowledged its setbacks in recent years and has set about innovating its tactics to counter the government's successes. Most notably, CPI–Maoist's highest-ranking leader (who had led the organisation since 2004) stepped down in September 2018 and was replaced by his younger second in command. Little evidence emerged in 2019, however, that the leadership shake-up or other measures were helping to reverse the Maoists' losses. Events in 2019 suggested that few civilians support CPI–Maoist or violence more generally. The insurgency also has no foreign patrons from which to draw support, and there is little risk that the conflict will become internationalised. Thus, though a resurgence cannot be ruled out, the eventual collapse of the CPI–Maoist appears increasingly likely.

Key statistics

Type	Internal
Start date	2004
IDPs total	No data
Refugees total	No data
People in need	No data

Key Conflict Parties

Various federal- and state-level law-enforcement agencies are responsible for combatting the Naxalite insurgency. Splinter groups have posed relatively little threat to the government and civilian communities. The most prominent of these, the People's Liberation Front of India (PLFI), suffered serious damage in 2017 when security forces killed its leader and several commanders in a string of successful combat operations. Despite losing a high-ranking leader to a police ambush in February 2019,[1] the PLFI was likely behind the assassination of a Jharkhand-based Bharatiya Janata Party (BJP) leader (along with several of his family members) in July 2019.[2]

Government of India

Strength
At least 87 federal law-enforcement battalions were deployed in the Red Corridor by the beginning of 2019 to strengthen state-level and district-level police forces. Indian military forces do not take part in combat, but have supported counter-insurgency operations.

Areas of operation
Law-enforcement units have been deployed to all areas where CPI–Maoist is known to operate. This encompasses many rural areas of central and eastern India, especially in Andhra Pradesh, Bihar, Chhattisgarh, Jharkhand, Maharashtra and Odisha states.

Leadership
India's Ministry of Home Affairs is responsible for the deployment of federal forces and for coordinating with individual state governments, each of which have raised their own paramilitary-style commando forces to deal with the insurgency.

Structure
The federal-level Central Reserve Police Force (CRPF) battalions undertake combat operations in coordination with local-level law-enforcement units. All 'Naxal-affected' states have built up their own anti-Naxalite paramilitary units modelled on the CRPF. Maharashtra's C-60 Commandos, for instance, have become competent enough to challenge CPI–Maoist forces without CRPF support.

History
Prior to 2014, the Indian government had little presence in the rural areas where CPI–Maoist rose to prominence. The central government began building up its security presence in these areas to combat Maoists and bolster local governance structures.

Government of India

Objectives
Since 2014, the government has attempted to defeat the insurgency through combat while also undermining its support among civilians. CRPF battalions, aided by local forces, continue to launch short- and long-range patrols. These forces also provide humanitarian assistance to marginalised communities and guard infrastructure and development projects.

Opponents
CPI–Maoist, and periodically small Maoist splinter groups, such as the PLFI.

Affiliates/allies
Not applicable.

Resources/capabilities
Government forces typically wield light machine guns during combat operations. They are most vulnerable to CPI–Maoist IED attacks while driving in unarmoured vehicles. Anti-mine vehicles have been sent to some units in the Red Corridor but remain relatively rare. The Indian Air Force has occasionally provided helicopter transport, especially when evacuating wounded personnel. Non-combat casualties among security forces (from harsh conditions) are common.

Communist Party of India–Maoist (CPI–Maoist)

Strength
Leaked Indian intelligence reports put the number of Maoist fighters at 3,722 in 2019, compared to 6,000 in 2017.[3] This number should be taken as an estimate, however, as CPI–Maoist conceals its troop strength. It is unclear whether the estimate includes part-time activists.

Areas of operation
Rural areas of central and eastern India, especially Andhra Pradesh, Bihar, Chhattisgarh, Jharkhand, Maharashtra and Odisha states.

Leadership
In 2018, Nambala Keshav Rao (alias 'Basavraj') became the leader of the Central Committee (CC) in an orderly transition of power. Due to the institutionalised nature of CPI–Maoist's leadership structure, Basavraj's authority is not absolute.

Structure
The CC is CPI–Maoist's highest-ranking leadership body and is responsible for formulating strategy and coordinating operations across central and eastern India. CPI–Maoist is a highly institutionalised group. The CC delegates authority to regional or zonal subcommittees who delegate authority to local bodies.

History
Formed from the 2004 merger of the People's War Group (PWG) and the Maoist Communist Centre (MCC). The group reached the height of its power in the early 2010s when it governed large swathes of 'liberated' territories but has been losing ground to security forces since at least 2014.

Objectives
Seeks to overthrow Indian parliamentary democracy in favour of a communist regime by means of a guerrilla-style insurgency. Attempts to create a power base by mobilising marginalised communities in India's hinterlands, though these efforts have proven increasingly ineffective in recent years. Continues to ambush Indian security forces with hit-and-run attacks.

Opponents
Primarily targets Indian federal- and state-level security forces, who are law-enforcement personnel trained to operate as paramilitary units. The Maoists also harass and kill individuals perceived to be working with police.

Affiliates/allies
Several splinter groups, such as the PLFI. The Maoists occasionally fight these groups over territory and the right to tax or extort local communities.

Resources/capabilities
Access to resources has eroded since it began losing ground to security forces in 2014. It currently arms itself primarily with home-made firearms, though its elite fighting squads wield AK-47s and semi-automatic weapons seized from police. The group also makes frequent use of IEDs.

Drivers

Social and economic grievances
Communist-inspired resistance movements have existed in central and eastern India since the 1940s. Proponents of 'left-wing extremism' (as the government calls it) argue that India's caste system creates and sustains social and economic inequalities. To challenge it, non-violent activists and violent insurgents have attempted to mobilise landless farmers in the hinterlands (and occasionally in urban areas) against their landlords, who are separated from their tenants by both class and caste cleavages.

Though with less success than in the past, CPI–Maoist continued efforts to mobilise communities in 2019 by leveraging grievances against the state and particularly against proposed or existing mineral-extraction projects. Traditionally, the group has recruited or intimidated villagers in order to gain food, shelter, information and taxes ('levy').

Since the mid-2000s, many CPI–Maoist members have come from rural tribal (or 'Adivasi') communities, such as the Dongria Kondhs and Gonds, who inhabit some of the least-developed and least-governed regions of India. For example, according to 2011 census data only 10% of households in Chhattisgarh's Dantewada district (in which 65% of the population is Gondi-speaking, according to the 2001 census) have access to treated drinking water, compared to 32% of all Indian households.

Police brutality

The government's counter-insurgency campaign itself is a secondary driver of the conflict. Federal- and state-level security personnel have used excessive and indiscriminate force over the years. Though hard to verify, allegations often portray police as too quick to fire on suspected militants and willing to cover up unjustified killings by falsely identifying victims as militants (a practice known as 'fake encounters'). In March 2019, a Greyhounds team (members of Andhra Pradesh's anti-Naxalite security agency) killed two men during a reported 'exchange of fire' with CPI–Maoist fighters in Visakhapatnam district. Local civilians (aided by the Human Rights Forum, a local watchdog) challenged the official account, claiming that the victims were civilian hunters upon whom the police illegally fired without warning or sufficient cause. A judicial inquiry was opened in July and remained open at the end of the year.[4] In another incident in August, a CRPF team member killed a three-year-old child by throwing her to the ground during a house search in Jharkhand's Palamu district. The accusation resulted in the arrest of several police officers.[5]

Allegations of police brutality have provoked public outrage. In September 2019, well-known activists Soni Sori and Bela Bhatia staged a demonstration around a police station in Chhattisgarh's Dantewada district to protest the killing of two civilians during an alleged fake encounter. The police used force to disperse the protest and arrest its leaders.[6] In November, villagers from Potaali, also in Dantewada district, surrounded and protested the opening of a local police station, fearing increased abuse and harassment. They dispersed after police officers fired into the air.[7]

Dwindling civilian support

Communities in the Red Corridor continue to hold serious grievances against the government, with regard to mineral extraction and heavy-handed policing in particular. CPI–Maoist has historically depended on police malfeasance to facilitate its own recruitment efforts, but evidence suggests that this is no longer the case. Since 2012, the government has sought to address civilians' grievances by providing public goods, especially transportation infrastructure, and services to remote communities. Signs of this strategy's success continued in 2019, especially as indicated by recent election results. High turnout rates for the 2018 state-level elections in Chhattisgarh State and national elections in 2019 indicated widespread support for parliamentary democracy, particularly because civilians who voted did so in spite of CPI–Maoist's calls for a polling boycott (and the risk of retaliation). The election results suggested that civilians' grievances no longer fuel mobilisation into the insurgency. Rather, communities have increasingly pursued their aims through other (usually non-violent) means, which likely led to the insurgency's loss of momentum in recent years.

Despite trying to co-opt popular movements, CPI–Maoist's support among tribal communities, for example, continued to erode. After government forces killed CPI–Maoist's last senior-ranking tribal commander during the Balimela Reservoir battle in 2016 (one of the government's most successful combat operations), Maoist efforts to recruit from tribal communities have met with little success. Instead, many tribal communities in Jharkhand State joined the 'Pathalgadi' movement in 2018, which opposes both Naxalite and government forces and denies the rights of both to enter Adivasi territories.[8] Though CPI–Maoist declared its support for the Pathalgadi movement in July 2019,[9] Pathalgadi activists never rescinded their opposition to the Maoists.

Political Developments

The government's greatest challenge in 2019 was the implementation of the elections to the Lok Sabha (the lower house of the Indian parliament) throughout the Red Corridor despite CPI–Maoist's violent opposition and attempts to disrupt the polling. Insurgents distributed pamphlets and posters threatening violence against voters in virtually all districts where they operated (areas of Andhra Pradesh, Bihar, Chhattisgarh, Jharkhand, Kerala, Maharashtra, Odisha and Telangana states). They planted IEDs (most of which were discovered before being detonated) near polling stations and even killed a candidate who campaigned in Chhattisgarh's Dantewada district in April.[10] The Maoists also attacked and killed polling officials,[11] sometimes stranding them in remote places after destroying or seizing their vehicles. Despite these intimidation tactics, affected communities participated in the election. Polling data showed that the 14 polling constituencies with the highest recent death tolls from Naxalite-related violence had an average voter turnout of 72.2%, higher than the national average of 68.7% (excluding constituencies in the Indian state of Jammu and Kashmir). Tellingly, the Naxal-affected precinct with the lowest turnout rate (Jharkhand's Chatra constituency) still had a reasonably high turnout rate of 65.1%.

Following the national elections, the incumbent BJP government retained its parliamentary majority with an average vote share of just under 65% across constituencies. BJP candidates' average vote share was consistent across Naxal-affected and unaffected constituencies (just over 66% compared to just under 65%, respectively), suggesting that Indian voters inside and outside the Red Corridor approved of the BJP's performance. The polling results gave the BJP little incentive to alter its counter-insurgency strategy in the future.

Naxalite-related violence has remained confined to rural and remote areas, as in the past decades. However, India's Minister for Home Affairs Amit Shah, who is responsible for federal counter-insurgency operations, signalled in November that he might redeploy the CRPF to fight Naxalism in urban centres. The BJP government has regularly claimed that many city-based intellectuals and activists have links with CPI–Maoist and work covertly to support the insurgency. The government caused a national controversy in August when it arrested nine activists alleged to be urban CPI–Maoists for their role in organising the Bhima Koregaon protests in January 2018 and for allegedly conspiring to assassinate Prime Minister Narendra Modi. The high-profile investigations continued into December, when charges were officially brought against the accused, paving the way for a trial in 2020.[12] There is little evidence to corroborate the claim that CPI–Maoist has a foothold in India's urban centres. In fact, Muppala Lakshman Rao (alias 'Ganapathi'), CPI–Maoist's commander until 2018, publicly lamented that his group had not been able to mobilise urban support.[13]

Military Developments

Government forces and CPI–Maoist fighters clashed occasionally throughout 2019. The police conducted numerous patrols in the Red Corridor in attempts to find and engage CPI–Maoist units (especially

Key Events in 2019

Political events

9 April — Maoists kill a Legislative Assembly member and several bodyguards as he campaigned for re-election in Chhattisgarh State.

11 April — Lok Sabha polling begins.

19 May — Lok Sabha polling ends.

Military/Violent events

7 February — Security forces attack a CPI–Maoist encampment, killing at least ten militants, in Chhattisgarh's Bijapur district.

1 March — Security forces kill eight CPI–Maoist militants, including five women, in Maharashtra's Gadchiroli district.

1 May — CPI–Maoist militants use an IED to ambush a C-60 Commandos team in Maharashtra's Gadchiroli district, killing 16 people.

People's Liberation Guerrilla Army units – CPI–Maoist's military wing), and used intelligence to organise large-scale attacks on Maoist encampments. The most successful attack, in Chhattisgarh's Bijapur district in February, killed ten Maoists. Similar attacks occurred in Maharashtra's Gadchiroli, Chhattisgarh's Jagadalpur and Rajnandgaon districts in March, July and August. Though CPI–Maoist can ill afford such losses, none of these incidents was as damaging as the April 2018 battle along the Indravati River, when a team of C-60 Commandos (Maharashtra's anti-Naxal police) killed at least 40 CPI–Maoist commanders and fighters.

The Maoists also targeted the police in 2019. Since 2016, the insurgents have increasingly turned to hit-and-run-style IED attacks, which are less risky than prolonged gun battles. Their most effective such attack in 2019 occurred in May in Gadchiroli district, when militants detonated an IED as a police transport vehicle drove by and killed 15 C-60 Commandos and their civilian driver. Despite this highly publicised incident, Maoists killed fewer police officers in 2019 (20) than in 2018 (25).

CPI–Maoist has suffered morale problems for several years and continued to grapple with desertions throughout the year. At least 163 Maoists, including 30 commanders, surrendered to authorities in 2019, a sharp decline (over 38%) in overall surrenders compared to 2018 but an increase in command-level surrenders (over 20%). Both combat losses and state-sponsored amnesty offers (usually accompanied by financial rehabilitation packages) incentivised the surrenders. The highest-profile surrender occurred in September, when Udaya, the secretary of the Andhra Odisha Border Special Zonal Committee (AOBSZ), defected to the government. The AOBSZ has been an important strategic and political component of CPI–Maoist since the group's emergence, but its importance has declined since most of its leaders were killed in the Balimela Reservoir Battle in 2016. Udaya's defection is the most recent indication that the AOBSZ never fully recovered from that setback.

Impact

CPI–Maoist's operations

By the end of 2018, it was clear that combat losses and defections had significantly reduced CPI–Maoist's fighting strength and leadership, but it was still possible that defections were syphoning off less-committed leaders, leaving fewer but highly committed and therefore more resilient leaders. By the end of 2019, however, it became clear that CPI–Maoist could not stop the flow of desertions. In fact, former leader Ganapathi stated publicly that the loss of so many leaders contributed to the group's diminished strength in 2019.

CPI–Maoist also signalled its intention to shift operations away from its traditional heartlands, where the government's security presence is most robust, to new and relatively undefended areas in Kerala, Madhya Pradesh, Maharashtra and Telangana states. Fatality data, however, showed no

23 May
Lok Sabha election results announced, confirming incumbent BJP government's re-election.

27 July
Security forces attack a CPI-Maoist encampment in Chhattisgarh's Jagadalpur district, killing seven militants.

3 August
Security forces attack a CPI-Maoist encampment in Chhattisgarh's Rajnandgaon district, killing seven militants.

16 November
Minister of Home Affairs Amit Shah declares intention to deploy CRPF to urban centres.

clear shift away from Chhattisgarh State (where 46% of fatalities occurred in 2018 as opposed to 40% in 2019). There were few indications that CPI–Maoist successfully infiltrated new areas, though attempts were made. For instance, the police killed four Maoists in Kerala's Palakkad district in late October after attacking their encampment, and captured an important CPI–Maoist arms instructor, sent to help establish a Maoist presence in the area.

Civilian safety and human rights

Violence in the whole Red Corridor, measured by annual deaths, dropped significantly from 2018. Civilians remained vulnerable, however, and at least 53 assassinations occurred in 2019. This figure is consistent with the previous year (49 killings), suggesting that security forces' combat operations did not make civilians significantly safer. Still, total civilian deaths (62 including civilians caught in crossfire) fell well below the 2017 toll (106 deaths). From a long-term perspective, 2019 was an unusually safe year for civilians in the Red Corridor.

Various human-rights organisations attempted to operate in the Red Corridor, using investigations and monitoring to pressure combatants into restraint. The federal government, often called out by these organisations, reacted by raiding Amnesty International's offices and freezing its assets in October 2018. A similar raid occurred again in November 2019, probably in retaliation for the organisation's critical reports on the Naxalite and Kashmir conflicts.

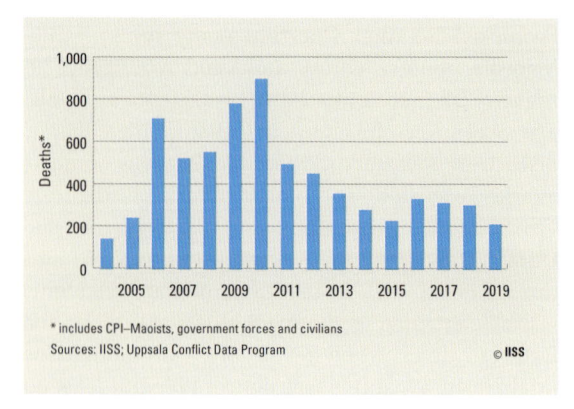

Figure 1: Total deaths since 2004*

* includes CPI–Maoists, government forces and civilians
Sources: IISS; Uppsala Conflict Data Program

Economic development

The government has invested heavily in economic development in the Red Corridor to tackle civilian discontent. Road construction, electrification, construction of cellular-communications infrastructure and other small-scale projects continued in 2019. The government has also attempted to expand mineral extraction in the Red Corridor as CPI–Maoist's influence has waned, but approved and ongoing operations remained bitterly contested by some communities.

Trends

Political trajectories

Despite losing the 2018 Chhattisgarh State legislative election to the Indian National Congress, the BJP had a strong showing in the Red Corridor in the 2019 general elections, which suggests that the BJP might have repaired its standing with the public. Even if voters in the Red Corridor disapprove of the government's handling of the insurgency, this concern was outweighed by other considerations. Regardless, the BJP's victory portends no drastic policy changes in the Red Corridor. The government's dual policy of securitisation and economic development will likely persist in the coming years.

Conflict-related risks

Though 2019 was the lowest-fatality year since 2004,[14] CPI–Maoist remained a dangerous group and few government officials predict a sudden collapse of the insurgency. In fact, the governments of Andhra Pradesh, Bihar, Chhattisgarh, Jharkhand and Odisha states requested increased troop deployments and funding from the central government to fight CPI–Maoist in 2020.[15]

Prospects for peace

The federal government has periodically offered to begin a political dialogue with CPI–Maoist on the condition that the group first disarm. However, no such offers were issued during 2019, suggesting that the government aims to achieve a complete military victory over CPI–Maoist rather than ending the conflict through negotiations. This may equate to a lost opportunity to bring violence in the Red Corridor to an end. Although highly speculative, peace talks might have incentivised the entire group (or at least a majority of the group) to disavow violence in the near term, potentially bringing the insurgency to a quick and relatively early end. While CPI–Maoist's leadership is aware of its decline, it has made no overtures to begin a peace process, nor have any of its surrendered militants and leaders advocated such a process (though they do encourage individual surrenders).

Notes

[1] 'PLFI rebel Bajiram killed in encounter', *Times of India*, 1 March 2019.
[2] 'Armed men kill BJP leader, family in Jharkhand', *Hindustan Times*, 24 July 2019.
[3] 'How forces neutralised Maoists in Andhra and Telangana', *Times of India*, 17 October 2019.
[4] 'Andhra adivasis' killing: Magisterial inquiry ordered', *Times of India*, 20 July 2019.
[5] 'Jharkhand cops, CRPF men booked for minor's death', *Hindustan Times*, 27 August 2019.
[6] 'FIR against Bela Bhatia & Soni Sori for "fake encounter"', *Times of India*, 22 September 2019.
[7] 'Dantewada police fires in air to disperse tribals protesting against security camp', *Hindustan Times*, 12 November 2019.
[8] 'The Pathalgadi rebellion', *Hindu*, 14 April 2018.
[9] 'Maoists back Pathalgadi movement, threaten to punish policemen for "repressing" activists', *Hindustan Times*, 22 July 2019.
[10] 'Chhattisgarh: BJP MLA, 4 cops killed in Maoist attack ahead', *Times of India*, 9 April 2019.
[11] 'Lok Sabha Phase 2 elections: Maoists gun down woman poll officer in Odisha', *New Indian Express*, 17 April 2019.
[12] The Battle of Koregaon (1818) is celebrated annually in large gatherings by the Dalit community. The celebration on 1 January 2018 became politicised and led to large protests against high-caste Hindu nationalism. Police suppressed the protests after they became violent, leading to the death of one Dalit protester and triggering similar protests across India. These events prompted law-enforcement agencies to investigate the organisers.
[13] 'Is Maoist movement losing steam?', *Hindu*, 16 September 2019.
[14] IISS and Uppsala Conflict Data Program's Georeferenced Event Dataset (GED) data.
[15] 'Don't downsize or withdraw forces from state for next 2–3 years, Das urges Centre', *Hindustan Times*, 27 August 2019; 'Nitish pitches for a bigger central role in fighting LWE', *Hindustan Times*, 27 August 2019; 'Need more funds to fight Maoists: CM Bhupesh Baghel', *Times of India*, 27 August 2019; 'Liberal help needed to develop tribal areas: CM', *Hindu*, 27 August 2019; 'Centre's help needed to check LWE', *Hindu*, 27 August 2019.

INDIA (NORTHEAST)

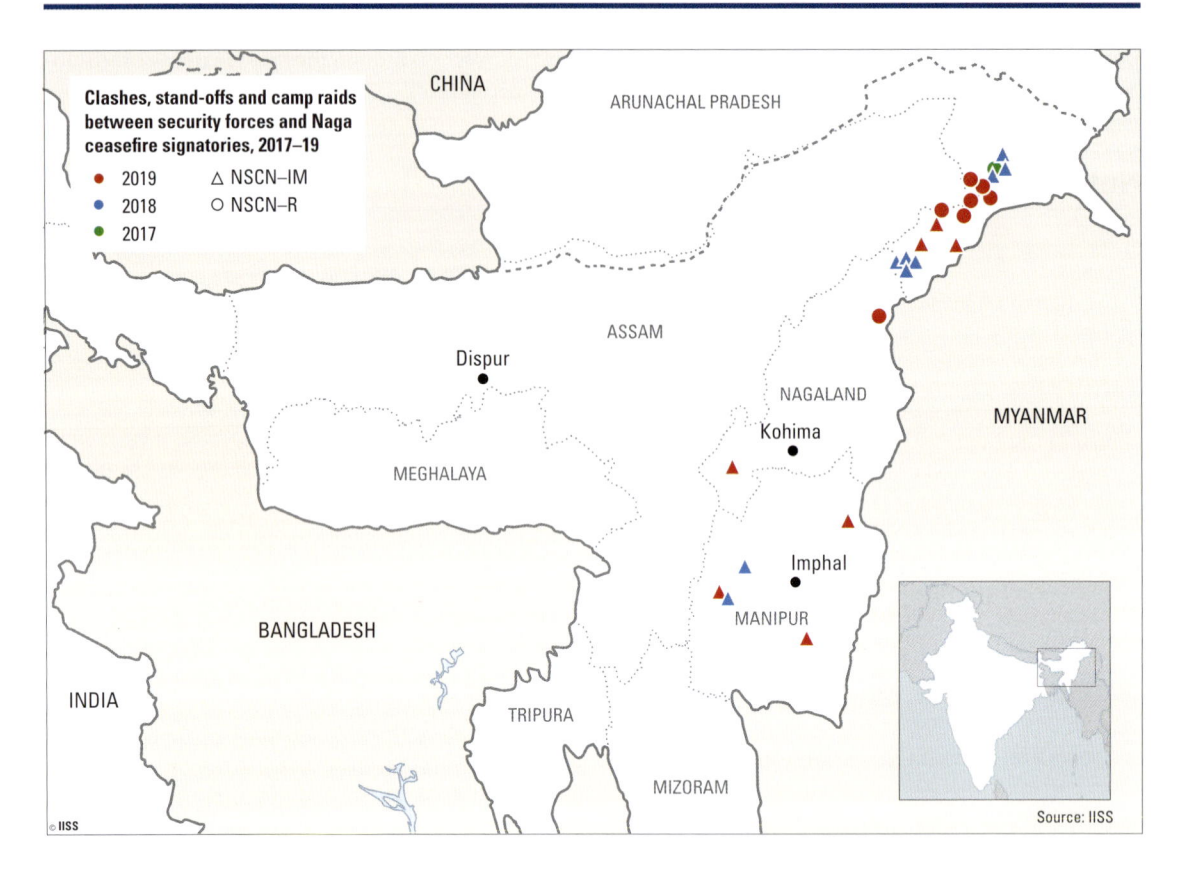

Clashes, stand-offs and camp raids between security forces and Naga ceasefire signatories, 2017–19
- 2019
- 2018
- 2017
- △ NSCN–IM
- ○ NSCN–R

Source: IISS

Overview

The conflict in 2019

There was a significant reduction in lethal violence in the three main armed conflicts in Northeast India (in the states of Assam and Manipur, and the Naga-inhabited areas of the region) in 2019, with 42 conflict-related fatalities, down from 78 in 2018 and 95 and 2017, continuing a trend that began in 2010. This decline marked the culmination of several years of counter-insurgency operations by Indian government forces against recalcitrant non-ceasefire signatory groups such as the National Democratic Front of Bodoland–Saoraigwra (NDFB–S). In the first six months of the year, the Myanmar military (Tatmadaw) conducted operations against the National Socialist Council of Nagaland–Khaplang/Yung Aung (NSCN–K/YA) – the group coordinating the activities of anti-talks factions – and significantly disrupted its ability to launch attacks into Indian territory.

The April–May elections for the Lok Sabha (the lower house of the Indian parliament) produced significant successes for the Bharatiya Janata Party (BJP) in the region, despite protests over New Delhi's proposals to grant citizenship to religious minorities from neighbouring communities. The eventual passage of the Citizenship (Amendment) Bill in December led to violence across the region, leaving five people dead in Assam. The elections

Key statistics

Type	Internal
Start date	1956
IDPs total	No data
Refugees total	No data
People in need	No data

further stalled the peace talks between the Indian government and Naga armed groups – 22 years after the first ceasefire with the most prominent of these, the National Socialist Council of Nagalim–Isak Muivah (NSCN–IM). Public disagreements increased in the months after the elections, highlighting the disunity of the armed groups in terms of their negotiating positions and deadlock over symbolic concessions, such as a separate Naga constitution and flag. The central government's decision to impose a deadline of 31 October for a final peace agreement led to panic amid rumours of mobilisation by Naga and Indian security forces. Rumours of an agreement, followed by reports that talks were continuing, however, suggested that both sides had climbed down to some extent, although no details of such an agreement were disclosed.

The conflict to 2019

Following a substantial escalation in counter-insurgency operations against Naga and Assam-based insurgents during the early to mid-1990s, the Indian government began drawing down its operations in Assam, Manipur and the Naga-inhabited areas in the late 1990s, leading to the creation of a diverse range of state–insurgent relationships.[1] In 1997 and 2001, the central government ended its operations against the NSCN–IM and NSCN–K respectively, leading to a violent but stable coexistence between the state and militant groups. Amnesty programmes tied to surrenders and peace deals in Assam and Manipur created a layered post-conflict architecture with varying disarmament, demobilisation and reintegration (DDR) arrangements. Although low-level violence between factions, and against civilians and state forces, has continued, the ceasefires de-incentivised full-scale operations and led to new informal social, economic and political structures that allow armed groups to continue to coerce civilians, rival factions and, to a lesser extent, the state.

While this strategy reduced violence, it also raised concerns that the state is using peace strategically, tiring the armed groups through protracted negotiations.[2] The armed groups, including the NSCN–IM – the most powerful in the region – have similarly taken advantage of the ceasefires to recruit, challenge rivals and consolidate their control of territory and resources. Although New Delhi and the NSCN–IM agreed in 2015 to negotiate a final peace deal (the Framework Agreement), neither party has altered its strategy since. Thus, lingering tensions, including over the status of Nagas beyond Nagaland state (in Arunachal Pradesh, Assam and Manipur), interpretations of sovereignty and the inclusion of other stakeholders (armed groups or civil-society bodies), have continued to plague the process.

Figure 1: History of the Naga insurgency

1956	Naga insurgency begins, led by Naga National Council (NNC)
1963	Creation of Nagaland state
1964–68	Peace Mission-brokered ceasefire
1975	Shillong Accord signed with NNC representatives
1980	National Socialist Council of Nagaland (NSCN) breaks away from NNC, becomes main rebel group
1988	NSCN splits into NSCN–Isak Muivah (NSCN–IM) and NSCN–Khaplang (NSCN–K)
1997	Ceasefire signed with NSCN–IM
2001	Ceasefire signed with NSCN–K
2001	Bangkok Agreement temporarily extends NSCN–IM ceasefire coverage 'without territorial limits', revoked following civil unrest
2007	Ceasefire with NSCN–IM extended indefinitely
2007	NSCN–Unification (NSCN–U) breaks from NSCN–IM
2011	NSCN–Khole-Kitovi (NSCN–KK) breaks from NSCN–K, amalgamating with NSCN–U
2015	NSCN–K withdraws from ceasefire agreement, conducts major ambush in Chandel, Manipur. Pro-talks NSCN–Reformation (NSCN–R) breaks away
2015	Government of India signs 'Framework Agreement' with NSCN–IM
2016	Working Committee (WC) of pro-talks Naga armed groups formed
2017	Government of India signs agreement with WC
2018	NSCN–K splits into Burmese and Indian factions
2019	Myanmar Army operations against anti-talks groups in Myanmar
2019	Bharatiya Janata Party (BJP) wins general election
2019	Interlocutor appointed governor of Nagaland, vows to resolve talks within three months
2019	Deadline for resolution passes amid tensions, parties claim to reach an agreement

Key Conflict Parties

Table 1: Indian government forces

Force	Organisation type	Role and deployment
Indian Armed Forces	Military force	Army: Counter-insurgency (Arunachal Pradesh, Assam, Manipur, Nagaland); border defence Air Force: Supply; logistics
Assam Rifles	Paramilitary force, officered by army personnel	Counter-insurgency (Arunachal Pradesh, Assam, Manipur, Nagaland); border defence
State police of Assam, Manipur, Nagaland	Local law enforcement	Counter-insurgency (Assam, Manipur); anti-extortion policing (Nagaland)
Central Reserve Police Force	Central police force	Policing support (Assam, Manipur)
Border Security Force	Central armed police force	Border defence; limited internal-security operations
Indo-Tibetan Border Police	Central armed police force	Border police; limited internal-security operations
Central Industrial Security Force	Central armed police force	Installation defence

Indian government forces

Counter-insurgency operations in Assam, Manipur and Nagaland are conducted by the Indian armed forces and five central police/paramilitary agencies, in addition to each state's law-enforcement agencies (see Table 1).

Coordination between these forces has long been a challenge, making the security approach to insurgency 'fragmented', according to Nagaland Governor R.N. Ravi. Unified command structures exist (in Assam, for example), but insurgent groups have continued to exploit the inter-state institutional boundaries between Arunachal Pradesh, Assam and Nagaland, particularly in recent years.

The structure of force deployments in the region remained largely unchanged in 2019, with only the phased addition of central paramilitary forces during the April–May elections. On 5 August, the central government moved 29 Central Reserve Police Force (CRPF) companies from Assam to Kashmir but relocated 51 back to Assam on 27 August. The additional 29 Border Security Force (BSF) companies deployed after the publication on 31 August of the National Register of Citizens (NRC) in the state brought the total number to 219 companies. As violence remained low after the NRC's publication, 10,000 of these forces were withdrawn again on 14 September.[3] On 14 October, the army announced that it would withdraw from 20 of the 33 districts in Assam, confirming the considerable improvements in the security situation.[4] During 11–13 December, the central government deployed 59 additional companies of paramilitary forces following the outbreak of massive protests against the Citizenship (Amendment) Act in Assam.

Non-state armed groups

Non-state armed groups in the region can be divided into those engaged in peace talks with the government (see Table 2) and those opposed to them (see Table 3).

Table 2: Armed groups in talks with the Indian government

Name	Formed	Strength (estimate)	Objectives	Areas of operation	Operations	Allies	Rivals
Government of the Democratic Republic of Nagaland/Naga National Council–Non-Accord (GDRN/NNC–NA)	2011 (split from NNC–Parent Body)	Minor	Solution within Indian constitution	Nagaland	Peace talks	Working Committee members (but rivalries with NNC factions)	NSCN–IM

Table 2: Armed groups in talks with the Indian government

Name	Formed	Strength (estimate)	Objectives	Areas of operation	Operations	Allies	Rivals
Kangleipak Communist Party–Lamphel (KCP–Lamphel)	1980 (KCP), date of breakaway unknown	Minor	Manipuri independence	Manipur plains	Armed operations suspended – formally surrendered	Unknown	Non-ceasefire signatory groups (e.g. UNLF)
Kuki National Organisation (KNO)	1988	1,122 (2018)	Kuki autonomy	Kuki-populated areas of Manipur	Umbrella organisation: no operations of its own	Local BJP, Moreh, Manipur	NSCN–IM, UPF
Kuki Revolutionary Army (KRA)	2000	40 (2010); 250 (2018)	Kuki autonomy	Kuki-populated areas of Manipur	Illicit economic activity including extortion	KNO constituent members	Rival Kuki armed groups
Naga National Council/Federal Government of Nagaland (NNC/FGN)	2005	Minor	Solution within Indian constitution	Nagaland	Peace talks	Working Committee members (but rivalries with NNC factions)	NSCN–IM
Naga National Council–Parent Body (NNC–Parent Body)	1991 (originally NNC–Khadao; rebranded in 1995 after defection to NSCN–IM)	Minor	Solution within Indian constitution	Nagaland	Peace talks	Working Committee members (but rivalries with NNC factions)	NSCN–IM
National Democratic Front of Bodoland–Progressive (NDFB–P)	2009	3,000	Bodo autonomy/ statehood	Western Assam	Ceasefire, peace talks	Bodo civil-society organisations	NDFB–S
National People's Government of Nagaland/Naga National Council–Non-Accord (NPGN/NNC–NA)	2014 (split from NNC–Parent Body)	Minor	Solution within Indian constitution	Nagaland	Peace talks	Working Committee members (but rivalries with NNC factions)	NSCN–IM
National Socialist Council of Nagaland–Khaplang/Khango Konyak (NSCN–K/KK)	2018	150 (2018)	Solution within Indian Constitution	Eastern Nagaland	Peace talks, extortion-related activity	Member of Working Committee. Clashes with NSCN–R in 2019	NSCN–IM, NSCN–K/YA
National Socialist Council of Nagaland–Kitovi-Neokpao/Unification (NSCN–KN/U)	2007 (NSCN–U formed); 2011 (NSCN–Khole-Kitovi formed. NSCN–KK rebranded NSCN–KN following Khole's defection to NSCN–IM in 2016)	1,800	Solution within Indian constitution	Arunachal Pradesh, Nagaland	Ceasefire, factional clashes	Working Committee members	NSCN–IM

Table 2: Armed groups in talks with the Indian government

Name	Formed	Strength (estimate)	Objectives	Areas of operation	Operations	Allies	Rivals
National Socialist Council of Nagaland–Reformation (NSCN–R)	2015	1,200 (2015)	Solution within Indian constitution	Arunachal Pradesh, Nagaland	Ceasefire, factional clashes	Working Committee members (however killed one NSCN K/KK member in 2019)	State forces (limited clashes), NSCN–IM
National Socialist Council of Nagalim–Isak Muivah (NSCN–IM)	1988	5,000	Sovereign 'Nagalim' through shared, but separate, sovereignty with the Indian government	Nagaland, Naga-populated areas of Arunachal Pradesh, Assam and Manipur	Peace talks, clashes with rival groups, limited clashes with state forces, illicit economic activity including extortion and kidnapping	Occasional tacit collaboration with security forces. Civil-society organisations (e.g. Naga People's Movement for Human Rights, United Naga Council Manipur)	State forces, NSCN–K, ZUF, Kuki armed groups, Working Committee
United Liberation Front of Asom–Pro-Talks Faction (ULFA–PTF)	2009	Transition to civil-society movement	Addressing implementation of the Assam Accord, social/political issues related to illegal migration, citizenship and the rights of former ULFA combatants	Assam	Peace talks, participates in peaceful protests	Assamese civil-society organisations (e.g. All Assam Students Union)	n/a
United People's Front (UPF)	1977	1,059 (2018)	Kuki autonomy (demand fluctuates)	Kuki-populated areas of Manipur	Umbrella organisation: no operations of its own	Alliance between constituent members	KNO, NSCN–IM
United Socialist Revolutionary Army (USRA)	Date of breakaway from ZRA unknown	Minor – member of KNO	Unknown	Hill areas of Manipur	Illicit economic activity including extortion	Unknown	Rival tribal factions
United Tribal Liberation Army (UTLA)	2002	Unknown – part of KNO	Kuki autonomy	Kuki-populated areas of Manipur	Clashes with UTLA–P/LTT	KNO constituent members	UTLA–P/LTT
Working Committee (WC)[a]	2016	Umbrella organisation – no estimates	Solution within Indian constitution	Nagaland	Peace talks, limited intra-factional clashes, extortion	Alliance between constituent members	NSCN–IM

[a] Membership: NSCN–KN/U, NSCN–R, NNC/FGN, NNC–Parent Body, NPGN/NNC–NA, GDRN/NNC–NA, NSCN–K/KK.

Table 3: Armed groups not in talks with the Indian government

Name	Formed	Strength (estimate)	Objectives	Areas of operation	Operations	Allies	Rivals
Coordination Committee (CorCom)	2011	Umbrella organisation – no estimates	Sovereign Manipur	Arunachal Pradesh, Manipur	Coordinated strikes, extortion	UNLFWESEA umbrella	State forces
Dimasa National Army (DNA)	Early 2000s	Minor	Political concessions (autonomy) to Dimasa community	Dima Hasao district, Assam	Extortion, limited clashes with security forces	Unknown	State forces
National Democratic Front of Bodoland–Saoraigwra (NDFB–S)	2012	150 (2016)	Sovereign Bodoland	Western Assam	Violence against perceived 'outsiders', clashes with security forces	CorCom, NSCN–K/YA, ULFA–I, UNLFWESEA	State forces
National Socialist Council of Nagaland–Khaplang (NSCN–K)	1988. In 2018 the original NSCN–K split into NSCN–K/YA and NSCN–K/KK	1,500 (2015)	Sovereign Nagaland (including Myanmar areas)	Arunachal Pradesh, Eastern Nagaland, Manipur, Myanmar	Cross-border strikes	CorCom, ULFA–I, UNLFWESEA	State forces NSCN–IM
National Socialist Council of Nagaland–Khaplang/Yung Aung (NSCN–K/YA)	2018	No estimates ~500 (based on NSCN–K/KK defection figures)	In talks with government of Myanmar	Arunachal Pradesh, Eastern Nagaland, Manipur, Myanmar	Cross-border strikes, joint operations with allies	CorCom, ULFA–I, UNLFWESEA	NSCN–K/KK
People's Liberation Army (PLA)	1978	1,500–3,000	Region-wide revolutionary front against Indian rule	Arunachal Pradesh, Manipur	Strikes in coordination with allies	CorCom, UNLFWESEA	State forces
People's Revolutionary Party of Kangleipak (PREPAK)	1977	500–650 (including both factions)	Expulsion of outsiders from Manipur	Plains of Manipur	Coordination with allies via CorCom	CorCom, UNLFWESEA	State forces
Thadou People's Liberation Army (TPLA)	2015	Minor	Defend rights of Thadou people, within Indian Constitution	Thadou-populated areas of Manipur	Clashes with security forces	Unknown	State forces
United Liberation Front of Asom–Independent (ULFA–I)	2009	100 (partial estimate, 2019), 500 (2017)	Sovereign, independent Assam	Arunachal Pradesh, northeastern Assam	Extortion, attacks on security forces, bombings	CorCom, NSCN–K/YA, UNLFWESEA	State forces
United National Liberation Front (UNLF)	1964	1,500–1,700 (2018)	Sovereign Manipur	Manipur	Limited strikes against security forces, moral-policing killings	CorCom, UNLFWESEA	State forces, rival Meitei groups (i.e. KCP–Lamphel)

Table 3: Armed groups not in talks with the Indian government

Name	Formed	Strength (estimate)	Objectives	Areas of operation	Operations	Allies	Rivals
United National Liberation Front of Western South East Asia (UNLFWESEA)	2015	Umbrella organisation – no estimates	Sovereign northeast India	Arunachal Pradesh, Assam, Manipur, Nagaland	Coordinated strikes, extortion	CorCom	State forces
United Tribal Liberation Army–Poukhai (UTLA–P)/ Liberation Tigers of Tribals (LTT)	2002 (UTLA), August 2018 (UTLA–P rebranded as LTT)	Minor	Tribal autonomy	Kuki-populated areas of Manipur	Clashes with rival armed groups, security forces	Unknown	Rival UTLA factions
Zeliangrong United Front (ZUF)	2011. Split a second time into ZUF–Kamson and ZUF–Jenchui Kamei (September 2019)	300 (2017)	Resistance to NSCN dominance in Zeliangrong areas	Assam, Nagaland, Zeliangrong-populated areas of Manipur	Clashes with NSCN–IM, security forces	Sporadic tacit collaboration with security forces	NSCN–IM
ZUF–Jenchui Kamei	Split from ZUF 2017, reconciliation 2018, split again from ZUF 2019	>300	Resistance to NSCN dominance in Zeliangrong areas	Assam, Nagaland, Zeliangrong-populated areas of Manipur	Clashes with ZUF–Kamson, NSCN–IM	Unknown	ZUF–Kamson
ZUF–Kamson	Split from ZUF 2017, reconciliation 2018, split again 2019. Merged with NSCN–KN/U (October 2019)	>300	Resistance to NSCN dominance in Zeliangrong areas	Assam, Nagaland, Zeliangrong-populated areas of Manipur	Clashes with ZUF–Jenchui Kamei, NSCN–IM	Unknown	ZUF–Jenchui Kamei

Many other smaller armed groups operate in the region, organised around unstable loyalties to factional leaders, which often shift their allegiance between broader alliances and umbrella organisations. The roughly 300-strong Zeliangrong United Front (ZUF), formed in 2011 to defend the Zeliangrong Naga-inhabited areas of Assam, Manipur and Nagaland against the NSCN–IM and to a lesser extent Indian security forces, split in August–September 2019. The two factions, formed around senior leaders Sinthuingam Kamson and Jenchui Kamei, had previously split in April 2017, but had reconciled in July 2018. Throughout summer 2019, a series of ZUF statements announced the expulsion of the other party and claimed sole leadership. On 30 October, the Kamson faction announced that it had ceased to exist in May and joined the NSCN–Kitovi-Neokpao/Unification (NSCN–KN/U). The group thus formally joined the peace talks under the umbrella of the seven-group Working Committee (WC), adding momentum to the WC's peace process with New Delhi, sidelining the Kamei faction and further damaging the NSCN–IM's claim to be the sole representative of the Naga population.

Drivers

Insurgent networks

Northeast India's geographical isolation from 'mainland' India has long played a critical role in sustaining the region's armed rebellions.[5] The region's strategic vulnerability has provided ample opportunities for Pakistan and China to arm, train and finance Naga, Assam-based and Manipuri insurgents,[6] while its porous borders have allowed armed groups to exploit ambivalent governments in Bangladesh (until 2009, when bilateral relations improved considerably) and Myanmar. In recent years, insurgents have increasingly relied on a network of over 50 camps along the border area of the Sagaing Region of Myanmar, launching operations into India via the corridor connecting Arunachal Pradesh, eastern Nagaland and upper northeastern Assam.[7] During the first six months of 2019, seven of the nine clashes between security forces and insurgents on Indian territory took place in the tri-junction between those three state – an area of strategic significance for insurgents. The Indian security forces are seeking to interdict the critical transit network in this area. It was Myanmar, however, that successfully disrupted that network, launching three operations against Indian-based insurgent camps in 2019.

Structural factors: unaddressed and exacerbated

Although ceasefires have introduced formal and informal rules of engagement since 1997, they have failed to address the structural drivers of the conflict. Peace accords have frequently resulted in organisational splintering as hardline factions pressed for further concessions.[8] Since the 1990s, armed groups have waited to join peace talks, while New Delhi has slowed the pace of concessions to armed groups.[9] Frustrated groups such as the United Liberation Front of Asom–Pro-Talks Faction (ULFA–PTF) and the NDFB–P have resorted to protests in response. On 10 September 2019, for example, the NDFB–P, All Bodo Students' Union and People's Joint Action Committee for Bodoland Movement held a rally threatening mass agitations if a separate state of Bodoland was not granted.

The passing of the Citizenship (Amendment) Bill in the Lok Sabha on 8 January 2019, which would grant citizenship to Hindu, Sikh and Christian minorities from Afghanistan, Pakistan and Bangladesh, fuelled fears of demographic engineering in Assam and Manipur. The ULFA–PTF warned on 12 January that it would abandon peace talks if the bill passed in the Rajya Sabha (the upper house). The Asom Gana Parishad (AGP), the political party of the former Assam movement, temporarily withdrew from the alliance with the ruling BJP. Although the bill was withdrawn in February, the BJP's resounding electoral success ensured its passage through the Lok Sabha and Rajya Sabha on 9 and 11 December respectively. The bill included exemptions to states falling under the purview of the Inner Line Permit (ILP) regime and tribal areas governed through the Sixth Schedule of the Indian Constitution, thus exempting Arunachal Pradesh, Nagaland and parts of Assam such as Karbi Anglong district.

However, widespread civil unrest broke out across Assam during 11–13 December, to which the Indian authorities responded with large police and army deployments, internet blackouts and curfews to curb further unrest. Four people were killed by police firing on 11–12 December,[10] with a fifth killed by protesters in Sonitpur the following day. Although curfews had been lifted by 17 December, massive protests continued across the state; on 19 December, tens of thousands of protesters held rallies across Dibrugarh, Tinsukia and Jorhat districts. In a bid to prevent any violent protests in Manipur, on 10 December the central government extended the ILP regime to the state, restricting the movement of non-locals into the area and thereby exempting the state from the Act's provisions. However, the state government imposed restrictions on large gatherings across Imphal West district for three months on 21 December, fearing further unrest.[11]

Political Developments

The Indo-Naga peace talks were put on hold during the run-up to the elections. Despite optimism that the talks would quickly regain momentum following the elections, they have made little progress since the central government signed the Framework Agreement with the NSCN–IM in 2015, and the equivalent with the WC in 2017.

In 2018, it became clear that the government would devise 'special arrangements' for and grant constitutional benefits to the Nagas of 'Nagalim' (addressing the NSCN–IM's demands for a 'Greater Nagalim' – a belt of territory encompassing all of Nagaland, the hills of Manipur, part of central Assam and northeastern Arunachal Pradesh – without making territorial changes to Assam, Manipur and Arunachal Pradesh). On 4 March 2019, the government's interlocutor for peace talks with the Nagas, R.N. Ravi, said that the only remaining stumbling blocks were symbolic issues, such as the NSCN–IM's demand for a separate Naga flag and constitution. In response, on 21 March, the NSCN–IM accused the central government of delaying a final settlement; and in February, civil-society organisations boycotted a meeting with Ravi.[12]

The 2019 general election generated some initial optimism – on 20 June, the NSCN–IM called the results 'heartening' and looked forward to a prompt return to the peace talks.[13] The appointment of Ravi as governor of Nagaland in August signalled political momentum for the peace process and Ravi declared on 17 August that Prime Minister Narendra Modi wanted it concluded within three months, by 31 October.

The optimism was short-lived. On 3 August, the NSCN–IM announced that talks with the government had not gone well, and denounced Ravi's 'capricious and bossy' attitude.[14] The NSCN–IM saw Ravi's appointment as a 'reduction' of the talks to a lower level. On 8 September, the group's chairman, Q. Tuccu, rejected the three-month deadline as an 'ultimatum' and a scheme by the government to force NSCN–IM concessions.

A separate Naga flag and constitution remained the sticking point of the negotiations until September, when government sources indicated that neither demand would be met, and the NSCN–IM threatened to abandon the peace process. In October, the central government announced there would be 'no more talk' after 31 October,[15] and accused the NSCN–IM of delaying and 'mischievously' misleading the public on the contents of the 2015 Framework Agreement.[16]

Divergences in the NSCN–IM's and the WC's negotiating positions became increasingly apparent during these months, and the two groups clashed in the press, casting doubt over the prospects of reconciliation. On 10 October, the WC requested that the NSCN–IM clarify its position on a Naga constitution, warning that Nagas would not accept an imposed constitution that would erode centuries of heritage. On 13 October, the NSCN–IM accused the WC of being 'confused' and manipulated by the Indian government.

The government's insistence on the final deadline applied considerable pressure to the NSCN–IM while bolstering the WC's claim to represent Nagas beyond Nagaland. On 14 October, NSCN–IM sources warned that any deal struck separately with the WC at the expense of the NSCN–IM would be 'suicidal' for the Indian government.[17] On 25 October, former senior NSCN–IM functionary Hukavi Yepthomi joined the NSCN–KN/U along with 16 senior NSCN–IM militants, while on 28 October a further 22 senior NSCN–IM militants defected to the NSCN–KN/U.[18]

Key Events in 2019

Political events

8 January — Passage of the Citizenship (Amendment) Bill in the Lok Sabha sparks protests across Arunachal Pradesh, Assam, Manipur and Nagaland.

13 February — Citizenship (Amendment) Bill is withdrawn from parliament.

4 March — Chief negotiator for Naga peace talks R.N. Ravi says that only symbolic issues remain. In response, the NSCN–IM accuses the central government of delaying the talks.

15 April — Ceasefires are renewed between the government and NSCN–K/KK, NSCN–KN/U and NSCN–R for one year.

Military/Violent events

11 January — Army personnel clash with NSCN–R militants in Namtok, Changlang, Arunachal Pradesh.

2 February — Myanmar military forces launch operations against ULFA–I, NDFB–S and KLO camps in Taga, Sagaing Region, Myanmar (one ULFA–I militant killed).

29 March — Suspected NSCN–IM militants kill an NPP candidate in Kheti, Tirap, Arunachal Pradesh.

6 April — ULFA–I militants kill three of their own cadres attempting to flee the group's camp in Taga, Myanmar.

21 May — NSCN–IM militants attack an NPP convoy in Khonsa, Tirap, Arunachal Pradesh, killing 11 people.

Military Developments

As frustrations grew over the Naga peace process, contentious interaction between ceasefire signatories intensified, even though operations by anti-talks groups declined. Stand-offs, clashes, raids and ambushes between security forces and ceasefire signatory armed groups rose from one in 2017, to nine in 2018, to 15 in 2019. This did not translate into more conflict-related fatalities though – security forces inflicted just one casualty on the NSCN–Reformation (NSCN–R) in 2019 – but rather reflected the parties' intention to strengthen their local leverage and negotiating position.[19] It also accounted for the intensified mobilisation across Nagaland in late October, as both central security forces and the NSCN–IM sought to signal the consequences of the failure to reach an agreement.

The recent violent incidents in the region primarily involved the two major ceasefire signatory groups, the NSCN–IM (17 incidents since 2017) and the NSCN–R (eight incidents over the same period). In 2019, incidents were more evenly split: seven involving the NSCN–R and eight involving the NSCN–IM. The stand-offs were clustered around Arunachal Pradesh and Manipur, with comparatively fewer incidents in Nagaland, which has been formally covered by ceasefire rules since 2001. These patterns thus reflected fluctuations in 'armed orders' (the diverse relationships between the state and armed groups),[20] with more contention emerging as tensions within the peace processes grew.

The NSCN–IM also continued to use its military power to shape local politics in the areas under its control. In the Tirap district of Arunachal Pradesh, the group killed a National People's Party (NPP) candidate on 29 March and kidnapped an NPP worker on 17 April. On 21 May, suspected NSCN–IM militants ambushed a convoy of NPP workers, killing Member of the Legislative Assembly (MLA) Tirong Aboh and ten others in one of the most lethal insurgent attacks in recent years.

Manipur accounted for 49 of the 81 violent incidents and 11 of the 42 total fatalities across the three conflicts during 2019. The high percentage of violent incidents and the comparatively small number of fatalities reflected the two dominant patterns of violence in Manipur. Five fatalities resulted from intra-factional clashes within the Kuki and Zeliangrong Naga communities, as on 15 October, for example, when the Kamson and Kamei factions of the ZUF clashed over intra-movement disputes. The remaining six fatalities were civilians, killed in relation to extortion demands or informal justice mechanisms. Most attacks in the state were nonlethal. Grenade attacks in the Imphal municipal area, for instance, are used as warnings related to extortion demands and typically target businesses or the gates of residential compounds.

---

23 May
The BJP-led alliance stays in power with 353 seats in the Lok Sabha. The party and its allies perform strongly in the northeast.

1 August
Ravi is appointed governor of Nagaland and tasked with resolving the peace process before 31 October.

19 November
Home Minister Amit Shah states that Arunachal Pradesh, Nagaland and Mizoram will be exempted from the Citizenship (Amendment) Bill.

2–13 December
The Citizenship (Amendment) Bill is passed in the Lok Sabha and Rajya Sabha. Five people are killed during major civil unrest in response across Assam.

8 June
Indian Army and Tatmadaw forces conclude a three-week joint operation against Indian insurgent groups.

22 July
Suspected Kuki militants kill a senior Kuki National Front (KNF) militant in Moltam, Kangpokpi, Manipur.

26 August
NSCN–R militants kill an NSCN–K/KK militant in Longlung, Changlang, Arunachal Pradesh.

28 September
Army personnel kill an NSCN–R militant in Kharsang, Changlang, Arunachal Pradesh.

30 November
Assam Rifles personnel clash with NSCN–R militants in Changlang, Arunachal Pradesh. One militant is killed.

Impact

More uncertainty in Naga-inhabited areas
The impending 31 October deadline for a final peace agreement and continued deadlock in the negotiations throughout August, September and October created a deep sense of unease in Nagaland and the surrounding states, leading to rumours that peace was on the verge of collapse. Government departments prepared for worst-case scenarios. On 22 October, the state government recalled its administrators and police officers from leave and two days later the Nagaland police directed its armed battalions to stockpile rations to last at least two months.[21] On 25 October, Nagaland police intercepted NSCN–IM communications regarding mobilisation in Dimapur, Zunheboto and other parts of Nagaland. The army and Assam Rifles began re-establishing a comprehensive counter-insurgency grid and reaching out to the Myanmar Army to ensure coordination in the event of NSCN–IM militants crossing the international border.[22]

The 31 October deadline passed and reports emerged that the NSCN–IM had agreed to sign a peace deal with the government, but there was no indication of whether either party had conceded on the flag and constitution issue.[23] Negotiations appeared to continue well beyond the deadline; on 8 November Ravi met NSCN–IM negotiators to discuss 'final loose ends'. On 18 December, NSCN–IM chairman Tuccu said that negotiations were making positive progress and that a final agreement was imminent following the 'breakthrough' of 31 October.[24] This return to optimistic statements, alongside the NSCN–IM's broad compliance with ceasefire regulations,[25] suggested that the talks had made enough progress to prevent their collapse. It remained unclear whether these talks had generated any substantive results, or whether the reported agreement offered a convenient face-saving mechanism allowing the parties to return to their status quo arrangement of limited cooperation and conflict.[26]

Relations with neighbouring and international partners
Myanmar's operations against Indian insurgents in its territory scattered non-signatory groups, forcing them to regroup and putting them under increased financial pressure. Although the NSCN–K/YA and the ULFA–Independent (ULFA–I) conducted multiple attacks in 2019, the groups killed only three members of the security forces, and 50 ULFA–I militants surrendered during the year (until 27 October),[27] suggesting that the groups' focus had shifted to regrouping and that the Tatmadaw operations had demoralised some members.

The coordination of counter-insurgency operations with Myanmar represents a significant development in India–Myanmar military and diplomatic relations. Yet triumphalist statements on the defeat of the insurgency should be taken with caution. Though weakened, insurgents continued to exploit limited state penetration in the India–Myanmar border area during 2019. Indian security sources estimated in June that up to 150 ULFA–I and 100 NDFB–S militants remained in Myanmar, while on 24 July intelligence sources told the media that more than 100 ULFA–I militants had relocated to new camps within 35 kilometres of the border.

Trends

Implications of a possible Naga talks collapse
The Naga conflict is but one of many low-level insurgencies across Northeast India, but it is by far the most significant due to the size of the groups involved, their strategic location along the India–Myanmar border and their historic role in arming, training and financing armed groups across the region.

Following the crisis during summer and autumn 2019, the collapse of the peace talks between the central government and the NSCN–IM remains a possibility for 2020. A return to hostilities would be costly for both parties. The NSCN–IM would need to relocate its assets from urban areas (its headquarters is outside Dimapur, Nagaland's commercial capital), engage in an expensive programme to maintain a combat-ready cadre base and work hard to justify a return to violence to its civil-society constituents.

Internal politics will be a key determining factor of whether the NSCN–IM will return to hostilities.

The group is dominated by the Tangkhul tribe of Manipur, whose fragile control over its members was demonstrated on 25 and 28 October when 39 NSCN–IM members defected to the WC.[28] Were WC groups to remain committed to the peace process, the NSCN–IM would face significant contestation over its support bases in Arunachal Pradesh, Assam and Nagaland. Any perceived confinement to Manipur would undermine the group's claim to leadership over the Naga movement and would benefit the Indian state attempting to contain the situation.

Continued Citizenship (Amendment) Act unrest likely

The passage of the Citizenship (Amendment) Act in December 2019 led to the eruption of large-scale civil unrest. Although the bulk of this took place in Assam, civil-society organisations in Manipur and Nagaland also took part in agitations in solidarity with those not exempted from the bill.[29]

The protests of late 2018 and early 2019 highlighted the potentially dangerous implications of the bill in terms of insurgent-group strength in the state. Although considerably weakened, the ULFA–I reportedly enjoyed a 'fresh lease of life' as a result of protests against the bill in 2018.[30] Indeed, on 11 December the group warned Assam police that any violence towards protesters in the state would be met with action.[31] With the bill's passage and the dramatic upswing in civil unrest in the state since December, the ULFA–I is likely to thrive in a political climate featuring high levels of emotionally charged hostility towards New Delhi and Guwahati. With this in mind, close attention should be paid to ULFA–I recruitment, extortion patterns and attempted attacks in 2019.

Notes

[1] See Paul Staniland, 'Armed Politics and the Study of Intrastate Conflict', *Journal of Peace Research*, vol. 54, no. 4, June 2017, pp. 459–67.

[2] Samrat Sinha, 'The Strategic Use of Peace: Non-State Armed Groups and Subnational Peacebuilding Mechanisms in Northeastern India', *Democracy and Security*, vol. 13, no. 4, 2017, pp. 273–303.

[3] '10,000 paramilitary troops deployed in Assam before NRC release withdrawn', *Economic Times*, 14 September 2019.

[4] 'After Decades, Army to Be Withdrawn from Several Districts of Assam', *Sentinel Assam*, 14 October 2019.

[5] Lawrence E. Cline, 'The Insurgency Environment in Northeast India', *Small Wars and Insurgencies*, vol. 17, no. 2, 2006, pp. 126–147 (p. 127).

[6] Gurudas Das, 'India's North-East soft underbelly: Strategic vulnerability and security', *Strategic Analysis*, vol. 26, no. 4, 2002, pp. 537–49; E.N. Rammohan, 'The Weapons Trail in India's Northeast', *United Services Institution of India Journal*, vol. 141, no. 587, 2012.

[7] Samudra Gupta Kashyap, 'Chinese agencies helping North East militants in Myanmar', *Indian Express*, 10 January 2017.

[8] Vivek Chadha, *Low Intensity Conflicts in India: An Analysis* (New Delhi: SAGE, 2005), pp. 426–7.

[9] Nani Gopal Mahanta, 'Conflict Management Vis-à-Vis Conflict Transformation: Some Reflections from Northeast India', in Wasbir Hussain (ed.), *Peace Tools and Conflict Nuances in India's Northeast* (Guwahati: Wordweaves, 2010), pp. 158–74.

[10] Munish Chandra Pandey, 'Assam CAA Protest: 4 dead in police firing, 175 arrested, more than 1400 detained', *India Today*, 16 December 2019.

[11] 'Section 144 Imposed', *Sangai Express*, 22 December 2019.

[12] 'Our demand is greater Nagaland with own flag & constitution: NSCN(I-M) leader', *Business Standard*, 21 March 2019.

[13] 'NSCN (IM) gives push for final pact', E-Pao!, 20 June 2019.

[14] 'RN Ravi Has Turned "Bossy": NSCN (IM)', *Nagaland Page*, 4 August 2019.

[15] R. Dutta Choudhury, 'Centre Sets Oct 31 Deadline to Conclude Naga Talks', *Assam Tribune*, 18 October 2019.

[16] 'No separate flag, Constitution for Nagas: talks can't be held under shadow of guns: Centre', *India Today*, 20 October 2019.

[17] 'GoI-NSCN (IM): No breakthrough in stalemate over flag & constitution', *Morung Express*, 14 October 2019.

[18] 'Naga Talks: NSCN-IM leader Hukavi Yepthomi quits to join NNPG', East Mojo, 25 October 2019; 'Split in NSCN-IM? After Hukavi, 22 eastern Nagaland leaders quit', East Mojo, 29 October 2019.

[19] M.A. Athul, 'Naga Talks: A Rising Desperation', *South Asia Intelligence Review*, vol. 18, no. 7, 12 August 2019.

[20] See Staniland, 'Armed Politics and the Study of Intrastate Conflict'.

[21] Ratnadip Choudhury, 'Nagaland Cancels Cops, Bureaucrats' Leaves Fearing Naga Process Breakdown', NDTV, 22 October 2019; 'Naga talks: IRBn unit heads told to keep 2-month stock of rations', East Mojo, 24 October 2019.

[22] Bhadra Gogoi, 'NSCN-IM mobilises cadres at strategic locations', *People's Chronicle*, 25 October 2019.

[23] Prabin Kalita, 'NSCN-IM agrees to sign peace deal; no clarity if demands met', *Times of India*, 31 October 2019.

[24] 'Final pact at hand: NSCN (IM)', *Sangai Express*, 18 December 2019.

[25] 'Another NPG camp shuts down in Jalukie', *Northeast Today*, 9 November 2019.

[26] Staniland, 'Armed Politics and the Study of Intrastate Conflict', p. 462.
[27] Sadiq Naqvi, 'Eight ULFA(I) militants surrender in Assam', *Hindustan Times*, 27 October 2019.
[28] 'Senior NSCN (I-M) leader, 16 others join GPRN/NSCN', E-Pao!, 25 October 2019; Rahul Tripathi and Bikash Singh, 'Govt firm on October 31 deadline; 22 NSCN–IM rebels join pro-talk group', *Economic Times*, 30 October 2019.
[29] 'Naga Students' Federation calls for 6-hour strike to protest against CAA', OrissaPOST, 14 December 2019; 'Anti-CAA protests in Manipur', *Business Standard India*, 20 December 2019.
[30] 'India (Northeast)', in *Armed Conflict Survey 2019* (Abingdon: Routledge for the IISS, 2019), p. 248.
[31] Biju Kumar Deka, 'ULFA-I Chief Paresh Baruah Warns Assam Police against Assaulting Anti-Citizenship Bill Protesters', News 18, 11 December 2019.

INDIA–PAKISTAN (KASHMIR)

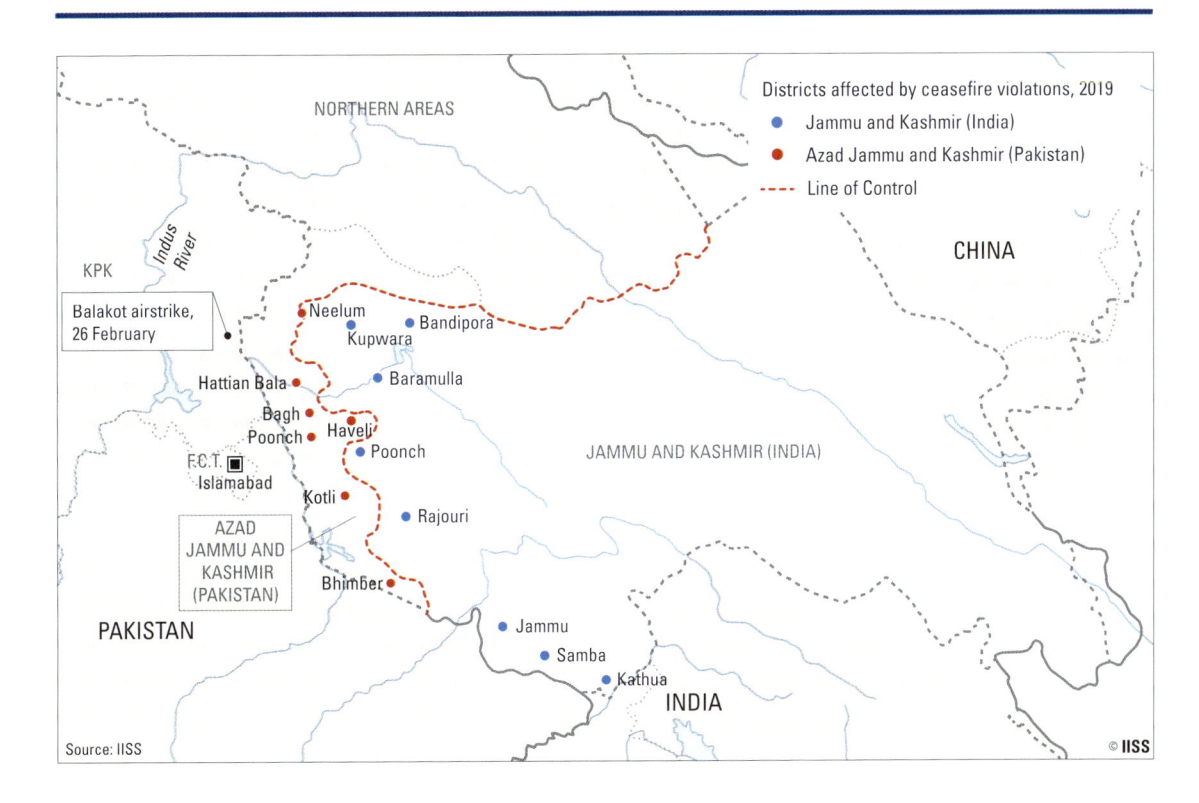

Overview

The conflict in 2019

The conflict in Jammu and Kashmir (India) continued to escalate in 2019, with violence breaking out between India and Pakistan after a suicide attack on 14 February on a Central Reserve Police Force (CRPF) convoy in Pulwama district that killed 40 troops. Airstrikes across and violence along the Line of Control (LoC) ensued and both nuclear-armed countries mobilised their armed forces to the front lines, raising concerns worldwide. The international community attempted to defuse the situation – China, the European Union, Russia, Saudi Arabia and the United States urged both sides to exercise restraint and offered diplomatic assistance to de-escalate the situation.

On 5 August, the Indian government unilaterally abrogated Article 370 of the Indian Constitution, thereby revoking the semi-autonomous status of the Indian state of Jammu and Kashmir. The revocation followed a previously imposed communication blockade, which also contributed to a serious deterioration of the security and humanitarian situation in the region. Ceasefire violations along the LoC spiked in 2019, with over 3,000 violations reported by the end of December.[1] While the number of fatalities in 2019 decreased compared to 2018, at least 280 people were killed.[2] By the end of 2019, Indian security forces had reportedly arrested 102 rebels, though approximately 250 (most of them local youth) were still active.[3]

Key statistics

Type	International
Start date	August 1947
IDPs total	No data
Refugees total	No data
People in need	No data

The conflict to 2019

The Kashmir dispute began after India and Pakistan became independent in 1947 and fought a war over the princely state of Jammu and Kashmir. Ultimately, a United Nations-brokered ceasefire in 1949 divided the formerly independent kingdom into India-administered and Pakistan-administered regions.[4]

Article 370 of the Indian Constitution limited the powers of the Indian parliament over the state of Jammu and Kashmir and exempted the state from the full applicability of the constitution. Jammu and Kashmir received a separate constitution and flag, and its chief executive was called the prime minister. In 1954, Article 35A to the Indian Constitution was introduced, which empowered the state legislature to define the state's permanent residents, who were given special rights and privileges. To safeguard the unique culture and identity of the state, non-permanent residents were barred from acquiring land in the state.

The political situation changed drastically after a popular anti-India armed uprising started in the late 1980s. India responded with violent security crackdowns that resulted in severe human-rights violations and pushed even more Kashmiris toward the guerrilla movement spearheaded by the pro-independence Jammu and Kashmir Liberation Front (JKLF). By the early 1990s, the JKLF had suffered causalities at the hands of both Indian security forces and rival insurgent groups. As a result, the pro-Pakistan groups Hizbul Mujahideen (HM) and Lashkar-e-Taiba (LeT) came to dominate the Kashmir insurgency.

After 9/11, the Kashmiri insurgent movement weakened as Pakistan began to withdraw its support gradually, and India and Pakistan started the Composite Dialogue Process in 2004. Annual fatalities decreased from over 3,000 in 2002 to approximately 450 in 2008,[5] while Kashmiris increasingly turned to non-violent demonstrations. Anti-India uprisings in 2008 and 2010 catalysed a 'new-age militancy' that emerged largely in response to India's violent crackdown on peaceful protests. Social media helped to further catapult this new-age militancy into the public eye.

Indian security forces have killed more than 1,000 rebels since 2010,[6] but local recruitment into the armed groups and infiltration from across the LoC has not ceased. Since 2016, the situation in Kashmir has been tense, with frequent gunfights and protests.

Key Conflict Parties

Hizbul Mujahideen (HM)

Strength
100–200 members active in the Kashmir Valley and over 1,000 members based in Azad Jammu and Kashmir (Pakistan). Additional overground workers – a term used by Indian security forces for people supporting insurgents and insurgent sympathisers – provide logistical support and information.

Areas of operation
Concentrated in Anantnag, Pulwama, Shopian and Kulgam districts, with marginal presence in northern Kashmir districts.

Leadership
Headed by Mohammad Yusuf Shah (alias Syed Salahuddin). Riyaz Naikoo is the chief commander in the Kashmir Valley, under whom area commanders for each district operate.

Structure
Headquarters in Muzaffarabad, Azad Jammu and Kashmir (Pakistan). Cadres comprise mostly local Kashmiris who receive rudimentary arms training from senior members. Divisional commanders work under a semi-autonomous structure, but also receive instructions from across the LoC via satellite communication.

History
Indigenous armed group with a pro-Pakistan ideology, founded in September 1989 by former JKLF member and Jamaat-e-Islami affiliate, Mohammad Ahsan Dar. Many JKLF members joined HM after 1994, when the JKLF suffered heavy losses and voluntarily quit the armed conflict to pursue non-violent means. Recruitment of local Kashmiri youth into HM also surged after the death of its commander Burhan Muzaffar Wani in July 2016.

Objectives
Dislodge Indian rule in Kashmir and merge the region with Pakistan. The group has supported negotiated settlement through dialogue.

Opponents
Indian government.

Affiliates/allies
LeT and JeM.

Resources/capabilities
Charities, mosque-based donations across Pakistan and the Pakistani military establishment.

Lashkar-e-Taiba (LeT)

Strength
Largest armed group in Kashmir in 2018, with around 141 members.

Areas of operation
Presence across the Kashmir Valley, but mostly active in the northern districts of Baramulla, Bandipora and Kupwara.

Leadership
Led by Hafiz Muhammad Saeed. Overall command is in the hands of a divisional commander, who is often a non-Kashmiri.

Structure
Headquarters in Muridke, Punjab province, Pakistan. Though banned by the Pakistani government in 2002, LeT is believed to maintain connections to Pakistani intelligence agencies. Valley-based cadres are mostly Pakistani nationals working under district commanders and trained in camps.

History
Created in the late 1980s by Pakistan-based cleric Hafiz Muhammad Saeed, who also heads the missionary organisation Jamaat-ud-Dawa (JuD). Since LeT entered Kashmir in the early 1990s, it has carried out several deadly attacks against Indian armed forces and political workers. Despite losing its commanders in quick succession over the past three years, the group has survived the Indian army's *Operation All Out* (launched in 2017) and still recruits local youth, though a shortage of arms and ammunition has limited its capacity to carry out major attacks.

Objectives
Merge Kashmir with Pakistan.

Opponents
Indian government.

Affiliates/allies
Jamaat-ud-Dawa.

Resources/capabilities
Fundraising through charities in Pakistan (e.g. Jamaat-ud-Dawa and Falah-e-Insaniyat), which receive government and public contributions, and social networks in Pakistan and Afghanistan.

Jaysh-e-Mohammad (JeM)

Strength
Strength unknown but believed to have fewer members than HM and LeT.

Areas of operation
Most attacks carried out in southern Kashmir. Indian security forces killed eight high-ranking JeM commanders between September 2017 and October 2018.

Leadership
Pakistani Hafiz Umar is the current chief operational commander.

Structure
Headquartered in Bahawalpur, Punjab province, Pakistan. JeM is Pakistan-based and its members are mostly Pakistanis. Divisional commanders work under the chief operational commander based in Kashmir.

History
Founded by Pakistani Masood Azhar in 2000. JeM entered Kashmir in the early 2000s and introduced suicide attacks. The Pakistani government banned the group in 2002. After a period of dormancy, JeM re-emerged in 2017 with an attack on a paramilitary camp in Pulwama. JeM is the most powerful insurgent group in Kashmir, with highly trained cadres and better resources than other insurgent groups. In 2018, more than 60 youths joined JeM, including Adil Ahmad Dar, who was responsible for the February 2019 suicide attack in Pulwama district.

Objectives
Merge Kashmir with Pakistan.

Opponents
Indian government.

Affiliates/allies
HM and LeT. Believed to have ties to the Afghan Taliban.

Resources/capabilities
Unknown.

Ansar Ghazwat-ul-Hind (AGH)

Strength
Believed to have been eliminated by October 2019. Fewer than ten members.

Areas of operation
Pulwama district.

Leadership
Commander Hameed Lelhari, who succeeded founder Zakir Rashid Bhat in May 2019, was killed in October 2019.

Structure
Composite organisation without defined structure.

History
In July 2017, Zakir Rashid Bhat (aka Zakir Musa) created AGH after growing ideological differences with his former organisation HM, which Musa accused of working towards the secular ideas of a nation-state and democracy. Known for his controversial anti-Pakistan rhetoric. Lack of resources made AGH a marginal group.

Ansar Ghazwat-ul-Hind (AGH)

Objectives
Independent Islamic state in Kashmir.

Opponents
Indian and Pakistani governments, HM and LeT.

Affiliates/allies
Al-Qaeda.

Resources/capabilities
Unknown.

Indian state forces

Strength
A counter-insurgency force in Kashmir of approximately 500,000 Indian security personnel – including over 200,000 army soldiers and approximately 58,000 infantry troops within the Rashtriya Rifles (RR), the special counter-insurgency unit – was augmented with circa 120,000 additional paramilitary personnel over the course of 2019.[7] Also includes the Central Reserve Police Force (CRPF), Border Security Force (BSF), Indo-Tibetan Border Police, Jammu and Kashmir Police (JKP), Special Police Officers and various intelligence wings.

Areas of operation
All districts of Jammu and Kashmir (India) and along the LoC.

Leadership
Indian troops in Kashmir are under the Northern Command based in Udhampur (Jammu and Kashmir union territory) and led by Lt-Gen. Ranbir Singh. The CRPF, the main paramilitary force, is under the Ministry of Home Affairs. A special director general has overall command of the CRPF in Jammu and Kashmir (India), while inspectors general command the respective sectors.

Structure
The Northern Command is composed of seven divisions, three corps and one brigade. The RR has 65 battalions, each comprising six infantry companies, and five headquarters. The CRPF's Jammu and Kashmir Zone Srinagar Sector covers Budgam, Ganderbal and Srinagar districts, with a strength of nearly 22,000 personnel. The CRPF's Kashmir Operations Sector covers Anantnag, Awantipora and Baramulla districts while the Jammu Sector covers the Jammu region.

History
After the UN-brokered ceasefire came into effect in 1949, both India and Pakistan maintained heavy troop presence along the LoC. After an anti-India armed rebellion broke out in the late 1980s, India sent thousands of troops to crush the popular uprising. Initially, paramilitary and regular army troops fought the Pakistan-backed insurgents, but in 1994 the RR was introduced, which coordinates with other security agencies, including the Special Operations Group (SOG), a counter-insurgency unit of the JKP.

Objectives
India maintains firm control over Jammu and Kashmir (India) with a superior military presence, both to guard the LoC and to defeat the armed opposition. India sees Pakistan as the main actor controlling the armed groups within the state, but it also faces hostility from local Kashmiris, most of whom seek either autonomy, independence or a merger with Pakistan.

Opponents
Armed groups (HM, LeT, JeM, AGH) and Pakistani military.

Affiliates/allies
Village Defence Committees, volunteer state-armed groups concentrated in hilly and border areas with sizeable Hindu populations (Doda, Kathua, Kishtwar, Poonch, Rajouri, Ramba and Reasi districts).

Resources/capabilities
Ministry of Defence and Ministry of Home Affairs budgetary funds, web-based public donations through portals like 'Bharat Ke Veer' (India's Bravehearts), and government contracts under *Operation Sadhbhavna*.

United Nations Military Observer Group in India and Pakistan (UNMOGIP)

Strength
44 observers from Croatia, the Philippines, South Korea, Sweden, Thailand, Switzerland, Uruguay, Chile, Italy and Romania (in descending order of troop numbers). 72 civilian staff, including Pakistanis, Indians and international members.

Areas of operation
UN field stations: six based in Azad Jammu and Kashmir (Pakistan) and four based in Jammu and Kashmir (India). The Sialkot field station in Pakistan monitors the working boundary, which is the international border between Punjab province, Pakistan and the disputed territory of Jammu and Kashmir.

Leadership
Maj.-Gen. Per Lodin from Sweden was appointed Chief Military Observer and Head of Mission on 3 July 2016. Deputy Chief Military Observer Col Davorko Jokic from Croatia, Chief of Mission Support Nester Odaga-Jalomayo from Uganda and Chief Security Officer Syed Capua from Bangladesh.

Structure
UNMOGIP is mandated by UNSC Resolution 91. Headquarters alternates between Islamabad in November–April and Srinagar in May–October.

History
In January 1948, the UN Commission for India and Pakistan (UNCIP) was created under UNSC Resolution 39. In January 1949, the first team of unarmed military observers arrived to supervise the ceasefire between India and Pakistan. Under UNSC Resolution 91 of March 1951, UNCIP was replaced by UNMOGIP. After UNSC Resolution 307 (1971), India and Pakistan made minor adjustments to the ceasefire line and in 1972 established the LoC to be supervised by UN military observers. To date, the mission has suffered 11 fatalities including two international civilians, three locals, five military personnel and one military observer.

United Nations Military Observer Group in India and Pakistan (UNMOGIP)

Objectives
Neutral observer. It monitors, investigates and reports ceasefire violations along the LoC and working boundary between India and Pakistan. It submits its findings to both parties and the UN Secretary-General.

Opponents
Not applicable.

Affiliates/allies
UN departments of Peace Operations and Operational Support.

Resources/capabilities
UN approved budget: US$19,754,400 for January 2018–December 2019.

Drivers

'New-age militancy'
The failed India–Pakistan Composite Dialogue Process (2004–08) and the violent suppression of the post-2008 mass protests have driven the current wave of armed insurgency in Kashmir. Emerging in 2013 mainly from southern Kashmir, the youth-led armed movement gained momentum and had turned into a full-blown insurgency by 2015. This was aided by a surging recruitment of local young men, many of whom had experienced police harassment for participating in anti-India street protests. Some recruits were influenced by insurgents hailing from their neighbourhoods, often strongholds of Jamaat-e-Islami. Funerals of killed rebels also became sites of recruitment, such as that of popular HM commander Burhan Muzaffar Wani in 2016.

BJP's hardline policies
The Bharatiya Janata Party (BJP) holds the Indian National Congress (commonly known as the Congress Party), which ruled India for 54 years between 1952 and 2014 (with interruptions), responsible for creating the Kashmir crisis. The BJP argues that by taking the issue to the UN, agreeing to the 1949 ceasefire and ceding the other half of Jammu and Kashmir to Pakistan, and giving autonomy to the state under Article 370, the Congress Party also nurtured the separatist sentiments in the region. However, when the August 2019 lockdown of Kashmir brought international attention to the issue and calls to resolve the conflict grew, the Congress Party criticised the BJP for internationalising the conflict. BJP leaders issued statements saying that Kashmir was an internal matter. Following the revocation of Article 370, many senior officials of the Narendra Modi administration, including Minister of External Affairs S. Jaishankar and Minister of State Jitendra Singh, said that India will seize Azad Jammu and Kashmir (Pakistan). Indian army chief Gen. Bipin Rawat also ratcheted up this rhetoric on 25 October 2019 during the KM Cariappa Memorial Lecture in New Delhi.[8] These recurrent statements caused concern in Pakistan and Pakistani Prime Minister Imran Khan described them as 'existential threats'. Khan referred several times to the BJP's policies, including the abrogation of Article 370, as part of the Hindutva (or Hindu nationalist) ideology, which believes in *Akhand Bharat* (a unified India that includes much of South Asia).

Kashmiris are concerned about losing their land and identity to a possible Indian settler colonial project, which drives the current unified resistance. The demotion of the Indian state of Jammu and Kashmir has now given New Delhi firm control through a centrally appointed lieutenant governor who is heading the Jammu and Kashmir union territory administration. With the removal of Article 35A, which debarred 'non-permanent' residents from acquiring immovable properties, the Indian government might be able to change the demographics of the region in the long term by encouraging non-Kashmiri businesses and investors to acquire land and exploit local resources.

Political Developments

Direct presidential rule and detentions
Following the collapse of coalition government between the People's Democratic Party (PDP) and the BJP in June 2018 in Jammu and Kashmir (India), the pro-BJP governor Satya Pal Malik, who was appointed by President Ram Nath Kovind,

dissolved the state assembly and assumed control of Jammu and Kashmir under the so-called governor's rule. In December 2018, under Article 356 of the Indian Constitution, the governor's rule was replaced by the president's rule, which was extended for another six months in June 2019. During the direct central rule, the Modi government used the National Investigation Agency (NIA) to summon prominent Kashmiri dissidents (both unionists and separatists) and local media owners to New Delhi in relation to 'terror funding'. Over 30 people were summoned in July 2019 alone, including close relatives of the separatist leader Syed Ali Shah Geelani. In an unprecedented crackdown around the 5 August revocation of the Indian state of Jammu and Kashmir's semi-autonomous status, India suspended civil liberties, imposed a communication blockade and detained approximately 3,500 people, including former chief ministers, legislators and political activists, including minors.[9]

Abrogation of Article 370

Article 370 of the 1950 Indian Constitution gave Jammu and Kashmir a certain level of autonomy within India. The ruling Hindu-nationalist BJP had long been opposed to the semi-autonomous status of the state, which has a Muslim-majority population. During the 2019 Indian general elections, which the BJP won with an absolute majority, the party proposed to remove the special status from the constitution. The Modi government revoked Article 370 on 5 August 2019, split the Indian state of Jammu and Kashmir into two federally administered union territories (Jammu and Kashmir, and Ladakh) and appointed two lieutenant governors to head the territories.

The Indian government justified the move by arguing that it would expedite the development of the region and end the separatist movement. The decision triggered protests in pockets of Kashmir, particularly in Srinagar's suburban Anchar neighbourhood, where more than 200 protesters were injured by pellet bullets during 9–16 August 2019. Protests and widespread civil disobedience ensued and continued for months.[10]

Military Developments

Troop surge

The presence of Indian security personnel in Jammu and Kashmir (India) has increased significantly, from 35,000 soldiers in 1989 to approximately 600,000 in 2019. In the run-up to the revocation of the state's semi-autonomous status, New Delhi sent 46,000 troops to the state within ten days. This troop surge excluded the 120,000 paramilitary forces already in the region, which included 55,000 troops sent for the April–May elections and the annual Hindu pilgrimage of Amarnath Yatra. *Operation All Out* – launched by the Indian armed forces in July 2017 to quell the new-age militancy – saw a momentary halt after the communication lockdown around 5 August hampered intelligence-gathering and electronic surveillance.

Key Events in 2019

Political events

- **23 February**: Police detain 150 political activists, mostly from Jamaat-e-Islami. Five days later, the central government bans Jamaat-e-Islami for five years.
- **22 March**: India bans the Jammu and Kashmir Liberation Front (JKLF).
- **3 April**: The Jammu and Kashmir (India) government imposes a ban on civilian traffic along the Srinagar–Jammu highway for two days a week in response to the suicide attack in Pulwama district.

Military/Violent events

- **14 February**: A militant suicide attack in Pulwama district kills 40 CRPF soldiers.
- **18 February**: Five Indian troops, three alleged JeM militants and a civilian are killed in a gunfight in Pulwama district.
- **26 February–1 March**: India reportedly launches an airstrike on Balakot, Pakistan. Pakistan downs an Indian MiG-21 *Bison* and captures its pilot (later released).
- **March**: Cross-LoC shelling and tensions increase. India and Pakistan mobilise troops to the front line.

South Asian arms race

The strained relationship between India and Pakistan and their failure to resume dialogue means that both states continue to amass weapons. Recent hostilities have driven both countries to sign new defence deals with a range of arms exporters, including Russia and Israel. In August 2019, Pakistan tested a short-range (290 kilometres) *Ghaznavi* ballistic missile, which many saw as part of its efforts to generate international attention around the India–Pakistan conflict over Kashmir. In November 2019, India scheduled back-to-back launches of four nuclear-capable missiles, including an intermediate-range (3,500 km) indigenous K-4 ballistic missile, which is capable of targeting all areas of Pakistan. In August, India's Defence Minister Rajnath Singh had hinted at the revision of the 'no-first-use' nuclear policy that provides for nuclear retaliation only in case of a nuclear attack by an adversary. These tests occurred against the backdrop of heightened tensions between India and Pakistan, and signalled to Pakistan India's preparedness for escalatory retaliation if Pakistan used its short-range nuclear-headed *Nasr* missiles during a conventional war. Pakistan developed the *Nasr* missile as a deterrent to India's 'Cold Start' military doctrine that envisages multiple Indian armed divisions rapidly capturing Pakistani territories and leveraging these at the negotiating table. India's new missile tests and development of nuclear-powered submarines put pressure on Pakistan to match India's arms build-up, thus potentially risking a new arms race that might further strain Pakistan's already sluggish economy.

Impact

Human rights and international attention

Human-rights abuses continued across the region in 2019, in particular following the security crackdown in August. Indian security forces were accused of torturing and intimidating citizens.[11] The police in Jammu and Kashmir (India) also admitted to detaining at least 144 minors,[12] while the Indian government put 450 Kashmiris on a 'no-fly list', barring them from leaving India.[13] In February, Kashmiri students living in other parts of India reportedly faced retributive assaults after the Pulwama suicide attack.[14]

Although India insists that Kashmir is an internal issue, the recent crisis has attracted increased international attention. On 8 July, the Office of the UN High Commissioner for Human Rights issued a report requesting that a commission of inquiry conduct a 'comprehensive, independent, international investigation' into allegations of human-rights violations in the region since July 2016.[15]

The Kashmiri diaspora also mobilised, especially in the US, where constituents called on their local representatives in Congress. The House Committee on Foreign Affairs held a congressional hearing on 22 October during which many voiced concerns at the situation in Jammu and Kashmir (India) and asked the Indian government to ease restrictions and allow international observers into the region.

---

11 April–19 May
Lok Sabha election takes place. Nearly 80% of voters in the Kashmir Valley boycott the ballot.

29 June
The Jammu and Kashmir (India) government issues restrictions for civilian traffic during the 46-day annual Hindu pilgrimage of Amarnath Yatra.

3 July
The president's rule in Jammu and Kashmir (India) stays in place for six additional months.

5 August
The Modi government revokes the semi-autonomous status of the Indian state of Jammu and Kashmir. Pakistan responds by downgrading diplomatic relations and suspending bilateral trade.

31 October
Jammu and Kashmir, and Ladakh officially become 'union territories' to be ruled directly by New Delhi.

23 May
The Indian army kills AGH leader Zakir Musa in Pulwama district.

12 June
Militants kill five CRPF members in Anantnag district. One militant is also killed.

23 October
Indian security forces kill Musa's successor, Hameed Lelhari. Police declare AGH eliminated.

24 December
The home ministry withdraws 72 paramilitary companies from the new Jammu and Kashmir union territory.

At the request of China, the UN Security Council (UNSC) convened a 90-minute closed-door meeting on the Kashmir crisis on 16 August. This was the first time in 50 years that the UNSC had listed Kashmir on its agenda. Although the UNSC issued no formal press statement, the meeting on Kashmir itself and critical statements made by politicians outside of India and international organisations undermined India's position that Kashmir was an internal matter.

Civilian and non-local casualties
Firing incidents across the 740-km LoC surged after the 14 February suicide attack in Pulwama district. In late July, cross-LoC shelling destroyed houses, killed civilians and displaced dozens of people. The Indian and Pakistani armies exchanged fire again after India revoked Jammu and Kashmir's special status. On the Pakistani side, Indian firing reportedly killed 59 people and wounded 281 others in 2019.[16] In September, India's Ministry of External Affairs said that in the cases of 2,050 ceasefire violations by Pakistan, 21 Indians were killed.[17] Later in October, heavy artillery exchanges killed at least ten people on both sides of the LoC.

In a series of attacks, unidentified gunmen targeted non-locals after India revoked Article 370. Non-Kashmiri labourers and traders had not been targeted prior to 5 August and the motive remains unclear. While the Indian government had issued a 'security advisory' on 2 August and asked its citizens to leave Kashmir 'as soon as possible', many non-locals had returned after restrictions had been partially lifted within the region.

Socio-economic consequences
According to the December 2019 report of the Kashmir Chamber of Commerce and Industry, since the lockdown on 5 August, the Kashmir Valley suffered an economic loss of up to NR178 billion (US$2.3bn).[18] The service sector was hit particularly hard and 500,000 jobs were lost during the period. Conflict-related mental-health issues, already prevalent in the region, were exacerbated by the prolonged lockdown in 2019. Doctors reported a significant increase in the number of patients with psychological concerns visiting their clinics.[19]

International diplomacy
The Kashmir crisis gives China, Russia, the US and the UK leverage to demand concessions from India, which has to tread cautiously for them to endorse its Kashmir policy. On 24 September 2019, US President Donald Trump offered to mediate the Kashmir crisis. While the offer was welcomed by Pakistan, it was met with rejection from India. India is an ally for the US in countering China but Pakistan is still an important partner, especially given its role in facilitating the Afghan peace process between the Taliban and the US. Trump's 'offer' allows the Khan government to assuage domestic audiences and counter the growing criticism of the opposition parties on its Kashmir policy.

Pakistan's ties with Russia have improved in recent years. The two countries held joint military exercises in 2016, signed a military–technical cooperation agreement in 2017 and a naval cooperation agreement in 2018. To balance against the possible China–Pakistan–Russia alliance, in September 2019, India signed 25 agreements with Russia and, in November 2019, made advance payments for five Russian S-400 air-defence systems (worth around US$5bn) despite the threat of US sanctions.

Trends

No India–Pakistan rapprochement in sight
The continuing escalation of the Kashmir conflict makes rapprochement between India and Pakistan unlikely. New Delhi's aggressive Kashmir policy undercuts Khan's overtures of peace, which have been conveyed through multiple offers of dialogue since 2018.[20] While Pakistan's efforts to enlist international diplomatic support have had some success, the general international opinion seems to have gradually tilted against India due to the Modi government's populist majoritarianism.

However, India's economic clout compensates for its diplomatic shortcomings. Several world powers (including from the Organisation of Islamic Cooperation) refrained from issuing strong statements and tempered their responses by reiterating that Kashmir is a bilateral issue between India and Pakistan. The United Arab Emirates' ambassador to

India, for example, said that the revocation of Article 370 was India's internal matter as stipulated by the Indian Constitution. It is doubtful that there will be any real external pressure in the near future, even as India is unlikely to restore Kashmir's autonomy or resume dialogue with Pakistan.

Risk of military crisis

The Modi government has publicly pledged that it would strike Pakistan again in the event of any aggression similar to the February 2019 Pulwama suicide attack. In the absence of a dialogue process, Pakistan (partly due to pressure from Kashmiris) will continue to allow armed groups to operate in Pakistani territory, which increases the likelihood of large-scale attacks on the Indian military. The risk of an Indian military incursion into Azad Jammu and Kashmir (Pakistan) remains possible, as India has not recalled its troops from the forward positions to which it mobilised them in February 2019. In December, India's army chief also suggested that the situation along the LoC could 'escalate any time'. Any Indian attempt to infiltrate Pakistan, however, would be thwarted by Pakistan's likely coalition with China, whose strategic interests in the region deepened with the China–Pakistan Economic Corridor passing through Azad Jammu and Kashmir (Pakistan).

United opposition in Kashmir

The revocation of Article 370 and the demotion of the Indian state of Jammu and Kashmir to two federally administered territories have left pro-India parties in Kashmir little choice but to align with the pro-independence groups. Their political survival will depend on whether they join the new Legislative Assembly (the decisions of which can be vetoed by New Delhi-appointed Lieutenant Governor of Jammu and Kashmir (India) and close Modi aide Girish Chandra Murmu) and strive for the restoration of Kashmir's statehood or if they are supplanted by the new political elite that the BJP is promoting in Kashmir to create a political bloc that is more amenable to its agenda.

Most Kashmiris fear that the BJP is changing the demography of the Muslim-majority Kashmir region through settlements. This continues to drive civil disobedience supported by parties across the ideological spectrum. The Indian government may try to normalise the political situation in Kashmir by offering special provisions that protect the region's economic and cultural interests, as changes in the domicile laws and land-ownership rights is what make people, including Hindus and Buddhists, in Jammu and Kashmir (India) the most apprehensive.

While Modi's Kashmir policy received wide support within India, it will ultimately be assessed on its ability to reduce the level of violence in the region. As Kashmir is now directly ruled by New Delhi, increased violence and instability within the region will ultimately be imputed to Modi and Minister of Home Affairs Amit Shah, thus giving the oppositional parties in India an opportunity to scrutinise the government. Now regrouped after a halt of *Operation All Out* after 5 August, and reinforced by newer recruits both from inside Kashmir and across the LoC, insurgent groups will feel emboldened and will likely attempt a wide range of attacks, including improvised explosive devices and assassinations on Indian settlers, pro-India campaigners and politicians.

Notes

[1] Ministry of Foreign Affairs Government of Pakistan, 'Text of Foreign Minister's letter to President of Security Council and UN Secretary General', 18 December 2019; '2019 recorded highest ever ceasefire violations by Pakistan in Jammu and Kashmir in last 16 years', *Economic Times India*, 5 January 2020.

[2] South Asia Terrorism Portal, 'Datasheet – Jammu & Kashmir'; Association of Parents of Disappeared Persons and Jammu Kashmir Coalition of Civil Society, 'Annual Review of Human Rights situation in Indian administered Jammu and Kashmir', 31 December 2019, p. 9.

[3] '160 terrorists killed and 102 arrested in J-K in 2019, decrease in number of local youths joining militancy: DGP', *India Today*, 31 December 2019.

[4] During the 1962 Indo-China war, China seized the northeastern area of Jammu and Kashmir, which is called Aksai Chin.

[5] South Asia Terrorism Portal, 'Datasheet – Jammu & Kashmir'.

[6] Ibid.

[7] Regular Indian deployment in Kashmir: author's own research, 2019. For 2019 troop build-up, see Zulfikar Majid, 'Troops deployed in Kashmir for Amarnath Yatra', *Deccan Herald*, 28

May 2019; 'Centre rushes 10,000 troops to Kashmir', *Economic Times*, 27 July 2019; Prabhash K. Dutta, 'Kashmir: Why Centre is sending additional 38,000 troops to J&K', *India Today*, 2 August 2019; Manjeet Singh Negi, '8,000 more troops deployed in Jammu and Kashmir after govt [sic] moves to revoke Article 370', *India Today*, 5 August 2019.

[8] 'Army chief Bipin Rawat hawkish on 370, PoK', *Telegraph India*, 26 October 2019.

[9] Peerzada Ashiq, 'Three months of spontaneous shutdown: 1,300 still under detention in Kashmir', *Hindu*, 5 November 2019. In the following months, 2,000 more people were arrested, taking the tally of detainees to over 6,000.

[10] Rahul Bedi, 'Kashmir in grip of civil disobedience over loss of autonomy', *Irish Times*, 12 September 2019.

[11] Niha Masih, Joanna Slater and Shams Irfan, 'The night the soldiers came: Allegations of abuse surface in Kashmir', *Washington Post*, 1 October 2019.

[12] Aneesha Mathur, '9-year-olds among 144 minors detained in Kashmir since Article 370 abrogation: Reports', *India Today*, 1 October 2019.

[13] Hakeem Irfan Rashid, '450 people on temporary No Fly List in Jammu & Kashmir after August 5', *Economic Times India*, 2 November 2019.

[14] Um Roommana, 'What the Pulwama Attack Means for Kashmiris', Diplomat, 26 February 2019.

[15] Office of the UN High Commissioner for Human Rights, 'Update of the Situation of Human Rights in Indian-Administered Kashmir and Pakistan-Administered Kashmir from May 2018 to April 2019', 8 July 2019.

[16] Tariq Naqash, 'Indian violations claimed 59 lives along LoC in 2019', Dawn, 1 January 2020.

[17] '21 Indians killed in 2,050 ceasefire violations by Pakistan this year: MEA', *Telegraph India*, 16 September 2019.

[18] 'Kashmir suffered losses worth up to Rs 18,000 crore due to Article 370 abrogation', *Indian Express*, 19 December 2019.

[19] Fahad Shah, '"People are panicked": Kashmir curfew takes toll on mental health', *Guardian*, 23 October 2019.

[20] Salman Masood and Maria Abi-Habib, 'Pakistan Leader Vents Frustration at India: "No Point in Talking to Them"', *New York Times*, 21 August 2019.

PAKISTAN

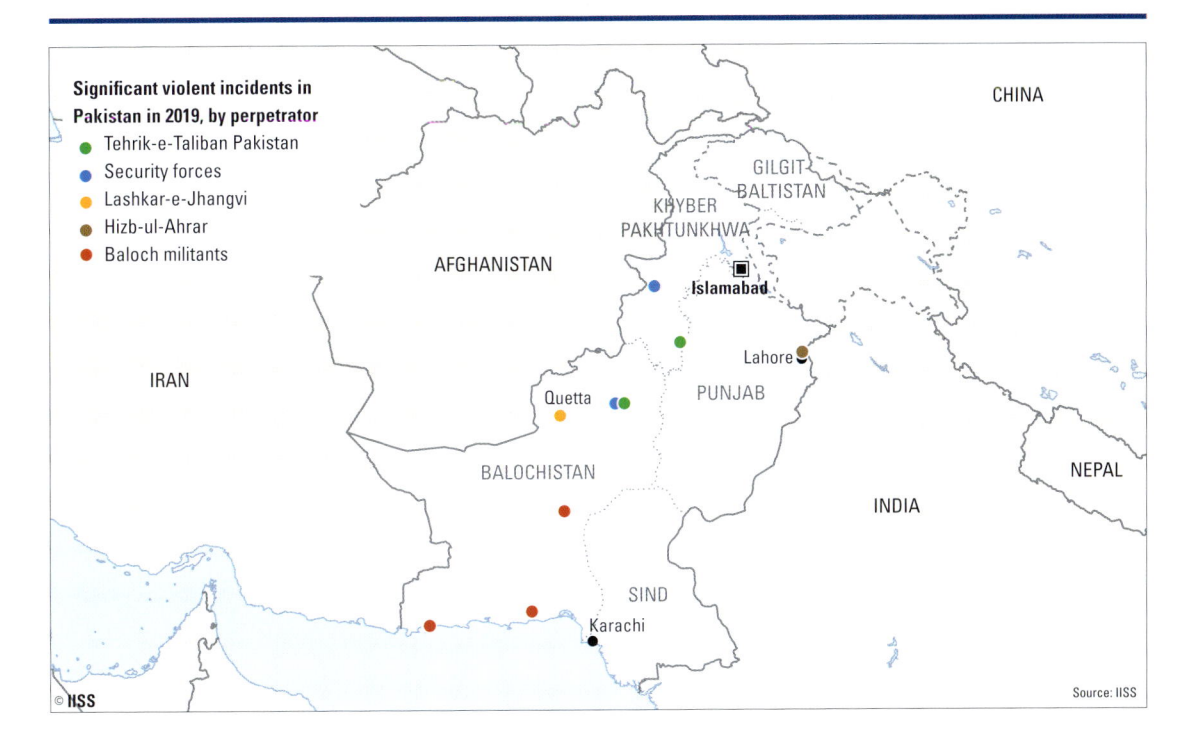

Significant violent incidents in Pakistan in 2019, by perpetrator
- Tehrik-e-Taliban Pakistan
- Security forces
- Lashkar-e-Jhangvi
- Hizb-ul-Ahrar
- Baloch militants

Source: IISS

Overview

The conflict in 2019

In 2019, Baloch insurgents continued attacks against the China–Pakistan Economic Corridor (CPEC). Ambushes, kidnappings and bombings targeted labourers, works sites and the Pearl Continental Hotel in Gwadar – a hotel in CPEC's flagship port city, which often hosts visiting Chinese. Measures by the Pakistani Armed Forces (PAF) and Civil Armed Forces (PCAF) to combat the insurgency are yet to yield results. By contrast, the jihadist and Pashtun insurgency, led by Tehrik-e-Taliban Pakistan (TTP), was at its lowest ebb since 2004, due in part to the success of the army's campaign against it. The TTP, under the relatively new leadership of Mufti Noor Wali Mehsud, also refocused its attacks on police and army targets, although civilians were frequently among the casualties of these attacks. 2019 was the first year since 2003 in which there were no United States or Pakistani airstrikes against militant groups. The total number of deaths across the country due to insurgency-related violence was markedly lower in 2019 than in 2018.

The incorporation of the former Federally Administered Tribal Areas (FATA) into Khyber-Pakhtunkhwa (KPK) continued to strain relations between Pashtun tribes and regional and national authorities. The Pashtun Tahaffuz Movement (PTM), a political movement, staged several protests against alleged abuses of Pashtuns' human, civil and political rights. A protest in Kharqamar, North Waziristan, in May met with a violent response by the Pakistani Army, which killed 13 civilians. Likewise, the Khasadar and Levies forces, tribal paramilitary forces in the former FATA, staged numerous demonstrations, strikes and sit-ins in

Key statistics

Type	Internal
Start date	June 2002
IDPs total	No data
Refugees total	No data
People in need (31 December 2019)	2,900,000

protest at the conditions of their amalgamation into the PCAF. Legislation for the amalgamation passed through the KPK Assembly in September and the merger took place over subsequent months, representing a significant step in the normalisation of the governance of the former FATA.

The conflict to 2019

Pakistan has struggled with ethnic and religious tensions since its foundation due to the perceived marginalisation of the Baloch, Pashtuns and Sindhis by the Punjabi majority. The Baloch have a long history of insurgency against state forces in pursuit of greater autonomy or the outright secession of Balochistan: they waged insurgencies in 1948, 1958, 1962 and 1973, and returned to violence in 2003, starting the ongoing insurgency. The Baloch insurgents have split on several occasions and some splinter groups have demobilised, but the Balochistan Liberation Army (BLA) has continued its attacks, increasingly against targets associated with CPEC. In 2016, under pressure from China, the Pakistani government raised a 15,000-strong Special Security Division to protect Chinese workers and businesses.

Meanwhile, armed groups originating in the Pashtun tribal areas of FATA and KPK have taken up arms against the Pakistani state, the Shia religious minority and Western targets. These tribal areas provided haven for Taliban and al-Qaeda militants ousted from Afghanistan following the US–United Kingdom invasion in 2001. Operations by US and Pakistani forces in the tribal areas against these groups stoked animosity and the creation of Pakistani Taliban factions, motivated by extreme Islamism and by resistance to outside interference in Pashtun tribal areas. These Pakistani Taliban groups came together as the TTP in 2007. Pakistani forces began a counter-insurgency campaign against the TTP in 2009 but the lack of coherent strategy brought the campaign little success. After the TTP attacked the Army Public School in Peshawar in December 2014, Pakistan drafted its first counterterrorism policy, the National Action Plan (NAP), and security forces launched concerted operations against the group: *Operation Zarb-e-Azb*, launched in 2014, and *Operation Radd-ul-Fasaad*, launched in 2017. Insurgent attacks decreased rapidly as a result between 2014 and 2018.

Key Conflict Parties

Pakistani Armed Forces (PAF)

Strength
The total number of active PAF personnel is 653,800, of which circa 60,000 are involved in *Operation Radd-ul-Fasaad* against terrorist groups and around 9,000 (nine infantry battalions) are assigned to the Special Security Division responsible for protecting CPEC projects. The creation of a further division to protect CPEC was announced in 2019.

Areas of operation
The PAF are deployed throughout Pakistan but the main areas of operation against insurgent groups are in KPK and Balochistan.

Leadership
The Chief of Army Staff, currently General Qamar Javed Bajwa, leads *Operation Radd-ul-Fasaad*, while a two-star army general, currently Maj.-Gen. Ahsan Gulrez, leads the Special Security Division.

Structure
Operation Radd-ul-Fasaad involves an array of PAF units supporting the police and PCAF in counter-terrorism operations. XI Corps is heavily involved due to the concentration of TTP forces in KPK.
The Special Security Division was formed as part of the Pakistani Army's X Corps and consists of nine army infantry battalions alongside 6,000 PCAF personnel. It is tasked to protect CPEC, particularly from attacks by the BLA. The Pakistani Navy deploys a number of vessels to Task Force-88, responsible for the seaward security of Chinese projects in Pakistan.

History
Operation Radd-ul-Fasaad was announced in 2017 and is the successor to *Operation Zarb-e-Azb* which ran from 2014 to 2017. It was launched in response to a resurgence in attacks by TTP splinter group Jamaat-ul-Ahrar.
The Special Security Division was formed in 2016 in response to pressure from China to step up protection of CPEC businesses and workers from terrorist attacks.

Pakistani Armed Forces

Objectives
The PAF's objective is to eliminate insurgent groups presenting a threat to the Pakistani state. It conducts raids and search operations against insurgent groups.

Opponents
TTP, Hizb-ul-Ahrar, BLA, IS–PP.

Affiliates/allies
PCAF, Pakistani Police.

Resources/capabilities
The PAF are well resourced with an array of weapons systems and equipment.

Pakistani Civil Armed Forces (PCAF)

Strength
Circa 175,000.[1] Of these, around 145,000 belong to divisions involved in security against insurgent groups in KPK and Balochistan.

Areas of operation
The PCAF are deployed throughout Pakistan but its main areas of operation against insurgent groups are in KPK and Balochistan provinces.

Leadership
The PCAF are funded by the Interior Ministry, although most divisions are commanded by officers seconded from the PAF.

Structure
The main divisions of the PCAF involved in conflict with insurgent groups are the Frontier Corps (Frontier Corps KPK and Frontier Corps Balochistan), the Frontier Constabulary, the Sindh Rangers and the Punjab Rangers. These forces participate in the PAF-led *Operation Radd-ul-Fasaad*. 6,000 members of the PCAF are deployed alongside nine infantry battalions (9,000 soldiers) as part of the Special Security Division to protect CPEC.

History
The PCAF have contributed to *Operation Radd-ul-Fasaad* since its establishment in 2017, and to the Special Security Division since 2016.

Objectives
The PCAF's objective is to eliminate insurgent groups presenting a threat to the Pakistani state. It runs checkpoints to interdict insurgent groups and conducts raids and search operations against them.

Opponents
TTP, Hizb-ul-Ahrar, BLA, IS–PP.

Affiliates/allies
PAF, Pakistani Police.

Resources/capabilities
The PCAF are primarily equipped with small arms and light weapons, with some shorter-range artillery and mortars. The Frontier Corps have an armoured corps, with armoured personnel carriers and tanks, and an aviation corps.

Tehrik-e-Taliban Pakistan (TTP)

Strength
Circa 3,000–5,000.[2]

Areas of operation
KPK, Balochistan.

Leadership
Mufti Noor Wali Mehsud is emir and the overarching leader, supported by a central shura council. The leadership is purportedly based in Kuran province, Afghanistan.[3]

Structure
Noor Wali has sought to re-establish a strongly hierarchical structure in the TTP after years of infighting. The organisation is divided by locality into factions, or constituencies, each of which is led by a local emir and supported by a local shura council, which report to the central shura council. Each faction has a judge or *qazi* to adjudicate local disputes.

History
Following the NATO invasion of Afghanistan in 2001, al-Qaeda and Taliban militants sought haven in the tribal areas of Pakistan. Operations by the Pakistani Army – and later by US forces – against al-Qaeda led to the formation of Pakistan Taliban groups, who opposed the army's presence. In 2007, these Taliban factions unified as TTP under the leadership of Baitullah Mehsud. After he was killed in a US airstrike in 2009, a TTP shura elected Hakimullah Mehsud, another member of the Mehsud clan, as the organisation's second emir. Divisions grew during Hakimullah's leadership over legitimate targets for attacks and peace talks with the Pakistani government, and worsened under the leadership of Fazal Hayat (Mullah Fazlullah) between 2013 and 2018. As a result, several factions splintered off, including the IS–KP in 2014. During Hayat's leadership, the TTP attacked the Army Public School in Peshawar, which brought about a major offensive against them by the PAF. Fractured and under attack, the TTP weakened. Following the death of Fazal Hayat in 2018, the leadership reverted to the Mehsud clan and sought to reunite and rebuild under Noor Wali.

Tehrik-e-Taliban Pakistan

Objectives
TTP aimed originally to defend and promote strict Islamism and Pashtunwali in Pakistan, but as the group has grown more ethnically diverse, it has focused increasingly on extreme Islamism. According to Noor Wali's 2018 guidelines, legitimate targets are the Pakistani state and militias supporting the state, and so-called non-believers or *kafir* (including Shia and Ahmadi Muslims, Westerners and NGOs). Mehsud ruled that deaths of other civilians should be avoided and suicide attacks reserved for high-value targets. The main means of attack are improvised explosive devices (IEDs).

Opponents
PAF, PCAF.

Affiliates/allies
Afghan Taliban, al-Qaeda.

Resources/capabilities
TTP has access to small arms and IEDs (including suicide vests).

Hizb-ul-Ahrar

Strength
Unknown, but likely fewer than 200 members.[4]

Areas of operation
KPK and Punjab provinces.

Leadership
Led by Mukarram Khan.

Structure
Unclear structure but likely led by a shura council.

History
In 2014, a faction of TTP calling itself Ahrar-ul-Hind broke away, rejecting TTP's talks with the government of Pakistan, and merged with other splinter groups to form Jamaat-ul-Ahrar. In November 2017, a faction of Jamaat-ul-Ahrar broke away, objecting to attacks on minority groups. This faction established Hizb-ul-Ahrar, which focuses its attacks on the Pakistani state and armed forces.

Objectives
Like the TTP from which it sprang, Hizb-ul-Ahrar's objective is to promote extreme Islamism in Pakistan. It furthers these objectives through attacks on the police and army with IEDs, and assassinations of politicians, officials and military and police personnel.

Opponents
PAF, PCAF.

Affiliates/allies
TTP.

Resources/capabilities
It has access to small arms and IEDs.

Balochistan Liberation Army (BLA)

Strength
Circa 2,000–3,000.

Areas of operation
Balochistan.

Leadership
The leadership of the BLA is contested between Hyrbyair Marri and Bashar Zaib.

Structure
The BLA is divided into two factions. The government of Pakistan alleges that one faction is led by the UK-based Hyrbyair Marri, the brother of BLA founder Balach Marri, and by associates in Balochistan. The second faction rejects leadership by Marri: it is instead led by Bashar Zaib and claims to have two central committees, the Senior Command Council and the Operation Core Committee.

History
The BLA was formed in 2000 under the leadership of Afghanistan-based Balach Marri, who was subsequently killed in an airstrike in Helmand in 2007.[5] Its leadership thereafter became unclear and probably contested, with many of the leading Balochi separatists exiled to the UK and Switzerland, including Hyrbyair Marri. In 2018, Aslam Baloch (a.k.a. Aslam Achu), leader of the BLA's constituent Majeed Brigade, rejected the leadership of Hyrbyair Marri and laid claim to leadership of the group as a whole.[6] He was subsequently killed in a suicide attack on his residence in a secure compound in Kandahar, Afghanistan, during a meeting with BLA members.[7] He was succeeded as leader of his faction by Bashar Zaib.[8] In July 2019, the US State Department listed the BLA as a Specially Designated Global Terrorist organisation.

Balochistan Liberation Army

Objectives
The BLA seeks greater autonomy for the region of Balochistan as a solution to perceived discrimination against Balochis. It opposes the extraction of natural resources in Balochistan by Pakistani and foreign actors, especially China (which one BLA commander has described as the group's 'number one enemy'), due to the implications of the China–Pakistan Economic Corridor for Balochi aspirations.[9] The BLA carries out ambushes and attacks involving small arms and IEDs against security personnel, workers and businesses in the region.

Opponents
PAF, PCAF.

Affiliates/allies
None.

Resources/capabilities
BLA attacks have involved the use of small arms and IEDs, including suicide vests and car bombs.

Islamic State – Pakistan Province (IS–PP)

Strength
Unclear.

Areas of operation
Balochistan, KPK, Punjab, Sindh.

Leadership
Daud Mehsud, Emir of IS–PP.[10]

Structure
The details of IS–PP's organisational structure are poorly understood. It is likely hierarchical, with an emir at the head, above provincial-level commanders and a shura council, in turn above district-level commanders and local commanders.[11]

History
The Islamic State announced the establishment of the Islamic State–KP in 2014 by former members of TTP to conduct operations in Afghanistan and Pakistan. Its first four emirs were all killed in US airstrikes in Afghanistan.[12] In May 2019, Islamic State's Amaq media outlet announced a rebranding of the group's operations in Pakistan as IS–PP.[13]

Objectives
Like all factions of the Islamic State, IS–PP seeks to establish a caliphate and introduce sharia law at a local level and ultimately at a national and regional level. To this end, it seeks to delegitimise the Pakistani state and force religious minorities out of Pakistan.

Opponents
PAF, PCAF.

Affiliates/allies
None.

Resources/capabilities
IS–PP attacks have involved the use of small arms and IEDs, including suicide vests.

Drivers

Ethnic grievances

Ethnic Pashtun, Baloch and Sindhi grievances drive part of the armed conflict in Pakistan. These grievances result from political and economic discrimination by a state in which the army and the government are largely dominated by Punjabis (the ethnic majority). The ethnic minorities accuse the Pakistani state forces, including the army and police, of violently repressing and marginalising them, and dissidents are often targets of extrajudicial killings and enforced disappearances.

A peaceful Pashtun Tahafuz Movement (PTM, also known as the Pashtun Protection Movement) emerged in January 2018 to protest the extrajudicial killing of a Pashtun youth, Naqeebullah Mehsud, by the Karachi police. Suspected of being a terrorist, Mehsud was in police custody for days prior to his death. PTM has staged several demonstrations criticising the army and police for harassment of Pashtuns, for abuse of their human rights and for forced disappearances. In 2018, two of its leading members were elected to the National Assembly. It staged further rallies in 2019, attracting tens of thousands of attendees. The PTM calls for equal rights for the Pashtuns in Pakistan, investigations into forced disappearances and missing persons, and the removal of mines from FATA, and denounces the TTP and the protection of certain TTP factions by the Pakistani security establishment. In 2018, the TTP attacked a PTM gathering in Wana, South Waziristan.

Baloch groups also allege violations of their civil, political and human rights by the government, but have drawn additional attention to grievances relating to the distribution of economic benefits from the extraction of natural resources in Balochistan. CPEC has become a lightning rod for these economic grievances. CPEC is a Chinese-driven infrastructure project worth around US$50 billion, part of China's larger development framework, the Belt and Road Initiative. As part of CPEC, Chinese businesses are involved in a variety of infrastructure projects in Balochistan, including power plants, mines, highways, railways and a port in Gwadar. Baloch groups question whether they will benefit at all from the projects or whether the benefits will instead accrue to China and its partners in the Pakistani government.

Religious divides

Pakistan has a Sunni majority (approximately 80% of the population) and a Shia minority (approximately 14%). The rise of Barelvi extremism in 2017 has increased sub-sectarian extremism within the Sunni population. Barelvi Sunnis are the majority within the Sunni population in Pakistan and are traditionally known to be moderate and non-violent, whereas Deobandi Sunni groups (such as the TTP) primarily fought state security forces. However, the issue of blasphemy – a chief cause advocated by Barelvi militants and hardliners – has become a driver of radicalisation and violence among Pakistan's Barelvi Sunnis.

Confrontations between Barelvi insurgents and the state began in 2017 with the advent of a new religio-political group, Tehrik-e-Labbaik (TLP), a staunch advocate of blasphemy laws formed to represent Barelvi Sunnis. In 2017, the TLP violently protested against a proposed electoral reform, shutting down one of the primary roads to the capital in a three-day-long sit-in that resulted in clashes with the police and the eventual resignation of the law minister.

Political Developments

In 2019, the Pakistani government pushed ahead with the merger of the former FATA into KPK province. Integrating the administrative and security apparatuses of the former FATA into those of KPK meant giving the tribal areas representation in the provincial assembly and regularising tribal paramilitary groups – the Khasadar and Levies forces – as part of the PCAF. The latter measure was particularly contentious, with disputes over status, pay levels and the appointment of new police commanders (district inspector generals) to former FATA districts. Numerous tribal jirgas (traditional decision-making assemblies) were convened, with tribal elders either rejecting certain police commanders or opposing the amalgamation of FATA into KPK altogether. The Khasadar and Levies forces staged protests, abandoning their posts and blocking roads in KPK, in attempts to extract better conditions for their regularisation. Those changes were pushed through in September and protests continued. Elections to the KPK provincial assembly took place successfully in July – a significant step forward in the alignment of the administrative system in the former FATA with the rest of the country.

Key Events in 2019

Political events

13 March
Khasadar and Levies forces personnel hunger strike and block the road between Peshawar and Turkham in protest at their merger into the KPK police force.

May
IS–PP separates from IS–KP, under the leadership of Daud Mehsud.

Military/Violent events

29 January
The TTP attacks the Deputy Inspector General's office in Loralai, Balochistan, killing eight police and a civilian.

2 February
A PTM leader is killed in the police response to a PTM sit-in in Loralai.

12 April
IS–KP affiliate Lashkar-e-Jhangvi kills 21 people in a suicide attack on a market in Quetta.

18 April
Militants in Balochistan shoot dead 14 non-Baloch bus passengers on the Makran Coastal Highway.

The federal government under Prime Minister Imran Khan announced a ten-year development plan for the former FATA, including a yearly investment of Rs100bn (US$645 million). In the annual budget, revealed in July, the government allocated Rs152bn (US$980m) to the region.[14] Similar pledges made by previous governments have not led to the actual release of funds. Were the former FATA to indeed receive its allocation, together with the normalisation of the regional administration, it would go some way towards addressing ethnic tensions between the Pashtun tribal communities and the Pakistani state.

However, progress in addressing the political and economic marginalisation of the former FATA was partly undermined by the police and army's aggressive response to the PTM protests. PTM's demands for an inquiry into forced disappearances and the dismantling of checkpoints present a challenge for the army which, in response, has sought to cast suspicion on PTM's motivations and play on fears that PTM could evolve into a secessionist movement, alleging foreign backing without presenting any evidence. Attempts by the KPK government to ban demonstrations, the imprisonment of the two PTM-affiliated members of the National Assembly and the violent suppression of the protests – including in Loralai where police beat a local PTM leader to death and in Kharqamar where the army killed 13 people – only reinforce the PTM's accusations and fuel perceptions of mistreatment of Pashtuns.

In 2018, the Financial Action Task Force (FATF) added Pakistan to its 'grey list' of states with structural deficiencies in anti-money laundering (AML) and countering the financing of terrorism (CFT). Pakistan had until September 2019 to implement the FATF's AML and CFT action plans but failed to do so. Despite government pledges of compliance, the Pakistani state remains riven by internal divisions over suppressing jihadist groups, with elements of the army and intelligence services sympathetic to the Taliban, Haqqani network and terrorist groups in Kashmir. Though the sympathy does not extend to the Balochistan Liberation Army and other factions opposed to the Pakistani state, resistance to the measures required for CFT has hamstrung the Pakistani government's efforts to comply with the FATF National Action Plan. As a result, at its October plenary meeting, the FATF sought to add Pakistan to its 'high-risk and non-cooperative jurisdictions' list (also known as the 'blacklist'), alongside Iran and North Korea, but after intensive lobbying by the Pakistani government, three FATF members – China, Turkey and Malaysia – voted against the blacklisting. Pakistan was rebuked for failing to deliver on 22 of the 27 targets in its action plan and received a four-month extension.

8 May
Hizb-ul-Ahrar kills 13 people in a suicide attack on Data Darbar shrine, Lahore.

11 May
The BLA attacks the Pearl Continental Hotel in Gwadar.

20 July
Provincial-assembly elections take place for the first time in the former FATA.

26 May
Pakistani security forces kill 13 PTM demonstrators in Kharqamar.

10 September
The US State Department adds TTP leader Mufti Noor Wali Mehsud to its list of specially designated global terrorists.

21 July
TTP militants stage a complex attack on police in Kotla Saidan and Dera Ismail Khan, killing ten officers.

18 October
The FATF decides to keep Pakistan on its grey list and review compliance with its National Action Plan in February 2020.

16 August
Balochistan National Party leader Mir Nawab Amanullah Zehri and three others are shot dead in Khuzdar.

Military Developments

Across the country, activity associated with insurgency and terrorism decreased in 2019. In Balochistan, the number of incidents involving the use of force (insurgent attacks and security-force operations) declined from 63 in 2018 to 51 in 2019, and the number of fatalities was considerably lower. (The 128 deaths in the July suicide attack on the Balochistan Awami Party political rally had contributed to an exceptionally high fatality count for 2018.) Likewise, the number of incidents declined from 58 in 2018 to 51 in 2019 in KPK (including the former FATA). The number of incidents in Sindh and Punjab remained very low, primarily involving operations by Pakistani security forces to capture or kill suspected militants.

Most notably, there was a decline in the number of suicide attacks in 2019, which reflected a change in TTP's practice. In late 2018, the new leader of the group, Mufti Noor Wali Mehsud, set out new guidelines on legitimate targets and preferred tactics, including the more limited use of suicide bombings and a focus on state rather than civilian targets. While the extent of Mehsud's authority over the TTP's many factions remains unclear, his tactical advice has been borne out over the year. Most attacks attributed to the TTP targeted police and army personnel (although still with many collateral civilian deaths). The most notable such incident was a successfully planned dual attack in Dera Ismail Khan in which TTP gunmen attacked a checkpoint and a suicide bomber detonated their device at the nearby hospital as the injured police arrived.

In 2019, there were no airstrikes by US forces for the first year since 2003, which reflects a number of political and security changes. Firstly, the Taliban controls growing swathes of territory in Afghanistan and so senior al-Qaeda figures have been able to return there from their havens in Pakistan. Secondly, the Pakistani security forces' campaign against jihadists in the tribal areas has brought some success and militancy there has declined. And thirdly, Prime Minister Khan strongly opposes US airstrikes in the country, leaving less political scope for the US to undertake any such attacks.

The Islamic State, also known as ISIS or ISIL, remained a minor player in Pakistan, despite its

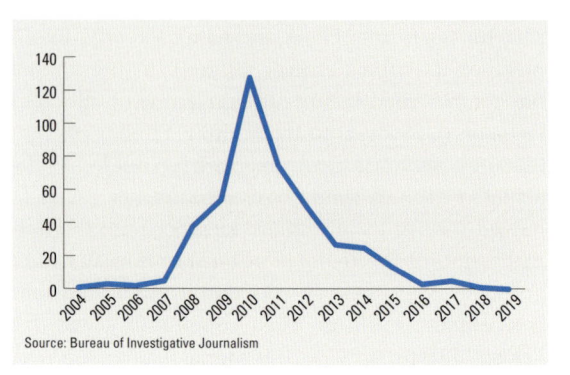

Source: Bureau of Investigative Journalism

Figure 1: Number of US airstrikes in Pakistan, 2004–19

growing significance elsewhere in South Asia. It staged no major attacks during 2019 and Pakistani security forces conducted a number of raids on suspected Islamic State militant bases. In May, the organisation divided itself into three separate South Asian *wilayat* or provincial branches: the Islamic State – Khorasan Province (IS–KP), previously responsible for the whole region, limited its activities to Afghanistan; the Islamic State – Pakistan Province (IS–PP) was established to coordinate activities in Pakistan; and the Islamic State – Hind Province (IS–HP) was established to coordinate activities elsewhere in the subcontinent. IS–KP and IS–HP were considerably more active than IS–PP. Although some 650 Pakistanis travelled to Iraq and Syria to fight for the Islamic State there, it is unclear how many are likely to return and bolster the ranks and capacity of IS–PP, with IS–KP more likely to draw experienced fighters into its own ranks.[15]

The attack on the Pearl Continental Hotel in Gwadar in May was perhaps the most significant incident of 2019, despite its low death toll (the BLA militants who attacked the hotel killed four hotel staff, including three security guards, and a Pakistani navy officer, and were themselves killed by security forces). It showed that, despite the very large presence of PAF and PCAF forces in Gwadar, the BLA could still puncture their defences. Staging such eye-catching attacks – and maintaining the same rate of attacks in Balochistan at a time when Pakistan is under pressure from China to address Baloch insurgency – gives the BLA the best prospect of extracting concessions from the government.

Impact

The insurgency in Balochistan and the threat it poses to Chinese businesses and workers, and the failure of the PAF and PCAF to address it effectively (despite the allocation of substantial resources), continued to frustrate China. Impatient for improvements, China has pressured Pakistan to address the threat. In the wake of the BLA's attack on the Pearl Continental Hotel in Gwadar, China reported that Pakistan would set up a special committee on the safety of Chinese personnel and CPEC projects, and the Director General of Inter-Services Public Relations, Major General Asif Ghafoor, announced that Pakistan would raise a second division to protect CPEC (supplementing the existing Special Security Division).[16] In addition, the government decided to divert funds from the PAF to finance development projects in Balochistan, which – with China's support – represented a small shift in the emphasis of CPEC, underscoring its potential benefits for the Baloch population in an effort to address the grievances underlying the insurgency there.

Despite China's impatience with Pakistan's failure to address militancy, it did prevent its blacklisting at the FATF. Being on the FATF's grey list has had little impact on Pakistan, despite increased due-diligence requirements making Pakistani banks' and businesses' access to foreign financing more difficult and more inconvenient. Were the FATF to add Pakistan to its blacklist and recommend countermeasures, the impact would be far greater, with an effect on Pakistani businesses' and individuals' access to international financial markets and on their ability to build relationships with foreign businesses. It might, in addition, lead to greater reluctance by the International Monetary Fund and other international financial institutions to lend to the Pakistani government. Given that Pakistan is currently reliant on lending from the IMF, this would have serious implications for the government's finances.

Trends

The PAF and PCAF's selective offensive against insurgent groups threatening the Pakistani state (and not against groups threatening neighbouring countries) has been successful in much of the country, with a significant decline in insurgent and terrorist attacks since 2014, which looks set to continue outside Balochistan. In Balochistan, however, the insurgency will likely continue at its current rate due to incentives to make its mark now.

All in all, there remains little prospect of Pakistan resolving the ethnic grievances underlying the insurgency in Balochistan and KPK. Doing so would require the army and police to acknowledge their role in fuelling ethnic grievances. Instead, by dismissing legitimate criticisms and vilifying and attacking civil-resistance groups such as the PTM, the security forces risk creating a far greater problem than they currently face. Harsh responses to peaceful protest inflame tensions and encourage rather than discourage violence.

Moreover, the intransigence of some factions within the Pakistani state on measures to address money laundering and terrorist financing risks the FATF blacklisting Pakistan. Despite its close relationship with Pakistan, China might yet abstain or vote in favour of blacklisting the country: it voted against Pakistan in June 2018 when the FATF added Pakistan to its grey list and since then China has grown still more impatient with Pakistan's failure to address militancy.

Notes

[1] Sadia Sulaiman, 'Ex-FATA budget allocation and structural deficiencies', *Express Tribune*, 19 June 2019.

[2] Richard Barrett, 'Beyond the Caliphate: Foreign Fighters and the Threat of Returnees', Soufan Center, October 2017, p. 13.

[3] 'Pakistan army plans new unit to protect CPEC projects', *Gulf News*, 19 May 2019.

[4] IISS, *The Military Balance 2020* (Abingdon: Routledge for the IISS, 2020); 'K-P FC seeks modern weapons', *Express Tribune*, 20 February 2019; Gilgit Baltistan Scouts, 2019; Iftikhar Firdous, 'FATA to integrate secretariat into K-P', *Express Tribune*, 25

June 2018; Saleem Shahid, 'Plan to re-organise Levies Force approved', Dawn, 12 September 2018.

5   US Department of Defense Office of the Inspector General, 'Operation Freedom's Sentinel: Lead Inspector General Report to the United States Congress, 1 January–31 March 2019', 17 May 2019, p. 25.

6   Zia Ur Rehman, 'The TTP: Cornered and desperate', Geo.tv, 16 October 2018.

7   Although no figure is available for Hizb-ul-Ahrar, the group splintered from Jamaat-ul-Ahrar, which was estimated by US Forces–Afghanistan (with a low degree of certainty) to have 200 fighters. See US Department of Defense Office of Inspector General, 'Operation Freedom's Sentinel: Lead Inspector General Report to the United States Congress, January 1, 2019–March 31, 2019', 17 May 2019, p. 25.

8   Saleem Shahid, 'Balach Marri killed: Violence in Quetta, schools closed', Dawn, 22 November 2007.

9   'BLA says it does not have any representatives in London, Europe or US', Balochistan Post, 17 August 2018; Fahad Nabeel, 'Aslam Baloch's killing: Implications for Balochistan Insurgency', Centre for Strategic and Contemporary Research, 28 December 2018.

10 Tahir Khan, 'Chinese consulate attack "mastermind" killed in Afghanistan', Daily Times, 26 December 2018.

11 Abdul Ghani Kakar, 'Pakistan welcomes US designation of BLA as terrorist group', Pakistan Forward, 8 July 2019.

12 Kaswar Klasra, '"The Chinese are our No 1 enemy": why Beijing's US$62 billion investment in Pakistan is the top target for Balochistan separatists', South China Morning Post, 16 May 2019.

13 Roohan Ahmed, 'Daesh looks to gain foothold in Balochistan under ex-Karachi cop', Samaa News Agency, 18 September 2019.

14 Amira Jadoon and Andrew Mines, 'Taking Aim: Islamic State Khorasan's Leadership Losses', CTC Sentinel, vol. 12, no. 8, September 2019, pp. 15–16.

15 Ibid., pp. 15–19.

16 Ayaz Gul, 'Islamic State Announces "Pakistan Province"', Voice of America, 15 May 2019; Robert Postings, 'ISIS announces new India and Pakistan provinces, casually breaking up Khorasan', Defense Post, 15 May 2019.

6 Sub-Saharan Africa

Cameroon	288	Lake Chad Basin (Boko Haram)	329	South Sudan	369
Central African Republic	298	Nigeria (Farmer–Pastoralist)	338	Sudan (Darfur, Blue Nile &	
Democratic Republic of the Congo	308	The Sahel (Mali & Burkina Faso)	347	South Kordofan)	381
Ethiopia	320	Somalia	360		

Protests against food shortages at a camp in Maiduguri, northeast Nigeria

Key trends

- Violence decreased in the conflicts in the Central African Republic, Nigeria (Farmer–Pastoralist), South Sudan and Sudan, while the Sahel registered unprecedented levels of violence and human displacement. Violence also continued in Cameroon, the Democratic Republic of the Congo, Ethiopia, the Lake Chad Basin and Somalia.

- ISIS offshoots are present to varying degrees in multiple conflicts: from ISWAP, the most successful splinter outside the Middle East, to the little-known Central Africa Province in the DRC.

- The numbers of refugees and IDPs remained high across all conflicts. Ongoing violence prevented effective emergency responses to humanitarian and health crises, including Ebola and measles outbreaks in the DRC.

Strategic implications

- Foreign powers are involved in almost all conflicts in the region. Russia's increased involvement in the CAR sparked concerns in Washington and Paris. Burundi, Rwanda and Uganda pursued their rivalries through armed groups in the DRC, over which the latter has no control.

- The ousting of President Omar al-Bashir prompted Western governments to re-engage with Sudan, while Bashir's traditional allies in the Gulf backed the new transitional government.

- The US revoked Cameroon's preferential trade status and withdrew a pledge of military aid. Washington also imposed sanctions on South Sudanese officials.

Prospects

- The implementation of various peace agreements will remain a key challenge across most conflicts because of limited capacity to reintegrate fighters (in the DRC, for example) and fragmentation within negotiating parties (in Cameroon).

- In Sudan, the consolidation of military power poses risks for a democratic transition and the peace process.

- The Sahel conflict shows signs of further expansion and threatens coastal West Africa.

- Somalia's prospects for a united government are poor. Unrestrained competition between wealthy global powers (of which the country has seen some signs) will exacerbate the problem and prolong the conflict.

CAMEROON

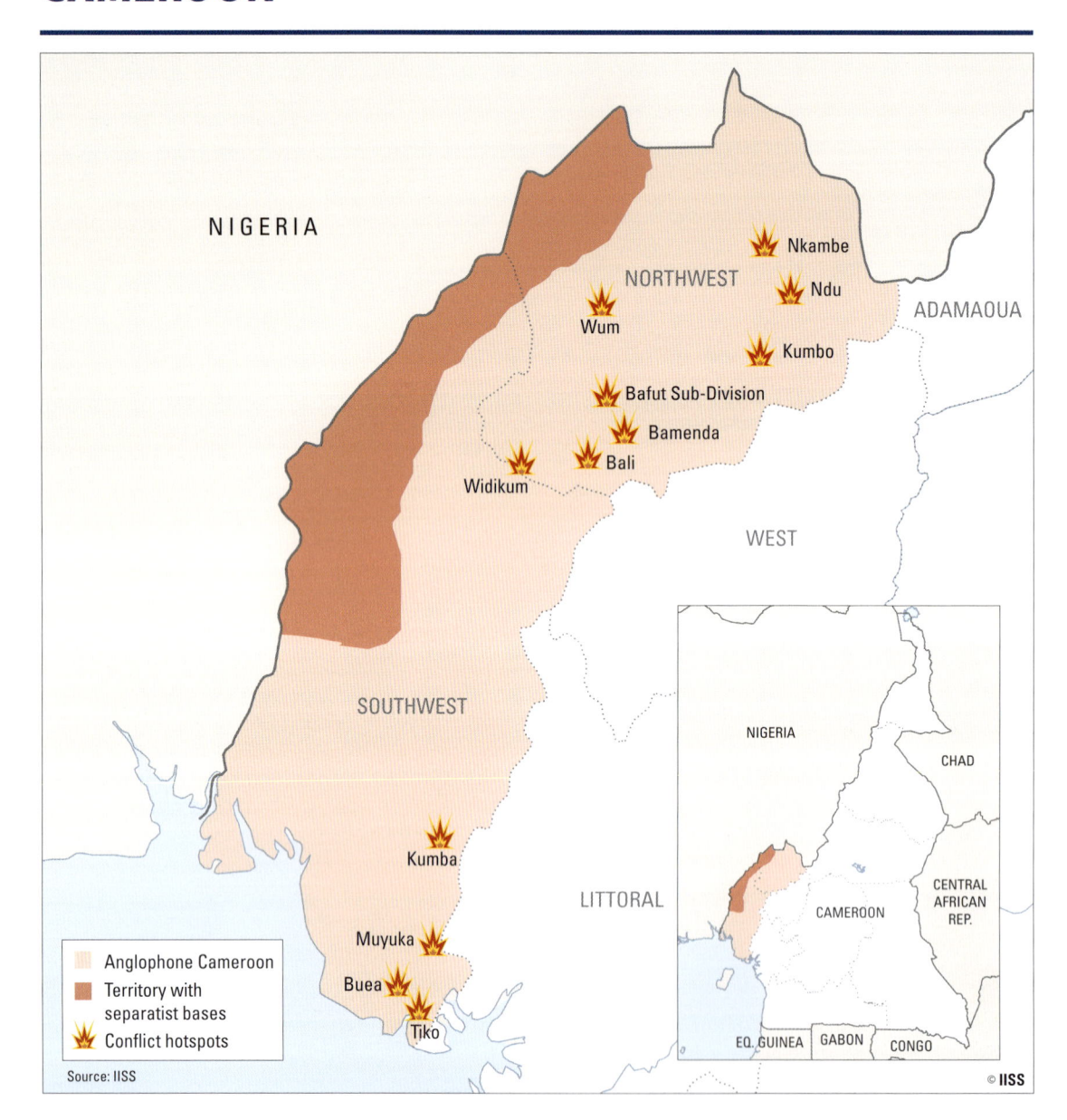

Map legend:
- Anglophone Cameroon
- Territory with separatist bases
- Conflict hotspots

Source: IISS

Overview

The conflict in 2019
In 2019, the conflict in Cameroon entered a state of stalemate and remained primarily confined within the regions of Northwest and Southwest Cameroon. Throughout the year, separatist groups and the Cameroonian security forces clashed regularly. Government forces continued a widespread counter-insurgency campaign, which at times included the use of indiscriminate violence against civilian populations. Nonetheless, armed separatist groups were able to launch attacks repeatedly (at times against high-profile targets), blockade major roads and interrupt commerce and education. They also increased their use of kidnappings for ransom, largely in response to dwindling donations from the Cameroonian diaspora. The fragmented nature

of the secessionist movement continued to inhibit reconciliation efforts, while new divisions within the secessionist leadership emerged. In contrast, the regime remained highly centralised.

International attention to the conflict increased in 2019, but peacemaking efforts remained largely ineffective. The United States reduced its security commitments and revoked Cameroon's preferential trade status. The United Nations Security Council held its first informal meeting on the crisis, and the Swiss government began mediation efforts. In early October, President Paul Biya convened a Major National Dialogue that brought together several Anglophone groups, but was boycotted by the main secessionist groups. In December, the Cameroonian Parliament approved a special status for Northwest and Southwest regions, but the provisions have yet to be implemented and were opposed in principle by the major Anglophone groups.

The crisis continued to take a large human and economic toll. As of December 2019, almost 680,000 people had been displaced and 52,000 had become refugees since the beginning of the conflict. Various sources indicate that approximately 1,000 people were killed in 2019. In total, approximately 500 security personnel, 1,000 separatists and 1,500 civilians have been killed since the start of the conflict in 2017.

The conflict to 2019

The conflict in Anglophone Cameroon (the Northwest and Southwest regions) began in late 2016 with a series of protests and general strikes led by lawyers, teachers and other civil-society organisations who sought to foreground issues affecting the Anglophone population in Cameroon. Anglophones, who constitute approximately 20% of the population, called for the redress of perceived policies of cultural, economic and political discrimination dating back to the abolishment of federalism in 1972. Groups such as the Cameroon Anglophone Civil Society Consortium (CACSC) supported political decentralisation or a return to federalism, while others such as the Southern Cameroons National Council (SCNC) advocated for self-determination

Key statistics	
Type	Internal
Start date	September 2017
IDPs total (31 December 2019)	679,393
Refugees total (31 December 2019)	52,000
People in need (31 December 2019)	4,400,000

in the form of an independent nation called 'Ambazonia'. The lack of sustained or credible efforts at political reconciliation created a dynamic of mutual escalation. Anglophone groups staged numerous protests and organised region-wide strikes. The government cracked down violently on demonstrators and arrested several members of the protest movement under charges of domestic terrorism.

An armed secessionist movement had developed by October 2017, with two rival political organisations – the Interim Government (IG) of Ambazonia and the Ambazonia Governing Council (AGC) – competing to lead it. The IG began to coordinate the activities of the Anglophone Self Defence Council (ASDC), which united several local self-defence groups. In January 2018, the IG's first president, Sisiku Julius Tabe, was arrested, along with other top leaders, and extradited from Nigeria.

The AGC began to operate a military wing called the Ambazonia Defence Forces (ADF). In addition, several smaller militias emerged, which gave the secessionist movement a very fractured character. These groups use guerrilla tactics to attack government forces and intimidate citizens to participate in boycotts of commerce and education. Likewise, many groups kidnap citizens for ransom as a way of raising funds.

In response to the secessionist movement, the Cameroonian government deployed parts of its elite force, the Rapid Response Brigade (BIR), which has been criticised for its harsh tactics and human-rights violations. Until 2018, the conflict took a significant toll on local populations but failed to draw much international attention.

Key Conflict Parties

Cameroonian Armed Forces

Strength
Approximately 25,400 regular army personnel and 9,000 paramilitaries. The scale of deployment in Anglophone Cameroon is unclear, but consists of elements of the military police (the gendarmerie) and the elite military force, the Rapid Response Brigade (BIR).

Areas of operation
Northwest and Southwest Cameroon, in a military region designated RMIA 5.

Leadership
Led by General Agha Robinson Ndong, but all of Cameroon's armed forces report directly to the president.

Structure
The BIR has no general staff and is under the authority of the chief of staff of the army. The gendarmerie is under the authority of the secretary of state in the Ministry of Defence.

History
The BIR was created in 2001 to combat banditry along Cameroon's frontiers, but has been used since as an elite intervention force. The gendarmerie was created in the early 1960s as a direct descendent of the French colonial-era force.

Objectives
Counter-insurgency against separatist groups in Northwest and Southwest regions, and restoration of the regular flow of commerce.

Opponents
The Interim Government of Ambazonia and the ASDC, the Ambazonia Governing Council and the ADF, various smaller militias.

Affiliates/allies
The Cameroonian armed forces receive military assistance from France and the US. In February 2019, the US government rescinded a pledge of US$17 million in military aid over human-rights abuses.

Resources/capabilities
The armed forces have access to advanced weaponry. In 2018, the BIR acquired a number of *Panthera* T6 armoured personal carriers to be used in urban areas in Northwest and Southwest Cameroon.

Interim Government of Ambazonia (IG) / Ambazonia Self Defence Council (ASDC)

Strength
The ASDC consists of several local self-defence groups (the Seven Karta Militia, the Ambazonia Restoration Army, the Tigers of Ambazonia, the Southern Cameroon Defence Force, the Manyu Ghost Warriors and possibly the Red Dragons). Collectively the ASDC can draw on some 1,000 to 1,500 fighters. The largest group is the Ambazonia Restoration Army.

Areas of operation
The ASDC operates throughout Northwest and Southwest Cameroon. The Ambazonia Restoration Army and the Southern Cameroon Defence Force operate in most divisions in Northwest and Southwest Cameroon. The Seven Karta is primarily present in Mezam Division, the Tigers in Manyu and Meme Division, the Ghost Warriors in Manyu and the Red Dragons in Lebialem.

Leadership
The IG is currently led from abroad by Samuel Ikome Sako. The links between the IG and the various groups within the ASDC are often tenuous. Leadership of many of the individual groups is also unknown. The Ambazonia Restoration Army is led by Paxton Agbor, the SCDF by Nso Foncha Nkem and the Red Dragons by Lekeaka Oliver. Since May 2019, there have been significant disputes between wings of the IG loyal to Tabe and those associated with Sako, as well as between the IG and the ASDC.

Structure
The IG operates a government structure that includes an executive and legislative body. The ASDC lacks a centralised command structure. The structure of the several localised self-defence organisations that compose it is unclear, yet many leaders are titled 'general'.

History
The IG emerged from the Southern Cameroons Ambazonia Consortium United Front (SCACUF), and declared Ambazonia's independence on 1 October 2017. The ASDC was created in March 2018 as a coordinating mechanism following a call for collective self-defence from the IG.

Objectives
Ambazonia's independence through a strategy of increased international pressure on the Cameroonian government and disruption of commerce.

Opponents
The Cameroonian armed forces.

Affiliates/allies
The IG coordinates with other groups through the Southern Cameroons Liberation Council (SCLC), and at times coordinates with the AGC/ADF.

Resources/capabilities
The IG and ASDC rely on makeshift weaponry and some imports of small arms from neighbouring Nigeria. Financing of the IG comes primarily from donors in the Cameroonian diaspora, while affiliates of the ASDC have been implicated in kidnapping for ransom as a means of funding their operations.

Ambazonia Governing Council (AGC) / Ambazonia Defence Forces (ADF)

Strength
Estimates place the group's strength between 1,500 and 3,000 fighters.

Areas of operation
Throughout Northwest and Southwest Cameroon, parts of Littoral Region.

Leadership
The AGC is led from abroad by Lucas Cho Ayaba, while the chairman of the ADF council is Benedict Kuah.

Structure
The AGC operates a government structure that includes an executive and a legislative branch. The specifics of the ADF's structure are not clear, but it likely operates between 30 and 50 camps. Various leaders in the ADF have the title of 'general'.

History
The AGC was created in 2013 as a merger of several other self-determination movements, and remains outside the IG. In September 2017, the AGC declared a war of independence against the Cameroonian government and the ADF was deployed as its official armed wing.

Objectives
The AGC seeks Ambazonia's independence through a strategy of insurgency and disruption of commerce. The AGC's goal is to make the Anglophone territory ungovernable and thus compel the Cameroonian government to concede.

Opponents
The Cameroonian armed forces.

Affiliates/allies
The AGC/ADF at times interacts with groups in the ASDC and coordinates with SOCADEF. It has a loose relationship with the IG. During 2019, the AGC appeared to support the Tabe faction of the IG.

Resources/capabilities
The ADF relies on makeshift weaponry and some imports of small arms from neighbouring Nigeria. Financing for the organisation comes primarily from donors in the Cameroonian diaspora, while some members have been implicated in kidnapping for ransom to fund their operations.

Southern Cameroons Defence Forces (SOCADEF)

Strength
Approximately 100 members.

Areas of operation
Meme Division, Southwest Region.

Leadership
Led from abroad by Ebenezer Derek Mbongo Akwanga and, until January 2019, on the ground by General Andrew Ngoe.

Structure
While SOCADEF is ostensibly the armed wing of the African People's Liberation Movement (APLM), the degree of coordination between the two is unclear. SOCADEF's organisation on the ground is unknown.

History
SOCADEF is an independent armed secessionist group that grew out of the APLM and the Southern Cameroons Youth League.

Objectives
SOCADEF seeks independence for Ambazonia through a strategy of insurgency and disruption of commerce.

Opponents
The Cameroonian armed forces.

Affiliates/allies
SOCADEF maintains a loose alliance with the AGC/ADF. In March 2019 its parent organisation, the APLM, joined the Southern Cameroons Liberation Council.

Resources/capabilities
SOCADEF relies on makeshift weaponry and some imports of small arms from neighbouring Nigeria.

Various small militias

Strength
Unclear, but approximately 100–150 members in total across nearly a dozen militias, including the Vipers, often going under the generic term 'Amba Boys'.

Areas of operation
Northwest and Southwest Cameroon.

Leadership
Unknown.

Structure
Unknown.

History
With the start of the conflict in October 2017, various small militias emerged whose operations blur the line between insurgency and crime.

Objectives
These groups share the goals of independence for Ambazonia through insurgency, but also seem to seek short-term material gains from the conflict and are responsible for many of the kidnappings for ransom in the region.

Opponents
The Cameroonian armed forces.

Affiliates/allies
The Vipers coordinate with the ADF and SOCADEF on an ad hoc basis.

Resources/capabilities
Makeshift weaponry and small arms imported from Nigeria.

Drivers

Historical perceptions of discrimination

The conflict's root causes date back to the colonial history of Cameroon. After independence, the country consisted of a larger French-speaking territory and a smaller English-speaking region, with the combined entity operating as a federation between 1962 and 1972. First president Ahmadou Ahidjo used the state machinery and his control of the budget to eliminate rival political parties and consolidate power in a single-party state under his ruling party, the Cameroonian National Union (CNU). In 1972, a referendum to abolish federalism and create a unitary state easily passed, but with significant opposition from Anglophone areas. Since then, Anglophone perceptions of cultural, economic and political discrimination have grown.[1] Common criticisms include the lack of major infrastructural investments in Northwest and Southwest Cameroon, disregard for bilingualism in the public sector and higher education, and the absence of a bench for common law on the Supreme Court.

Patronage, corruption and weak democratic accountability

Rampant corruption and weak democratic accountability have also significantly elevated the Anglophone sense of alienation. The office of the presidency, which oversees a vast state apparatus used to distribute patronage to supporters, dominates the Cameroonian political system. The president can single-handedly appoint most government positions, including influential regional governors and district officers. He can also dissolve parliament and commands all the armed forces. In 1992, Cameroon transitioned to multi-party democracy, but the ruling Cameroon People's Democratic Movement (CPDM) has continued to dictate politics, in part through electoral manipulation and violence. A process of gerrymandering and a disproportionate electoral system have also increasingly disadvantaged opposition parties, who only constitute 18% of parliamentary seats. In 2008, Biya changed the constitution to abolish term limits and in 2018 won a seventh consecutive term in power. The perception of an entrenched status quo and powerful elite has pushed many Anglophones to consider full autonomy as the only solution.

Imposition of French-speaking magistrates

The initial protests in Anglophone areas were against the increase in the number of French-speaking magistrates appointed in Anglophone areas in late 2015. While common law is recognised in English-speaking regions, the country's legal system is based primarily on French civil law. At the time there was no common-law bench on the Supreme Court, and no common-law Bar association. Anglophone lawyers further complained that many essential laws were never translated into English, and that French-speaking magistrates pushed cases into the French legal system because they were unfamiliar with common law. On 11 October 2016, Anglophone lawyers began a 72-hour strike in Buea and Bamenda. Shortly thereafter, the Common Law Bar Association was created to advocate for their interests. These strikes extended throughout 2016 and expanded into a protest movement that included the major teacher associations and student groups from the University of Buea and the University of Bamenda.[2]

Dynamics of mutual escalation

The government's aggressive response to the protest movement created a dynamic of mutual escalation that increased the odds of armed conflict. Ad hoc negotiations led by the prime minister were met with distrust and failed to make headway after government forces violently dispersed protesters on several occasions in late 2016. After negotiations collapsed, the CACSC began to coordinate wider-scale strikes known as ghost-town campaigns. In response, on 17 January 2017 the government used its authority under a 2014 anti-terrorism law to ban the SCNC and the CACSC and arrest its central leadership, although the charges were later dropped.[3] Many Anglophone advocates began to shift their position towards secession. In response, the government started to frame the Anglophone issue as a direct threat to the stability of the country and made only conciliatory concessions, such as the creation of a National Commission for Bilingualism and Multiculturalism and the designation of a common-law bench in the Supreme Court. Anglophones saw these measures as insincere, while the government continued to use indiscriminate violence against protesters.

Permissive international environment
Cameroon enjoys a unique status in international circles given its historical ties to France and its role in regional national-security concerns. Cameroon's relationship with France dates back to the post-colonial period, when important military and economic partnerships developed. Since 2001, Cameroon has also occupied an important position in security circles as the gateway to Central Africa and a member of the Joint Force of the G5 Sahel (FC-G5S) and the Multinational Joint Task Force (MNJTF), which fights Boko Haram. In part due to these relationships, the international response to the crisis has been muted. During the protests, many countries – including Canada, the European Union, France, Germany and the United Kingdom – made no public statements on the increasing violence. The US and the African Union expressed concern and encouraged dialogue but took no concrete diplomatic steps to resolve the conflict. In 2019, international scrutiny increased, but still did not translate into concerted peacemaking efforts.

Political Developments

New fissures within the Anglophone movement
The Anglophone movement continued to fragment in 2019, despite efforts to bring greater cohesion. In April 2019, the Southern Cameroons Liberation Council (SCLC) was formed in yet another attempt to create an umbrella organisation to coordinate the various Anglophone advocacy groups, but the AGC did not recognise the SCLC and other Anglophone entities spurned the SCLC's decision-making (on 9 April, for example, the ASDC rejected the SCLC's decision to end a ghost-town campaign in Fako Division). There also appeared to be growing fissures with the major Anglophone political party, the Social Democratic Front (SDF). In 2019, SDF founder and chairman John Fru Ndi was kidnapped twice by separatists seeking to pressure him into removing representatives from the National Assembly and the Senate.

The January 2018 arrest and extradition of the senior leadership of the IG created rifts within the IG as well. On 2 May, the jailed former president of the IG, Sisiku Julius Ayuk Tabe, ordered the dissolution of the new cabinet formed by Samuel Ikome Sako. Later, the Ambazonia Restoration Council (the legislative branch of the IG) impeached Tabe. The AGC, which is not affiliated with the IG, has continued to recognise Tabe as the IG's president. The two IG factions issued contradictory statements and guidance in response to events and ghost-town campaigns.[4] On 20 August, Tabe and the other jailed IG leaders were sentenced to life in prison by a military tribunal.

Growing international attention and Swiss mediation
Throughout 2019 there was increased international attention to the Cameroonian crisis, but not to a degree that would significantly impact the conflict. The US, which is a key security partner of Cameroon's, rescinded a pledge of US$17m of military aid in February. The US also sent its first congressional delegation in July, which called for talks between the government and the separatist group. In November, the US terminated Cameroon's preferential trade status. While not a major US trade partner, this limited Cameroon's duty-free access for specific exported products. In May, the UN Security Council began an informal debate of the Cameroonian crisis, after South Africa opposed formal discussions. In February, the Vatican offered to act as a mediator to the conflict but received little response from the Cameroonian government or the separatist groups. In June, the Swiss government announced that it had begun mediation efforts, with the support of eight separatist groups, but not the AGC, while it remained unclear whether the IG or the government of Cameroon were committed to the process. By the end of 2019, the Swiss mediation had not produced any results.

The Major National Dialogue
On 10 September 2019, President Paul Biya offered a pardon for more than 300 detained separatists and announced plans for a 'major national dialogue' to be held in Yaoundé between 30 September and 5 October. There were, however, severe disagreements over who should be invited, what the parameters of debate should be and who should moderate the proceedings. While there were more than 1,000 participants from several Anglophone groups, the major separatist groups boycotted

the proceedings, while the SDF only gave partial endorsement to them.

Eight commissions focused on multiculturalism and bilingualism, the education and the judicial systems, refugees, reconstruction, disarmament, the rights and representation of the diaspora, and decentralisation. The dialogue endorsed a number of broad resolutions that were criticised by many Anglophones as being too vague and not far-reaching enough.[5] The most important resolutions were the recommendation of a special status for Northwest and Southwest regions, the proposed election of regional governors and a change of Cameroon's name from the Republic of Cameroon back to the United Republic of Cameroon.

'Special status' bill
In recognition of their unique cultural and linguistic heritage, on 19 December the Cameroonian Parliament approved a 'special status' for Northwest and Southwest regions. The bill included the creation of assemblies of chiefs, regional assemblies and regional councils. The bill was controversial because it required the president and vice-president of the regional executives to be composed of 'indigenous personalities', without any clear definition of what that meant. Importantly, no timeline for implementation was provided. The main separatist groups, along with the SDF, rejected the bill and continued to maintain that federalism must be the starting condition for negotiations.

Military Developments

No clear victory in the field
The government's concerted counter-insurgency effort did not lead to any military progress against the secessionist movement. Throughout 2019 there were numerous raids against suspected insurgent camps, which reportedly killed between 500 and 1,000 separatists. A number of key figures in the secessionist movement were killed, including General Andrew Ngoe, a top leader of SOCADEF, in January. Nonetheless, secessionist groups and affiliated militias continued to operate freely in many rural areas in Northwest and Southwest Cameroon and were still able to launch numerous attacks in major urban areas surrounding Buea and Bamenda. These activities also grew in sophistication and included, among others, multiple attacks on the convoys of the governors of Northwest and Southwest regions.[6] On 16 June, separatists used a roadside bomb for the first time. In one of the more brazen attacks of the year, separatist forces ambushed a military boat on the Manyu River on 3 July.

Increased separatist targeting of civilian populations
Separatist intimidation and targeting of civilian populations increased dramatically. In 2019, there were at least 70 incidents of kidnapping for ransom, the majority of which targeted individuals in the education system (including schoolchildren), clergymen and journalists. However, there were also high-profile kidnappings such as that of the President

Key Events in 2019

Political events

- **7 February**: US rescinds a pledge of US$17m of military aid to Cameroon.
- **29 March**: The IG creates the SCLC to coordinate international advocacy efforts.
- **5 May**: UN Security Council holds its first informal meeting about the Cameroonian crisis.
- **27 June**: The Swiss government begins mediation efforts, but is unsuccessful in engaging the government or the IG.

Military/Violent events

- **January**: The government escalates counter-insurgency activities, killing three separatist generals and a SOCADEF leader.
- **5 February**: Separatist groups begin to enforce a ten-day region-wide economic lockdown.
- **4 April**: Separatist groups declare a six-day region-wide economic lockdown, but disagreement between the IG and SCLC leads to weak enforcement.
- **16 June**: Separatist forces use a roadside bomb for the first time to attack policemen.

of the Bangem High Court in April, and that of the Archbishop of the Catholic Diocese of Bamenda in June. There was also a notable increase in the use of regional economic lockdowns, which took place in February, April, June and August. Separatists attacked civilians perceived to be violating these lockdowns or suspected of being government collaborators. Separatists enforced shutdowns of local schools for nearly the entire year.

Evidence of ethnic clashes in Menchum Division (Wum)

Wum, in Menchum Division in the Northwest Region, was the site of several government raids on suspected separatist camps and hideouts between May and June 2019. On two occasions, there were reports of ethnic clashes between migrant Fulani herdsmen and civilians that led to at least a dozen deaths. In both instances, the Fulani herdsmen were reportedly encouraged and supported by government forces to engage in violence.[7]

Prison riots in Yaoundé and Buea

On 22 July, a major riot broke out in Kondengui Central Prison in Yaoundé. While the riot was ostensibly over prison conditions, the large proportion of Anglophone detainees gave the event a broader political context. The riot was broadcast over social-media feeds and culminated in the injury of several inmates and four deaths. On 24 July, prisoners in Buea (Southwest Region) staged a similar protest in a show of solidarity. Subsequently there were reports of more than 100 inmates being moved to unknown locations, which led to calls for investigation from human-rights groups.[8]

The Red Dragons claim leadership in Lebialem

In October 2019, Lekeaka Oliver, the head of the Red Dragons militia, proclaimed himself the paramount ruler of Lebialem Division, Southwest Region. This followed a concerted attack by the Red Dragons against traditional rulers in the region, who were perceived as collaborators with the central government. The government struggled to regain control of the territory and return power to the traditional chiefs. In the battles that ensued, 11 separatist fighters were killed and a police officer was beheaded. Lekeaka was not apprehended, however, and the Red Dragons continued to operate in the division.

Conflict outside of Anglophone regions

As in 2018, there were reports of clashes and separatist activities outside the Northwest and Southwest regions, but the ADF only formally endorsed expanding the conflict in March 2019. On 1 April, separatist forces attacked a military checkpoint in Penda Mboko, Littoral Region. On 4 August, separatist forces killed a solider and his driver in the same area. On 7 April, separatists kidnapped a number of internally displaced children from the Anglophone region, who had relocated to Fongo Tongo in the West Region.

---

22 July
A riot breaks out in Kondengui Central Prison in Yaoundé.

26 July
Separatist groups begin a ten-day region-wide lockdown, but disagreement between IG factions leads to weak enforcement.

26 August
Separatist forces begin to enforce a three-week lockdown.

30 September
The Major National Dialogue begins with over 1,000 attendees, but is boycotted by major separatist groups.

1 October
Red Dragons leader Lekeaka Oliver proclaims himself leader of Lebialem Division.

8 November
US rescinds Cameroon's preferential trade access due to human-rights violations.

14 October
Separatist 'general' Ekeom Polykarb surrenders to government forces but is assassinated soon after by separatist forces.

19 December
Cameroonian National Assembly approves special status for Northwest and Southwest regions.

Impact

Human rights
Numerous reports have alleged severe human-rights violations by both the government's security forces and separatist groups. Human-rights organisations reported that government forces destroyed approximately 134 villages in 2019, bringing the total number to more than 200.[9] The separatist focus on disrupting the educational system and limiting commerce with French companies has also had a profound impact. In Northwest and Southwest regions, 90% of public primary schools and 77% of secondary schools remained closed throughout 2019, and universities in Buea and Bamenda have been targeted for kidnappings. The UN Office for the Coordination of Humanitarian Affairs (OCHA) estimates that the educational crisis, which has now continued for several years, has led to an increase in sexual exploitation, gender-based violence, early marriage and forced labour.[10] In 2019, separatist groups also increased the use of kidnapping for ransom, greatly affecting the safety and well-being of citizens in Anglophone Cameroon.

Humanitarian
While there was no dramatic change in conditions in 2019, the situation has deteriorated. The conflict and the government's use of harsh counter-insurgency tactics have taken a significant humanitarian toll. There were more than 300 reported violent incidents, while OCHA reported in December 2019 that at least 668,000 people had been internally displaced, up from 437,000 in 2018. The UN High Commissioner for Refugees (UNHCR) assessed that in 2019 there were an additional 10,000 refugees in Nigeria, bringing the total to more than 45,000. More than 4m people are in need of humanitarian aid.

Economic
There is no systematic assessment of the economic costs of the conflict, but agricultural exports of cocoa and coffee declined by approximately 25% between September 2017 and September 2018.[11] The conflict has led the state-run palm-oil company Pamol to shut down mills in Ndian and Meme and the Cameroonian Development Corporation (CDC) to dismiss nearly 20,000 workers. There has been a slowdown in trade of basic goods such as fabrics, electronics and foodstuffs along the Cameroon–Nigeria border.[12] The only economic estimate of the cost of the conflict comes from September 2018, and totalled half a billion dollars.[13] Frequent internet shutdowns have brought investments into the IT sector to a halt, and many enterprises have moved to Douala or Yaoundé.[14]

Political
The Major National Dialogue was a missed opportunity for resolving the crisis, and Biya has offered no tangible concessions to Anglophone demands for third-party mediation. The creation of a special status for Northwest and Southwest regions was not supported by the major Anglophone groups and was seen as purely symbolic.

The conflict has also worsened democratic processes in Cameroon. Legislative elections have been postponed for nearly two years, and the 2018 presidential election was marred by violence and fraud, particularly in Northwest and Southwest regions. Many members of the main opposition party, the Cameroon Renaissance Movement (MRC), and its leader Maurice Kamto were controversially imprisoned in a military tribunal without effective representation until October 2019. The MRC remains a target of government repression.[15] While the MRC is not part of the immediate Anglophone movement, the regime's increased sensitivity to political opposition is due to the conflict.

Relations with neighbouring and international partners
Cameroon plays an important role in regional security cooperation, which the Anglophone conflict might threaten. Cameroon is a member of the MNJTF and contributes troops to the UN's stabilisation mission in Central African Republic. Moreover, Cameroon patrols a lengthy border with Chad and Central African Republic that is porous to smuggling and other illicit activities. While the Cameroonian armed forces have made significant advances against Boko Haram, continued conflict in Anglophone regions could divert crucial military resources and lead to a resurgence of the group in the frontier areas in the North and to increased criminal activity along its long rural borders.

Trends

Political trajectories

The 2020 legislative elections, already postponed for two years, will be an opportunity for the regime to strengthen its ruling coalition and position strong supporters in public institutions. There is not likely to be any public opposition to the government's strategy from members of the ruling party, and Biya will easily be able to pass legislative measures that could shield the regime from scrutiny and perpetuate the crisis.

Conflict-related risks

The conflict will likely remain in the condition of stalemate. The government will not reduce its counter-insurgency efforts but will instead seek to consolidate the control gained over areas in Anglophone Cameroon. Nonetheless, separatist groups will continue to operate with ease in many rural areas where infrastructure is poor. The insurgents will likely increasingly rely on tactics such as kidnappings for ransom to supplement financing from the diaspora community in Nigeria, France and the US.

Prospects for peace

Throughout 2019, the IG and the ADF eclipsed the civil-society-based protest movement that was still paramount in 2017. There are now numerous armed groups with different political aims, and deep divisions between the political and armed opposition. The fragmentation of the Anglophone movement will remain a key impediment to conflict resolution. Although international attention to the conflict has increased, unless there is greater concerted effort and the use of stronger measures, the conflict is likely to continue in 2020.

Notes

[1] Piet Konings and Francis B. Nyamnjoh, 'The Anglophone Problem in Cameroon', *Journal of Modern African Studies*, vol. 35, no. 2 (1997).

[2] Moki Edwin Kindzeka, 'Lawyers, Teachers in Cameroon Strike for More English in Anglophone Regions', VOA News, 29 November 2016.

[3] Amnesty International, 'Cameroon: Release of Anglophone Leaders a Relief but Others Still Languish in Prison', 30 August 2017.

[4] 'Ambazonia Generals Reject 10-Day Shutdown in Restive NW Region', *Journal du Cameroun*, 5 August 2019.

[5] 'Key Resolutions of the Major National Dialogue', CRTV, 6 October 2019.

[6] 'Governor of Crisis Hit NW Region on Peace Campaign in Bui', *Journal du Cameroun*, 30 July 2019; 'Two Wounded in Amba Fighters' Attack on NW Governor Convoy', *Journal du Cameroun*, 23 October 2019; Eric Tataw, 'Ambazonia Fighters Attack Cameroon Governor's Convoy, Injure Four Soldiers', *National Telegraph*, 12 February 2019; 'Gunmen Attempt to Burn Residence of Biya Aid', *Journal du Cameroun*, 20 February 2019; 'Ambazonia Fighters Attack Convoy of Meme SDO', *Journal du Cameroun*, 25 October 2019.

[7] 'Government Condemns Ambazonia Attack on Fulani Camp in Bamenda', *Journal du Cameroun*, 1 June 2019; International Crisis Group, '*Crisis Watch*', June 2019.

[8] Moki Edwin Kindzeka, 'Whereabouts of 100s Unknown After Cameroon Prison Riot', VOA News, 5 August 2019.

[9] Center for Human Rights and Democracy in Africa, 'Cameroon's Unfolding Catastrophe: Evidence of Human Rights Violations and Crimes Against Humanity', 3 June 2019; International Crisis Group, 'Cameroon's Anglophone Dialogue: A Work in Progress', 26 September 2019.

[10] OCHA, 'Cameroon: North-West and South-West Situation Report No. 11', 30 September 2019.

[11] International Monetary Fund, 'Third Review Under Extended Credit Facility Agreement', IMF Country Report 18/378, December 2018.

[12] 'Cameroon's Palm Oil Cocoa Sectors Worst Hit by Crisis', *Journal du Cameroun*, 19 July 2018; Amindeh Blaise Atabong, 'Cameroon's Nigerian business community is fleeing as the Anglophone crisis deepens', Quartz, 7 July 2018.

[13] Groupement Inter-Patronal du Cameroun, 'Consequences Economiques et Impacts Sur L'activite des Entreprises', July 2018.

[14] Abdi Latif Dahir, 'How do you build Africa's newest tech ecosystem when the government shuts the internet down?', Quartz, 3 February 2017.

[15] Jeffrey Smith, 'The US Should Bid Biya Goodbye', *Foreign Affairs*, 10 July 2019.

CENTRAL AFRICAN REPUBLIC

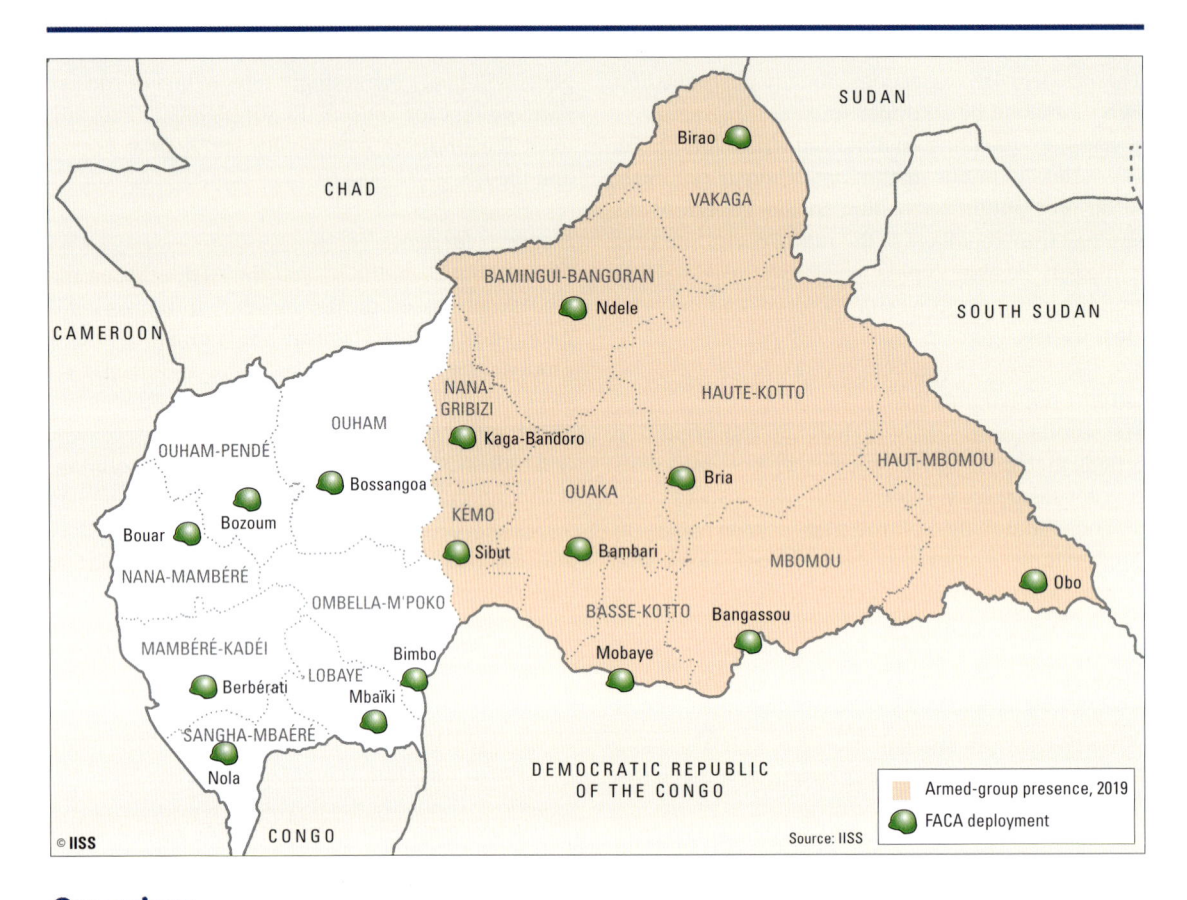

Overview

The conflict in 2019

After multiple uncoordinated and unsuccessful mediation attempts, the African Union (AU) negotiated a peace deal concerning the conflict in the Central African Republic (CAR) that was signed in Khartoum in February 2019. The main provisions were the inclusion of 14 armed groups into the government, a disarmament, demobilisation and reintegration (DDR) programme for militia fighters, and the creation of mixed units with the CAR Army (FACA). In exchange, the armed groups promised to end violence and hand over their territory to the state's representatives and security forces.

The Khartoum agreement did not significantly change the balance of power between the government and the armed groups in the CAR. Most of the country remained under the control of armed groups which lacked any political agenda and whose main activities are extortion and banditry.

There were, however, signs of progress: though the groups did not disarm and at times violated the agreement, they were not involved in any serious fighting. As a result, violence significantly decreased in 2019, with the conflict remaining confined to three hotspots: northwest (one armed group versus the United Nations Multidimensional Integrated Stabilization Mission in the Central African Republic (MINUSCA)); northeast (fighting

Key statistics	
Type	Internationalised
Start date	December 2012
IDPs total (30 September 2019)	600,136
Refugees total (31 December 2019)	591,712
People in need (31 December 2019)	2,600,000

between two ethnically based armed groups); and the capital Bangui (confrontations between traders and militiamen).

The conflict to 2019

The current conflict in the CAR broke out at the end of 2012 when a coalition of armed groups known as the Séléka formed in the Muslim-majority northern part of the country with the objective of ousting then-president François Bozizé. When a peace deal mediated by the Economic Community of the Central African States (ECCAS) failed, the Séléka rebel coalition marched into Bangui and overthrew Bozizé on 24 March 2013. The Séléka coalition, however, proved unable to establish a functional government, leading to the collapse of the state and proliferation of armed groups in the security vacuum.

Exploiting the situation of anarchy, a self-defence group called the 'anti-balaka' emerged in western CAR in 2013 and marched on Bangui. To avoid a massacre (and protect its citizens), France launched *Operation Sangaris* on 5 December 2013.

The Séléka coalition was chased away from Bangui and fragmented but left behind some fighters in the main trade district, PK5. As Muslims were perceived as Séléka supporters, the violence assumed religious and inter-communal dimensions. Most of the Muslims fled to Cameroon and Chad, but others remained trapped in enclaves surrounded by the anti-balaka. A peacekeeping force deployed (first by the AU then by the UN) and a transitional government was established in early 2014, but by 2015 the initial confrontation between the anti-balaka and the Séléka coalition had turned into a chaotic fight between many armed groups vying for territorial control and economic resources.

Elections were organised in 2016 under international supervision. Faustin-Archange Touadéra, former prime minister under Bozizé, won and formed a government. *Operation Sangaris* ended in October 2016 and 11,000 UN peacekeepers deployed throughout the country, but in 2017, the conflict spread from the west to the centre and the southeast of the country.

Key Conflict Parties

Union for Peace in the Central African Republic (UPC)

Strength
Approximately 5,000.

Areas of operation
Central and southeastern CAR (Ouaka, Kémo, Mbomou, Haut-Mbomou, Basse-Kotto and Haute-Kotto provinces). At the end of 2019, the UPC extended its control to the border with South Sudan. Its fighters moved into the Haut-Mbomou Province and took control of the border post of Bambouti.

Leadership
Ali Darassa, a Fulani long-term rebel and bandit, formerly a commander of the Baba Ladde militia. The rest of the leadership (comzones) comprises professional bandits and mercenaries.

Structure
Not known.

History
The UPC was the first group to split from the Séléka coalition in 2014.

Objectives
Officially, the UPC protects Fulani communities but its main objective is to control natural resources and the trade routes between the CAR and neighbouring countries.

Opponents
The expansion of the UPC in 2015 and 2016 caused the creation of an anti-UPC coalition (FPRC, MPC and some anti-balaka groups). In 2017 and 2018, the UPC fought against those armed groups on several fronts in the east and the south of the CAR, and also opposed government forces.

Affiliates/allies
3R.

Resources/capabilities
Involved in cattle trade, minerals smuggling and weapons trafficking between Chad, the DRC and South Sudan.

United Nations Multidimensional Integrated Stabilization Mission in the Central African Republic (MINUSCA)

Strength
As of 31 December 2019, MINUSCA had 13,312 personnel.

Areas of operation
All CAR.

Leadership
In February 2019, Mankeur Ndiaye was appointed head of MINUSCA, replacing Parfait Onanga-Anyanga. Lt-Gen. Balla Keita is the Force Commander.

United Nations Multidimensional Integrated Stabilization Mission in the Central African Republic (MINUSCA)

Structure
MINUSCA comprises 10,835 military personnel, 1,162 civilians, 146 experts on mission, 2,067 police, 303 staff officers and 216 volunteers. (Civilian data as of May 2018.)

History
MINUSCA was authorised by the UN Security Council on 10 April 2014; its mandate was extended for one year on 15 November 2019.

Objectives
MINUSCA's highest priority is the protection of civilians. Other tasks include support for the transition process; facilitating humanitarian assistance; promotion and protection of human rights; support for justice and the rule of law; and disarmament, demobilisation, reintegration and repatriation processes.

Opponents
Various armed groups, including 3R.

Affiliates/allies
CAR government.

Resources/capabilities
Approved budget for mid-2019–mid-2020: US$976.4 million.

Popular Front for the Renaissance in the Central African Republic (FPRC)

Strength
Not known.

Areas of operation
Northeastern CAR (Vakaga, Haute-Kotto and Bamingui-Bangoran provinces). In 2019, the FPRC lost control of part of Vakaga Province.

Leadership
Abdoulaye Hissène is the FPRC's military leader; Noureddine Adam is the political leader.

Structure
Made up of Rounga, Goula, Chadian and Sudanese fighters, but most Goula elements left after internal fighting in 2017–18 and joined another armed group (RPRC NAME).

History
Emerged after the fall of the Séléka coalition in 2014. Leading Séléka members Hissène and Adam created a new group to maintain control of the northeast.

Objectives
FPRC's political agenda focuses on protecting Muslim communities and partitioning the country. In 2015, Adam briefly proclaimed the creation of an independent state, the Logone Republic, and subsequently tried to re-unite the former Séléka groups, with no success.

Opponents
MLCJ and government forces.

Affiliates/allies
Loose alliance with the UPC in the southeast.

Resources/capabilities
FPRC controls some of the trade and cattle routes between Chad, Sudan and the CAR and thus can count on significant financial resources. It is well connected in Chadian and Sudanese circles, from which it receives mercenaries as well as military equipment.

3R (Retour, reclamation et rehabilitation)

Strength
Approximately 800, according to a UN estimate.

Areas of operation
Ouham-Pendé Province; the group's headquarters are in De Gaulle town.

Leadership
Fulani warlord Abass Sidiki.

Structure
Not known, but recruitment is Fulani-based.

History
Emerged in late 2015 at the northwest border between the CAR and Cameroon. The group was originally mandated by Fulani cattle-owners based in Cameroon to protect their cattle during the transhumance.

Objectives
Protection of Fulani cattle and economic predation. The group launches indiscriminate retaliatory attacks against villages in case of cattle theft or when Fulani herders are attacked.

Opponents
MINUSCA and anti-balaka groups.

Affiliates/allies
UPC.

Resources/capabilities
Economic resources come from the taxation of Fulani pastoralists and weapons smuggling between Chad and Cameroon. Most of its military equipment comes from Chad.

Movement of Central African Liberators for Justice (MLCJ)

Strength
Not known.

Areas of operation
Vakaga Province.

Leadership
Gilbert-Toumoudeya, a relative of a Kara traditional leader, is the president.

Structure
Not known.

History
The Kara-based MLCJ broke away from the Union of Democratic Forces for Unity (UFDR) in 2008, and therefore precedes the Séléka rebellion. It remained dormant until 2019.

Objectives
Controlling the Kara territory.

Opponents
FPRC.

Affiliates/allies
In the fight against the FPRC, the MLCJ receives support from Goula militiamen traditionally opposed to the Rounga. Government support cannot be ruled out.

Resources/capabilities
Not known.

Central African Patriotic Movement (MPC)

Strength
Not known.

Areas of operation
Ouham and Nana-Gribizi provinces; the group's headquarters are in Sido (at the border between Chad and the CAR).

Leadership
The MPC's leader is Mahamat Al-Khatim, a Chadian whose family has settled in the CAR. He was appointed special advisor to Prime Minister Firmin Ngrébada after the Khartoum agreement but resigned in August 2019. The rest of the leadership (comzones) are all Chadian fighters.

Structure
Mostly made up of Chadian fighters from the Salamat region. The Salamat traditional leaders have a strong influence over Mahamat Al-Khatim.

History
The MPC splintered from the FPRC in mid-2015.

Objectives
Securing the interests of the Salamat communities in the Ouham and Nana-Gribizi provinces (cattle migration, access to land and markets).

Opponents
UPC and anti-balaka.

Affiliates/allies
Chadian security forces.

Resources/capabilities
Not known.

Lord's Resistance Army (LRA)

Strength
Approximately 200.

Areas of operation
Haut-Mbomou and Haute-Kotto provinces.

Leadership
Joseph Kony (if alive).

Structure
Small groups of bush fighters scattered between the DRC, South Sudan and the CAR.

History
Formed in northern Uganda in the late 1980s, by 2005 the LRA had been pushed to the DRC, South Sudan and the CAR. In 2005, the International Criminal Court (ICC) issued arrest warrants for Kony and several commanders for crimes against humanity and war crimes. A joint Uganda–US mission between 2011 and 2017 failed to capture Kony.

Objectives
The LRA is infamous for its forced recruitment of child soldiers. It now survives by looting villages and trading gold and ivory. LRA activity surged since the withdrawal of the US and Ugandan forces from southeastern CAR in 2017.

Opponents
Zande communities.

Affiliates/allies
Fulani pastoralists.

Resources/capabilities
Small-scale trade of gold and ivory.

Anti-balaka groups

Strength
Not known.

Areas of operation
Active in front-line areas (southeast and central CAR), with some residual groups in western CAR.

Leadership
No central leadership or chain of command. Two coordination branches (run by Maxime Mokom and Sebastien Wenezoui respectively) present themselves as interlocutors for the movement and have signed the Khartoum agreement (Mokom consequently became DDR minister).

Structure
Loose network of anti-Muslim local militias.

History
Emerged as a self-defence movement against the Séléka in western CAR in late 2013. Entered Bangui in December 2013 to chase away the Séléka coalition. In 2014 they became infamous for their attacks against Muslim communities. By 2017, the movement's territorial reach extended with the emergence of self-defence groups in southeastern CAR.

Objectives
No clear agenda. Initially, anti-balaka fighters sought to drive Muslims out of the CAR but quickly turned to violent economic predation (looting and extortion). Each anti-balaka group sets up specific predation mechanisms at the local level, and, despite the initial anti-Séléka motive, some allied with Muslim armed groups.

Opponents
Muslim armed groups and other anti-balaka groups.

Affiliates/allies
Government forces.

Resources/capabilities
Artisanal arms, few automatic weapons. No organised control of natural resources and trade routes.

Drivers

Widespread economic predation
According to UN estimates, armed groups control 70% of the country, where they compete for territory and resources. Armed groups are self-funded and have economic ties with national political and economic actors. They generate revenues through predation on trade routes and natural resources (diamonds, gold, wildlife and cattle), through roadblocks, pastoralism and trade in minerals.

The sophistication of their predatory strategies varies but all groups use violence to control resource-rich territories. The anti-balaka are notorious for their infighting over revenues, while the most powerful Muslim armed groups (UPC, FPRC and MPC) have set up taxation mechanisms and rely on a diversified revenue base. Ex-Séléka and anti-balaka roadblocks are widespread and are at the core of the political economy of the CAR's conflict: without these revenues, armed groups would struggle to retain their rank and file. The MPC, UPC and FPRC together generate at least €3.6m (US$3.9m) a year from taxing cattle routes, and another €2.5m (US$2.7m) along Sudanese trade routes.

Social and economic rivalries under religious disguise
Since the start of the conflict, hate speech and incitement to ethnic and religious-based violence have been widespread, and some anti-balaka groups have carried out targeted attacks against the Muslim population. Despite many mixed marriages, relations between Muslims and the rest of the population are often tainted by social jealousy, particularly in regard to Muslim control over commerce. In the CAR, traders are mostly Muslim, and Muslim entrepreneurs dominate business sectors including the cattle trade, clothing, transportation, gold and diamond artisanal trade. The real-term decline of civil-servant wages and the Séléka takeover in 2013 exacerbated that economic domination.

Revival of an historic divide
The Séléka power grab in March 2013 marked a fundamental change in national politics. Since the CAR's independence in 1960, the struggle for power was the prerogative of military officers from savanna and riverside communities (central and southern CAR). Previous coups were carried out by senior army officers, sometimes supported by Chadian mercenaries, as in 2003. Dissatisfied with the Bozizé regime, the mercenaries in the 2003 coup became the coup leaders in 2013 and a rebel force composed of Muslims from the north and east of the country took power for the first time.

This violent emergence of new protagonists in the CAR's power game was literally seen as an 'invasion' by the rest of the country. It also awakened the collective memory of Muslim slaving raids that depopulated entire regions and sent captives to Nigeria and Sudan between the sixteenth and nineteenth centuries, when the CAR territory was seen as the slave trade's 'El Dorado'. With the slave trade still very much alive in the collective memory, politicians have used fears of the Muslim 'invasion' to mobilise support.

Environmental degradation
The cattle migration from Cameroon, Chad and Sudan to the CAR is a key economic issue, while the migration's militarisation is a key driver of the violence in rural areas in north and central CAR. Each year during the dry season, thousands of cows move from Chad, Cameroon and Sudan to the grazing fields in the CAR. The Chadian and Sudanese pastoralist communities have progressively encroached further into the CAR territory to escape desertification and natural-resources scarcity, pushing out other pastoralist communities such as the Fulani, who have crossed into the DRC with their cattle, fuelling land conflicts between pastoralist and farming communities in the CAR as well as in northeast DRC.

Political Developments

Khartoum peace agreement
The signing of the Khartoum peace agreement was the most significant political development in 2019. Signed on 6 February in Khartoum, Sudan, it was negotiated by the AU with the blessing of the UN and the discreet support of Russia (with high-ranking officials attending the negotiations). While the AU was in charge of the peace negotiations, the AU, UN and European Union were in charge of implementing the peace deal, with a clear division of labour: the AU would provide political supervision, the UN technical and logistical support, while the EU was the main funder.

Since armed groups control most of the CAR territory, the government accepted a power-sharing agreement in exchange for a halt to the violence and a DDR process. The agreement stipulates the formation of a new government that would include the leaders of the armed groups, as well as mandating the dismantlement of taxation checkpoints, a stop to the violence, the deployment of state personnel throughout the country and a DDR process. Militiamen would also join together with state security forces to form 'mixed units' in Bouar (west), Ndele (north) and Bangassou (south) to provide security and secure borders, mining areas and the cattle migration. The first mixed unit formed in Bouar and began training in October.

By the end of 2019, however, little progress had been made. The leaders of the armed groups received official positions and ceased violence but did not reduce their forces and kept control of their economic resources. Thanks to the momentum of the peace deal, MINUSCA convinced some small armed groups in western CAR to join the DDR process (FDPC, Revolution and Justice), but only the Bouar mixed unit has been set up (supervised by the UN) and in some cases, the rank and file and their leaders split over the DDR process.

Two governments were formed in the space of a few weeks in March, as some armed-group leaders were unhappy with the positions offered. Abdoulaye Miskine (FDPC) disavowed the agreement immediately and refused his ministerial position, while Sidiki Abass (3R) blocked the implementation of the DDR process in the area under his control (he then agreed in November). The peace agreement also had little domestic support. CAR elites, the public and even some members of the government opposed the power-sharing agreement with the armed groups, which they saw as engineered by international actors. The political opposition tried to launch a parliamentary debate on the peace deal and religious leaders and civil-society organisations publicly expressed their concerns.[1] The power-sharing arrangement also compromised post-conflict justice initiatives, including ongoing criminal proceedings by the Special Criminal Court and the ICC, as most of the armed-group leaders have obtained official appointments.

In terms of implementation, the peace agreement was violated twice (firstly, the killing of civilians around Paoua, and secondly with the fighting between the FPRC and MLCJ) without significant reactions from the AU, UN, EU or the government. The UPC has extended its territorial control from the centre to the southeast of CAR without encountering any resistance from MINUSCA or government forces. At the end of October, a group of UPC militiamen took over Bambouti, the border post between the CAR and South Sudan, and asserted its authority in the area.

Preparations for elections in 2020

The faulty implementation of the peace agreement will likely become a key campaign issue ahead of the elections to be held on 27 December 2020. The opposition was divided over participation in the electoral process: some members were ready to participate, while others feared that the president and the armed groups would prevent them from campaigning in many provinces. A civil-society platform called E Zingo Biani voiced its opposition to the Khartoum peace agreement and blamed the president for the lack of development. The movement gathered civil-society activists and some disgruntled politicians, including some former members of the government, and positioned itself as the main opposition. The government banned its first demonstration in June but allowed the second in September.

Adding a further complication, former president Bozizé made a surprising comeback after six years of exile in Uganda. Despite the international warrant issued by the CAR authorities in 2013, his political party, the Kwa Na Kwa (KNK), helped him to secretly return in December 2019 and organised a public meeting in Bangui in which he declared his intention to challenge the incumbent president in 2020. Bozizé met with opposition leaders and will tour the country in 2020. The Touadéra government did not try to arrest him for fear of triggering a popular uprising, but the risk of a military coup cannot be ruled out (Bozizé has widespread support in military circles).[2]

The UN and the EU will support the electoral process. On 15 November, the UN Security Council extended MINUSCA's mandate for a year to include electoral assistance for the government. The EU will provide most of the funding as it did in 2011 and 2016. By the end of 2019, the composition of the electoral commission had yet to be decided and is likely to remain a highly contentious issue.

The new 'Cold War'

The CAR remained caught between international rivalries in 2019. Since strengthening ties with Touadéra in late 2017, Russia has continued providing military equipment and instructors for the FACA and close protection for the president through a private military company (Wagner).[3] It discreetly supported the deployment of FACA units

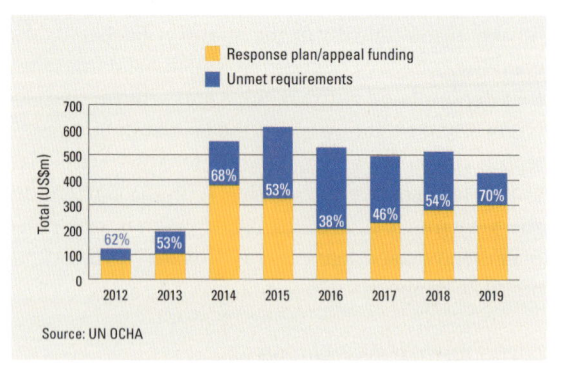

Figure 1: Received and required humanitarian funding, 2012–19

Key Events in 2019

Political events

- **11 January**: New US Ambassador to the CAR Lucy Tamlyn is sworn in.
- **6 February**: The government and 14 armed groups sign a peace deal in Khartoum.
- **April**: Russian President Vladimir Putin authorises the deployment of up to 30 military personnel with MINUSCA.
- **3 March**: First government including leaders of armed groups is formed, led by new Prime Minister Firmin Ngrébada.
- **22 March**: Ngrébada forms second government, including more leaders of armed groups.

Military/Violent events

- **22 May**: 3R militiamen attack three villages (Koundjili, Bohong and Ndjondjon) in Ouham-Pendé Province.

in some provinces, sent 15 personnel to MINUSCA, appointed a new ambassador in Bangui and increased the embassy staff.

While the Wagner group was the first Russian entity to set foot in the CAR in 2018 through locally created companies, the state-to-state relationship grew in 2019. On 23–24 October, Touadéra attended the Russia–Africa Summit in Sochi and requested more weapons for his army. After the signing of a military-cooperation agreement, there were talks of a military base and an economic agreement. Russia has supported the CAR government's requests to lift the UN arms embargo.

France and the United States paid close attention to the growing influence of Russia in the CAR in 2019. French authorities worried about the sponsoring of anti-French rhetoric and the spreading of anti-French sentiments in CAR social-media networks, while the US government appointed an ambassador in Bangui in January 2019, having failed to do so for several years. In the following months, the US also increased its diplomatic staff in Bangui and its financial assistance.

Diplomatic dialogue with neighbouring countries
Following the peace deal, the CAR government re-established diplomatic dialogue with Cameroon and the Republic of Congo by reviving two bilateral commissions that had not met for years. The CAR–Cameroon and the CAR–Congo Brazzaville commissions both met in Bangui in 2019 to deal with border security and refugee returns, among other issues.

In October 2019, the Chadian government announced the appointment of an ambassador in Bangui (diplomatic relationships between the CAR and Chad were suspended after the start of the conflict in 2013 and the closure of the border in 2014). In December, CAR Minister for Foreign Affairs Sylvie Baïpo-Témon went to N'Djamena to start discussions for reopening the border between the two countries.

Military Developments

FACA deployment
As stipulated in the peace agreement, FACA units continued to deploy across the CAR in 2019, with more than 1,300 troops based in provincial cities by the end of the year. Training by the EU and Russia continued, while troops also received support from MINUSCA and were accompanied and mentored by Wagner personnel. Since the FACA lacked vehicles and logistical capacity, its role was mainly to secure the entry points to the cities. In 2019, there was only one confrontation between the FACA and the UPC (on 27 November in Bambari, Ouaka Province), with no casualties.

3R killings
The first violation of the Khartoum agreement occurred in early May, when 3R fighters killed at least 40 civilians in the villages of Koundjili, Bohong and Ndjondjon in the northwest (close to the Chadian border) in retaliation for the killing of Fulani herders

---

15 June
Demonstration by opposition platform E Zingo Biani is banned. Two French journalists are beaten and arrested.

30 September
Demonstration by E Zingo Biani in Bangui is authorised.

17 October
First mixed unit starts training in Bouar, Nana-Mambéré Province.

23–24 October
President Touadéra attends the Russia–Africa Summit in Sochi.

15 November
UN Security Council extends MINUSCA mandate for a year and includes electoral assistance for 2020.

November
Registration of 3R militiamen for the DDR process starts in their stronghold (Koui, Ouham-Pendé Province).

June
Clashes begin between FPRC and MLCJ in Vakaga Province.

September
MINUSCA launches *Operation Enclume* against 3R.

27 November
Clash between UPC and the FACA in Bambari, Ouaka Province.

25–26 December
Fighting between militiamen and traders in Bangui's PK5 district.

in the same area. The killings terrorised the communities in northwestern CAR, shocked the public and increased hatred for the Fulani people.

In response, MINUSCA and the government opted for a combination of negotiations and military pressure. In September and October 2019, MINUSCA launched several operations against the 3R. *Operation Enclume* aimed to contain the 3R before the cattle-migration season and urge the group to join the DDR programme. At the end of October, negotiations restarted between the government, MINUSCA and Sidiki, who pledged to respect the peace agreement, allow his fighters to join the DDR programme and relocate to Bouar under the protection of government forces.

Fighting between two armed groups in Vakaga
The FPRC and MLCJ began fighting in Vakaga Province in June 2019 in what appeared to be a community war fought through armed groups. The fighters of the MLCJ and FPRC belong to different northeastern CAR communities – the MLCJ to the Kara; the FPRC to the Rounga – although some Goula militiamen also sided with the MLCJ because they are traditional rivals of the Rounga.

At stake was the control of local resources, notably land and the city of Birao, which hosts the main market in the province. As the gateway to South Darfur, Birao is also of strategic importance for the trade between Sudan and the CAR, including the flow of weapons between the two countries. The FPRC was ousted by the MLCJ from three cities (Tissy, Birao and Am-Dafock, a border post with Sudan) but launched a new offensive in mid-December and retook control of Am-Dafock.[4] Busy fighting the 3R, MINUSCA adopted a wait-and-see strategy towards the conflict in the northeast and did not deploy more troops to the area.

Fighting between militiamen and traders
At least 30 people were killed in fighting between militiamen and traders in the main market neighbourhood of Bangui, PK5, on 25–26 December 2019. The fighting began after traders in the district took up arms to oppose taxes levied by local militia groups. Some shops and houses were burned down.

Impact

Humanitarian
The humanitarian situation in the CAR in 2019 did not change significantly compared to 2018. Some 2.6m people – half of the population – still depended on humanitarian assistance by December 2019,[5] and by September 2019 around 600,000 people were internally displaced and there were 590,000 refugees in Cameroon, the DRC, Chad, the Republic of Congo, Sudan and South Sudan.[6]

In 2019, the first spontaneous returns of refugees began since the 2014 mass displacements, mostly comprised of several hundred Muslim refugees coming back to western CAR from northern Congo-Brazzaville and Cameroon (the country hosting the most CAR refugees).[7] Most of these are Fulani pastoralists, whose cattle need grazing land. In the southwestern CAR provinces (Mambéré-Kadéï and Sangha-Mbaéré) their return was peaceful, but in the northwestern provinces (Nana-Mambéré and Ouham-Pendé) they sought 3R's protection for the annual cattle migration, causing tensions with local communities. Other returnees were traders, who came back without any significant incident.

Two agreements for the repatriation of refugees were signed in 2019: between the UN High Commissioner for Refugees (UNHCR), Cameroon and the CAR on 29 June; and between UNHCR, the CAR and the Republic of Congo on 6 August.[8] The agreement with Cameroon set out the terms for the voluntary return of 285,000 refugees; UNHCR should start repatriations in 2020.

Trends

Political trajectories
The implementation of the peace deal will be central in the coming electoral campaign and its progress or failure will have a major impact on electoral strategies. The unexpected return of former president Bozizé is a major setback for the government and

compromises Touadéra's strategy for re-election. Even if Bozizé cannot register as a candidate, he will put his political weight behind the opposition and rally important support in military circles.

Conflict-related risks

Despite the breakthrough in Khartoum in February, some signatories demonstrated a lack of commitment to the peace deal, tensions remain and fighting between the FPRC and MLCJ in particular could escalate during the dry season (December to March). Territorial and economic rivalries could trigger fighting between other armed groups, especially as the UPC tries to expand its territorial control.

Strategic implications and global influences

A stateless country in the centre of Africa constitutes an international security risk that is underestimated. Conflict actors from the region can infiltrate and settle down in the CAR as they wish, pastoralist communities are gradually relocating from the Sahel to the CAR and the DRC, and opportunistic and shadowy businessmen can take advantage of the very weak governance of the CAR. This failed state can become a platform for criminal networks of regional and international dimension. The Russian government will continue to play a role behind the scenes as part of its attempt to regain diplomatic influence in world affairs.

Notes

[1] 'RCA: la confusion autour du nouveau gouvernement inquiète la société civile', Radio France Internationale, 6 March 2019.

[2] 'Centrafrique: L'armée met en garde contre la manipulation', Radio Ndeke Luka, 26 December 2019.

[3] Dionne Searcey, 'Gems, Warlords and Mercenaries: Russia's Playbook in Central African Republic', *New York Times*, 30 September 2019.

[4] 'Vakaga: Nouveau combats entre FPRC et MLCJ á Am-Dafock', Radio Ndeke Luka, 17 December 2019.

[5] United Nations Office for the Coordination of Humanitarian Affairs, 'Central African Republic'.

[6] United Nations High Commissioner for Refugees, 'Refugees Operational Portal: Central African Republic'.

[7] 'Plusieurs centaines de réfugiés centrafricains quittent le Congo-Brazzaville', Radio France Internationale, 20 October 2019.

[8] Lassaad Ben Ahmed, 'Cameroun: accord tripartite pour rapatrier 285 mille réfugiés centrafricains', Anadolu Agency, 1 July 2019; 'Nouvel accord pour le rapatriement volontaire des réfugiés centrafricains du Congo', centrafrique-presse.com, 8 August 2019.

DEMOCRATIC REPUBLIC OF THE CONGO

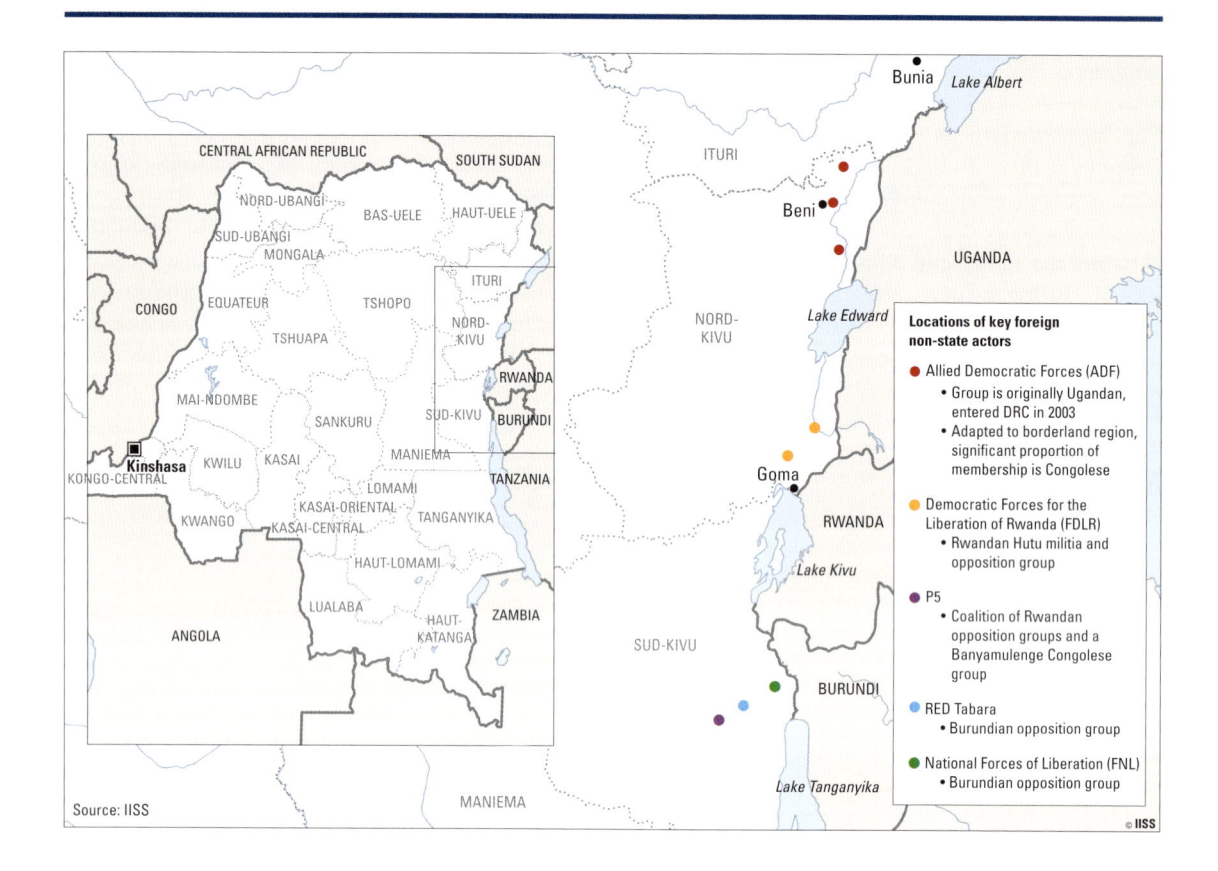

Locations of key foreign non-state actors

- **Allied Democratic Forces (ADF)**
  - Group is originally Ugandan, entered DRC in 2003
  - Adapted to borderland region, significant proportion of membership is Congolese
- **Democratic Forces for the Liberation of Rwanda (FDLR)**
  - Rwandan Hutu militia and opposition group
- **P5**
  - Coalition of Rwandan opposition groups and a Banyamulenge Congolese group
- **RED Tabara**
  - Burundian opposition group
- **National Forces of Liberation (FNL)**
  - Burundian opposition group

Source: IISS

Overview

The conflict in 2019

January 2019 witnessed what appeared to be dramatic changes in the political landscape of the Democratic Republic of the Congo (DRC), when it was announced that opposition candidate Félix Tshisekedi had won the fraught December 2018 election. However, it rapidly became clear that Tshisekedi's victory was fraudulent and conditional on outgoing president Joseph Kabila's Common Front for Congo (FCC) parliamentary group retaining maximum influence in Congolese politics. Throughout 2019, the FCC entrenched its position through a series of sub-national elections and the acquisition of key cabinet posts in a nominal coalition with Tshisekedi. The hopes for change – and their subsequent dampening – among Congolese affected the country's many conflicts.

Early 2019 was marked by a surge of armed-group disarmaments in both the east and west of the country, mostly in reaction to the change in leadership. However, these steps towards stabilisation either stagnated or reversed by the end of the year, largely due to a lack of strategy and resources, as well as broader mismanagement by the Congolese government. Meanwhile, a new phase of an old conflict between Lendu and Hema ethnic groups in Ituri had devastating humanitarian consequences, including the displacement of several hundred thousand

Key statistics

Type	Internationalised
Start date	November 1996
IDPs total (31 December 2019)	5,000,000
Refugees total (31 December 2019)	526,171
People in need (31 December 2019)	15,900,000

people. Other armed groups such as the Allied Democratic Forces (ADF) have remained extremely violent. In the case of the ADF, international concern heightened following claims by official Islamic State (also known as ISIS or ISIL) media that the group was part of a so-called Central Africa Province. The possibility of transnational militancy in the DRC – and its associated risks – continued to worry observers throughout the year, particularly as relations between Uganda, Rwanda and Burundi soured even as multinational military cooperation was discussed. The Ebola crisis was declared a public health emergency of international concern on 17 July, but efforts to address it were hampered by high levels of violence.

The conflict to 2019

It is inaccurate to speak of a single conflict in the DRC. There are well over a hundred localised conflicts in the country, with wave after wave of new armed groups forming since the early 2010s. Groups fight not only the government, but also each other, and ethnic rivalries are a frequent factor in these conflicts. Likewise, foreign insurgencies' activity in the DRC have shaped the country's modern history. After the Rwandan genocide in 1994, Rwandan President Paul Kagame remained fearful of the Hutu militants opposed to his government that were still operating in the DRC's eastern Kivu provinces. Ugandan insurgencies have also made use of the Congolese borderlands to hide from Kampala's reach. These security concerns and the lucrative trade opportunities in natural resources have long incentivised Rwandan and sometimes Ugandan military activity on Congolese soil, whether through their own troops or by backing local armed groups. These dynamics have caused much bloodshed in the DRC and left a legacy of suspicion of foreign intervention, a suspicion which still drives the militarisation among communities in eastern Congo.

After the formal conclusion of the Second Congo War in 2003, the main source of instability was the disagreement between Joseph Kabila's government and the new rebel group National Congress for the Defence of the People (CNDP) led by Laurent Nkunda. A peace deal was eventually reached in 2009, by which the CNDP was integrated into the national army. CNDP officers mutinied in 2012 and formed a new armed group known as M23, which wreaked a devastating military campaign in North and South Kivu. M23 eventually broke down, but its defeat did not bring stability. Smaller groups emerged, large enough to impose their will on civilians and to organise attacks against them and other groups, but not large enough to force the government to deal with them. The weak national army (FARDC) even found some groups to be helpful temporary partners in operations for both military and personal gains.

Joseph Kabila's tenacity also shaped the conduct of the conflict in several ways. Kabila's refusal to leave government after his constitutional mandate and his continuous curtailing of political participation generated widespread grievances and led many to take up arms. His strategy of repeatedly delaying the election became popularly known as '*glissage*' (slippage). Kabila was also directly implicated in igniting violence between the Lendu and Hema groups in Ituri in 2017–18, and even recruited former M23 members to repress political protesters. Likewise, he prevented the United National Stabilization Mission in Congo (MONUSCO) from exercising its mandated political role, allowing him instead to shape the government to protect his position.[1]

Key Conflict Parties

The Armed Forces of the Democratic Republic of the Congo (FARDC)

Strength
Approximately 135,000.

Areas of operation
The FARDC operates across the country in 11 Military Regions, but operations mainly focus on North and South Kivu provinces and (to a lesser extent in 2019) Kasai Province.

Leadership
Lt-Gen. Célestin Mbala Munsense is Chief of the General Staff.

Structure
The FARDC is very large but poorly structured, with perhaps as many as 65% of its troops being officers, 26% of whom are high-ranking.[2] This is partly the result of regularly awarding officer positions to defecting rebels.

The Armed Forces of the Democratic Republic of the Congo (FARDC)

History
The FARDC was created by the 2003 Sun City Peace Agreement, which stipulated that all parties to the conflict contribute troops to the national army, an integration process known as *brassage*. Despite international efforts at security-sector reform, the FARDC remains a mix of feuding militias.

Objectives
While formally the FARDC fulfils national-security objectives, many officers and soldiers pursue their own agendas, particularly wealth-seeking through illicit trade and mining, or enacting the violent demands of political patrons.

Opponents
The majority of armed groups in the DRC (except those with which the FARDC has an alliance of convenience).

Affiliates/allies
The FARDC frequently uses armed groups to do its fighting and sometimes allies with them for political and economic opportunities.

Resources/capabilities
The FARDC suffers from chronic resource shortages (including salaries) due to political and military corruption and is weak and ineffective. It is predominantly armed with small arms and light weapons, but also has artillery, 430 armoured fighting vehicles, anti-aircraft guns and surface-to-air missiles.

United Nations Stabilization Mission in Congo (MONUSCO)

Strength
As of 31 December 2019, MONUSCO had 15,346 personnel. While most MONUSCO troops do not have an offensive mandate and are tasked with protection of civilians, the mission also has a Force Intervention Brigade (FIB) to allow the use of force against armed actors.

Areas of operation
The mission headquarters and the political unit are based in Kinshasa. MONUSCO's military component is predominantly concentrated in North and South Kivu provinces, though it has a presence in Kasai and was also forced to surge its presence in Ituri Province this year.

Leadership
Lt-Gen. Ricardo Augusto Ferreira Costa Neves is MONUSCO's Force Commander, while Leila Zerrougui is the Special Representative of the Secretary General.

Structure
The contingents are spread out over a number of bases (sometimes temporary bases) and operate in clusters of forces, with units from several contingents per base.

History
MONUSCO replaced the United Nations Organization Mission in the Congo (MONUC) in July 2010 with an enhanced peacekeeping mandate that would allow protection of civilians. The FIB was mandated in 2013 with the aim of strengthening peacekeeping operations.

Objectives
To stabilise the situation in the DRC and improve governance.

Opponents
Non-state armed groups in its areas of operation.

Affiliates/allies
MONUSCO does periodically conduct joint operations with the FARDC, but relations are often tense.

Resources/capabilities
MONUSCO is relatively well equipped and has air assets (including four combat jets and seven helicopter gunships) as well as armoured personnel carriers and artillery. However, intermittent donor funding complicates its ability to resource its operations effectively.

Cooperation for the Development of Congo (CODECO)

Strength
Believed to be around 500 people, but estimates should be treated with caution. Uncertainly over who perpetrates the attacks against Hema residents in Ituri persists.

Areas of operation
Djugu, Mahagi and Irumu territories in Ituri Province.

Leadership
A man named Ngujolo is the recognised leader of CODECO, although his first name has not been confirmed.

Structure
Unclear, but given CODECO's repeated engagements in violence over several decades, and the fact that the widespread violence of 2019 is believed to have been well coordinated, the group likely coordinates its activity through cells.

History
CODECO formed in the 1970s, originally as a farming collective, but developed both mystical and militant dimensions over time. It has since engaged in numerous bouts of violence against the Hema.

Objectives
While CODECO's objective appears to be ethnic violence against the Hema population, ethnicity is not the main driver, and conflict is tied to political circumstances. The group is expressing willingness to enter a peace process, and better food provision for the area is one of the conditions for its participation.

Opponents
Hema individuals and self-defence groups, FARDC.

Affiliates/allies
CODECO is believed to have links with the Iturian groups Front of Integrationist Nationalists (FNI) and Ituri Patriotic Resistance Force (FPRI).

Resources/capabilities
Much of CODECO's fighting is done with bladed weapons or small arms and light weapons.

Allied Democratic Forces (ADF)

Strength
Likely around 1,000–1,200, although not all its personnel are combatants.

Areas of operation
Beni Territory (particularly Beni town), Eringeti, Mbau and (increasingly) in Kamango, close to the border with Uganda.

Leadership
Seka Musa Baluku is the overall leader.

Structure
The ADF is divided between several main camps, each of which houses between 150 and 200 fighters. Its principal base near Eringeti is known as Madina Camp. Each camp has recognised military leaders and ranks, although it is unclear if the ranks follow a conventional military structure.

History
Created in 1995 from a merger between Ugandan Tabliqh Islamists and the remnants of a Ugandan secessionist movement in the Uganda–Congo border area. Over time the group has increasingly adopted jihadist rhetoric and ideology. It referred to itself as Medina al-Tauheed wa Mujahedeen, and in April 2019 official ISIS media began claiming some of its attacks.

Objectives
The ADF regularly attacks and kills civilians in the Beni area, but has no clearly articulated political plans other than vague Salafi-jihadist statements. While ISIS has claimed credit for its attacks, it has not expressed specific plans in relation to the DRC.

Opponents
The FARDC and MONUSCO have engaged in numerous operations against the ADF for several years.

Affiliates/allies
The ADF has been known to form temporary alliances or bargains with local armed actors, including elements of the FARDC.

Resources/capabilities
The ADF is well integrated into the borderland landscape and can draw on a number of sources to sustain itself, including agriculture and illicit trade. While it is armed largely with light weapons, ISIS media has regularly claimed that the group steals weapons from the FARDC.

RED Tabara

Strength
Unclear, but RED Tabara claims to have 2,000 recruits.[3]

Areas of operation
Uvira Territory and the Ruzizi Plain.

Leadership
'General' Birembu Melkiade is the recognised leader of RED Tabara, but is currently believed to be in Congolese custody. 'Colonel' Raymond Lukondo is Melkiade's deputy and is the interim military leader.

Structure
Unclear, but presence of designated ranks suggests the group is mimicking a conventional military structure.

History
RED Tabara is believed to be the military wing of the Movement for Solidarity and Democracy (MSD) party led by Alexis Sinduhije, which was formed in response to Burundian President Pierre Nkurunziza's refusal to give up power in 2015.

Objectives
The overthrow of the Nkurunziza regime in neighbouring Burundi.

Opponents
The Burundian armed forces (FDN), which have made several incursions into Congolese territory to fight RED Tabara. A Burundian youth group known as Imbonerakure has been known to fight RED Tabara alongside the FDN.

Affiliates/allies
Other Burundian opposition groups including the National Forces of Liberation (FNL) operate in the same area, but it is unclear whether they cooperate.

Resources/capabilities
The group is believed to receive some funding from the Burundian diaspora, and also some support from Burundi.

Raia Mutomboki

Strength
As a decentralised franchise rather than a single armed group, it is not possible to give clear numbers, though there are likely several thousand Raia Mutomboki affiliates across several dozen groups. However, many of these individuals are not solely combatants, and only take up arms at specific times.

Areas of operation
Raia Mutomboki are historically a phenomenon of South Kivu and are still most active in the Katchungu, Shabunda and Walungu areas, as well as in Kahuzi-Biega National Park. However, there is some limited Raia Mutomboki activity in North Kivu as well.

Leadership
While the Raia Mutomboki were launched around a pastor named Jean Musumbu, Raia Mutomboki groups have since proliferated and each group has different leadership structures.

Structure
Groups are largely informally structured given their ideological foundation as citizens' movements, although this causes tension with military objectives and there are individuals who attempt to structure and lead the groups. However, these structuring efforts are transient.

Raia Mutomboki

History
Formed in 2005 in order to combat FDLR violence, but also as a form of protest against state violence and neglect. The name Raia Mutomboki means 'angry citizens', and the groups largely continue to style themselves as grassroots defenders.

Objectives
The political demands vary from group to group. Broadly, they aim to fight the FDLR, counter state violence and advocate for the inclusion of their area's citizens into state services. They also function as local defence militias.

Opponents
FDLR, FARDC.

Affiliates/allies
Alliances tend to be localised and short-term.

Resources/capabilities
Raia Mutomboki largely draw on the same revenue sources as ordinary people, including agriculture and artisanal mining. Their weapons are limited to small arms and bladed weapons.

Mai-Mai groups

Strength
There are over 50 known Mai-Mai groups in the Kivu provinces. Some groups have formed large coalitions of several hundred fighters (such as the Mai-Mai Mazembe or Yakutumba), but the majority of groups tend to comprise fewer than 200 fighters.

Areas of operation
Present in most of North and South Kivu.

Leadership
Each group has its own leadership arrangements, with some groups being more centralised around a single leader, while others have a less defined leadership.

Structure
Largely informal and non-hierarchical.

History
Mai-Mai groups mostly formed as self-defence militias. A majority have anti-Tutsi or anti-Rwandan sentiments, and see themselves as indigenous defenders against Rwandan foreigners.

Objectives
While the groups are styled as community-protection groups, usually around a particular ethnicity and locality, they often collaborate with each other, or with larger armed actors, for both defensive and opportunistic reasons.

Opponents
Typically groups are of Rwandan origin or Banyamulenge groups. However, localised territorial struggles are also common.

Affiliates/allies
Alliances of convenience are periodically formed, including between Mai-Mai groups.

Resources/capabilities
Mai-Mai weapons are usually limited to small arms or machetes and other bladed weapons. A number of groups take part in artisanal mining and periodically exercise control over mining sites.

The Democratic Forces for the Liberation of Rwanda (FDLR)

Strength
While the FDLR was believed to number between 500 and 1,000 combatants in 2017, several hundred fighters demobilised in 2018. In 2019, the FDLR likely had fewer than 500 combatants. Following the leadership crisis of 2019, it is possible that numbers will fall further.

Areas of operation
Rutshuru and Kitchanga (North Kivu Province).

Leadership
The FDLR lost its most senior leaders in 2019 and it is unclear what effect the leadership change will have on the group's cohesion. FDLR president Ignace Murwanashyaka died in April 2019 in hospital in Germany. In September 2019, the FDLR's military commander Sylvestre Mudacumura was killed by the FARDC. The current leader is believed to be Pacifique Ntawunguka.

Structure
The FDLR mimics a conventional military structure, with specialised units for particular missions. However, the reduction in numbers and loss of long-standing leaders may see a gradual informalisation of the group.

History
Former officers from the army of Rwandan president Juvénal Habyarimana fled to the DRC (then known as Zaire) after the 1994 genocide and remobilised in refugee camps. The group changed its name to the FDLR in 1999. Individuals involved in the genocide are still believed to be with the movement.

Objectives
The FDLR's stated aim is to ensure the repatriation of Rwandan refugees displaced during the genocide. However, Rwanda insists that the FDLR aims to overthrow the Kagame government in Rwanda. The FDLR is ideologically divided along these lines, and has previously suffered splits.

Opponents
The government of Rwanda, the Nduma Defence of Renovated Congo (NDC–R).

Affiliates/allies
Mai-Mai Nyatura.

Resources/capabilities
The FDLR has developed a sophisticated financing scheme over years of operation, through involvement in the trade of local goods, agriculture and looting. They have also been known to trade cannabis and charcoal and to oversee the exploitation of gold and tin mines, as well as receiving funding from the Rwandan diaspora.

P5

Strength
Around 400 fighters, but its political support network is larger.

Areas of operation
Bijabo in Fizi Territory (South Kivu Province).

Leadership
Rwandan political dissident Kaymba Nyamwasa is believed to be the group's political leader, but he lives in exile in South Africa. The military leader is Shaka Nyamusharaba, the head of a Congolese Banyamulenge militia Ngumino, which is one of the P5 component groups.

Structure
Umbrella group of anti-Kagame Rwandan and Burundian fighters and Congolese Banyamulenge militias, particularly Ngumino. Some of the Rwandan groups involved are alleged to be militant wings of opposition political parties.

History
Probably created in 2014 by former Rwandan military and intelligence officers. The composition of groups operating under the P5 umbrella is subject to some change, particularly with the inclusion of Congolese groups.

Objectives
While the leadership of the group predominantly aims to challenge the Rwandan government, the group is also fighting Burundian rebel groups on Congolese soil.

Opponents
The Rwandan government, anti-Tutsi/Banyamulenge ethnic militias, Mai-Mai Yakutumba, Burundian armed groups.

Affiliates/allies
Elements of the Burundian state, individuals in the Rwandan diaspora, and the Banyamulenge ethnic militias Ngumino and Twiganeho.

Resources/capabilities
The group receives funding from Burundi, allegedly from the Burundian government in exchange for fighting Burundian rebels on Congolese soil. It is also alleged to receive funding from Rwandan business figures opposed to the Kagame regime.

The Nduma Defence of Renovated Congo (NDC–R)

Strength
Not known. While less than 200 when the NDC–R split from its parent Mai-Mai Sheka group in 2013, it has undoubtedly grown in 2019 with the absorption of small groups and the conquest of new territory and mining sites. It now likely has more than 500 combatants.

Areas of operation
Masisi, Rutshuru, Lubero and Walikale territories, North Kivu Province.

Leadership
The NDC–R is led by Guidon Shimiray Mwissa, former deputy commander of Mai-Mai Sheka.

Structure
Not known.

History
NDC–R splintered from the Mai-Mai Sheka group in 2014.

Objectives
NDC–R claims to be a necessary counter to FDLR activity in the area, and has contributed to pushing both FDLR and the FDLR splinter group the National Council for Renewal and Democracy (CNRD) out of the areas of Masisi, Rutshuru and Walikale. However, NDC–R has also fought for control of mining sites in the area, particularly gold.

Opponents
The FDLR and the Mai-Mai Nyatura and Mazembe factions.

Affiliates/allies
Temporary alliances are sometimes struck with local Mai-Mai factions.

Resources/capabilities
Draws income from its control over gold, tin and tungsten mines. Also has an extensive tax and forced-labour system in the areas that it controls. It is known to have procured light weapons from the FARDC and other armed groups.

Drivers

Armed groups' motivations vary. Crucially, local factors mediate national political grievances, including government favouritism towards ethnic groups or traditional leaders and competition over territory and resources.

Ethnicity and land
The legacy of the DRC's colonial past is a lasting driver of the DRC's conflicts. Under the Congo Free State (1885–1908), ruled entirely by the Belgian King Leopold II, loose ethnic groupings were solidified through territorial divisions. The idea was to administer particular groups via their own customs and 'traditional leaders', but the system left some ethnicities de facto stateless and created a legacy of land conflict between groups, as well as questions about which people were 'indigenous' to Congo and which were not.

After the atrocities of the Congo Free State were exposed, the Belgian Parliament took responsibility for the Congolese territory and sought to rule the colony indirectly by co-opting local authorities. Under the Belgian system, association with an ethnic group and a 'traditional' territory became necessary for receiving government resources. Groups believed to be 'indigenous' were prioritised, while groups believed to have originated from outside of Congo saw their citizenship questioned.

The Banyamulenge are one such group, who were classified as non-indigenous to Congo because their ancestors had migrated from Rwandan territory several generations earlier, although they were settled in Congo by the time the state boundary was drawn. As a result of this, many locals still see the Banyamulenge as Tutsis or Rwandans rather than Congolese, which keeps them dependent on a mix of patronage and militancy to survive. These ethnic divisions exacerbate other conflicts, over land between farmers and pastoralists, or over water and other natural resources. Unable to rely on state security forces for protection, rival communities arm themselves to ensure their own security and to control local resources (agricultural and mineral).

Mistrust of government
Violence has continued in the aftermath of the 2003 peace process in large part because political elites – both local and national – find armed groups to be useful tools to achieve their political ends, as does the FARDC. This has undermined the credibility of the FARDC in the eyes of citizens, who see it as yet another armed actor that frequently engages in abuses. This perception is a critical obstacle to state-building. At the national level, violence served to divide communities and prevent them from forming coherent opposition fronts. More broadly, local people (particularly in the Kivu provinces) feel both forced and incentivised to form their own militias. The communities of Minembwe, the home of the aforementioned Banyamulenge, are an acute example of this cycle of militarisation. The communities that see the Banyamulenge as enemy invaders justify mobilising their own militias on the grounds that the Banyamulenge have them, and vice versa.[4]

Failed demobilisations
While demobilisation, disarmament and reintegration (DDR) is necessary in conflict resolution, the incentives given to combatants to demobilise risk inspiring new recruits, who may conclude that violence leads to rewards. Likewise, the reintegration process must be managed well enough to prevent former combatants from taking up arms again. In the DRC, both scenarios have repeatedly materialised and served to perpetrate the armed conflicts. During the creation of the FARDC, high ranks were promised to armed-group commanders if they agreed to integrate their forces into the army. Not only did this factionalise the new army from the start, but the focus on commanders also failed to satisfy the grievances of the rank and file, leading to widespread desertions. In general, DDR efforts have been systematically plagued by chronic shortages of resources caused by embezzlement and corruption.

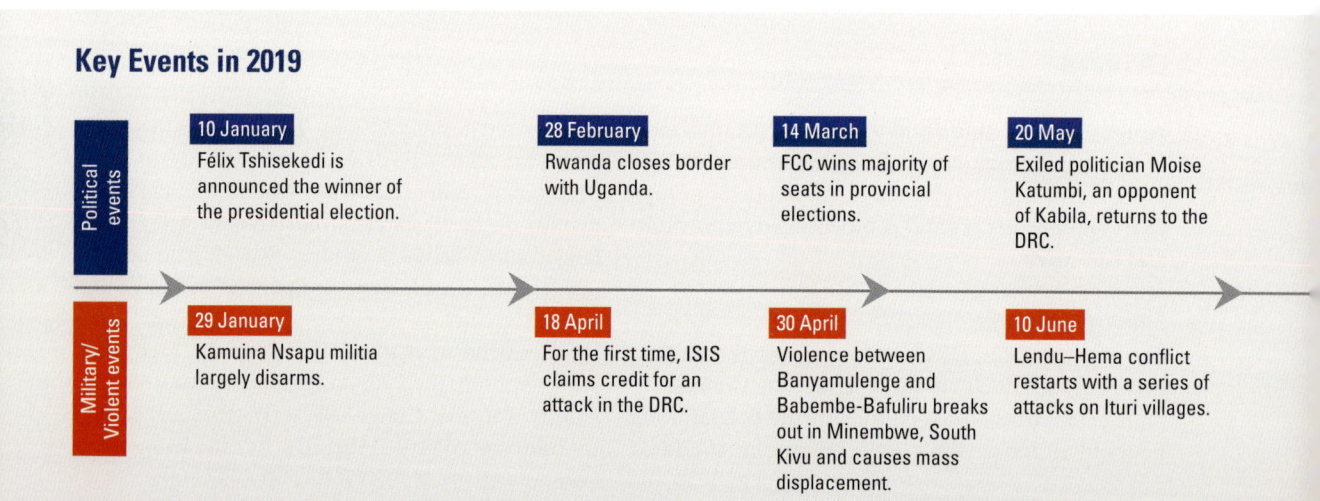

Key Events in 2019

Political events

- **10 January** — Félix Tshisekedi is announced the winner of the presidential election.
- **28 February** — Rwanda closes border with Uganda.
- **14 March** — FCC wins majority of seats in provincial elections.
- **20 May** — Exiled politician Moise Katumbi, an opponent of Kabila, returns to the DRC.

Military/Violent events

- **29 January** — Kamuina Nsapu militia largely disarms.
- **18 April** — For the first time, ISIS claims credit for an attack in the DRC.
- **30 April** — Violence between Banyamulenge and Babembe-Bafuliru breaks out in Minembwe, South Kivu and causes mass displacement.
- **10 June** — Lendu–Hema conflict restarts with a series of attacks on Ituri villages.

Political Developments

Contested elections

Despite formally stepping down from the presidency in January, Joseph Kabila maintained his enormous influence over Congolese politics throughout 2019, including keeping many of his patronage structures intact, thanks to a complex series of local elections and brokered agreements with other parties.

Kabila's likely influence over the outcome strained the credibility of the 30 December 2018 election long before voting took place, with numerous accusations of malpractice both in its preparation and its unfolding. The exclusion of the three provinces of Beni, Butembo and Yombe only a few days before the rest of the nation cast its vote further discredited the election in the eyes of many Congolese. The expectation was that Kabila's FCC would use any means necessary to instal Emmanuel Ramazani Shadary, its candidate of choice, as president. However, on 10 January 2019, Félix Tshisekedi of the Union for Democracy and Social Progress (UDPS) and leader of the Cape for Change (CACH) opposition coalition was announced as the winner. The official result defied the data recorded by electoral observation bodies and a data leak on 15 January made it clear that Martin Fayulu, leader of the opposition Lamuka coalition, was the real winner.[5]

While a victory for the opposition candidate was unexpected, the FCC had struck a deal with Tshisekedi when it became clear that Shadary could not conceivably fake a victory, reportedly in exchange for Tshisekedi guaranteeing the preservation of much of the FCC's power. The official apportioning of National Assembly seats reflected the probable deal: Tshisekedi's CACH coalition took only 46 seats (out of 485) in the National Assembly, while the FCC secured 337 and Lamuka 102. In the remainder of the year, the FCC proceeded to secure control of most government bodies though a CACH–FCC coalition. In the senatorial elections on 14 March, the FCC claimed 99 out of 109 seats, while Tshisekedi's CACH took only three seats and the Lamuka coalition six. In June, the Constitutional Court – where six of the nine judges were appointed by Kabila – invalidated 23 of Lamuka's 102 National Assembly seats, on the grounds of alleged electoral malpractice, and reallocated them to FCC members without an election.

Given that he depended on the FCC for his position and his limited power, Tshisekedi struggled to balance public expectations for him to resist FCC entrenchment in 2019, although he exercised his will to modest effect on some occasions. On 4 July, the Constitutional Court restored 19 of the 23 invalidated Lamuka deputies after Tshisekedi branded the decision 'scandalous'. (Fears of action by Lamuka coalition members Moise Katumbi and Jean-Pierre Bemba, whose deputies were among the affected, may also have influenced the reversal.)[6] Tshisekedi also prevented the appointment of some of Kabila's candidates in cabinet positions. The post of prime minister went to Ilunga Ilunkamba, an FCC politician of Kabila's Lunga ethnic group, but still a compromise choice, as Tshisekedi vetoed candidates closer to Kabila. Yet when the joint FCC–CACH cabinet was finally announced in August

---

22 July — Health minister Oly Ilunga resigns in protest over Ebola crisis management.

26 August — Coalition government finalised by FCC and CACH parties.

18 September — FDLR's military commander Sylvestre Mudacumura is killed by the FARDC.

25 October — New cross-regional military initiative is thwarted by Uganda's refusal to participate.

29 October — Major new operation against ADF announced, involving FARDC with MONUSCO support.

25 November — Protesters burn a UN military base and the Beni Town Hall in protest over insecurity.

2019 – eight months after the elections – the FCC remained clearly in charge, claiming 42 out of 65 cabinet posts, including the lucrative finance and natural-resource ministries.

Military Developments

Regional tensions and cooperation
The involvement of the DRC's neighbours on its soil increased in 2019, with the tense relationship between Rwanda and Uganda having the most impact. In February, Rwanda closed its border with Uganda after an attack by suspected P5 militants on its territory. The attack was launched from the DRC, but Rwanda was suspicious of Uganda's links with businessman Tribert Rujugiro, whom Kigali believed financed a P5 subgroup. Rwanda and Uganda appeared to have reconciled by August, when they signed a memorandum to ensure free movement of people and trade across their borders.

Cross-regional cooperation looked set to improve in October when Rwanda, Uganda, Tanzania and Burundi announced that they would join the DRC's army in an operation against armed groups in North and South Kivu. Working plans suggested the creation of an integrated command structure, but whether the foreign troops would be invited to operate on Congolese territory remained unclear and highly contentious, given the history of intervention in the area. The plan for inviting in foreign military cooperation also met domestic resistance in the DRC, with the FCC suggesting that the responsibility for countering armed groups should be left to Congolese troops. Unexpectedly, however, Uganda refused to sign the regional cooperative agreement after the final meeting on 25 October, likely for fear of strengthening Rwandan influence in the DRC.[7]

Allied Democratic Forces remain a threat
The ADF was targeted in several large-scale offensives in 2019, including one initiated by the FARDC on 30 October that was aimed at the rebels' main base, Madina Camp. This widely publicised offensive brought more than 21,000 FARDC soldiers to Beni, the epicentre of the ADF's violence, but did not bring relief for the residents of the area between the towns of Beni, Eringeti and Mbau (known as the 'triangle of death'). The Kivu Security Tracker recorded 77 civilian deaths in ADF attacks during the first two weeks of the operation and suggested that the ADF was drawing the FARDC back to the urban centres and away from Madina Camp. Given the asymmetry of forces, it is unlikely the ADF can repel the FARDC's advance in the medium term. However, even if Madina Camp is taken, the ADF has proven resilient to similar attacks in the past thanks to its mobility. The temporary loss of its base will not affect the group's survival so long as it escapes with most of its combatants. The ADF also succeeded in inflicting heavy casualties on the FARDC. An army spokesman said in late December that in the two months of the campaign so far, 60 soldiers had been killed and 175 wounded.

The first official ISIS claim of an ADF attack took place in April 2019 via the official ISIS media outlet Amaq. The article referred to ISIS's presence in a 'Central Africa Province' in the DRC. However, ADF's loose affiliation to ISIS did not significantly alter its size or practices in 2019, while its international connections and recruitment structures predate the ISIS claims for its attacks. ISIS's Arabic-language propaganda claiming ADF's attacks for ISIS does not refer to killings of civilians, and focuses instead on attacks on the FARDC and MONUSCO, who are described as 'crusaders'. This narrative is unlikely to be meaningful to most Congolese, but seems rather aimed at gaining international attention.

Violence in Ituri
The relative stability of Ituri Province was shattered in June 2019 with a spike in the violence between the Lendu and Hema ethnic groups. The violence primarily took the form of Lendu attacks on Hema settlements. The conflict is not new, with a wave of violence between December 2017 and May 2018 having resulted in the displacement of 100,000 people. However, the 2019 outbreak was even more severe, with UN sources estimating more than 360,000 internal displacements in the month of June

alone. At least 701 people had been killed between the start of the violence in December 2017 and September 2019.[8]

The Lendu militant group CODECO was widely reported in the media to be the key perpetrator of violence. A later UN investigation added that while sporadic attacks from 2017 to 2018 appeared to have been perpetrated by members of the community, violence post-September 2018 is the work of an organised armed group.[9] MONUSCO established three temporary bases in Ituri in June in response to the violence in Djugu, Mahagi and Irumu territories and CODECO leader Ngujolo expressed willingness to demobilise, but while attacks decreased, they had not ceased by the end of the year.

DDR failures

DDR programmes continued to be hampered by a lack of sufficient resources and effective implementation, despite promising signs early in the year. In January, for example, Kamuina Nsapu militants voluntarily surrendered after Tshisekedi was declared president, but a number of them subsequently returned to the bush after a demobilisation plan failed to materialise and relations with the FARDC remained hostile. On several occasions in 2019, fighters walked out of government-run DDR centres because they were not being adequately fed. In late December, the North Kivu Provincial Assembly announced a number of defections from different groups and urged the government to better fund the DDR programmes in order to avoid recidivism.

Impact

Human rights

The right to assembly and political membership was still ignored by the Congolese state, despite the change in administration. Excessive use of force was regularly deployed against protesters in 2019, with little indication that the new administration would rein in law enforcement. On 30 June, supporters of the Lamuka coalition were fired upon with live ammunition during a demonstration in Kinshasa, with one person killed. Meanwhile, all armed actors in the conflict continued to engage in myriad human-rights violations and attacks on civilians, including widespread sexual and gender-based violence. Beni territory experienced the greatest number of attacks on civilians, largely perpetrated by the ADF, but the FARDC and other armed groups were also known to attack civilians in the area.

Humanitarian

Internal displacement in the DRC remained high, with around five million internally displaced persons (IDPs) as of December 2019. The problem was particularly acute in Beni in North Kivu, Fizi Territory in South Kivu and Djugu in Ituri. The June violence in Ituri caused the largest displacement of the year, with more than 300,000 people displaced in a few days. The DRC remained an extremely volatile place for aid workers, particularly for those involved in the Ebola relief efforts, who suffered numerous attacks by armed groups and civilians alike in 2019.

Social

The World Health Organization declared the Ebola outbreak in the DRC a public health emergency of international concern in July 2019, but responses to the outbreak faced extreme challenges. The epicentre of the epidemic was located in Beni in 2019, where high levels of violence frequently forced aid agencies to suspend their efforts. These interruptions were particularly damaging because Ebola can only be countered through containment. Moreover, extremely low social trust in authority facilitated disinformation around Ebola and the relief efforts in eastern DRC. A Lancet study released in March 2019 found that 25.5% of people surveyed in the region did not believe Ebola existed, while over 80% of respondents had heard rumours that the government was manufacturing the disease to destabilise the area.[10] As a result, ordinary people resisted, sometimes violently, the efforts of relief workers to vaccinate or contain potential patients. Four Ebola responders were killed in November during attacks on their camps and workstations.[11]

Economic

The DRC's economy remained dependent on mineral and rare-earth exports, with cobalt accounting for 26% of total exports. However, the price of cobalt crashed in 2018, leading to a reduction in growth projections for the DRC in 2019, from 5.8%

to 4.3%.[12] More worryingly for Kinshasa, in early 2019 the London Metal Exchange – the world's largest metal-trading organisation – threatened to ban the trading of cobalt that was being sold at too low a price, given the probability of human-rights abuses in the supply chain. The plans were abandoned in April after concerns were raised about the exclusion of artisanal miners who depend on the practice for their livelihood, but the possibility of tighter regulation remained. In December, the IMF approved a US$368m loan to the DRC, suggesting that Tshisekedi may have persuaded investors that he represents a fresh financial start.[13]

Relations with neighbouring and international partners

Despite decrying electoral fraud, the international community decided that it needed to work with Tshisekedi. Beyond limited sanctions, the DRC did not lose international partners, and even tried to become a counter-terrorism partner to the Trump administration on the grounds that ISIS was active in the DRC. Tshisekedi has tried to reset relations with the DRC's neighbours, but with Kabila's powerful influence behind the scenes, he is unlikely to change the status quo substantially. The FCC opposed the proposed regional task force to fight armed groups in North and South Kivu, a factor that may well have reduced the ambition of the plan. Uganda agreed to pursue a bilateral agreement with the DRC to take on the ADF, but will not cooperate with Rwanda. Meanwhile, there is little Kinshasa can do to prevent Rwanda, Burundi and Uganda from pursuing their disputes through armed groups on Congolese soil. Tshisekedi had greater success with Angola in 2019, however. Tshisekedi discreetly allowed Angolan raids on Kongo Central in pursuit of Angolan rebels, an accommodation that fostered goodwill in Luanda. However, the unresolved issue of the two countries' maritime border, and the oil deposits beneath it, will likely raise tensions when and if it is addressed.

Trends

Political trajectories

Trapped in the difficult marriage between the FCC and CACH, Tshisekedi will struggle to create the substantial change the Congolese population wants and needs. Contentious mega-projects, such as the construction of the Inga hydroelectric dam on the Congo River, have yet to advance as political parties jostle to control them. The FCC, for its part, needs to maintain the appearance of Tshisekedi as a legitimate president for its arrangement to work. As a result, they will continue to allow Tshisekedi certain concessions, so long as they do not damage the FCC's overall hold on power. The disagreements between FCC and CACH are publicly known, but Tshisekedi did not win the popular vote and thus his limited efforts to distance himself from Kabila will not satisfy voters who wanted a drastic transformation of the political system. He may begin looking for ways to secure his position in office over the long term and would need FCC cooperation for that, further limiting his options for independent action. Meanwhile, if an angered population engages in more civil disobedience to make their feelings known, Tshisekedi may make further use of the repressive measures he once promised to stop.

Conflict-related risks

The conflict in 2019 has vastly exacerbated the public-health crises in the DRC. Ebola is the most extreme case, with violence preventing an effective emergency response. A vast measles epidemic also broke out in 2019, killing more than 5,000 people in the period to November 2019.[14] This is double the 2,228 deaths recorded between the start of the Ebola outbreak in August 2018 and December 2019.[15] Some of the areas with the highest transmission rates are the camps for people displaced by conflict, where healthcare and sanitation are extremely poor. Ongoing displacement risks spreading the measles outbreak even further if not countered, and vaccination campaigns are regularly interrupted by violence.

Prospects for peace

Some groups, including the Lendu militants CODECO, expressed a willingness to enter a peace process initiated by the provincial government in 2019, on the condition that certain social services are provided in their community. However, meeting this condition will require improved local governance which will remain challenging in the unstable eastern provinces. In any case, the challenge for solving the DRC's conflicts lies less in brokering local peace accords than in sustaining the ones that already exist. For instance, the opportunity to make peace with the Kamuina Nsapu militia in Kasai in 2019 was not used effectively.

Strategic implications and global influences

The risk of tensions between Rwanda, Uganda and Burundi rising and playing out through armed groups in the DRC remains high. A resumption of fighting will have knock-on effects, sparking even greater militarisation in the Kivus and undermining efforts to contain the Ebola crisis. While the epidemic has already spilled over to Uganda, it has so far been controlled. Further violence, however, would damage the ability of health workers to track suspected patients, and thus heighten the risk of cross-border transmission and of the virus reaching other countries' major cities.

Notes

[1] 'The art of the possible: MONUSCO's new mandate', Congo Research Group, March 2018.

[2] James Barnett, 'DR Congo in crisis: Can Kabila trust his own army?', African Arguments, 20 September 2016.

[3] Elsa Buchanan, '"We are ready for war" – Burundi's rebel groups and how they plan to topple President Nkurunziza', International Business Times, 2 March 2017.

[4] 'Atrocities, Populations Under Siege and Regional Tensions: What is Happening in Minembwe?', Kivu Security Tracker, 29 October 2019.

[5] David Blood, David Pilling and Tom Wilson, 'Congo voting data reveal huge fraud in poll to replace Kabila', Financial Times, 15 January 2019.

[6] 'RDC : l'invalidation de l'élection de députés de l'opposition annulée', Jeune Afrique, 5 July 2019.

[7] 'Foreign Troops Enter DRC: Why the Goma Meeting Failed', Kivu Security Tracker, 18 November 2019.

[8] 'Rapport public sur les conflits en territoire de Djugu, province de l'Ituri Décembre 2017 à septembre 2019', UN Office of the High Commissioner for Human Rights, 10 January 2020.

[9] Ibid.

[10] P. Vinck et al., 'Institutional trust and misinformation in the response to the 2018–19 Ebola outbreak in North Kivu, DR Congo: a population-based survey', The Lancet, vol. 19, no. 5, May 2019.

[11] World Health Organization, 'Dead and injured following attacks on Ebola responders in the Democratic Republic of the Congo', 28 November 2019.

[12] 'Falling cobalt prices add fresh challenges to DRC's economy', Mining.com, 24 June 2019.

[13] IMF, 'Five takeaways from Democratic Republic of the Congo's IMF Program', 23 December 2019.

[14] UNICEF Representative in the DRC Edouard Beigbeder, '4,500 children under the age of five died from measles in the Democratic Republic of the Congo so far this year', UNICEF, 27 November 2019.

[15] Médecins Sans Frontières, 'DRC Ebola outbreaks: Crisis update – 27 December 2019', 27 December 2019.

ETHIOPIA (COMMUNAL VIOLENCE)

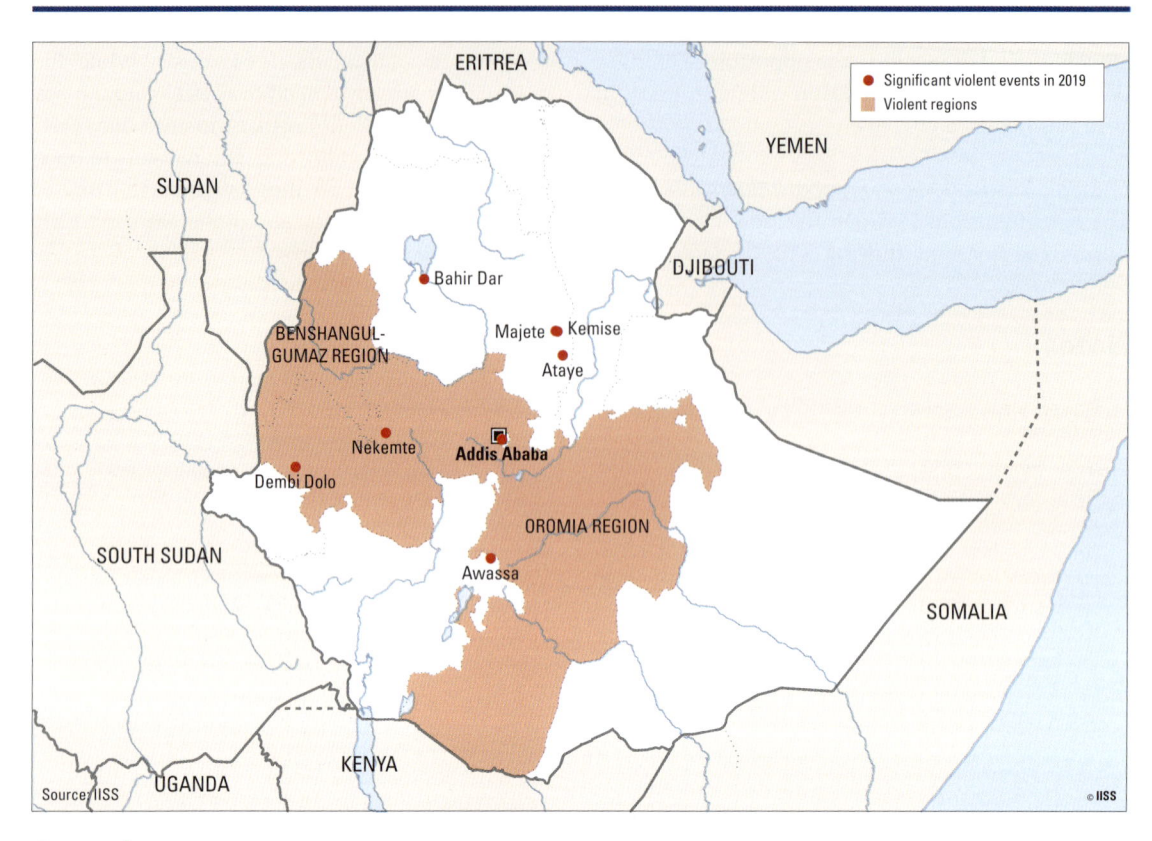

Overview

The conflict in 2019
Ethiopia experienced violence among ethnic groups and between armed groups and the central government in 2019. Ethnic groups continued to seek greater political autonomy at the regional level, while violence was also a consequence of historical ethnic divides being re-ignited by Prime Minister Abiy Ahmed's 2018 reforms. In Oromia Region, there was a surge in violence between the Oromo Liberation Army (WBO) and the federal and regional security forces, with the WBO overrunning ten districts in west Oromia in August, while in November large-scale anti-government protests broke out, leaving 86 people dead. In the Sidama Zone, Southern Nations, Nationalities and Peoples Region (SNNPR), at least 17 people were killed in clashes between Ethiopian security forces and activists in July 2019 after a referendum on autonomy for the Sidama failed to take place by the constitutionally stipulated deadline. On 20 November 2019, the rearranged referendum saw 98.5% voting in favour of self-administration.[1]

There were also signs of internal friction within the security architecture. On 22 June, regional security forces killed the Amhara regional president Ambachew Mekonnen in Bahir Dar, Amhara Region and Ethiopia's Army Chief General Seare Mekonnen in Addis Ababa. The government continued to clamp down on corrupt officials in 2019. This included the arrest of 59 government officials

Key statistics

Type	Internal
Start date	2015
IDPs total (31 December 2019)	2,600,000
Refugees total	Not applicable
People in need (31 December 2019)	8,000,000

on suspicion of corruption and economic sabotage in April. The head and other staff of the government's Public Procurement and Property Disposal Service were also detained, while staff attached to the Finance, Economics and Cooperation Ministry were arrested. However, many consider the arrests to be politically motivated and designed to remove officials opposed to Abiy's administration.

The International Organization for Migration (IOM) Round 20 report assessed that there were 1.73 million internally displaced people (IDPs) in Ethiopia in the period November–December, the majority of whom (1.14m) had been displaced as a result of conflict.[2] The number of IDPs peaked at 3.04m in March 2019.

The conflict to 2019

Decades of repressive rule by the Provisional Military Government of Socialist Ethiopia (the Derg) ended in 1991 after an uprising by the Ethiopian People's Revolutionary Democratic Front (EPRDF), a coalition of resistance groups led by Meles Zenawi that championed multicultural federalism. In 1995, Ethiopia became a federation of nine regions created along linguistic lines, but over the next 20 years the central state (directed by the EPRDF) nevertheless became stronger than ever, greatly diminishing the autonomy of the regions.

Zenawi died in 2012 and was succeeded by Hailemariam Desalegn, who soon had to contend with rising anti-government sentiment. In April 2014, the Addis Ababa city administration launched a plan to expand Addis Ababa by 1.1m hectares into Oromia Region, a move that triggered several youth-led protests in Oromia Region. The protests built upon long-standing Oromo grievances about land, socio-economic development and identity issues, as well as exclusion from political power. The narrative of Tigray dominance was the main rallying point, with discontent focused against the Tigray People's Liberation Front (TPLF), which was considered the core of EPRDF.

In early 2015 the protests died down after the government halted the urban-expansion plan, but flared up again in 2015. Protests also broke out in Amhara region in mid-2016, also on a platform of political marginalisation and land issues, reinforcing the sense of solidarity between the Oromo and Amhara against the central government which had formed after the widely criticised 2005 election. The government responded violently to the protests, killing thousands and arresting tens of thousands, and declared a state of emergency in October 2016 that lasted for ten months. During this time, the political situation also became more confrontational, with opposition politicians charged under counter-terrorism laws. With tension across the country and pressure within the party mounting due to the protests, Desalegn resigned in April 2018, handing over power to Abiy Ahmed, the country's first Oromo leader, who enacted sweeping reforms under the banner of *medemer* (synergy), which attempted to reconcile federalism and the unitary state. Abiy lifted the state of emergency in June 2018, ordered the release of 10,000 political prisoners and unblocked hundreds of websites. In July, the Ethiopian government removed three armed opposition groups – the Ogaden National Liberation Front (ONLF), Ginbot 7 and the Oromo Liberation Front (OLF) – from its list of terrorist organisations and welcomed opposition leaders back to Ethiopia where they could register as political parties.

However, Abiy's reformist agenda paradoxically also served to re-ignite old tensions between various ethnic groups. Most of the tension between groups has been a result of opposition to some of Abiy's policies and the fact that many of Abiy's policies have been implemented very quickly, opening political space for ethnic nationalism in a context of weak local institutions that are unable to provide a stabilising counterweight. Ethnic opposition groups returning from exile in 2018 took up arms to fight both for regional autonomy and against other ethnic groups. Disputes over boundaries between regions have also increased, in particular between Oromo and Somalis, Amhara and Tigray, Somali and Afar, and Amhara and Benishangul Gumuz, with levels of violence rising due to the influx of arms from neighbouring countries and the associated militarisation of civilians.

Key Conflict Parties

Ethiopian National Defense Force (ENDF)

Strength
The ENDF has 138,000 active military personnel (army 135,000, air 3,000), the highest in the region, although voluntary-recruitment campaigns in previous years have not reached their objectives.

Areas of operation
Amhara, Oromia, Somali and SNNPR (Welaita and Sidama zones) regions.

Leadership
The Chief of the General Staff, Seare Mekonnen, was killed in June 2019. General Adem Mohammed, chief of the National Intelligence and Security Service, was appointed as new chief six days later.

Structure
The ENDF is designed to be able to conduct both a conventional war (using infantry, armoured vehicles and artillery) and counter-insurgency missions (both inside Ethiopia and across borders). At the regional level, the security forces are represented by specialised units such as the *Liyu* ('special' in Amharic) Police in all regional states of Ethiopia.

History
The ENDF grew out of a coalition of former guerrilla armies, mainly the TPLF and the EPRDF. Since the EPRDF took power in 1991, the armed forces have relied on volunteers, but over the past two decades have still undergone a transformation from militia force to one of the major military powers in Africa. Because of the ethnic constitution of TPLF and EPRDF, more than 90% of ENDF generals and senior officers are ethnic Tigrayan, while the rank and file are drawn from other communities.

Objectives
Keep order and fight secessionist movements in Ethiopia.

Opponents
Secessionist movements in Ethiopia.

Affiliates/allies
United States, Israel, France.

Resources/capabilities
The ENDF is the most powerful army in the region, with a defence budget of US$518m in 2019. Elite units, such as Special Forces, represent several thousand men, and armoured and mechanised units are generally good. The ENDF has excellent support capabilities (logistics, training, maintenance), but efficiency fluctuates greatly between units.

Oromo Liberation Front (OLF)

Strength
It is estimated that 2,800 OLF fighters are based mainly in the western and southern parts of Oromia regional state, the principal operating ground of OLF.

Areas of operation
Oromia Region.

Leadership
Dawud Ibsa.

Structure
The army of the OLF – also known as Waraana Bilisummaa Oromoo (WBO) – officially separated from the political OLF party in April 2019.

History
The OLF was established in 1973 by Oromo nationalists and participated in the Provisional Government in 1991–92. The OLF made a deal with the government in 2018 to lay down arms but there have been reports that factions still control part of Guji.

Objectives
OLF seeks self-determination for the Oromo people against what they see as Amhara colonial rule.

Opponents
Ethiopian government.

Affiliates/allies
Eritrea-based OLF branch, founded in 2006 (nearly 200 soldiers).

Resources/capabilities
OLF acts clandestinely, especially in the diaspora, but is very weak in Ethiopia.

Ogaden National Liberation Front (ONLF)

Strength
The ONLF's armed wing comprises 1,500 members.

Areas of operation
The ONLF operates in the Ogaden desert, Somali Region, in eastern Ethiopia, which is inhabited by ethnic Somali from the Ogaden clan.

Leadership
Admiral Muhammad Omar Osman.

Structure
Political party with armed branch.

Ogaden National Liberation Front (ONLF)

History
Founded in 1984. Attacks have decreased in recent years, and especially after a ceasefire was agreed with the government in August 2018, but could rise again if the government refuses a self-determination referendum called by the group.

Objectives
Its aims have varied over time but centre around defending the human and civil rights of the Ogadeni people, protecting the region's natural resources from perceived exploitation by the state and campaigning for self-determination.

Opponents
Ethiopian government.

Affiliates/allies
Not known.

Resources/capabilities
Not known.

Ginbot 7 (G7)/ Arbegnoch (Patriot) Ginbot 7 for Unity and Democratic Movement (AGUDM)

Strength
Not known.

Areas of operation
Amhara State's Gonder Zone.

Leadership
Berhanu Nega and Andargachew Tsige, but there appear to be disputes within the group over its leadership.

Structure
Not known.

History
Founded by Nega and Tsige in 2008. They returned to Ethiopia from their base in Eritrea in September 2018. In May 2019, G7 joined six other opposition groups to form the Ethiopian Citizens for Social Justice political party.

Objectives
The group calls for 'the realisation of a national political system in which government power and political authority are assumed through peaceful and democratic process based on the free will and choice of the citizens of the country'.

Opponents
Ethiopian government.

Affiliates/allies
The group is largely based outside of Ethiopia and has close relations with the Eritrean government.

Resources/capabilities
Not known.

Drivers

Weak institutions

The division of political control between the regional states and central government has long stoked tensions, and the recent violence has been facilitated by weak institutions at both local and central-government levels. At the central-government level, this fragility is a result of the divergences between the four parties of the ruling EPRDF coalition, each of which represents different ethnic groups. At the local level, state fragility is a result of how regional state security forces respond to ethnic tensions between local groups, as these responses can cause nationalist antagonisms. Institutions have also helped to shape contentious ethnic nationalisms that in turn weaken those institutions, leading to further nationalist competition between regions and communities, leading to surges in the number of IDPs.

Ethnic tensions amid political reform

The historical divisions between Ethiopia's different ethnic communities have long fuelled violence in Ethiopia. The country is dominated by four main ethnic groups, the Oromo (which make up 34% of Ethiopia's population), the Amhara (27%), the Tigrayan (6%) and the Somalis (6%).[3] The ruling EPRDF coalition was (until late 2019) comprised of four parties, with three representing the major ethnic groups – the Tigray People's Liberation Front (TPLF), the Oromo People's Democratic Organization (OPDO) and the Amhara National Democratic Movement (ANDM) – together with the Southern Ethiopian People's Democratic Movement (SEPDM). While the Tigrayan ethnic community, based in the north, are a minority in the country, they are perceived in some quarters to have dominated the business and political elite since leading the overthrow of the Derg in 1991, while the Oromo were perceived by some to have been politically marginalised until Abiy's accession in 2018. The Amhara were the rulers of Ethiopia under the monarchical system that ended in 1974, but now claim to be increasingly marginalised.[4]

Abiy's unprecedented series of reforms initiated in 2018 was intended to open the political space in

Ethiopia, but the reforms proved divisive, including among those who saw them as a tool to consolidate the prime minister's power. Some believe that Abiy's reforms did not go far enough, with the Oromo community perceiving Abiy's commitment to reduce Tigrayan influence within the business elite as ineffective. In addition, the return of various opposition parties from exile in 2018 has resulted in the expression of the ethnic frustrations of the past and their exacerbation by the sudden irruption of radical activists, ready to fight for the supremacy of their group or 'nationality' and seize power. This rise in 'ethnic nationalism' has been the main driver behind violence in 2019.

There are also divisions within ethnic communities over the best path of travel in response to Abiy's reforms. Some Oromo protesters have pushed for a more legitimate and inclusive political and social system, even if the OPDO is part of the EPRDF, while others continue to argue for the protection of the region's autonomy and borders in the face of Addis Ababa's urban expansion.

Increasing militarisation

The rise in violence can be linked to the shift from peaceful to armed demonstrations in retaliation for the state's heavy-handed response to protests, as well as the perceived need among some protesters to take back control of their areas through violent means. This has been facilitated by the flow of weapons from Sudan and Uganda via South Sudan, particularly into northern Amhara Region.

Political Developments

Attempts to harmonise governance

In March 2019, the EPRDF and 107 Ethiopian political parties (mostly regional parties) signed a code of conduct intended to guide their operations and political activities. The document also established a joint council in which every party would be represented. The chair will be elected every six months and is tasked to settle disputes arising between political parties.

On 1 December, Abiy launched the Prosperity Party, which aimed to refound the EPRDF as a single inclusive national political party in an attempt to transcend the ethnic divisions between its constituent parties. The Prosperity Party also incorporated five smaller parties formerly marginalised in the political space. However, the TPLF – for many years the most powerful party within the EPRDF – refused to join, signifying a schism within the ruling coalition.

Sidama referendum

The Sidama demand for statehood presented one of the greatest challenges to Ethiopia's federal system since the system's inception in 1995. The Sidama, who comprise about 5% of Ethiopia's population and are the south's largest ethnic group, have long sought greater autonomy, and on 18 July 2018 formally passed a motion via the Sidama district assemblies requesting that the central government arrange a referendum on the subject of autonomy within a

Key Events in 2019

Political events

- **February**: Ethiopia formally establishes national reconciliation commission.
- **March**: Code of Conduct signed between EPRDF and 107 Ethiopian parties.
- **May**: G7 joins six other opposition groups to form the Ethiopian Citizens for Social Justice political party.

Military/Violent events

- **19 March**: Unidentified gunmen kill five employees (including two foreign nationals) of a copper-mining company.
- **5–7 April**: Unidentified gunmen kill 15 civilians in Majete, Kemise and Ataye in Amhara Region.
- **23 June**: Amhara militia fighters kill more than 50 people in Benshangul-Gumaz Region.
- **22–24 June**: Foiled coup in Addis Ababa and Bahir Dar, Amhara Region, kills four government officials.

year, as constitutionally stipulated. As the deadline approached, the Sidama officials announced that in the absence of a referendum they would unliterally establish an autonomous region on 18 July 2019 (one year after the initial request).[5]

Citing security concerns, the government failed to arrange a referendum by the deadline, leading to a series of clashes breaking out on 18–19 July between security forces and Sidama activists which left at least 17 dead. On 20 July, the Sidama Liberation Movement, which had been spearheading the drive for the new region, accepted the government's proposal for a referendum to take place before the end of the year. On 20 November 2019, the Sidama finally went to the polls and voted overwhelmingly for a new federal region, with 98.5% voting for autonomous rule and turnout at 99.7%. There were similar demands for self-administration by almost all ethnic communities in South Ethiopia.

Military Developments

Inter-ethnic violence

Inter-ethnic tension, particularly between Somali and Oromo, and Afar and Somali, continued in 2019, with internal border disputes between sub-national units and local groups pushing for more power within their respective states. Key hotspots in 2018–19 included northeastern, northwestern and western Amhara Region; several woredas in the Benishangul-Gumuz Region; western, southern and central Oromia; several border areas between Oromia and Somali regions; and eastern and northeastern parts of the SNNPR.

Violence in Oromia Region

In February 2019, more than 1,000 OLF fighters were admitted to government camps for rehabilitation, and on 29 March, OLF leader Dawud Ibsa declared the group no longer had any fighters.[6] However, Ibsa's path towards rapprochement with the regional government in Oromia was rejected by the WBO, the armed wing of the OLF, which formally declared that it had split from the OLF in April 2019. Violence escalated in Oromia Region in the first half of 2019, fuelled by hardline tactics from the security forces as they sought to crack down on suspected OLA militants, as well as regional authorities repeatedly obstructing the opening of OLF offices and the organisation of public meetings and arresting OLF representatives. The Kelem area near the town of Nekemte witnessed repeated grenade attacks between mid-January and mid-April.[7]

Later in the year, large protests broke out in Addis Ababa after Jawar Mohammed, an Oromo activist and leader of the Oromo protests in Addis Ababa, unexpectedly found his house in Addis Ababa surrounded by the police. (Mohammed alleged on social media that his security detail had been changed as part of a plot by the prime minister to have him killed.) Protests later spread to many areas of Oromia Region, but quickly devolved into intercommunal violence. According to Abiy, some

18–19 July
Clashes between the ENDF and Sidama activists near Awassa city, SNNPR, leave at least 17 people dead.

23–25 October
Protests take place in Oromia Region, with reports of intercommunal violence killing 67 civilians.

November
Civil unrest spreads across main cities of the Oromia Region, leading to the deaths of 19 civilians.

20 November
Referendum in Sidama Zone results in overwhelming support for creation of new autonomous region.

1 December
Abiy launches Prosperity Party; the TPLF refuses to join.

76 were killed in communal clashes, with a further ten people dying in clashes with the security forces. The government was criticised for not responding quickly enough to the outbreak of violence, though Abiy defended his stance, stating that the government had 'opted for dialogue and education instead of using force, however those who think patience is fear or magnanimity is weakness should know they are mistaken'.[8]

Al-Shabaab in Ethiopia

In September 2019, Ethiopian government officials reported that several people suspected of belonging to al-Shabaab had been arrested while plotting to launch a wave of attacks in Addis Ababa and Oromia and Somali regions.[9] The arrest of al-Shabaab militants in Ethiopia potentially signals a shift in the group's focus from Kenya to Ethiopia, which would have serious security implications for Addis Ababa.

Impact

Humanitarian

Ongoing insecurity continues to impact the humanitarian situation in western and southern Oromia Region; in Gedeo Zone, SNNPR; and in the regions of Gambela and Somali, although government efforts did help people return home. Approximately 3m people were recorded as displaced in March 2019 until the government organised a return operation which saw approximately 815,000 people returning to their homes in June, although there were reports that some of the returns were involuntary.[10]

As of December 2019, 2.6m people remained internally displaced in Ethiopia. The scale of displacement has tested the capacity of local and central government to provide essential services to people in need, a situation compounded by the fact that as of December 2019 Ethiopia also hosted 735,00 refugees, mainly from South Sudan, Somalia, Eritrea and Sudan.[11] In February 2019, Ethiopia hosted the two-day African Union summit in Addis Ababa, which focused on finding solutions for the issue of refugees, returnees and IDPs.

Economic

Two five-year plans – the Growth and Transformation Plans I and II (GTP I and II) – were adopted in 2010 and 2015 respectively, intended to facilitate Ethiopia becoming a middle-income state by 2025. Despite being one of the region's fastest-growing economies (with growth averaging 9.5% between 2010 and 2019),[12] the country is facing high inflation (approximately 14% in 2019) and is struggling to recover from the economic downturn in 2018.

The economic downturn has played a role in stoking anti-government grievances and helped to facilitate ethnic mobilisation, lowering the opportunity cost of engaging in violence since some feel that they have little to lose. The government did not appear to have a clear economic programme to ameliorate the economic crisis in Ethiopia in 2019 and overcome problems such as the persistent shortage of foreign-exchange reserves, inflation, unemployment and low wages. After a flurry of optimism in mid-2018 following Abiy's successful peace overtures, relations with Eritrea remained bogged down in 2019, with the border remaining closed and a failure to regularise cross-border trade impacting the Ethiopian economy.[13] However, Abiy met with Kenyan President Uhuru Kenyatta at the two-day Kenya–Ethiopia high-level trade forum in Addis Ababa in March 2019, with a view to strengthening economic ties between the two countries.

Human rights

In April 2019, Reporters Without Borders placed Ethiopia at 110 out of 180 countries, up from 150 in 2018, but questions remained about the actual progress made in terms of freedom of expression since 2018. The Ethiopian government blocked access to the internet on nine occasions in 2019 in the wake of public protests and in the aftermath of the June assassinations of the Amhara regional president and the army chief of staff in order to control the flow of information. In March–April 2019, a controversial media-reform project by Abiy Ahmed – nominally designed to tackle the 'dangerous surge' of 'fake news' – raised concerns about a covert attempt to reinstate state censorship, while in February 2019, Mohammed Ademo, founder of the site OPride (Oromo Pride), which is very critical of the EPRDF, resigned just a few months after his return to the country and his appointment as head of the Oromo regional television network.

The government also continued to use the 2009 Anti-Terrorism Proclamation (ATP) to silence dissenting voices and arrest journalists and activists in 2019 after the June coup attempt and the violence in the Sidama Zone in July, raising concerns about a potential return to the repressive methods of the previous government. In March 2019, the United Nations Human Rights Council expressed its concern that the ATP 'was incompatible with international human rights standards'.[14]

Relations with neighbouring and international partners
No state in the Horn of Africa appears able to play the role of stabiliser in the Ethiopian crisis. Sudan, South Sudan and Somalia have their own internal difficulties, Uganda and Kenya are focused on their own development and the Djibouti government is playing a long-term strategy. The Intergovernmental Authority on Development (IGAD), the eight-country regional bloc, is an instrument of Ethiopian foreign policy, and therefore cannot bring any influence to bear on the country itself, while international actors also appear disinclined to engage, being preoccupied with internal matters: the United States, for example, will be entering an election year in 2020. In recent years, the Gulf states have amplified their influence in the region, in large part due to the war in Yemen (the United Arab Emirates, for example, has a military presence in Eritrea), but it is unlikely that they will involve themselves in Ethiopia's security situation.

The European Union, however, has indicated a greater willingness to assist in Ethiopia's situation. On 7 December 2019, President of the European Commission Ursula von der Leyen visited Addis Ababa and announced a €170m (US$190m) package to support the country's economic reforms and health service and boost its technical and administrative capacity during the 2020 elections.[15] In addition, in December 2019 the International Monetary Fund approved a US$2.9 billion programme designed to support Ethiopia's economic reforms and make the private sector the engine of the economy.[16]

Trends

Political trajectories
The political context in Ethiopia is characterised by ineffectiveness at the federal level and a power vacuum at the regional level (except in Tigray Region). Abiy's reforms have opened the political space to groups formerly kept on the outside of the political process, but balancing the demands of ethnic nationalism and greater regional autonomy with a coherent federal government will continue to pose challenges.

Abiy appears to represent the best chance for the EPRDF to reinvent itself (and distance itself from its association with historical human-rights abuses), but the refusal of the TPLF to join Abiy's new Prosperity Party may point to a fissure in the current power structure that could lead to a more antagonistic political landscape in the run-up to the elections scheduled for 29 August 2020. Given the government response to protests in 2019, the possibility of state repression becoming more prevalent cannot be discounted during the election period.[17]

At the regional level, the Sidama referendum also poses several questions for the year ahead. The federal government will want to ensure that the area is sufficiently stable before establishing the new region, but any delay to the implementation of the referendum result may cause further instability and questions raised about the government's good faith towards respecting the result. The initial success of the Sidama referendum has also galvanised other ethnic groups to seek their own autonomy, potentially presenting a tumultuous time ahead at the regional level, further exacerbating insecurity.

Conflict-related risks
The presence of al-Shabaab in Ethiopia in 2019, while not directly connected to the pattern of conflict in Ethiopia in 2019, may point to the prospect of Islamist terrorism establishing a base on Ethiopian soil. The group may exploit Ethiopia's unemployed youth as it seeks to recruit new members and take advantage of the flow of weapons entering the country.

The elections in 2020 may also represent a potential flashpoint for violence, with Abiy's pan-Ethiopian political party likely to come under strain if ethnic groups attempt to manoeuvre for influence. Any anti-government protests in the run-up to the election may, as in 2019, be met by a state crackdown. The government's responsiveness to new referendum demands put forward by various ethnic groups seeking autonomy will also be under scrutiny, with any delay (as occurred in Sidama Zone in July 2019) potentially leading to outbreaks of violence.

Prospects for peace
Deep divides between ethnic groups, at times divisive state leadership, widespread economic inequality and a lack of institutional credibility at the regional level mean that the fundamental drivers of violence will likely persist in 2020. The national reconciliation commission, formally established in February 2019, could pave the way for greater social cohesion and the setting aside of historical disputes, but it faces a legitimacy crisis and lacks broad-based support for its mandate. Armed groups and militias will in all probability continue to resort to violence as they attempt to further their own specific agendas.[18]

Strategic implications and global influences
Climatic change is likely to compound issues that overlap with the conflict, such as displacement, high unemployment and competition over resources at the local level. Likewise, the continuing instability in South Sudan and Somalia and the rise in instability in Sudan could impact Ethiopia, particularly if regional trade suffers and economic performance drops.

Notes

[1] Giulia Paravicini, 'UPDATE 1–Ethiopia's Sidama vote overwhelmingly to form autonomous region', Reuters, 23 November 2019.

[2] International Organization for Migration (IOM), 'Ethiopia National Displacement Report 3: Round 20: November–December 2019', 7 February 2020.

[3] Minority Rights, 'Ethiopia: Minorities and Indigenous peoples', updated January 2018.

[4] Aaron Maasho, 'Factbox: Ethiopia's main ethnic groups', Reuters, 16 February 2018.

[5] International Crisis Group, 'Time for Ethiopia to Bargain with Sidama over Statehood', Briefing 146, 4 July 2019.

[6] Ermias Tasfaye, 'Two steps forward, one step back for Oromia?', Ethiopia Insight, 7 June 2019.

[7] OCHA, 'Ethiopia: Humanitarian Access Situation Report', April 2019.

[8] 'Ethiopian PM Abiy defends response to ethnic clashes', AFP News, 3 November 2019.

[9] Martina Schwikowski, 'Is al-Shabab looking to Ethiopia?', Deutsche Welle, 16 October 2019.

[10] International Organization for Migration (IOM), 'Ethiopia Publishes First Ever National Displacement Report', 25 October 2019; Tom Wilson, 'Ethnic violence in Ethiopia has forced nearly 3 million people from their homes', LA Times, 20 May 2019.

[11] UNHCR, 'Ethiopia Fact Sheet, December 2019', 31 December 2019; UNCHR, 'Operational Portal: Refugee Situations: Ethiopia', 20 January 2020.

[12] Sam Kisika, 'Yes, Ethiopia "the fastest growing economy globally" – but it's all in the details', Africa Check, 17 December 2019.

[13] 'Ethiopia–Eritrea relations hampered by closed borders, stalled trade deals', Africanews.com, 24 July 2019.

[14] UNHCR, 'Compilation on Ethiopia: Report of the Office of the United Nations High Commissioner for Human Rights', 1 March 2019.

[15] European Commission, 'EU strengthens cooperation with Ethiopia', 7 December 2019.

[16] International Monetary Fund, 'IMF Executive Board Approves US$2.9 Billion ECF and EFF Arrangements for Ethiopia', 20 December 2019.

[17] Lefort René, 'A flicker in the gloom', Ethiopia Insight, 31 October 2019.

[18] Solomon Ayele Dersso, 'Ethiopia's Experiment in Reconciliation', United States Institute of Peace, 23 September 2019.

LAKE CHAD BASIN (BOKO HARAM)

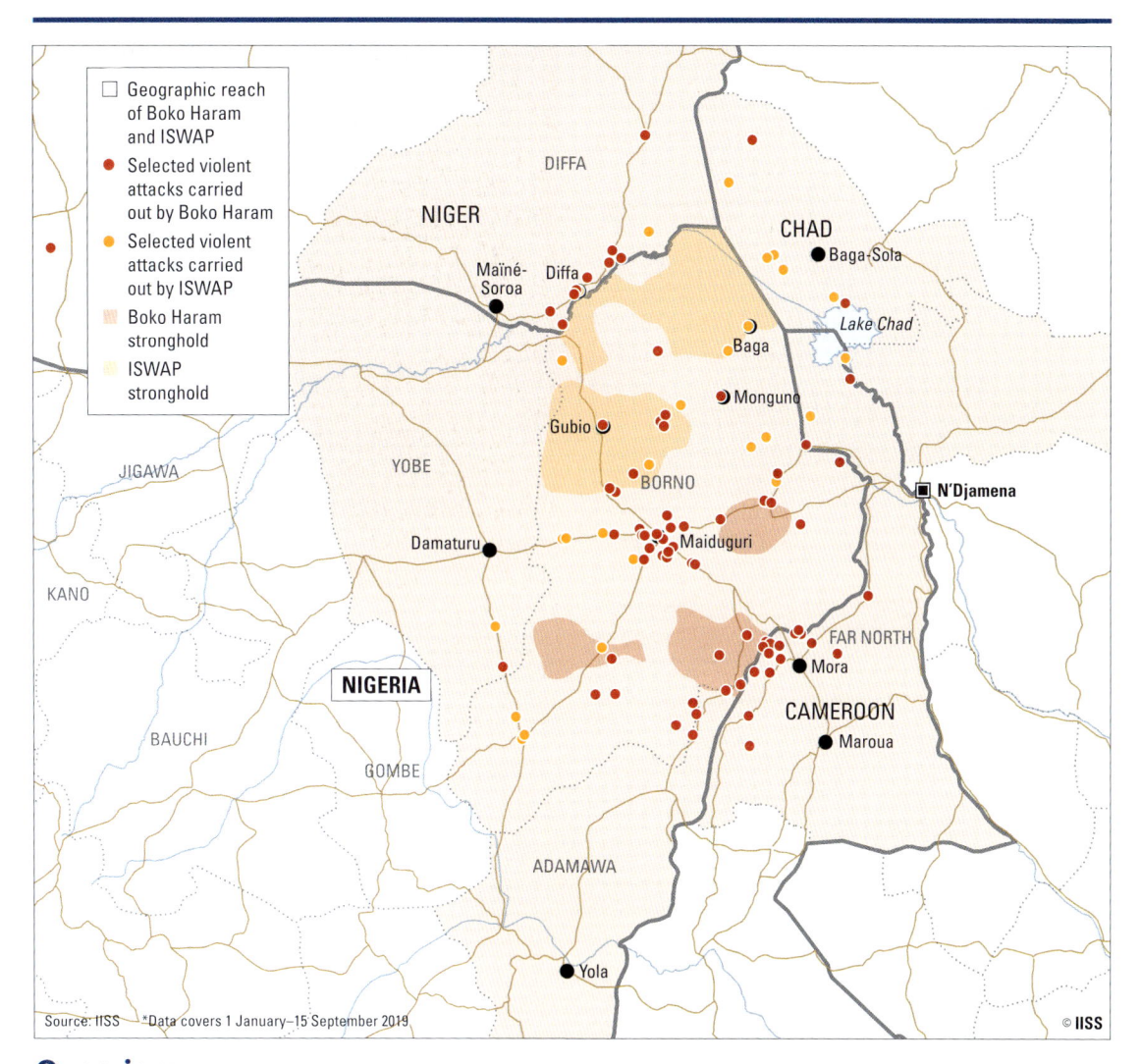

Map legend:
- Geographic reach of Boko Haram and ISWAP
- Selected violent attacks carried out by Boko Haram
- Selected violent attacks carried out by ISWAP
- Boko Haram stronghold
- ISWAP stronghold

Source: IISS *Data covers 1 January–15 September 2019

Overview

The conflict in 2019

Ten years after the start of Boko Haram's violent insurgency, the group remains a major security threat to the Lake Chad Basin. Despite Nigerian President Muhammadu Buhari's recurrent claims of victory since 2015, Boko Haram and the Islamic State West Africa Province (ISWAP), a splinter group, continued to target communities, humanitarian workers and military positions in 2019. ISWAP has proven to be resilient and has grown in power and influence within the local communities, who perceive it as a better alternative to Boko Haram or the Nigerian authorities.

The Multinational Joint Task Force (MNJTF), a regional body that coordinates counter-insurgency operations against Boko Haram, was revived in 2019. It conducted large-scale operations in the first part of the year that made inroads into Boko Haram and ISWAP's core territory. The MNJTF, however, could not prevent ISWAP from looting and destroying poorly constructed military barracks on a regular basis, forcing the Nigerian Army to abandon some of its positions in rural areas and adopt a new strategy of concentrating its presence in 'Super Camps'. This change resulted in fewer clashes between ISWAP and the armed forces, and fewer casualties in the second half of 2019, but also allowed ISWAP to roam freely and strengthen its ties with the local population.

The conflict to 2019

Boko Haram was established in impoverished northeast Nigeria in early 2002 by the charismatic preacher Mohammed Yusuf. The group's goal was to establish sharia law in Nigeria and destroy the country's Western-influenced institutions, including education and democracy. In July 2009, the Nigerian security forces killed Yusuf and the group appeared to be declining.

However, the desire to revenge Yusuf's extrajudicial killing became a powerful rallying call for Boko Haram. In 2010 the group reorganised and transitioned from religious movement to insurgent organisation under the leadership of former second-in-command Abubakar Shekau. This was a major turning point: the group escalated its violent campaign and broadened its influence and territorial control, extending into neighbouring Cameroon, Chad and Niger, which it previously only used as safe havens.

The widespread violence that followed prompted the Nigerian government to launch the largest military deployment in the country since the civil war (Biafra War) of 1967–70. Despite some progress, however, the violence did not diminish. In 2015, Boko Haram pledged its allegiance to the emir of the Islamic State (also known as ISIS or ISIL) and adopted the new name ISWAP. This development added to the complexity of the conflict and produced frictions within the group regarding different methods and targeting strategies. The group eventually split in 2016 when Abu Musab al-Barnawi, son of Boko Haram's late founder Mohammed Yusuf, was appointed leader of ISWAP and broke away from Boko Haram.

Key statistics

Type	Internationalised
Start date	July 2009
IDPs total (31 December 2019)*	2,587,438
Refugees total (31 December 2019)*	243,404
People in need (31 December 2019)	9,900,000

*IDPs/Refugees in the Lake Chad Basin, a region spanning Cameroon, Chad, Niger and Nigeria.

Key Conflict Parties

Nigerian armed forces

Strength
143,000, of which 100,000 in the army. The Nigerian armed forces are one of the largest in Africa and the principal military power in West Africa.

Areas of operation
Northeast of Nigeria (Adamawa, Yobe, Borno states) as well as regions not related to this conflict (Niger Delta, Middle Belt Region).

Leadership
The president of Nigeria, Muhammadu Buhari, is the commander-in-chief of the armed forces. The Army Chief of Staff is Lt-Gen. Tukur Yusuf Buratai.

Structure
The Nigerian armed forces comprise the army, the air force and the navy. The army is organised into headquarters, divisions, brigades, battalions, companies, platoons and sections.

History
The Nigerian armed forces have been fighting Boko Haram since 2009. Their strategy has evolved drastically over time, including an expansion from five to eight divisions and the relocation of its headquarters to Maiduguri, the capital of Borno State, closer to the epicentre of the insurgency, in 2015.

Objectives
Secure Nigeria's territorial integrity and end the threat to the populations in the Lake Chad Basin.

Opponents
Boko Haram/ISWAP.

Affiliates/allies
Multinational Joint Task Force, Civilian Joint Task Force, international partners (United States, United Kingdom, France).

Resources/capabilities
Heavy and light weaponry in land, air, sea and cyber spheres. The Nigerian armed forces have significantly improved the resources and capabilities of the army, the air force and Cyber Warfare Command over the past five years. However, morale remains low and there have been complaints about poor equipment and training.

Boko Haram

Strength
Between 1,500 and 2,000 fighters.[1]

Areas of operation
Lake Chad Basin region spanning Nigeria, Cameroon, Chad and Niger. Core area of control in Sambisa forest and southern Borno State.

Leadership
Led by Abubakar Shekau since 2010.

Structure
Highly decentralised structure with weak command chain, various offshoots and cells that can act independently.

History
Boko Haram was established in the early 2000s by Mohammad Yusuf. After he was killed in 2009, Shekau escalated its violent campaigns and broadened its influence and territorial control in northeast Nigeria and neighbouring countries. In 2015, Boko Haram pledged allegiance to ISIS.

Objectives
Boko Haram's goals have remained the same over time and across leaders: to establish an Islamic caliphate in the northeast of Nigeria.

Opponents
Nigerian armed forces, Multinational Joint Task Force, Civilian Joint Task Force, Western institutions and representatives.

Affiliates/allies
ISIS, al-Qaeda.

Resources/capabilities
Stolen weaponry from military bases and acquisitions from the black market, including assault rifles, tanks, rocket-propelled grenades, improvised bombs, mortars and armoured personnel vehicles. It has a limited anti-aircraft capability. Boko Haram has reportedly used drones since 2018.

Islamic State West Africa Province (ISWAP)

Strength
Between 3,500 and 5,000 fighters.[2]

Areas of operation
Lake Chad Basin region spanning Nigeria, Cameroon, Chad and Niger. Core area of territorial control on the islands of Lake Chad and the forests of northern Borno State and eastern Yobe State.

Leadership
Abu Abdullah al-Barnawi replaced previous leader Abu Musab al-Barnawi in March 2019.

Structure
ISIS and ISWAP drew closer in 2019 as the former's caliphate collapsed in the Middle East. Reports of transfers of money and soldiers, however, remain unclear and limited.

History
ISWAP split from Boko Haram in 2016 following clashes between Shekau, Nur (a senior founder of the group) and al-Barnawi. ISIS recognises this new faction and its leader in August 2016. After a few clashes with Boko Haram, both factions agreed to a ceasefire.

Objectives
Establish an Islamic caliphate in the northeast of Nigeria. It aims at consolidating its territorial control and expanding its network. ISWAP largely abstains from targeting civilians, appeals to local community networks and harnesses local grievances for its own ends.

Opponents
Nigerian armed forces, Multinational Joint Task Force, Civilian Joint Task Force, Western institutions and representatives.

Affiliates/allies
ISIS.

Resources/capabilities
While ISWAP initially suffered from a lack of weaponry, its tactic of attacking military bases has proven useful. Since mid-2018, the group has attacked large military bases and stolen weaponry such as assault rifles, rocket-propelled grenades, mortars and armoured personnel vehicles.

Multinational Joint Task Force (MNJTF)

Strength
Approximately 8,700 troops from Benin, Cameroon, Chad, Niger and Nigeria.

Areas of operation
Lake Chad Basin. The MNJTF's headquarters is in N'Djamena, Chad.

Leadership
Maj.-Gen. Ibrahim Manu Yusuf became MNJTF Force Commander in November 2019, taking over from Maj.-Gen. Chikeze Onyeka Ude, who had been in post since August 2018.

Structure
Four sections: Mora in Cameroon, Baga-Sola in Chad, Diffa in Niger and Baga in Nigeria, each led by a commander with wide ambit to manoeuvre. The force promotes cooperation over integration. The command chain is a complex balance between the multinational command and the individual armies with their chiefs of staff.

Multinational Joint Task Force (MNJTF)

History
The MNJTF was first created in 1998 to tackle cross-border crimes and banditry affecting the Basin area, but the force had become largely inactive by the time Boko Haram militants overran the headquarters in Baga in 2015. In response, the African Union's Peace and Security Council agreed to revive the MNJTF to focus its efforts on neutralising Boko Haram.

Objectives
Coordinate the regional counter-insurgency efforts and restore security in the areas affected by Boko Haram in the Lake Chad Basin. Also involved in non-military operations, such as stabilisation programmes and displaced-people returns.

Opponents
Boko Haram/ISWAP.

Affiliates/allies
Nigerian armed forces, international partners (US, UK, France).

Resources/capabilities
Lack of adequate funding has hampered the MNJTF's ability to fulfil its mandate. The operational budget when the force was put in place in 2015 was US$700 million, but actual available funds were significantly below this level.

Civilian Joint Task Force (CJTF)

Strength
Around 26,000 (in 2016).[3]

Areas of operation
Northeastern Nigeria (Borno, Yobe and Adamawa states).

Leadership
The army (through MNJTF commanders) commands, supervises and monitors CJTF activities.

Structure
Organised in four sectors – Mora (Cameroon), Baga-Sola (Chad), Baga (Nigeria), Diffa (Niger) – each under the supervision of an MNJTF commander. Some MNJTF officers select CJTF sector leaders and some state officials hold CJTF positions. Approximately 500 members have been incorporated into the Nigerian armed forces and some MNJTF checkpoints have been transferred to the CJTF.

History
CJTF was formed in 2013 as a response to Boko Haram in Borno State, Nigeria. It began as a popular youth movement, protecting people from Boko Haram and the brutality of Nigerian state authorities.

Objectives
Assist the Nigerian armed forces in the fight against Boko Haram; protect local communities from attacks; and free villages and towns from insurgent control. The CJTF patrols the streets, establishes checkpoints and provides intelligence to the security forces.

Opponents
Boko Haram/ISWAP.

Affiliates/allies
Nigerian armed forces; Multinational Joint Task Force.

Resources/capabilities
Bows and arrows, swords, machetes, axes, daggers, cutlasses, handmade muskets and sticks. Most fighters have never received formal military training.

Drivers

Radical ideology
Boko Haram and ISWAP are Salafi-jihadi groups, and radical ideologies still provide a strong motivation for the insurgency. The immediate driver of the conflict is the quest to create an Islamic caliphate based on sharia law and to erase 'Western' influence in the region.

From its early days, Boko Haram has strived to present its radical version of Salafism as the antidote to societal 'evils' represented by Westernised, corrupted elites; inequality and poverty; and Islamic religious leaders who, in the eyes of Mohammed Yusuf, had gone astray by adopting moderate positions. ISWAP appears to be more flexible and open to negotiations with the governments of the region compared with Boko Haram, which has from its inception attacked government institutions and the United Nations.

Socio-economic grievances
The North East of Nigeria has one of the highest rates of poverty in the country, along with high levels of illiteracy and a significant number of out-of-school children – schools in the North East have on average an attendance rate of 53%, compared to 61% nationwide.[4] In Far North Cameroon, the young generation has the highest unemployment rate and the lowest level of education in the country (54% against 81% nationwide).[5] Poverty is highly concentrated, with 56% of the poor located in the northern regions.[6] Faced with limited opportunities, the youth in the Lake Chad area are easy targets for

recruitment into criminal activity or armed groups. Boko Haram and ISWAP have taken advantage of this situation and recruited many youths into their cause by offering them a mix of spiritual glorification and financial rewards.

While the leadership of the two groups believes in the ideology of radical Salafi-jihadism, the rank-and-file members of the group seem more driven by opportunism (joining criminal networks to make money) or pragmatism (joining armed groups for their own security). Given Boko Haram's highly decentralised structure, some of its members might not even adhere to Salafist ideology and are instead motivated by local grievances. Defeating the group thus requires not only a military campaign but also a multifaceted approach centred on the socio-economic challenges that continue to fuel the conflict.

Political Developments

Nigeria decides

The first quarter of 2019 was a crucial period for Nigeria's democracy. Presidential elections originally scheduled for 16 February were postponed a mere five hours before the polls opened and were eventually held a week later on 23 February. While the elections featured 73 candidates, the two main challengers were incumbent President Muhammadu Buhari, of the All Progressives Congress (APC), and former vice-president and opposition leader Atiku Abubakar from the People's Democratic Party (PDP). Increasing security and tackling corruption were the issues that dominated the campaign, as both candidates used the counter-insurgency operations against Boko Haram as a rallying point. Buhari repeatedly cited his success in 'decimating' Boko Haram, while Abubakar pledged that he would end the insurgency in Borno State.

On 27 February, Buhari was officially declared the winner with 56% of the votes, despite expectations of a very close race. There were numerous reports of intimidation, violence towards voters and vote-buying – recurrent issues in Nigeria's elections.[7] Abubakar immediately contested the results, describing them as a 'throwback to jackboot era of military dictatorship', and challenged them in court. The ensuing months-long legal battle ended when both the election tribunal (in September) and the Supreme Court (in October) dismissed Abubakar's appeals.

Change in ISWAP leadership

An internal crisis within ISWAP prompted the replacement of Abu Musab al-Barnawi as leader of the group on 3 March. This change occurred in the context of a purge following the reported execution of Mamman Nur, one of ISWAP's most senior leaders, by the group in late 2018. Barnawi was reportedly replaced by Abu Abdullah al-Barnawi, a relatively unknown figure, and it is unclear whether the decision came from the central ISIS leadership or from within ISWAP itself. The succession did not affect ISWAP's capacity. The group continued to launch weekly attacks on military outposts, forcing the Nigerian Army to reorganise.

Military Developments

Insurgent attacks during the election

In the hours before voting finally commenced on 23 February, both main candidates promised Nigerians that security would be tight and urged them to go to the polls. In the run-up to the elections, both Boko Haram and ISWAP increased their attacks in order to disrupt the electoral process or to claim more territory. Numerous towns were reported as being captured. On 5 February, the Nigerian armed forces were forced to deny claims that Boko Haram had occupied five villages (Baza, Gulak, Madagali, Michika and Shuwa) in Adamawa State.

On polling day, insurgents targeted Maiduguri in a series of rocket attacks. The Nigerian armed forces denied the existence of the attacks and claimed that the rockets were part of training exercises. But the insurgent violence was widespread. Boko Haram's attacks in Yobe State even prevented State Governor Ibrahim Gaidam from casting his vote. This level of violence is in line with previous electoral processes (democracy being one of the 'Western-imported' values that Boko Haram opposes as incompatible with Islam).

Greater regional cooperation

In 2019 the MNJTF was revived with the launch in March of *Operation Yancin Tafki*, a series of coordinated intelligence, surveillance and reconnaissance missions. MNJTF troops made some progress in Boko Haram and ISWAP core territory, thanks to better coordination among the four member countries (Cameroon, Chad, Niger and Nigeria), but particularly between Chad and Nigeria. Chad agreed to deploy troops in Borno State as part of the operation and participated in numerous joint operations with Nigerian troops over the year.

Attacks in the Lake Chad Basin

Boko Haram and ISWAP continued to ramp up attacks in the Lake Chad Basin in 2019, from southwestern Borno to the eastern side of Lake Chad. Boko Haram was mainly active in central and southern Borno, while ISWAP was present in the northern part of the state and eastern Yobe. Both groups used the same tactics – hiding in forest or marsh areas and consolidating their rural strongholds – but differed when it came to targeting. Boko Haram continued to use improvised explosive devices (IEDs) and suicide attacks against civilians, conducting mass killings and abductions of civilians and attacking places such as mosques and markets. For example, on 27 July, Boko Haram conducted its deadliest attack of the year, killing at least 65 civilians who were returning from a mourning ceremony in the Nganzai area of Borno State. Meanwhile, ISWAP largely targeted military positions in northern Borno as well as on the shores of Lake Chad. On 22 March, ISWAP conducted its deadliest attack ever in Chad, killing 26 Chadian soldiers in Dangdala. Following the attack, Chad President Idriss Déby sacked the chief of armed forces, Brahim Seid Mahamat, in post since 2013.

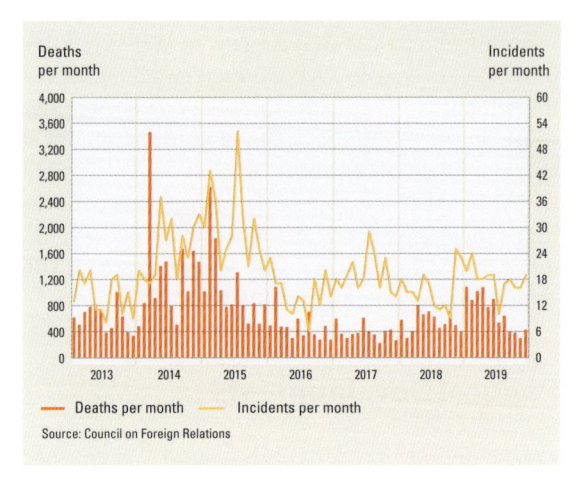

Figure 1: Deaths in Nigeria, and violent incidents related to the Boko Haram insurgency, Jan 2013–Dec 2019

The new 'Super Camp' strategy

The Nigerian Army announced a new strategy against Boko Haram in the northeast of the country, which consisted of concentrating its troops in strongholds, or 'Super Camps'. This change was part of a series of new initiatives over the year, including the revival of the MNJTF's activities in the first quarter of 2019 and the deployment of Chadian troops in Nigeria in late February.

Key Events in 2019

Political events

- **27 February**: President Buhari is officially declared winner of the election with 56% of the vote.
- **March**: MNJTF launches *Operation Yancin Takfi*.
- **4 April**: Fifth anniversary of the kidnappings of 267 Chibok girls by Boko Haram; 112 are still missing.
- **15 June**: ISWAP video shows Mali and Burkina Faso fighters renewing allegiance to ISIS leader Abu Bakr al-Baghdadi.

Military/Violent events

- **28 January**: Boko Haram attacks Rann, Borno State, killing at least 60 people and displacing tens of thousands.
- **February**: Boko Haram and ISWAP increase attacks in northeastern Nigeria ahead of the presidential elections.
- **22 March**: ISWAP kills 23 Chadian soldiers in Dangdala, on the northeastern banks of Lake Chad.
- **26 April**: Boko Haram attacks MSF office in Diffa Region. MSF subsequently suspends operations.

The new strategy is designed to boost the protection of the armed forces and to limit military casualties and the looting of weapons and equipment. The construction of enhanced camps aims to enable the Nigerian armed forces to dominate the territory, respond quickly to threats, raid militant camps and conduct more effective clearance operations.

The strategy has been heavily criticised as the army's withdrawal overlapped with numerous insurgent raids on towns that were left undefended, allowing militants to man checkpoints and deprive thousands of civilians of access to aid. On 21 August, hundreds of ISWAP militants stormed Magumeri and Gubio, two key towns near Maiduguri, the capital of Borno State. They destroyed houses, government buildings, health centres and schools and looted food, fuel and supplies. Thousands of residents fled to Maiduguri. Similar attacks happened on a weekly basis during the second half of the year in Gubio and Magumeri, but also Gajiram and Gajigana. The armed forces had recently left their barracks in these towns as part of the Super Camp strategy and the militants were able to raid the towns for hours, facing no resistance. So far, the new strategy has only led to the absence of the Nigerian armed forces in the area between Damasak and Maiduguri, thus enabling ISWAP and Boko Haram to roam freely and take control of the territory.

The Super Camp strategy also resulted in a much lower number of armed clashes between ISWAP and the armed forces in the second half of 2019. ISWAP moved more freely in rural areas but had far fewer encounters with the armed forces. In return for fewer casualties, however, the authorities have effectively ceded control over areas of Borno State to ISWAP and allowed the group to tighten its hold on the local population.

Impact

Human rights

The insurgency in northeast Nigeria continues to severely affect the human-rights situation. Weak state authority and the corruption of local governments hinder the protection of civilians. All actors involved in the conflict – Boko Haram, ISWAP, the CJTF and the Nigerian security forces – were responsible for gross human-rights violations in 2019. The Nigerian armed forces were accused of arbitrary detention and extrajudicial killings; Boko Haram of killing and kidnapping civilians and using children and women as suicide bombers. In the attack near Maiduguri in June, Boko Haram used three children as suicide bombers, who killed 30 and injured 40 people who had gathered to watch football.

Humanitarian

As of December 2019, almost 10m people were in need of life-saving assistance[8] and 2.5m internally displaced persons (IDPs) were registered across the Lake Chad Basin region. Various factors exacerbated the humanitarian crisis in 2019. In August, the rainy season and the consequent heavy flooding triggered

---

17 July — UNDP launches US$100m Regional Stabilization Facility to improve stabilisation, peacebuilding and sustainable development in Lake Chad.

17 August — Meeting of governors of the eight Lake Chad Basin regions to improve cross-border security.

September — The Nigerian Army closes the offices of two international aid groups in northeastern Nigeria.

30 October — Nigeria's Supreme Court dismisses Abubakar's appeal against the results of the presidential election in February.

10 May — The CJTF releases 894 children in Maiduguri to prevent the recruitment of children to armed groups.

10 June — More than 300 ISWAP fighters attack Darak, Cameroon, killing 16 MNJTF soldiers and eight civilians.

16 June — Boko Haram launches a triple suicide bombing by children, killing 30 people and injuring 40.

27 July — Boko Haram militants kill at least 65 civilians in Nganzai area of Borno State.

25 September — ISWAP beheads one of the six Action Against Hunger workers abducted on 18 July.

further displacement and food insecurity. The Super Camp strategy also indirectly impeded the delivery of humanitarian aid due to growing insecurity in vulnerable areas.

The humanitarian space in the northeast shrunk over 2019. The continuous targeting of humanitarian workers by Boko Haram forced some organisations to suspend their operations – Médecins Sans Frontières (MSF) closed its office in Maïné Soroa, Diffa Region, in August, three months after a violent attack on the office. The Nigerian Army also closed the offices of two international aid groups that were active in northeastern Nigeria on the basis that they were providing assistance to Boko Haram. Action Against Hunger's office in Maiduguri was shut down on 18 September – just a week before ISWAP executed one of the six Action Against Hunger workers whom it had abducted on 18 July – while Mercy Corps suspended its operation in Borno and Yobe states on 23 August after the army closed four of its offices in the region.

Economic
Nigeria's economy has not yet recovered from the 2016 recession, and half of its population still lives in extreme poverty. The unemployment rate has doubled since Buhari assumed office in 2015, reaching more than 35% youth unemployment in 2019. In October, Buhari closed all of Nigeria's land borders in an attempt to control smuggled goods and foster domestic production, but the tactic only led to rising food prices. Particularly in the northeast, closing trade routes often results in further alienating the population and driving communities into the militants' hands.

Relations with neighbouring and international partners
Regional cooperation continued this year through military operations and through wider diplomatic efforts. The second meeting of the Lake Chad Basin Governors' Forum – a framework to unite local governors of the eight regions of the Lake Chad Basin – took place in Niamey, Niger. During the meeting, the governors committed to improving cross-border security. On 17 August, the UN Development Programme launched a Regional Stabilization Facility for Lake Chad with a planned budget of US$100m (September 2019 to August 2021) to improve stabilisation, peacebuilding and sustainable development.

In 2019, the United States conducted operations in Cameroon and Nigeria as well as Mali, Burkina Faso and Niger, but is planning on reducing – or withdrawing – its troops from West Africa in 2020. While it considers that Boko Haram and ISWAP are still a threat for the region, these groups do not represent a threat for the US as they do not intend (nor are they capable of) attacking the US.

Meanwhile, the UK reaffirmed its support to Nigeria in the fight against Boko Haram. British foreign secretary Jeremy Hunt stated that the UK could scale up its support (which in 2019 amounted to £240m (approximately US$315m) in aid to the country, including £100m (US$130m) for the northeast). Russia also announced its willingness to help Nigeria in its fight against militants and to sign a military technical cooperation deal; in October 2019, Russia and Nigeria signed a deal for Moscow to provide 12 Mi-35 attack helicopters.

Trends

Political trajectories
The 2019 presidential election represented a setback to Nigerian democracy after the first peaceful transition of power in 2015. Along with widespread abuses and violence and an eight-month legal battle over results, only 36% of the electorate voted – the lowest turnout since the transition to democracy in 1999. The poor turnout was due to Buhari's disappointing first term and widespread disenchantment with democratic politics amid a system widely perceived as corrupt.

Conflict-related risks
The Super Camp strategy is likely to backfire in early 2020. Fewer clashes and casualties should not be interpreted as signifying the Nigerian government's victory over ISWAP. In fact, the group does not need to launch regular attacks, as the Super Camp strategy is providing them with the space and time to deepen their control of extended swaths of territory and rural areas. ISWAP will likely adapt its military strategy: it will save its strength for large-scale attacks against military positions and bases,

while remaining prepared to ambush and attack convoys and patrols in its territory. The group will also strengthen its ties with and support from local communities, increase recruitment and eventually attack more forcefully. Boko Haram, meanwhile, appears likely to retain its strongholds and continue its attacks on civilians, and will perhaps benefit from the Nigerian armed forces' focus on ISWAP.

Prospects for peace

While Boko Haram is no longer able to wage large-scale attacks as it did before 2015, the group is far from being defeated, despite Buhari's claims. Additionally, ISWAP has grown in power in the past few years and poses a major security threat to the Lake Chad Basin area. ISWAP in particular has been successful in earning the support of local populations – more than Boko Haram ever did – by providing state services and filling gaps in governance in the northeast. The Nigerian government will not ensure stability and peace through counter-insurgency alone. The underlying drivers of the violence – inequality, poverty, unemployment and marginalisation – need to be addressed, along with state legitimacy being re-established in the region.

Strategic implications and global influences

When Boko Haram and ISWAP split in 2016, ISWAP attracted many fighters. ISIS began promoting ISWAP's victories as its own, a trend which increased after ISIS's collapse in Iraq and Syria. For similar reasons, in 2019 ISWAP started claiming victories by the ISIS branch in central Sahel as its own and published videos of fighters in Mali renewing allegiance to ISIS. Yet despite reports of financial and strategic ties and fighter movements from the Middle East to northern Nigeria, the full extent of the links between ISWAP and ISIS remains unclear. What is certain is that ISWAP is by far the most successful ISIS offshoot outside the Middle East. The group has grown strong over the past two years and will continue to do so, probably with increased support and attention from ISIS.

Notes

[1] International Crisis Group, 'Facing the Challenge of the Islamic State in West Africa Province', 16 May 2019.
[2] Ibid.
[3] International Crisis Group, 'Watchmen of Lake Chad: Vigilante Groups Fighting Boko Haram', Report no. 244, 23 February 2017.
[4] UNICEF, 'Nigeria: Education'.
[5] Norwegian Refugee Council, 'Thousands of children out of school', 12 June 2018.
[6] World Bank, 'Cameroon: Overview'.
[7] European Union Election Observation Mission Nigeria, 'Final Report', June 2019.
[8] UN Office for the Coordination of Humanitarian Affairs (OCHA), 'Nigeria and the Lake Chad Region: Situation'.

NIGERIA (FARMER–PASTORALIST)

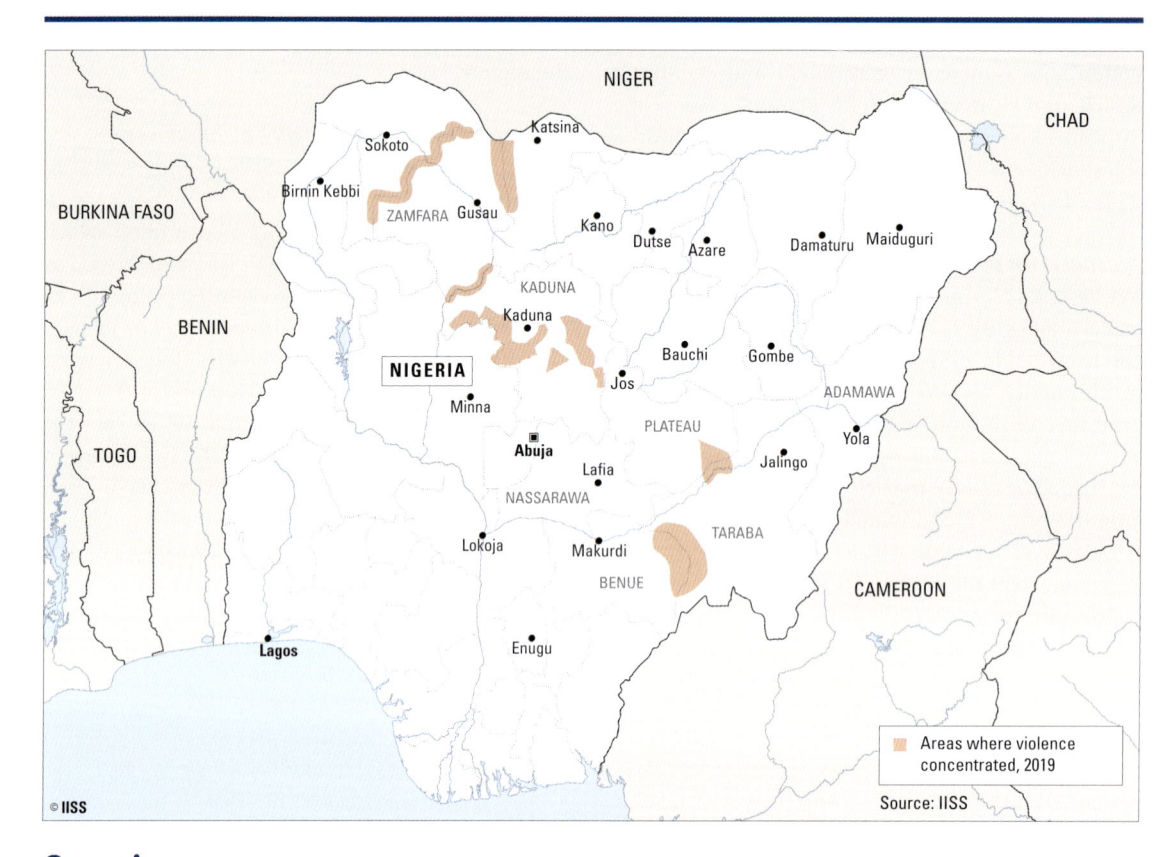

Overview

The conflict in 2019

Violence between farmers and pastoralists in Nigeria decreased significantly in 2019 compared to the previous year, in part due to the conclusion of the electoral cycle in the first quarter as well as various peacebuilding initiatives. State and federal governments became more proactive in negotiations, resulting in a marked drop in violence in Zamfara and Katsina states in the latter part of the year, although military operations continued.

The anti-open grazing laws implemented in Ekiti in 2016, Benue and Taraba in 2017 as well as Edo in July 2018 continued to generate passive and active resistance from herdsmen in 2019. Violence was concentrated in Adamawa, Benue, Kaduna, Nasarawa, Plateau, Taraba and Zamfara states. Political interests also exacerbated the volatile situation. An attack by armed men from the Adara ethnic group on the Fulani community on 11 February, which killed at least 66 Fulani, was only discussed by Kaduna State Governor Nasir el-Rufai on the eve of the presidential election. (Incumbent President Muhammadu Buhari is Fulani.) The governor later doubled the death toll to 130, saying that it appeared to have been a clear and deliberate plan to 'wipe out certain communities'.[1] Various Christian and Adara organisations accused the governor of inciting violence to influence votes ahead of the elections and creating unnecessary confusion around the attack. The Nigerian election took place on 23 February and resulted in a victory for Buhari.

Key statistics	
Type	Internal
Start date	2014
IDPs total	No data for 2019
Refugees total	Not applicable
People in need	No data

The conflict to 2019

The pastoral-transhumant group, which controls the livestock economy, and the sedentary grain producers, who grow grains (millet, maize and sorghum), vegetables and fruit, have a long history of coexistence in Nigeria. In recent years, however, cooperation between the two groups disintegrated and led to conflict, driven by climate change, poverty, corruption, inequality, violent extremism and the proliferation of small arms and light weapons, as well as divisive national and local politics. Violence often manifests as a series of attacks and counter-attacks over a short period, resulting in spiralling insecurity and rapidly mounting fatality numbers.

Farmer–herder violence spiked after Nigeria's return to democratic rule in 1999, when both herder and farmer communities took up arms, allegedly for self-defence. In 2001, Muslim–Christian violence between Fulani herders and local farmers in Plateau State began during the 7–12 September riots in Jos, as violence spread from urban to rural areas of the Jos Plateau. The conflict spiralled into reprisals on Berom and Irigwe villages over subsequent years, a situation that successive governments not only failed to resolve but also at times inflamed. There was a resurgence of mass violence in January 2010 that has continued intermittently ever since. The violence also affected stability in neighbouring states due to the displacement of pastoralists from Plateau.

In neighbouring Kaduna State, riots against the results of the 2011 presidential election also spread from urban to rural areas, leading to violence between pastoralists and farmers in the south of the state. Fulani agro-pastoralists were not involved in the post-election riots but were targeted due to their religious and ethnic identities. The rioting had spread across towns and cities in northern Nigeria, where both Christians and supporters of the then-ruling People's Democratic Party (PDP) were targeted. This rekindled long-standing ethno-religious tensions in Kaduna city and Kafanchan town, where the violence precipitated retaliatory attacks on Muslims in majority Christian areas of southern Kaduna.

Benue State has also seen high levels of violence (especially since 2016), in which herders have attacked many villages and destroyed crops, while in some areas farmers and militias have killed herders and stolen cattle. The state also introduced an anti-open grazing law that effectively banned pastoralism in Benue State and in 2017 established the Livestock Guards militia to enforce the law. The militia clashed with Fulani pastoralists and expelled them from large areas of Benue, seizing and shooting cattle in the process, triggering large-scale attacks by herders on farmers. Since then, violence has been concentrated in rural areas and is mostly perpetrated by ethnic-based local militias and bandits, but cattle rustlers, pastoralists and farmers also support vigilante groups attacking the other communities. Benue State witnessed especially high levels of violence in the first half of 2014, when hundreds of men, women and children were killed and their villages sacked. The crisis spread to neighbouring Kogi, Plateau and Nasarawa states.

Reports by Amnesty International and International Crisis Group estimated the fatality figures for the conflict at 1,229 for 2014, 2,500 for 2016 and 1,867 for 2018.[2] These figures are likely to be significant underestimates, however, as the remote rural areas where the violence takes place are seldom reached and the central government has strong incentives to downplay its impact. In terms of domestic and international attention, the conflict also remains somewhat in the shadow of Boko Haram, despite the fact that it claims far more lives. In the first six months of 2018, for example, the farmer–herder conflict resulted in almost six times more fatalities than the Boko Haram insurgency within the same period.[3]

Key Conflict Parties

Pastoral Fulani

Strength
Not known.

Areas of operation
Adamawa, Benue, Kaduna, Katsina, Nasarawa, Plateau, Sokoto, Taraba and Zamfara states and some parts of Kebbi State.

Leadership
No formal leadership.

Structure
Fulani groups are highly decentralised, being divided into clans (*leyyi*) and sub-clans. Individuals have significant autonomy on whether to fight or retaliate for perceived wrongs, decisions that may be made without community leaders knowing. For some conflicts, mobilisation happens more officially.

History
Pastoral Fulbe, known as Fulani in the Nigerian context, mostly live in dispersed settlements. Their life centres on cattle, and they possess 19.5 million cattle (about 90% of the country's total), making them the major provider of meat in the country.[4]

Objectives
To protect their traditional 'cattle culture' from banditry and cattle rustling.

Opponents
Sedentary farmer militias, bandits, government forces.

Affiliates/allies
None.

Resources/capabilities
AK-47s, G3s, Mark 4 rifles, locally made single-barrel shotguns (Dane guns), 'Lebanons' (double-barrel shotguns), and a variety of other locally made guns.

Farmers, ethnic militias and vigilante groups

Strength
Not known.

Areas of operation
Adamawa, Benue, Kaduna, Nasarawa, Plateau, Taraba, Zamfara, Katsina and Sokoto states and some parts of Kebbi State.

Leadership
Within several communities in the conflict areas, there are active mobilisations mainly driven by traditional rulers and local community leaders.

Structure
Farming communities mobilise on an ethnic basis, but unlike Fulani combatants, in some cases they also form alliances across ethnic lines, using a Christian religious identity to mobilise members. Main militias include the Mambila and Militant Vigilante Group, while main ethnic units include Berom, Irigwe, Eggon, Tarok, Adara, Alago, Tiv, Idoma, Igede and Agatu.

History
Some farmer communities took up arms in 1999 in self-defence, a trend that broadened due to successive waves of violence in the next two decades.

Objectives
To protect against raids by Fulani pastoralists and bandits.

Opponents
Fulani pastoralists, bandits.

Affiliates/allies
Government forces.

Resources/capabilities
The Hausa vigilante groups rely heavily on locally made weapons.

Armed bandits and cattle rustlers

Strength
The number of bandit gangs decreased to 35 in 2019 from 60 in 2018 due to several peace and dialogue initiatives by the state governments and continued military operations in the affected areas.

Areas of operation
Northwest Nigeria (Kaduna, Kano, Katsina, Sokoto and Zamfara states and some parts of Kebbi State).

Leadership
No generally recognised leader.

Structure
No formal structure.

History
Roving bandits have killed several thousand people in the northwest since 2012. Buharin Daji was recognised as the leader of bandits in Zamfara State but was killed by his fellow bandits on 10 March 2018 following an internal rift. He was the main link between the Zamfara State government and other bandits, but since his death there has been no generally recognised leader of the bandit groups.

Objectives
Rustling is a criminal syndicate involving different ethnic groups and nationalities. Cattle-rustling attacks are sometimes justified as reprisals against Hausa vigilante groups.

Armed bandits and cattle rustlers

Opponents
Fulani pastoralists, Hausa sedentary farmers.

Affiliates/allies
Other bandit groups in neighbouring states in the country as well as those in Niger and Mali.

Resources/capabilities
Due to their financial resources from cattle rustling, pillaging and kidnapping, bandits can purchase more sophisticated weaponry, including small arms and light weapons. They often carry out attacks while riding motorbikes.

Nigerian armed forces

Strength
143,000 military personnel, including 100,000 army personnel. Paramilitary forces number approximately 80,000.

Areas of operation
Benue, Kaduna, Katsina, Nasarawa, Plateau, Taraba and Zamfara states.

Leadership
Nigerian President Muhammadu Buhari is the commander-in-chief of the armed forces. Lt-Gen. Tukur Yusuf Buratai is the Army Chief of Staff.

Structure
The Nigerian armed forces comprise the army, the air force and the navy. The army is organised into headquarters, divisions, brigades, battalions, companies, platoons and sections.

History
Operation Sharan Daji was launched in May 2016 to fight armed banditry and cattle rustling in northwest Nigeria, with the main focus on Zamfara State, while *Operation Diran Mikiya* – an air-force operation – commenced on 31 July 2018 against armed bandits in northwest Nigeria.

Objectives
Establish and/or maintain security across Nigeria.

Opponents
Violent actors from the pastoralist and farmer communities; bandits; Boko Haram.

Affiliates/allies
International partners include the US, UK and France, while Nigeria also participates in the Multinational Joint Task Force (MNJTF) along with Chad, Niger, Cameroon and Benin, although the MNJTF is focused on fighting Boko Haram. Some vigilantes work with the army, air force and police to provide information on the location of belligerents.

Resources/capabilities
Heavy and light weaponry in land, air, sea and cyber spheres. The Nigerian armed forces have significantly improved the resources and capabilities of the army, the air force and Cyber Warfare Command over the past five years, but morale remains low and there have been complaints about poor equipment and training.

Drivers

Breakdown of farmer–pastoralist arrangements
Pastoralism generally requires transhumance – the movement of herders and their animals, often on a seasonal basis between dry and rainy seasons, as well as the daily journeys between pastures and water points. Historically, mutually beneficial rules and regulations guided the interaction between farmers and pastoralists, enabling them to coexist in the same rural space. Conflicts arising from farm destructions were amicably resolved by chieftaincy institutions and the warring parties had an unconditional respect for the community mediators. The system began declining in the 1970s with the active involvement of the police, army and lower courts, which the communities perceived as having no moral justification to settle such disputes. Furthermore, these new institutions frequently turned out to be agents of coercion and exploitation, often arresting and charging Fulani pastoralists and forcing them to sell their cattle to pay bribes. As a result, many pastoralists lost their stock and became destitute. The anti-open grazing laws implemented in the states of Benue, Edo, Ekiti and Taraba in 2016–18 further compounded the problem by restricting the movement of herders, making it impossible for them to carry out their livelihoods.

Increasing competition over land and water
Nigeria's population quadrupled in 60 years, from about 46m people in 1960 to more than 200m in 2019, leading to increased demand for agricultural land and by extension increased pressure on the pastoralists' grazing areas. In the 1960s, Nigeria's northern government established 415 grazing reserves, but only 114 of these were formally delineated.[5] Many of the unformalised reserves were subsequently lost, particularly in Jigawa and Yobe states, with land often appropriated by traditional leaders, politicians and other influential elites in the society.

Climate change has also driven increasing competition for land and water. Decreasing rainfall has contributed to the desertification in central and northern Nigeria, causing pasture and agricultural lands to shrink and agricultural productivity to fall. Pastoralists have been forced to move to the country's central and southern areas from December to May (the dry season) in search of pasture. Some of the herders settled permanently and became a major source of tension, mainly due to crop damage by livestock. The pressure of climate change has also led to land traditionally assigned to grazing being brought into agricultural production. The World Bank has initiated a series agricultural-development projects collectively known as 'Fadama' – a Hausa word for low-lying swampy areas – designed to bring formerly overlooked land under cultivation. As a result of these efforts, high-yield agriculture is now taking place around these sources of dry-season water, meaning that cattle can no longer access water and grass in these areas.

Insecurity

Insecurity resulting from Boko Haram's activities in the Lake Chad Basin has exacerbated tensions between farmers and pastoralists. Pastoralists from the Lake Chad Basin and those who use the area for dry-season grazing have altered their migrations to safer environments, raising competition with farmers over land in these new areas. Likewise, kidnapping and cattle rustling have rendered areas in Katsina, Sokoto and Zamfara states hostile for pastoralists and made cattle rearing unprofitable due to the large quantity of livestock stolen. Banditry, rustling and kidnapping have also affected the historical grazing zone of the Dandume/Birnin–Gwari area, Kaduna State. Herdsmen have instead migrated to southern Benue, Kaduna, Kogi and Nasarawa states, areas that have become hotspots for farmer–herder clashes in the past five years.

Climate of impunity

Nigeria's court system is dysfunctional and corrupt, and police capacity is limited. When disputes arise, such as over land ownership, crop damage or theft of livestock, it is very difficult and expensive to resolve them through the police or judiciary. This leads people to disregard the law and creates an incentive for using violence to resolve disputes. The perpetrators of violent attacks are almost never prosecuted. The ready availability of illegal weapons further exacerbates the consequences of this turn to violence, increasing the number of fatalities in farmer–pastoralist conflicts.

Ethnic and religious prejudice

Nigeria is the most populous state in Africa and the most ethnically and linguistically diverse. It is also about half Muslim and half Christian. There is much coexistence and amity across ethnic and religious lines, but there is also prejudice and animosity between some communities. This is partly historical and contextual and partly ideological. In central and southern Nigeria, a widespread Christian viewpoint is that Fulani pastoralists are vanguards of a northern Islamisation agenda, with conflicts perceived as being religious rather than resource-based. The Fulani still often refer to non-Fulani as *haabe* (plural) or *kaado* (sing.), pejorative terms denoting non-Muslim 'blacks' (and often used for non-Fulani Muslims such as Hausas too). In contrast, a view among the pastoral Fulani is that they are attacked and denied access to land by some ethnic groups due to their

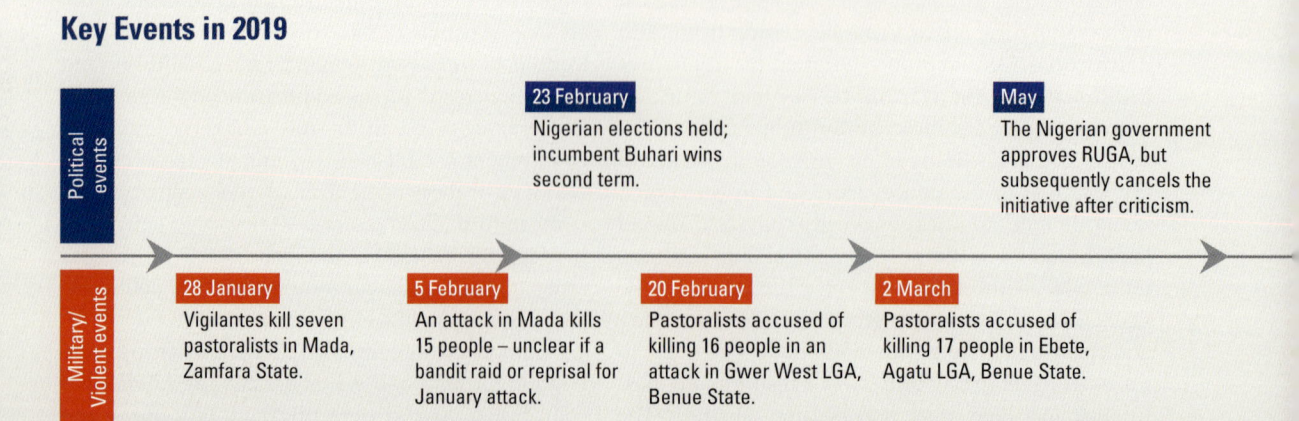

Key Events in 2019

Political events

- **23 February**: Nigerian elections held; incumbent Buhari wins second term.
- **May**: The Nigerian government approves RUGA, but subsequently cancels the initiative after criticism.

Military/Violent events

- **28 January**: Vigilantes kill seven pastoralists in Mada, Zamfara State.
- **5 February**: An attack in Mada kills 15 people – unclear if a bandit raid or reprisal for January attack.
- **20 February**: Pastoralists accused of killing 16 people in an attack in Gwer West LGA, Benue State.
- **2 March**: Pastoralists accused of killing 17 people in Ebete, Agatu LGA, Benue State.

Muslim religious identity and their status as Fulani nomads. Their self-perception is of a socio-cultural crisis and vulnerability, which is also a problem in far northern states, with grazing land and pastoral livelihoods not well protected. Land disputes are often articulated in ethnic terms between farmers and pastoralists, with assertions that the Fulani have neither tenure nor user rights on land as they are 'outsiders' or 'latecomers' to areas to which they have migrated, even in cases where they purchased land or had been settled or grazing on it for generations.

Political Developments

Elections

The violence between farmers and pastoralists became highly politicised in the build-up to the elections on 23 February 2019, with many believing that the conflict had either been instigated by the PDP opposition or overblown to discredit incumbent President Buhari, a Fulani from Daura, Katsina State. A cross-section of the Nigerian population believed that the conflict was initially between farmers and herders but was later hijacked by violent actors from other ethnic groups to make Buhari unpopular. At the polls, however, Buhari secured a second four-year term, with his All Progressives Congress (APC) party winning 19 of the 36 states, although the result was rejected by Atiku Abubakar, leader of the PDP. The election was also notable for the lowest voter turnout since Nigeria became democratic in 1999 – only 36% – indicating widespread apathy towards the political establishment, which has failed to address the multiple security issues facing the country. At the state level in 2019, various governments continued to blame political opponents rather than address security challenges on the ground, and some of these challenges were seen as being instigated from within. The governor of Zamfara State, for example, was accused of making inflammatory statements on the eve of the national elections, as well as exacerbating insecurity in the state.

RUGA and NLTP

In May 2019, Buhari approved the implementation of the Rural Grazing Area settlement (RUGA), which attempted to address the challenges of farmer–herder conflict by creating designated reserved communities for pastoralists. The settlements will house both nomadic herdsmen and animal farmers regardless of their ethnicity. The RUGA plan is founded on the belief that the settlement of nomadic herdsmen is the sole way to end the clashes. To encourage the herders to settle, the government will provide necessary amenities (water, pasture, schools, security and veterinary clinics) to add value to animal products. This decision provoked an immediate reaction from political actors. The Southeast Governors' Forum, Afenifere (Yoruba) and Ohanaeze (Igbo) organisations and the Middle Belt Forum, among others, all contested the plan, stating that they would never give any land to such settlements and this was a move by Buhari to import 'criminal' Fulani and 'colonise' the country. The government was forced

6 May
Armed bandits attack villages in Ardo-Kola and Jalingo LGAs, Taraba State, killing 11 people.

8 September
Governors of Katsina, Sokoto and Zamfara states sign MoU with governor of Maradi, Niger, on cross-border cooperation.

16 June
Pastoralists attack suburbs in Jalingo, state capital of Taraba State.

13 September
Northwest governors adopt NLTP.

17 July
Bandits attack several villages in Goronyo area, Sokoto State, killing 39.

19 September
The National Economic Council approves N100 billion (US$275m) initial budget for NLTP.

3 November
Vigilantes attack suspected Fulani bandits in Gummi area of Zamfara State, killing nine.

to suspend RUGA two months later after it was criticised as being a land-seizure policy that would mainly benefit pastoralists.[6]

After the failure of RUGA, in September 2019 Buhari relaunched the National Livestock Transformation Plan (NLTP), a ten-year plan aimed at modernising Nigeria's livestock sector and resolving the farmer–pastoralist conflict. Adamawa, Nasarawa and Plateau were the first pilot states for the programme and, unlike RUGA (which was a federal initiative launched by the Ministry of Agriculture without the approval of state governors), each state will determine its own implementation model, with support from the federal government. The NLTP also sparked controversy, with some calling it 'RUGA in disguise'.[7] Despite this, the implementation continued in the pilot states.

Progress on tackling rural banditry

Conflict-management measures and peacebuilding initiatives gained momentum in 2019. Katsina and Zamfara states made concerted efforts to negotiate with the bandits in the last quarter of the year, resulting in fewer violent incidents, and villages and roads that were formerly under bandit control returning to normal life. In August, the governors of Kaduna, Katsina, Kebbi, Sokoto and Zamfara states met in Katsina to discuss strategy and coordination efforts to tackle the security issues facing the states. On 8 September, the governors met with the governor of Maradi region, Niger, to discuss how to curb cross-border banditry and other related criminal activities, resulting in the signing of a Memorandum of Understanding (MoU) on cross-border cooperation. In September, Sanusi Muhammad Kotorkoshi, executive secretary of the Zamfara State Emergency Agency, said that 25,000 internally displaced persons (IDPs) had returned to their homes as a result of the peacebuilding initiatives.[8]

Controversy over anti-open grazing laws

The anti-open grazing laws, which were implemented between 2016 and 2018 in Benue, Edo, Ekiti and Taraba states, continued to generate controversy and became a politicised issue in the run-up to the election. Buhari repeatedly criticised the law as being discriminatory against Fulani herders. In January, a few weeks before the election, opposition candidate Atiku Abubakar, also a Fulani, pledged to review the laws in terms of their compatibility with the Nigerian Constitution, which enshrines freedom of movement. In October, Fulani herdsmen pledged to seek legal redress if Oyo State continued with its plan to implement an anti-open grazing law.

Military Developments

State operations

The government continued several military operations in 2019. On 10 May, the Nigerian Army-led *Operation Sharan Daji* (targeting banditry and cattle rustling in the northwest states) was reorganised and expanded to include the Nigerian police and Civil Defence Corps and became *Operation Hadarin Daji*. Elsewhere, *Operation Safe Haven* continued, mainly focused on Plateau State and the Plateau–Taraba state boundary, and achieved a major success in December 2019 with the negotiated surrender of weapons and ammunition by former militias. *Operation Whirl Stroke* – set up in May 2018 to address insecurity associated with farmer–pastoralist violence in Benue, Nasarawa and Taraba states – also continued in 2019. The operation reported arresting and killing bandits and recovering weapons and ammunition.

Impact

Human rights

The failure of the authorities to intervene in clashes between farmers and pastoralists and bring the culprits to justice has created a climate of impunity that has allowed situations to escalate unchecked. In a 2018 report, Amnesty International claimed that the Nigerian security forces had prior warning of an attack but did not intervene; in other instances, the security forces were slow to respond to incidents or abandoned their posts before or during the attack.[9] Vigilante groups have stepped into this security vacuum, nominally to provide stability and protection, but in practice they also perpetrate attacks and human-rights abuses.[10]

Humanitarian
The conflict has created a major humanitarian crisis in Nigeria, with 200,000 people displaced due to the conflict in 2018 alone.[11] IDPs, most of whom are women and children, often live in severely overcrowded camps with poor sanitation and lack safe drinking water. Makurdi, the capital of Benue State, houses an estimated 35,000 people. In April 2019, at least seven children died from measles at the Abagena camp in Makurdi, while malaria and diarrhoea also pose health risks.[12] The camps are not segregated, leaving girls and women vulnerable to sexual violence. Resources for IDPs are severely overstretched, especially in Benue and Plateau, challenging state capability to deliver basic necessities in the camps. On 18 July, the World Health Organization announced plans to construct provisional health centres and offer routine immunisation for children under five in the Plateau State camps.

Economic
The conflict has severely impacted economic activities, resulting in the loss of livelihood for both farmers and pastoralists. Research from 2018 demonstrated that conflict and subsequent displacement disrupted agricultural work for communities living in Benue, Kaduna, Nasarawa, Plateau, Taraba and Zamfara states, resulting in sharp drops in food production.[13] In 2019, violence discouraged farmers from planting crops in border areas between Plateau and Taraba in Wase (Langtang South local-government area (LGA) in Plateau State and Ibi LGA in Taraba State).

The costs of doing business have also risen due to the conflict.[14] Transport across the country has become a fraught undertaking due to the high level of insecurity in some areas: there have been reports of farmer communities stopping commercial buses and killing travellers suspected of being Fulani. Travellers and transport companies have therefore become warier of travelling through these communities; trips must often be undertaken only in daylight hours and with an armed guard in place, raising costs and hindering the efficacy of the transport network.

Trends

Political trajectories
Buhari's re-election is unlikely to bring about a radical change in the government's approach to the conflict from a security standpoint, although there is some cause for optimism with its political initiatives, despite serious obstacles ahead. As with RUGA, the relaunched NLTP aroused controversy, and the plan's success (or otherwise) will be heavily dependent on the ability of the federal government and participating states to engage with the pastoralists and farmers to the point where both groups buy into the government's proposed modernisation programme. However, the government appears to have learned from past failures and the approach in the implementation of the NLTP is slowly gaining the trust of local populations in the designated pilot states. The NLTP is a ten-year framework, however, so competition over land and water will only continue in the immediate term and will likely escalate. Buhari's victory also in no way reverses the growing stigma of the Fulani within Nigerian society and the prominence of pastoralism as a political issue. Indeed, the politicisation of ethnic and religious difference in Nigeria, the intersection of rural violence with other forms of insecurity (including urban riots) and the perceived links with Boko Haram's violent activities in the northeast of the country will likely continue to fuel public mistrust of Fulani pastoralists.

Conflict-related risks
The proposal to withdraw the armed forces from parts of the country was criticised in some quarters, particularly by the state governors in the northwest and central regions of the country. There is still a lack of confidence in the capacity of the police to fill the void, despite promises by Chief of Naval Staff Admiral Ibok Ekwe Ibas Obok that the police would be supported by the Nigeria Security and Civil Defence Corps, and that a recruitment drive for an additional 10,000 police personnel had been approved. Elsewhere, states that implemented anti-open grazing laws will likely witness renewed violence not directly related to farmer–pastoralist conflict, but by Fulani bandits who are completely against the law.

Despite the success of the amnesties brokered with bandits in Katsina and Zamfara states, progress will be short-lived unless all armed groups are included in a comprehensive deal, but the sheer number of bandit groups makes this a daunting diplomatic challenge. In 2019, there were already reports of friction between the bandits and their representatives at the negotiating table with the government. Implementation will also continue to be difficult, particularly in terms of the disarmament process, with ex-bandits still seen in local markets and other public places carrying weapons. Failing to agree a comprehensive deal may lead to bandits migrating to neighbouring states. In 2019, states as far as Adamawa started complaining of new forms of rural insecurity partly associated with bandits coming from Zamfara. However, most of the farming communities, especially in Zamfara, consider the peace initiative to be lopsided in favour of Fulani bandits. These dynamics could lead to a renewal of violence in Katsina and Zamfara.

Prospects for peace
The underlying drivers of the conflict between pastoralists and farmers in Nigeria – increasing competition for land and water – will continue to pose fundamental challenges to any initiative that seeks to resolve the conflict. In addition, the cycle of attacks and counter-attacks has created a legacy of animosity between farmers and pastoralists that will be difficult to defuse, especially in the context of a climate of widespread impunity and government inaction. In the short term, violence will most likely continue, although the frequency and intensity of such violence depends on many factors, particularly the success of the NLTP in the pilot states.

Strategic implications and global influences
The impacts of global climate change may force pastoralists to take their herds further afield into new territories in Nigeria, bringing them into confrontation with farming communities there. Conversely, insecurity in Nigeria may continue to drive pastoralists out into neighbouring countries, where they may settle if safe return is not possible. On a regional level, countries around the Lake Chad Basin (Cameroon, Chad, Niger and Nigeria) all host pastoralist communities, and so are vulnerable to tensions that may result when herders and farmers clash over land and/or water, and therefore all have a stake in attempting to find a resolution to the seemingly intractable clash between these different ways of life.

Notes

[1] 'Death Toll From Northwest Nigeria Attack Doubles to 130', Voice of America, 19 February 2019.
[2] Amnesty International, 'Nigeria: Government failures fuel escalating conflict between farmers and herders as death toll nears 4,000', 17 December 2018.
[3] International Crisis Group, 'Stopping Nigeria's Spiralling Farmer–Herder Violence', Report no. 262, 26 July 2018.
[4] International Crisis Group, 'Herders against Farmers: Nigeria's Expanding Deadly Conflict', Report no. 252, 19 September 2017.
[5] Ibid.
[6] Samson Totomade, '7 things you should know about Buhari's controversial RUGA settlements', Pulse Nigeria, 1 July 2019.
[7] Femi Ibirogba, 'National livestock plan is RUGA in disguise, Nigerians warn', *Guardian* (Nigeria), 16 September 2019.
[8] Mohammed Munirat Nasir, 'Homecoming for displaced persons', *Sun* (Nigeria), 16 September 2019.
[9] Amnesty International, 'Nigeria: Government failures fuel escalating conflict between farmers and herders as death toll nears 4,000'.
[10] Tim McDonnell, 'Herders Vs. Farmers: A Deadly Year In Nigeria', NPR, 17 December 2018.
[11] IDMC, 'Excerpt from 2019 Global Report on Internal Displacement: Spotlight Nigeria: Floods and conflict converged to deepen an existing crisis', 2019.
[12] 'Measles outbreak in IDP camp kills seven children', *Guardian* (Nigeria), 6 April 2018.
[13] International Crisis Group, 'Stopping Nigeria's Spiralling Farmer–Herder Violence'. International Crisis Group, 'Stopping Nigeria's Spiralling Farmer–Herder Violence'.
[14] SBMIntel, 'Growing impact of the Pastoral Conflict', 4 July 2018.

THE SAHEL (MALI & BURKINA FASO)

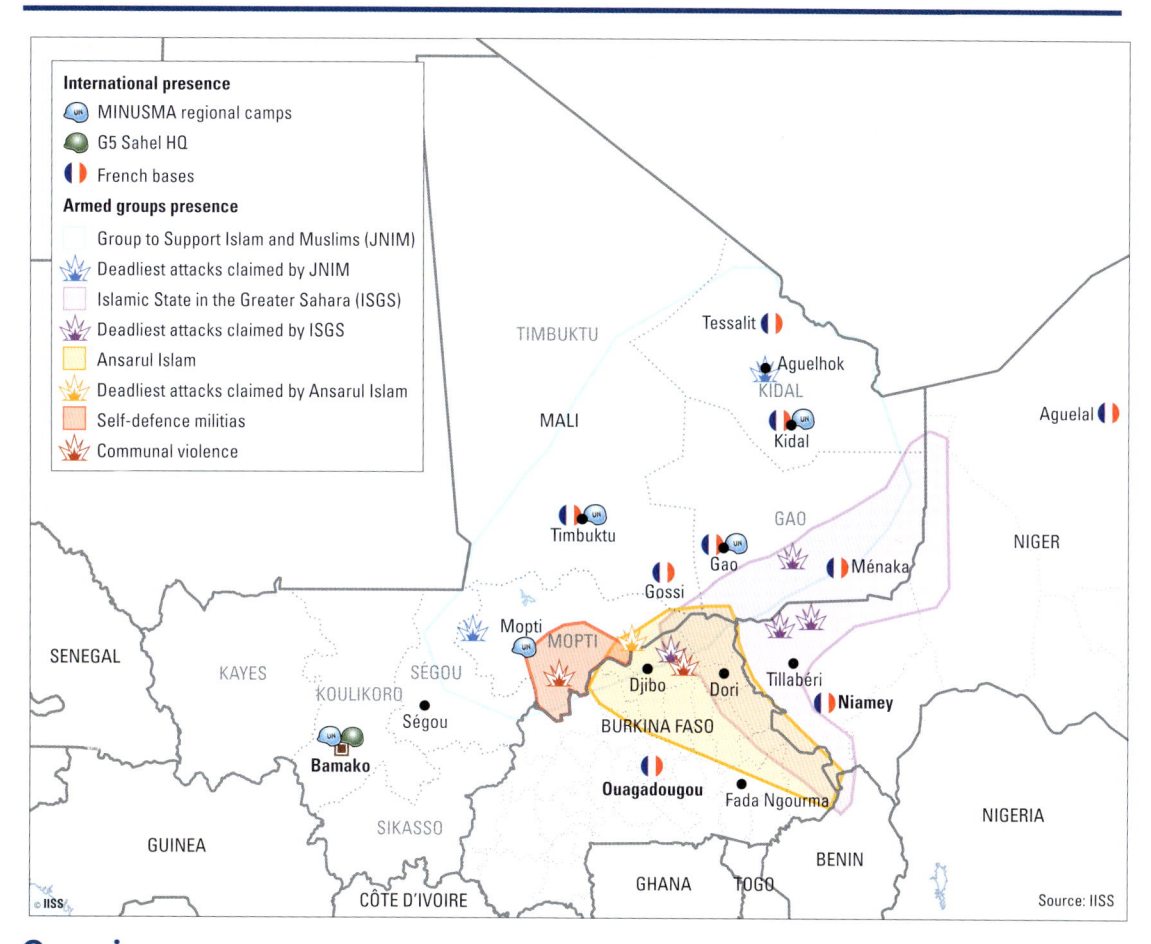

International presence
- MINUSMA regional camps
- G5 Sahel HQ
- French bases

Armed groups presence
- Group to Support Islam and Muslims (JNIM)
- Deadliest attacks claimed by JNIM
- Islamic State in the Greater Sahara (ISGS)
- Deadliest attacks claimed by ISGS
- Ansarul Islam
- Deadliest attacks claimed by Ansarul Islam
- Self-defence militias
- Communal violence

Source: IISS

Overview

The conflict in 2019

The conflict in the Sahel in 2019 was characterised by an unprecedented level of violence in northern and central Mali, northern and eastern Burkina Faso and western Niger. Communal violence spiralled, jihadist attacks rose sharply and counter-terrorism operations by regional and international actors intensified. Civilians were the main victims of the crisis, not only directly targeted by all sides (militant groups, local self-defence groups and security forces) but also suffering from the indiscriminate nature of the violence. By June 2019, the number of civilian deaths had already exceeded the total fatality count for 2018, hitherto the deadliest year since the conflict began in 2012.

Burkina Faso was hit particularly hard as the two main groups – the Group to Support Islam and Muslims (known by its Arabic acronym JNIM) and the Islamic State in the Greater Sahara (ISGS) — continued to spread from Mali's eastern and southern border areas, targeting military positions but also

Key statistics

Type	Internationalised
Start date	January 2012
IDPs total* (31 December 2019)	840,430
Refugees total** (31 December 2019)	138,603
People in need (November 2019)	6,100,000

*Total IDPs for the affected areas in Mali, Burkina Faso and Niger.
**Malian refugees in neighbouring countries

schools, public buildings and churches. The violence disrupted socio-economic life and had dramatic humanitarian consequences. Across the country, the number of internally displaced persons (IDPs) increased tenfold, from 47,000 in January 2019 to 560,000 in mid-December 2019.[1] This level of insecurity is unprecedented in Burkina Faso, and the authorities struggled to manage and contain the situation, leaving the region with deep concerns about a potential spillover of militant groups to coastal West African countries.

The conflict to 2019

The conflict in Mali began in January 2012, when Tuareg groups in the north rebelled against marginalisation and neglect by the capital Bamako, the fourth such rebellion since the country's independence in 1960. Led by the National Movement for the Liberation of Azawad (MNLA), the separatists sought to establish the independent state of 'Azawad' and were initially supported by extremist groups, namely Ansar Dine and the Movement for Oneness and Jihad in West Africa (MUJAO), a splinter group of al-Qaeda in the Islamic Maghreb (AQIM). In March 2012, Malian soldiers mutinied over the mismanagement of the Tuareg rebellion, leading to the *coup d'état* that ousted president Amadou Toumani Touré.

Within three months, the joint forces of the separatist and extremist groups had won significant territory, including the three largest cities in northern Mali – Gao, Kidal and Timbuktu. Eventually, the former allies split over ideological differences and by July 2012, northern Mali had fallen into the hands of extremist groups. When extremist groups began moving southwards towards Bamako in January 2013, and following Mali's request for assistance, the French forces launched *Operation Serval* (the predecessor of the current *Operation Barkhane*, which was launched in August 2014). The Economic Community of West African States (ECOWAS) also deployed the African-led International Support Mission to Mali (AFISMA) – a military mission authorised by the UN Security Council in December 2012 – which initially had been expected to start later in 2013. Within a month, French forces had retaken the extremist-controlled areas of northern Mali.

After various failed attempts, a peace agreement was signed between the government, the Coordination of the Movement of Azawad (CMA) – a coalition of predominantly Tuareg separatist movements – and the Plateforme, a coalition of groups that professed loyalty to the state after the rebellion. The 2015 Algiers Accord officially ended the rebellion of 2012–15 and provided a way forward for Mali, including provisions for a disarmament, demobilisation and reintegration (DDR) programme; security-sector reforms; greater representation of northern populations in national institutions; decentralisation; and socio-economic initiatives such as the development of northern zones. In April 2013, the United Nations Security Council mandated the UN Multidimensional Integrated Stabilization Mission in Mali (MINUSMA) to implement the peace deal and stabilise the north. Over the next five years, however, extremist groups evolved, reorganised and spread from northern Mali to central Mali, then to western Niger and northern and eastern Burkina Faso.

Key Conflict Parties

Malian armed forces (FAMa)

Strength
13,000 active military personnel and 7,800 paramilitary personnel (1,800 gendarmerie, 1,000 national police, 3,000 militia and 2,000 national guard).

Areas of operation
Northern and central Mali. In 2019, particularly in the Gourma (border with Burkina Faso) and the Liptako (border with Niger) areas.

Leadership
Led by Abdoulaye Coulibaly, appointed Chief of the General Staff in March 2019 after a leadership reshuffle in the wake of the Ogossagou attack.

Structure
FAMa consists of the army (under the Ministry of Armed Forces and Veterans) and the gendarmerie (under the Ministry of Interior and Security).

History
Created in October 1960. FAMa now focuses on countering militant groups. With international support, a defence reform is under way. Efforts to improve training and air-force capability are priorities.

Malian armed forces (FAMa)

Objectives
FAMa plays the primary role in responding to security incidents around the country, including jihadist activity, and in maintaining internal security.

Opponents
JNIM, ISGS, Ansarul Islam.

Affiliates/allies
EU, France, US, Burkina Faso, Niger, G5 Sahel Joint Force, MINUSMA.

Resources/capabilities
Mali's defence budget for 2019 was US$727 million (4.12% of GDP), up from US$726m in 2018, and compared to US$467m in 2015 and US$208m in 2010.

Niger armed forces

Strength
5,300 active military personnel (5,200 army and 100 air force) and 5,400 paramilitary (1,400 gendarmerie, 2,500 republican guard and 1,500 national police).

Areas of operation
Western Niger, regions of Tahoua and Tillabéri. The country is also confronted by another jihadist threat, Boko Haram, in the southeast (Diffa Region).

Leadership
Led by General Ahmed Mohamed, appointed General Chief of Staff in January 2018.

Structure
The armed forces are comprised of the army, the air force, the national gendarmerie and the national guard, and the national police.

History
Founded in 1961 from French Colonial Forces companies and officered by the French until the 1974 military coup. It was reorganised in 1970, and again in 2003 to integrate the Niger Air Force.

Objectives
The Niger armed forces are responsible for maintaining internal and border security in light of regional jihadist threat.

Opponents
JNIM, ISGS, Ansarul Islam.

Affiliates/allies
France, Mali, Burkina Faso, G5 Sahel Joint Force, MINUSMA.

Resources/capabilities
Niger's defence budget for 2019 was US$176m (1.86% of GDP), up from US$230m in 2018 and compared to US$166m in 2015 and US$47m in 2010.

Burkina Faso armed forces

Strength
11,200 active military personnel (6,400 army, 600 air force, 4,200 gendarmerie). There are also 45,000 personnel in the People's Militia (reserve military/conscripts) and 250 active paramilitary personnel.

Areas of operation
In 2019, northern and eastern Burkina Faso, and the border area with Mali (the Gourma).

Leadership
Led by Brig.-Gen. Moise Minoungou, appointed General Chief of Staff in January 2019 after a military reshuffle prompted by the security situation.

Structure
The armed forces are comprised of the army, the air force, the gendarmerie and the People's Militia.

History
Created in its current form in 1985 with the inauguration of the air force.

Objectives
Burkina Faso's armed forces are responsible for maintaining security in the country and countering jihadist groups.

Opponents
Ansarul Islam, JNIM, ISGS.

Affiliates/allies
France, Mali, G5 Sahel Joint Force, MINUSMA.

Resources/capabilities
Burkina Faso's defence budget for 2019 was US$361m (2.47% of GDP), up from US$313m in 2018 and compared to US$148m in 2015 and US$126m in 2010.

French armed forces (*Operation Barkhane*)

Strength
Approximately 4,500 soldiers.

Areas of operation
Active across Mali, Burkina Faso, Chad, Mauritania and Niger.

Leadership
Pascal Facon succeeded Frédéric Blachon as commander of *Operation Barkhane* in July 2019.

Structure
Permanent structures include the headquarters in N'Djamena (Chad), a regional base in Gao (Mali), a special-forces base in Ouagadougou (Burkina Faso), and an intelligence and surveillance base in Niamey (Niger). Smaller bases include Aguelal, Gossi, Kidal, Ménaka, Tessalit and Timbuktu. The operation also relies on three logistical hubs: Dakar, Abidjan, Douala.

French armed forces (*Operation Barkhane*)

History
French forces entered the conflict in 2013 with *Operation Serval*, responding to an official request for assistance by the Malian government following the jihadist occupation of many Malian cities, including Timbuktu. After quickly driving the insurgency out of the most populous areas, *Operation Serval* was replaced by the stabilisation-focused *Operation Barkhane* in 2014.

Objectives
Operation Barkhane's mandate is to support counter-terrorism efforts across the Sahel, both by conducting missions and by building capacity in the Malian security forces, with a focus on fighting the terrorist threat directly and supporting partner forces, including the FC-G5S and the Malian Army.

Opponents
JNIM, ISGS, Ansarul Islam.

Affiliates/allies
Malian armed forces, G5 Sahel Joint Force, MINUSMA.

Resources/capabilities
Operation Barkhane is France's largest overseas military operation, with an estimated budget of €600m (approximately US$670m) per year. French forces benefit from good equipment and technology, such as three MQ-9A *Reaper* uninhabited aerial vehicles (UAVs), seven *Mirage* aircraft, between six and ten transport aircraft, 19 helicopters and nearly 500 armoured vehicles.

United Nations Multidimensional Integrated Stabilization Mission in Mali (MINUSMA)

Strength
As of December 2019, MINUSMA had 13,695 personnel. The main troop contributions were from Bangladesh (1,260), Burkina Faso (1,071) and Chad (413).

Areas of operation
Northern and central Mali.

Leadership
Lt-Gen. Dennis Gyllensporre (Force Commander).

Structure
MINUSMA deploys regular military units, special forces and a helicopter detachment under the direct command of the Force Commander.

History
Established by UN Security Council (UNSC) Resolution 2100 in April 2013 to support Malian authorities and stabilise the country after the 2012 Tuareg rebellion. MINUSMA has one of the highest mortality rates among peacekeeping missions in the world.

Objectives
The first strategic priority is the implementation of the 2015 peace agreement. In June 2019, the UNSC renewed MINUSMA's mandate and added the protection of civilians, the reduction of communal violence and the restoration of state presence in central Mali as its second strategic priority.

Opponents
JNIM, ISGS, Ansarul Islam.

Affiliates/allies
Malian armed forces, French armed forces, G5 Sahel Joint Force.

Resources/capabilities
Approved budget for July 2019 to June 2020 is US$1.2 billion.

G5 Sahel Joint Force (FC-G5S)

Strength
Approximately 5,000 troops, provided by the five member countries, Burkina Faso, Chad, Mali, Mauritania and Niger.

Areas of operation
Border areas of Burkina Faso, Chad, Mali, Mauritania and Niger.

Leadership
General Oumarou Namata, Nigerien deputy chief of staff, was appointed Force Commander in July 2019, succeeding Mauritanian General Hanena Ould Sidi.

Structure
Includes troops across seven battalions in three sectors in Burkina Faso, Chad, Mali, Mauritania and Niger.

History
Created in March 2017, with French support.

Objectives
A joint counter-terrorism task force, the FC-G5S is designed to address threats across the Sahel, including terrorism, transnational organised crime and human trafficking. Its first objective is to improve security along the shared borders of the member countries through cooperation between their security forces and the deployment of joint patrols.

Opponents
JNIM, ISGS, Ansarul Islam.

Affiliates/allies
Foreign and regional armed forces, MINUSMA. FC-G5S is intended to complement both MINUSMA and *Operation Barkhane*.

Resources/capabilities
The G5 Sahel countries face budget shortages and a lack of predictable financing, as pledges of hundreds of millions of dollars by international partners have not materialised. Troop deployment is slow due to a lack of operating bases, capacity and equipment.

Group to Support Islam and Muslims (JNIM)

Strength
Approximately 1,000–2,000 fighters.

Areas of operation
Northern and central Mali, northern and eastern Burkina Faso and (to a limited extent) western Niger.

Leadership
Led by Tuareg militant Iyad Ag Ghali.

Structure
JNIM was created as a collaborative structure but has become a more rigid hierarchy, led by AQIM.

History
JNIM formed in March 2017 as a merger of AQIM, Ansar Dine, Macina Liberation Front and Al Mourabitoun. The group is responsible for the majority of attacks in the region.

Objectives
JNIM aims to drive foreign forces out of Mali, replace existing governments in its area of operations, establish a *wilayat* (province) of the Islamic State in the Sahel and impose sharia law.

Opponents
Malian armed forces, MINUSMA, G5 Sahel Joint Force, foreign forces (including France's *Operation Barkhane*).

Affiliates/allies
Al-Qaeda, Ansarul Islam. JNIM operates in proximity to and cooperates with ISGS fighters.

Resources/capabilities
Heavy weaponry; improvised explosive devices (IEDs) including vehicle-borne IEDS (VBIEDs), suicide-vehicle-borne IEDs (SVBIEDs).

Islamic State in the Greater Sahara (ISGS)

Strength
Between 200 and 500 fighters.

Areas of operation
Mali (Mnaka and Gao regions), western Niger (Tillabéri and Tahoua regions) and Burkina Faso (Sahel and East regions).

Leadership
Adnan Abu Walid al-Sahraoui.

Structure
No defined structure and loose hierarchy.

History
The group split from Movement for Oneness and Jihad in West Africa (MUJAO), when Sahraoui declared adherence to the Islamic State (also known as ISIS or ISIL) in May 2015.

Objectives
Restore the Islamic caliphate. ISIS sets the strategic direction and ideological goals.

Opponents
Malian armed forces, MINUSMA, G5 Sahel Joint Force, foreign forces (i.e. French armed forces and allies).

Affiliates/allies
ISIS, Katiba Salaheddine. While not affiliates, the group operates in proximity to and cooperates with JNIM fighters.

Resources/capabilities
IEDs and light weapons.

Ansarul Islam

Strength
Approximately 200 fighters.

Areas of operation
Northern and eastern Burkina Faso and the border area with Mali (the Gourma).

Leadership
Jafar Dicko replaced his brother and original leader, Malam Ibrahim Dicko, upon his death in 2017.

Structure
No clearly defined structure. The group is part social uprising, part religious movement. Lacking an ethnic base, it primarily recruits within Fulani and Rimaibe communities but does not pursue identity-based grievances.

History
Formed in Burkina Faso in 2016 as a localised insurgency against the Soum province's social-order structures and inequalities, Ansarul Islam has quickly expanded in cooperation with Malian jihadist groups. Today, the group carries out most of the attacks in northern Burkina Faso.

Objectives
Ibrahim Dicko was a prominent preacher in radical Islam who vowed to resurrect the ancient kingdom of Djeelgodji. While linked to other jihadist groups, Ansarul Islam is primarily focused on challenging the social order in northern Burkina Faso.

Opponents
Burkina Faso armed forces, Malian armed forces, foreign forces (i.e. French armed forces and allies), G5 Sahel Joint Force.

Affiliates/allies
JNIM.

Resources/capabilities
IEDs and light weapons.

Self-defence groups

Strength
Numbers vary and depend on groups, and even the number of groups is unclear.

Areas of operation
Mali, mainly Bankass, Bandiagara, Koro and Mondoro districts, but also Douentza, Djenné and Ségou.

Leadership
Most groups do not have a clear leadership structure. Dan Na Ambassagou's leader is Youssouf Toloba.

Structure
Groups are divided along ethnic lines, with the Dogon and Bambara on one side, the Fulani on the other. Most groups are fluid and do not possess military organisation. Dan Na Ambassagou is one of the few armed groups that is organised and hierarchical, and mainly recruits Dogon, who are sedentary farmers.

History
Originally set up to manage areas where state presence is limited, the groups became widespread and turned violent in central Mali as jihadist groups moved south, heightening communal tensions and threatening their livelihoods.

Objectives
To defend and protect their villages and communities against bandits, jihadist groups, rebel groups or other ethnic militias (the enemy depends on the group).

Opponents
Bambara and Dogon groups oppose jihadist groups and hence Fulani, whom they accuse of allying with jihadist groups. Fulani groups oppose Bambara and Dogon.

Affiliates/allies
Bambara and Dogon groups cooperate – to various degrees – with the Malian authorities (who sometimes fully delegate security responsibilities to these groups).

Resources/capabilities
Light weapons such as guns and rifles.

Coordination of Azawad Movements (CMA)

Strength
CMA groups were estimated to have between 800 and 4,000 fighters in 2012. After the 2015 Algiers Peace Agreement, the number of fighters is unclear.

Areas of operation
Northern Mali, including Kidal, Timbuktu, Gao and Ménaka, Tessalit, Aguelhok and Diré.

Leadership
The position of president rotates between the various CMA components. The current leader since February 2018 is the MNLA leader Bilal Ag Acherif.

Structure
The CMA is an umbrella group which includes the National Movement for the Liberation of Azawad (MNLA), the High Council for Unity of Azawad (HCUA) and the CMA-affiliated faction of the Arab Movement of Azawad (MAA–CMA).

History
The CMA is a Tuareg-dominated coalition of separatist movements created in 2014 to represent the separatists' views in the peace negotiation in the aftermath of the 2013 French intervention. The CMA is a signatory of the 2015 Algiers Peace Agreement.

Objectives
The loose coalition of former rebel groups has shared interests such as self-determination. Independence is no longer an objective.

Opponents
Before the 2015 peace agreement, the group opposed the Plateforme and the Malian government. Fighting still occurs with the Plateforme, as well as among the groups in the coalition and with jihadist groups.

Affiliates/allies
CMA groups allied with jihadist groups in the 2012 rebellion. Since 2015, the government, the Plateforme and the CMA have worked together towards the implementation of the agreement. There are still allegations that some parts of the CMA cooperate with jihadist groups.

Resources/capabilities
Small arms and light weapons from the Libyan military arsenal as Tuareg fighters came back to Mali after the fall of former Libyan leader Muammar Gadhafi, but also rockets and rockets launchers.

The Plateforme

Strength
Not known.

Areas of operation
Northern Mali, including Ménaka, Gao, Timbuktu, Bourem, the Gourma, Gossi and Tilemsi.

Leadership
The Plateforme is a loose collection of autonomous armed movements.

Structure
The Plateforme is an umbrella group which includes the Imghad Tuareg Self-Defence Group and Allies (GATIA), the Arab Movement of Azawad–Plateforme (MAA–PF) and the Coordination for Movements and Fronts of Patriotic Resistance (CMFPR-1).

The Plateforme

History
The Plateforme coalition was created in June 2014 during the peace negotiations to represent the views of groups which claimed loyalty to the Malian state after the 2012 rebellion.

Objectives
These groups formed to support Mali's territorial integrity. The armed groups have different local agendas – some are engaging in local disputes while others are supplementing the depleted army.

Opponents
Before the 2015 peace agreement, the Plateforme opposed the CMA and jihadist groups. Fighting still occurs with the CMA and with jihadist groups.

Affiliates/allies
Government and foreign forces (France) until 2015 peace agreement. The MAA–PF has been accused of having close ties with the jihadist groups.

Resources/capabilities
Small arms and light weapons, as well as heavy machine guns and rocket launchers.

Drivers

A constellation of violent actors

The presence and strength of many jihadist and self-defence groups is the most immediate driver of violence and insecurity in Mali. After being defeated by French forces in 2013, militant groups reorganised successfully, formed a coalition (JNIM) and expanded their territorial reach by exploiting local grievances and widespread mistrust of the central authorities.

As jihadists spread to central Mali in 2015, Bambara and Dogon ethnic groups organised self-defence militias. However, attempting to defend communities quickly turned into launching pre-emptive attacks against neighbouring communities – especially the Fulani – to neutralise the perceived jihadist threat. Instead of taking responsibility and addressing communal tensions, Malian, Nigerien and Burkinabe authorities delegated security responsibilities to these communal militias. At the Mali/Niger border, France and Niger worked with groups such as GATIA and the Movement for the Salvation of Azawad (MSA) – both Tuareg self-defence groups – to fight against ISGS. In Mali, the authorities have relied on communal militias such as Dozo groups – most notably Dan Na Ambassagou – which have become paramilitaries and established bases in full view of the Malian authorities. Similarly, in Burkina Faso, the government has so far failed to seriously condemn the vigilante justice conducted by the Koglweogo, self-defence groups similar to Dozo hunters in central Mali. Cooperating with – or sometimes completely relying on – the militias for counter-terrorism operations fuelled communal violence and undermined state legitimacy.

While tensions between ethnic groups existed for decades, and skirmishes occurred regularly, this dynamic has deteriorated in recent years. In 2019, intercommunal violence reached unprecedented levels in both Mali and Burkina Faso, with dozens of retaliatory attacks erasing villages and killing hundreds, and the militias being responsible for more violence and casualties than jihadist groups.

Failed institutions

Extremism has flourished in part because the state is absent in northern and central Mali. Military presence is concentrated in major cities, leaving isolated villages vulnerable to jihadist attacks or influence. The borders of Mali, especially in the north and east, are notoriously porous and allow for many illicit trade routes that provide both funding and fighters from regions around West and North Africa.

Even when it is present, the state is unable to provide the needed public services. The stabilisation and restoration of state authority in northern and central Mali, a key aspect of the 2015 Algiers Agreement, remains limited as the precondition – namely the reduction of violence and communal tensions – has not been met yet. As of December 2019, only 23% of civil administrators were in their posts in northern Mali mainly due to insecurity.[2]

Additionally, rather than strengthening state capacity, foreign interventions reinforced these perceptions and their own legitimacy at the expense of the local authorities. When *Operation Barkhane* engages in the development side of its operation to address the root causes of conflict – for example, building wells in Gao – or when MINUSMA increases its patrols in rural areas and engages with local communities, the population perceives the central state as inactive and unresponsive. Such distrust and discontent provide fertile ground for the spread of jihadist groups.

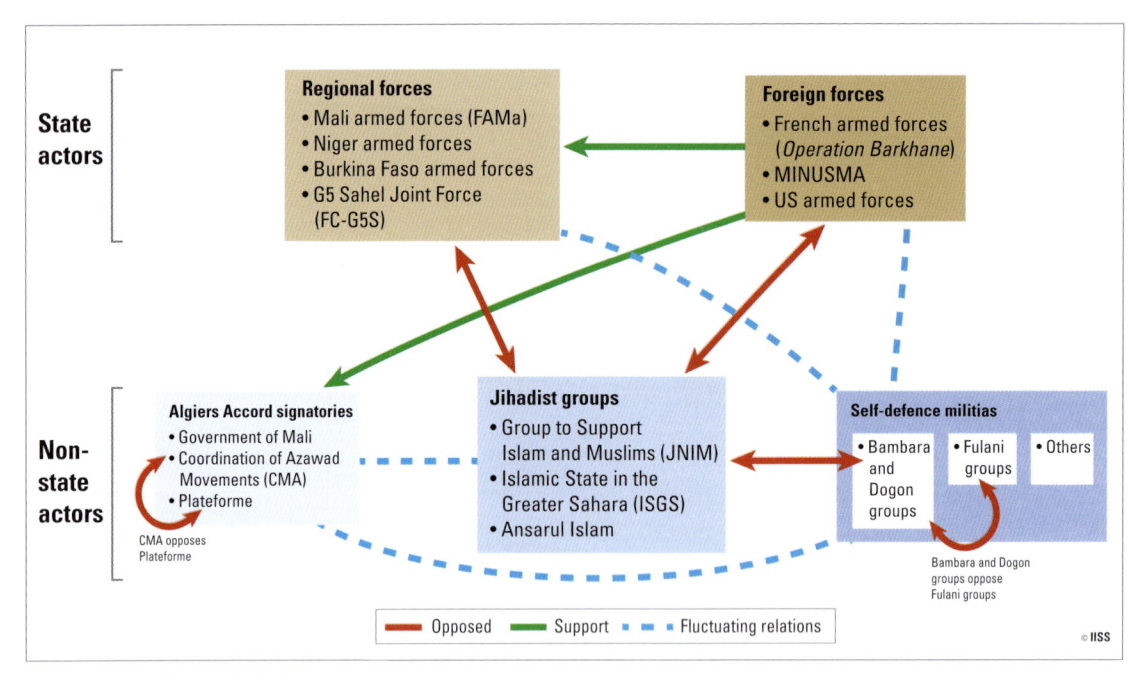

Figure 1: Armed actors' relations

State actors
- Regional forces
  - Mali armed forces (FAMa)
  - Niger armed forces
  - Burkina Faso armed forces
  - G5 Sahel Joint Force (FC-G5S)
- Foreign forces
  - French armed forces (*Operation Barkhane*)
  - MINUSMA
  - US armed forces

Non-state actors
- Algiers Accord signatories
  - Government of Mali
  - Coordination of Azawad Movements (CMA)
  - Plateforme
  - *CMA opposes Plateforme*
- Jihadist groups
  - Group to Support Islam and Muslims (JNIM)
  - Islamic State in the Greater Sahara (ISGS)
  - Ansarul Islam
- Self-defence militias
  - Bambara and Dogon groups
  - Fulani groups
  - Others
  - *Bambara and Dogon groups oppose Fulani groups*

Legend: Opposed — Support — Fluctuating relations

© IISS

Lack of structural reform

The conflict in the Sahel is a multifaceted one, driven by climate change, a growing population, competition over land, arms proliferation, unemployment, marginalisation, corruption and failed institutions. Only a coordinated and comprehensive strategy addressing these multiple drivers can contain the violence and eventually stabilise the region. The national and international responses to the crisis, however, have so far focused on its security dimension, including anti-radicalisation measures and counter-terrorism operations, thus diverting attention and funds from the underlying causes of the conflict.

Since the 1990s and the transition to democracy, Malian history has been one of failed promises. Notably, greater autonomy for northern Mali and decentralisation for the rest of the country were promised by then-president Alpha Oumar Konaré in 1992 but never fully implemented. In 2012, the Malian government announced a comprehensive decentralisation plan. This plan is part of the implementation stage of the peace agreement, but so far the politico-institutional reform has only resulted in the launch of the inclusive national dialogue and talks around the constitutional reform. In addition, the level of funds transferred to local authorities remains a major concern (only 21% of the state budget allocated in June 2019 instead of the 30% goal for December 2018 as mandated by the peace agreement) and the establishment of the northern economic-development zone still remains incomplete, despite a step forward in July when President Ibrahim Boubacar Keïta signed decrees establishing the legislation for its creation. The resumption of the constitutional review and the future establishment of the northern economic-development zones provide an opportunity to address the root causes of the conflict, but could also lead to further frustration and violence if not fully implemented.

Political Developments

Malian government resigns

In April 2019, prime minister Soumeylou Boubèye Maïga's government came under increasing pressure over its mismanagement of the economic situation and the escalating insecurity in central Mali. On 5 April, 15,000 people rallied in Bamako at the call of religious leaders against the authorities' alleged inaction towards escalating violence. Opposition parties and civil-society organisations representing civil servants and teachers followed, protesting their working conditions. On 19 April, Maïga and his government resigned, hours before the parliament was set to vote on a no-confidence motion filed jointly by the ruling coalition and opposition parties.

Three days later, President Keïta appointed former minister of economy and finance Boubou Cissé as the new prime minister and tasked him with forming a politically inclusive government. Cissé accordingly signed a 'historic' political agreement with several opposition parties to agree on the conditions for the new government. On 5 May, the new government was announced, composed of 37 ministers under the prime minister (including nine women): 18 from the ruling coalition, three from the opposition, seven from the civil society and ten technocrats. Out of the three opposition members, Tiébilé Dramé – campaign director of opponent Soumaïla Cissé during the 2018 presidential election – was appointed foreign minister.

The legislative elections, originally scheduled for November 2018, were postponed to April and then June 2019, but the National Assembly further extended its mandate to May 2020, until 'optimal conditions' existed to conduct elections.

Faltering peace process

Some progress on the implementation of the 2015 Algiers Agreement was made in 2019, particularly with the resumption of the constitutional review process (suspended since August 2017) and the launch of an inclusive national dialogue on the constitution, a dialogue which included discussion of all major reforms provided for in the peace agreement. On 1 April, the expert committee in charge of amending the constitution submitted a draft proposal after conducting extensive consultations. Progress was also made in the accelerated DDR programme, under which 1,000 former combatants (of the 4,000 identified) officially joined the armed forces in September.

Implementation advanced at a slow pace, however, and several stakeholders repeatedly expressed impatience and frustration over the year. At a briefing at the UN Security Council in October 2019, the United States declared that 'it cannot continue to support a peacekeeping mission where the signatory parties enjoy security provided by international forces while refusing to fully implement their own agreement'.[3] Other Security Council members, including France, urged the Malian authorities and the signatory parties to update their road map and warned that failure to implement the agreement could lead to sanctions. In July 2019, following France's recommendation, the UN Security Council added five people to the sanctions list – all important members of armed groups operating in northern Mali – accusing them of hampering the peace process, drugs and arms trafficking, supporting terrorist groups and diverting humanitarian aid.[4] A month later, the UN Security Council extended the sanctions regime for Mali until August 2020, reaffirming its frustration with delays and the lack of sufficient progress in the implementation.[5]

Status of Kidal fuels tensions

Tensions surrounding Kidal, the northeastern regional capital, re-emerged in the second half of the year. Despite the presence of French and UN bases, the Malian state has never been able to establish a presence in the town after it was seized by Tuareg rebels in 2012. As one of the key aspects of the peace agreement is the restoration of the state's presence in northern Mali, Kidal's status – as a town still controlled by the CMA – has been a contentious issue ever since the agreement was signed.

On 1 July, 18 Nigerien soldiers were killed in an ISGS attack in Inates, western Niger, at the border with Mali – an attack supposedly launched from a CMA base in Mali – reviving the controversy around Kidal's status. In September, Niger's President Mahamadou Issoufou accused the HCUA, a member of the CMA and as such a signatory of the peace agreement, of being directly or indirectly involved in several jihadist attacks in Niger. The G5 Sahel secretary-general, Maman Sidikou, made similar accusations, stating that Kidal was a rear base and a launch pad for multiple terrorist attacks. The tensions surrounding Kidal and the alleged complicity of the CMA with jihadist groups led to the cancellation of a meeting of the Agreement Monitoring Committee (CSA) – scheduled for the first time in Kidal as a sign of progress in the implementation and the restoration of Malian state presence – a decision that led to the CMA suspending its participation in the CSA.

Military Developments

Violence on the rise

Throughout 2019 the security situation remained volatile in northern Mali and deteriorated in central Mali as well as across the border in Burkina Faso and Niger. Communities were trapped between attacks by jihadist groups, self-defence militias and government counter-terrorism operations. According to the UN, more than 4,000 civilians were killed in terrorist attacks in the region in 2019, representing a fivefold increase since 2016; in Burkina Faso, for example, terrorist attacks killed 80 in 2016 and 1,800 in 2019.[6]

Jihadist violence

The jihadists' main target remained Malian, Burkinabe and Nigerien defence and security forces, MINUSMA and international troops. While militant groups – especially JNIM – increasingly targeted civilians in a bid to disrupt communities and fuel local conflict, self-defence groups were responsible for most civilian casualties.

To contain JNIM and ISGS, regional and international security forces partnered up and focused on border areas, in particular the region of Liptako-Gourma. Joint operations were conducted at an unprecedented rate in 2019. Burkina Faso opened up to more cooperation and asked for more support from *Operation Barkhane* in its northern area. French, Malian, Nigerien and Burkinabe troops conducted joint operations, either in bilateral or multilateral coalitions, to maintain pressure on extremist groups, with the objective of detecting and neutralising bases across borders. On 30 March, for example, the Malian and Burkinabe security forces launched the joint cross-border *Operation Kapigdou*.

The second half of the year, however, was particularly deadly for the armed forces, with both JNIM and ISGS stepping up attacks in the Liptako-Gourma, the tri-border area between Mali, Burkina Faso and Niger. In the last three months of the year, more than 200 soldiers were killed in large-scale attacks against military positions. The ISGS's December attack on Inates, western Niger, killed 71 soldiers – the deadliest attack on Niger's armed forces since the conflict began. This series of attacks resulted in the retreat of the Malian military from two strategic frontier posts (Labbezanga and Anderamboukane), leaving this area at the border with Niger open to infiltration by jihadist groups.

In March 2019, ISIS merged ISGS with Islamic State in West Africa Province (ISWAP) – an ISIS branch active in the Lake Chad Basin – from a propaganda perspective (ISWAP claiming ISGS attacks). Since then, ISGS has received more attention from ISIS central – it was until then a branch that rarely featured in ISIS channels and newspapers – and it became one of the most active and deadly ISIS offshoots as of December 2019.

Communal violence

In the first half of the year, communal violence escalated in central Mali, particularly in Bankass, Bandiagara and Koro districts between Dogon and Fulani communities. The highest number of attacks against civilians were recorded in these areas, mainly due to intercommunal clashes and activities

Key Events in 2019

Political events

1 January	24 March	5 April	19 April	22 April
A six-month state of emergency enters into force in 14 provinces.	Following the Ogossagou attack, Keïta sacks three chiefs of the armed forces.	15,000 people demonstrate in Bamako against the mismanagement of the escalating violence in central Mali.	Prime minister Maïga and his government resign.	Keïta appoints Boubou Cissé as new prime minister.

Military/Violent events

20 January	17 March	23 March	31 March–2 April	14 May
AQIM claims an attack on a MINUSMA camp in Aguelhok, Kidal Region, killing ten Chadian peacekeepers.	A Dioura jihadist attack kills 23 Malian soldiers.	Dan Na Ambassagou kills 157 Fulani in Ogossagou, Mopti Region in retaliation for 17 March attack.	62 civilians are killed in tit-for-tat attacks between communities in Arbinda, northern Burkina Faso.	ISGS militants ambush and kill 28 Nigerien soldiers in Tongo-Tongo, Tillabéri Region, western Niger.

of self-defence militias, exacerbated by the presence and violence of jihadist groups. On 23 March, Dan Na Ambassagou waged the deadliest attack against civilians since the conflict began, killing at least 157 Fulani, including 46 children, and burning down the village of Ogossagou in the Mopti Region. In response to the surge of communal violence in Mopti, on 30 March MINUSMA launched *Operation Oryx* and created a new 'Sector Central' command post in Mopti to be closer to the epicentre of communal violence and provide a deterrent presence, allowing FAMa to focus on border areas.

The level of communal violence decreased in the second part of 2019, thanks to joint patrols of *Operation Oryx* I in Bandiagara and Bankass districts and *Operation Oryx* II in Koro district. Local and international mediation efforts were also productive, resulting in the signing of various ceasefires between Dogon and Fulani militias in Mopti and Ségou regions in July and August. However, while large-scale attacks decreased, small-scale retaliatory attacks continued throughout the year and in November a series of attacks against Fulani villages killed almost 40 civilians.

Impact

Human rights

Human-rights violations occurred through the year, particularly in central Mali and in the border areas with Burkina Faso and Niger. Self-defence ethnic and communal militias were responsible for most abuses, followed by jihadist groups and armed forces during counter-terrorism operations. Both Dogon and Fulani militias increased their participation in retaliatory attacks after the attack on the Fulani village of Ogossagou in March 2019, with the two most significant occurring in June 2019, when members of the Fulani community attacked Sobane Da (killing 35 civilians), and then Yoro and Gangafani villages (killing 32 civilians).

In an incident in February, the Burkinabe Movement for Human and Peoples' Rights (MBDHP) accused security forces of killing 60 civilians in Kain town, mostly Fulani, while the armed forces declared that they killed 146 militants. Allegations of indiscriminately targeting Fulani communities were also made against Malian troops and Dozo militias in Mopti Region.

Humanitarian

The humanitarian situation deteriorated throughout 2019. Communal violence displaced unprecedented numbers of people in all countries in central Sahel, while no state had adequate infrastructure or resources to address the sudden rise in IDPs. Access to food and basic services has become increasingly difficult. In Burkina Faso, more than a million people have no or almost no access to healthcare after 95 facilities closed over the past two years.[7]

Burkina Faso saw more than a tenfold increase in IDPs, from 47,000 to 560,000, 88% of whom are in Sahel and Centre-Nord regions in local communities. In Mali, the number of IDPs increased from 120,000 to more than 200,000, mostly in Mopti and

---

28 June MINUSMA's mandate is renewed, with the security situation in central Mali as new strategic priority.

9 July UNSC sanctions five members of Malian armed groups for hampering the peace process.

14 September ECOWAS members pledge US$1bn to eradicate terrorism in the region.

16 September Cissé officially launches the inclusive national dialogue.

20 May–3 June First joint Burkinabe–French operation launched; 450 Barkhane soldiers deployed and dozens of militants killed.

19 August Unidentified militants attack a military detachment in Koutougou, Sahel Region, northern Burkina Faso, killing 24 soldiers.

18 October Mali's ministerial council approves a year-long extension of nationwide state of emergency, starting 31 October 2019.

1 November ISGS fighters kill 53 Malian soldiers in Indelimane, Liptako Region, Mali.

10 December Militants attack a military camp in Inates, western Niger, killing 71 soldiers. ISWAP claims the attack.

Ségou regions, central Mali. In Tillabéri and Tahoua regions in western Niger, violence raised the number of IDPs from 53,000 to 80,000.

The total funding requirement for the UN Office for Coordination of Humanitarian Affairs (OCHA) Humanitarian Response Plan (HRP) for Mali in 2019 was increased to US$324m in July, aimed at reaching 3m people, but only 51% had been received as of December 2019.[8] The HRP requirement for Burkina Faso is US$187m (48% funded), while the HRP requirement for Niger is US$383m (59% funded).

Socio-economic
Insecurity in the Sahel has severely restricted access to education. Militant groups directly attacked, burned or occupied schools and targeted teachers and pupils. As of December 2019, more than 900 schools were closed in Mali (compared to 700 in December 2018) and more than 2,000 in Burkina Faso (compared to 400 in December 2018).[9]

Strikes have been common in Mali since the 2015 peace agreement. Hospital workers, teachers, bankers and police continued to join mass strikes in 2019 to protest widespread insecurity and the scant progress made on social and economic issues. One of the most noteworthy events was the 72-hour strike initiated by the National Union of Workers of Mali (UTM) on 9 January to demand better working conditions and salary rises.

Relations with neighbouring and international partners
Worsening security and the potential spread of jihadist groups to coastal West Africa has fostered cooperation between leaders in the region and their international partners and led to more information sharing. At the ECOWAS Summit on Terrorism in September, regional leaders pledged US$1bn to tackle terrorism and planned to send ECOWAS troops to Mali, Niger and Burkina Faso in 2020. France advocated for increased support from European countries to the G5 Sahel and MINUSMA as well as bringing together contingents of European special forces for a Combined Joint Special Operations Task Force (called *Operation Takuba*) by mid-2020.

Meanwhile, the US announced that it was creating a special envoy for the Sahel and an inter-agency task force, coordinating efforts from the State Department, the Defense Department and the intelligence agencies. However, the Trump administration was also reportedly evaluating plans for a major reduction, or even withdrawal, of its 7,000 troops in West Africa. At a time of more comprehensive and concerted effort between all stakeholders, the United States' decision to remain involved will be crucial for international engagement in the Sahel.

Trends

Political trajectories
The creation of a broad-based government and the launch of a national dialogue are important steps towards stability in Mali. Stakeholders from across the political spectrum have the opportunity to agree on future reforms, concrete measures for the constitutional review, and the process towards legislative elections in May 2020. These, however, are just the first steps and significant hurdles lie ahead. Some parties are already withdrawing from the national dialogue and some opposition figures are leaving the ruling coalition over disagreements on its inclusivity.

Conflict-related risks
The security situation in the Sahel will remain volatile in 2020. Communal violence decreased in the second part of 2019 and ethnic militias agreed on a ceasefire, but the root causes of the violence have not been addressed. Jihadist groups have gained momentum in the past two years, and are likely to continue to flourish. They have proven to be resilient and capable of conducting large-scale, sophisticated attacks, despite increased pressure from regional and international forces. In 2020, several West African countries will hold contentious elections in 2020 (presidential elections in Côte d'Ivoire, Guinea and Togo; parliamentary elections in Burkina Faso and Mali) which might potentially create further destabilisation and violence, and distract leaders from the jihadist threat.

Prospects for peace
The security challenges in northern Mali are different from those in central Mali. A crucial factor driving

violence in both regions, however, is limited state authority. In 2019, the government deployed interim administrations to the north, but restoring state presence remains a challenge, though a necessary condition for regaining the trust of local communities and stopping the spread of militant groups. The Mali government has also not devised a clear plan to implement key provisions of the 2015 Algiers Agreement concerning decentralisation, economic development, justice and security-sector reform. If progress is not forthcoming, frustration will likely grow among signatory parties and international partners, but most importantly in the communities bearing the brunt of the violence in both northern and central Mali.

Strategic implications and global influences

The strengthening and spreading of jihadist groups, especially JNIM and ISGS, now threatens coastal West African countries as the groups move southwards from Mali and Burkina Faso into Benin, Togo, Ghana and Côte d'Ivoire. They may soon be able to establish cells and bases in these countries and gain access to the Gulf of Guinea, providing a rear base to rest and a launch pad to attack major coastal cities, while also obliging regional and international forces to disperse their efforts. The Burkina Faso intelligence service stated in April 2019 that members of jihadist groups operating in eastern Burkina Faso had moved to Benin, Togo and Ghana after the launch of *Operation Otapuanu* ('Rain of fire' in Gulmacema), designed to contain militant groups from spreading to the Eastern and Centre-Eastern regions. Regional leaders are well aware of the potential spillovers, but despite public declarations to pursue further regional security coordination, their security apparatuses at present lack the capacity to contain the cross-border expansion of extremist violence.

Notes

[1] UN High Commissioner for Refugees (UNHCR), 'Operational Portal: Refugee Situations: Refugees in Burkina Faso'.

[2] UN Security Council, 'Report of the Secretary-General on the Situation in Mali', S/2019/983, 30 December 2019.

[3] United States Mission to the UN, 'Remarks at a UN Security Council Briefing on the Situation in Mali and the MINUSMA', 8 October 2019.

[4] UN Security Council, 'Security Council 2374 Committee Adds Five Entries to Its Sanctions List', SC/13878, 10 July 2019.

[5] UN Security Council, 'Security Council Renews Mali Sanctions, Panel Monitoring Implementation, Unanimously Adopting Resolution 2484 (2019)', CS/13933, 29 August 2019.

[6] Briefing of Mohamed Ibn Chambas, UN Special Representative and Head of UNOWAS to the Security Council, January 2020.

[7] OCHA, Burkina Faso, 'Aperçu de la situation humanitaire au 9 Décembre 2019'.

[8] OCHA, 'Financial Tracking Service', December 2019 (fts.unocha.org).

[9] UNICEF, 'L'éducation en péril en Afrique de l'Ouest et centrale', August 2019.

SOMALIA

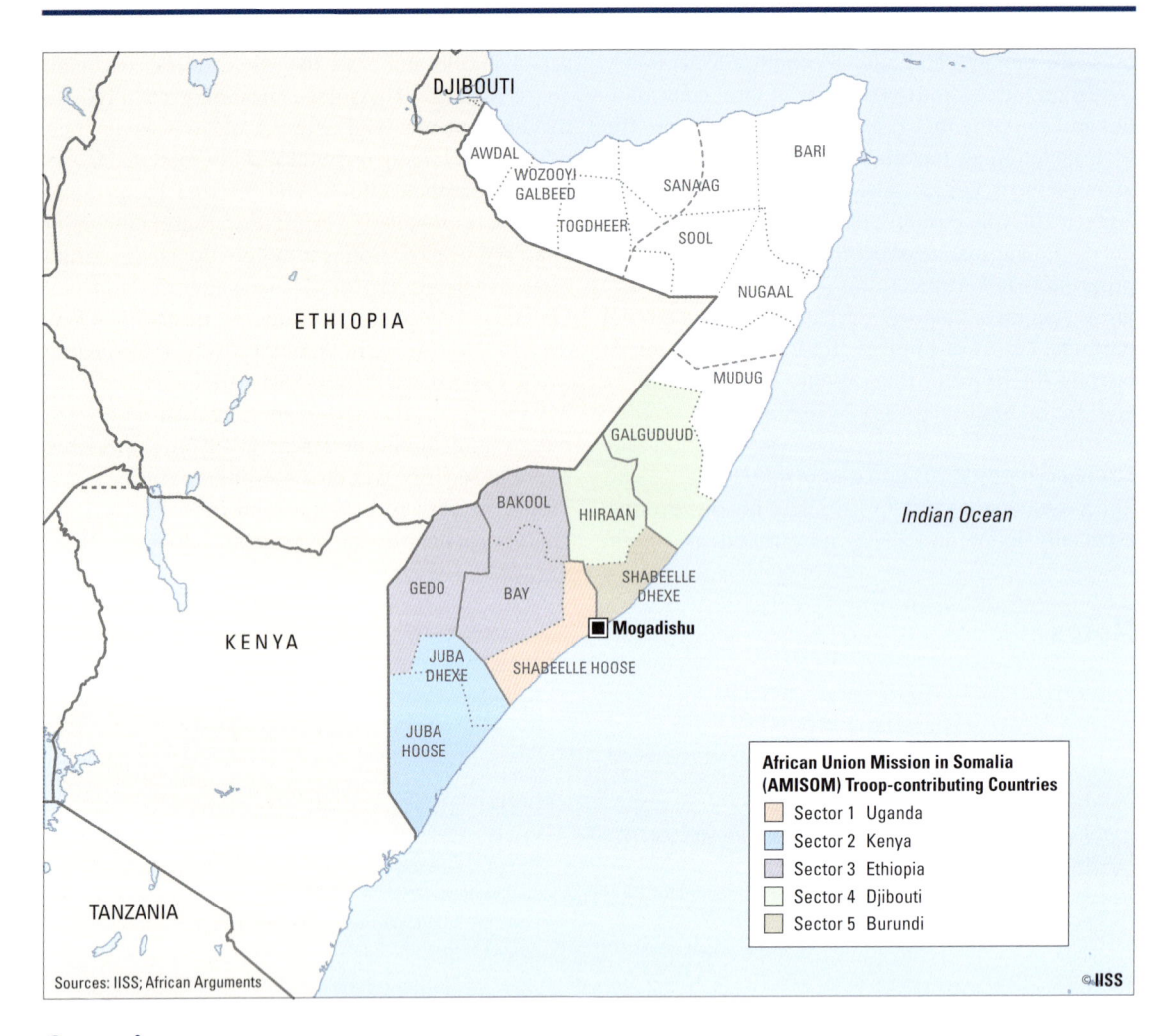

Overview

The conflict in 2019
In 2019 the Somali conflict saw the continuation of the stalemate between al-Shabaab and the Somali federal government, both of whom are fighting for control of the country. While Mogadishu remained in government hands in 2019, al-Shabaab perpetrated several large-scale attacks on the capital, including a bombing on 28 December that killed over 80 people. Al-Shabaab also remained active across borders, particularly in Kenya, where it conducted several attacks, including against the DusitD2 hotel complex in Nairobi.

The persistent challenge facing both the Somali National Army (SNA) and the African Union Mission in Somalia (AMISOM) is not retaking Somali territory from al-Shabaab, but rather maintaining control over it. AMISOM and SNA troops are thinly stretched over southern Somalia, so once

Key statistics

Type	Internationalised
Start date	January 1991
IDPs total (31 December 2019)	2,600,000
Refugees total (31 December 2019)	752,038
People in need (31 December 2019)	5,200,000

they withdraw from retaken areas to their forward operating bases, al-Shabaab rapidly re-enters the territory and re-establishes its control. The group provides a degree of governance and security for the population that the federal government cannot.

Efforts to increase the responsibilities of the troubled SNA and decrease its reliance on AMISOM stalled. This situation leaves the planned transition of security responsibility from AMISOM to the SNA in 2020, and the intended AMISOM withdrawal in 2021, in doubt. Over the year the few occasions in which AMISOM forces withdrew showed that al-Shabaab was ready to retake the territory it abandoned. Troop-contributing countries' (TCCs) opposition has so far stalled the planned drawdown of 1,000 AMISOM troops that was intended for 2019. Though AMISOM's mandate explicitly states that its deployment must be reduced by 1,000 troops by May 2020, the United Nations Security Council emphasised that withdrawal must be subject to conditions on the ground. Mostly likely, AMISOM's present plans will change.

The conflict to 2019
At its core, the Somali conflict is a contestation for governance between the al-Shabaab insurgency and the federal government. The ultimate solution to this conflict will be political rather than military, implemented through the provision of much-needed services to the Somali population. However, the federal government remains in an extremely weak position to do this.

When the authoritarian regime of Siad Barre collapsed in 1991, a devastating civil war ensued that lasted over a decade. In the mid-2000s, a combination of Islamist militias and grassroots authorities formed the Union of Islamic Courts (UIC), a system of Islamist rule that restored order in Mogadishu. International suspicion that the UIC was in the grip of al-Qaeda led to an invasion by neighbouring Ethiopia in 2006, supported by the United States. The UIC was shattered, but its enforcement wing regrouped and joined other militia fragments to form the insurgency presently known as al-Shabaab.

The Transitional Federal Government (TFG) established in 2007 lacked legitimacy from the start given its reliance on Ethiopia, a nation with which Somalia has a troubled history. The Ethiopian connection also proved critical to al-Shabaab's early recruitment efforts, which played on nationalist sentiment. As the TFG took its seat in Mogadishu and became the federal government of Somalia, it also relied on the AMISOM mission, which was created in 2007 but continued to expand.

The federal government is not only unable to rule Somalia because of al-Shabaab. It has a persistent constitutional struggle for authority over the five federal member states of Somalia (Galmudug, Hirshabelle, Jubaland, Puntland and South West State; the state of Somaliland declared itself an independent nation, although Mogadishu does not recognise it). Since each federal state has its own president, administration and territorial ambitions, reaching a comprehensive security agreement for the whole nation has proven extremely difficult, and so far impossible.

Key Conflict Parties

Somali National Army (SNA)

Strength
Officially listed at 22,000 but official records are known to be inflated by 'ghost soldiers',[1] veterans and the registering of soldiers' dependents. The number of able troops is unclear but an Operational Readiness Assessment in 2017 established that battalions had, on average, 63% of their authorised strength.

Areas of operation
All five federal states of Somalia (excluding self-declared independent Somaliland, which the government still sees as a federal state).

Leadership
General Odawaa Yusuf Rageh is Army Chief of Staff, having been appointed in August.

Structure
The SNA is divided into four command divisions and spread across Somalia's operational sectors. It has associated special-forces units such as the US-trained Danaab.

Somali National Army (SNA)

History
Attempts to reconstruct the SNA began in 2008. Given the lack of existing national forces it had to be built through both new recruitment and the incorporation of existing armed actors such as clan militias. The lack of a national-security framework agreed on between the government and member states led to highly fragmented international efforts, and soldiers are trained in different fashions by different countries. As a result, the present SNA has severe internal cleavages and problems of cohesion.

Objectives
Securing the territorial authority of the federal government of Somalia, primarily through the defeat of al-Shabaab.

Opponents
Al-Shabaab, the Islamic State (also known as ISIS or ISIL) in Somalia, militias and criminal actors.

Affiliates/allies
AMISOM; international trainers including Turkey, the United Kingdom, the US and the European Union.

Resources/capabilities
The SNA suffers from severe shortages of resources, particularly small arms. This challenge is in significant part due to internal corruption, with soldiers selling their arms (including to al-Shabaab), which in turn is due to irregular and low salaries.

Harakat al-Shabaab al-Mujahideen (al-Shabaab)

Strength
Believed to have an active fighting force of at least 5,000 men in Somalia, not including fighters' families, networks and those living in their controlled areas.

Areas of operation
Strongest in southern Somalia (Jubaland, South West and Hirshabelle states). Presence is more limited in Galmudug and Puntland. No full control over any areas of Mogadishu, but the city's northern peripheries and economic hotspots (e.g. Bakara Market) are subject to al-Shabaab authority for much of the time, particularly at night.

Leadership
Ahmad Umar Diriye, better known as Abu Ubaidah, is the current leader, or emir.

Structure
The conventional military wing (*Jahabaat*) is divided into six regional fighting units (*jaysh*, pl. *juyush*) and two special units. A large intelligence wing (*Amniyat*) has a transnational reach.

History
The group was formed in response to the Ethiopian invasion of Somalia in 2006, through the fusion of the al-Itihaad al-Islamiya group with al-Qaeda elements. Subsequent recruitment was heavily dependent on Somali nationalist sympathies, thanks to which al-Shabaab grew into a major challenger to the TFG. Although its military fortunes have declined since 2011, al-Shabaab remains a highly effective insurgency.

Objectives
Defeat the Federal government and establish Islamist rule in Somalia.

Opponents
Federal government, Somali National Army, ISIS Somalia.

Affiliates/allies
Periodic alliances of convenience with militias and organised-crime syndicates.

Resources/capabilities
Al-Shabaab has considerable resources thanks to its diverse funding strategy, which includes taxation of the population and illicit trade.

African Union Mission in Somalia (AMISOM)

Strength
19,625 troops.

Areas of operation
The five TCCs' (Burundi, Djibouti, Ethiopia, Kenya and Uganda) forces are each responsible for a sector of central and southern Somalia, including Jubaland, South West and Hirshabelle states, and the Galguduud region of Galmudug State.

Leadership
There is no centralised command-and-control structure, which makes coordinating operations difficult. Each sector's forces operate under their own command and are ultimately responsible to their own governments.

Structure
AMISOM contingents function as conventional militaries.

History
The UN authorised the African Union's peacekeeping deployment in February 2007 with a six-month mandate. The force was composed of Ugandan troops. As the situation failed to stabilise AMISOM expanded.

Objectives
Defeat al-Shabaab, retake its territory and protect the federal government of Somalia.

Opponents
Al-Shabaab.

Affiliates/allies
AMISOM is supported by numerous international governments and periodically by military contingents from allied countries, who deliver training.

Resources/capabilities
AMISOM lacks critical resources such as air assets, but its key challenge is the unpredictability of donor funding, which makes strategic planning difficult.

ISIS Somalia

Strength
Between 250 and 300 fighters.

Areas of operation
Based in the Galgala mountain region of Puntland, but periodically conducts assassinations in Bosaso and Mogadishu.

Leadership
Believed to be led by elderly Abd al-Qadir Mumin, who was reported killed in an airstrike in March 2019. Later video footage, however, suggests he is still alive and remains leader.[2]

Structure
Little is known about its internal structure but, given the group's small size and the regular targeting of senior figures by both Somali and US forces, it is likely relatively decentralised.

History
Mumin broke away from al-Shabaab with a small group of fighters in October 2015 and pledged allegiance to ISIS. Al-Shabaab has repeatedly vowed to eliminate the rival group.

Objectives
In the near term, to spread ISIS's ideology within Somalia and neighbouring countries, such as Ethiopia, and to attract broader support.

Opponents
Al-Shabaab, Somali and Puntland security forces.

Affiliates/allies
Believed to have limited support networks in Yemen, but details are unknown.

Resources/capabilities
Small arms.

Drivers

Limited governance

The federal government suffers from a severe lack of national legitimacy due to numerous factors, including its historical relation with Ethiopia, its domination by Somalis from the diaspora and widespread corruption, but above all its inability to provide public services and to exercise its authority outside Mogadishu.

Rural Somalis rarely interact with representatives of the state other than the SNA, which has a poor reputation among many civilians. Meanwhile, al-Shabaab's hold over rural southern Somalia, although not constant, is more consistent than that of the government and gives them the chance to provide services. Although rudimentary and largely limited to justice mechanisms and Koranic education, al-Shabaab service provision and the less-frequent violent contestations lead the areas under its control to be perceived as more stable than those under government control.

Clan divisions

Somali clans challenge all political structures aimed to transcend their authority. There are four major clans in Somalia – Darod, Dir, Hawiye and Rahanweyn – which framed the '4.5' power-sharing system used in the 2017 election. 'Major clans' are better comprehended as clan families, stemming from a common patrilineal ancestor, each with myriad sub-clans. At a local level, the most significant clan unit is the Diya group, whose members share a common customary-law system (*xheer*) and are socially contracted to pay *mag* (compensation) in the event of crimes against each other.

At the macro level, clan loyalties can fracture political arrangements or beget unstable, exclusionary arrangements, while clan competition inhibits the development of a functioning political system. To understand the enduring importance of clans, however, it is crucial to recognise the benefits that clans offer on an everyday basis. Mutual assistance between members of a Diya group is socially mandated: if a member of a Diya is killed, their fellow members are obliged to seek revenge or compensation for their death. Likewise, when seeking protection or favours from someone more powerful, a shared clan identity invokes mutual responsibility. Clan leaders also tend to be the most effective dispute mediators at a local level. Members of minority clans (those who do not trace their ancestry to a major clan family) suffer from frequent discrimination, and often become targets for militant recruitment since they have fewer support networks.

Climate change

Somalia is uniquely vulnerable to the effects of climate change, with its surface temperature predicted to warm between 3.2 and 4.3 degrees Celsius by 2100.[3] The climate varies between semi-arid and desert, leaving the population highly dependent on the two rainy seasons each year – the Gu', from April to June, and the Deyr, from October to December.

The rains are becoming increasingly unpredictable, however. 2019 was the second year in a row where the Gu' failed. The Deyr, by contrast, was exceptionally heavy and led to catastrophic flooding. The increasingly unpredictable conditions put communities at risk, as 70% of the Somali population depends on agriculture for its livelihood.

The changing climate is also presenting much broader national-security threats.[4] Communal conflicts over resources such as water and fertile land are increasingly common, particularly between farmers and herders. This competition exacerbates inter-clan violence. For instance, 30 people were killed in Burdere, Middle Shabelle in March in clan clashes over grazing land.[5] Likewise, the high rates of displacement, caused by agriculture becoming impossible in certain areas, have led to significant rural-to-urban migration and worsened the humanitarian and security situations in cities like Mogadishu and Baidoa. Displaced people are vulnerable to lack of food, water and sanitation, but also to recruitment by al-Shabaab.

Political Developments

Tense relations between the federal government and the federal states

Relations between the federal government and the federal member states have long been complicated, but in September 2018, the states officially severed relations with Mogadishu. This move ended the so-called security pact – a plan for a national-security architecture meant to guide cooperation between the government and the member states. Since then, cooperation has been ad hoc and no official reconciliation has followed.

One of the biggest obstacles to Somalia's political reconciliation is a lack of constitutional clarity over the relative power of the federal government vis-à-vis the member states, each of which has its own administration and president. In 2019, the troubled relationship was put under further strain during member-state elections. National elections are planned for 2020, with many believing these will not be the universal vote that the international community had hoped for, but rather another selection of a president by lawmakers. If this is the case, then the composition of the state governments – which will have a hand in arranging lawmakers' votes – could well affect the choice of national president. The incumbent Somali President Mohamed Abdullahi Mohamed, popularly known as 'Farmaajo', is widely suspected of trying to rig the member-state elections so as to produce favourable regional governments and obtain a second term.

Galmudug elections

Tensions mired the Galmudug state election throughout 2019, to the point that the Electoral Commission failed to select the new administration within the year. Galmudug President Ahmed Duale Gelle (known as 'Xaaf') suspended cooperation with Somali President Farmaajo in July over a disagreement about when the election should take place. Xaaf argued he still had two years to serve,

Key Events in 2019

Political events

Military/Violent events

15 January
21 people are killed in an al-Shabaab attack on the DusitD2 hotel complex in Nairobi, Kenya.

12 July
26 people are killed in an al-Shabaab attack on the Asasey Hotel in Kismayo.

as he only assumed responsibility from the previous president in 2017. He eventually agreed to hold elections in 2019, but the influence of Ahlu Sunna wal Jamaa (ASWJ), a Sunni-Sufi militant group and political party whose fighters are technically part of Galmudug's security forces, complicated the matter. ASWJ made a deal in July with Galmudug and the federal government and obtained 35 seats out of 89 in the regional administration. However, Mogadishu later indicated it would retract the deal and create a different electoral board, prompting a tense stand-off in Dhusamareb between ASWJ and SNA troops.

A new agreement struck in September helped ease the situation, and in December the federal government confirmed that the election would happen on 25 December. However, the election was delayed again after ASWJ boycotted it over disagreement on the candidate qualifications. It is unclear when the election will take place, but angering ASWJ – a powerful force in Galmudug – will further strain relations between the state government and the federal government.

Jubaland elections

Another tense state election, and one significantly influenced by regional concerns, was that of Jubaland in August. The incumbent, Ahmed Madobe, was re-elected president, but the federal government refused to recognise the result. Kenya considers Madobe a reliable ally who helps maintain a security buffer along the border. Ethiopia, ever mindful of secessionist sympathies in its ethnic-Somali Ogaden region, views a strong Somali federal government as key to its own security, and is therefore suspicious of Madobe's protectiveness over his autonomy, as well as of his Ogadeni heritage.

At the end of the year, Mogadishu appeared to have accepted the need to deal with Madobe's new term. Yet Madobe may face internal resistance within the state. Jubaland's regional governors refused to accept his order for their dismissal in December, saying that they were loyal to the federal government. These fragmentations of authority are unlikely to cease in 2020 without a constitutional reform that clarifies the relative authority of political powers throughout Somalia.

Military Developments

Al-Shabaab proved its significant transnational reach again on 15 January when it attacked the DusitD2 Hotel inside the 14 Riverside Drive complex in Nairobi. A suicide bomber and five gunmen entered the building and killed 21 people. The attack was far from the most deadly committed by al-Shabaab on Kenyan soil, but it was striking in the fact that all the attackers were Kenyans of non-Somali heritage. While previously young Kenyan-Somalis had been the key targets of al-Shabaab recruitment, the DusitD2 attack forced Kenyan authorities to confront the fact that citizens from all over the country were vulnerable to extremism. Some of the Dusit attackers had been involved with al-Shabaab since at least 2016, proving that cross-ethnic recruitment in Kenya is a long-running phenomenon.[6]

22 August
Ahmed Madobe is re-elected as South West State president following a disputed voting process.

25 December
The Galmudug election is postponed after ASWJ boycotts the process.

24 July
A suicide bomber kills seven people including Mogadishu Mayor Abdirahman Omar Osman.

22 August
General Odawaa Yusuf Rageh is appointed the new Army Chief of Staff.

30 September
Al-Shabaab attacks a US military base in Baledogle, Lower Shabelle.

28 December
At least 80 people are killed in an al-Shabaab truck bombing in Mogadishu.

Al-Shabaab also pulled off several complex terror attacks in Mogadishu. On 24 July, a female suicide bomber attacked the offices of the mayor of Mogadishu, Abdirahman Omar Osman. The bomber was in fact aiming to kill the new UN envoy to Somalia, James Swan, who had already left at the time of the attack. Six people were killed and the mayor, severely injured, died from his wounds days later. The attack was perpetrated by employees in the mayor's office, demonstrating al-Shabaab's continued ability to access secured buildings through corruption. In July, the group also struck the relatively peaceful port of Kismayo, targeting the Asasey hotel in a complex wave attack involving a suicide bomber and gunmen which killed 26 people.

A further, devastating attack in Mogadishu occurred on 28 December, when at least 80 people were killed when a truck bomb exploded at the Ex-Control Afgoye junction. Remarkably, al-Shabaab apologised for there having been civilian victims in the bombing and said that it had in fact been targeting Turkish and foreign forces. The group is aware that its level of sympathy among Somalis is damaged by large-scale attacks. Indeed, the group did not claim responsibility for the Zoobe Junction bombing in 2017, which killed 587 people.

Nevertheless, the group is unlikely to prevent further civilian casualties as its attacks aim to make government-controlled areas insecure and thus to present al-Shabaab as the only credible security provider.

While urban areas are the more visible target of violence, rural areas continue to be critical to al-Shabaab's power and survival. In rural areas, al-Shabaab perpetrates attacks almost exclusively against military bases, convoys and patrols. Attacks on bases – particularly SNA and AMISOM ones – are not uncommon. The September attack on the American uninhabited aerial vehicle (UAV) base in Baledogle was widely reported, for example.

In rural areas, therefore, the key concern for government and international security forces is not simply to clear al-Shabaab from an area, but rather to retain control of it ('clear and hold'). In October and November, Somali forces engaged in operations to expel al-Shabaab from the lands surrounding Mogadishu and the nearby Afgoye area. The strategy behind the operations was to better safeguard Mogadishu, since it is from outside the city that al-Shabaab plans complex attacks on it. However, such strategies will remain temporary fixes until security forces can also win the sympathies of the local population and control the area permanently.

Impact

Human rights
The ongoing fighting and al-Shabaab's continued bombings and attacks have killed and injured many civilians, exacerbating the country's already dire human-rights situation. Human-rights breaches stem from violence by all conflict parties as well as clan rivalries. In 2019, the US conducted 60 airstrikes against al-Shabaab and ISIS Somalia, more than in any previous year. While the AFRICOM command often denies its attacks leading to civilian casualties, several human-rights groups have claimed the opposite. In April, after pressure from Amnesty International, AFRICOM admitted that one of its 2018 strikes caused two civilian deaths.

Humanitarian
The humanitarian crisis in Somalia remains alarming, with approximately 5.2 million people in need of humanitarian assistance. Ongoing violence in Shabelle Hoose caused the displacement of roughly 60,000 people to nearby cities during the first half of 2019. But climate is driving even more displacement than violence. The unpredictable, short and uneven Gu' rains and the floods caused by the Deyr rains exacerbated the humanitarian situation in 2019. In late October, flooding displaced another 270,000 people, who remain in need of basic services and food supplies. In the first six months of 2019, the Norwegian Refugee Council reported that 100,000 of the 244,000 newly displaced people in Somalia were displaced because of drought.[7]

Social
Years of conflict had devastating effects on Somalia's schooling system, leading to low enrolment, which in 2019 stood at 33% for children aged six to 13, with a strong disparity between urban and rural areas. In Mogadishu and other cities, the enrolment rate is

twice as high as in rural areas or IDP settlements.[8] Men are also more likely to have attended school than women. As a result, more than half of Somali women in rural areas are illiterate. These disparities reflect broader gender and rural–urban inequalities in Somali society.

Economic

The national economy has suffered heavily from years of conflict and roughly 69% of the population lives in poverty.[9] Poverty affects IDPs particularly, who are forced to leave behind their livelihoods and their means of income. While agricultural products account for more than 90% of Somalia's exports, repeated droughts and general instability makes dependence on crops extremely volatile. Despite these challenges, Somalia made incremental progress in stabilising its economy in 2019, with projected GDP growth of circa 3–3.5%. In December, the International Monetary Fund (IMF) approved a plan that would help mobilise funding to relieve some of the country's debt, currently at US$5.3 billion.

Relations with neighbouring and international partners

The conflict continues to pose a threat to Somalia's neighbours, most notably Kenya, where several al-Shabaab attacks took place throughout the year. In January 2019, al-Shabaab attacked the DusitD2 hotel in Nairobi killing 21 people. In December 2019, al-Shabaab attacked Manda Bay airfield on Kenya's coast, which is used by US counter-terrorism forces. Given the threat al-Shabaab poses to its stability, Kenya remains an invested partner in AMISOM despite escalations in the dispute over its maritime border with Somalia. Throughout 2019, rivalries among Gulf countries continued to play out in Somalia. Turkey remains one of Somalia's main partners with regards to humanitarian assistance and security and responded quickly with aid deliveries following the November floods.

Trends

Political trajectories

There is little to suggest that the federal government and member states will establish a productive working relationship in 2020, particularly as President Farmaajo becomes increasingly focused on ensuring his next term. A larger regional dispute with Kenya over its maritime boundary, which is set to be decided in June 2020 by the International Court of Justice (ICJ), will have a significant impact – not just on regional relations, but also on Somalia's domestic politics. The dispute over the contested sea area intensified after the discovery of oil deposits. Somalia took the case to the ICJ in 2014, while Kenya is hoping for an out-of-court settlement. The case has several key implications for Somalia. If the dispute is resolved in its favour and oil exploration begins, there will likely be a series of new disputes with member states, and particularly semi-autonomous Puntland, over how to distribute oil revenues. However, an ICJ ruling can only be enforced by the parties in question. If either Kenya or Somalia chooses to ignore it and tensions rise, this may jeopardise Kenya's contribution to AMISOM, as well as broader security cooperation around the border region. How President Farmaajo handles the dispute with Kenya, as well as the potential management of oil revenues, will have significant implications for his national credibility.

Conflict-related risks

Lack of clarity over the future of the AMISOM mission is the most significant conflict-related risk at present. UN and African Union leaders have remained committed in principle to the 2021 withdrawal deadline, but this posture has put them at odds with the TCCs, and arguably also with the reality on the ground. Given that the TCCs have ultimate authority over their forces in Somalia, they are decisive stakeholders in the process – a point clearly made by Uganda and Burundi in 2019, when they threatened to withdraw all of their troops after AMISOM attempted to withdraw 1,000 Burundian personnel. Brief withdrawals by Kenyan forces in March saw al-Shabaab retake the same territories within hours. The mission also faces considerable fatigue from its donors, as AMISOM sustains government control of major cities but still fails to defeat al-Shabaab. 2020 may force donors to take a more decisive stance – either enhancing AMISOM's capacity to seriously disadvantage al-Shabaab, or to explore alternative options for ending the conflict (or a combination of both). They may also choose to extend AMISOM's mandate with limited structural change, which will make for a continuation of the stalemate.

Prospects for peace

While the international community has so far avoided discussing the prospects for negotiation with al-Shabaab, Somalis are largely cognisant that such a settlement will be inevitable. Indeed, it is widely known in Somalia that al-Shabaab and government officials do negotiate on an individual basis. In Somalia, the question is when official negotiations will happen rather than if. Whether this scenario will play out in the near or far future depends on various factors. The first is the balance of power on the battlefield. It would be a mistake for the federal government to enter decisive negotiations with al-Shabaab before securing the upper hand militarily and being able to exercise influence. Al-Shabaab will insist on a degree of Islamist governance in Somali public life. This position will present difficult choices for Somalia and alarm increasingly powerful regional actors, such as the Gulf states, who may try to prevent negotiations reaching that point.

Strategic implications

The strategic value of the coastline along the Red Sea and the Horn of Africa, particularly for Gulf states but also for China, puts Somalia in a vulnerable position. Both Gulf and neighbouring African countries have taken advantage of the ambiguous status of federal states to bypass the central government's approval of infrastructure projects. For instance, the federal government banned the Dubai company DP World from operating in Somalia after it struck a deal with the breakaway region of Somaliland, but DP World developed the Puntland port of Bosaso undeterred. Competition led to the adoption of extreme tactics. In July, the *New York Times* reported that a Qatari businessman organised a bombing in Bosaso to drive out the Emirati company, already fearful after the assassination by al-Shabaab of one of its executives in February.[10] Somalia's prospects for a united government are already poor, but unbridled competition between wealthy global powers will exacerbate the problem and prolong the conflict.

Notes

[1] 'Ghost soldiers' are fake names listed as active-duty soldiers for the corrupt collection of salaries.

[2] Christopher Anzalone (@IbnSiqilli), 'The latest installment in IS media's ongoing bay'a [oath of allegiance] renewal series comes from Somalia & shows small groups of IS-Somalia militants. Most noteworthy is the first new substantial footage of IS-Somalia chief 'Abdi Qadir Mu'min in years, who [sic] the film claims is still alive', 21 July 2019, Tweet.

[3] 'Climate-related Security Risks and Peacebuilding in Somalia: SIPRI Policy Paper 53', Stockholm International Peace Research Institute, p. 12, October 2019.

[4] See *Ibid*.

[5] 'Calm Returns to Somalia Town Following Deadly Clan Clashes', Radio Shabelle, 18 March 2019.

[6] Matt Bryden and Premdeep Bahra, 'East Africa's Terrorist Triple Helix: The Dusit Hotel Attack and the Historical Evolution of the Jihadi Threat', *CTC Sentinel*, vol. 12, no. 6, July 2019.

[7] Norwegian Refugee Council, 'Drought and conflict displace quarter of a million people in Somalia', 10 September 2019.

[8] World Bank Group, 'Somali Poverty and Vulnerability Assessment', April 2019, p. xvii.

[9] *Ibid.*, p. 126. Poverty in this assessment was defined as living on less than US$1.90 per day.

[10] Ronen Bergman and David K. Kirkpatrick, 'With Guns, Cash and Terrorism, Gulf States Vie for Power in Somalia', *New York Times*, 22 July 2019.

SOUTH SUDAN

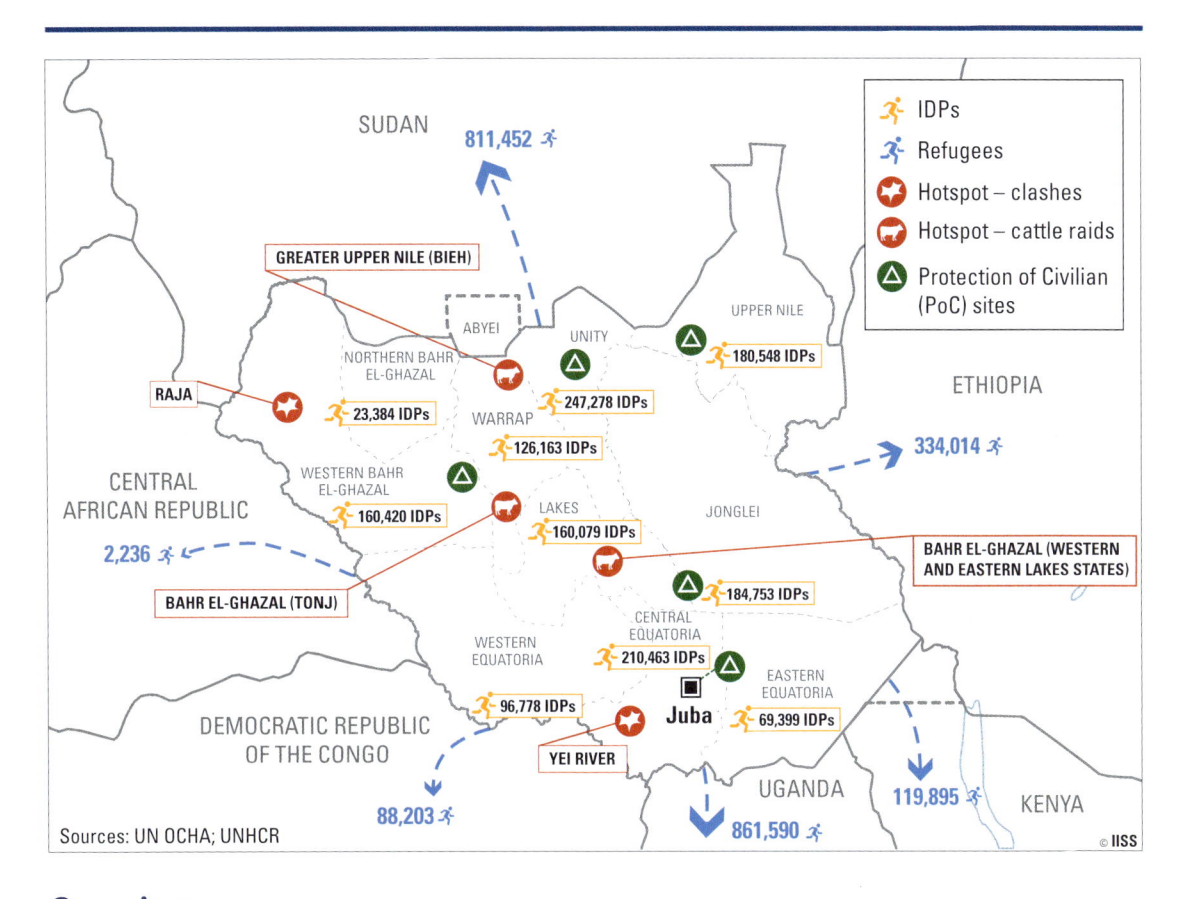

Overview

The conflict in 2019
The implementation of the Revitalized Agreement on the Resolution of the Conflict in South Sudan (R-ARCSS), signed by the main conflict parties on 12 September 2018, progressed slowly in 2019. While the formation of a government of national unity was scheduled to take place on 12 May, the parties postponed the start of the transitional period twice (first to November 2019 and then to February 2020). Several unresolved issues, including the number and boundaries of the states and security provisions for the capital Juba, cast doubt on the sustainability of the peace process. Violence significantly decreased under the ceasefire, but clashes between government forces and rebel groups who rejected the R-ARCSS were frequent in Central Equatoria, while intercommunal fighting also continued across the country. The South Sudanese economy began to recover, especially after the resumption of oil production in Unity region in January, but years of violence pose immense challenges for economic reconstruction. The humanitarian, human-rights and food-security situations also remained dire. While the overall displacement situation improved and spontaneous waves of voluntary returns occurred throughout the year, continued conflict in Equatoria led to further civilian casualties and displacement.

Key statistics

Type	Internationalised
Start date	December 2013
IDPs total (31 December 2019)	1,470,000
Refugees total (31 December 2019)	2,215,037
People in need (31 December 2019)	7,500,000

The conflict to 2019

South Sudan gained independence from Sudan in 2011 but plunged into conflict in 2013 after President Salva Kiir accused then-vice president Riek Machar of attempting a *coup d'état*. The ruling Sudan People's Liberation Movement/Army (SPLM/A) subsequently split: soldiers affiliated with Machar formed the SPLM–In Opposition (SPLM–IO), while those loyal to Kiir searched the streets, hunting for ethnic Nuer thought to be loyal to Machar. Fighters from both sides went on a killing rampage, raping and pillaging their way through towns and villages. As reports of massacres spread, so did revolts across the country. The violence split the country along ethnic lines and deepened rifts between tribes.

The two main fighting groups signed the Agreement on the Resolution of the Conflict in the Republic of South Sudan (ARCSS) on 17 August 2015, but this agreement fell apart as security worsened. Kiir formed a Transitional Government of National Unity (TGoNU) in April 2016 with SPLM–IO General Taban Deng Gai as vice-president and without opposition leader Machar. In July 2016, Machar returned to Juba to join the government, but fighting broke out again between his and Kiir's forces, leaving 300 people dead and starting a new wave of displacement and violence. In 2017, the eight-country regional bloc Intergovernmental Authority on Development (IGAD) began mediating to revitalise the 2015 ARCSS. Negotiations culminated in the signing of the R-ARCSS in September 2018, which provided for a permanent ceasefire and an eight-month pre-transitional period, during which time a unified national army would be created and internal boundaries settled.

Key Conflict Parties

Since the outbreak of conflict and the formation of the SPLM–IO in December 2013, a large number of rebel armed groups have emerged, as well as smaller local self-defence militia groups that operate as community-protection forces against the SPLM/A. In 2018, some of South Sudan's main opposition groups renounced armed struggle to join the R-ARCSS, including the coalition of opposition groups called the South Sudan United Alliance (SSOA). The section below only features armed groups that were involved in fighting in 2019.

South Sudan People's Defence Force (SSPDF), formerly Sudan People's Liberation Movement/Army (SPLM/A)/Transitional Government of National Unity (TGoNU)–South Sudan Armed Forces

Strength
The SSPDF has approximately 185,000 soldiers. Its precise size is unknown, after alliances shifted and various militias were integrated into it.

Areas of operation
Presence throughout the country, except for pockets in opposition areas (Central Equatoria).

Leadership
Salva Kiir.

Structure
Nine territorial divisions and three services (ground force, air force and defence, and navy). Hierarchical leadership including the commander-in-chief, the minister of defence and veteran affairs, the chief of defence force, the deputy chief of defence force and the inspector general.

History
Founded in 1983 by generals who defected from the Sudanese army to fight for South Sudan's autonomy. In 2018, the SPLA was renamed the South Sudan People's Defence Forces. In 2019, the SPLM was reunified to include the Former Detainees (FD) group and the SPLM–IO faction led by Taban Deng Gai.

Objectives
Governing South Sudan and defeating armed opposition groups.

Opponents
NAS–TC, SSNDA.

Affiliates/allies
Uganda People's Defence Force (UPDF), Justice and Equality Movement (JEM), Sudan People's Liberation Movement–North (SPLM–N).
Tribal militias: Maban Defence Force (MDF), Mathiang Anyoor, Gelwent.

Resources/capabilities
Equipped with heavy artillery, tanks, armoured fighting vehicles and attack helicopters. The 2019 defence budget was US$70.1 million, or 1.9% of the country's GDP. In 2019, the EU and UN have maintained their arms embargos on South Sudan and expanded them to include all types of military equipment in 2018.

Sudan People's Liberation Movement/Army (SPLM/A)–In Opposition (SPLM/A–IO)

Strength
Unknown. In 2019, increased recruitment was reported (but denied by Machar) ahead of the planned unification of the army.

Areas of operation
Cantonment across the country, fighting against the NAS–TC in Central Equatoria.

Leadership
Riek Machar.

Structure
Loose grouping of fragmented armed groups, low institutionalisation.

History
Founded in 2013 following the split between Kiir and then vice-president Machar. Ethnically dominated by the Nuer. In 2018, the SPLM–IO signed the R-ARCSS with the government and has largely respected the ceasefire but has also cooperated with the SSPDF against the NAS–TC.

Objectives
Prior to the R-ARCSS: removing Kiir from power and governing South Sudan. After the R-ARCSS: securing a favourable position in the new government and the new unified army.

Opponents
NAS–TC.

Affiliates/allies
The group cooperated with the SSPDF against the NAS–TC in 2019.

Resources/capabilities
Assault rifles, mortars, rockets, grenades, pistols and machine guns. Ammunition mostly from China and Sudan. In 2018, Conflict Armament Research revealed that since 2014, the SPLM/A–IO has mostly been relying on weapons captured after battles or brought in by SPLA defectors, rather than external arms supplies (except for Sudanese weapons).

National Salvation Front–Thomas Cirillo (NAS–TC)

Strength
Not known.

Areas of operation
Central Equatoria.

Leadership
Thomas Cirillo Swaka.

Structure
Not known.

History
Formed in March 2017 by General Thomas Cirillo Swaka, who defected from the SPLA in February 2017. The NAS–TC mostly appeals to members of the Bari community in the Equatoria region. After its creation, the group was joined by officials of the SPLM–IO, who accused Machar of disenfranchising non-Nuers.

Objectives
The NAS–TC calls for a renegotiation of the R-ARCSS. It seeks to establish a federal state, reinstitute South Sudan's original ten states and overthrow Kiir.

Opponents
SSPDF, SPLM–IO.

Affiliates/allies
Cirillo is also chair of the South Sudan National Democratic Alliance (SSNDA), a coalition of non-signatories to the R-ARCSS. In August 2019, the SSNDA formed an alliance with a new opposition group called the Real Sudan People's Liberation Movement (R–SPLM) and the SSUF/A.

Resources/capabilities
The NAS–TC possesses equipment looted from the SSPDF, mainly during ambushes. Weapons include AK-47s and AKM general-purpose machine guns. The group has a small supply of uniforms and ammunition. It also takes part in forced recruitment and kidnappings.

South Sudan United Front/Army (SSUF/A)

Strength
Not known.

Areas of operation
Western Bahr el-Ghazal (Raja town).

Leadership
Paul Malong Awan.

Structure
Not known.

History
Created in April 2018 under the leadership of Paul Malong Awan, former chief of staff of the SPLA and former governor of Northern Bahr el-Ghazal State. Excluded from the 2018 R-ARCSS, though Malong expressed his willingness to join the peace process.

Objectives
'Arrest the carnage' of the conflict and overthrow Kiir, whom Malong accuses of mismanaging the country and looting its resources. The SSUF also calls for the establishment of a federal state.

Opponents
SSPDF.

Affiliates/allies
SSNDA, R–SPLM.

Resources/capabilities
Exact supplies are unknown – the SSUF most likely possesses weapons formerly belonging to the SPLA, including machine guns, assault rifles, pistols and ammunition.

South Sudan National Movement for Change (SSNMC)–Unvuas

Strength
Unknown.

Areas of operation
Central Equatoria.

Leadership
Vakindi Unvuas.

Structure
Not known.

History
Created by Joseph Bangasi Bakosoro, former governor of Western Equatoria State. In September 2018, a faction of the group rejected Bakosoro's support of the R-ARCSS. The splinter faction, led by Vakindi Unvuas, later joined the SSNDA, the group of non-signatories led by Cirillo. In July 2019, UNMISS cited the SSNMC as one of the groups responsible for atrocities against civilians in Central Equatoria between September 2018 and April 2019.

Objectives
Reject the R-ARCSS and obtain a 'meaningful negotiated settlement to the crisis in South Sudan that will fulfil the aspirations of the people'.

Opponents
SSPDF.

Affiliates/allies
Part of the SSNDA.

Resources/capabilities
Not known.

South Sudan National Democratic Alliance (SSNDA)

Strength
Not known.

Areas of operation
Western and Central Equatoria.

Leadership
Thomas Cirillo Swaka.

Structure
The SSNDA is composed of the NAS–TC, the United Democratic Republic Alliance (UDRA), the New Democratic Movement (NDM) faction led by Emanuel Aban, the People's Democratic Movement (PDM) led by Hakim Dario, and the SSNMC–Unvuas.

History
The SSNDA is an offshoot from the South Sudan Opposition Alliance (SSOA). After the SSOA signed the R-ARCSS in September 2018, holdout groups split up to form their own coalition, the SSNDA, in November 2018.

Objectives
Reject the R-ARCSS and obtain a renegotiation of the agreement to achieve 'fundamental Democratic Transformation change in South Sudan'.

Opponents
SSPDF.

Affiliates/allies
In August 2019, the SSNDA allied with the SSUF/A and a new opposition group called the Real SPLM to form a new coalition, the United South Sudan Opposition Movements, with the aim of engaging international support for the holdout groups' cause.

Resources/capabilities
Not known.

Mathiang Anyoor

Strength
In 2015, Mathiang Anyoor was estimated to comprise between 3,000 and 15,000 fighters.[1]

Areas of operation
Northern Bahr el-Ghazal, Central Equatoria.

Leadership
Santino Deng Wol.

Structure
Loose collection of militias trained by the SSPDF 3rd Infantry Division.

History
Group of Dinka militiamen from the Aweil region in Northern Bahr el-Ghazal, who defended the South Sudanese border with Sudan in 2011–12 and protected local communities. When the civil war started in 2013, the Mathiang Anyoor were mobilised by Paul Malong to contribute to the defence of Kiir's government. After Malong's sacking in 2017, many Mathiang Anyoor remained loyal to Kiir and continued to fight on the SPLA payroll. In 2019, the Mathiang Anyoor fought alongside the SSPDF against the NAS–TC in Central Equatoria.

Objectives
Protecting Dinka communities, supporting the SSPDF and defending Kiir's presidency.

Opponents
NAS–TC (in 2019).

Affiliates/allies
SSPDF.

Resources/capabilities
Mathiang Anyoor has access to SSPDF weapons, as the army equips the militia.

United Nations Mission in South Sudan (UNMISS)

Strength
16,761 personnel as of 31 December 2019.

Areas of operation
Presence across the country. Protection of Civilian (PoC) sites in Central Equatoria (Juba UN House), Unity (Bentiu), Upper Nile (Malakal), Jonglei (Bor) and areas adjacent to UNMISS in Wau.

Leadership
Special Representative David Shearer.

Structure
As of September 2019, UNMISS was comprised of 14,275 military personnel, 2,275 civilians, 228 Experts on Mission, 1,738 police, 430 staff officers and 398 UN volunteers.

History
Established on 8 July 2011 by UNSC Resolution 1996 to consolidate peace and security and to help establish conditions for development.

Objectives
After civil war broke out in 2013, UNSC Resolution 2155 (2014) updated the UNMISS mandate to prioritise civilian protection and human-rights monitoring, as well as supporting the delivery of humanitarian aid and the ceasefire implementation. The UN Security Council also authorised the Regional Protection Force (RPF) 'to use robust action to facilitate safe and free movement around Juba' (Resolution 2459 (2019)).

Opponents
n/a

Affiliates/allies
n/a

Resources/capabilities
Approved budget (July 2019–June 2020): US$1.27 billion.

Drivers

SPLM/A infighting

Since its foundation in 1982, the SPLM/A suffered from infighting over the leadership style, the overall aim of the group and power sharing. Fundamental differences emerged regarding the desirability of maintaining a united Sudan or campaigning for secession of the south. When the planned transfer of power from Kiir to then-vice-president Machar failed to take place in 2013, the group split. The SPLM's political and structural divisions led fighters to mobilise and target communities along ethnic lines (Kiir is a Dinka; Machar, a Nuer). However, the relationship between ethnicity and violence in South Sudan is more complex than a Nuer–Dinka dichotomy.

Creation of states

A major cause of conflict is Kiir's practice of signing peace agreements and then decreeing the creation of new states that benefit the Dinka communities. Kiir increased the number of states from ten to 28 in December 2015, and then to 32 in January 2017, without consulting the parties to the August 2015 peace agreement, opposition groups or local communities. This practice is likely a consequence of the pressure the Jieng Council of Elders, a group of Dinka leaders who advise Kiir, is able to exert on the president.

The creation of additional states along ethnic lines exacerbated further division among the ethnic communities, while allowing tribal areas to be consolidated to preserve indigenous majority rule. The practice had caused considerable tensions at the national level and fuelled local conflicts, particularly for communities in the Shilluk Kingdom in the former states of Upper Nile, in Equatoria and Western Bahr el-Ghazal. It eroded the capacity of local chiefs, state institutions and local government systems and led local rebel groups to reject the R-ARCSS in order to claim lands that they see as rightfully theirs.

Abuse of power

The SPLM/A political leaders have focused on their own short-term political gains rather than addressing the needs of the South Sudanese people. The SPLM/A has absolute control over the executive and legislative arms of government: all policies that the government implements come from its political programme. Within this framework, supporting the government agenda rather than having political experience or any relevant competency are the criteria for appointments. Governors were nominated to the 32 states because they were active generals or returning political defectors, not because they could manage public affairs. Many became ministers or legislators overnight, without any formal experience. Thus, as capacity in the local councils and districts suffered, the SPLM/A's political power strengthened.

Weak leadership

Since 2005, South Sudan has experienced a combination of disintegration of local institutions and communal networks and ethnic segmentation. South Sudan's 2005 Interim Constitution provided for a decentralised system based on three levels of governance (national, state and local). The local level is itself divided into three levels (county, *payam* and *boma*), and involves traditional leaders. While most of this system was retained by the 2011 Transitional Constitution, decentralisation is mostly not applied in practice. Across South Sudan, county-level legislative assemblies are not established, county commissioners are mostly selected from the central government and local taxation and service provision is not clearly defined, which is worsened by limited-resource constraints.[2] Weak local governance dates back to when South Sudan was still part of Sudan. In particular, the Sudanese civil war (1983–2005) displaced and fragmented local communities across South Sudan, and led traditional leaders to lose influence over their constituencies due to the establishment of parallel authorities by armed groups. During 2019, weak leadership at both the national and local levels continued to erode the few existing governance systems. Since the signing of the Comprehensive Peace Agreement in 2005, the South Sudan government and the UN Mission in Sudan (UNMIS) – later renamed UNMISS – have lacked a strategy for resolving local tensions and intercommunal pastoral infighting, focusing instead on building the new state from the centre.

Political Developments

Implementation delays

The R-ARCSS provides for an eight-month pre-transitional period and the holding of elections 60 days before the end of a 36-month transition. On 3 May 2019, IGAD agreed to prolong the pre-transitional period by six months to complete pending tasks, including the formation of a unity government and the incorporation of the agreement into a Transitional Constitution. Despite the implementation of some of the provisions of the R-ARCSS, delays continued, mainly due to logistical challenges, resource constraints and disagreements over security arrangements. Many parties also continued to reject the agreement's provisions on the number and boundaries of states. These delays created fears that Machar and other opposition groups were using the additional time to build up their capacities for renewed fighting.

SPLM/A's faltering commitment to peace

Responding to criticisms that the government was allocating insufficient funds to the peace process, Kiir pledged US$100m to accelerate implementation. However, donors remained reluctant to increase their support to a government lacking transparency and a genuine commitment to the agreement. Their suspicions deepened when the SPLM/A used US$135,000 of the National Pre-Transitional Committee's (NPTC) budget to renovate two politicians' houses. Donors' mistrust

Key Events in 2019

Political events

- **21 January**: Oil extraction fully restarts in Unity region, in accordance with the R-ARCSS.
- **3 May**: The R-ARCSS signatories agree to prolong the pre-transitional period until 12 November.
- **16 May**: Anti-government protests by the youth coalition RCM take place outside various South Sudanese embassies.
- **3 July**: An UNMISS report documents human-rights violations by government forces and rebel groups between September 2018 and April 2019.

Military/Violent events

- **January**: The NAS–TC clashes with both the SSPDF and the SPLM–IO in Central Equatoria.
- **14 January**: Cattle raiders attack herders in Tonj State, killing at least 105 people.
- **31 January**: The SSNDA repels a 'coordinated heavy attack' by the SSPDF in Central Equatoria.
- **9 April**: Cattle raids in Luwaacodou, Boma State leave at least 50 people dead. The state minister says that a Murle youth militia perpetrated the attacks.

also increased after public documents disclosed that the South Sudanese government collaborated with a US lobbying agency to prevent the formation of a Hybrid Court for South Sudan intended to investigate war crimes.[3]

Continued mediation

In 2019, international mediators remained committed to implementing the peace agreement. IGAD repeatedly convened the R-ARCSS parties but could not forge a consensus on pending issues. The regional bloc also reached out to non-signatories, including SSUF leader Paul Malong, who expressed interest in direct discussions with the government. Talks with Thomas Cirillo were less successful, with Cirillo maintaining that the agreement needed to be revised to address the root causes of the conflict. The Catholic Church also attempted to foster dialogue. In April, Pope Francis called on Kiir, Machar, Rebecca Garang and Taban Deng Gai to increase cooperation during a spiritual retreat in the Vatican. Face-to-face meetings between Kiir and Machar in Juba were also a positive step towards peace. In September, Machar visited the capital for the first time in 2019, and, together with Kiir, vowed to solve all the pending issues by November. However, Machar noted that his freedom of movement was still restricted – according to the SPLM–IO, he was under effective house arrest in Khartoum. The two leaders met multiple times afterwards. In December, they again failed to reach a consensus on the number and boundaries of states, but insisted on forming a transitional government within the new 100-day period even if outstanding issues remained.

Internal disagreements

The death of SSOA and South Sudan United Movement (SSUM) leader Peter Gatdet in April 2019 exacerbated disputes within the SSOA, an R-ARCSS signatory, and prevented the coalition from agreeing on key implementation tasks, including the nomination of a vice-president and appointments to ministerial positions. In February 2019, the SPLM announced its reunification with the SPLM–IO faction led by Taban Deng and the FD group, but the SPLM–IO rejected this move, saying it had different priorities. Disagreements within the SPLM also emerged, and Pagan Amum, former SPLM secretary-general of the party, resigned in June to protest against the reunification process.

Thwarted protests

On 16 May, youth groups under the Red Card Movement (RCM) umbrella protested outside various South Sudanese embassies. The RCM also sought to organise an anti-government march in Juba to protest against the slow implementation of the peace process, but cancelled the plan after receiving threats by government officials and being harassed by the security forces.[4]

---

30 August
The SSNDA, SSUF/A and R–SPLM create a new coalition (the United South Sudan Opposition Movements) to coordinate opposition efforts.

9 September
Riek Machar meets Salva Kiir in Juba for the first time since 2018.

7 November
Kiir and Machar agree to extend the deadline for the formation of a unity agreement by 100 days.

25 November
The US temporarily recalls its ambassador following Kiir and Machar's failure to form a unity government.

16 December
The US imposes sanctions on two South Sudanese officials accused of spoiling the peace process.

30 May
The UN Security Council renews the arms embargo imposed on South Sudan in 2018 until 2020.

21 August
The NAS–TC clashes with the SSPDF in Loka West, Central Equatoria, killing 20 soldiers according to the NAS–TC.

7 October
SPLM–IO troops arrive for training to become a new protection force with SSPDF soldiers.

27–29 November
Clashes among the Pakam Dinka clan kill 79 people in Maper town near Rumbek, Lakes State.

Military Developments

Fighting in Central Equatoria
The ceasefire established by the R-ARCSS held in 2019, reducing violence significantly. However, fighting involving holdout groups, especially the NAS–TC, continued, with the SSPDF and SPLA–IO jointly gaining control over multiple NAS–TC-held territories in Central Equatoria until the rainy season slowed down fighting from April. In particular, the SSPDF and NAS–TC clashed frequently in Yei River State, where violence peaked at the beginning of 2019 following the government offensives against rebels in December 2018. The National Security Service (NSS) and SSPDF detained many individuals suspected of cooperating with the NAS–TC.

Security arrangements
Uncertainty and delays surrounded the implementation of the peace agreement's security arrangements throughout 2019. The demilitarisation of cities remained incomplete, with the SSPDF continuing to occupy civilian buildings. As in 2016, the government (which controls the main urban centres) is reluctant to implement this provision because it would benefit the opposition in the case of a return to conflict. Kiir has little incentive in applying other provisions that would diminish his power, such as reducing the Dinka domination of the army by including opposition groups.[5] Machar also has an interest in slowing down the implementation of security arrangements, because longer cantonments allow him to increase the number of his troops and their military capabilities.

In August, only 23 out of the 35 cantonment sites set up by the Joint Defence Board (JDB) were verified as operational, and the cantonment process had been slowed down by the rainy season that made the movement of troops difficult. In addition, peace monitors reported that opposition soldiers deserted cantonment sites in October due to lack of food and medicine.[6] For opposition armed groups, the prospect of being integrated into the official army and having access to its resources has led to more recruitment, including of child soldiers. The SSPDF, which also has an interest in inflating its number of troops, has likewise reportedly sought to widen its recruitment, which has also included child soldiers.[7]

Intercommunal fighting
Cattle raids, inter-clan clashes and other violent incidents involving ethnic militias remained frequent and caused the most civilian casualties in 2019, enabled by the widespread availability of weapons among civilian communities, grievances over the destruction of livelihoods and continued disagreements over resources and territory. The Greater Bahr el-Ghazal region, in particular Lakes State, was the most affected by intercommunal conflicts. In this area, the government's operations to disarm civilians involved killings and the displacement of those who refused to lay down their weapons.

Impact

Human rights
The human-rights situation improved across the country after the signing of the R-ARCSS, but abuses against civilians remained at particularly alarming levels in Central Equatoria. In July 2019, UNMISS published a report documenting human-rights violations perpetrated by government forces and rebel groups in the region, recording 104 killings of civilians, 187 abductions and 99 rapes and other forms of sexual violence between September 2018 and April 2019.[8] Human Rights Watch also reported that government soldiers 'shot at civilians, looted extensively, burned homes and crops, and chased thousands of residents from their villages'.[9] While government soldiers were the main perpetrators of abuses, Human Rights Watch said that opposition groups (including the NAS–TC, the SSNMC and SPLM–IO) also attacked and abducted civilians and prevented humanitarian access to civilians in need.

Humanitarian
The number of refugees from South Sudan stood at 2.22m at the end of December 2019,[10] while in August 2019 the UN Office for the Coordination of Humanitarian Affairs (OCHA) revised down the number of internally displaced people (IDPs) from 1.83m to 1.47m.[11] Despite reduced violence,

PERMANENT CEASEFIRE
In place since 1 July 2018

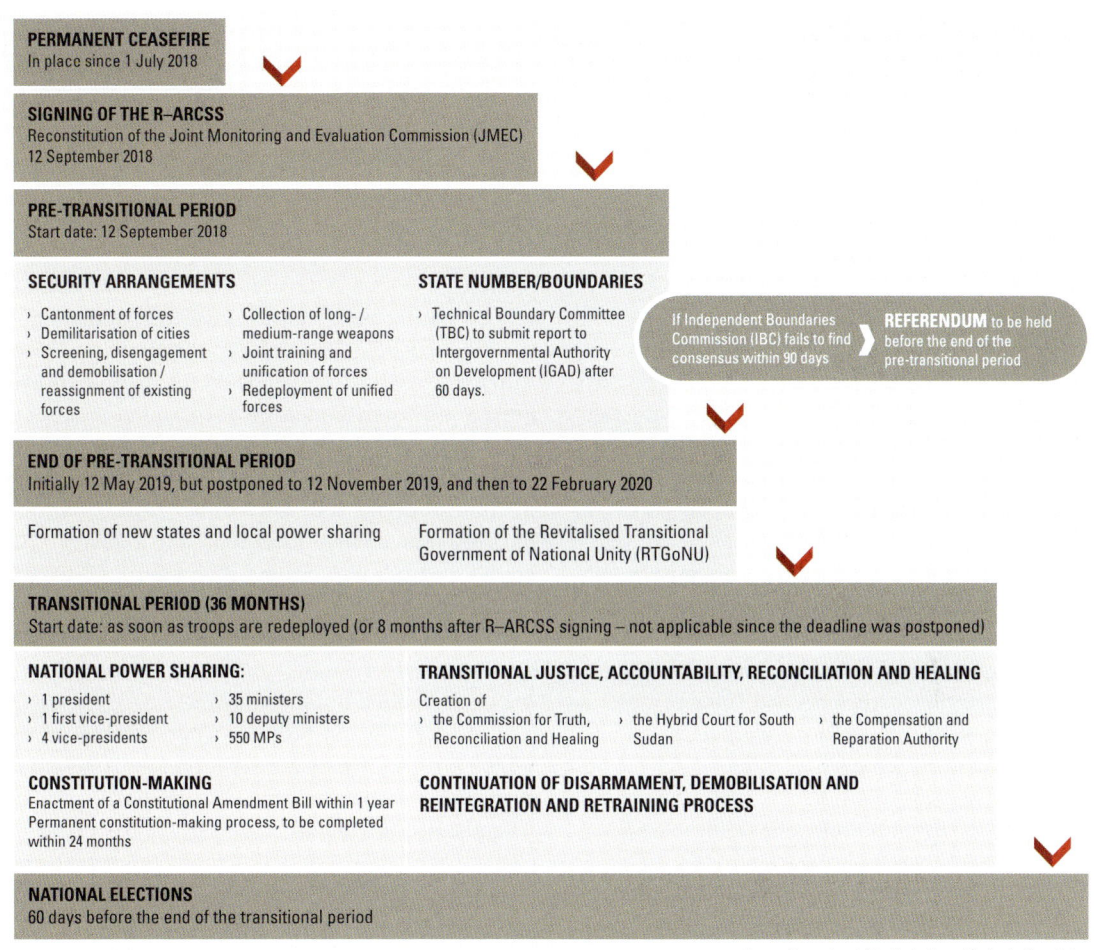

SIGNING OF THE R–ARCSS
Reconstitution of the Joint Monitoring and Evaluation Commission (JMEC)
12 September 2018

PRE-TRANSITIONAL PERIOD
Start date: 12 September 2018

SECURITY ARRANGEMENTS
› Cantonment of forces
› Demilitarisation of cities
› Screening, disengagement and demobilisation / reassignment of existing forces
› Collection of long- / medium-range weapons
› Joint training and unification of forces
› Redeployment of unified forces

STATE NUMBER/BOUNDARIES
› Technical Boundary Committee (TBC) to submit report to Intergovernmental Authority on Development (IGAD) after 60 days.

If Independent Boundaries Commission (IBC) fails to find consensus within 90 days › **REFERENDUM** to be held before the end of the pre-transitional period

END OF PRE-TRANSITIONAL PERIOD
Initially 12 May 2019, but postponed to 12 November 2019, and then to 22 February 2020

Formation of new states and local power sharing

Formation of the Revitalised Transitional Government of National Unity (RTGoNU)

TRANSITIONAL PERIOD (36 MONTHS)
Start date: as soon as troops are redeployed (or 8 months after R–ARCSS signing – not applicable since the deadline was postponed)

NATIONAL POWER SHARING:
› 1 president
› 1 first vice-president
› 4 vice-presidents
› 35 ministers
› 10 deputy ministers
› 550 MPs

TRANSITIONAL JUSTICE, ACCOUNTABILITY, RECONCILIATION AND HEALING
Creation of
› the Commission for Truth, Reconciliation and Healing
› the Hybrid Court for South Sudan
› the Compensation and Reparation Authority

CONSTITUTION-MAKING
Enactment of a Constitutional Amendment Bill within 1 year
Permanent constitution-making process, to be completed within 24 months

CONTINUATION OF DISARMAMENT, DEMOBILISATION AND REINTEGRATION AND RETRAINING PROCESS

NATIONAL ELECTIONS
60 days before the end of the transitional period

Source: Reconstituted Joint Monitoring and Evaluation Commission

Figure 1: Key steps of the Revitalised Agreement on the Resolution of the Conflict in the Republic of South Sudan

new displacement continued within and outside the country. Thousands of people were displaced within Central Equatoria and into the Democratic Republic of the Congo due to escalating fighting between the SSPDF and the NAS–TC. In June, approximately 30,000 persons were displaced in Eastern Equatoria, Upper Nile and Warrap as a result of intercommunal clashes and cattle raids. The overall decrease of violence has also encouraged displaced people and refugees to return home: the International Organization for Migration (IOM) recorded 534,082 returns since the signing of the R-ARCSS.[12] The Office of the United Nations High Commissioner for Refugees (UNHCR) reported more than 39,000 returns of refugees between May and July, most (33,095) being to Unity due to insecurity in Sudan.[13] The returns created urgent needs for food, protection and shelter, new demands for healthcare and education, and increased requests for reconstruction materials.

Humanitarian access to populations in need has improved since the signing of the agreement. Confidence-building activities between the government and opposition groups allowed the opening of roads and facilitated the movement of goods and people. By the end of June 2019, 4.1m people had received aid, or 72% of people targeted in 2019.[14] However, violence against humanitarian personnel and facilities continued, as did the bureaucratic obstacles, harassment, detentions and confiscations of assets.

In 2019, an unprecedented number of people suffered from food insecurity in South Sudan. In June, at least 6.96m people (more than half of the population) were estimated to be severely food insecure, despite humanitarian aid. However, the proportion of people who are severely food insecure has decreased compared to the previous year, mainly due to the reduction of violence and increased access to livelihood across the country, including returnees' ability to cultivate their land.

Economic
The South Sudanese economy remained fragile in 2019. Years of conflict and mismanagement have hampered the productive capacity of the country, which remains heavily dependent on oil-related activities. Oil production increased after the January 2019 opening of oilfields that had been closed due to conflict. The projected increase in revenue contributed to a 155% projected increase in public expenditure from 2018, which was mostly allocated to building new infrastructure or refurbishing existing infrastructure.[15] In June, the International Monetary Fund warned the government against oil-backed payment advances and loans prior to the production of oil, a costly and non-transparent practice that remained pervasive in 2019.

Relations with neighbouring and international partners
The April 2019 ousting of then Sudanese president Omar al-Bashir, one of the main mediators of the R-ARCSS who had leverage over both Kiir and Machar, deprived the peace process of a key guarantor. The crisis in Sudan also threatened the sustainability of the deal by disrupting Sudan's transportation system, which is key to South Sudan's oil exports. However, the establishment of a new civilian government in Khartoum offered new prospects for rapprochement with Juba. In April, Kiir offered to mediate in negotiations for the Sudanese transition, and in September, he agreed with new Sudanese Prime Minister Abdalla Hamdok to reopen border zones to improve the circulation of goods and people. This trend could provide momentum for renewed discussions on the disputed Abyei area, a territory claimed by both Sudan and South Sudan since 2011.

The United States, an active diplomatic actor in the conflict as member of the Troika that also includes the United Kingdom and Norway, has largely withdrawn from diplomatic efforts to sustain the peace process in recent years; tellingly, US President Donald Trump has not appointed a special envoy for South Sudan. Nonetheless, in 2019, the US continued to push for sanctions against Juba and in May, the UN Security Council renewed the arms embargo it had imposed on South Sudan in 2018. In November 2019, the US temporarily recalled its ambassador to Juba 'as part of the re-evaluation of the U.S. relationship' with South Sudan following the parties' failure to establish a unity government. In December, the US imposed sanctions on two South Sudanese officials accused of undermining the peace process.

Trends

Political trajectories
The continued delays in the implementation of the peace agreement generated new fissures between the SPLM and other signatories. Even after the formation of a unity government, tensions are likely to re-emerge in the run-up to the 2022 elections, which will likely pit Kiir and Machar against each other. This competition involves high risks, as the peace agreement does not include mechanisms to mitigate future incompatibilities between the two rivals. The winner-takes-all nature of South Sudan's presidential system also raises the stakes of the election. In addition, Machar promised his followers that he would address their demands for federalism and resources sharing after the elections, but his supporters could resort to violent tactics again if these demands are not addressed.

Conflict-related risks
Disagreements over security arrangements hamper the return of opposition leaders to Juba and the formation of a unity government. Conditioning the government formation on the cantonment completion (a complex process struggling with limited capacity) will cause further delays. The control of Juba also remains a sticking point in the implementation of the peace process. The 2015 agreement established a force made up of distinct units from Kiir's and Machar's camps tasked with protecting the capital, but this arrangement contributed to the

eruption of new clashes between security guards in 2016 and the scenario could be repeated if Machar is allowed to return to Juba with his own troops.[16]

The R-ARCSS provides for the establishment of a Hybrid Court for South Sudan, a Commission for Truth, Reconciliation, and Healing, and a Compensation and Reparation Authority. All these bodies are yet to be established, as the government requires a functioning legislature to be in place before the justice mechanisms are set up. The absence of a meaningful commitment to bring perpetrators of war crimes to justice is likely to foster resentment among the population, which will in turn create new tensions.

While officially committed to the army integration, most parties to the peace deal still rely on affiliated militias to retain military strength and to protect their constituent communities and leaders.[17] For this reason, instead of weakening the NAS–TC, the SSPDF's ongoing offensive in Central Equatoria might have the opposite effect and encourage more people to join Cirillo's forces.

Prospects for peace

Despite implementation delays, financial strains and fighting in Central Equatoria, the continued holding of the ceasefire, the multiplication of confidence-building initiatives and population returns offered encouraging signs in 2019. The agreement, however, fails to address the most contentious issues (particularly the number and boundaries of states) and thus cannot ultimately solve the underlying tensions between the conflict parties. For instance, while a referendum should take place in case of no agreement on the number of states, logistical challenges make a nationwide consultation highly unlikely. Deadlock appears to be the most probable outcome for the implementation process in the near future.

Another inherent shortcoming of the agreement is that it does not include all warring parties. Holdout groups, especially the NAS–TC, will continue to use violence and reject the peace process if the deal is not reopened for amendments. Among the main grievances of NAS–TC supporters is the persistence of a centralised system of governance in South Sudan, which will remain a source of tensions, as minority regions continue to push for more decentralisation. Any unity government comprised of competing ethnic factions and operating in the context of the existing centralised system will likely implode.[18]

Strategic implications and global influences

Donor fatigue (partially caused by the government's lack of transparency in allocating donor funds and by the exclusion of the Troika and the European Union from the peace talks led by Sudan) will continue to threaten the sustainability of funding for peace implementation.[19] Meanwhile, political developments in the Horn of Africa, including the government transition in Sudan and increased rivalry between Ethiopia (an important mediator in South Sudan's peace process) and Egypt, have diminished IGAD's mediation capacity. While strong regional pressure is needed to push the R-ARCSS parties to accelerate implementation of the agreement, changing regional dynamics could hamper the ability of IGAD members to coordinate their diplomatic efforts.

Notes

[1] 'Generals say Juba massacres done by private militia, not SPLA', Radio Tamazuj, 9 March 2015.

[2] Louise Aalen, 'The Paradox of Federalism and Decentralisation in South Sudan: An Instrument and an Obstacle for Peace', Sudan Brief (2019:01), Chr. Michelsen Institute, September 2019.

[3] Robbie Gramer, 'Former U.S. Diplomats Lobby to Stop South Sudan War Crimes Court,' Foreign Policy, 29 April 2019.

[4] Amnesty International, 'South Sudan: Authorities crackdown on critics in cross-border campaign of intimidation', 18 July 2019.

[5] Klem Ryan, 'Taking Stock of the Revitalized Agreement on the Resolution of the Conflict in South Sudan,' African Center for Strategic Studies, 12 January 2019.

[6] 'Peace monitors say S. Sudan forces leaving cantonment sites over lack of food, medicines', Sudan Tribune, 29 October 2019.

[7] Emma Farge, 'United Nations sees increase in child soldiers recruited in South Sudan', Reuters, 16 September 2019.

[8] United Nations Mission in South Sudan (UNMISS), 'Conflict-related violations and abuses in Central Equatoria, September 2018–April 2019', 3 July 2019.

[9] Human Rights Watch, 'South Sudan: Government Forces Abusing Civilians', 4 June 2019.

[10] UN High Commissioner for Refugees (UNHCR), Operations Data Portal: South Sudan.

[11] The decrease is mainly due to the review and verification of previously cumulated data, rather than reflecting an actual

change in the number of IDPs. UN Office for the Coordination of Humanitarian Affairs (OCHA), 'South Sudan Humanitarian Snapshot (August)', 27 September 2019.

[12] International Organization for Migration (IOM), 'IOM's New Report Documents Need for Improved Service Delivery in Conflict Affected Areas', 30 August 2019.

[13] UN Security Council, 'Situation in South Sudan – Report of the Secretary-General', S/2019/722, 10 September 2019.

[14] OCHA, 'South Sudan Humanitarian Response Dashboard (June 2019)', 15 August 2019.

[15] UN Security Council, 'Situation in South Sudan', 10 September 2019.

[16] Alan Boswell and Alex de Waal, 'South Sudan: The Perils of Payroll Peace', London School of Economics Conflict Research Programme, March 2019.

[17] Ryan, 'Taking Stock of the Revitalized Agreement'.

[18] International Crisis Group, 'Salvaging South Sudan's Fragile Peace Deal', Report no. 270, 13 March 2019.

[19] Lasuba Memo, 'Misused Donations Hurt Global Trust in South Sudan, Officials Say', *VOA News*, 16 September 2019.

SUDAN (DARFUR, BLUE NILE & SOUTH KORDOFAN)

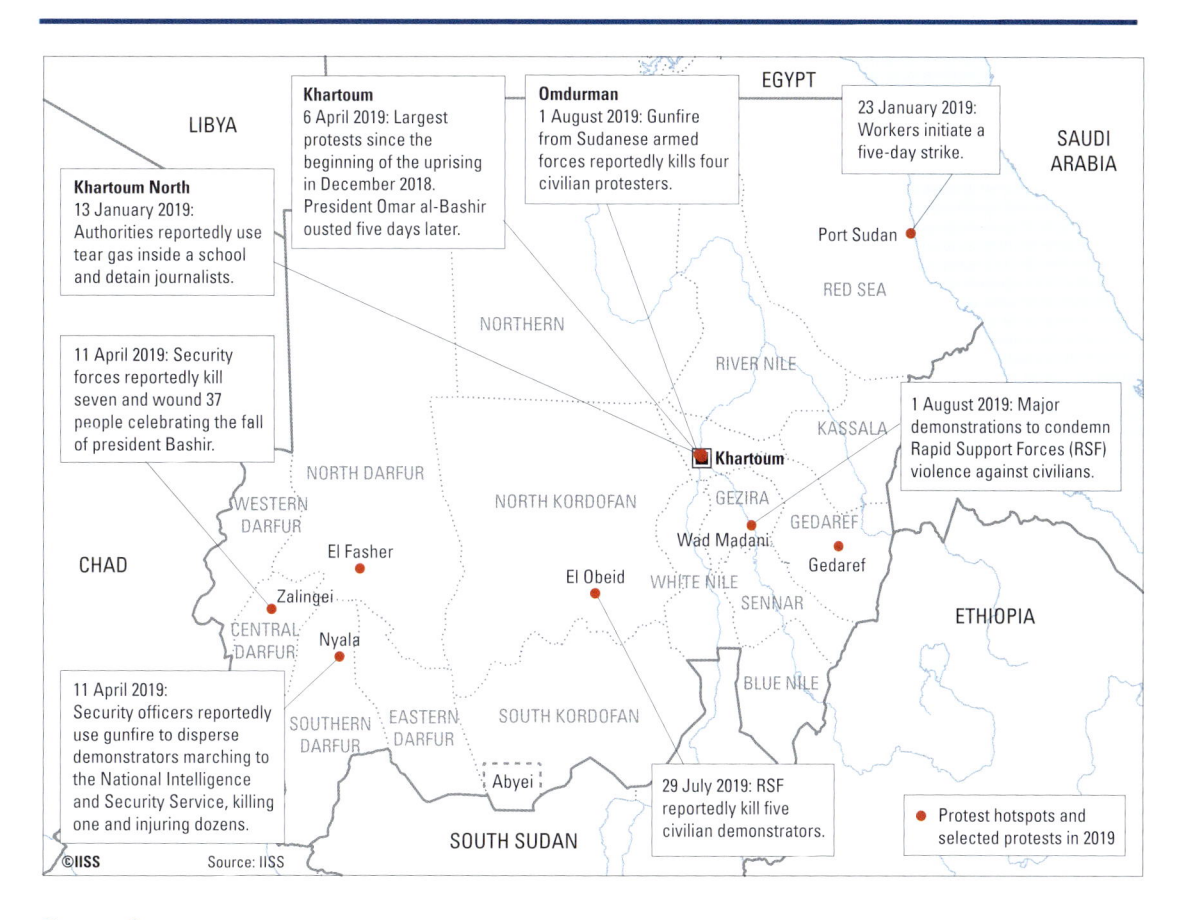

Khartoum North — 13 January 2019: Authorities reportedly use tear gas inside a school and detain journalists.

Khartoum — 6 April 2019: Largest protests since the beginning of the uprising in December 2018. President Omar al-Bashir ousted five days later.

Omdurman — 1 August 2019: Gunfire from Sudanese armed forces reportedly kills four civilian protesters.

23 January 2019: Workers initiate a five-day strike.

11 April 2019: Security forces reportedly kill seven and wound 37 people celebrating the fall of president Bashir.

1 August 2019: Major demonstrations to condemn Rapid Support Forces (RSF) violence against civilians.

11 April 2019: Security officers reportedly use gunfire to disperse demonstrators marching to the National Intelligence and Security Service, killing one and injuring dozens.

29 July 2019: RSF reportedly kill five civilian demonstrators.

● Protest hotspots and selected protests in 2019

Source: IISS

Overview

The conflict in 2019

A large wave of anti-government protests in 2019 ended the 30-year rule of Omar al-Bashir. A turbulent period followed Bashir's ouster, during which protests continued against the new military regime. Mediation led by both the African Union and Ethiopia established a civilian–military transitional regime in August. The political turmoil brought the peace talks in the framework established by the Doha Document for Peace in Darfur (DDPD) to a halt but violence in Darfur and the Two Areas (the states of Blue Nile and South Kordofan) continued to decline significantly in 2019.

In Darfur, fighting remained limited to the Jebel Marra area, where the Sudan Liberation Movement/Army faction led by Abdel Wahid al-Nur (SLM/A–AW) and the Sudanese armed forces engaged in hit-and-run attacks against each other. Armed clashes were less frequent than in 2018 but violence by the security forces against civilians and anti-government protesters continued.

The ousting of Bashir and the establishment of a transitional government offered Sudan a renewed opportunity for peace. Specifically, the signing of the Juba Declaration between the Sudanese government and rebel-group coalition the Sudan Revolutionary Front (SRF) in September laid the foundations for the continuation of peace negotiations. Talks between the parties continued in December 2019. A framework agreement was signed between most Darfur-based armed movements and the transitional authorities,[1] while the Sudan People's Liberation Movement–North (SPLM–N) postponed its talks with the government because of disagreements over the relationship between religion and the state.

The conflict to 2019

Multiple civil wars have been fought in Sudan since independence in 1956. The current conflict consists of protracted rebellions in Darfur and the Two Areas waged by non-state armed groups against the marginalisation of 'non-Arab' tribes under Bashir's policies of Arabisation.[2]

In Darfur, rebel groups took up arms against the government and its allies in 2003. Government forces and the paramilitary Janjaweed (a militia composed of nomadic, mostly Arab tribesmen) responded with indiscriminate violence, killing at least 300,000 civilians since the start of the conflict and displacing more than 2 million people.[3] The violence led to an International Criminal Court (ICC) indictment against Bashir for war crimes and crimes against humanity in 2009, and for genocide in 2010, both of which remain outstanding.

In Blue Nile and South Kordofan states, the conflict originated from the 1983–2005 war between the central government in Khartoum and the Sudan People's Liberation Movement/Army (SPLM/A) over the independence of southern Sudan. The signing of the Comprehensive Peace Agreement (CPA) in 2005 led to the referendum that established the independence of South Sudan in 2011. However, the referendum was not held in the Two Areas, despite the identification of people from the Nuba Mountains and Blue Nile with the south. In a context of unresolved issues, fighting broke out following the disputed election of a governor from the ruling National Congress Party (NCP) in South Kordofan in May 2011. The remaining SPLM/A fighters in the Two Areas formed the SPLM/A–North and continue to fight the government for greater autonomy and reforms. Khartoum responded with counter-insurgency tactics similar to those employed in Darfur, including aerial bombings followed by ground attacks in civilian areas.

Fighting intensified in both conflict areas in 2013–14 when the government used local militias for a series of dry-season offensives, in which several villages were shelled. Violence has decreased since the government and the rebel groups agreed a ceasefire in both Darfur and the Two Areas in mid-2016, but peace talks have not yet led to a substantive agreement.

Key statistics

Type	Internationalised
Start date	2003 (Darfur); 2011 South Kordofan/ Blue Nile
IDPs total (December 2019)	1,100,000
Refugees total (31 December 2019)	1,870,000
People in need (31 December 2019)	9,300,000

Key Conflict Parties

Sudanese armed forces

Strength
104,300 active military personnel (100,000 army, 1,300 navy, 3,000 air force).

Areas of operation
Darfur, South Kordofan and Blue Nile states. In 2019 operations focused on the remaining SLM–AW strongholds in Jebel Marra.

Leadership
Lt-Gen. Abdel Fattah al-Burhan is commander-in-chief of the armed forces and chairman of the transitional sovereign council.

Structure
More than 20 divisions: 15 infantries, armoured, mechanised, artillery, engineering and marine units, and residential guard formations, air assault, counter-terrorism and special forces. The military chain of command has been restructured since Bashir's ousting and replaced with an advisory general staff system.

History
While Islamist-oriented army officers carried out the coup that brought Bashir to power in 1989, the armed forces became weaker as they gradually lost Bashir's trust and paramilitaries were increasingly used instead. In April 2019, army members deposed Bashir and formed a military junta, which was then replaced by the civil–military transitional government in August.

Objectives
Suppress rebel insurgencies and their supporters in Darfur and the Two Areas. Attempted to maintain public order during the 2019 protests.

Opponents
Rebel groups in Darfur and the Two Areas. Sudanese forces also fight the Houthis in Yemen as part of the Saudi-led coalition.

Sudanese armed forces

Affiliates/allies
Collaborates with paramilitary forces (e.g. the RSF) and the National Intelligence and Security Service (NISS), which collectively make up the Sudanese security apparatus.

Resources/capabilities
Mostly financed from the state budget. Additional revenue is generated by producing and trading arms and ammunition through the state-run Sudanese Military Industrial Corporation (MIC). The armed forces have recently acquired aircraft, artillery and tanks from Russia and China.

Rapid Support Forces (RSF)

Strength
10,000–40,000 combatants.

Areas of operation
Primarily active in the capital, Khartoum, and the peripheral regions of Darfur, South Kordofan and Blue Nile. Additional forces active in southern Libya and Yemen.

Leadership
General Mohamed Hamdan Dagalo (Hemeti) heads the RSF and the transitional sovereign council. His extensive political influence and personal wealth make him one of the most powerful individuals in Sudan.

Structure
After being formally integrated into the Sudanese armed forces and removed from the NISS in 2017, the RSF continued to operate as a semi-autonomous force.

History
The RSF is a paramilitary group set up by the government in 2013 to fight anti-regime rebel groups. It is mainly composed of former Arab pastoralist militias (predominantly the Janjaweed) involved in the Darfur conflict.

Objectives
No clear ideological objectives. Supportive of government goals under Bashir, through counter-insurgency, bombardments and scorched-earth operations in the conflict areas. Since Bashir's ousting, the group has focused on law enforcement.

Opponents
Rebel groups in Darfur and the Two Areas.

Affiliates/allies
The RSF and the Sudanese armed forces have maintained a contentious though relatively stable alliance since the fall of Bashir's regime. Hemeti maintains ties with General Khalifa Haftar in Libya and the Popular Front for the Renaissance of Central African Republic (FPRC) in the CAR, as well as with Saudi Arabia and the United Arab Emirates.

Resources/capabilities
Income derived from the state budget; exporting gold from Hemeti's mines; and from mercenary activities in Yemen and Libya.

Sudan Liberation Movement/Army–Abdel Wahid al-Nur (SLM/A–AW)

Strength
1,000–2,000 active fighters.

Areas of operation
Its traditional stronghold of Jebel Marra. Its territory has shrunk considerably after clashes with government forces in recent years.

Leadership
Founder Abdel Wahid al-Nur still heads the group. He has lived in self-imposed exile in France and Kampala since 2006 and his influence among members has waned. In May 2019, factions within the group challenged Nur's leadership and attempted to remove him from power. General Commander Abdelgadir Abdelrahman Ibrahim ('Gaddura') leads the military branch.

Structure
The SLM/A–AW is one of two main SLM/A factions (the other is led by Minni Minnawi). Despite Gaddura's presence, Nur's long-term absence has blurred the group's chain of command and overall cohesion. The SLM/A–AW is now composed of loosely coordinated local groups.

History
The SLM/A formed in 2002 and split in 2006 when Nur rejected the Darfur Peace Agreement. The group then established itself in the Jebel Marra area in Darfur. Members are predominately Fur, one of the largest non-Arab ethnic groups in Darfur.

Objectives
The SLM/A–AW is the only active armed group operating in Darfur. Before April 2019, it sought the removal of Bashir and the establishment of a secular and decentralised governance system. The faction has refused to engage in peace talks with the transitional authorities as it considers them to be a continuation of the Bashir regime.

Opponents
Despite signing a three-month ceasefire agreement with the government in September 2018, the SLM/A–AW has repeatedly clashed with government forces and the RSF and publicly rejected the Transitional Military Council.

Affiliates/allies
Member of the Sudan Revolutionary Front alliance. The SLM/A–AW has reportedly received military support from the Justice and Equality Movement (JEM), South Sudan and Uganda.

Resources/capabilities
The SLM/A–AW enforces a taxation system in the areas under its control in Jebel Marra, but its territory is shrinking. The group also relies on ammunition seized after clashes with the Sudanese armed forces and the RSF.

Sudan Liberation Movement/Army–Minni Minnawi (SLM/A–MM)

Strength
800–1,000 fighters, predominantly active in Libya.

Areas of operation
No territorial presence in Sudan but has established the largest Darfuri presence in Libya, where it fights alongside the LNA.

Leadership
Headed by Suliman Arcua Minnawi, more commonly known as Minni Minnawi.

Structure
Composed primarily of ethnic Zaghawa fighters. The exile of Minnawi in 2010 has affected command and control and led to multiple internal divisions. After suffering many defeats against government forces, the group fragmented and some troops moved into South Sudan and Libya.

History
The SLM/A–MM split in 2006 from the SLM/A when Minnawi signed the Darfur Peace Agreement with Khartoum and began working as senior assistant to Bashir. Minnawi moved to Juba in 2010 and the SLM/A–MM denounced the agreement and took up arms again.

Objectives
Like the rest of the SRF, the group called for the dissolution of the Islamist ruling party (NCP), the ousting of Bashir and the establishment of a secular and liberal state. Involved in peace talks with transitional government.

Opponents
Bashir's government and the national security forces. Involved in peace talks with transitional government.

Affiliates/allies
Member of the SRF alliance with close ties to the JEM. Military partnership with General Khalifa Haftar's LNA in Libya.

Resources/capabilities
The Libyan National Army (LNA) is an important source of financing for the SLM/A–MM through mercenary and criminal activities.

Justice and Equality Movement (JEM)

Strength
Once among the strongest rebel groups in Darfur, the JEM now has approximately 100–200 active fighters.

Areas of operation
No territorial presence in Sudan but has active fighters in Libya.

Leadership
Headed by Gibril Ibrahim since 2012.

Structure
In September 2012, a group of JEM members defected and established a new faction led by Mohamed Bashar (JEM–Bashar), who signed a peace agreement with Khartoum in April 2013. After Bashar's assassination in 2015, Bakheit Abdallah Abdel-Karim 'Dabajo' has led the faction (JEM–Dabajo).

History
Founded in August 2001 by Darfuris affiliated with the Popular Congress Party (PCP), the JEM initially primarily comprised members of the Kobe Zaghawa community. The Islamist group has been a major actor in the Darfur conflict. It used to enjoy support from Chadian President Idriss Déby before it was expelled from Chad in 2010.

Objectives
Opposition to the Sudanese government. As a member of the SRF, the JEM called for Bashir's ousting. As an Islamist group, however, it has rejected the alliance's demands for a secular state. More broadly, it seeks to end the imbalance of power and wealth between the country's north and its peripheral regions.

Opponents
Sudanese government forces and militias, with which it has been under a unilateral ceasefire (signed collectively with the SRF) since October 2015.

Affiliates/allies
Member of the SRF.

Resources/capabilities
Before suffering heavy military losses, the JEM had seized air-defence systems, rocket-propelled grenades, hundreds of vehicles and at least two tanks from the Sudanese armed forces. The Bashir government said that the group received weapons, vehicles and fuel from the Chadian and Libyan governments.

Sudan People's Liberation Movement/Army North (SPLM/A–N)

Strength
Unknown.

Areas of operation
Hilu's faction operates primarily from its stronghold in South Kordofan but has also engaged in clashes in Blue Nile State. The group has an ongoing ceasefire with the government.

Leadership
Abdelaziz al-Hilu (SPLM/A–N al-Hilu) and Malik Agar (SPLM/A–N Agar).

Sudan People's Liberation Movement/Army North (SPLM/A–N)

Structure
Comprises two rival factions that generally operate in separate areas but have repeatedly engaged in clashes with each other. The largest faction is headed by Abdelaziz al-Hilu and based in South Kordofan. Malik Agar leads the smaller 'Blue Nile' faction.

History
Formed in the 1980s from a tribal self-defence militia opposed to Khartoum in the fight for self-determination in the south. The SPLM/A–N faction formed upon the independence of South Sudan.

Objectives
Topple Bashir, disband government forces and militias, and establish a secular, democratic state. Hilu demands self-determination, and Agar regional autonomy for South Kordofan and Blue Nile states. Involved in peace talks with transitional government.

Opponents
Sudanese government forces and paramilitaries. Despite both factions signing and renewing a unilateral ceasefire agreement, the group claims to have been subjected to attacks and detentions by the RSF.

Affiliates/allies
Member of the SRF coalition. South Sudan has reportedly supported the faction.

Resources/capabilities
Upon the independence of South Sudan in 2011, the SPLM/A sent thousands of soldiers, weapons and vehicles to the SPLM/A–N but most were seized in skirmishes with the Sudanese armed forces.

Drivers

Subnational and ethnic cleavages
The current rebellions in Darfur and the Two Areas originate from the grievances of marginalised non-Arab tribes over the political, cultural and socio-economic domination by Arab elites in central Sudan. The 30-year rule of Bashir's NCP centred on a national Muslim Arab identity founded by politician Hassan al-Turabi, who codified sharia law in Sudan in 1983 and enforced aggressive policies of Arabisation of non-Arabs. The regime used local governments across the country to spread Islam and handed over local services to Islamic organisations.[4] The alienation of peripheral tribes fuelled insurgent political agendas aimed at overthrowing the regime and establishing a multi-ethnic state. The 'New Sudan' ideology, promoted by SPLM founder John Garang in the 1980s, which advocated national reforms and ethnic diversity, still inspires the rebellion in the Two Areas.

Competition over land and resources
Sudan has a long history of intercommunal disputes over land and natural resources, which have often pitted nomadic herders against sedentary farmers. Competition over land and water has intensified since the second half of the twentieth century as the Sahel desert began spreading into Darfur.[5] In the 1970s, traditional local mechanisms of conflict resolution and land allocation began to be undermined as the central government increasingly enforced its authority. The influx of foreign pastoralists from Chad further contributed to this erosion.[6]

The conflict over resources intertwines with the fight of peripheral tribes against Khartoum: non-Arab tribes accuse the central government of reaping the benefits from natural resources, leaving only marginal returns for local communities. Darfuri armed groups accuse Khartoum of allowing Arab pastoralists to displace non-Arab farmers.[7] In Blue Nile and South Kordofan, rebels resist local taxation and denounce the government's failure to fairly distribute revenues from oil extraction in these areas among local populations.[8]

Regional relations
Relations between Khartoum and Juba have recently improved thanks to the role Khartoum played in negotiating the 2018 peace deal in South Sudan. Unresolved border issues and regional instability, however, continued to fuel the conflicts in Sudan. After South Sudan's independence in 2011, tensions remained between Khartoum and Juba over the oil-rich border area of Abyei. The two sides still disagree on Abyei's eligibility for a referendum. Khartoum exerts de facto administrative control, while the United Nations Interim Security Force in Abyei (UNIFSA) provides security in the region.

Khartoum and Juba have repeatedly accused each other of backing rebellions against their respective governments.[9] Similar accusations

Political Developments

The ouster of President Bashir

2019 was a turbulent year in Sudanese politics. Anti-government protests took place throughout 2018 following years of economic decay and violent repression but began to accelerate in December 2018. Further increases in bread and fuel prices and a severe cash shortage triggered the initial demonstrations. Citizens from all social groups – regardless of gender, ethnicity or religion – participated in protests against the regime's repressive policies. Opposition parties, labour unions, armed groups and civil society united under the umbrella of the Forces of Freedom and Change (FFC) on 1 January 2019.

Bashir's initial response was to deploy the Sudanese security forces – the use of force to curb protests being a trademark technique of his rule. But his allies, from the Gulf as well as in the national-security apparatus, turned against him after a five-day sit-in protest at the army headquarters in Khartoum that began on 6 April. The security forces ousted him on 11 April.[11] Following the coup, a military junta, the Transitional Military Council (TMC), initially headed by Gen. Ahmed Awad Ibn Auf, sought to consolidate power, but protests continued.

have been levelled at other regional states, Libya and Chad in particular, as the shared ethnicity of Darfuri tribes with Chadian groups and support of Arab militias in the region by former Libyan leader Muammar Gadhafi favoured the spread of insurrections across borders.[10] After the improvement in Sudan's relations with Chad in 2010 and the fall of Gadhafi in 2011, sources of support for Darfuri armed groups subsided. However, Darfuri rebels have been cooperating with Libyan militias since 2015, thereby accessing new equipment and personnel.

Lt-Gen. Abdel Fattah al-Burhan and his deputy, RSF commander Mohamed Hamdan Dagalo (Hemeti), replaced the junta's leadership after one day, on 12 April. Saudi Arabia and the UAE, increasingly seeking partnerships in the broader region to counter Qatari influence, were quick to show their support for the transitional government, pledging US$3 billion in aid only a few days after the military took control.

Protesters saw the TMC as a continuation of the previous regime, as Hemeti's RSF were among the worst perpetrators of atrocities in the conflict areas. Countrywide protests continued, now aimed at the new ruling council. The crackdown by the security forces continued and intensified following the TMC takeover. On 3 June, security forces killed more than 100 protesters while dispersing the ongoing sit-in at the army headquarters.[12]

Transitional government

After the coup, the TMC and opposition coalition the FFC engaged in several rounds of negotiations on the establishment of a civilian-led transitional government. On 15 May, the parties agreed to the formation of a three-year transitional government

Key Events in 2019

Political events

- **1 January**: The opposition alliance signs the Declaration of Freedom and Change.
- **22 February**: President Omar al-Bashir dissolves the government and declares a state of emergency.
- **11 April**: The Sudanese army ousts Bashir and establishes a Transitional Military Council (TMC).
- **20 April**: Talks begin between the civilian opposition and the TMC on a transitional period.

Military/Violent events

- **28 January**: President Omar al-Bashir extends a ceasefire in the Two Areas.
- **9 February**: The SRF extends the ceasefire for three months to allow humanitarian access.
- **3 June**: Security forces kill more than 100 protesters at the army headquarters in Khartoum.

headed by a sovereign council prior to holding elections. However, disagreements over the distribution of seats between military and civilian representatives ultimately led to the suspension of the talks on 15 May. Suspicions that the TMC intended to cling on to power grew and sparked further protests and general strikes. The largest protest, the 'march of millions', took place on 30 June, when tens of thousands of Sudanese citizens took to the streets, increasing pressure on the TMC to hand over power to civilians. Violence against protesters – particularly on 3 June when the sit-in protest at the army headquarters was dispersed – also increased pressure from the international community for negotiations to continue. In early June the African Union (AU) suspended Sudan's membership until the formation of a civilian-led transitional government. Following the instalment of the transitional government in September 2019, the AU lifted the suspension.

In July, FFC representatives and the TMC returned to the negotiating table under the auspices of an AU–Ethiopia-led mediation effort. In mid-July the parties reached a political agreement and drafted a constitutional declaration that laid out a legal framework for a 39-month transitional period. The parties agreed to an 11-member sovereign council composed of five military and five civilian appointees and one jointly appointed civilian. The military will lead the sovereign council for the first 21 months and the civilians for the following 18 months. After further negotiations, a civilian-led cabinet headed by economist Abdalla Hamdok took office on 8 September, embarking on the challenging task of stabilising Sudan's economy, preparing the country for democratic elections and engaging in peace talks with the armed groups in Darfur and the Two Areas. Peace talks resumed in December 2019 and led to the signing of a framework agreement setting out the topics to be discussed in direct peace negotiations between Darfur-based rebel groups and the transitional government. Talks in the Two Areas were however suspended until January 2020 because of disagreements over the role of religion within the state.

Military Developments

SLM/A–AW activity in Jebel Marra

The SLM/A–AW is the only active armed group with a territorial foothold in Darfur, though its presence was heavily reduced following clashes with government forces in 2018 and the first quarter of 2019 – mostly small-scale hit-and-run attacks in the Jebel Marra area of Central Darfur.[13] The SLM/A–AW attacked UN–African Union Hybrid Mission in Darfur (UNAMID) and humanitarian-organisation offices in the area where the group remains active. In July the group abducted six aid workers in two separate attacks in the vicinity of Golo, Central Darfur.

A rift between factions following either Mubarak Aldouk or Salih Borsa over Aldouk's plan to sign a peace agreement with the government sparked clashes that killed 42 combatants between 17 January

30 June
The 'march of millions' takes place across Sudan.

17 July
The civilian opposition and the TMC sign a political declaration detailing transitional political institutions.

20 August
The sovereign council takes office for a 39-month transitional period.

8 September
An 18-member cabinet headed by Prime Minister Abdalla Hamdok is sworn in.

28 November
The transitional government approves a law that will dismantle the former ruling NCP.

11 September
The sovereign council, the SRF and the SPLM–N al-Hilu sign the Juba Declaration, paving the way for peace talks.

28 October
Lt-Gen. Abdel Fattah al-Burhan issues a decree reforming the structure of the Sudanese armed forces.

28 December
The transitional government and Darfuri armed groups sign a framework agreement on issues to be discussed in peace talks.

29 December
An attack on a refugee camp in West Darfur kills dozens of people, leading to the suspension of the Juba peace talks.

and 26 March 2019, according to UNAMID reports.[14] The violence continued throughout 2019.

Juba peace talks

The ousting of Bashir created space for engagement between the transitional government and the armed groups, but relations between the parties were rocky at the start of the transitional period. Rebel-group coalition the SRF complained that the FFC did not prioritise peace in its transitional agreement with the TMC, despite the fact that the FFC and the SRF signed an agreement in July in Addis Ababa stipulating the demands that the FFC would present to the military part of the transitional government.[15]

In early September, South Sudan intervened as a mediator in the ongoing conflict, meeting with several armed groups and Hamdok. On 11 September, the sovereign council, the SRF,[16] the SPLM–North faction of Abdelaziz al-Hilu, the Beja Congress and Tahir Hajer's Sudan Liberation Forces Alliance signed the Juba Declaration, which provided a road map for negotiations and the establishment of confidence-building measures. Subsequent negotiations started in December. However, the most active armed group, the SLM–AW, remained absent from the negotiating table. The parties agreed on a cessation of hostilities for humanitarian purposes and the government committed to delivering humanitarian aid to the conflict-affected areas.

UNAMID withdrawal postponed

UNAMID delayed the drawdown of its forces, fearing the consequences of the changed political landscape on Darfur's stability. The UN Security Council extended UNAMID's mandate until 31 October 2020 and tasked it with focusing on curbing violence in Jebel Marra. The mission will retain 4,050 military and 2,500 police personnel until at least 31 March when the Security Council will review its mandate again.

Impact

Human rights

The security forces, particularly the RSF, dispersed protests violently throughout the year, using tear gas and rubber bullets, mostly in Khartoum and in Darfur. Violence against protesters increased when the TMC took over after ousting Bashir. The opposition Central Committee of Sudan Doctors, an association that has recorded injuries and fatalities throughout the protests, estimated that 246 people had been killed by mid-July (when the wave of major protests had ended).[17] Furthermore, many journalists were arrested and detained. Reporters Without Borders reported in February that at least 79 journalists had been arrested during the first two months of protests.[18]

Humanitarian

Despite a decline in violence, humanitarian issues persisted in conflict-affected areas, particularly internal displacement, floods, inflation and challenges to aid delivery. The fighting between government forces and the SLM/A–AW in early 2019 caused the displacement of at least 2,600 people from northern Jebel Marra to Kurmul and Thurragway villages in central Jebel Marra.[19]

The government and armed groups have repeatedly disagreed over the routes for aid delivery, limiting access to the conflict areas, particularly those under the control of the SPLM–N factions and sporadically the SLM/A–AW areas in central Jebel Marra. The Juba Declaration included a provision on opening rebel-held territories to humanitarian organisations. In late October, the executive director of the World Food Programme (WFP) visited Kauda, a rebel-held city in South Kordofan, to discuss humanitarian-aid access with the SPLM–N. This was the first UN humanitarian mission in more than eight years to reach the area.

Severe flooding in August exacerbated the humanitarian situation, affecting 364,000 people[20] and causing a cholera outbreak in central and southern Sudan. The continued inflation of prices of basic commodities has contributed to increased levels of food insecurity in Sudan. In November 2019 the UN identified 9.3m people as needing humanitarian assistance, up from 5.7m in January 2019.

However, the changing political and military landscape also provided a new opening for

LEGISLATIVE COUNCIL

Will consist of a maximum of 300 members. The opposition Forces of Freedom and Change (FFC) will appoint 67% and 33% will be selected by other groups that are not part of the FFC. The legislative council had not been formed by the end of 2019. In the meantime, the sovereign council and the cabinet will exercise legislative powers.

SOVEREIGN COUNCIL

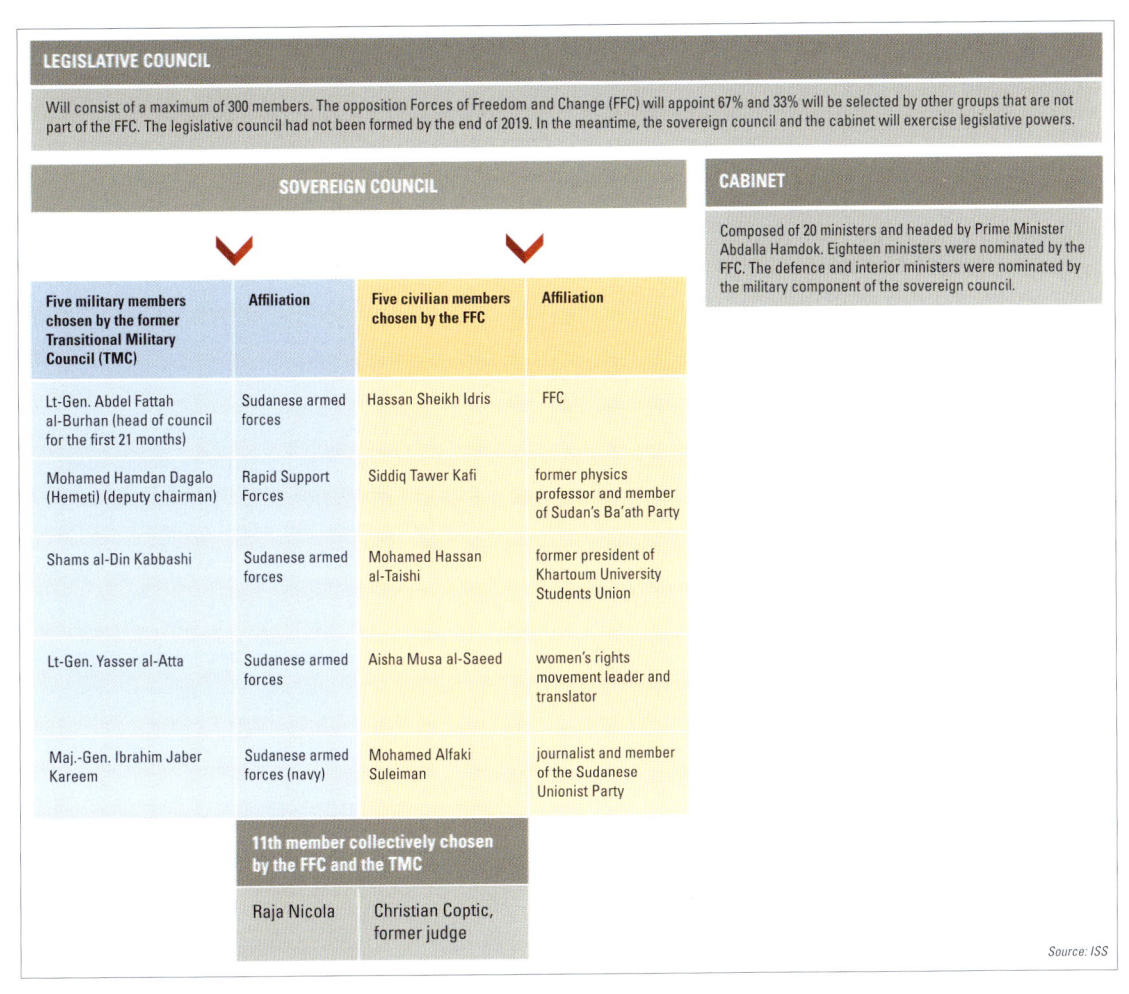

Five military members chosen by the former Transitional Military Council (TMC)	Affiliation	Five civilian members chosen by the FFC	Affiliation
Lt-Gen. Abdel Fattah al-Burhan (head of council for the first 21 months)	Sudanese armed forces	Hassan Sheikh Idris	FFC
Mohamed Hamdan Dagalo (Hemeti) (deputy chairman)	Rapid Support Forces	Siddiq Tawer Kafi	former physics professor and member of Sudan's Ba'ath Party
Shams al-Din Kabbashi	Sudanese armed forces	Mohamed Hassan al-Taishi	former president of Khartoum University Students Union
Lt-Gen. Yasser al-Atta	Sudanese armed forces	Aisha Musa al-Saeed	women's rights movement leader and translator
Maj.-Gen. Ibrahim Jaber Kareem	Sudanese armed forces (navy)	Mohamed Alfaki Suleiman	journalist and member of the Sudanese Unionist Party

11th member collectively chosen by the FFC and the TMC

Raja Nicola	Christian Coptic, former judge

CABINET

Composed of 20 ministers and headed by Prime Minister Abdalla Hamdok. Eighteen ministers were nominated by the FFC. The defence and interior ministers were nominated by the military component of the sovereign council.

Source: ISS

Figure 1: Sudan's 39-month transitional period government structure

the delivery of aid in conflict-affected areas. On 18 December 2019, the WFP carried out its first food-distribution operation since 2011 in the conflict-affected Yabus area, Blue Nile State.

Social

The protests in Sudan were predominantly led by civil-society organisations and labour unions, notably umbrella group the Sudanese Professionals Association (SPA), which voiced demands for a more inclusive government. The labour unions mobilised followers across ethnic, religious and gender lines, exposing grievances shared across Sudanese society. The wide range of social groups involved in the protest movement was only partially reflected in the composition of the new government, however. Only two sovereign-council members are women and one is from the Copt minority community. Hamdok is from Kordofan, a reversal of the 30-year trend of leaders from central Sudan.

Several universities across Sudan functioned as flashpoints for protests by students and staff. The security forces' attempts to disperse the protests included targeting universities. On 27 June, the RSF detained many students from East Nile University College in Khartoum. At least seven universities suspended studies as a result of the insecurity, among them the large University of Khartoum, which only reopened in October. Soon after taking office, Hamdok dismissed 35 university vice chancellors to reduce the presence of officials with links to the former regime.

Economic

Inflation continued to peak in 2019, reaching 53.1% in August and hitting the remote conflict areas particularly hard.[21] Hopes remained high that the new government would stabilise and improve the economy. An economic emergency plan was introduced to address structural deficiencies, but much more is still required. Rehabilitating Sudan's economy will require significant international support. In August, Hamdok declared that the country needed US$8bn in foreign aid to cover import costs and economic recovery and another US$2bn to stop the currency spiralling.[22] The IMF is willing to support Sudan, conditional on a commitment to repay arrears of around US$16bn.

Relations with neighbouring and international partners

The political changes of 2019 provided an opportunity for Sudan to redefine its relations with international partners. The new regime realised it required the support of regional powers and the international community to address the multiple transitional challenges and sought to balance its developmental goals with broader geopolitical agendas.

Saudi Arabia and the UAE were quick to announce their support for the TMC after Bashir was ousted, offering it an aid package of US$3bn. While this support could be a move to counter the influence of rivals Qatar and Turkey in Sudan, keeping the TMC as a close ally also benefits Saudi Arabia's war efforts in Yemen, where RSF troops have been deployed since 2015. Protesters strongly opposed the 'meddling' by Gulf countries and obtained support from Saudi Arabia and the UAE for the AU–Ethiopia-led mediation following the events of 3 June in Khartoum.

Various Western governments – traditionally wary of engaging with Sudan, given its designation by the US Department of State as a sponsor of terrorism – welcomed the transition and expressed support. For example, France offered to organise a conference on Sudan's debt if the US lifted its sanctions. Hamdok's visit to the US towards the end of 2019 – the first visit to Washington by a Sudanese head of state since 1985 – indicated a first step towards rapprochement between the US and Sudan.

Trends

Political trajectories

Organising elections in three years will be challenging for a government apparatus that ruled with little opposition and dominated economic and security decision-making for 30 years. Dismantling this system will face resistance from actors who have personally benefited from it. The most immediate risk to a democratic transition in Sudan will be the military's consolidation of power during its time at the helm of the sovereign council. Hemeti, a member of the council who has numerous vested business and security interests in the country (his troops serve as mercenaries in conflicts in Libya and Sudan and he and his brother own gold mines across Sudan), may try to sideline and divide the civilian forces on the council. While Hemeti officially claims otherwise, he has so far demonstrated little commitment to a future civilian-led government. Another risk could emerge from Islamist allies of Bashir, who are currently being sidelined. The dissolution of the former ruling NCP has fostered resentment among the party's supporters, who took to the streets in December in support of Bashir.

Prospects for peace

The rise to power of RSF commander Hemeti presents a serious challenge to the peace process set up by the Juba Declaration. Hemeti's troops stand accused of carrying out attacks after signing the declaration, thereby reneging on agreed confidence-building measures. In October, the SPLM/A–N al-Hilu suspended negotiations with the transitional government after an attack by the RSF in South Kordofan.[23]

The other main conflict-related risks come from the SLM/A–AW, and from SLM/A–MM and JEM-affiliated mercenaries returning from southern Libya, where they conduct mercenary activities for the LNA led by Khalifa Haftar. The resources and training gained there would potentially allow these groups to resume their fight upon their return to Darfur.

The SLM/A–AW has rejected the transitional government as not genuinely civilian. The group, the only one still regularly clashing with state forces in Darfur, has also boycotted the ongoing talks in Juba. Feelings of exclusion, coupled with perceptions of the current government as a continuation of the Bashir regime, fuel resentment towards a transition led by a body including the RSF and create fertile ground for further hostilities.

Despite significant challenges, on 28 December Darfur-based armed groups and the transitional government signed a framework agreement that demonstrated commitment from both sides of the conflict to peace talks. The prospect of peace in the Two Areas looks less likely, as the SPLM–N al-Hilu and the government have yet to reach an agreement due to outstanding disagreements over the relationship between religion and the state. Talks are expected to continue in January 2020.

Strategic implications and global influences

The political transition will enable Sudan to rethink its role in the region and provide opportunities for other countries to (re-)engage with it, as in the case of the financial support from the UAE and Saudi Arabia. The Gulf countries will continue to pursue a close alliance with Sudan given its strategic importance to them as a Red Sea state, and to avoid the return of Islamist parties to power. Sudan will also likely increase its ties to Western governments, most notably the US. Its removal from the sponsors-of-terrorism list and shedding its status as an international pariah would give Sudan access to much-needed debt relief. Hamdok's visit to the US in November did not result in Sudan's removal from the list but provided a positive basis for rapprochement between the two countries.

Notes

[1] The Darfur-based armed groups engaging in talks with the transitional sovereign council include the Sudan Liberation Movement–Minni Minnawi (SLM–MM), Justice and Equality Movement (JEM), Sudan Liberation Movement–Transitional Council (SLM–TC) and the Sudan Liberation Forces Alliance.

[2] The division between 'Arabs' and 'non-Arabs' in Sudan is the outcome of an ideological political construct that simplifies a complex history of flexible ethnic identities. See Alex de Waal, *Famine That Kills: Darfur, Sudan* (Oxford: Oxford University Press, 2005), p. iv.

[3] Estimates of the fatality count in Darfur vary widely. The former UN head of humanitarian affairs, John Holmes, said that an estimated 300,000 people have died as a result of the conflict.

[4] Alex de Waal, 'Sudan: The Turbulent State', in *War in Darfur and the Search for Peace* (Cambridge, MA: Harvard University Press, 2007), pp. 14–15.

[5] Jeffrey Mazo, 'Darfur: The First Modern Climate-change Conflict', in *Climate Conflict: How global warming threatens security and what to do about it* (Abingdon: Routledge for the IISS, 2009), pp. 73–86.

[6] United Nations Environment Programme (UNEP), 'Sudan: Post-Conflict Environmental Assessment', June 2007.

[7] *Ibid.*, p. 78.

[8] International Crisis Group, 'Sudan's spreading Conflict (I): War in South Kordofan', Africa Report No. 198, February 2013, p. i.

[9] United Nations Security Council Report, 'Sudan and South Sudan, June 2015 Monthly Forecast', 1 June 2015.

[10] Ahmad Sikainga, 'The World's Worst Humanitarian Crisis: Understanding the Darfur Conflict', *Origins: Current Events in Historical Perspective*, vol. 2, no. 5, February 2009.

[11] 'Abandoned by the UAE, Sudan's Bashir was destined to fall', Reuters, 3 July 2019.

[12] The opposition Central Committee of Sudan Doctors (CCSD) has documented fatalities throughout the protests. It put the number of fatalities on 3 June at 128. The Sudanese Ministry of Health put the number at 61.

[13] UN Security Council, 'African Union–United Nations Hybrid Operations in Darfur: Report of the Secretary-General', 10 April 2019.

[14] *Ibid.*

[15] See, for example, 'Sudan Revolutionary Front rejects Constitutional Declaration', Radio Dabanga, 5 August 2019.

[16] Excluding the Sudan Liberation Movement/Army led by Abdel Wahid al-Nur, who has rejected engagement with the sovereign council on the grounds that the new government is not 'civilian-led'.

[17] 'More than 240 people killed in Sudan uprising', Radio Dabanga, 20 July 2019.

[18] 'At least 79 journalists arrested in two months of protests in Sudan', Reporters Without Borders, 14 February 2019.

[19] UN Office for the Coordination of Humanitarian Affairs, 'Sudan Humanitarian Bulletin', no. 4, 25 March–12 May 2019.

[20] United Nations Office for the Coordination of Humanitarian Affairs, 'Sudan Situation Report', 26 September 2019.

[21] 'Sudan's inflation rate rises to 53.13 pct in Aug', Xinhua, 10 September 2019; 'Food prices soar in Sudan', Radio Dabanga, 19 July 2019.

[22] Khalid Abdelaziz, 'Exclusive: Sudan needs up to $10 billion in aid to rebuild economy, new PM says', Reuters, 24 August 2019.

[23] 'Sudan rebels suspend Juba peace talks after militia ambush in South Kordofan', Radio Dabanga, 16 October 2019.

Index

A

al-Abadi, Haider 167, 172
Abbas, Mahmoud 181–184, 187
Abdi, Mazlum Kobani 206, 216
Abdul-Mahdi, Adil 168, 171, 172, 173, 175
Abiy Ahmed 320–327
Abubakar, Atiku 333, 343, 344
Abu Dar 108, 110, 112
Abu Dhabi (UAE) 194, 196, 224
Abu Sayyaf Group (Philippines) 90, 104–114
Abyan (Yemen) 226, 228
Abyei 378, 385
Adamawa (Nigeria) 330, 332, 333, 338, 339, 340, 344, 346
Addis Ababa (Ethiopia) 320, 321, 324–388
Aden (Yemen) 222, 223, 224, 226–231
Afghanistan 7, 14, 19, 24, 25, 27, 139, 140, 204, 234–242, 259, 267, 272, 276–279, 282
   Afghan National Defense and Security Forces 237, 238
   Bonn Conference 237, 238
African Union 196, 198, 293, 298, 299, 303, 326, 332, 360, 362, 367, 381, 387, 390
   Mission in Somalia 360, 361, 362, 366, 367
Agar, Malik 384, 385
Aguelhok (Mali) 352, 356
Akar, Hulusi 205, 215
Al-Bukamal (Syria) 204, 211
Aleppo (Syria) 20, 202, 203, 204, 209, 212
Algeria 24, 27, 195, 198, 199
Al-Islah (Yemen) 224, 225, 226
Aliyev, Ilham 138, 140, 142, 143
All Burma Students' Democratic Front (Myanmar) 93, 94
Allied Democratic Forces (DRC) 309, 311, 316
al-Qaeda 15, 109, 168, 169, 193, 205, 224, 236, 238, 268, 239, 276, 277, 282, 351, 361, 362
al-Qaeda in the Arabian Peninsula 224, 225
al-Qaeda in the Islamic Maghreb 191, 192, 193, 194, 239, 348, 351, 356
al-Shabaab (Somalia) 19, 32, 239, 326, 327, 360–368
Amazonas (Brazil) 41, 44
Ambazonia Defence Forces (Cameroon) 289, 290, 291, 295, 297, 309, 311, 315–318
Amhara (Ethiopia) 320–326
Amnesty International 47, 339, 344, 366
Amsterdam (Netherlands) 117, 121
Anantnag (India) 266, 268, 271
Anbar (Iraq) 167, 168, 169, 170, 173–176
Andhra Pradesh (India) 245–248, 250
Anglophone Self Defence Council (Cameroon) 289, 290, 291, 293
Angola 318
Ansar al-Sharia (Yemen) 224, 225, 226
Ansar Dine (Mali) 348, 351
Ansar Ghazwat-ul-Hind (India) 267, 268, 271
al-Ansari, Abu Jafar 160, 163
Ansar Khalifah Philippines 105, 106, 107, 108, 114
Ansarul Islam (Mali) 349, 350, 351
Ansarullah (Yemen) 6, 20, 173, 222–232
Antioquia (Colombia) 51, 52, 54, 55, 56, 57
Applied Economic Research Institute (Brazil) 45, 49
Aquino III, Benigno 105, 117

Arab League 184, 211
Arab Movement of Azawad–Plateforme (Mali) 352, 353
Arab Spring 159, 223
Arakan Army (Myanmar) 92–102
Arakan Liberation Party (Myanmar) 93, 95
Arauca (Colombia) 52, 54
Argentina 43
Arias, Jaime 56, 58
Arish (Egypt) 158, 159, 161, 162, 164
Armenia 136, 138–145
Arunachal Pradesh (India) 253–261, 263
Asia Foundation 239, 240
al-Assad, Bashar 16, 17, 171, 201–212, 220
Assam (India) 252–261, 263
Association of Southeast Asian Nations 131, 132
Atlas of Violence 45, 46
Aung San Suu Kyi 93, 94, 97, 98, 99, 100
Austria 31, 35
Azad Jammu and Kashmir (Pakistan) 266, 268, 269, 273
Azerbaijan 136, 138–145

B

Badiya desert (Syria) 206, 209, 213
Baga (Nigeria) 331, 332
Baghdad (Iraq) 168, 169, 171–176, 211
al-Baghdadi, Abu Bakr 24, 109, 114, 169, 206, 209, 212, 238, 334
Baghouz (Iraq) 167, 202, 206, 209
Bahrain 185, 211
Baja California (Mexico) 19, 80, 81
Baku (Azerbaijan) 144
Balochistan (Pakistan) 5, 276–283
Balochistan Liberation Army (Pakistan) 276–283
Bamako (Mali) 348, 354, 356
Bamenda (Cameroon) 292, 294, 295, 296
Bandiagara (Mali) 352, 356, 357
Bangkok (Thailand) 90, 126, 128–132
Bangladesh 97, 100, 101, 102, 259, 268
Bangsamoro Islamic Armed Forces (Philippines) 107, 111
Bangsamoro Islamic Freedom Fighters (Phiippines) 104–112, 114
Bangui (CAR) 299, 302, 304, 305, 306
Banguingui (Philippines) 105, 112
Bankass (Mali) 352, 356, 357
Baramulla (India) 267, 268
Barisan Revolusi Nasional (Thailand) 90, 126–129, 131–134
Barisan Revolusi Nasional–Coordinate (Thailand) 128, 129
al-Barnawi, Abu Musab 330, 331, 333
Barrio 18 (El Salvador) 61, 62, 64
al-Bashir, Omar 286, 378, 381–386, 388, 390
Basilan (Philippines) 105, 106, 109, 110, 112, 114
Basra (Iraq) 168, 173, 174, 175
Bayda (Yemen) 224, 225, 226
Belgium 121, 313, 314
Beltrán Leyva Organisation (Mexico) 79, 80
Benghazi (Libya) 190, 192, 195
Beni (DRC) 311, 315, 316, 317
Benin 331, 341, 359
Benue (Nigeria) 338–342, 344, 345
Berlin (Germany) 131, 132

Bhat, Zakir Rashid 267, 271
Biden, Joe 151
Bihar (India) 245, 246, 248, 250
Bijapur (India) 248, 249
bin Laden, Osama 239
Bir al-Abd (Egypt) 159, 163, 164
Biya, Paul 289, 292, 293, 296, 297
Blue Nile (Sudan) 381–385, 389
Bogotá (Colombia) 52, 56, 58
Boko Haram (Nigeria) 17, 19, 31, 293, 296, 329–337, 339, 341, 342, 345, 349
Bolivia 42, 43, 44
Bolsonaro, Jair 40, 46, 49
Borno (Nigeria) 330–336
Bosnia-Herzegovina 17
Bouar (CAR) 303, 305, 306
Bozizé, François 299, 302, 304, 306, 307
Braga, Wellington da Silva 43
Brazil 38, 40–45, 48, 49, 50, 53
B'Tselem 178, 186
Buea (Cameroon) 292, 294, 295, 296
Buhari, Muhammadu 329–334, 336, 337, 338, 341–345
Bukele, Nayib 60, 62–67
Bukidnon (Philippines) 120, 122
Buratai, Tukur Yusuf 330, 341
al-Burhan, Abdel Fattah 382, 386, 387
Burkina Faso 334, 336, 347–351, 353, 356, 357, 358, 359
Burundi 286, 309, 311, 313, 316, 318, 319, 362, 367
Bush, George W. 184

C

Cairo (Egypt) 162, 163, 198
Calderón, Felipe 76, 77, 84
California (US) 61, 69, 77, 80
Cameroon 5, 7, 31, 286–300, 303, 305, 306, 330–336, 341, 346
  Ambazonia Governing Council 289, 290, 291, 293
  Interim Government of Ambazonia 289, 290, 291, 293, 294, 295, 297
  Major National Dialogue 289, 293, 295, 296
Camp David (US) 236, 241
Camp David Peace Accords 161
Camp David Summit 184
Canada 26, 34, 77, 84, 293
Caquetá (Colombia) 53, 56
Castro, Fidel 53
Catatumbo (Colombia) 53, 54, 57, 58
Cauca (Colombia) 51, 52, 53, 54, 55, 57
Ceará State (Brazil) 38, 40, 41, 42, 44, 45, 46, 47, 48, 49, 50
Celebes Sea 113, 114
Central African Patriotic Movement (CAR) 299, 301, 302
Central African Republic 7, 31, 286, 296, 298–307, 383
Central Equatoria (S Sudan) 369–377, 379
Chad 14, 31, 191, 192, 194, 198, 296, 299–303, 305, 306, 330, 331, 332, 334, 341, 346, 349, 350, 356, 384, 385, 386
Chhattisgarh (India) 245–250
Chihuahua (Mexico) 81, 84
Chile 268
China 5, 20, 21, 49, 67, 78, 80, 90, 94, 97, 98, 99, 101, 102, 118, 130, 184, 195, 211, 234, 259, 265, 272, 273, 275, 276, 279–283, 368, 371, 383
Chin National Front (Myanmar) 93, 95
Chin State (Myanmar) 93, 95, 96, 99, 100
Chocó (Colombia) 52, 53, 54, 56, 57
Cilo, Sahin 206, 216
Cirillo Swaka, Thomas 371, 372, 375, 379
Civilian Joint Task Force 330, 331, 332
Clement, Noel 105, 117
Clinton, Bill 184
Clinton, Hillary 184
Coahuila (Mexico) 78, 81, 84
Cold War 52

Collective Security Treaty Organisation 139, 141
Colombia 6, 14, 38, 42, 43, 51–59, 77, 78, 79, 83, 120
Communist Party of India–Maoist (India) 234–251
Conseil du Commandement Militaire pour la Salut de la République (Libya) 191, 198
Cooperation for the Development of Congo (DRC) 310, 317, 318
Coordination of the Movement of Azawad (Mali) 348, 352, 353, 355
Copán (Honduras) 69, 70
Córdoba (Colombia) 54, 57
Cotabato (Philippines) 90, 106, 109, 110, 111, 112
Côte d'Ivoire 358, 359
Cox's Bazar (Bangladesh) 101, 102
Croatia 268
Cuba 53
Culiacán (Mexico) 76, 77, 85
Cyrenaica (Libya) 190, 193, 198

D

Dagalo, Mohamed Hamdan 383, 386, 390
Dakar (Mali) 349
Damascus (Syria) 180, 204, 208, 210, 211
Dan Na Ambassagou (Mali) 352, 353, 356, 357
Dantewada (India) 247, 248
Darfur (Sudan) 306, 381–385, 387, 388, 390, 391
Davao (Philippines) 111, 120
Deir ez-Zor (Syria) 204, 211, 213
Democratic Forces for the Liberation of Rwanda (DRC) 312, 313, 315
Democratic Karen Benevolent Army (Myanmar) 93, 95
Democratic Republic of the Congo 7, 31, 286, 287, 299, 301, 303, 306–314, 316, 317, 318, 319, 377
  Common Front for Congo 308, 314, 315, 316, 318
  Ginbot 7 321, 323, 324
  Ogaden National Liberation Front 321, 322, 323
Deraa (Syria) 203, 204
Dera Ismail Khan (Pakistan) 281, 282
Derna (Libya) 190, 192, 193
Diffa (Niger) 331, 332, 334, 336, 349
Diyala (Iraq) 167, 168, 169, 173, 176
Djibouti 327, 362
Djugu (DRC) 310, 317
Donbas (Ukraine) 19, 136, 146, 147, 149–154
Donetsk (Ukraine) 146, 147, 148, 151, 153, 154
Donetsk People's Republic (Ukraine) 147–154
Douala (Cameroon) 296, 349
drug-trafficking organisations 68, 70, 72, 76, 77, 78, 81–87
Dubai (UAE) 368
Duque, Iván 51, 52, 53, 56, 57, 58, 59
Durazo, Alfonso 82, 85
Duterte, Rodrigo 105, 108–113, 116, 117, 119–124

E

East Jerusalem 179, 181, 182, 185, 186
ebola 286, 309, 315, 317, 318, 319
Ebrahim, Al Haj Murad 104, 105, 107, 109, 110, 111, 113
Economic Community of West African States 348, 357, 358
Edo (Nigeria) 338, 341, 344
Egypt 7, 24, 31, 156, 158, 159, 160, 161, 163, 164, 165, 179, 181, 184, 185, 187, 190, 192, 198, 379
  Directorate of Military Intelligence 160, 162, 165
  Supreme Council of the Armed Forces 159, 160, 162
Ekiti (Nigeria) 338, 341, 344
El Salvador 17, 34, 38, 60, 61, 62, 63, 64, 65, 66, 67, 69, 71, 72, 74
El Tambo (Colombia) 55, 57
El Tarra (Colombia) 55, 58
Equatoria (S Sudan) 369, 371, 373
Erbil (Iraq) 173, 174
Erdogan, Recep Tayyip 23, 26, 34, 195, 199, 205, 208, 209, 211, 215, 217, 218, 219
Erekat, Saeb 184, 185

Eringeti (DRC) 311, 316
Eritrea 322, 323, 326, 327
Escobar, Pablo 45
Esperon, Hermogenes 120, 121
Estrada, Joseph 117
Ethiopia 164, 286, 320–328, 361, 362, 363, 365, 379, 381, 387, 390
Ethiopian People's Revolutionary Democratic Front 321, 322, 323, 324, 326, 327
Euphrates River 23, 206, 209
Eurasian Economic Union 141
European Union 6, 26, 27, 33, 34, 35, 100, 120, 121, 122, 123, 124, 147, 149, 150, 160, 164, 165, 179, 180, 184, 187, 209, 210, 214, 293, 303, 304, 305, 327, 349, 362, 370, 379
ExxonMobil (US) 173, 174

F
Fatah 180, 186, 187
Federally Administered Tribal Areas (Pakistan) 275, 276, 279, 280, 281, 282
Félix, Ágatha 47, 48
Fezzan (Libya) 193, 194, 197
Financial Action Task Force 281, 283
First Command of the Capital (Brazil) 40, 41, 42, 43, 44, 46, 47, 49, 50
Fizi (DRC) 313, 317
Fortaleza (Brazil) 41, 48
France 17, 27, 139, 146, 151, 160, 174, 190, 194, 195, 196, 198, 203, 217, 219, 290, 292, 293, 296, 297, 299, 305, 322, 330, 332, 341, 348–357, 358, 383, 390
    Operation Barkhane 348, 349, 350, 351, 353, 356
Free Syrian Army (Syria) 204, 205, 209, 216
Friends of Friends (Brazil) 41, 42, 43, 44

G
G5 Sahel Joint Task Force 6, 293, 349, 350, 351, 355, 358
Gadchiroli (India) 248, 249
Gadhafi, Muammar 14, 16, 190, 191, 199, 352, 386
Gai, Taban Deng 370, 375
Galmudug (Somalia) 361, 362, 364, 365
Galvez, Carlito 111, 120
Gao (Mali) 348, 349, 351, 352, 353
Gaza 159, 160, 161, 165, 178–183, 185, 186
Germany 146, 151, 160, 196, 217, 219, 293, 312
Ghani, Ashraf 237, 241
Gharyan (Libya) 192, 194, 195, 197, 198
Golan Heights 179, 181, 182, 209
Gorbachev, Mikhail 138
Gossi (Mali) 349, 352
Gourma (Mali) 348, 349, 351, 352, 356
Government of the Democratic Republic of Nagaland/Naga National Council–Non-Accord (India) 254, 256
Griffiths, Martin 223, 227
Group to Support Islam and Muslims (Mali) 347, 349, 350, 351, 353, 356, 359
Guanajuato (Mexico) 19, 78, 80, 86
Guardians of the State (Brazil) 40, 41, 42, 44, 46, 47
Guatemala 34, 61, 62, 63, 66, 68, 69, 71, 72, 74, 78, 79, 83
Guerrero (Mexico) 78, 79, 80, 81, 87
Guler, Yasar 205, 215
Gulf Cartel (Mexico) 78, 79
Gulf Clan (Colombia) 52, 53, 54, 56, 57
Gulf Cooperation Council 223
Guzmán, Joaquín 76, 78, 85
Guzmán, Ovidio 76, 78, 85
Gwadar (Pakistan) 275, 280, 281, 282, 283

H
Hadhramaut (Yemen) 224, 226
Hadi, Abdu Rabbu Mansour 169, 222–231
Haftar, Khalifa 16, 163, 189, 190, 191, 192, 194–199, 383, 384, 390

Haiti 70
Hama (Syria) 204, 209, 210
Hamas (PT) 179, 180, 182, 183, 185, 186, 187
Hamdok, Abdalla 378, 387, 388, 389, 390, 391
Haqqani network (Afghanistan) 238, 281
Haute-Kotto (CAR) 299, 300, 301
Haut-Mbomou (CAR) 299, 301
Hayat Tahrir al-Sham (Syria) 21, 203, 204, 205, 206, 208, 209, 210
Helmand (Afghanistan) 238, 278
Hernández, Juan Orlando 68, 70, 71, 73, 74
Hernández, Tony 70, 71, 73
High Council for Unity of Azawad (Mali) 352, 355
al-Hilu, Abdelaziz 384, 385
Hirshabelle (Somalia) 361, 362
Hizb-ul-Ahrar (Pakistan) 277, 278
Hizbullah (Lebanon) 20, 21, 174, 175, 179, 203, 204, 206, 209, 224
Hizbul Mujahideen (India) 266, 267, 268, 269
Homs (Syria) 203, 204
Honduras 34, 38, 61, 62, 66, 67, 68, 69, 70–75
al-Houthi, Abdul Malik 223, 224, 228
Hudaydah (Yemen) 222, 223, 224, 226, 227, 228, 229, 230, 231
Human Rights Watch 73, 132, 376
Hungary 31, 34, 150, 151

I
Idlib (Syria) 201, 202, 204, 205, 208–214, 216, 219, 220, 221
improvised explosive devices 19, 20, 99, 106, 107, 112, 116, 118, 120, 121, 122, 126, 127, 129, 130, 131, 132, 133, 158, 162, 170, 205, 244, 246, 248, 249, 273, 278, 279, 334, 351
Inates (Niger) 355, 356, 357
India 5, 14, 27, 95, 97, 98, 99, 101, 211, 234, 235, 239, 244–273
    Assam Rifles 254, 261, 262
    Bharatiya Janata Party 245, 248, 249, 250, 252, 253, 255, 259, 261, 269, 270, 273
    Border Security Force 254, 268
    Central Reserve Police Force 245–249, 254, 265, 268, 270, 271
    Citizenship (Amendment) Bill 252, 254, 259, 263, 260, 261
    Composite Dialogue Process 266, 269
    Constitution 259, 265, 266, 270, 273
        Article 370 265, 266, 269, 270, 272, 273
    Red Corridor 244, 245, 246, 247, 248, 250
Indonesia 25, 107, 109, 112, 113, 114, 129
intelligence, surveillance and reconnaissance 19, 20, 21, 179, 205, 215, 224, 226
Intergovernmental Authority on Development 327, 370, 374, 375, 379
internally displaced persons 92, 100, 104, 113, 117, 126, 138, 144, 146, 153, 158, 167, 174, 178, 190, 198, 202, 210, 214, 222, 236, 242, 245, 252, 265, 275, 286, 289, 298, 308, 317, 320, 321, 323, 326, 330, 335, 338, 344, 345, 347, 348, 357, 358, 360, 367, 369, 376, 382
International Committee of the Red Cross 17, 228
International Court of Justice 93, 99, 100, 367
International Criminal Court 99, 301, 303, 382
International Monetary Fund 162, 163, 283, 318, 327, 367, 378, 390
International Organization for Migration 35, 230, 321, 377
Interpol 25, 27, 122, 219
Iran 16, 20, 21, 139, 145, 156, 168, 169, 171, 173, 174, 175, 176, 179, 180, 187, 201–205, 207–213, 217, 223, 224, 226, 228, 229, 232, 281
    Islamic Revolutionary Guard Corps 21, 168, 169, 171, 203, 204, 206, 209
Iraq 6, 19, 20, 21, 23, 24, 25, 26, 27, 28, 109, 156, 157, 160, 164, 167–176, 179, 202, 204, 205, 206, 210, 211, 214, 215, 217–221, 239, 282
    Popular Mobilisation Units 20, 168, 169, 170, 171, 173, 174, 175
Irumu (DRC) 310, 317
ISIS Somalia 362, 363, 366
Islamic Jihad (PT) 180, 185
Islamic State 6, 14, 16, 20–28, 31, 32, 90, 104–109, 111–114, 118, 123, 134, 156–160, 164, 167–171, 173–175, 176, 189, 191–195, 199, 202–213, 216–219, 221, 223–226, 228, 234, 236, 238, 239, 241, 279, 282, 286, 309, 311, 314, 316, 318, 330, 331, 333, 334, 337, 351, 356, 362, 363

Islamic State in the Greater Sahara 347, 349, 350, 351, 353, 355, 356, 357, 359
Islamic State in Yemen 224, 225, 226, 228, 229, 231
Islamic State – Khorasan Province 236, 237, 238, 239, 241, 242, 277, 280, 282
Islamic State – Pakistan Province (Pakistan) 277, 279, 280, 282
Islamic State West Africa Province 286, 329–337, 356, 357
Israel 20, 34, 94, 127, 156, 157, 159, 160, 161, 178–183, 185, 186, 187, 201, 202, 207, 208, 209, 213, 271, 332
Italy 17, 19, 31, 35, 190, 195, 196, 199, 268
Ituri (DRC) 308, 309, 310, 314, 316, 317

J

Jabhat al-Nusra (Iraq) 205, 207
Jalisco (Mexico) 78, 81, 82
Jalisco New Generation Cartel (Mexico) 78, 79, 80, 81
Jamaat-e-Islami (Pakistan) 266, 269, 270
Jamaat-ul-Ahrar (Pakistan) 276, 278
Jammu and Kashmir (India) 248, 265, 266, 268, 269, 270, 271, 272, 273
Jammu and Kashmir Liberation Front 266, 270
Janjaweed (Sudan) 382, 383
Japan 19, 108, 174
Jaysh-e-Mohammad (Pakistan) 266, 267, 268, 270
Jebel Marra (Sudan) 381, 382, 383, 387, 388
Jerusalem 178, 179, 181, 185, 186, 187
Jharkhand (India) 245, 246, 247, 248, 250
Jolo (Philippines) 105, 110, 112
Jordan 143, 167, 175, 178, 184, 195, 210, 211
Juarez Cartel (Mexico) 78, 85
Juba (S Sudan) 369, 370, 373, 375, 378, 379, 381, 384, 385, 387, 388, 390
Jubaland (Somalia) 361, 362, 365
Jufra (Libya) 191, 193, 197
Justice and Equality Movement (S Sudan) 370, 383, 384, 390

K

Kabila, Joseph 308, 309, 314, 315, 318
Kabul (Afghanistan) 237, 240, 241
Kachin (Myanmar) 93, 94, 95, 96, 100, 102
Kachin Independence Army (Myanmar) 94, 95, 96, 98
Kaduna (Nigeria) 338, 339, 340, 341, 342, 344, 345
Kagame, Paul 309, 312, 313
Kampala (Uganda) 309, 383
Kamuina Nsapu (DRC) 314, 317, 319
Kana, Ali 191, 197
Kandahar (Afghanistan) 237, 238, 278
Kangleipak Communist Party–Lamphel (India) 255, 257
Kani Brigade (Libya) 192, 195, 197
Kara (CAR) 301, 306
Karbala (Iraq) 169, 173, 175
Karen National Liberation Army–Peace Council (Myanmar) 93, 95
Karen National Union (Myanmar) 93, 94, 95, 98
Karen State (Myanmar) 94, 95, 100
Kasai (DRC) 309, 310, 319
Kashmir Valley 266, 267, 271, 272
Kataib Hizbullah (Iraq) 20, 174, 175
Katsina (Nigeria) 338, 339, 340, 341, 342, 343, 344, 346
Katumbi, Moise 314, 315
Kazakhstan 210
Kebbi (Nigeria) 339, 340, 344
Keïta, Ibrahim Boubacar 354, 355, 356
Kenya 326, 327, 360, 362, 364, 365, 367
Kerala (India) 248, 249, 250
Kerry, John 179, 185
Khalilzad, Zalmay 236, 241
Khamenei, Ali 209, 226
Khan, Imran 269, 281, 282
Khan Sheikhoun (Syria) 209, 210
Kharqamar (Pakistan) 275, 281
Khartoum (Sudan) 298, 301–305, 307, 375, 378, 382–386, 388, 389, 390

Khyber-Pakhtunkhwa (Pakistan) 275–283
Kidal (Mali) 348, 349, 352, 355, 356
Kiev (Ukraine) 150, 151, 154
Kiir, Salva 370–376, 378
al-Kilani, Abdel Rahman Hashim 192
King Abdullah II (Jordan) 184
Kinshasa (DRC) 310, 317, 318
Kirkuk (Iraq) 167, 168, 169, 170, 173, 174, 175
Kismayo (Somalia) 364, 366
Kivu (DRC) 309, 312, 314
Knights Templar Cartel (Mexico) 78, 80
Kogi (Nigeria) 339, 342
Kongsompong, Apirat 127, 130
Kordofan (Sudan) 381, 382, 383, 384, 385, 388, 389, 390
Koro (Mali) 352, 356, 357
Kosovo 5
Kuki National Organisation (India) 255, 256
Kurdish People's Protection Units (Syria) 16, 202–207, 209, 211, 212, 214, 215, 216, 218, 219, 221
  Women's Protection Units 206, 216
Kurdistan 16, 20, 168, 169, 170, 174, 202, 206, 207, 209, 211, 212, 214–219, 221
  Kurdistan Democratic Party 170
  Kurdistan Regional Government 217, 220
  Kurdistan Region of Iraq 168, 170
  Patriotic Union of Kurdistan 170
  Peshmerga 20, 168, 169, 170
Kurdistan Workers' Party (Turkey) 156, 205, 206, 207, 214–221
Kushner, Jared 183
Kuwait 175

L

Ladakh (India) 270, 271
Lahij (Yemen) 224, 226, 230
Lahu Democratic Union (Myanmar) 93, 95
Lake Chad 286, 329–337, 342, 346, 356
Lakes State (S Sudan) 375, 376
Lanao del Norte (Philippines) 108, 109
Lanao del Sur (Philippines) 105, 108, 109, 110, 112, 114
Laos 97
Lashkar-e-Taiba (India) 266, 267, 268
Latakkia (Syria) 204, 209
Lazaro Cardenas (Mexico) 78, 80
Lebanon 20, 143, 179, 180, 204, 212
Lebialem (Cameroon) 290, 295
Lelhari, Hameed 267, 271
von der Leyen, Ursula 327
Libya 14, 15, 16, 17, 24, 25, 27, 28, 34, 35, 156, 157, 159, 160, 163, 164, 165, 189–199, 352, 383, 384, 386, 390
  Government of National Accord 190–195, 197, 198, 199
  Libyan Armed Forces 190, 191, 195, 197, 198, 199
  Libyan National Army 16, 190–199, 384, 390
  Operation Flood of Dignity 189, 194, 196, 197, 198
Line of Contact (Armenia–Azerbaijan) 139, 140, 142, 143, 144, 147
Line of Control (India–Pakistan) 235, 265, 266, 268, 269, 270, 272, 273
Liptako (Mali) 348, 356, 357
Littoral Region (Cameroon) 291, 295
López Obrador, Andres Manuel 76, 77, 83, 84, 85, 86, 87
Loralai (Pakistan) 280, 281
Los Zetas Cartel (Mexico) 78, 79, 80, 81, 83
Luhansk (Ukraine) 146, 147, 148, 150, 151, 153, 154
Luhansk People's Republic (Ukraine) 147, 148, 149, 153, 154
Luna, García 84, 85
Luzon (Philippines) 118, 124

M

Machar, Riek 370, 371, 373–379
Macron, Emmanuel 194
Maduro, Nicolás 59

Maguindanao (Philippines) 105–112, 114
Mahagi (DRC) 310, 317
King Maha Vajiralongkorn (Thailand) 126, 130
Maharashtra (India) 245, 246, 248, 249
Mahrah (Yemen) 224, 226, 230
Mahwit (Yemen) 224, 230
Maiduguri (Nigeria) 286, 330, 333, 335, 336
Maïga, Soumeylou Boubèye 354, 355, 356
Mai-Mai (DRC) 312, 313
Malaysia 25, 106, 107, 109, 113, 114, 126, 127, 129, 131, 132, 134, 151, 281
Mali 6, 7, 14, 15, 334, 336, 337, 341, 347–359
Malong, Paul 372, 375
Mamlouk, Ali 207, 210
Manama (Bahrain) 183, 185, 187
Manbij (Syria) 208, 218, 219
Manila (Philippines) 117
Manipur (India) 95, 252–261, 263
Maradi (Niger) 343, 344
Mara Salvatrucha (El Salvador) 38, 60–75
Marawi (Philippines) 24, 25, 27, 105–109, 111, 112, 113, 114
Marcos, Ferdinand 105, 107, 117, 123
Marib (Yemen) 224, 225, 226
Márquez, Iván 52, 53, 55, 56, 57, 58
Marxism 52, 117, 119
Mathiang Anyoor (S Sudan) 370, 372
Mauritania 349, 350
Maute Group (Phiippines) 104–110, 112, 114
Mazar-e Sharif (Afghanistan) 237
Mbau (DRC) 311, 316
Médecins Sans Frontières 334, 336
Medellín Cartel (Colombia) 45, 78
Mediterranean Sea 35, 157, 165, 195, 199
Megawer, Khaled 160, 162, 165
Mehdiyev, Ramiz 141, 143
Mehsud, Daud 279, 280
Mehsud, Noor Wali 275, 277, 281, 282
Mekonnen, Seare 320, 322
Meme (Cameroon) 290, 291, 296
Ménaka (Mali) 349, 352
Meta (Colombia) 53, 56
Mexico 19, 34, 35, 38, 55, 61, 62, 66, 68, 69, 71, 72, 74–87
Mexico City (Mexico) 79, 82, 85
Mexico State (Mexico) 79, 80
Michoacán (Mexico) 78, 80, 81, 82
Michoacán Family Cartel (Mexico) 78, 80
Middle Belt (Nigeria) 330, 343
Min Aung Hlaing 94, 97, 99, 102
Mindanao (Philippines) 104–119, 122, 123, 124
Minnawi, Minni 383, 384
Misrata (Libya) 14, 15, 16, 190, 191, 192, 193, 197, 199
Misuari, Nur 105, 107, 108, 110, 111, 114
Modi, Narendra 248, 260, 269, 270, 271, 272, 273
Mogadishu (Somalia) 360, 361, 362, 363, 364, 365, 366
Mohamed, Mohamed Abdullahi 364, 367
Mongolia 101
Mon State (Myanmar) 93, 95
Mopti (Mali) 356, 357
Mora (Cameroon) 331, 332
Morocco 27, 112, 190
Moro Islamic Liberation Front (Philippines) 104–111, 113, 114
Moro National Liberation Front (Philippines) 105–111, 114
Morsi, Muhammad 159, 162, 163, 181
Mosul (Iraq) 168, 170, 173, 174
Movement for Oneness and Jihad in West Africa (Mali) 348, 351
Movement of Central African Liberators for Justice (CAR) 300, 301, 303, 305, 306, 307
Mubarak, Hosni 160, 184

Mudacumura, Sylvestre 312, 315
Mukallah (Yemen) 224, 226
Multinational Joint Task Force 293, 296, 329–335, 341
Murzuq (Libya) 192, 193, 194, 195, 197, 198
Muslim Brotherhood (Egypt) 159, 160, 180, 192, 193, 225
Myanmar 5, 90, 92–102, 234, 252, 253, 257, 259, 260, 262
   Federal Political Negotiation and Consultative Committee 95, 96, 97, 98, 99, 102
   Nationwide Ceasefire Agreement 93–99
Myanmar National Democratic Alliance Army 95, 96, 97, 98, 99

N

Nagaland (India) 95, 252–263
Naga National Council/Federal Government of Nagaland (India) 255, 256
Nagorno-Karabakh 6, 136, 138–145
Nairobi (Kenya) 360, 364, 365, 367
Najaf (Iraq) 169, 172, 174, 175
Nana-Mambéré (CAR) 305, 306
Narathiwat (Thailand) 126–132
Nariño (Colombia) 55, 57
Nasarawa (Nigeria) 338, 339, 340, 341, 342, 344, 345
Nasser, Gamal Abdel 159, 160
National Democratic Front of Bodoland–Progressive (India) 255, 259
National Democratic Front of Bodoland–Saoraigwra (India) 252, 255, 257, 260, 262
National Front for Liberation (Syria) 205, 216, 219
National Liberation Army (Colombia) 51–59
National Liberation Front (Syria) 203, 204, 205, 211
National Movement for the Liberation of Azawad (Mali) 348, 352
National People's Government of Nagaland/Naga National Council–Non-Accord (India) 255, 256
National Salvation Front–Thomas Cirillo (S Sudan) 370, 371, 372, 374, 375, 376, 377, 379
National Socialist Council of Nagaland–Khaplang (India) 95, 98, 99, 101, 252, 253, 255, 256, 257, 260, 261, 262
National Socialist Council of Nagaland–Khaplang/Khango Konyak (India) 255, 256, 257, 260, 261
National Socialist Council of Nagaland–Khaplang/Yung Aung (India) 252, 255, 257, 260, 262
National Socialist Council of Nagaland–Kitovi-Neokpao/Unification (India) 255, 256, 258, 260
National Socialist Council of Nagaland–Reformation (India) 253, 255, 256, 260, 261
National Socialist Council of Nagalim–Isak Muivah (India) 253–258, 260, 261, 262, 263
NATO 5, 6, 14, 15, 127, 139, 140, 156, 205, 215, 217, 218, 220, 221, 237, 238, 277
Naxalites (India) 244, 245, 247, 248, 250
N'Djamena (Chad) 305, 349
Nduma Defence of Renovated Congo (DRC) 312, 313
Negros Island (Philippines) 116, 118, 122, 123, 124
Negros Occidental (Philippines) 118, 120, 121, 122, 123
Negros Oriental (Philippines) 118, 120, 121, 122, 123, 124
Nepal 14
Netanyahu, Benjamin 178, 182, 183, 184, 185
Netherlands 55, 118, 122, 124
New Mon State Party (Myanmar) 93, 95, 99
New People's Army (Philippines) 90, 105, 116–124
New York (US) 73, 77, 78, 142
Nganzai (Nigeria) 334, 335
Ngoe, Andrew 291, 294
Ngujolo 310, 317
Niamey (Niger) 336, 349
Nicaragua 71
Niger 194, 330, 331, 334, 336, 341, 343, 344, 346–351, 353, 355, 356, 357, 358
Nigeria 7, 17, 19, 32, 286, 289, 290, 291, 296, 297, 303, 330–346
   National Livestock Transformation Plan 343, 344, 345, 346

Rural Grazing Area settlement 342, 343, 344, 345
9/11 236, 239, 266
Nineva (Iraq) 167–171, 173, 175, 176
Norte de Santander (Colombia) 51, 55, 57, 58
North American Free Trade Agreement 83, 84
North Cotabato (Philippines) 106, 109, 110, 112, 114
Northern Alliance (Myanmar) 94, 95, 96, 98
Northern Bahr el-Ghazal (S Sudan) 371, 372
Northern Family (Brazil) 40, 41, 44, 46, 47
North Kivu (DRC) 309, 311, 312, 313, 316, 317, 318
North Korea 281
North Sinai (Egypt) 158, 159, 160, 161, 162, 163, 164, 165
Northwest region (Cameroon) 288–292, 294, 295, 296, 340, 343
Norway 173, 174, 184, 208, 378
Noscué, Navides Chilhueso 56, 57
al-Nur, Abdel Wahid 381, 383
Nur, Mamman 333, 383

O

Obama, Barack 184, 207, 237
Odisha (India) 245, 246, 248, 249, 250
Ogossagou (Mali) 348, 356, 357
Olmert, Ehud 184
Omoa (Honduras) 69, 73
O Povo 41, 44
Orbán, Viktor 34
Organisation for Security and Co-operation in Europe 6, 139, 141, 143, 144, 151, 153
    Minsk Group 139, 141, 146, 151–154
Organization of American States 47, 48, 72
    Inter-American Commission on Human Rights 47, 70
Oromia (Ethiopia) 320, 321, 322, 325, 326
Oromo Liberation Army (Ethiopia) 320, 322, 325
Oromo Liberation Front (Ethiopia) 322, 325
Oslo (Norway) 117, 121
Oslo Accords 179, 181, 182, 184, 187
Osman, Abdirahman Omar 365, 366
Ouaka (CAR) 299, 305
Ouham-Pendé (CAR) 300, 304, 305, 306

P

P5 (DRC) 313, 316
Pakistan 7, 24, 27, 204, 234, 235, 237, 238, 239, 240, 259, 265–283
    China–Pakistan Economic Corridor 273, 275, 276, 277, 280, 283
Palermo (Italy) 195, 196
Palestinian Liberation Organization 184, 187
Palestinian Territories 156, 157, 165, 178–187
Panama 210
Pa-O National Liberation Organisation (Myanmar) 93, 96
Paraguay 42, 43, 49
Paris (France) 142, 151, 196
Pashinyan, Nikol 138, 139, 141, 142, 143, 144
Pashtun Tahaffuz Movement (Pakistan) 275, 279, 280, 281, 283
Patani United Liberation Organisation (Thailand) 127, 128, 129
Patikul (Philippines) 105, 110, 112, 113
Pattani (Thailand) 127–133
Peace and Solidarity Committee/National Democratic Alliance Association–East Shan State (Myanmar) 96
Peña Nieto, Enrique 76, 77, 84
Pence, Mike 211
People's Liberation Front of India 245, 246
Peru 43, 44
Peshawar (Pakistan) 240, 276, 277, 280
Petrivske (Ukraine) 146, 151, 153, 154
Philippines 14, 24, 25, 27, 90, 104–125, 268
    Autonomous Region in Muslim Mindanao 104, 105, 109, 110, 113, 114
    Bangsamoro Autonomous Region in Muslim Mindanao 104, 105, 107, 109, 110, 111, 113, 114
    Bangsamoro Organic Law 104, 105, 109, 110, 111, 114
    Bangsamoro Transition Authority 104, 110, 111, 113, 114
    Communist Party of the Philippines 116–124
    National Democratic Front of the Philippines 116, 117, 118, 120, 121, 122, 124
Plateau (Nigeria) 338, 339, 340, 341, 344, 345
Poland 147, 218
Pompeo, Mike 26, 183
Popular Front for the Renaissance in the Central African Republic 299–307, 383
Popular Liberation Army (Colombia) 52–58
Poroshenko, Petro 146, 149, 150, 151
Portugal 43, 49
Prayut Chan-o-cha 126, 130, 133
Puerto Rico 78
Pulwama (India) 265, 266, 267, 270, 271, 272, 273
Punjab (Pakistan) 267, 268, 278, 279, 282
Puntland (Somalia) 361, 362, 363, 367, 368
Pure Third Command (Brazil) 41, 42, 43, 44, 45
Pushilin, Denis 148, 150, 154, 208, 211, 304
Putumayo (Colombia) 52, 53, 55

Q

Qandil Mountains (Iraq) 217, 218
Qatar 182, 207, 225, 368, 386, 390
Quetta (Pakistan) 238, 240, 280
Quezon (Philippines) 105, 117
Quiroz, Juan Gabriel Villa 53, 56
al-Qurayshi, Abu Ibrahim al-Hashimi 160, 169, 206, 225

R

Rabin, Yitzhak 184
Rafah (Egypt) 159, 161, 162, 164, 165
Rageh, Odawaa Yusuf 361, 365
Raia Mutomboki (DRC) 311, 312
Rakhine (Myanmar) 92–102
Rao, Muppala Lakshman 248, 249
Raqqa (Syria) 206, 211, 218
Ravi, R.N. 254, 260, 261, 262
Red Command (Brazil) 41, 42, 43, 44, 45, 46, 47
Red Dragons (Cameroon) 290, 295
Red Sea 160, 230, 368, 391
Reporters Without Borders 326, 388
Republic of Congo 305, 306
Restoration Council of Shan State (Myanmar) 93, 96
Revolutionary Armed Forces of Colombia 6, 14, 38, 51–59
Revolutionary Proletarian Army–Alex Boncayao Brigade (Philippines) 118, 119, 122, 123, 124
Rio de Janeiro (Brazil) 40, 41, 42, 43, 45, 46, 47, 48, 49, 50
Riyadh (Saudi Arabia) 195, 228
Romania 268
Rome (Italy) 117
Rouhani, Hassan 209
Rugsanaoh, Wanlop 126, 131
Runda Kumpulan Kecil (Thailand) 128, 129
Russia 19, 21, 24, 25, 27, 136, 139, 140, 141, 142, 144–156, 159, 160, 164, 184, 189, 199, 201–214, 216–221, 240, 265, 271, 272, 286, 303, 304, 305, 307, 336, 383
Rutshuru (DRC) 312, 313
Rwanda 286, 309, 312, 313, 314, 316, 318, 319

S

Saada (Yemen) 224, 229, 230
Sabah (Malaysia) 106, 113
Sabha (Libya) 192, 197
Sabratha (Libya) 192, 197
al-Sadr, Muqtada 173, 175
Sagaing (Myanmar) 95, 101, 259, 260
al-Saharoui, Adnan Abu Walid 351

Salahaddin (Iraq) 167, 168, 169, 173
Salamé, Ghassan 190, 194, 196, 199
Saleh, Agila 192, 198
Saleh, Ali Abdallah 223, 224, 226, 227
Salih, Barham 173, 174
King Salman bin Abdulaziz Al Saud 194
bin Salman, Mohammed 194, 224
Samar (Philippines) 116, 118, 120, 121, 122
Sanaa (Yemen) 223, 224, 227, 228, 230
Sanjuan, Luis Antonio Quiceno 56, 57, 58
San Pedro Sula (Honduras) 68, 69, 70
Santana, Camilo 48, 50
São Paulo (Brazil) 41, 49
Sardinata (Colombia) 55, 57, 58
al-Sarraj, Fayez 190, 191, 194, 195, 196, 197, 199
Saudi Arabia 6, 20, 24, 157, 163, 171, 173, 175, 194, 195, 207, 222–232, 382, 383, 386, 390, 391
Sawadjaan, Hatib Hajan 104, 106, 112
Second World War 108, 117
Ségou (Mali) 352, 357, 358
Séléka (CAR) 299, 300, 301, 302
Sergiwa, Seham 195, 198
Shabwah (Yemen) 224, 226
Shah, Amit 248, 249, 261, 273
Shan State (Myanmar) 93, 94, 95, 96, 99, 100, 102
Sharon, Ariel 181, 184
Sheikh Zuweid (Egypt) 159, 161, 164
Shekau, Abubakar 330, 331
Sidama (Ethiopia) 320, 322, 324, 325, 327, 328
Sidiki, Abass 300, 303, 306
Sinai (Egypt) 7, 24, 28, 156, 158, 159, 160, 161, 163, 164, 165
Sinaloa (Mexico) 77, 79, 85
Sinaloa Cartel (Mexico) 68, 69, 74, 76, 77, 78, 79, 80, 81, 83, 84, 85, 86
Sinaloa Federation (Mexico) 61, 66
Sindh (Pakistan) 277, 279, 282
Singapore 99
Sirte (Libya) 193, 197
Al-Sisi, Abdel Fattah 160, 161, 162, 163, 164, 165, 181, 192, 198
Sison, Jose Maria 117, 118, 119, 120, 121, 122, 124
al-Sistani, Ali 168, 169
SNNPR (Ethiopia) 320, 322, 325, 326
Sochi (Russia) 212, 305
Sokoto (Nigeria) 339, 340, 342, 343, 344
Soleimani, Qasem 204, 209
Somali (Ethiopia) 322, 325, 326
Somalia 19, 24, 32, 239, 286, 287, 326, 327, 328, 360–368
Somaliland (Somalia) 361, 368
Songkhla (Thailand) 127, 128, 129
Sonora (Mexico) 81, 85, 86
South Africa 17, 43, 293, 313
South Kivu (DRC) 309, 310, 311, 312, 313, 314, 316, 317, 318
South Kordofan (Sudan) 381, 382, 383, 384, 385, 388, 390
South Korea 268
South Protection Force (Libya) 191, 194
South Sudan 7, 224, 286, 299, 301, 304, 306, 324, 326–379, 382, 383, 384, 385, 388
   Agreement on the Resolution of the Conflict 369–379
   South Sudan National Democratic Alliance 370–375
   South Sudan People's Defence Force 370–377, 379
South Sudan United Front/Army (S Sudan) 371, 372, 375
Southern Cameroons Defence Forces (Cameroon) 291, 294
Southern Cameroons Liberation Council (Cameroon) 290, 293, 294
South West (Somalia) 361, 362, 365
Southwest region (Cameroon) 288, 289, 290, 291, 292, 294, 295, 296
Soviet Union 138, 139, 140, 184, 238, 239, 242
Spain 49, 53, 55, 105, 108, 184
Sri Lanka 27
Srinagar (India) 268, 270

Stanytsia Luhanska (Ukraine) 146, 150, 151, 153, 154
Sudan 7, 31, 191, 192, 194, 286, 287, 300, 303, 306, 324, 326, 327, 328, 370–374, 377, 378, 379, 381–391
   National Congress Party 382, 384, 385, 387, 390
   Transitional Military Council 383, 386, 387, 388, 390
Sudan Liberation Movement/Army–Abdel Wahid al-Nur (Sudan) 192, 381, 383, 387, 388, 390
Sudan Liberation Movement/Army–Minni Minnawi (Sudan) 192, 384, 390
Sudan People's Liberation Movement/Army–North (Sudan) 382, 384, 385, 390
   SPLM–N al-Hilu (Sudan) 387, 388, 390, 391
Sudan People's Liberation Movement/Army (S Sudan) 370, 371, 373, 374, 382, 385
Sudan People's Liberation Movement–In Opposition (S Sudan) 370, 371, 374, 375, 376
Sudan Revolutionary Front (Sudan) 381, 383, 384, 385, 386, 387, 388
Sultan Kudarat (Philippines) 106, 111
Sulu (Philippines) 104–114, 123
Sulu Sea 106, 114
Sweden 268
Switzerland 49, 268, 278, 289, 293, 294
Syria 5, 6, 15, 16, 17, 20–28, 34, 106, 109, 114, 139, 142, 145, 156, 157, 160, 164, 167, 168, 169, 171, 175, 179, 180, 201–221, 239, 282
   Geneva process 201, 208, 211, 213
Syrian Democratic Forces 16, 23, 25, 26, 156, 167, 174, 202, 203, 205, 206, 209, 212, 214, 215, 216, 217, 218, 219, 220, 221
Syrian National Army (Syria) 205, 206, 209, 211, 215, 216, 218, 219

T

Ta'ang National Liberation Army (Myanmar) 95, 96, 97, 98, 99
Tabe, Sisiku Julius 289, 290, 291, 293
Tahoua (Mali) 349, 351, 358
Taiwan 67
Taizz (Yemen) 223, 224, 225, 226, 227, 230, 231
Tajoura (Libya) 191, 195
Taliban (Afghanistan) 7, 14, 234, 236–242, 267, 272, 275, 276, 277, 278, 281, 282
Tamah, Mohammad Saleh 228, 229
Tamaulipas (Mexico) 38, 78, 79, 81, 84
Tanzania 316
Taraba (Nigeria) 338, 339, 340, 341, 343, 344, 345
Tarhouna (Libya) 192, 194, 197
Tartous (Syria) 210, 212
Tawi-Tawi (Philippines) 105, 106, 109, 110, 112, 114
Tegucigalpa (Honduras) 70, 71, 72
Tehrik-e-Taliban Pakistan 7, 234, 238, 275–282
Telangana (India) 248, 249
Tel Aviv (Israel) 185, 186
Tel Rifaat (Syria) 218, 219
Tessalit (Mali) 349, 352
Texas (US) 78, 79, 81
Thailand 90, 97, 98, 99, 126–131, 133, 134, 268
3 R (CAR) 299, 300, 303, 304, 305, 306
Tigray People's Liberation Front (Ethiopia) 321–325, 327
Tijuana (Mexico) 80, 83
Tijuana Cartel (Mexico) 78, 80
Tikrit (Iraq) 168, 170
Tillabéri (Niger) 349, 351, 356, 358
Timbuktu (Mali) 348, 349, 350, 352
Togo 358, 359
Touadéra, Faustin-Archange 299, 304, 305, 307
Transparency International 54
Tripoli (Libya) 16, 189, 190, 191, 192, 193, 194, 195, 196, 197, 198, 199
Trump, Donald 65, 66, 67, 74, 77, 83, 84, 85, 86, 87, 151, 154, 157, 164, 171, 182, 183, 185, 186, 187, 199, 209, 211, 217, 228, 231, 236, 237, 241, 242, 272, 318, 358, 378
Tshisekedi, Félix 308, 314, 315, 317, 318
Tuareg Self-Defence Group and Allies (Mali) 352, 353

Tuccu, Q. 260, 262
Tumaco (Colombia) 55, 57
Tunisia 27, 195, 198
Turkey 5, 17, 23, 25, 26, 27, 31, 34, 136, 139, 140, 141, 142, 145, 156, 157, 165, 167, 171, 175, 189, 195, 197, 198, 199, 201–221, 281, 362, 366, 367, 390
  Operation Peace Spring 23, 209, 211, 214, 218, 219, 220
Two Areas (Sudan) 381, 382, 383, 385, 386, 387, 391

U

Uganda 268, 286, 301, 304, 309, 311, 314, 315, 316, 318, 319, 324, 327, 362, 367, 370, 383
Ukraine 6, 19, 20, 94, 136, 146, 147, 149, 150, 151, 153, 154
  Trilateral Contact Group 150, 151, 152, 153, 154
uninhabited aerial vehicles 6, 19, 20, 21, 144, 147, 148, 195, 197, 198, 204, 205, 215, 223, 224, 226, 228, 229, 231, 366
Union des Forces de la Résistance (Libya) 191, 198
Union for Peace in the Central African Republic 299–305, 307
United Arab Emirates 20, 163, 165, 173, 189, 190, 195, 197, 211, 222, 224, 225, 226, 228–232, 272, 327, 386, 390, 391
United Kingdom 17, 19, 26, 27, 31, 157, 179, 210, 231, 272, 276, 278, 293, 330, 332, 336, 341, 362, 378
United Liberation Front of Asom–Independent (India) 257, 260, 262, 263
United Liberation Front of Asom–Pro-Talks Faction (India) 256, 259
United National Liberation Front (India) 255, 257
United National Liberation Front of Western South East Asia (India) 257, 258
United Nations 6, 20, 23, 24, 26, 31, 33, 34, 48, 49, 52, 55, 57, 63, 73, 97, 139, 162, 163, 174, 175, 179, 181, 184, 185, 186, 189, 190, 193, 194, 195, 196, 198, 199, 201, 207, 208, 209, 210, 211, 213, 219, 223, 227, 228, 229, 230, 231, 238, 242, 266, 268, 269, 271, 293, 294, 296, 298, 299, 300, 302, 303, 304, 305, 306, 310, 315, 316, 317, 327, 332, 336, 348, 350, 355, 356, 358, 362, 366, 367, 370, 373, 374, 375, 376, 377, 378, 385, 387, 388
  African Union Hybrid Mission in Darfur 387, 388
  Assistance Mission in Afghanistan 238
  Commission for India and Pakistan 268
  Convention against Transnational Organized Crime 31
  Food and Agriculture Organization 101
  Geneva Convention 181
  Global Compact on Refugees 33
  High Commissioner for Human Rights 153
  High Commissioner for Refugees 219, 296, 306, 377
  Human Rights Monitoring Mission in Ukraine 153
  Interim Security Force in Abyei 385
  International Tribunal for the Law of the Sea 151
  Military Observer Group in India and Pakistan 268, 269
  Mission in South Sudan 372, 373, 374, 376
    Regional Protection Force 373
  Mission to Support the Hudaydah Agreement 227
  Multidimensional Integrated Stabilization Mission in Mali 348, 349, 350, 351, 353, 356, 357, 358
    Operation Oryx 357
  Multidimensional Integrated Stabilization Mission in the Central African Republic 298, 299, 300, 303, 304, 305, 306
    Operation Enclume 305, 306
  Office for the Coordination of Humanitarian Affairs 57, 100, 113, 185, 219, 230, 296, 358, 376
  Office on Drugs and Crime 34, 55, 57, 97
  Organization Mission in the Congo 310
  Relief and Works Agency for Palestine Refugees 186
  Security Council 23, 25, 26, 31, 34, 152, 234, 272, 289, 293, 294, 300, 304, 305, 348, 350, 355, 361, 373, 375, 378, 388
    Resolution 39 268
    Resolution 91 268
    Resolution 307 268
    Resolution 1996 373
    Resolution 2100 350
    Resolution 2155 373
    Resolution 2178 23, 26
    Resolution 2216 223
    Resolution 2254 208
    Resolution 2265 210
    Resolution 2396 23, 25
    Resolution 2459 373
    Resolution 2462 25
  Stabilization Mission in Congo 309, 310, 311, 315, 316, 317
  Support Mission in Libya 194, 198
  Sustainable Development Goals 34
  Universal Declaration of Human Rights 33
  World Food Programme 230, 388, 389
  World Health Organization 317, 345
United People's Front (India) 255, 256
United Self-Defence Forces of Colombia 52, 54, 55, 57
United States 7, 14, 16, 19, 23, 25, 26, 31, 34, 35, 38, 49, 52, 53, 55, 56, 61–87, 94, 99, 101, 105, 108, 113, 117, 118, 127, 128, 136, 139, 142, 143, 145, 147, 150, 151, 154, 156, 157, 160, 161, 164, 165, 167, 168, 169, 170, 171, 173, 174, 175, 176, 179, 180, 183, 184, 185, 186, 187, 189, 193, 199, 201, 202, 203, 204, 206–214, 216, 217, 219, 220, 223, 226, 228, 229, 231, 234, 236–242, 265, 271, 272, 275–279, 281, 282, 286, 289, 290, 293, 294, 295, 297, 301, 304, 305, 322, 327, 330, 332, 336, 341, 349, 355, 358, 361, 362, 363, 365, 366, 367, 375, 378, 390, 391
  Africa Command 193, 195, 366
  Agency for International Development 183, 186
  Caesar Syria Civilian Protection Act 211, 212
  Central Intelligence Agency 128
  Combined Joint Task Force 168, 169, 170
  Convention on Human Rights 33
  Defense Intelligence Agency 78
  Drug Enforcement Administration 78, 81
  FBI 85
  Operation Enduring Freedom 238
  Operation Freedom's Sentinel 237, 238
  Operation Inherent Resolve 23, 24, 25, 168, 169
United Tribal Liberation Army (India) 256, 258
United Tribal Liberation Army–Poukhai (India) 256, 258
United Wa State Army (Myanmar) 93, 94, 95, 96, 97, 98
Unity (S Sudan) 301, 323, 352, 369, 370, 373, 374, 377
Upper Nile (S Sudan) 373, 377
Uruguay 87, 268
Úsuga, Dairo Antonio 54, 57

V

Vakaga (CAR) 300, 301, 305, 306
Velásquez, Hernán Darío 56
Venezuela 43, 52, 53, 56, 58, 59
Veracruz (Mexico) 78, 84
Vietnam 101
Vintém, Celsinho da Vila 42, 43

W

Wagner Group 199, 304, 305
Wani, Burhan Muzaffar 266, 269
Washington DC (US) 184, 185
West Bank 178, 179, 180, 181, 182, 183, 184, 185, 186
Western Bahr el-Ghazal (S Sudan) 371, 373
Western Desert (Egypt) 159, 165
Western Visayas (Philippines) 118, 123
Wilayat Sinai (Egypt) 159, 160, 161, 162, 163, 164
Witzel, Wilson 40, 46, 47, 48, 49
Women, Peace and Security Index 100
World Bank 70, 101, 154, 181, 182, 231, 236, 242, 342
World Press Freedom Index 100

X

Xi Jinping 97

Y

Yakutumba (DRC) 312, 313
Yala (Thailand) 126, 127, 128, 129, 130, 131, 132
Yanukovych, Viktor 147, 149, 150
Yaoundé (Cameroon) 293, 295, 296
Yemen 6, 19, 20, 24, 25, 157, 173, 222–232, 327, 363, 382, 383, 390
  Southern Transitional Council 222–231
  Stockholm Agreement 157, 222, 223, 227, 228, 231, 232
Yobe (Nigeria) 330, 331, 332, 333, 334, 336, 341
Yushchenko, Viktor 149
Yusuf, Mohammed 330, 331, 332

Z

Zamfara (Nigeria) 338, 339, 340, 341, 342, 343, 344, 345, 346
Zari, Sama-ae Kho 128, 131, 132
Zawiya (Libya) 191, 197
Zelensky, Volodymyr 146, 147, 150, 151, 153, 154
Zeliangrong United Front (India) 256, 258, 261
Zintan (Libya) 190, 191, 192, 197, 199
Zolote (Ukraine) 146, 149, 151, 153, 154

IISS

THE
ARMED CONFLICT SURVEY
2020

The worldwide review of
political, military and humanitarian
trends in current conflicts

published by

Routledge
Taylor & Francis Group

for

The International Institute for Strategic Studies

The International Institute for Strategic Studies
Arundel House | 6 Temple Place | London | WC2R 2PG | UK

THE ARMED CONFLICT SURVEY 2020

First published May 2020 by **Routledge**
4 Park Square, Milton Park, Abingdon, Oxon, OX14 4RN

for **The International Institute for Strategic Studies**
Arundel House, 6 Temple Place, London, WC2R 2PG, UK

Simultaneously published in the USA and Canada by **Routledge**
52 Vanderbilt Avenue, New York, NY 10017

Routledge is an imprint of Taylor & Francis, an Informa business

© 2020 The International Institute for Strategic Studies

DIRECTOR-GENERAL AND CHIEF EXECUTIVE Dr John Chipman
EDITORS Virginia Comolli, Dr Francesca Grandi
ASSOCIATE EDITOR Alice Aveson
ASSISTANT EDITOR Gabriel Everington
EDITORIAL Alex Goodwin, Sara Hussain, Michael Marsden, Jack May, Bao-Chau Pham, Jonathan Stevenson, Jessica Watson
DESIGN AND PRODUCTION John Buck, Carolina Vargas, Kelly Verity

CONFLICTS Adam Wunische (Afghanistan), Dr Laurence Broers and Jenny Tobias (Armenia-Azerbaijan (Nagorno-Karabakh)), Cecília Oliveira (Brazil (Rio De Janeiro & Ceará)), Dr Yonatan Morse (Cameroon), Thierry Vircoulon (Central African Republic), Gonzalo Croci (Colombia (BACRIMs)), Dr Eleanor Beevor (Democratic Republic of the Congo and Somalia), Douglas Farah and Caitlyn Yates (El Salvador and Honduras), Dr Sonia Le Gouriellec and Dr Mehari Taddele Maru (Ethiopia (Communal Violence)), Christopher Wiley Shay (India (CPI–Maoist)), Dr Alex Waterman (India (Northeast)), Dr Mohd Tahir Ganie (India–Pakistan (Kashmir)), Dr Grace A. Wermenbol (Israel–Palestine), Flore Berger (Lake Chad Basin (Boko Haram) and The Sahel (Mali & Burkina Faso)), Dr Umberto Profazio (Libya), Dr Raul Benitez-Manaut (Mexico (Cartels)), Elliot Brennan (Myanmar (EAOs)), Dr Jimam T. Lar and Dr Murtala Ahmed Rufa'i (Nigeria (Farmer–Pastoralist)), Nicholas Crawford (Pakistan), Michael Hart (Philippines (ASG & Moro) and Philippines (NPA)), Nina Pouls (Somalia and Sudan (Darfur, Blue Nile & South Kordofan)), Jeremy Walden-Schertz (Southern Thailand), Chedine Tazi (South Sudan), Elliot Dolan-Evans (Ukraine)

GLOBAL TRENDS Dr Brian McQuinn and Laura Courchesne (Armed-Group Proliferation: Origins and Consequences), Dr Eleanor Beevor and Dhia Muhsin (Non-state Armed Groups and UAVs: Uptake and Effectiveness), Dr Francesco F. Milan (ISIS Foreign Fighters after the Fall of the Caliphate), Tuesday Reitano (Human Trafficking in Conflict)

THE CHART OF ARMED CONFLICT Flore Berger, Andrei Cursaru, Max Frank, Stephanie Mayne-Flood, Dhia Muhsin, Zaynab Olyabek, Toby Smith, Dr Andrew Tchie, Peppi Vaananen

COVER IMAGES Getty

All rights reserved. No part of this book may be reprinted or reproduced or utilised in any form or by any electronic, mechanical, or other means, now known or hereafter invented, including photocopying and recording, or in any information storage or retrieval system, without permission in writing from the publisher.

British Library Cataloguing in Publication Data
A catalogue record for this book is available from the British Library

Library of Congress Cataloguing in Publication Data

ISBN 978-0-367-54150-7
ISSN 2374-0973